liquid metal

THE SCIENCE FICTION FILM READER

3.2008

liquid metal

THE SCIENCE FICTION FILM READER

EDITED BY SEAN REDMOND

WALLFLOWER PRESS

LONDON and NEW YORK

First published in Great Britain in 2004, reprinted 2007
Wallflower Press
6 Market Place, London W1W 8AF
www.wallflowerpress.co.uk

A catalogue record for this book is available from the British Library.

ISBN 978-1-903364-87-1 (pbk)
       978-1-903364-88-8 (hbk)

Printed by Replika Press Pvt. Ltd. (India)

CONTENTS

Acknowledgements

All the articles and essays in this Reader have been previously published in a variety of journals and anthologies. Thanks go to all the authors, editors and publishers of the following publications who have permitted the reproduction of these works: Vivian Sobchack (1997) 'Images of Wonder: The Look of Science Fiction' (pp. 64–87 only) and 'Postfuturism' (pp. 223–41 only) *Screening Space: The American Science Fiction Film*, second edition, New York: Rutgers University Press; Steve Neale (1990) 'You've Got To Be Fucking Kidding!: Knowledge, Belief and Judgement in Science Fiction', in Annette Kuhn (ed.) *Alien Zone*, London: Verso, pp. 160–8; Barry Kieth Grant (1999) 'Sensuous Elaboration: reason and the Visible in the Science Fiction Film', in Annette Kuhn (ed.) *Alien Zone II*, London: Verso, pp. 16–29; Warren Buckland (1999) 'Between Science Fiction and Science Fact: Spielberg's Digital Dinosaurs, Possible Worlds and the New Aesthetic Realism', *Screen*, vol. 40, no. 2, pp. 177–92; Susan Sontag (1994) 'The Imagination of Disaster', in *Against Interpretation*, London: Vintage Press, pp. 209–25; Linda Ruth Williams (1999) 'Dream Girls and Mechanic Panic: Dystopia and its Others in *Brazil* and *Nineteen Eighty-Four*', in I. Q. Hunter (ed.) *British Science Fiction Cinema*, London: Routledge, pp. 153–69; Michael Ryan and Douglas Kellner (1988) 'Technophobia/Dystopia', in *Camera Politica*, Indiana: Indiana University Press, pp. 224–58; Eric Avila (2001) 'Dark City: White Flight and the Urban Science Fiction Film in Postwar America', in Daniel Bernardi (ed.) *Classic Hollywood: Classic Whiteness*, Minneapolis: University of Minnesota Press, pp. 52–71; Vivian Sobchack (1999) 'Cities on the Edge of Time: The Urban Science Fiction Film', in Annette Kuhn (ed.) *Alien Zone II*, London: Verso, pp. 123–43; Isolde Standish (1998) '*Akira*, Postmodernism and Resistance', in D. P. Martinez (ed.) *The Worlds of Japanese Popular Culture*, Cambridge: Cambridge University Press, pp. 56–74; Wong Kin Yuen (2000) 'On the Edge of Spaces: *Blade Runner*, *Ghost in the Shell* and Hong Kong's Cityscape', *Science Fiction Studies*, vol. 27, no. 1, pp. 1–21; Andrew Gordon (1987) 'Back to the Future: Oedipus as Time Traveller', *Science Fiction Studies*, vol. 14, no. 3, pp. 372–85; Constance Penley (1991) 'Time travel, Primal Scene and the Critical Dystopia', in Constance Penley (ed.) *Close Encounters: Film, Feminism and Science Fiction*, Minneapolis: University of Minnesota Press, pp. 63–80; Jonathan Bignell (1999) 'Another Time, Another Space: Modernity, Subjectivity and The Time Machine', in Deborah Cartmell, I. Q. Hunter, Heidi Kaye and Imelda Whelehan (eds) *Alien Identities*, London: Pluto Press, pp. 87–103; Carol Schwartz Ellis (1995) 'With Eyes Uplifted: Space Aliens as Sky Gods', in Joel W. Martin and Conrad E. Ostwalt (eds) *Screening the Sacred: Religion, Myth and Ideology in Popular American Film*, Boulder CO: Westview Press, pp. 83–93; Donna J. Haraway (1991) 'A Manifesto for Cyborgs: Science, Technology and Socialist Feminism in the 1980s', in *Simians, Cyborgs and Women: The Reinvention of Nature*, London: Free Association Books, pp. 149–81; Mary Ann Doane (1990) 'Technophilia, Representation and the Feminine', in Mary Jacobus, Evelyn Fox Keller and Sally Shuttleworth (eds) *Body/Politcs: Women and the Discourses of Science*, London: Routledge, pp. 163–76; Doran Larson (1997) 'Machine as Messiah: Cyborgs, Morphs and the American Body Politic', in *Cinema Journal*, vol. 36, no. 1, pp. 57–75; Susan J. Napier (2001) 'Ghosts and Machines: The Technological Body', in *Anime: From Akira to Princess Mononoke*, New York: Palgrave, pp. 85–102; Scott Bukatman (1990) 'Who Programs You? The Science Fiction of the Spectacle', in Annette Kuhn (ed.) *Alien Zone*, London: Verso, pp. 196–213; J. P. Telotte (1983) 'Human Artifice and the Science Fiction Film', *Film Quarterly*, vol. 36, no. 3, pp. 44–51; Alison Landsberg (1995) 'Prosthetic Memory: *Total Recall* and *Blade Runner*', in Mike Featherstone and Roger Burrows (eds) *Cyberspace/Cyberbodies/Cyberpunk*, London: Sage, pp. 175–89; Henry Jenkins III (1988) 'Star Trek Rerun, Reread, Rewritten: Fan Writing as Textual Poaching', *Critical Studies in Mass Communication*, vol. 5, no. 2, pp. 85–107; John Tulloch (1995) "We're Only a Speck in the Ocean': The Fan as Powerless Elite', in John Tulloch and Henry Jenkins (eds) *Science Fiction Audiences: Watching Doctor Who and Star Trek*, London: Routledge, pp. 144–72; Will Brooker (1997) 'New Hope' The Postmodern Project of *Star Wars*', Will and Peter Brooker (eds) *Postmodern After-Images*, London: Arnold, pp. 101–12; Kurt Lancaster (2001) 'Web of Babylon' (pp. 128–36 only) in *Fan Performances in a Media Universe: Interacting with Babylon 5*, Austin, TX: MIT; Peter Biskind (1983) "The Russians are Coming, Aren't They?' *Them!* and *The Thing*', in *Seeing is Believing: How Hollywood Taught Us to Stop Worrying and Love the 1950s*, London: Pluto Press, pp. 123–36; Mark Jancovich (1996) 'Re-examining the 1950s Invasion Narratives', in *Rational Fears*, Manchester: Manchester University Press, pp. 26–49; Peter Hutchings (1999) "We're the Martians Now': British SF Invasion Narratives of the 1950s and 1960s', in I. Q. Hunter (ed.) *British Science Fiction Cinema*, London: Routledge, pp. 33–48.

I would like to thank David, Deborah, Su, Karen, Cathy, John B., Peter, John H., Belinda and Annabel at Southampton Institute for their help, support and camaraderie during the composition of this Reader. I would also like to thank my cinefantastic classes for their conditional love of the sci-fi cinema machine and for their fancy dress seminar presentations. Never have so many superheroes looked so incapable of action! I would like to thank all at Wallflower Press for their support of this project.

… And thanks to Steven T. 'all the best directors have beards!' Hanley for the Anime reference.

Where would the cinema be without time travel and alien invaders? Nowhere that interesting, really…

For Caitlin and Joshua and those beams of light we never quite catch.
For Mum and Dad – for letting me watch too much television.

Preface
Sean Redmond

We live in a science fiction textured world. A world where a sense of the impossible, the fantastic, the spectacular finds its way into the architecture and design of everything from shopping malls, hospitals and office blocks to art galleries, restaurants and nightclubs. In these futuristic places and spaces, aluminium clad interiors, (hidden) surveillance cameras, robotic displays, retro sci-fi design and 'impossible' lines, shapes and vanishing points seemingly allow the wanderer to time travel and see beyond or rather to enter into the future. For example, in the modern nightclub interior, space can suddenly change or metamorphose, creating the impression that one is caught in a state of spatial flux. Floors move, lighting and laser rigs are in perpetual motion, video projection creates the sense that one is being immersed in the holodeck, and 'special effects', whether it be water emerging from beneath the floor or a space craft descending from the rotating ceiling, make the club space unstable – outside the physical laws of gravity. Of course, the cyborg clubber 'plugs' herself into this liquid machine and by so doing becomes a vital part of its futuristic circuitry.

We live in a world where the everyday stories that people tell one another – over dinner, in the school playground, on the front of newspapers and in the soundbites of television – border on the wondrous and the terrifying in equal measure. For example, tabloid and broadsheet newspapers are full of 'science fiction' stories such as the alien invasion scenarios that make it into print on almost a daily basis. The mysterious and scientifically unexplainable appearance of corn circles in England is one 'seasonal' example. Or newspapers are full of science fact stories that are written as impossible stories so they become interchangeably science

fact/fiction narratives. The recent, although still unconfirmed, genetic cloning of baby girl 'Eve' by the Raelians (a religious cult who believes that Aliens begat the human race), is one example where elements of science fact and fiction collide. It is an example that points to the way the borders of science fiction and science fact actually merge and ultimately collapse in the postmodern world – where the real is as much (science) fiction as the fiction itself, and where the (science) fiction is – or becomes – as credible or authentic as fact. Through this type of simulation, even Jean Baudrillard's (1994) meta-concept of hyperreality, from which this idea is borrowed from, seems little removed from the pages of Philip K. Dick or Robert A. Heinlein.

The television representation of war is another example of the way in which science fiction's codes and conventions in part provide the audio soundtrack, the special effects and the spectacular action sequences for the 'actual' conflict that takes place. Computer-generated missiles, spectacular explosions, doomsday scenarios and evil dictators planning biological attacks, are borrowed or re-imagined from the science fiction lexicon and drawn into the way war is imaged and narrated on factual television programmes. As this Reader was being composed, news programmes across the world spectacularly prepared their people for another horrifying invasion narrative as the US and UK fire-up for a terribly real sci-fi war in Iraq.

We live in a world where the mass media in general calls upon the science fiction text to sell cinema seats, boost ratings or to connect or engage people from across the globe. Today when one goes to the multiplex or to the video/DVD rental store, or when one switches on the television or scans the latest listings magazines, one expects to find either the latest science fiction blockbuster showing, or a recent science fiction hit or television series being rented or premiered, or a golden oldie sci-fi flick getting a repeat airing, often as part of some sci-fi mini-season, on late-night television. Whole digital channels are dedicated to its fare. Numerous magazines and journals speak its name. Bookshops dedicate whole sections to the science fiction text. Science fiction websites connect millions of fans across the globe. Science fiction-based conventions and conferences populate the entertainment and academic landscape, for many people structuring or mapping out the year for them. Science fiction is a religion for some, a big, fat dollar sign for others. Science fiction is everywhere in the postmodern world.

Science fiction film and television is everywhere and yet never really totally at home in the academic world today, ignored or scorned and critiqued as it so often is. In terms of cinema, science fiction is often in part blamed for the infantilism of New Hollywood and named as the motor for childish and vulgar cinematic display. As Thomas Schatz naively bemoans:

From *The Godfather* to *Jaws* to *Star Wars*, we see films that are increasingly plot-driven, increasingly visceral, kinetic, and fast-paced, increasingly reliant on special effects, increasingly 'fantastic' (and thus apolitical), and increasingly targeted at younger audiences. (1993: 23)

Or else science fiction is seen as one of the apocalyptic catalysts for real cinema's imminent death. So the argument runs, science fiction film fills the movie world with too many special effects and set-piece moments at the expense of narrative development or meaningful characterisation, or so relies on CGI or the digital aesthetic that reel film dies in the antiquated chemical process to which it clings to. Or finally, science fiction cinema is seen as the ultimate commodity intertext, a marketplace for selling games, toys, theme park rides and product tie-ins,

and its own endless stream of remakes and sequels – in what therefore becomes an over-determining and all-devouring franchise system. Television-based science fiction is seen to be central to this commodity-synergy footprinting: uniting the second, third, fourth etc. series of say, *Star Trek*, with their cinematic interpretations, year after year after year.

And yet science fiction film and television is in another sense valorised by the academic community since it is seen as a cohering genre that is best able to articulate contemporary fears, such as those that presently exist over genetic engineering and nuclear war, and to play out ideological tensions around class, race, gender and sexuality. As Annete Kuhn summarises,

... there is the idea that science fiction films relate to the social order through the mediation of ideologies, society's representation of itself in and for itself – that films speak, enact, even produce certain ideologies, which cannot always be read directly off films' surface contents. (1990:10)

The science fiction text, so seemingly far fetched and non-realistic, is here seen as an allegorical or metaphorical or mythical meaning-making system that directly interprets or questions or provides healing solutions to the everyday issues and problems that people face on the planet. Here the argument runs: if you want to know what really aches a culture at any given time don't go to its art cinema, or its gritty social realist texts, but go to its science fiction. This is precisely the destination of this Reader.

Liquid Metal: The Science Fiction Film Reader is the very first extended collection of previously published essays on science fiction film and, to a lesser extent, television. The Reader brings together a great number of what are regarded to be 'seminal' essays that have opened up the study of science fiction to serious critical interrogation. The essays in this collection understand science fiction either as a destructive genre, in the senses outlined above, or as culturally central to the transmission of dominant ideology or counter-hegemony, to identity formation, and to the political wounds that mark any age or society at any given time.

The essay choices in this Reader have not only been made on the quality and the importance of the writing to an understanding of how science fiction functions, but in terms of a loose histography, so that arguably the 'best' of the writing on science fiction, over the last thirty or so years, is represented. However, choices have also been predicated on two other factors. First, essays have been chosen so that across the Reader the film and television texts that are discussed cover science fiction from America, Europe and Asia – although, as might be expected, American cinema dominates. Second, essays have been chosen in terms of their centrality to the themes that structure and sub-divide the book, themes that themselves have been chosen on the basis of how they have come to dominate the major concerns of science fiction writing in recent academic history.

The Reader is divided into eight distinct themed sections, each section containing three or four key essays that explore in different and sometimes contradictory ways the theme that heads the section. The Reader, forgive the pun, takes the reader on an intellectual, textual and contextual journey, beginning with an exploration of the generic specificities of its form, and ending with a historically specific case-study section: the 1950s invasion narratives. Along the way cyborgs are encountered and dispatched; great metropolis are visited and destroyed; the world ends and is reborn; fan's poach around for deeper meaning; aliens arrive and issue grave warnings; and people stand and stare, in awe and wonder, at the liquid textures of the science fiction text.

Given the 'popular' dominance of science fiction cinema within Hollywood filmmaking, given the dramatic rise in the number of film courses (in Britain, Europe and North America) that take science fiction cinema as a key area of study, and given a current academic marketplace where only separately themed books on science fiction exist, *Liquid Metal* is a timely and necessary addition to the literature on science fiction cinema. I hope you enjoy the Reader.

References

Baudrillard, Jean (1994) *Simulacra and Simulation*. London: University of Michigan Press.

Kuhn, Annette (1990) *Alien Zone*. London: Verso.

Schalz, Thomas (1993) 'The New Hollywood', in Jim Collins, Hilary Radner and Ava Preacher Collins (eds) *Film Theory Goes to the Movies*. London: Routledge.

THE WONDER OF SCIENCE FICTION

ONE | THE WONDER OF SCIENCE FICTION

Science fiction can be set in the past, present and future. It can involve futuristic gadgets, weaponry, clothing, housing and transportation, including silver suits, inter-galactic space crafts, flying cars and light sabres. But science fiction can also involve the mere 'copying' of existing social and cultural relations so that what the audience sees and hears in part resembles closely the world as it is experienced on a daily basis. Science fiction can be special effects-laden with marvellous and miraculous worlds conjured up in instantaneous, seamless and seemingly effortless strokes of realism, but it can just as easily be technology free with the absence of special effect an eerie marker of malaise in the sci-fi narrative. Science fiction can be about mad scientists, bad science, alien invaders, nuclear or biological catastrophe, time travel, psychosexual lack and terror, space travel, prophecy and apocalypse, utopia, dystopia, technophobia, technophilia, racial and national identity, the family and corporate capitalism. Science

fiction can be driven by display, spectacle and wonderment, but it can also be motored by melancholy and introspection. Science fiction is like the western, the noir, and often borrows or shares its codes and conventions with the horror film, in hybrid exchanges and articulations. Science fiction is, as a consequence, particularly difficult to pin down generically. Science fiction shape-shifts and transmogrophies just like the best traditions of its narrative. Nonetheless, there is something *wonderful* about the science fiction text.

In an extract from Vivian Sobchack's 'Images of Wonder: The Look of Science Fiction', the visual surfaces of science fiction cinema are shown to be inconsistent, at least in terms of narrative meaning and context. Drawing on the work of Jim Kitses and Colin McArthur, Sobchack examines the iconography of the spaceship and the robot to see if they hold the same generic weight as that of the railroad in the western. Sobchack concludes that these two potential 'icons' are in fact so fluid in their textual uses within science fiction that 'it is the very plasticity of objects and settings in SF films which help define them as science fiction, and not their consistency. And it is this same plasticity of objects and settings that deny the kind of iconographic interpretation which critically illuminates the essentially static worlds of genres such as the western and gangster film'.

Steve Neale locates the cohering parameters of science fiction film in terms of the 'special effects effect'. This is the self-conscious response that is elicited from audiences the moment they are faced with a particularly astonishing or horrifying science fiction event that has been conjured up from the seamless magic of the special effects department. According to Neale, special effects not only have direct and involuntary cerebral or physical effects on the audience but they also simultaneously involve audiences in a three-way dialogue about the very nature of special effects as they happen in a film. Audiences are aligned with the (sometimes incredulous) characters in the film, with the makers of the special effect (who are 'showing off' their spectacular capabilities at the moment the special effect is revealed), and the cinema as institution, that is also drawing attention to its machinery and commercial nature more widely. According to Neale, special effects involve audiences in a self-conscious process: while audiences may stare in wonder at a city suddenly, supposedly, crafted out of thin air, they may at the same time utter 'what an amazing special effect', acknowledging the magic hand of the special effects department and filmmaking in the very moment that it is witnessed.

In contrast, Barry Keith Grant argues that 'the pleasure of science fiction is deter-mined by the quality (synonymous with believability) of the special effects. For these viewers, nothing destroys the pleasure of a science-fiction movie than seeing the 'seams' in a matte shot or glimpsing the zipper on an alien's bodysuit'. Grant begins his essay by comparing horror with science fiction, arguing that the appeal of science fiction is cognitive and cerebral, driven as it so often is by 'heady issues' and a sense of wonder. The science fiction texts looks to the stars, to parallel worlds, to 'alternative possibilities', while its narratives and thematics are conjured up out of the alchemy and the discoveries of chemistry and physics. Consequently, for Grant, the best (recurring) textual and reception symbol or image for the 'scopophilic pleasure' of science fiction is the wide-eyed child, repeatedly caught in the sensory overload of science fiction's possible futures.

Warren Buckland's essay initiated a heated exchange with J. P. Telotte in the pages of the journal *Screen*. Buckland also acknowledges the centrality of special effects to science fiction cinema, arguing that they are not just conduits of spectacle and display but representational devices for the creation of what he calls (borrowing from modal logic studies) 'possible worlds', or 'a modal extension of the 'actual world''. Buckland then goes on to develop a more controversial argument around the digital image, digital special effects and realism. In his reading of *Jurassic Park* and *The Lost World*, Buckland argues that 'The interactions created between the digital dinosaurs and live action/real backgrounds within a single shot help to create a new realism in the digital image, for the effects create the illusion of spatial and diegetic unity'.

Images of Wonder:
The Look of Science Fiction
Vivian Sobchack

Although a great deal has been written about the images in science fiction (SF) films, most often that writing has been more descriptive than analytic. There has been only minor consideration of the nature of SF images and their function in the creation of a film genre which in photographic content is unlike any other. Instead, discussions of the visual surface of the films have usually seemed to degenerate into a delightful but critically unproductive game film enthusiasts play: 'Swap that Shot' or 'The Robot You Love to Remember'. Although there is absolutely no reason to feel guilty about swapping nostalgically remembered images like baseball trading cards, it does seem time to go beyond both gamesmanship and nostalgia toward a discovery of how SF images in content and presentation function to make SF film uniquely itself. What, if anything, do all the films have in common in their visual surface?

Iconography

One approach to the images in genre films (most often the western or gangster film) has been iconographic. Jim Kitses, one of first film critics to discuss the relationship of iconography to the genre film in his *Horizons West*, explains the basis of the approach: 'As a result of mass production, the accretions of time, and the dialectics of history and archetype, characters, situations and actions can have an emblematic power.'[1] And Colin McArthur, in *Underworld U.S.A.*, emphasises the 'continuity over several decades of patterns of visual imagery, of recurrent objects and figures in dynamic relationship' which 'might be called the iconography of the genre.'[2] McArthur goes on to say: 'The recurrent patterns of imagery can be usefully divided into three categories: those surrounding the physical presence, attributes and dress of the actors and the characters they play; those emanating from the milieux within which the characters operate; and those connected with the technology at the characters disposal.'[3]

In certain groupings of films, then, the visual units which manifest – and often dictate – character, situation and action have been examined as those elements which not only link the films together, but which also carry meaning and emotional nuance beyond their physical particularity in any one film. Because these elements of visual content appear again and again in film after film, they have become visual conventions or icons, pictorial codes which are a graphic shorthand understood by both filmmaker and audience.[4] The western topography (whether photographed in the United States or Spain) is not just any place; beyond the specificity of badlands, mountains, rangeland, desert, its appearance evokes associations in the viewer which are, perhaps, more metaphysically than historically based. The same could be said of the city of the gangster film; buildings and alleys, rooftops and fire escapes surround themselves with clusters of meaning and yet-unplayed actions, with emotional reverberations which have little connection with the same physical objects represented, for example, in an urban comedy like Preston Sturges' *Christmas in July* (1940), or an urban musical like Robert Wise's *West Side Story* (1961). Costumes and tools also become objects of totemic significance in certain film genres; the gun of the western is different in significance as well as in kind from the gun of the gangster film.

This recognition of iconography is, perhaps, what Michael Butor was trying to indicate when, attempting to define science fiction, he felt it was sufficient to say: 'You know, those stories that are always mentioning interplanetary rockets.'[5] His statement, however, brings us to a crucial issue regarding any iconographic consideration of the SF film. Butor, himself, acknowledges that rocketships are not in themselves necessary to science fiction.[6] And one could create a list of such SF 'objects' as the spaceship which do indeed evoke the genre, but which are specifically and physically not *essential* to it: the New Planet, the Robot, the Laboratory, Radioactive Isotopes and Atomic Devices. On the other hand, it is extremely difficult to think of a western which does not take place in a visually represented 'West' with guns and horses, or to recall a gangster film which does not show a nightclub or which has no guns and no automobiles. These settings and objects seem physically essential to these genres and their iconographic significance seems readily approachable and comprehensible because they appear and send the same messages to us in almost every film.

It is also highly significant that both these genres are visually circumscribed by an awareness of history, the western even more so than the gangster film. This linkage of situation and character, objects, settings and costumes to a specific *past* creates visual boundaries to what can be photographed and in what context. This historical awareness, which leads at least to an imaginative if not actual authenticity, demands repetition and creates consistency throughout these genres. This is not true, however, of the SF film, a genre which is unfixed in its dependence on actual time and/ or place. There is, then, a very obvious reason for the fact that most iconographic analysis has focused on the western and the gangster film. Simply, these genres play out their narrative in a specific, visually identifiable and *consistent* context, and the objects of these films accrue their meaning not only from repetitious use, but also because they function in a much more circumscribed and limited way than do objects in other genres. This limitation of meaning should in no way be considered a cinematic, aesthetic, or thematic liability – but it should point to why iconographic analysis serves a less potent critical function when it is used as a method to seek meaning in settings and objects in other film genres less affixed to history.

Consider, for example, the railroad – a frequent, although not mandatory, icon in the western. The meanings which are suggested by its appearance on the screen are both complex and richly paradoxical, yet they are also circumscribed in scope from movie to movie. The railroad is not merely its physical manifestation; it *is* progress and civilisation. It threatens the openness and freedom of the West and individual enterprise, but it also promises the advantages of civilised life and brings the gentling influence of the Eastern heroine who plays the piano and uses an English saddle if she rides horses at all. The ambiguity and paradox contained in the western's images of the Iron Horse are as rich as our mixed feelings about civilisation and progress, but they are also limited to those feelings and those feelings only. The railroad is not interchangeable with other means of transportation in the western; its meanings

are not those which surround the images of a stagecoach, horse or covered wagon. From its first silent chugging to its clangorous present, the railroad in the history of the western film has not altered in its physical particularly or its specific significance; it is, indeed, an icon.

Now let us examine one of the most potential icons of SF cinema: the spaceship. Any inspection of the genre leads one inevitably to the conclusion that there is no *consistent* cluster of meanings provoked by the image of a spaceship. The visual treatments of the ship vary from film to film – and sometimes even vary within a single film. Beyond the fact that seeing a spaceship on the screen signals to the viewer that he is watching a film which does not take place in the present (and even that signal is weakening since space flight is now a reality), there is no constant meaning generated by that image; because there is no consistent meaning, there is little accumulation of 'emblematic power' carried by the object from movie to movie.

There are those films, for example, which treat the spaceship lovingly, positively, optimistically. There is no doubt as to the 'goodness' of a technology which can produce such a magnificent toy (although this goodness does not necessarily extend to the men who created the technology nor to the men who employ it). The ship itself is 'good'. It is aesthetically beautiful. It is fun to play with. It promises positive adventure, an ecstatic release from the gravitational demands of Earth, and it can remove us from ourselves and the complexity of life on our planet, taking us to new Edens and regeneration. In *Destination Moon* (Irving Pichel, 1950), the silvery sleekness of Ernest Fegté's single-stage spaceship almost palpably glows against the velvet black and star-bejewelled beauty of a mysterious but non-hostile space; it is breathtakingly beautiful, awe inspiring and yet warmly comforting like the night light in a child's bedroom. In the interior of the ship the crew delights in its weightlessness, playing games with gravity like children released in a schoolyard for recess. *When Worlds Collide* (Rudolph Mat, 1951), although its plot and themes evoke what John Baxter sees as 'a 1930s vision of Armageddon',[7] presents us with the positive image of a spaceship as an 'interplanetary Noah's Ark',[8] destined to carry a group of potential colonists from a doomed Earth to a new world. The spaceship, plumper and looking more fecund than its predecessor in *Destination Moon*, is visually divorced from the chaos and squabbling on Earth. Completed, it sits horizontally on its launching pad on a mountainside high above the confusion and it 'glows like gold, while the sky is in perpetual sunset'.[9] It visually promises, in contrast to the orange and dying hues of Earth, a golden dawn. Among other films which visually celebrate the spaceship and dwell on its surfaces with a caressive photographic wonder which precludes any ambiguous interpretation of its essential worth are *Conquest of Space* (Byron Haskin, 1955), with its lavish treatment of takeoffs, manueverings and landings, and *Forbidden Planet* (Fred Wilcox, 1956), whose 'palatial flying saucer'[10] operates 'via quanto-gravitetic hyperdrive and postonic transfiguration'.[11]

There is, however, a demonic side to the spaceship. In many films it is a trap from which there is little hope of escape. Its sleekness is visually cold and menacing, its surfaces hostile to human warmth. It functions mechanically and perfectly, ignorant of its creators and operators – or it malfunctions with malice, almost as if it could choose to do otherwise but prefers to rid itself of its unsleek and emotionally tainted human occupants. Instead of glowing like a night light, it coldly glitters like the blade of a stiletto. Instead of humming, it ticks. It evokes associations not of release, but of confinement. The womb-like and protective warmth of a positive visual treatment is nowhere apparent; rather, the ship is seen negatively, viewed with anti-technological suspicion, the images of it suggesting a tomb-like iciness, a coffin-like confinement. Its corridors and holds echo the sounds of human isolation or provide a haven for alien and lethal dusts and slimes; in unseen corners the subversion of human life begins.

In *20 Million Miles to Earth* (Nathan Juran, 1957), a spaceship returning to Earth from Venus crashes into the sea, carrying aboard the gelatinous embryo of an alien monster who subsequently hatches and proceeds, after growing, to terrorize Rome. The ship of *Mutiny in Outer Space* (Hugo Grimaldi, 1964), harbours a deadly fungus and transports it to a space station from whence it threatens to infect the Earth. These rockets and countless others harbour, support and transport alien 'things' which ultimately threaten not only Earth, but life itself as we know it. Even more menacing is the ship 'Discovery' which is to take astronauts Bowman and Poole to Jupiter in *2001: A Space Odyssey* (Stanley Kubrick, 1968). Although the film does not in any way deny the aesthetics of technology, it gives us in 'Discovery' a mechanism which barely tolerates and finally rejects human existence. Despite the vastness of the ship, the visual treatment impresses upon us a sense of claustrophobic and stifling confinement, cold and death. Most of the crew are temporarily frozen in cryogenic beds which resemble the sarcophagi of 'Egyptian mummies'.[12] Their movement from life to death because of a computer malfunction is discernable only through the impersonal and yet somehow malevolent red lights and computer print which let us know that their life support systems are no longer operative, and by the needles on the screens above their glass coffins which 'run amok on the graphs and then record the straight lines of extinction'.[13] Vast as it is, the ship allows no room for privacy; Bowman and Poole attempt to hide from the main computer HAL's omnipresent eyes and ears and unctious voice so they can discuss a possible solution to their predicament, but HAL can read lips and we are given a subjective camera shot to prove it. The astronauts are forced into their bulky and oppressive space-suits by the ship and its computer's increasing rejection of biological existence; HAL's paranoia is the ship's madness as well. This sense of entrapment and confinement is echoed in a more 'realistically' plotted film, *Marooned* (John Sturges, 1969), which 'was released during the week the world waited for Apollo 13'.[14] Three astronauts are confined in a malfunctioning space capsule; almost all the visuals are in close-up, showing the men cramped in their potential coffin orbiting the moon. The capsule is dubbed 'Ironman One', a name perhaps suggestive of the medieval torture chamber, called the 'Iron Maiden', in which the victim was most securely confined. And, in *Silent Running* (Douglas Trumbull, 1972), the space freighter 'Valley Forge' literally becomes a coffin for its crew, murdered by Freeman Lowell (the ecologically-minded protagonist) to protect his specimens of plant life from destruction. In this film, the visuals emphasise the vastness of solitary confinement, the deadness of a hermetically sealed existence which is silent and unyielding in its evocation of eternal loneliness.

The spaceship need not, however, be treated either positively or negatively. In numerous SF films, it is seen and used neutrally; its wonders are de-emphasised visually, made to seem commonplace, accepted not only by the characters but by the camera as well – matter-of-factly. The ship is merely a means to get from here to there – and has about as little visual impact and iconic power as a Greyhound bus. The dials and lights and switches are neither warmly supportive nor coldly sinister. They exist – like an automobile dashboard – as something familiar, conquered and forgotten. The complex workings of the ship pose no problems to the garage-mechanic confidence aboard. In *Marooned*, when the capsule malfunctions, one astronaut helplessly and impotently refers to the good old days in contrast to a present whose technology no longer admits salvation through tinkering: 'We used to fix the planes we flew with paperclips', he says, frustration apparent on his face. In those films which treat the spaceship like a Ford, repairs on malfunctions can be affected with the equivalents of paperclips and hairpins – or the problem is so 'understood' by the crew in their mechanic-like overalls that there is no mystery whatsoever connected to the malfunction. Films like *Rocketship X-M* (Kurt Neumann, 1950), *The Angry Red Planet* (Ib Melchior, 1959) and *Queen of Blood* (Curtis Harrington, 1965) treat the spaceship as a mechanical convenience which, devoid of wonder, will carry the crew to visually exciting adventures having little to do with a technology already accepted and dismissed. To be nostalgic for a moment, but also to the point, I fondly remember a scene aboard the spaceship in *The Angry Red Planet* in which the attitude toward the voyage to Mars is visually encapsulated: one sees the hero shaving with an electric razor and the heroine putting perfume behind her ears while a tape bank records a mundane log entry. This domestication of the spaceship leads one to recall the recent terminology used by actual astronauts on the various moon flights and aboard Sky Lab, their references to 'housekeeping'. Perhaps no film to date, however, has visually evoked the reduction of space flight to 'the ultimate in humdrum'[15] as has *2001: A Space Odyssey* in the section in which space-scientist Floyd flies Pan American to an orbiting spaceport and from there to the moon. As Joseph Morgenstern aptly comments: 'We see that space has been conquered. We also see it has been commercialised and … domesticated. Weightless stewardesses wear weightless smiles, passengers diddle with glorified Automat meals, watch karate on in-flight TV and never once glance out into the void to catch a beam of virgin light from Betelgeuse or Aldebaran'.[16]

The spaceship of the SF film, then, is in no way comparable to the railroad of the western in the latter's ability to communicate by its standard physical presence a constant and specific cluster of meanings throughout an entire genre. Unlike the railroad, in so far as the spaceship is a means of getting from here to there, it is, at times, functionally interchangeable with other modes of transportation like the time machine. In films such as *The Time Machine* (George Pal, 1960) and *The Time Travelers* (Ib Melchior, 1964), there are definite mechanisms which are at least physically differentiated from the spaceship, but in *World Without End* (Edward Bernds, 1956) and *Planet of the Apes* (Franklin Schaffner, 1968), the spaceship is the time machine. Unlike the railroad, not only can the spaceship's meanings and functions change from film to film and from decade to decade, but its very shape and colour are plastic and inconstant – ergo, the sleek and silver body of the ship in *Destination Moon*, the circular perfection of the flying saucer in *Forbidden Planet*, the bright yellow of the minaturised submarine in *Fantastic Voyage* (Richard Fleischer, 1966), and the combination of dark awkward bulk with the latticed delicacy of the plant domes on the 'Valley Forge' of *Silent Running*.[17] In addition, one can draw no conclusions from the films as to a tendency to visualise positively those ships which belong to us (Earthlings) and to visualise negatively those ships which belong to 'them' (aliens). Treated as a thing of beauty, the alien Klaatu's 350-foot flying saucer in *The Day the Earth Stood Still* (Robert Wise, 1951), is so pure in line, so ascetically designed by Lyle Wheeler and Addison Hehr, that it concretises the Platonic virtues of clarity, sanity, reason – virtues sadly lacking in the Washington, D.C., *mise-en-scène* in which the saucer comes to rest.[18] On the other hand, the Martians' individual war ships in *War of the Worlds* (Byron Haskin, 1953), could hardly be more sinister (and eerily beautiful) in their realisation; their shape suggests a cobra or the ocean's deadly manta ray, their silent movement over city and countryside metaphorically turns Earth's atmosphere turgid, their inexorable progress is punctuated only by the hissing of their incinerating rays.[19] The morally ambiguous and finally reprehensible Metalunans of *This Island Earth* (Joseph Newman, 1955) kidnap two Earth scientists and transport them to another world aboard a spaceship which is pointedly emphasised as a marvel of design, containing as it does such visual delights as a main control centre composed of a brightly-lit and revolving replica of the atom, and a series of translucent tubes which transform their occupants' molecular structure before our eyes.

Even more obvious in their capacity to change shape and colour and evocative power than spaceships are SF robots, all too frequently considered *en masse*, lumped together superficially and erroneously for critical convenience as emblematic of that vague term 'SF technology'. Yet, again, after seeing robots in a wide range of films, the viewer must be drawn inevitably to a recognition of their essentially expressive singularity. Gort, the huge intergalactic 'policeman' of *The Day the Earth Stood Still*, is definitely mysterious and menacing. Shot much of the time from a low angle, he is faceless; the otherwise smooth and metallic impenetrability of his blank visage is broken only by a visor which slowly opens to reveal a pulsing light or to emit incinerating rays after which it silently closes. His metallic surface, that visor, is a perverse visualisation of the medieval knight in shining armor, and the images of Gort are far removed from those of the lumbering but pleasant clumsiness of *Tobor the Great* (Lee Sholem, 1954), devised as the 'answer to the problem of human space flight'.[20] Tobor is treated with the reverence one usually reserves for a can opener, and in one highly comic scene, the robot – operated by a scientist's young grandson – walks stiff-leggedly about the house crashing into furniture and through doors in what amounts to a parody of Frankenstein's Monster. Tobor becomes a mindless hero because of his inexplicable emotional attachment to the little boy, explained away in the film as 'a new synthetic instinct, race-preservational concern for the young'.

Perhaps the most celebrated robot of all SF film, Robby of *Forbidden Planet*, bears no resemblance whatsoever to either Gort or Tobor. He was 'one of the most elaborate robots ever built for a film production. More than two months of trial and error labour were needed to install the 2,600 feet of electrical wiring that operated all his flashing lights, spinning antennae and the complicated gadgets that can be seen moving inside his transparent dome-shaped head'.[21] Visually, Robby looks like the offspring of some mad mating between the Michelin tire man and a juke box. He is 'a phenomenal mechanical man who can do more things in his small body than a roomful of business machines. He can make dresses, brew bourbon whiskey, perform feats of Herculean strength and speak 187 languages … through a neon-lit grille. What's more, he has the cultivated manners of a gentleman's gentleman'.[22] Although essentially a servant and programmed according to Isaac Asimov's famous Robotic Laws of SF literature (whose prime directive is that robots shall not harm human beings), Robby has a distinct personality. He is comically humourless and proud. ('This is my morning's batch of Isotope 217. The whole thing hardly comes to ten tons', he says, carrying the 'whole thing' around.) He is alternately petulant and helpful; 'when Francis [Anne Francis, who plays the role of Alta in the film] asks him for star sapphires, he croaks, 'Star sapphires take a week to crystallise. Will diamonds or emeralds do?' 'So long as they're big ones', Francis says. 'Five, ten, fifteen carats are on hand', Robby replies smugly'.[23] Robby's personality – although treated positively – prefigures to a degree the more sinister HAL of *2001: A Space Odyssey*, the computer (an immobile robot) who pushes Robby's comic *hubris* over the edge of reason. 'It is when HAL cannot admit he has made a mistake that he begins to suffer a paranoid breakdown, exhibiting overanxiety about his own infallible reputation and then trying to cover up his error by a murderous attack on the human witnesses.'[24] Ultimately, despite their similarity of manner, Robby and HAL are decades apart in both visualisation and meaning. Even if HAL were physically realised as more than 'a bug-eyed lens, a few slabs of glass',[25] it is hard to imagine him becoming the darling of the toy industry as Robby was to become after the release of *Forbidden Planet*. Robby's cute rotundity and comic primness, however, did not influence the subsequent screen images of robots. He was revived the following year in *The Invisible Boy* (Nicholas Nayfack, 1957), as 'the playmate of his inventor's ten-year-old son'[26] and then he disappeared.

Through the 1950s and 1960s, mobile robots continued their singular ways, sometimes visualised negatively, sometimes positively. And they also occasionally functioned interchangeably with other SF manifestations. In *Kronos* (Kurt Neumann, 1957), the robot is not an instrument of an alien race as was Gort in *The Day the Earth Stood Still*; brought to Earth by a fireball, Kronos *is* the alien, a 'strange machine, half creature, half construction'.[27] The huge electronic robot of *The Colossus of New York* (Eugene Louri, 1958), is a monster also, but his technologically-devised exterior is motivated by impulses found in the most traditional horror films. The robot's brain is not a complex gadget or an incomprehensible alien mind; it is the transplanted human brain of a scientist's son and it turns against its father, its creator, as Frankenstein's monster had done years before.

Perhaps the most innovative and intellectually complex treatment of robots was in the low budget *Creation of the Humanoids* (Wesley Barry, 1962), a film which considers the robot both positively and negatively. Here is posited and visualised a 'history' of robotics which leads to the creation of humanoids. The rationale for making the machines look and act human is that 'Humans found it psychologically unbearable to work side by side with machines'. Finally, the dividing line between robot and human is totally extinguished. Interpreting Asimov's Robotic Laws literally, the robots have been transferring and duplicating sick humans and accident victims into perfect mechanical bodies; as one robot says, 'Humanity doesn't always know what is in its best interest.' The film's protagonist, antirobot and member of the Order of Flesh and Blood, turns out to be a humanoid himself and – along with the heroine – is finally raised to the humanoid level R100 by undergoing an operation which will enable him to 'humanly' contribute to the reproductive process, a function which the robots see as crude but which 'fulfills a psychological need'. The film ends with a close-up of a pleasant-looking 'man' – our narrator – who smiles directly at the viewer and says, 'Of course the operation was a success or *you* wouldn't be here.'

The mixed treatment of robots is still apparent in the 1970s, in the new group of SF films which followed the commerical success of *2001*. The mechanical 'drones' of *Silent Running* are affectionately named Huey, Louey and Dewey, but although they waddle, their visual realisation reminds one less of Disney than of Tolkien. (Paul Zimmerman has aptly called them 'iron hobbits'.[28]) They are unaesthetic squat boxes on stumpy short legs, neither marvelous nor sinister in their physical realisation. It is their very ordinariness which makes them endearing. The drones are not superhuman like Gort or Robby, nor are they capable of insubordination like HAL; they don't even talk and their literal interpretation of the English language results occasionally in functional *faux pas*. And yet, as the film progresses and they are programmed to play poker, to perform a surgical operation, to be 'companions' to the isolated Lowell, the camera's treatment of them becomes progressively sympathetic and subjective, suggesting the merest hint of an animate life of some kind tucked away in their circuitry. As William Johnson points out in an excellent review of the film: 'They are machines with at least as much claim to animate being as a responsive and well-trained pet.'[29] The subjective camera lets us see out of their monitor-screen 'eyes' in a way which does not deny their machineness (the images are obviously poor TV quality and in black and white), but promotes as well a feeling of sentient watchfulness. 'When two drones, standing side by side, bury a dead crewman, Lowell sees part of the body through one drone's eye and part through the other's. Later, this odd subjectivity is taken a stage further: when Lowell is talking to the two drones, we (the audience) are shown their monitor screens, through which we look at Lowell and Lowell looks at us … Here, through the drones eyes, 'man is linked with his creation in a single circuit of consciousness'.[30]

Such is not the case in *Westworld* (Michael Crichton, 1973). The subjective camera may let us in one instance look through the scanner-eyes of the robot gunfighter (coldly played to mechanical perfection by Yul Brynner), but what we see is so remote from human vision that we are emphatically made aware not of a 'single circuit of consciousness', but of the vast separation between man and his creations. The little colored cubes which move geometrically over a graph paper-like grid may be aesthetically pleasing in their pastel visualisation, but they deny any but the most tenuous connection between the robot's vision and our (the audience) vision of a warm-blooded and un-geometric human being trying to escape from mechanical retribution. The robots which run amok in this nightmarish extension of Disneyland do so for no known reason. The initial competence of the scientific staff who run the resort, the calm and often boring visual emphasis on computers and monitor screens under expert control, the close-ups of mechanical 'operations' and repairs which in their detail suggest a technology thoroughly understood, routinised and conquered, all are quickly subverted by images which emphasise chaos and claustrophobia in the control centre, and a world outside which has been stolen from its anthropomorphic gods in white lab coats. The robots' malevolence which goes beyond mere malfunction is inexplicable in scientific terms. And Asimov's Robotic Laws seem purposefully mocked by the mechanical creations turned perfect and skilled killers.

The fluctuating meanings of what super-ficially seem to be iconic objects in SF films can be demonstrated many times over. Time and place are not constants either. The temporal setting of science fiction has no obligation to history; it may be a speculative past (*Creation of the Humanoids*), the present (*Seconds*, [John Frankenheimer, 1966]), the immediate future (*The Andromeda Strain*, [Robert Wise, 1971]), the distant future (*Forbidden Planet*), or a combination of times as in the *Planet of the Apes* series. As well, the settings of science fiction know no geographical boundaries and may be found literally anywhere – from smalltown USA, to distant and undiscovered galaxies, to the interior of a human body. Inevitably, then, we must be led away from a preoccupation with a search for consistent visual emblems into more ambiguous territory. It is the very plasticity of objects and settings in SF films which help define them as science fiction, and not their consistency. And it is this same plasticity of objects and settings that deny the kind of iconographic interpretation which critically illuminates the essentially static worlds of genres such as the western and gangster film.

Notes

1 Jim Kitses, *Horizons West* (Bloomington, IN.: Indiana University Press, 1969), p. 25.
2 Colin McArthur, *Underworld U.S.A.* (New York: The Viking Press, 1972), p. 24.
3 Ibid., p. 25.
4 For further discussion of the theoretical aspects of iconography in genre films, see Edward Buscombe's 'The Idea of Genre in the American Cinema', John Cawelti's *The Six-Gun Mystique* and Tom Ryall's 'The Notion of Genre'.
5 Michael Butor, 'Science Fiction: The Crisis of its Growth', *SF: The Other Side of Realism*, ed. Thomas D. Clareson (Bowling Green: Bowling Green Popular Press, 1971), p. 157.
6 Ibid.
7 John Baxter, *Science Fiction in the Cinema* (New York: Paperback Library, 1970), p. 150.
8 Jacques Siclier and Andrew S. Labarthe, *Images de la Science-Fiction* (Paris: Les Editions du Cerf, 1958), p. 62.
9 Baxter, *Science Fiction in the Cinema*, p. 151.
10 Ibid., p. 13.
11 Denis Gifford, *Science Fiction Film* (London: Studio Vista/Dutton Pictureback, 1971), p. 118.
12 Renata Adler, Review of *2001: A Space Odyssey* in *A Year in the Dark* (New York: Random House, 1969), p. 103.
13 Penelope Gilliatt, Review of *2001: A Space Odyssey* in *Film 68/69*, eds Hollis Alpert and Andrew Sarris (New York: Simon and Schuster, 1969), p. 56.
14 Gifford, *Science Fiction Film*, p. 130.
15 Gilliatt, in *Film 68/69*, p. 55.
16 Joseph Morgenstern, Review of *2001: A Space Odyssey* in *Film 68/69*, pp. 61–2.
17 For more information on the design these spaceships, see John Brosnan, *Movie Magic* (New York: St. Martin's Press, 1974).
18 Brosnan, *Movie Magic*, p. 197.
19 Ibid., pp. 191–4.
20 Gifford, *Science Fiction Film*, p. 54.
21 Brosnan, *Movie Magic*, pp. 198–9.
22 Bosley Crowther, Review of *Forbidden Planet* in the *New York Times*, (4 May 1956).
23 Baxter, *Science Fiction in the Cinema*, p. 113.
24 Alexander Walker, *Stanley Kubrick Directs* (New York: Harcourt, Brace, Jovanovich, 1971), p. 255.
25 Ibid., p. 258.
26 Gifford, *Science Fiction Film*, p. 59.
27 Baxter, *Science Fiction in the Cinema*, p. 136.
28 Paul D. Zimmerman, Review of *Silent Running* in *Newsweek* (20 March 1972), p. 113.
29 William Johnson, Review of *Silent Running* in *Film Quarterly* 25 (Summer 1972), p. 55.
30 Ibid.

'You've Got To Be Fucking Kidding!': Knowledge, Belief and Judgement in Science Fiction
Steve Neale

In John Carpenter's version of *The Thing* (1982), there is, as Philip Brophy has pointed out, one particularly telling line uttered during the course of one particularly telling and spectacular scene.[1] *The Thing* concerns an alien that first invades and then imitates both human and animal forms. It has infiltrated the base camp – and the crew – of a scientific observation post in Antarctica. At one point, in the guise of the body of an ailing crew member, it tears off the hands of the doctor who attempts to revive him; then, awakened, sprouts all manner of tentacles and limbs through the muscles and flesh of its host. It is shot down in flames. But one of its tentacles latches on to the crew member's head, which is now lying under the table:

> the tentacle lashes out of the head onto a door, and drags itself on its side. Just as it reaches the doorway, the crew see it and are transfixed by it. The head slowly turns upside down and, suddenly, eight insect-like legs rip through the head using it like a body. The sight is of an upside-down severed human head out of which have grown insect feet. As it 'walks' out the door, a crew member says *the* line of the film: 'You've got to be fucking kidding!'[2]

As Brophy goes on to show, the significance of this line lies in its twofold status. It is on the one hand a narrative event: a fictional remark made by a fictional character about a specific, fictional entity. As such it is a sign of the character's astonishment, an acknowledgement of what is for him the reality of the creature and its powers. On the other hand, it is what one might call both a 'textual' and an 'institutional' event: a remark addressed to the spectator by the film, and by the cinematic apparatus, about the nature of its special effects. As such it is the sign of a number of things. It is a sign that the film is, at this point at least, 'violently selfconscious' (to use Brophy's words):[3] it is aware that the Thing (and the world it inhabits) are cinematic fabrications, the product, in particular, of an up-to-date regime of special effects; it is aware that the powers of this regime have here been stretched to their limit; and it displays both those powers – and that awareness – to the full. It is a sign also of an awareness on the part of the spectator (an awareness often marked at this point by laughter): the spectator knows that the Thing is a fiction, a collocation of special effects; and the spectator now knows that the film knows too.

Despite this awareness, the special effects have had an effect. The spectator has been, like the fictional character, astonished and horrified. An effect of this kind is fundamental to science fiction in the cinema. So too, though, is the awareness. In fact, as I shall go on to argue, the effect and the awareness are interdependent. Indeed, one of the keys to understanding the attraction, the pleasure, the lure of science fiction lies precisely in the intricate intercalation of different forms, kinds and layers of knowledge, belief and judgement that a line like the one from *The Thing*, together with the effect it accompanies, serves both to correlate and mark. In order to identify a little more precisely the nature and function of these forms, kinds and layers, it is necessary to say something about narrative fiction and genre, about cinema and the nature of its images and sounds, and about the status and role of its special effects.

All narratives involve the representation of events and their agents. The primary purpose of these agents and events is to provide links in a narrative chain (a plot) on the one hand, and to occasion a range of aesthetic effects (like suspense, surprise and pathos) on the other. Narrative events and their agents are understood and adjudged on the basis of a variety of types of knowledge, and in accordance with a variety of different criteria. This knowledge and these criteria can either be internal and overt or external and implicit. Thus on the one hand the narrative can have its characters comment on one another, on the world they inhabit, and on the events that they encounter, thereby providing the spectator with an array of explicit information and judgements. Alternatively, it can rely on the spectator's own knowledge and values, appealing implicitly to information and criteria of judgement it presumes it shares with its audience. Most narratives in most genres in the cinema involve both kinds of knowledge and judgement. Thus, for example, two of the members of the crew in *The Thing* are called doctors, but the film does not at any point explain what a doctor is or does. It assumes we will know. However, soon after the Thing's first transformation on the base, one of the doctors performs an autopsy on its partially incinerated body. He is needed to provide both spectator and crew with the kind of information that the narrative cannot presume. He says:

'You see what we're talking about: here is an organism that imitates other life forms. And it imitates them perfectly. When this thing attacked our dogs it tried to digest them, absorb them, and in the process shape its own self to imitate them.'

This information is treated as authoritiative, in part because it is delivered, precisely, by an expert, and in part because it remains uncontested: it is the only explanation we are offered. However, a little later in the film there is both speculation and dispute. Two members of the crew are sent out onto the ice to investigate what looks like the remains of some kind of spaceship:

– 'Jesus, how long you figure this has been in the ice?'
– 'I'd say the ice this is buried in is a hundred thousand years old. At least.'

They return to base. The helicopter pilot, MacReady, explains what he thinks might have happened; and crewmen Childs and Palmer comment on what he says:

– 'I don't know. Thousands of years ago it crashes and this thing gets thrown out, or crawls out, and it ends up freezing in the ice.'
– 'I just can't believe any of this voodoo bullshit.'
– 'Happens all the time, man. They're falling out of the sky like flies. Government knows all about it. Right, Mac?'
– 'You believe any of this voodoo bullshit, Blair?'
– 'Childs, Childs. Chariots of the gods, man.'

In line with Colin MacCabe's argument that in conventional narrative films (or what he calls 'classic realist texts') the truthful view is the

view confirmed by the camera, by what we ourselves see, it is significant that we tend here to accept MacReady's account.[4] We do so not only because it is the only coherent account we are given but because all Childs offers is doubt, though this is important. Nor do we do so only because MacReady is played by the star of the film, Kurt Russell, though this is important too. We do so primarily because we have been shown MacReady actually looking at the spaceship's remains, and because we have been shown, in a pre-credit sequence, the spaceship crash. Thus this particular conversation, and the judgement it involves, is significant for what it can tell us about the articulation and acquisition of knowledge in any kind of narrative film. It is significant also, though, for what it can tell us about the nature and function of knowledge in science fiction in particular.

All fiction to some extent involves what has traditionally been called 'suspension of disbelief', by virtue of the fact that its agents and events are, by definition, unreal. In actual fact, while disbelief may well be involved, it is often knowledge and judgement that the spectator is required to suspend, as Ben Brewster has pointed out.[5] Thus in Vincent Minnelli's film, *The Cobweb* (1955), we have no choice but to accept the judgement of the film and of a number of the characters that the designs for a new set of curtains show artistic promise and skill, whether or not we may personally like them.[6] Similarly, we have no choice but to accept that the unconventional behaviour of many of the film's characters is due to neurosis, whether or not we have any precise knowledge of mental states and conditions, and whether or not we agree with the way they are portrayed and explained in the film. In *The Thing*, we have no choice but to accept the doctor's explanation that the Thing can absorb and imitate other life forms, and MacReady's thesis that it came from outer space, crashing to Earth in a spaceship. However, while *The Cobweb* is a contemporary drama, *The Thing* is science fiction. The cultural status of the events and narrative agents involved in the two films are therefore distinct. While they are in both films equally unreal, spaceships and shape-changing aliens – unlike curtains, neurotically inspired artistic talent and mentally disturbed behaviour – are conventionally adjudged in our culture as also inherently improbable.[7]

It is in this context that the conversation between Childs, MacReady and Palmer is particularly significant. For what is at stake here is precisely the improbability, not only of the film's own events, but of the reasons it gives for their occurrence. Childs's scepticism is especially important. For it articulates a position of doubt, a refusal to suspend disbelief, that is shown to be mistaken. But Palmer's ready acceptance of MacReady's explanation is also important. If Childs is sceptical, Palmer is naive (and slightly deranged). His enthusiastic evocation of the 'Chariots of the gods' is thus merely the equally unacceptable obverse of Childs's dismissive evocation of voodoo. MacReady's position, based as it is on direct observation and a coherent assessment of the facts – not on a refusal to face those facts, or on an acceptance of them only because they fit neatly into a pre-existing framework of irrational beliefs – emerges, therefore, by contrast, as all the more balanced, all the more credible, all the more convincing; all the more probable.

Like MacReady, *The Thing* is here engaged in a process of persuasion. Major aspects of its fictional world are, from a general cultural point of view, not only unlikely or impossible, but also, therefore, unknowable in advance and thus in need of explanation. The film is therefore involved both in establishing its own credibility, and in establishing its own regime of credence – the rules, the norms and the laws by which its events and agents can be understood and adjudged. What is probable or possible in this world? How does it operate? What is regarded within it as unusual, unlikely, inexplicable? How do we know when the explanations we are offered for the events that occur are right or wrong? And so on.

Such a process is of course very common in science fiction (as it is in other genres, like the horror film, which involve the depiction of improbable or 'marvellous' events). Common also is the twofold nature of this process, one in which exposition, explanation and the establishment of internal norms are coincident with the negotiation of a position of credibility – and the acknowledgement of positions of incredulity and doubt. Thus in *Close Encounters of the Third Kind* (1977), Roy Neary tries to explain to his wife what it is that he has witnessed. 'You're not going to believe what I saw', he says. And in the 1978 remake of *Invasion of the Body Snatchers*, Elizabeth Driscoll and others try to explain to a sceptical David Kibner that human beings are somehow being copied. 'Don't you think we know how insane this sounds?', she says. 'But what do you think we're doing? Do you think we're making it up?'

One of the reasons why we know that Elizabeth and the others are not 'making it up', one of the reasons why we, at least, believe what Roy has to say, is that, as in *The Thing*, we ourselves have seen what it is that is being referred to, what it is that is being explained. Inasmuch as this is the case, the processes and issues of judgement and belief are ultimately focused – and founded – on what it is we see, and hence ultimately also on the cinematic image and its powers.

In his essay 'The Imaginary Signifier', the film theorist Christian Metz has addressed in general terms the nature and the powers of the cinematic image – and cinematic sound – and the extent to which they involve, and depend on, specific regimes and structures of knowledge and belief.[8] Metz points out that the cinema is in many ways 'more perceptual' than other arts like music, literature, sculpture, painting and photography. It involves both vision and audition, and it involves the representation, in detail, of sound, of speech, of objects in space, and of movement and temporal progression. However, this 'numerical superiority' disappears when cinema is compared to arts like opera and theatre. For opera and theatre, too, involve several axes of perception, and are possessed of similar representational capacities.

> Their difference from the cinema lies elsewhere: they do not consist of *images*, the perceptions they offer to the eye and the ear are inscribed in a true space (not a photographed one), the same as that occupied by the public during the performance; everything the audience hear and see is actively produced in their presence, by human beings or props which are themselves present.[9]

In the cinema, by contrast, 'everything is recorded',[10] everything, therefore, is absent:

> Thus the cinema, 'more perceptual' than certain arts according to the list of its sensory registers, is also 'less perceptual' than others once the status of these perceptions is envisaged rather than their number of

diversity; for its perceptions are all in a sense 'false'. Or rather, the activity of perception it involves is real (the cinema is not a phantasy), but the perceived is not really the object, it is its shade, its phantom, its double, its *replica* in a new kind of mirror. It will be said that literature, after all, is itself only made of replicas (written words, presenting absent objects). But at least it does not present them to us with all the really perceived detail that the screen does ... The unique position of the cinema lies in this dual character of its signifier: unaccustomed perceptual wealth, but at the same time stamped with unreality to an unusual degree, and from the very outset.[11]

In the cinema, therefore, a dual and contra-dictory status is accorded its images and sounds. These images and sounds thus incrementally redouble the already contradictory status of any fiction they may be used to present: 'In the cinema it is not just the fictional signified, if there is one, that is thus made present in the mode of absence, it is from the outset the signifier.'[12]

Inasmuch as this is the case, the 'suspension of disbelief' required by any fiction – or more accurately, the suspension of judgement, on the one hand, coupled with a splitting or division of knowledge on the other (as can be encapsulated in a formula like 'I know this is fictional, unreal, but will nevertheless treat it as worthy of judgement, and therefore as worthy of credence') – is given, in the cinema, an additional twist ('I know that what is presented by means of these images and sounds is not really there, but nevertheless...'). Yet further twists are added when it comes to a genre like science fiction, which by definition deals, as we have seen, with the unlikely, and hence the unbelievable; and when it comes to the mobilisation, in cinematic science fiction, of a regime of special effects, of specially fabricated images and sounds, both to present and to authenticate its events, its agents and its settings.

Metz has discussed special effects in the cinema in '*Trucage* and the Film'.[13] He points out that '*trucages*' in the cinema are of various kinds, and can operate in a variety of different ways at a variety of distinct and different levels. Some, like the effects involved in fades and dissolves, are meant to be perceived. Others,

like the use of stuntmen and stand-ins, are not. Some, like back projection, are involved at the point of filming. Others, like wipes, are not. Some, like the use of models and make-up, are primarily profilmic (effects produced in front of the camera, but without the aid of its own particular technological capabilities). Others, like slow-motion and mattes, depend either upon the specific capacities of the camera, or upon other cinematographic devices and processes. And so on. At the moment of viewing, as opposed to the moment of production, the spectator is engaged in a number of mental operations. In the case of 'visible *trucages*' 'the spectator undertakes a type of spontaneous sorting out of the visible material of which the text is composed and ascribes only a portion of it to the diegesis [the fictional world]'.[14] In the case of the majority of effects usually termed, and regarded, as 'special effects', by contrast (the use of mattes, make-up, back projection, models and the like), 'the spectator *ascribes to the diegesis the totality of the visual elements furnished him*'.[15] Metz goes on to argue:

> In films of the fantastic, the impression of unreality is convincing only if the public has the feeling of partaking, not of some plausible illustration of a process obeying a nonhuman logic, but of a series of disquieting or 'impossible' events which nevertheless unfold before him in the guise of eventlike appearances.[16]

Thus here, once again, the spectator's credibility is subject to division: 'The spectator is not the victim of the machination to the point of being unaware that it exists, but he is not sufficiently conscious of it for it to lose its impact.'[17]

With this particular combination of forms of awareness and 'impact', we are back again at the point in *The Thing* at which the character utters his self-reflexive line. Here it is worth stressing, once more, the element of display the line involves. As Metz himself points out, while there is always a degree of duplicity, of secrecy, of the hidden attached to the use of special effects, there is always also 'something which flaunts itself'.[18] This flaunting both caters to – and counters – the spectator's awareness, while ensuring at the same time that cinema will take the credit for the impact. Either way, cinema gains. It is worth also stressing that, of course, both the impact itself, and hence the particular – and delicate – balance between impact and awareness, is always relative both to the capacities of cinema's special effects regimes as they exist at any point in time, and to the amount of capital expended on effects in production. As has already been pointed out, *The Thing* is concerned, among other things, not only to display the latest special effects, but also to display an awareness that they *are* the latest. It is also concerned, like other, often cheaper, science fiction and horror films to build in an element of camp, a tongue-in-cheek knowingness. This element is designed to protect the spectator (and hence the film) both from disappointment, should the effects fail to convince, or should their convincingness serve merely to highlight the improbable nature of that which they are used to represent; and also from genuine trauma, should the effects and what they represent be taken too seriously.

Metz draws on the psychoanalytic concept of disavowal, and on its model of the fetish, to pinpoint the nature of the divisions of knowledge and belief that the cinema, its fictions, and its special effects all, in their various ways, involve. Just as the fetish both avows and disavows an absence, a lack (the lack, for the fetishist proper, of the phallus wished for in the object of sexual desire), so the fictional representation, the cinematic image, and the special effect both avow and disavow something that does not actually exist.[19] Although, as a clinical perversion, fetishism is a specific psychic formation (and practice), it is, like all perversions, only a particular response to a universal human experience (in this case the experience of castration of insufficiency, loss and lack); only a particularised extension of a universal disavowal (the disavowal of the lack of the phallus the mark of power and selfsufficiency initially imagined as belonging to the mother). It thus provides a paradigm for

> all the splittings of belief which man will henceforth be capable of in the most varied domains, of all the infinitely complex unconscious and occasionally conscious interactions which he will allow himself between 'believing' and 'not believing' and which will on more than one occasion be of great assistance in resolving (or denying) delicate problems.[20]

Inasmuch as the institution of the cinema is one of the 'domains' to which Metz goes on to refer, a thesis such as this accounts both for the spectator's general capacity to believe (and at the same time to know), and for the extent to which that capacity can be exercised, multiplied, doubled and redoubled in a genre like science fiction. It accounts, too, for the extent to which knowledge and belief are foregrounded – highlighted as issues – in science fiction films, the extent to which, for instance, as we have seen, the characters themselves have often to suspend disbelief, have often to undergo a process of learning, have often to revise the habitual basis of the judgements that they make. What it cannot do, though, is predict how any one individual film will draw on this capacity and deal with these issues. As a final comment, it is perhaps worth suggesting in this context that the more interesting films will be those which work not, like *E.T.* (1982), simply to affirm belief (and the cinema's capacity to feed it), but those which, like *Invasion of the Body Snatchers* (in particular the 1956 version), work instead to link habitual perceptions, assumptions and judgements to issues and forms of social conformity – and in the process offer a challenge to both.

Notes

1 Philip Brophy, 'Horrality – the Textuality of Contemporary Horror Films', *Screen*, vol. 27, no. 1, 1986.

2 Ibid., p. 11.

3 Ibid.

4 Colin MacCabe, 'Realism and Cinema: Notes on Some Brechtian Theses', *Screen*, vol. 15, no. 2, 1974.

5 Ben Brewster, 'Film' in Dan Cohn-Sherbok and Michael Irwin, eds, *Exploring Reality*, London: Allen & Unwin, 1987, p. 153.

6 Ibid., pp. 152–3.

7 It is worth pointing out here that the problem of improbability is common to a number of genres, including the horror film and what might be termed the fantasy-adventure film (films like *Jason of the Argonauts*, *Clash of the Titans* and so on). It is no accident, therefore, that these genres often overlap (as in *The Thing* itself, on the one hand, and a film like *Star Wars* on the other). What, in part at least, distinguishes these genres from one another is the degree and the type of motivation, of justification, they offer for the extraordinary events and agents they portray. Science fiction, of course, justifies its improbabilities on 'scientific' (or quasi-scientific) grounds. It is worth pointing out also, though, that such a justification is as conventional, and itself as subject to judgements of improbability, as the supernatural

justifications of the gothic horror film, and that in the end, in any case, motivation is merely an alibi for the elaboration of aesthetic effects. (See Gerard Genette, 'Vraisemblance et motivation', in Genette, *Figures*, 11, Paris: Seuil, 1969.)

8 Christian Metz, 'The Imaginary Signifier', trans. Ben Brewster in Metz, *Psychoanalysis and Cinema*, London: Macmillan, 1982.

9 Ibid., p. 43.

10 Ibid.

11 Ibid., pp. 44–5.

12 Ibid., p. 44.

13 Christian Metz, '*Trucage* and the Film', trans. Françoise Meltzer, *Critical Inquiry*, vol. 3, no. 4, 1977.

14 Ibid., p. 667.

15 Ibid.

16 Ibid.

17 Ibid.

18 Ibid. p. 665.

19 Metz, 'The Imaginary Signifier', pp. 69–78. I have here tended to give a Lacanian account, using the term phallus, rather than a Freudian account, using the term penis, though Metz himself tends to use Freudian terms.

20 Ibid., p. 70.

'Sensuous Elaboration': Reason and the Visible in the Science Fiction Film

Barry Keith Grant

In this essay I want to explore the relation of science fiction to the cinema – that is to say, the relation between the genre of science fiction and the medium of film.[1] As I shall argue, the inherent nature of cinema as a visual medium has tended to work against the distinctive dynamics of science fiction as a genre. However, my intention is not to claim, as indeed some critics have, that 'science fiction film … is an intellectual impossibility'.[2] Clearly such a sweeping claim would be absurd, yet fans of science-fiction literature have lodged this complaint against science-fiction film frequently.

For my purpose here, we might begin to hack our way through what Darko Suvin calls the 'genealogical jungle' of science fiction by distinguishing it from horror.[3] Although the two genres share some of the same generic elements (iconography, character types, conventions), their treatment is notably different. So while the genres of science fiction and horror often overlap, even more so in film than in literature, the contrasts between them are rooted in the particular nature of science-fiction *film*.

Both science fiction and horror, along with fantasy, are types of narrative that have been called speculative fiction or structural fabulation.[4] Horror and science fiction are both rooted in the real world: the former works by positing something as horrifying in contrast to the normal, quotidian world; the latter by acknowledging to some extent contemporary scientific knowledge and the scientific method. Hence the close relationship between the two genres. Such works as Mary Shelley's novel *Frankenstein* (1817), Ridley Scott's *Alien* (1979), and the two versions of *The Thing* (1951, 1982) have been categorised as both science fiction *and* horror, for all employ iconography and conventions found in both genres. By contrast, fantasy narratives are based neither in the natural world nor in the supernatural, but the *supra*natural. As Robert Heinlein notes,

Science fiction and fantasy are as different as Karl Marx and Groucho Marx. Fantasy is constructed either by denying the real world *in toto* or at least by making a prime basis of the story one or more admittedly false premise – fairies, talking mules, trips through a looking glass, vampires, seacoast Bohemia, Mickey Mouse.[5]

The distinctive aim of fantasy, then, according to Lester del Rey, is to present 'alternative *impossibilities*'.[6]

Despite the narrative relation between horror and science fiction, the two genres offer experiences and pleasures strikingly different, in fact almost opposite, in nature. As such critics as Robert Scholes and Bruce Kawin have argued, the appeal of science fiction is primarily cognitive, while horror, as the genre's very name suggests, is essentially emotional.[7] Linda Williams has discussed the horror film as a 'body genre' – that is, one of those genres (like pornography and melodrama) that works by eliciting pronounced emotional and physiological excitation. Science-fiction, by contrast, is often defined more cerebrally as a philosophical openness described as a 'sense of wonder'. Science fiction critic Sam Moskowitz, quoting Rollo May, for example, invokes the phrase as the essential quality of science fiction and defines this sense of wonder as a heightened awareness and open attitude to new ideas.[8] Science fiction, quite unlike fantasy and horror, works to entertain alternative *possibilities*.

Perhaps, then, the fundamental distinction between the two genres is one of attitude: a closed response in horror, an open one in science fiction. Horror seeks to elicit terror and fear of something unknown or unacknowledged. According to Robin Wood's highly influential Freudian/Marxist analysis of the horror film, the genre's monsters represent a 'return of the repressed', forbidden desire disowned and projected outward by the protagonist.[9] Accordingly, in horror stories narrative consciousness is often trapped or contained, set in claustrophobic, enclosed places, as in the countless castles, vaults, tombs and chambers that typify the genre's dramatic spaces. And vision is often obscured, from Poe's 'The Pit and the Pendulum' (1843) to John Carpenter's *The Fog* (1979). Because the sleep of reason breeds monsters, horror tales emphasise darkness and night (Stephen King's *The Dark Half* [1990], the numerous movies entitled *Night of ...*) and superstition (*Halloween* [1978], *Friday the 13th* [1980] and the various *Curse(s) of ...*).

Tellingly, the narrator's struggle in Poe's story 'Descent into the Maelstrom' (1841) to employ empirical reasoning to prevent himself from being sucked below the surface is paradigmatic of the horror tale. By contrast, the rapt upward gaze of faces bathed in beatific light in Steven Spielberg's *Close Encounters of the Third Kind* (1977) is emblematic of the expansive thrust of science fiction. Vision in horror tales tends to focus down and inward, as in Poe's 'The Premature Burial' (1844) or David Cronenberg's *Parasite Murders* (a.k.a. *Shivers/They Came From Within*, 1975), while science fiction gazes up and out – from man's one small step in Jules Verne's *From the Earth to the Moon* (1865) to the giant step for mankind through the stargate in Stanley Kubrick's *2001: A Space Odyssey* (1968). Kawin sums up the difference by comparing the last lines of *The Thing* – the dire warning 'Keep watching the skies!' – and *Brainstorm* (1983) – the hopeful and expansive invitation to 'Look at the stars!'[10] It is no coincidence that one of the first science fiction movies of the sound era was entitled *Just Imagine* (1930).

For Damon Knight, 'Some widening of the mind's horizons, no matter in what direction' is what science fiction is all about.[11] In this sense science fiction narratives are, to use Méliès's own phrase, *voyages extraordinaires* which, befitting their frequent setting in the future and/or on parallel worlds, emphasise the vastness of space and the fluidity of time. Thus in science fiction, narrative point of view expands to entertain rather than contain new possibilities. As in, say, Olaf Stapledon's novel *Last and First Men* (1930) or H. G. Wells' *The Shape of Things to Come* (1933) and the film version *Things to Come* (1936), which Wells scripted, the dramatic conflict in science fiction is quite often exactly this: the difficulty of accepting rather than combating forces larger than the individual will. According to Suvin, the genre works by providing us with an experience of 'cognitive estrangement': as in Russian Formalism, our attention is returned to reality by the premises of science fiction tales, which make us question the givens of our world.[12]

In both Richard Matheson's *The Shrinking Man* (1956) and the film adaptation *The Incredible Shrinking Man* (1957), the mental perspective of the protagonist expands even as his body dwindles. At first Scott Carey is terrified by the new, challenging world in which he finds himself, but ultimately he achieves spiritual transcendence. His epiphanic perception, on the novel's final page, is that he has moved from the 'universe without' to the 'universe within': 'Why had he never thought of it; of the microscopic and the submicroscopic worlds? ... He'd always thought in terms of man's concept, not nature's ... But to nature there was no zero. Existence went on in endless cycles' (or, as the film concludes: 'To God there is no zero').[13]

The horrible dangers of an enlarged world are embodied in both novel and film in the spectacular form of a spider that comes to seem monstrously large. Both horror and science fiction make generic claims to monster movies – 'the Creature film sits (awkwardly, for some) between horror and SF', observes Vivian Sobchack[14] – but they are represented quite differently in the two genres. This difference follows from their respective orientations of vision. In horror, creatures are monstrous violations of ideological norms, while in science fiction monsters are often simply a different life form. Because of this difference in the treatment of the Other, as Sobchack observes, horror monsters threaten the disruption of moral and natural order, while those of science fiction address the disruption of the social order.[15]

So the monsters of horror are typically abject, sometimes explicitly unnameable, as in Stephen King's *It* (1986); but in science fiction they may be subjects of rational scrutiny, as in John W. Campbell Jr's novella 'Who Goes There?' (1938), the source of both versions of *The Thing*. Because the monsters of horror commonly represent 'the return of the repressed', they tend to be anthropomorphic (the vampire, the zombie, the mummy) and animalistic (the wolf man, cat people), to spring from our physical nature, albeit in unnatural or 'interstitial' form.[16] The Other of science fiction, however, frequently takes non-humanoid forms, whether animal (*War of the Worlds*, 1953), vegetable (*The Andromeda Strain*, 1970) or mineral (*The Monolith Monsters*, 1957).

The fundamental difference between science fiction and horror is conventionally represented within the two genres themselves as a differing emphasis on the mind (science fiction) and the body (horror). Science fiction focuses on heady issues, as in such movies as *The Brain from Planet Arous* (1958) and *The Mind of Mr Soames* (1969). The premiss in Poul Anderson's novel *Brain Wave* (1954) is that the human race is suddenly confronted with a quantum leap in intelligence. By contrast, horror commonly evokes our anxiety about the body, so vividly invoked in such horror films as *I Dismember Mama* (1972) and *The Texas Chain Saw Massacre* (1974). Indeed, many horror movies focus on the graphic spectacle of the violated body to such an extent that they have been referred to as 'meat movies'. For Philip Brophy, they tend 'to play not so much on the broad fear of Death, but more precisely on the fear of one's own body, of how one controls and relates to it'.[17] In many of these movies, such as the *Hellraiser* series, evisceration and flaying – that is, exposing the body as a visible site, are treated as the privileged moments of horror, the generic 'money shots'. (Indeed, it might even be argued that the history of the horror film traces a trajectory of gradual, inexorable surrender to the allure of the visible, and that the genre had reached an aesthetic impasse as a result of its wholesale capitulation to the representation of horror as that which is corporeal, physical – that is, *seen*.)

For Christian Metz, the chronological development from Lumière to Méliès marks an evolution of 'cinematography to cinema' – that is, from a conception of film as a recording tool to an artistic medium.[18] But it is perhaps more accurate to say that cinema is simultaneously Lumière and Méliès, science *and* fiction, for the film image is at once a concrete, scientific record of things in the real world ('*actualités*') and a selected account of that world ('*artificially arranged scenes*'). Dziga Vertov's Kino Eye, that unblinking machine capable of perceiving the world with a greater objective fidelity than the human eye, always open to that which is placed before it, would suggest that the cinema would be an ideal medium for conveying science fiction's sense of wonder. Indeed, cinema as a medium displays three central aspects central to the genre of science fiction: space, time and the machine – or the apparatus, in the terms of materialist film theory. (We might note in passing that these themes appear much less often in the horror genre.)

In cinema, narration proceeds by manipulating time and space, elongating and condensing both for dramatic and affective purposes. The techniques for achieving such spatial and temporal distortions constitute the foundation of classic narrative film, but such manipulations are central to documentary and experimental cinema as well. Across the range of different film practices the camera, the recording apparatus itself, seems capable of moving through both dimensions at once. Terry Ramsaye has noted how much the cinema resembles a time machine in his discussion of H. G. Wells's description of travelling through time in *The Time Machine* (1895).[19] (Later in the year Wells's book was published, inventor William Paul, whom Wells knew, applied for a patent for a machine that would provide simulated voyages through time.)

The cinematic machine, like the Constructors in Stanislaw Lem's novel *The Cyberiad* (1967), is a device capable of imagining and 'building' (through special effects) other machines infinitely more sophisticated than itself. Science fiction film has relied heavily on special effects, and these effects in turn constitute one of the particular pleasures of the genre. The genre's reliance on special effects is itself an enactment of science fiction's thematic concern with technology. It is therefore understandable that for many viewers the value of (that is to say, the pleasure derived from) science fiction movies is determined by the quality (synonymous with believability) of the special effects. For these viewers, nothing destroys the pleasure of a science fiction movie more than seeing the 'seams' in a matte shot or glimpsing the zipper on an alien's bodysuit. Even Richard Hodgens, an apparent purist who bemoans the lack of scientific knowledge in science fiction movies, seems to confuse the failure of some films' special effects to be 'convincing' with the plausibility and consistency of their narrative premises.[20]

Special effects are 'filmic moments of a *radically* filmic character',[21] for they seek to achieve unreality as realistically as possible – to engage 'our belief, not our suspension of disbelief', as Sobchack puts it. We marvel at special effects images at once for their fantastic content and for the power of their realisation. They announce the powers of cinema while, paradoxically, taming the imagination through the very fact of visual representation. This visualisation for the camera pulls the images from speculation to spectacle – in Sobchack's terms, it transforms the poetry of the possible into the prosaic realm of the visible.[22]

Because of the science fiction film's emphasis on special effects, the genre's primary appeal has been the kinetic excitement of action – that 'sensuous elaboration' which Susan Sontag describes as 'the aesthetics of destruction ... the peculiar beauties to be found in wreaking havoc, making a mess'.[23] (This pleasure is itself visualised in the 'bird's-eye view' shot in Alfred Hitchcock's 1963 (science fiction?) thriller *The Birds*, as the viewer is placed with the hovering birds looking down in seeming satisfied contemplation of the picturesque destruction they have wrought in the town below.) At least one subgenre of the science fiction film, the apocalyptic film, is founded on the promise of scenes of mass destruction. In these films, from *When Worlds Collide* (1951) to the more recent *Armageddon* and *Deep Impact* (both 1998), we eagerly await the climactic tidal wave that will sweep over New York and its famous landmarks of Western civilisation.

The paradigmatic example of this difference between science fiction in the two media is, perhaps, *Frankenstein*. Shelley's novel is a central early text in the history of science fiction literature – the 'first great myth of the Industrial age', in the words of Brian Aldiss[24] – while James Whale's 1931 movie is a classic horror film. In the film, philosophy is replaced by *frisson*, and the white magic of science becomes black.[25] Dr Frankenstein's laboratory, with its battery of crackling generators and steaming German Expressionist beakers – clearly influenced by Rotwang's laboratory in *Metropolis* (1926) – evokes not enlightened scientific inquiry but the dark supernatural world of the Gothic. The creature is transformed from a nimble and articulate being, an effective metaphor for Romantic *hubris* and encroaching industrialisation, into a lumbering, grunting monster. The movie is less interested in the moral implications of human artifice than in the frightening spectacle of Boris Karloff's stiff-legged strut, and so shifts the focus from, as it were, the doctor's dilemma to the revenge of the creature. The doctor's famous cackle, 'It's alive, it's alive', as uttered by actor Colin Clive, unmistakably marks him as an unhinged man – the familiar mad scientist of horror who has committed the hubristic sin of investigating phenomena 'Man was not meant to know'.

Monsters, phaser-gun gadgetry and large-scale destruction are staple motifs of science fiction literature, but they have been more prominent in science fiction cinema. If the cinema's BBBs (big-bosomed babes, in the jargon of the genre), as represented by *Fire Maidens From Outer Space* (1956) and Jane Fonda as *Barbarella* (1967), cannot hope to match the depictions in the science fiction pulps in the 'Golden Age' (approximately 1938 to 1950), it is only that actresses of flesh and blood could never equal the damsels in the fantastically stylised illustrations of the pulp covers – although Russ Meyer's amply-endowed women in *Dr Breedlove* (1964) come close.

Because film is primarily a visual medium, it tends to concentrate on the depiction of visual surfaces at the expense of contemplative depth. Science fiction's characteristic sense of wonder thus works differently in film than in literature. According to Cyril Kornbluth, 'The science fiction writer churns out symbols every time he writes of the future or an alternate present; he rolls out symbols of people, places, things, relationships, as fast as he can work his typewriter or his pen.'[26] Indeed, writing in the interrogative mode of science fiction rather than the declarative mode of realism is necessarily to write symbolically, for it is the extrapolative kind of writing that contemplates the potential of things, how things *might* be regarded (Suvin's 'cognitive estrangement'). Unlike words, which are rendered either as sounds or marks on paper, representational images are by contrast first and always objects in the material world, the things themselves before being symbolic of something else.[27]

In other genres, inherent symbolism is provided by visual icons which carry 'intrinsic charges of meaning independently of whatever is brought to them by particular directors'.[28] But, as Sobchack notes, the common objects in science fiction films, like spaceships, lack the iconographic consistency of other genres and are relatively 'unfixed'.[29] Still, science fiction films are shaped by the ideological constraints of the genre system, which typically features comfortable narrative closure. Even though science fiction movies allow us the anarchic pleasure of witnessing civilisation's destruction, the genre also offers us, at least in its classic form (similar to the gangster film, to which monster movies are closely related), the satisfaction of the restoration of social order. So in the monster movies that typified science fiction film during the 1950s (the period John Baxter refers to as 'Springtime for Caliban'),[30] the creatures, which almost always appear as the result of nuclear testing, are often finally destroyed with an 'ultimate weapon' that uses similar technology. In other words, the unfortunate results of sophisticated and potentially lethal technology are defeated by the creation of even more sophisticated and lethal technology.

In *The Beast from 20,000 Fathoms* (1953), for example, one of the movies that initiated the 1950s monster cycle, the elegiac atmosphere that informs Ray Bradbury's 1951 source story, 'The Fog Horn', is emphatically sacrificed for visual spectacle. The story is a mood piece about a lonely prehistoric creature drawn from the sea to a lighthouse by the melancholy sound of its horn. Bradbury's prose is more suggestive than concrete in its description, but the movie features a radioactive, mutated Rhedosaurus that wreaks havoc in New York City, with the requisite shots of physical destruction and stampeding pedestrians. In the film's climax, the army pursues the creature to Coney Island, for no particular reason other than the visual interest in showing the creature in proportion to the famous Cyclone roller coaster, where it is killed with a new nuclear warhead. Thus our fears about the possibility of nuclear holocaust are at once aroused and assuaged in a narrative trajectory that in short order became a soothing ritual in the myriad movies featuring genetically altered insects, reptiles and other asserted BEMs ('bug-eyed monsters') that soon followed. Of course, the ideological assurance of such narrative closure works across numerous genres, but in the specific case of science fiction it compromises the radical potential of the genre's extrapolative, speculative dynamic.

In recent years, the science fiction film has placed great emphasis upon the child, and this is no accident. Robin Wood has argued convincingly that recent American cinema generally has tended to construct the viewer as childlike,[31] in thrall to the illusion. In science fiction specifically, the generic sense of wonder, and by extension the position of the spectator, has been located in the image of a wide-eyed child. This development, of course, is largely

the result of the huge commercial success of George Lucas's *Star Wars* trilogy and Steven Spielberg's *Close Encounters* and *E.T.: The Extraterrestrial* (1982), all of which rank among the top box-office winners in film history. (The *Star Wars* cosmology became even more firmly entrenched in American cultural consciousness when former President Ronald Reagan named his national defence programme after Lucas's film and referred to the Soviet Union as the 'Evil Empire'.) Subsequent science fiction movies such as *Starman* (1984), *The Explorers* (1985), *Short Circuit* (1986), *Tron* (1982) and *The Last Starfighter* (1984) exhibited a new adolescent orientation, clearly showing the influence of the Lucas and Spielberg films. *Cocoon* (1985), with its premiss of alien lifeforms that change a swimming pool into a fountain of youth, even manages to make children of senior citizens.

Before Spielberg and Lucas, children were as sparse in science fiction films as in the stylised towns of the classic western. Aside from such rare exceptions as *Invaders From Mars* (1953) and *Village of the Damned* (1960, based on John Wyndham's *The Midwich Cuckoos*, 1957), until recently children tended to be neither heard nor seen in science fiction. In horror, however, children have been presented frequently as figures of evil rather than innocence. From *The Bad Seed* (1956) to Stephen King's *Pet Sematary* (1983), horror tales have depicted children as figures of demonic possession. Many of these movies, following upon the popularity of *Rosemary's Baby* (1968) and *The Exorcist* (1973), may be read as embodying adult fears of being 'possessed by children' – that is, of being obligated to them, an expression of cultural backlash against the centrality of the nuclear family in a period of dissolving marriages and more open sexual mores.

Discussing the infantilisation that informed much of Hollywood cinema in the 1980s, Wood refers to special effects as the exhibition of technological 'magic'. Tellingly, Lucas's special effects company is called Industrial Light and Magic – the name itself suggesting the kind of totemic power the popular audience ascribes to the sophisticated technology required to produce such visual illusions. As Carl Freedman notes, special effects tend to 'overwhelm the viewer, to bathe the perceptual apparatus of the filmgoer in the very 'filmicness' of film'.[32] This position is literalised by the placement of the camera (and hence the position of the spectator) in the genre's now-conventional special effects image described by Martin Rubin as 'a shot ... of an enormous spacecraft rumbling over the camera position, so that the entire underside passes overhead, massive, ominous, bristling with special effects paraphernalia'.[33] (The convention is nicely parodied in the opening shot of Mel Brooks's 1987 science fiction parody *Spaceballs*, with its enormous ship that rumbles past – and past, and past.)

The scopophilic pleasure of cinema is mobilised most intensely in special effects images, as viewers are swathed in their power. This wondrous dependence on special effects imagery is itself the subject of Paul Verhoeven's *Total Recall* (1990), based on Philip K. Dick's short story 'We Can Remember It For You Wholesale' (1966). Like Dick's story, the movie is a reflexive science fiction film about the extent to which we look to the image to provide our reality. The protagonist, Douglas Quaid, because of his memory implant, becomes incapable of distinguishing reality from fantasy: he does not know whether his adventure is the program he requested at Rekall, Inc, or if his actual identity has been accidentally uncovered. Viewers share Quaid's lack of epistemological certainty since they are incapable of detecting – indeed, are virtually challenged to detect – a flaw in the state-of-the-art special effects, that is, of distinguishing between what is 'real' and what is 'imagination'. Inevitably, the viewer regresses to that earliest phase of childhood Jacques Lacan calls the pre-Oedipal Imaginary, unable to distinguish the nature of the visual field. The world of the film, with its domestic wall projections of make-believe environments, mechanical taxi drivers and holographic projections, is a postmodern simulacrum, just as the visual media are for us in the real world. The landscape of recent popular cinema offers ample evidence that, like Quaid, we enjoy imagining ourselves as Arnold Schwarzenegger in non-stop action movies – just like *Total Recall*.

Verhoeven follows the same approach in his more recent *Starship Troopers* (1997), based on Heinlein's 1959 novel. The book is a rather straightforward account of the military mindset and values in the future when the human race is threatened by an extraterrestrial army of giant intelligent insects. Without a trace of irony, Heinlein uses the story to offer extended passages about the benefits of a social order organised by militaristic principles. The film, however, completely subverts the book's conservative ideology by deconstructing military guts and glory even as it provides it so completely. Again with state-of-the-art effects, Verhoeven shows us graphic battles between bugs and humans as soldiers are impaled, eviscerated and dismembered. The protagonists are all played by beautiful young actors with whom the audience can easily identify. But these scenes alternate with images of official government propaganda films (obviously inspired by the nationalistic fervour of Frank Capra's *Why We Fight* documentaries from World War Two) that clearly contradict the bloody truths of the war. In the film, the young people still march off to war full of optimistic faith, just as audiences flocked to the film to see the much-touted violence of its battle scenes.

Apart from Verhoeven's postmodern critiques, much of contemporary science fiction cinema has replaced the sense of wonder with the awe of mystification. Popular science fiction movies like *The Terminator* (1984) and *Predator* (1987), offering almost continuous spectacular action, seem to have succumbed fully to the siren call of the sensuous spectacle. Other science fiction films like *Alien*, *Blade Runner* (1982, based on Dick's 1968 *Do Androids Dream of Electric Sheep?*) and John Carpenter's 1982 version of *The Thing*, which propound ostensible humanist messages, are devoid of rounded characters and overwhelmed by production design and special effects, thus contradicting their own themes.

The starchild of *2001* looking down at Earth, returning our gaze to us for self-scrutiny, has become the regressive child/man of *Close Encounters* who, wanting to escape his adult responsibilities and enter the womb of the 'Mother' ship, gazes upwards, as if in religious devotion. If the reverential awe we accord science fiction images is a debasement of science fiction's distinctive philosophical attitude, it is because the film medium, and the generic system which organises so much of popular cinema, work to discourage the kind of speculative narrative that has challenged us to embrace what Arthur C. Clarke calls *Childhood's End*. Embodied in science fiction films most fully in special effects, the genre's characteristic sense of wonder is perhaps the ontological fulfilment of the nature of science fiction *cinema*.

Notes

1 This essay originally appeared in different form in *Literature/Film Quarterly*, vol. 14, no. 3, 1986, pp. 154–63. It is here reprinted from *Alien Zone 2*, ed. Annette Kuhn (London: Verso, 1999), pp. 16–29, with slight revisions.

2 John Baxter, *Science Fiction in the Cinema* (New York: Paperback Library, 1970), p. 8.

3 Darko Suvin, *Metamorphoses of Science Fiction* (New Haven, CT: Yale University Press, 1979), pp. 16–36.

4 Science fiction author Robert A. Heinlein uses the term 'speculative fiction' in his essay 'Science Fiction: Its Nature, Faults, and Virtues', in Basil Davenport, ed., *The Science Fiction Novel: Imagination and Social Criticism* (Chicago: Advent, 1969), pp. 14–48. 'Structural fabulation' is Robert Scholes's term in *Structural Fabulation: An Essay on Fiction of the Future* (Notre Dame, IN: University of Notre Dame Press, 1975).

5 Robert Heinlein, 'Preface' to *Tomorrow, the Stars*, New York: Doubleday, 1967, p. 8. See also Heinlein, 'Science Fiction'.

6 Lester del Rey, *The World of Science Fiction, 1926–1976: The History of a Subculture* (New York: Ballantine, 1979), pp. 6–9.

7 Scholes, *Structural Fabulation*; Bruce Kawin, 'Children of the Light', in Barry Keith Grant, ed., *Film Genre Reader II* (Austin: University of Texas Press, 1995), pp. 308–29.

8 Linda Williams, 'Film Bodies: Gender, Genre, and Excess', in Barry Keith Grant, ed., *Film Genre Reader II*, pp. 140–58; Sam Moskowitz, *Seekers of Tomorrow* (Westport, CT: Hyperion Press, 1974), p. 211.

9 Robin Wood, 'An Introduction to the American Horror Film', in Barry Keith Grant, ed., *Planks of Reason: Essays on the Horror Film* (Metuchen, NJ: Scarecrow Press, 1984), pp. 164–200.

10 Kawin, 'Children of the Light', p. 256.

11 Damon Knight, *In Search of Wonder*, 2nd edn. (Chicago: Advent, 1967), p. 13.

12 Suvin, *Metamorphoses of Science Fiction*

13 Richard Matheson, *The Shrinking Man* (New York: Bantam, 1969), p. 188.

14 Vivian C. Sobchack, *The Limits of Infinity: The American Science Fiction Film* (New York: A. S. Barnes, 1980), p. 47.

15 Ibid., p. 30.

16 For a discussion of Julia Kristeva's concept of abjection as applied to the horror film, see Barbara Creed, *The Monstrous-Feminine: Film, Feminism, Psychoanalysis* (London and New York: Routledge, 1993). On monsters as interstitial beings, see Noel Carroll, *The Philosophy of Horror, or Paradoxes of the Heart* (New York and London: Routledge, 1990), pp. 31–5.

17 Philip Brophy, 'Horrality – The Textuality of Contemporary Horror Films', *Screen*, vol. 27, no. 1, 1986, p. 8.

18 Christian Metz, *Film Language: A Semiotics of the Cinema*, trans. Michael Taylor (New York: Oxford University Press, 1974), p. 44.

19 Terry Ramsaye, *A Million and One Night: A History of the Motion Picture through 1925* (New York: Touchstone, 1986), pp. 153–4.

20 Richard Hodgens, 'A Brief and Tragical History of the Science Fiction Film', *Film Quarterly*, vol. 13, no. 2, 1959, p. 31.

21 Carl Freedman, 'Kubrick's *2001* and the Possibility of a Science Fiction Cinema', *Science Fiction Studies*, no. 75, 1998, p. 305.

22 Sobchack, *The Limits of Infinity*, p. 88.

23 Susan Sontag, 'The Aesthetics of Destruction', in *Against Interpretation* (New York: Delta, 1966), p. 212.

24 Brian Aldiss, *Billion Year Spree: The True History of Science Fiction* (New York: Schocken Books), 1974, p. 23.

25 Hodgens, 'A Brief and Tragical History'.

26 C. M. Kornbluth, 'The Failure of the Science Fiction Novel as Social Criticism', in Davenport, ed., *The Science Fiction Novel*, p. 54.

27 Of course, the recent use of Computer Generated Imagery in science-fiction special effects complicates such claims about cinema's indexical fidelity to the real world.

28 Colin McArthur, *Underworld USA* (New York: Viking Press, 1972), p. 19.

29 Sobchack, *The Limits of Infinity*, pp. 64–87.

30 Baxter, *Science Fiction in the Cinema*, p. 100.

31 Robin Wood, *Hollywood from Vietnam to Reagan*, New York: Columbia University Press, 1986, p. 163.

32 Freedman, 'Kubrick's *2001*', p. 306.

33 Martin Rubin, 'Genre and Technology: Variant Attitudes in Science Fiction Literature and Film', *Persistence of Vision*, nos 3/4, 1986, p. 107.

Between Science Fact and Science Fiction: Spielberg's Digital Dinosaurs, Possible Worlds, and the New Aesthetic Realism

Warren Buckland

The film's screenwriter, David Koepp, doubling as an extra, gets gobbled up by the T-Rex in San Diego. He is listed as 'Unlucky Bastard' in the credits, and that could stand for the writer in this sort of movie, destined to be upstaged by Spielberg and special effects.[1]

This is not science fiction; it's science eventuality.[2]

Why do Spielberg's dinosaurs hold our attention and fascination? One potential answer is that they are not simply fictional, but exist in what philosophers of modal logic call a 'possible world'. A possible world is a modal extension of the 'actual world'. Fiction, on the other hand, we can think of as a purely imaginary world that runs parallel to, but is autonomous from, the actual world. Due to the scientific research underlying both *Jurassic Park* (Steven Spielberg, 1993) and *The Lost World* (Steven Spielberg, 1997) – extraction of prehistoric DNA from insects fossilised in amber – I will argue that both films articulate a possible world because they show one possibility that can emerge from a state of affairs in the actual world. Moreover, beyond Spielberg's dinosaurs, possible world theory can enable film theorists to rethink the nature of filmic fictionality and representation by clarifying both the meaning of concepts such as mimeticism, realism, depiction, deception, and illusion, and the way these are actualised in the cinema by techniques and technologies such as linear perspective, editing and special effects.

This process of rethinking and clarification is timely because of the transition taking place in the film industry – from cinema's nineteenth-century technologies (optics, mechanics, photochemistry) to digital technology. I shall limit myself to: examining the unique way special effects in the post-photographic (that is, digital) image articulate possible worlds;

identifying the aesthetics of this digital image – or, more precisely, an image that is a composite of the photographic and the digital. I also want to argue that special effects in the digital image have a function to perform beyond the creation of spectacle. Of course, special effects are employed in many films precisely for this purpose. They are also employed to create funny ridiculous effects (as in Tim Burton's *Mars Attacks!* [1996]). But some films, such as *Jurassic Park* and *The Lost World*, go beyond spectacle by employing special effects to articulate a possible world. Yet critics and theorists of contemporary Hollywood cinema ignore this difference and see no function to special effects beyond the creation of spectacle. Such critics and theorists are unwittingly reproducing the rhetoric of auteur criticism of the late 1950s (particularly the extreme positions of François Truffaut and Fereydoun Hoveyda in *Cahiers du cinéma*) who fetishised *mise-en-scène*, except that contemporary Hollywood critics are fetishising digital special effects. To divorce digital special effects from their representational function in films such as *Jurassic Park* and *The Lost World* negates their articulation of a possible world.

Mise-en-scène and special effects

Contemporary Hollywood cinema is frequently identified as promoting the image at the expense of narrative. Typical of this approach is the following comment by Jean Douchet: '[Today] cinema has given up the purpose and the thinking behind individual shots [and narrative], in favour of images – rootless, textureless images – designed to violently impress by constantly inflating their spectacular qualities'.[3] In this recent statement, Douchet is being dismissive of a cinema that, for him, emphasises the image over narrative. This is quite unusual, because in the 1960s he advocated, along with other critics writing for *Cahiers du cinéma*, a reading strategy that placed emphasis on *mise-en-scène* rather than narrative, or the script:

Auteur criticism : mise-en-scène/script

The exemplary instance of this exclusive emphasis on *mise-en-scène* is Fereydoun Hoveyda's paper on Nicholas Ray's *Party Girl* (1958). Hoveyda wrote: '*Party Girl* has an idiotic story. So what? If the substratum of cinematic work was made up simply of plot convolutions unravelling on the screen, then we could just annex the Seventh Art to literature, be content with illustrating novels and short stories ... and hand over *Cahiers* to literary critics'.[4] This type of extreme argument extends from Truffaut's paper, 'A certain tendency of the French cinema',[5] in which he attacked the French 'cinema of quality' for its privileging of the script rather than the cinematic dimensions of film (precisely, *mise-en-scène*, or *mise-en-shot*, if we want to be pedantic). In the 1970s, contemporary film theory translated the auteurists' opposition between *mise-en-scène* and script into the opposition between image (or spectacle) and narrative:[6]

'contemporary' film : image-spectacle/
narrative   theory

The views of the extreme elements within auteurism are too well known and would be of little importance today if their views were not being reproduced in critical discourse on contemporary Hollywood cinema. In other words, many of today's critics and reviewers are unwittingly reproducing the same rhetoric that Truffaut, Hoveyda and others used to discuss Hollywood cinema in the early 1960s, except that today's critics have replaced a fetishisation of *mise-en-scène* with a fetishisation of special effects and spectacular action sequences. The rhetoric from Hoveyda that I have just quoted can be found in numerous reviews and essays on films such as those of Spielberg. Representative of this position is Derek Malcolm's review of *The Lost World*: 'But the special effects brook no argument, being marginally better than those of the first time round and wrapped around the camera like chocolate around an ice-cream. That is all. The rest is amazing dross from the man who made *Jaws*, *Close Encounters* and *ET* – and *Schindler's List*'.[7] However, that is not all. The critics' almost exclusive emphasis on *mise-en-scène* and special effects is specious at best. It clouded Hoveyda's judgements, since he ended up arguing that '*Party Girl* is Ray's most interesting film to date'[8] – that is, better than *They Live by Night* and *Rebel Without a Cause*. The elements of *mise-en-scène* that make *Party Girl* an important film for Hoveyda include the following: the moment when Canetto goes into Vicki's dressing room and burns himself on one of the light bulbs that decorate the mirror; the

shot of the man sketching during the courtroom scene; the drops of water from the bouquet of roses that cling to Vicki's face; the little flame in the grate reflected in the corner of the mirror as Vicki and Farrell kiss; the scene where Vicki visits Farrell in his apartment: soon after Vicki arrives, Farrell has to leave in order to meet his gangster boss Rico; when Farrell returns later in the evening, Vicki comes out of the bedroom wearing all her clothes but is barefoot.[9]

In contrast to contemporary critics and reviewers, I will attempt to argue here that *Jurassic Park* and *The Lost World* cannot be reduced to special effects. To reduce it in this way is similar to Hoveyda talking about light bulbs, drops of water, flames reflected in mirrors and Vicki barefoot in *Party Girl*.[10] In *Jurassic Park* and *The Lost World*, an emphasis on special effects divorced from narrative ignores the film's articulation of a possible world:

Contemporary : special effects/
Hollywood   possible worlds criticism

Moreover, I shall be arguing that the film's representation of a possible world motivates the special effects and action sequences.

'To be existent without existing'
                                    – Thomas Pavel

The theory of possible worlds challenges the philosophy of logical positivism. For logical positivists, the actual world is all there is, and non-actual objects or possible states of affairs are meaningless because they do not correspond to immediate experience. It was only with the rise of modal logic (the study of possibility and necessity) that analytic philosophers broadened their horizons to analyse the possible as well as the actual.

Modal logic studies the range of possible – that is, non-actual – states of affairs that emerge from an actual state of affairs. These possible states of affairs have a different ontological status, or mode of being, to the actual state of affairs. Possible worlds form part of the actual world but have a different ontological status to the actual world. Whereas logical positivists would argue that non-actual possibilities are meaningless, because they do not correspond to the actual world, possible world theorists argue that non-actual possibilities correspond to an abstract, hypothetical state of affairs, which has an ontological status, but one different to the actual world.[11]

The basic premiss of possible world theory is that the world could have been otherwise. David Lewis argues that:

> It is uncontroversially true that things might be otherwise than they are. I believe, and so do you, that things could have been different in countless ways ... I therefore believe in the existence of entities that might be called 'ways things could have been'. I prefer to call them 'possible worlds'.[12]

Possible world theory has also entered the historian's domain. It may seem paradoxical that a discipline concerned with what has been can learn anything from the counterfactual philosophical position of possible world theory. Yet the work of R. W. Fogel in the 1960s and, more recently, Niall Ferguson's *Virtual History: Alternatives and Counterfactuals*,[13] propose that possible world theory is able to illuminate what actually happened, propositions that cannot be drawn from the consultation of historical records alone. For example, the proposition that 'Napoleon did not die on St Helena but escaped to New Orleans' contradicts a fact in the actual world (that Napoleon did die on St Helena). For this reason, logical positivists would classify this proposition as empty and meaningless. But in possible world history, that proposition is meaningful in an alternative possible world – a world in which Napoleon escaped to New Orleans. This possible world is not simply fictional because it is grounded in the actual world – namely, the historical figure of Napoleon; and arguably, he remains the same historical figure in the alternative possible world, even though his life story is altered. Because they are grounded in the actual world, possible worlds cannot simply be dismissed as a *jeux d'esprit*, an entertaining diversion from the determinism of thinking only about what already exists or existed. Possible world theory enables us to see the contingency of both historical and cultural events, and even natural laws such as biological evolution.

From the perspective of possible worlds, reality is not simply made up of a fixed realm of facts open to immediate experience, but a complex structure of sub-systems, only one of which is actual. In opposition to logical positivism, the theory of possible worlds stipulates that 'non-actual possibilities make perfectly coherent systems which can be described and qualified, imagined and intended and to which one can refer'.[14] The notion that one can refer to a non-actual – possible – world has a significant number of consequences for theories of filmic representation, some of which I shall examine later in this paper.

The actual and the possible

Michael Crichton's novels *Jurassic Park* and *The Lost World*, as with most of his other novels (such as *Congo* and *Disclosure*, as well as his films *Westworld* [1973] and *Coma* [1978]), do not operate in the realm of pure fantasy, imagination or fiction, but present a possible world, by drawing out extreme consequences from a non-fictional state of affairs in the actual world. When Spielberg's film of *Jurassic Park* was released in Britain in July 1993, much of the media speculated on the actual possibility of cloning dinosaurs. In the BBC programme *Spielberg and the Dinosaurs* one of the first questions asked was: 'With genetic engineering advancing at a startling speed, what if scientists were able to recreate the extinct species?'[15] The programme suggested that *Jurassic Park* is based upon a credible scientific foundation – the extraction of prehistoric DNA from bloodsucking insects fossilised in amber. In the *New Scientist*, the palaeontologist Douglas Palmer briefly summed up the research carried out by George Poinar of insects trapped in amber, and noted that: 'There is an enormous potential for research in molecular palaeontology ... two American research teams have independently extracted tiny fragments of insect DNA from fossils embedded in amber. ... Just a few weeks ago, one of the teams led by Poinar obtained fragments of the oldest yet known DNA, extracted from a Cretaceous plant-eating beetle found in amber from Lebanon'.[16] However, he sounded a sceptical note concerning the possibility of extracting dinosaur DNA from bloodsucking insects and genetically engineering dinosaurs from it: 'Speculation on the viability of recreating dinosaurs from fossil DNA endures despite its extreme improbability'.[17] Nonetheless, in *The Times* Ben Macintyre wrote: 'Despite the assurances of experts that the 'science' expounded [in] *Jurassic Park* is only tenuously based on reality, the film has had an effect on America in some way reminiscent of Orson Welles's 1938 broadcast of *War of the Worlds*'. He went on to write 'Even the relentlessly serious-minded *New York Times* felt moved to reassure its readers in an editorial that 'scientists will not have the capability any time soon of resurrecting the dinosaurs".[18]

The reason for this intense media speculation is that dinosaurs (unlike many aliens and monsters found in other films) did actually exist, and the research into fossilised DNA is actually being carried out, only not on the level articulated in Crichton's novels and Spielberg's films. For Nigel Hawkes: 'The power of the book [*Jurassic Park*] rests not on puff but plausibility. Like most of the best science fiction, it hovers on the very edge of science fact, creating a nightmare out of the kind of gentle speculation that scientists enjoy'.[19] It is this non-fictional dimension to *Jurassic Park* and *The Lost World* that enables us to characterise them as articulating a possible world. Both the novels and the films are taking new scientific ideas to their logical (or illogical) conclusions. In other words, *Jurassic Park* and *The Lost World* begin from scientific fact (the actual), and then take these facts to their furthest consequences (the possible). Because it takes as its starting point the actual, then it is not pure fantasy (the impossible). The novels and the films therefore present a possible world, which exists between science fact and science fiction. Below I shall begin to distinguish the presentation of a possible world in novels and films, since film (or, at least, the post-photographic, or digital image) has the unique capacity to present access to possible worlds, and to combine seamlessly the actual with the possible, by means of digital special effects. The specificity of film's presentation of possible worlds therefore lies in its digital capacity.

Others have theorised a similar concept to possible worlds. In *Hauntings* Joseph Natoli outlines the relation between the inconceivable and conceivable in popular film, and suggests that the ability to make the inconceivable appear conceivable is one of the main attractions of a film. He writes:

the film [can make] conceivable what the culture had not itself held as conceivable. The film [can bring] to the level of representation what has not already existed as a 'something' within the culture. The culture couldn't give us the means to categorise ... popular

films do put off and play with the as-yet inconceivable. And we are, as viewers, the ones toward whom all of this putting off and taking on is directed.[20]

Similarly, in a discussion of the difference between imagination and fantasy, Ernst Bloch argues that only imagination possesses what he calls 'an expectable not-yet existence ... [that] anticipates a real potentiality'.[21] Likewise, in *The Fantastic* Todorov identifies a form of literature he calls the 'instrumental marvellous', in which 'we find gadgets, technological developments unrealised in the period described but, after all, quite possible'.[22]

The reference world in *Jurassic Park* and *The Lost World* is not the actual world (these films are not documentaries), nor is it a purely imaginary world (these films are not purely fictional either). Their reference world is a possible world that is very similar to the actual world. Previously we saw how possible world historians altered the laws of historical fact to produce counterfactual histories. *Jurassic Park* and *The Lost World* mark their difference to the actual world by altering a scientific law of nature – namely, biological evolution by means of genetic engineering. The fact that this genetic engineering is being carried out in the actual world, only not on the scale depicted in *Jurassic Park* and *The Lost World*, demonstrates that there is a strong accessibility relation, or compatibility, between the actual world and the possible world of *Jurassic Park* and *The Lost World*. The research in molecular palaeontology mentioned previously has not discovered any dinosaur DNA; it has discovered prehistoric insect DNA. *Jurassic Park* and *The Lost World* represent a possible world from the extremely small probability in the actual world of eventually finding dinosaur DNA in a blood-sucking insect fossilised in amber and then 'growing' dinosaurs from this DNA. However, Spielberg has actualised this extremely small probability on the movie screen with the aid of digital special effects.[23]

Contemporary Hollywood: a composite cinema

We currently see before our very eyes in contemporary Hollywood cinema a composite – a composite of the optical (or photographic) and the digital (or post-photographic) image. In the following section. I shall attempt to determine the aesthetics and epistemic status of the composite.

Photography is dependent upon the presence of pre-existing real objects, whose appearance is automatically reproduced by means of optics and photochemistry (or electronics, in the case of video). The photographic image is therefore indexically bound to the actual world. The photographic is an analogue of the real. However, the digital (or post-photographic) image is not determined or limited to the actual world in the same way. Whereas the photographic image is an analogue of the pre-existing real objects whose appearance it reproduces automatically, the digital image is produced by numerical digital codes, each of which is then realised on screen as a pixel, on point of light. The continuous lines, masses and contours of the analogue are divided up into discontinuous, discrete fragments of information, or pixels, on a monitor. Lucia Santella Braga points out that:

Each pixel corresponds to numerical values that enable the computer to assign it a precise position in the two dimensional space of the screen, within a generally Cartesian coordinate system. To those coordinates are added chromatic coordinates. The numerical values [the digital code] transform each fragment into entirely discontinuous and quantified elements, distinct from the other elements, over which full control is exercised.[24]

The crucial phrase here is 'over which full control is exercised'. The 'filmmaker' has the potential to transform each pixel into an entirely different value, for each pixel is defined in terms of a numerical matrix that can be modified and transformed by a mathematical algorithm. 'The result', writes Braga, 'is that the numerical image is under perpetual metamorphosis, oscillating between the image that is actualised on the screen and the virtual image or infinite set of potential images that can be calculated by the computer'.[25]

Practitioners of the special effects industry distinguish between invisible and visible special effects. Invisible special effects, which constitute up to ninety percent of the work of the special effects industry, simulate events in the actual world that are too expensive or inconvenient to produce, such as the waves in James Cameron's

Titanic (1997). As their name implies, invisible special effects are not meant to be noticed (as special effects) by film spectators. Visible special effects, on the other hand, simulate events that are impossible in the actual world (but which are possible in an alternative world), such as the dinosaurs in *Jurassic Park* and *The Lost World*. The crucial aesthetic point in relation to the digital special effects in these two films in particular is that, while clearly visible, these effects attempt to hide behind an iconic appearance; that is, they are visible special effects masquerading as invisible effects. In other words, the digital images combine the aesthetics of both visible and invisible special effects, since they have the potential to replicate the realism and illusionism of the photographic image by conferring a perfect photographic credibility upon objects that do not exist in the actual world.

From this discussion it is possible to determine the motivation for the digital special effects in Spielberg's *Jurassic Park* and *The Lost World*: namely, to simulate the actuality of dinosaurs living in the present day. This actuality is of course an illusion – or, more accurately, what Richard Allen calls a sensory deception,[26] which shows dinosaurs inhabiting a world that otherwise looks like the actual world. In accordance with Allen's term, we see something that does not exist, but this does not necessarily lead us to believe that it actually exists. Of course, such deceptions have been created before by optically printing two separately filmed events onto the same strip of film. The result is a composite, or layered image. In theory, this optically produced composite fabricates a spatio-temporal unity, giving the impression that the two separate events are taking place at the same diegetic space and time. The first event may be of live actions, and the second event may consist of stop-motion animation. However, the optical and photochemical equipment used in this process has inherent limitations that cannot be disguised, such as loss of resolution, grain and hard edge matte lines. Therefore, although optical composites can always give the impression that the two separate events occupy the same screen space, they eventually fall short in convincing the increasingly sophisticated spectator that the separate events occupy the same diegesis. Digital compositing equipment does not have the technical limitations inherent in optical printers, and so it can create a more seamless blend of live action and animation, leading to the deception that the composited events do occupy the same diegesis.

In *Jurassic Park* and *The Lost World*, this deception is heightened even further in the moments when the digital dinosaurs and live-action characters interact. In these shots, Industrial Light and Magic (ILM) has created a seamless fusion of live action and computer-generated dinosaurs. Such a fusion and interaction greatly contributes to the realism of these films. We can even argue that (however paradoxical it may sound) the shots showing the humans and digital dinosaurs interacting are the digital equivalent of the long takes and deep focus shots praised by André Bazin for their spatial density and surplus of realism, in opposition to the synthetic and unrealistic effects created by editing. According to Bazin, there are three types of realism in the cinema: an *ontological* realism, which (to paraphrase Bazin) restores to the object and the decor their existential density, the weight of their presence; a *dramatic* realism, which refuses to separate the actor from the decor, the foreground from the background; and a *psychological* realism, which brings the spectator back to the real conditions of perception, a perception which is never completely predetermined.[27] For Bazin, all three types of realism are achieved via the long take and deep focus, because these techniques maintain spatial unity.

In light of the exponential advances in film theory since Bazin, we need to discuss a fourth type of realism in the cinema: the impression of reality, developed in the 1970s within a psychoanalytic (read Lacanian) framework, of which Stephen Heath's work on suture is representative.[28] As is well known, suture designates a process whereby the spectator is continually positioned and repositioned in an imaginary, as opposed to symbolic, relation to the image. Positioned in an imaginary relation to the image, the spectator enjoys a sense of mastery and pleasure, since she/he gains the impression of being an all-perceiving eye (analogous to the child at the mirror phase). The result of this imaginary positioning is that the spectator perceives the space of the image as unified and harmonious. For Heath, this position of imaginary plenitude and spatial unity constitutes the cinema's impression of reality. This impression is not, therefore, based on the

image's relation to profilmic reality, but on the cinema's ability to conceal from the spectator the symbolic dimension of the image (the image as signifier, as representing lack). Inevitably, the symbolic dimension of the image becomes apparent to the spectator when this illusion of all-seeingness is broken – most notably, when attention is drawn to offscreen space. The spectator's perception of spatial unity and harmony in the image is similarly broken. But a cut to this offscreen space realigns the spectator to an imaginary relation to the image (that is, sutures the spectator back into the film), and restores to the image the sense of unity and harmony – at least until the symbolic dimension of the image becomes noticeable to the spectator once more. According to this theory, realism is nothing more than an effect of the successful positioning of the spectator into an imaginary relation to the image, a position which creates a sense that the film's space and diegesis is unified and harmonious.

Heath and Bazin share this privileging of spatial and diegetic unity, despite the many differences that otherwise distinguish their respective accounts (Heath's emphasis that this unity is imaginary, that it has ideological effects, and so on). Bazin privileges spatial unity throughout his work, but I shall look at the long footnote to his essay 'The virtues and limitations of montage'.[29] He refers to a scene from the film *Where No Vultures Fly* (Harry Watt, 1951). The film is about a young family who set up a game reserve in South Africa. In the scene that Bazin discusses, the young son of the family picks up a lion cub in the bush and takes it home. The lioness detects the child's scent and begins to follow him. The lioness and the child with the cub are filmed separately, and the shots are simply edited together. But as the child reaches home, the director abandons his montage of separate shots that has kept the protagonists apart and gives us instead parents, child and lioness all in the same full shot. 'This single frame', writes Bazin, in 'which trickery is out of the question gives immediate and retroactive authenticity to the very banal montage that preceded it'.[30] In this particular example, the realism of the shot for Bazin is a matter of spatial unity, in which the child and the lioness clearly occupy the same diegetic space. Indeed, Bazin concludes his footnote by writing that: 'Realism here resides in the homogeneity of space'.[31] More specifically, the realism resides in the fact that this homogeneity of space is created optically.

In the digital images of Spielberg's dinosaur films, trickery is of course employed to bring together in the same full shot humans and dinosaurs. The first sighting of the digitally created dinosaurs in *Jurassic Park* is significant in this respect. Approximately twenty minutes into the film, Grant (Sam Neil) and Sattler (Laura Dern) are given a tour of the park, where they see the dinosaurs roaming around. The dinosaurs, however, do not simply 'appear' in the film; instead, they are depicted through a strongly orchestrated point-of-view sequence. The jeep transporting Grant and Sattler is brought to a sudden halt. In the back, Grant looks off-screen right and the camera dollies in on his face. The camera cuts to a new position as he then jumps out of his seat, takes off his hat and sunglasses, maintaining his face full frame. But instead of cutting to what he sees, the camera instead cuts to Sattler, sitting in the front seat of the jeep looking at a large leaf. Two additional shots then depict Grant's hand as he forcefully turns her head away from the leaf and towards off-screen space. She similarly jumps out of her seat, mouth agape, and takes off her sunglasses. Only then do we cut to this off-screen space – of a brachiosaur. Furthermore, Grant and Sattler appear in the shot, which therefore only represents their awareness, rather than their actual point of view. Or, in Edward Branigan's terms, the shot is externally (rather than internally) focalised around the collective gaze of Grant and Sattler, since they are present in the shot of the brachiosaur.[32] Numerous shots of other interactions between humans and dinosaurs populate both *Jurassic Park* and *The Lost World*. What this means is that ILM has created a seamless composite of both the digital and analogue image in the same shot – that is, layers, combines and merges the digital and the analogue into a single coherent image, resulting in a unified diegetic space. The films that ILM has worked on during the 1990s (not only Spielberg's dinosaur films, but also *Hook* [1991], *Terminator 2* [1991], *Death Becomes Her* [1992] and *Dragonheart* [1996]) constitute an authentic composite – or a mixed-media – cinema.

Contemporary Hollywood has thus combined features of digital special effects with narrational procedures of illusionist realism. Another instance of this can be seen in respect of camera movement which, rather as it did with the advent of sound, poses special problems for the composite mode. Initially, it was impossible to use camera movement when compositing live action with special effects or animation. But ILM was able to overcome this fundamental principle of compositing in their breakthrough film *Who Framed Roger Rabbit?* (Robert Zemeckis, 1988). This film created a seamless fusion of cel animation and live action while using extensive camera movement:

> The commandment of locking down cameras [that is, keeping them stationary] for effects photography was particularly strict in filming and compositing live action and animated elements. *Who Framed Roger Rabbit?* would not only break the mold and have a lively camera tracking both live actors and animated cartoon characters, it would be up to ILM to see that the twain would meet to create through optical alchemy a world where humans and cartoons could live together.[33]

In previous attempts to combine live action and cel animation, the live action had to be filmed using a stationary camera to provide the animators with fixed reference points around which to integrate the animation. However, this resulted in a static composite in which the live action and animation, although occupying the same screen space did not fabricate the impression that they are interacting with one another in the same diegesis. With *Who Framed Roger Rabbit?*, ILM created a more believable composite partly by means of camera movement, which gave the impression that the camera is equally following the live action and cartoons, resulting in the illusion that they are occupying the same diegesis. This impression is created through the compositing of digital special effects and live action by means of motion control.[34]

Advances in computer technology and software enabled Spielberg to use more complex camera movements in *The Lost World* that in *Jurassic Park*, as well as more intricate interactions between the digital dinosaurs and the live action. The result was a believable composite of live action and computer-generated dinosaurs. *The Lost World* begins with an intricate interaction between a young girl and dozens of small compys. When Ian

Malcolm (Jeff Goldblum) and his team visit Site B on Isla Sorna, they first encounter a herd of stegosauruses which, significantly, pass in front of, as well as behind the team. And when the second team, headed by Roland Tembo and Peter Ludlow, invade the island in an attempt to catch the dinosaurs we see 3-D interaction between them and the digital dinosaurs. And this is the primary difference between *Jurassic Park* and *The Lost World*: it is not a matter of fifty percent more dinosaurs in the second film, but a more complex series of composited interactions between the live action and computer-generated dinosaurs.

What are the consequences of this process of compositing the photographic and post-photographic images using digital rather than optical technology? The interactions created between the digital dinosaurs and live action/real backgrounds within a single shot help to create a new realism in the digital image, for the effects create the illusion of spatial and diegetic unity. This is analogous to Bazin's discussion of spatial unity in the shot from *Where No Vultures Fly*. Moreover, ILM's digital compositing creates all three types of realism identified by Bazin: ontological realism, in that the digital dinosaurs appear to have equal weight and density as the photographic background and live action characters; dramatic realism, in that they are seamlessly blended into, and interact with, the photographic background and live-action characters; and psychological realism, in that they are seen to occupy the same space as the photographic background and live-action characters. Finally, Heath's discussion of the impression of reality – in which this impression is created by suturing the spectator into an imaginary relation to the image, producing the impression that the image's space is unified and harmonious – is also applicable to the new digital technology, since it conceals the symbolic mechanisms from the spectator more seamlessly than optical technology, thus suturing the spectator into this imaginary relation. It is in the reproduction of the three types of realism central to the Hollywood feature film as conceived by Bazin, together with Heath's theory of suture, that digital cinema continues the practices of realism and illusionism.

As a final point, the composite mode has also developed a digital effect that reinforces the impression that digital and analogue events take place in the same unified space and diegesis:

the illusion that spectators are watching movement. This effect is the motion blur. In live-action shots, when people and objects move, they become blurred. However, when objects are moved via stop-motion animation they are not blurred; instead, the animated model simply consists of quick, hard movements. As each frame is exposed, it photographs a still model. Before the next frame is exposed, the model is moved very slightly. The next frame then records the result of that motion, but it does not photograph the motion itself. The result is that the model is always pin sharp, however fast it is meant to be moving. But in producing motion in Spielberg's digital dinosaurs, motion blur is added to the image. In the composites, the live action characters have optical blur when they move, and the digital dinosaurs have digital blur when they move. This 'limitation', which is automatically generated in the photographic image and simulated in the digital image, strengthens the illusion that the humans and dinosaurs occupy the same diegesis.

We are now in a better position to consider the spectator's investment in the realism and illusionism of the image in the composite mode. As we have already seen, the special effects in films such as *Jurassic Park* and *The Lost World* attempt to combine the aesthetics of both visible and invisible digital special effects – to repeat what I said above, they have the potential to replicate the realism and illusionism of the photographic image by conferring a perfect photographic credibility upon objects that do not exist in the actual world. In other words, digital special effects simulate realism and illusionism as theorised by both Bazin and Heath, whereas in other films, visible special effects by themselves are used to create totally synthetic, futuristic worlds. For the moment, we are only concerned with the digital image's simulation of realism and illusionism and, more particularly, in the way spectators react to this simulation.

Firstly, we can look at the two approaches to the way the film spectator's set of beliefs regarding the realism and illusionism of the fiction film have been theorised – the psychoanalytic theory (epitomised in Heath's theory of suture, discussed above) and the more recent cognitive theory (of Joseph Anderson, David Bordwell, Noel Carroll, Murray Smith and Ed Tan).[35] The difference between these two theories of fictional representation concerns the ontological commitment the spectator is regarded as investing in the fictional objects. In psychoanalytic theory the investment is high, to the extent that it involves a modification of consciousness (the spectator is positioned in an imaginary relation to the image), whereas in cognitive theory the investment is low or zero. For cognitivists, the spectator simply knows that fictional objects are unreal; there is no need to resort to systems of belief regarding the spectator's investment in the ontology of fictional objects. For this reason, cognitivists tend to reject the illusionistic theory of realism altogether.

Whether either the psychoanalytic or the cognitive theory offers an accurate or plausible account of fiction is a moot point. What I want to emphasise here is that theories of fictional representation cannot adequately characterise the belief system that spectators require to comprehend the worlds articulated in films such as *Jurassic Park* and *The Lost World*. When presented with a possible world on screen, spectators do not make a high ontological commitment to the reality of the objects on screen, but neither do they simply reject them as imaginary. The digital image can, by means of special effects, make the possible believable. The spectator's system of belief can be characterised in terms of 'What if', 'As if', or 'What might have been' propositional attitudes. The modality of these propositions indicate that (*pace* the modal realism of David Lewis), the existence of possible worlds is mind dependent. This conceptual approach to possible worlds reveals the hierarchy set up by possible world theorists, which posits that only actual states of affairs exist – that is, are mind independent. Possible, or unactualised states of affairs are mind dependent. Possible worlds exist in so far as they are thought of, hypothesised, imagined or assumed. Nonetheless, possible world theory is not merely concerned with the possibility in thought of unactualised states of affairs, but with the probability of occurrence of the unactualised but possible state of affairs. This is what makes films that articulate a possible world so compelling: the probability of occurrence of scientists finding dinosaur DNA and 'growing' dinosaurs from it, are presented as if they were mind independent – that is, actual states of affairs. The power in the presentation of a possible world is increased when it is actualised on the movie screen with

the aid of digital special effects, which create the perceptual illusion that the possible world is actual. The spectator's belief system regarding films that articulate possible worlds can therefore be characterised as a combination of modal propositions (descriptions of possible worlds) and declarative propositions (which describe the actual world).

One advantage of the theory of possible worlds to film theory is that it explores the interface between a film and social reality, but without returning to any naive theories of mimeticism. Marie-Laure Ryan points out that: 'The pragmatic purpose of counterfactuals is not to create alternative possible worlds for their own sake, but to make a point about [the actual world]',[36] namely, to emphasise that the actual world is not necessarily the best of all possible worlds, and that the actual world can be otherwise if a different set of conditions prevail.

Hopefully, the value of the theory of possible worlds in understanding the huge attraction of Crichton's novels and Spielberg's films is more evident. *Jurassic Park* and *The Lost World*, the books and the films, represent a possible world, which can be summarised as follows: 'If dinosaurs could be resurrected by scientists using dinosaur DNA extracted from prehistoric blood-sucking insects fossilised in amber, then these books or films show one possible outcome'. Spielberg's films go one step further than Crichton's novels because digital special effects create a new aesthetic realism by making visible and believable a possible world.

As with the best science fiction, Spielberg's *Jurassic Park* and *The Lost World* are grounded in science fact, but they go beyond those facts to create a possible world where the extreme consequences of the social and economic exploitation of contemporary technology are graphically illustrated using digital special effects.

Many film critics and theorists give the impression that special effects and action sequences are unmotivated in contemporary Hollywood cinema. In some films, of course, they are. But in *Jurassic Park* and *The Lost World*, digital special effects are motivated by the attempt to make the possible believable. Critics who discuss these films in terms of unmotivated special effects are unwittingly continuing the auteur criticism of the early

1960s by ignoring or by-passing the script in favour of *mise-en-scène*. The extremist members of *Cahiers du cinéma* fetishised *mise-en-scène*. In a similar vein, contemporary film critics and theorists fetishise special effects.

Spielberg's two films are not representing in a neutral manner the world of Crichton's novels, since the production technology of the digital image is actualising that world through the process of visual concretisation and intensification. In the end, Spielberg's two films are not only representing what is technologically possible in genetic engineering in another world, but also what is possible in digital special effects technology in the actual world.

I would like to thank Thomas Elsaesser for his comments on an earlier draft of this paper.

Notes

1 Quentin Curtis on *The Lost World*, *Daily Telegraph*, 18 July 1997, p. 24.

2 Steven Spielberg, quoted in the press kit for *Jurassic Park* (Universal Studios, 1993).

3 Jean Douchet, quoted in Thomas Elsaesser, 'Louis Lumière: the cinema's first virtualist?', in Thomas Elsaesser and Kay Hoffmann (eds), *Cinema Futures: Cain, Abel or Cable? The Screen Arts in the Digital Age* (Amsterdam: Amsterdam University Press, 1998), p. 45.

4 Fereydoun Hoveyda, 'Nicholas Ray's reply: *Party Girl*', in Jim Hillier (ed.), *Cahiers du cinéma: The 1960s* (Cambridge, MA: Harvard University Press, 1986), p. 123.

5 François Truffaut, 'A certain tendency of the French cinema', in Bill Nichols (ed.), *Movies and Methods* (Berkeley, CA: University of California Press, 1976), pp. 224–37.

6 Stephen Heath, 'Narrative space', in Philip Rosen (ed.), *Narrative, Apparatus, Ideology: A Film Theory Reader* (New York: Columbia University Press, 1986), pp. 379–420; editors of *Cahiers du cinéma*, 'John Ford's *Young Mr Lincoln*', in Rosen (ed.), *Narrative, Apparatus, Ideology*, pp. 444–82.

7 Derek Malcolm, 'Monster munch'. *The Guardian*, 18 July 1997, p. 8.

8 Hoveyda, 'Nicholas Ray's reply', p. 130.

9 Ibid., p. 125.

10 Leland Poague has developed a deconstructionist type of film criticism that also concentrates on 'inessential' details. See 'Links in the chain: *Psycho* and film classicism', in Marshall Deutelbaum and Leland Poague (eds). *A Hitchcock Reader* (Ames, IA: Iowa State University Press, 1986), pp. 340–9. See also Tom Conley, *Film Hieroglyphs: Ruptures in Classical Cinema* (Minneapolis: University of Minnesota Press, 1991).

11 The issue is more complex, because different philosophers ascribe a different ontological status to possible worlds. At one extreme, modal realists such as David Lewis argue that possible worlds have the same physical status as the actual world. At the other extreme, antirealists such as Nelson Goodman argue that all worlds only have a virtual existence. The view of possible worlds I outline in the text is called moderate realism, and is developed by Alvin Plantinga, Robert Stalnaker and Saul Kripke, among others. They avoid the extreme claims made by modal realists and antirealists by setting up a hierarchy between actual and possible worlds. See the authors' contributions in Michael Loux (ed.), *The Possible and the Actual: Readings in the Metaphysics of Modality* (Ithaca, NY: Cornell University Press, 1979).

12 David Lewis, 'Possible worlds', in Loux (ed.), *The Possible and the Actual*, p. 182.

13 Robert W. Fogel, *Railroads and American Economic Growth: Essays in Econometric History* (Baltimore: Johns Hopkins University Press, 1964); Niall Ferguson (ed.), *Virtual History: Alternatives and Counterfactuals* (London: Picadox, 1997).

14 Auth Ronen, *Possible Worlds in Literary Theory* (Cambridge: Cambridge University Press, 1994), p. 25.

15 *Spielberg and the Dinosaurs*, tx 12 July 1993, BBC1.

16 Douglas Palmer, 'Dr Faustus meets the dinosaurs', *New Scientist*, vol. 139, no. 1880 (1993), p. 43.

17 Ibid.

18 Ben Macintyre, 'Mad scientists on the loose', *The Times*, 25 June 1993, p. 14.

19 Nigel Hawkes, 'Reviving rex', *The Times Magazine*, 12 June 1993, p. 32.

20 Joseph Natoli, *Hauntings: Popular Film and American Culture 1990–1992* (Albany, NY: SUNY Press, 1994), pp. 3–4.

21 Ernst Bloch, *The Utopian Function of Art and Literature: Selected Essays* (Cambridge, MA: MIT Press, 1988), p. 105.

22 Tzvetan Todorov, *The Fantastic* (Ithaca, NY: Cornell University Press, 1973), p. 56.

23 Of course, Spielberg also employed the Stan Winston Studio to design and build the five action dinosaurs. However, these are 'profilmic' special effects that can also be found in theme parks; here I am only concerned with specifically filmic special effects.

24 Lucia Santella Braga, 'The prephotographic, the photographic, and the postphotographic', in Winfried Nöth (ed.), *Semiotics of the Media* (Berlin: Mouton de Gruyter, 1997), p. 125.

25 Ibid., p. 126.

26 Richard Allen, *Projecting Illusion: Film Spectatorship and the Impression of Reality* (Cambridge: Cambridge University Press, 1995).

27 André Bazin, *Orson Welles: A Critical View* (Los Angeles: Acrobat Books, 1991), p. 80.

28 Stephen Heath, *Questions of Cinema* (London: Macmillan, 1981), esp. Chapter 3.

29 André Bazin, 'The virtues and limitations of montage', in *What is Cinema?* Volume 1, trans. Hugh Gray (Berkeley, CA: University of California Press, 1967), pp. 41–52.

30 Ibid, p. 49.

31 Ibid, p. 50.

32 Edward Branigan, *Narrative Comprehension and Film* (London and New York: Routledge, 1992), pp. 100–7.

33 Mark Cotta Vaz, *Industrial Light and Magic: Into the Digital Realm* (London: Virgin Publishing, 1996), p. 123.

34 Motion control is a technique that creates repeatable camera movement by programming the movement into a computer. For an account of the way motion control is combined with live action and digital special effects, see Alison McMahan, 'E-motional control', *Millimeter* (November 1989), pp. 123–32.

35 Joseph Anderson, *The Reality of Illusion: An Ecological Approach to Cognitive Film Theory* (Carbondale, IL: Southern Illinois University Press, 1996); David Bordwell, *Narration in the Fiction Film* (London: Routledge, 1985); Noël Carroll, *Theorizing the Moving Image* (New York: Cambridge University Press, 1996); Murray Smith, *Engaging Characters: Fiction, Emotion, and the Cinema* (Oxford: Clarendon Press, 1995); Ed Tan, *Emotions and the Structure of Narrative Film: Film as an Emotion Machine* (New Jersey: Lawrance Erlbaum Associates, 1996).

36 Marie-Laure Ryan, *Possible Worlds, Artificial Intelligence and Narrative Theory* (Bloomington, IN: Indiana University Press, 1991), p. 48.

SCIENCE FICTION'S
DISASTER IMAGINATION

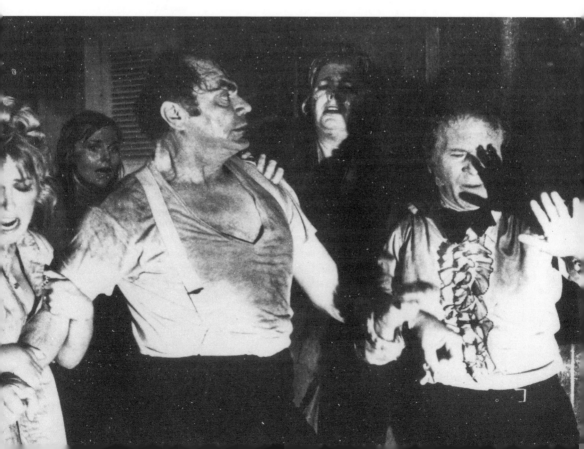

TWO | SCIENCE FICTION'S DISASTER IMAGINATION

While a great deal of science fiction is marked by its sense of wonder and, at least by its narrative closure, utopian idealism, there is much science fiction that is haunted by dystopian sentiments and apocalyptic scenarios. Above any comparable genre, science fiction seems to be able to represent and reproduce the individual and collective fears, paranoias and cultural and political transformations that exist in society. Science fiction can do this because by its definition it is delineated by the word 'fiction', and because its landscapes, narratives and ideological centres are seemingly so far removed from the 'realism' of the actual world by its time travel and future technology metaphors. Science fiction exists in possible worlds and imaginable futures, but the myths that are (barely) buried in its fantastic belly are ones that speak to people in the signs and codes of their everyday lives.

Science fiction's disaster imagination, to appropriate the title of Susan Sontag's seminal essay that heads this section, produces a vision of the (sometimes immediate) future that has gone badly wrong. Totalitarian regimes have taken over, big business has strangled individual sovereignty to death, technology has produced a race of clones or is on the verge of exterminating humanity or has laid waist to crops and fields, or bugs, bacteria, viruses and experiments have resulted in some disastrous meddling with nature, where humankind is just about to be wiped out. On the one hand, these critical dystopias can be seen to be a challenge to dominant ideology, offering its audiences powerful glimpses of where current forces and developments are taking them so that they can begin to get a critical and potentially oppositional view on it. On the other hand, such disaster narratives can be seen to be healing scenarios, ideological playgrounds for the airing and sharing of contests and conflicts that are only ever represented as such to smooth over the cracks and sutures of the modern world. In this conception the science fiction disaster scenario provides an arena for a type of social glue to be applied.

Susan Sontag looks at what she calls a sub-genre of science fiction films from the 1950s to the time the essay was written in 1965. Sontag argues that these science fiction films are about the 'aesthetics of destruction, with the peculiar beauties to be found in wreaking havoc, making a mess. And it is in the imagery of destruction that the core of a good science fiction lies.' Sontag goes on to argue that these images and scenarios of destruction serve two complimentary functions. First, they work to explore the 'deepest anxieties about contemporary experience'. Second, they are 'strongly moralistic' fables that in their representations and resolutions provide a 'utopian fantasy' space where all problems are easily resolved. As a consequence, Sontag concludes, 'there is absolutely no social criticism, of even the most implicit kind, in science fiction films'.

Michael Ryan and Douglas Kellner's position on this is more complex. They argue that there are two types of dystopian/technophobic text: there are those texts that work to a conservative and essentialist paradigm and which often involve a terrifying anti-humanist technology being counter-posed against an idealistic 'natural'; and there are those texts that project liberal-critical viewpoints around technology and nature and which consequently challenge the conservative binary oppositions that structure such relationships. Ryan and Kellner argue that Blade Runner works in this way: 'the film deconstructs the opposites – human/technology, reason/feeling, culture/nature – that underwrite the conservative fear of technology by refusing to privilege one pole of the dichotomy over another'. For Ryan and Kellner, 'dystopias or negative utopias' cluster together in the 1970s and 1980s because there is a particular 'crisis of confidence' in this period of American society.

J. P. Telotte examines the significance of what he calls the 'doubling process' in science fiction. This 'alluring and potentially destructive' desire to reproduce oneself 'seems to promise a reduction of man to no more than artifice' but which nonetheless holds 'man' in its spell because of the promise of 'bringing us back to ourselves, making us at home with the self and the natural world in spite of ourselves'. This doubling process, then, is on the one hand a death drive, 'a desire for oblivion', the snuffing out of humanness, but on the other it is a necessary quest to find oneself in the contradictions that life (and death) brings to the human world.

Linda Ruth Williams suggests that dystopian scenarios are always bound up with utopian sentiments, and as a consequence dystopia needs utopia and vice versa to be given definition and meaning. In a textual, contextual and comparative analysis of Brazil and Nineteen Eighty-Four, Williams suggests that both films' dystopian vision is interrupted by the utopian 'vision of a woman' who functions as a 'spectacle of interruption, an escape from the dark dystopian terrain. In both films it is the woman's face which functions as the utopic image, freezing 'the flow of action''.

The Imagination of Disaster
Susan Sontag

The typical science fiction film has a form as predictable as a western, and is made up of elements which, to a practiced eye, are as classic as the saloon brawl, the blonde schoolteacher from the East, and the gun duel on the deserted main street.

One model scenario proceeds through five phases:

(i) The arrival of the thing. (Emergence of the monsters, landing of the alien spaceship, etc.) This is usually witnessed or suspected by just one person, a young scientist on a field trip. Nobody, neither his neighbours nor his colleagues, will believe him for some time. The hero is not married, but has a sympathetic though also incredulous girlfriend.

(ii) Confirmation of the hero's report by a host of witnesses to a great act of destruction. (If the invaders are beings from another planet, a fruitless attempt to parley with them and get them to leave peacefully.) The local police are summoned to deal with the situation and are massacred.

(iii) In the capital of the country, conferences between scientists and the military take place, with the hero lecturing before a chart, map or blackboard. A national emergency is declared. Reports of further destruction. Authorities from other countries arrive in black limousines. All international tensions are suspended in view of the planetary emergency. This stage often includes a rapid montage of news broadcasts in various languages, a meeting at the UN, and more conferences between the military and the scientists. Plans are made for destroying the enemy.

(iv) Further atrocities. At some point the hero's girlfriend is in grave danger. Massive counter-attacks by international forces, with brilliant displays of rocketry, rays and other advanced weapons, are all unsuccessful. Enormous military casualties, usually by incineration. Cities are destroyed and/or evacuated. There is an obligatory scene here of panicked crowds stampeding along a highway or a big bridge, being waved on by numerous policemen who, if the film is Japanese, are immaculately white-gloved, preternaturally calm, and call out in dubbed English, 'Keep moving. There is no need to be alarmed.'

(v) More conferences, whose motif is: 'They must be vulnerable to something.' Throughout the hero has been working in his lab to this end. The final strategy, upon which all hopes depend, is drawn up; the ultimate weapon – often a super-powerful, as yet untested, nuclear device – is mounted. Countdown. Final repulse of the monster or invaders. Mutual congratulations, while the hero and girlfriend embrace cheek to cheek and scan the skies sturdily. 'But have we seen the last of them?'

The film I have just described should be in colour and on a wide screen. Another typical scenario, which follows, is simpler and suited to black-and-white films with a lower budget. It has four phases:

(i) The hero (usually, but not always, a scientist) and his girlfriend, or his wife and two children, are disporting themselves in some innocent ultra-normal middle-class surroundings – their house in a small town, or on vacation (camping, boating). Suddenly, someone starts behaving strangely; or some innocent form of vegetation becomes monstrously enlarged and ambulatory. If a character is pictured driving an automobile, something gruesome looms up in the middle of the road. If it is night, strange lights hurtle across the sky.

(ii) After following the thing's tracks, or determining that 'It' is radioactive, or poking around a huge crater – in short, conducting some sort of crude investigation – the hero tries to warn the local authorities, without effect; nobody believes anything is amiss. The hero knows better. If the thing is tangible, the house is elaborately barricaded. If the invading alien is an invisible parasite, a doctor or friend is called in, who is himself rather quickly killed or 'taken possession of' by the thing.

(iii) The advice of whoever further is consulted proves useless. Meanwhile, 'It' continues to claim other victims in the town, which remains implausibly isolated from the rest of the world. General helplessness.

(iv) One of two possibilities. Either the hero prepares to do battle alone, accidentally discovers the thing's one vulnerable point, and destroys it. Or, he somehow manages to get out of town and succeeds in laying his case before competent authorities. They, along the lines of the first script but abridged, deploy a complex technology which (after initial setbacks) finally prevails against the invaders.

Another version of the second script opens with the scientist-hero in his laboratory, which is located in the basement or on the grounds of his tasteful, prosperous house. Through his experiments, he unwittingly causes a frightful metamorphosis in some class of plants or animals which turn carnivorous and go on a rampage. Or else, his experiments have caused him to be injured (sometimes irrevocably) or 'invaded' himself. Perhaps he has been experimenting with radiation, or has built a machine to communicate with beings from other planets or transport him to other places or times.

Another version of the first script involves the discovery of some fundamental alteration in the conditions of existence of our planet, brought about by nuclear testing, which will lead to the extinction in a few months of all human life. For example: the temperature of the earth is becoming too high or too low to support life, or Earth is cracking in two, or it is gradually being blanketed by lethal fallout.

A third script, somewhat but not altogether different from the first two, concerns a journey through space – to the moon, or some other planet. What the space-voyagers discover commonly is that the alien terrain is in a state of dire emergency, itself threatened by extra-planetary invaders or nearing extinction through the practice of nuclear warfare. The terminal dramas of the first and second scripts are played out there, to which is added the problem of getting away from the doomed and/or hostile planet and back to Earth.

I am aware, of course, that there are thousands of science fiction novels (their heyday was the late 1940s), not to mention the transcriptions of science fiction themes which, more and more, provide the principal subject-matter of comic books. But I propose to discuss science fiction films (the present period began in 1950 and continues, considerably abated, to this day) as an independent subgenre, without reference to other media – and, most particularly, without reference to the novels from which, in many cases, they were adapted. For, while novel and film may share the same plot, the fundamental difference between the resources of the novel and the film makes them quite dissimilar.

Certainly, compared with the science fiction novels, their film counterparts have unique strengths, one of which is the immediate representation of the extraordinary: physical deformity and mutation, missile and rocket combat, toppling skyscrapers. The movies are, naturally, weak just where the science fiction novels (some of them) are strong – on science. But in place of an intellectual workout, they can supply something the novels can never provide – sensuous elaboration. In the films it is by means of images and sounds, not words that have to be translated by the imagination, that one can participate in the fantasy of living through one's own death and more, the death of cities, the destruction of humanity itself.

Science fiction films are not about science. They are about disaster, which is one of the oldest subjects of art. In science fiction films disaster is rarely viewed intensively; it is always extensive. It is a matter of quantity and in-genuity. If you will, it is a question of scale. But the scale, particularly in the widescreen colour films (of which the ones by the Japanese director Inoshiro Honda and the American director George Pal are technically the most convincing and visually the most exciting), does raise the matter to another level.

Thus, the science fiction film (like that of a very different contemporary genre, the Happening) is concerned with the aesthetics of destruction, with the peculiar beauties to be found in wreaking havoc, making a mess. And it is in the imagery of destruction that the core of a good science fiction film lies. Hence, the disadvantage of the cheap film – in which the monster appears or the rocket lands in a small dull-looking town. (Hollywood budget needs usually dictate that the town be in the Arizona or California desert. In *The Thing From Another World* [1951] the rather sleazy and confined set is supposed to be an encampment near the North Pole.) Still, good black-and-white science fiction films have been made. But a bigger budget, which usually means colour, allows a much greater play back and forth among several model environments. There is the populous city. There is the lavish but ascetic interior of the spaceship – either the invaders' or ours – replete with streamlined chromium fixtures and dials and machines whose complexity is indicated by the number of colored lights they flash and strange noises they emit. There is the laboratory crowded with formidable boxes and scientific apparatus. There is a comparatively old-fashioned-looking conference room, where the scientists unfurl charts to explain the desperate state of things to the military. And each of these standard locales or backgrounds is subject to two modalities -- intact and destroyed. We may, if we are lucky, be treated to a panorama of melting tanks, flying bodies, crashing walls, awesome craters and fissures in the earth, plummeting spacecraft, colorful deadly rays; and to a symphony of screams, weird electronic signals, the noisiest military hardware going, and the leaden tones of the laconic denizens of alien planets and their subjugated earthlings.

Certain of the primitive gratifications of science fiction films – for instance, the depiction of urban disaster on a colossally magnified scale – are shared with other types of films. Visually there is little difference between mass havoc as represented in the old horror and monster films and what we find in science fiction films, except (again) scale. In the old monster films, the monster always headed for the great city, where he had to do a fair bit of rampaging, hurling busses off bridges, crumpling trains in his bare hands, toppling buildings, and so forth. The archetype is King Kong, in Schoedsack and Cooper's great film of 1933, running amok, first in the native village (trampling babies, a bit of footage excised from most prints), then in New York. This is really no different in spirit from the scene in Inoshiro Honda's *Rodan* (1957) in which two giant reptiles – with a wingspan of 500 feet and supersonic speeds – by flapping their wings whip up a cyclone that blows most of Tokyo to smithereens. Or the destruction of half of Japan by the gigantic robot with the great incinerating ray that shoots forth from his eyes, at the beginning of Honda's *The Mysterians* (1959). Or, the devastation by the rays from a fleet of flying saucers of New York, Paris and Tokyo, in *Battle in Outer Space* (1960). Or, the inundation of New York in *When Worlds Collide* (1951). Or, the end of London in 1966 depicted in George Pal's *The Time Machine* (1960). Neither do these sequences differ in aesthetic intention from the destruction scenes in the big sword, sandal and orgy color spectaculars set in Biblical and Roman times – the end of Sodom in Aldrich's *Sodom and Gomorrah*, of Gaza in De Mille's *Samson and Delilah*, of Rhodes in *The Colossus of Rhodes*, and of Rome

in a dozen Nero movies. Griffith began it with the Babylon sequence in *Intolerance*, and to this day there is nothing like the thrill of watching all those expensive sets come tumbling down.

In other respects as well, the science fiction films of the 1950s take up familiar themes. The famous 1930s movie serials and comics of the adventures of Flash Gordon and Buck Rogers, as well as the more recent spate of comic book super-heroes with extraterrestrial origins (the most famous is Superman, a foundling from the planet Krypton, currently described as having been exploded by a nuclear blast), share motifs with more recent science fiction movies. But there is an important difference. The old science fiction films, and most of the comics, still have an essentially innocent relation to disaster. Mainly they offer new versions of the oldest romance of all – of the strong invulnerable hero with a mysterious lineage come to do battle on behalf of good and against evil. Recent science fiction films have a decided grimness, bolstered by their much greater degree of visual credibility, which contrasts strongly with the older films. Modern historical reality has greatly enlarged the imagination of disaster, and the protagonists – perhaps by the very nature of what is visited upon them -- no longer seem wholly innocent.

The lure of such generalised disaster as a fantasy is that it releases one from normal obligations. The trump card of the end-of-the-world movies -- like *The Day the Earth Caught Fire* (1962) – is that great scene with New York or London or Tokyo discovered empty, its entire population annihilated. Or, as in *The World, The Flesh, and The Devil* (1957), the whole movie can be devoted to the fantasy of occupying the deserted metropolis and starting all over again, a world Robinson Crusoe.

Another kind of satisfaction these films supply is extreme moral simplification – that is to say, a morally acceptable fantasy where one can give outlet to cruel or at least amoral feelings. In this respect, science fiction films partly overlap with horror films. This is the undeniable pleasure we derive from looking at freaks, beings excluded from the category of the human. The sense of superiority over the freak conjoined in varying proportions with the titillation of fear and aversion makes it possible for moral scruples to be lifted, for cruelty to be enjoyed. The same thing happens in science fiction films. In the figure of the monster from outer space, the freakish, the ugly, and the predatory all converge – and provide a fantasy target for righteous bellicosity to discharge itself, and for the aesthetic enjoyment of suffering and disaster. Science fiction films are one of the purest forms of spectacle; that is, we are rarely inside anyone's feelings. (An exception is Jack Arnold's *The Incredible Shrinking Man* [1957].) We are merely spectators; we watch.

But in science fiction films, unlike horror films, there is not much horror. Suspense, shocks, surprises are mostly abjured in favor of a steady, inexorable plot. Science fiction films invite a dispassionate, aesthetic view of destruction and violence – a *technological* view. Things, objects, machinery play a major role in these films. A greater range of ethical values is embodied in the décor of these films than in the people. Things, rather than the helpless humans, are the locus of values because we experience them, rather than people, as the sources of power. According to science fiction films, man is naked without his artifacts. *They* stand for different values, they are potent, they are what get destroyed, and they are the indispensable tools for the repulse of the alien invaders or the repair of the damaged environment.

The science fiction films are strongly moralistic. The standard message is the one about the proper, or humane, use of science, versus the mad, obsessional use of science. This message the science fiction films share in common with the classic horror films of the 1930s, like *Frankenstein*, *The Mummy*, *Island of Lost Souls*, *Dr. Jekyll and Mr. Hyde*. (Georges Franju's brilliant *Les Yeux Sans Visage* [1959], called here *The Horror Chamber of Doctor Faustus*, is a more recent example.) In horror films, we have the mad or obsessed or misguided scientist who pursues his experiments against good advice to the contrary, creates a monster or monsters, and is himself destroyed – often recognising his folly himself, and dying in the successful effort to destroy his own creation. One science fiction equivalent of this is the scientist, usually a member of a team, who defects to the planetary invaders because 'their' science is more advanced than 'ours'.

This is the case in *The Mysterians*, and, true to form, the renegade sees his error in the end, and from within the Mysterian space ship

destroys it and himself. In *This Island Earth* (1955), the inhabitants of the beleaguered planet Metaluna propose to conquer earth, but their project is foiled by a Metalunan scientist named Exeter who, having lived on earth a while and learned to love Mozart, cannot abide such viciousness. Exeter plunges his spaceship into the ocean after returning a glamorous pair (male and female) of American physicists to Earth. Metaluna dies. In *The Fly* (1958), the hero, engrossed in his basement-laboratory experiments on a matter-transmitting machine, uses himself as a subject, exchanges head and one arm with a housefly which had accidentally gotten into the machine, becomes a monster, and with his last shred of human will destroys his laboratory and orders his wife to kill him. His discovery, for the good of mankind, is lost.

Being a clearly labeled species of intellectual, scientists in science fiction films are always liable to crack up or go off the deep end. In *Conquest of Space* (1955), the scientist-commander of an international expedition to Mars suddenly acquires scruples about the blasphemy involved in the undertaking, and begins reading the Bible mid-journey instead of attending to his duties. The commander's son, who is his junior officer and always addresses his father as 'General', is forced to kill the old man when he tries to prevent the ship from landing on Mars. In this film, both sides of the ambivalence toward scientists are given voice. Generally, for a scientific enterprise to be treated entirely sympathetically in these films, it needs the certificate of utility. Science, viewed without ambivalence, means an efficacious response to danger. Disinterested intellectual curiosity rarely appears in any form other than caricature, as a maniacal dementia that cuts one off from normal human relations. But this suspicion is usually directed at the scientist rather than his work. The creative scientist may become a martyr to his own discovery, through an accident or by pushing things too far. But the implication remains that other men, less imaginative – in short, technicians – could have administered the same discovery better and more safely. The most ingrained contemporary mistrust of the intellect is visited, in these movies, upon the scientist-as-intellectual.

The message that the scientist is one who releases forces which, if not controlled for good, could destroy man himself seems innocuous enough. One of the oldest images of the scientist is Shakespeare's Prospero, the overdetached scholar forcibly retired from society to a desert island, only partly in control of the magic forces in which he dabbles. Equally classic is the figure of the scientist as satanist (*Doctor Faustus*, and stories of Poe and Hawthorne). Science is magic, and man has always known that there is black magic as well as white. But it is not enough to remark that contemporary attitudes – as reflected in science fiction films – remain ambivalent, that the scientist is treated as both satanist and savior. The proportions have changed, because of the new context in which the old admiration and fear of the scientist are located. For his sphere of influence is no longer local, himself or his immediate community. It is planetary, cosmic.

One gets the feeling, particularly in the Japanese films but not only there, that a mass trauma exists over the use of nuclear weapons and the possibility of future nuclear wars. Most of the science fiction films bear witness to this trauma, and, in a way, attempt to exorcise it.

The accidental awakening of the super-destructive monster who has slept in the earth since prehistory is, often, an obvious metaphor for the Bomb. But there are many explicit references as well. In *The Mysterians*, a probe ship from the planet Mysteroid has landed on Earth, near Tokyo. Nuclear warfare having been practiced on Mysteroid for centuries (their civilisation is 'more advanced than ours'), ninety percent of those now born on the planet have to be destroyed at birth, because of defects caused by the huge amounts of Strontium 90 in their diet. The Mysterians have come to Earth to marry earth women, and possibly to take over our relatively uncontaminated planet … In *The Incredible Shrinking Man*, the John Doe hero is the victim of a gust of radiation which blows over the water, while he is out boating with his wife; the radiation causes him to grow smaller and smaller, until at the end of the movie he steps through the fine mesh of a window screen to become 'the infinitely small' … In *Rodan*, a horde of monstrous carnivorous prehistoric insects, and finally a pair of giant flying reptiles (the prehistoric Archeopteryx), are hatched from dormant eggs in the depths of a mine shaft by the impact of nuclear test explosions, and go on to destroy a good part of

the world before they are felled by the molten lava of a volcanic eruption … In the English film, *The Day the Earth Caught Fire*, two simultaneous hydrogen bomb tests by the United States and Russia change by eleven degrees the tilt of the Earth on its axis and alter the Earth's orbit so that it begins to approach the Sun.

Radiation casualties – ultimately, the conception of the whole world as a casualty of nuclear testing and nuclear warfare – is the most ominous of all the notions with which science fiction films deal. Universes become expendable. Worlds become contaminated, burnt out, exhausted, obsolete. In *Rocketship X-M* (1950) explorers from Earth land on Mars, where they learn that atomic warfare has destroyed Martian civilisation. In George Pal's *War of the Worlds* (1953), reddish spindly alligator-skinned creatures from Mars invade Earth because their planet is becoming too cold to be inhabitable. In *This Island Earth*, also American, the planet Metaluna, whose population has long ago been driven underground by warfare, is dying under the missile attacks of an enemy planet. Stocks of uranium, which power the force field shielding Metaluna, have been used up; and an unsuccessful expedition is sent to Earth to enlist earth scientists to devise new sources for nuclear power. In Joseph Losey's *The Damned* (1961), nine icy-cold radioactive children are being reared by a fanatical scientist in a dark cave on the English coast to be the only survivors of the inevitable nuclear Armageddon.

There is a vast amount of wishful thinking in science fiction films, some of it touching, some of it depressing. Again and again, one detects the hunger for a 'good war', which poses no moral problems, admits of no moral qualifications. The imagery of science fiction films will satisfy the most bellicose addict of war films, for a lot of the satisfactions of war films pass, untransformed, into science fiction films. Examples: the dogfights between Earth 'fighter rockets' and alien spacecraft in the *Battle in Outer Space* (1960); the escalating firepower in the successive assaults upon the invaders in *The Mysterians*, which Dan Talbot correctly described as a non-stop holocaust; the spectacular bombardment of the underground fortress of Metaluna in *This Island Earth*.

Yet at the same time the bellicosity of science fiction films is neatly channeled into the yearning for peace, or for at least peaceful coexistence. Some scientist generally takes sententious note of the fact that it took the planetary invasion to make the warring nations of Earth come to their senses and suspend their own conflicts. One of the main themes of many science fiction films – the colour ones usually, because they have the budget and resources to develop the military spectacle – is this UN fantasy, a fantasy of united warfare. (The same wishful UN theme cropped up in a recent spectacular which is not science fiction, *Fifty-Five Days in Peking* [1963]. There, topically enough, the Chinese, the Boxers, play the role of Martian invaders who unite the Earthmen, in this case the United States, England, Russia, France, Germany, Italy and Japan.) A great enough disaster cancels all enmities and calls upon the utmost concentration of earth resources.

Science – technology – is conceived of as the great unifier. Thus the science fiction films also project a Utopian fantasy. In the classic models of Utopian thinking – Plato's Republic, Campanella's City of the Sun, More's Utopia, Swift's land of the Houyhnhnms, Voltaire's Eldorado – society had worked out a perfect consensus. In these societies reasonableness had achieved an unbreakable supremacy over the emotions. Since no disagreement or social conflict was intellectually plausible, none was possible. As in Melville's *Typee*, 'they all think the same'. The universal rule of reason meant universal agreement. It is interesting, too, that societies in which reason was pictured as totally ascendant were also traditionally pictured as having an ascetic or materially frugal and economically simple mode of life. But in the Utopian world community projected by science fiction films, totally pacified and ruled by scientific consensus, the demand for simplicity of material existence would be absurd.

Yet alongside the hopeful fantasy of moral simplification and international unity embodied in the science fiction films lurk the deepest anxieties about contemporary existence. I don't mean only the very real trauma of the Bomb – that it has been used, that there are enough now to kill everyone on Earth many times over, that those new bombs may very well be used. Besides these new anxieties about physical disaster, the prospect of universal mutilation and even annihilation, the science fiction films reflect powerful anxieties about the condition of the individual psyche.

For science fiction films may also be described as a popular mythology for the contemporary *negative* imagination about the impersonal. The other-world creatures that seek to take 'us' over are an 'it', not a 'they'. The planetary invaders are usually zombie-like. Their movements are either cool, mechanical, or lumbering, blobby. But it amounts to the same thing. If they are non-human in form, they proceed with an absolutely regular, unalterable movement (unalterable save by destruction). If they are human in form – dressed in space suits, etc. – then they obey the most rigid military discipline, and display no personal characteristics whatsoever. And it is this regime of emotionlessness, of impersonality, of regimentation, which they will impose on the Earth if they are successful. 'No more love, no more beauty, no more pain', boasts a converted earthling in *The Invasion of the Body Snatchers* (1956). The half-earthling, earthling, half-alien children in *The Children of the Damned* (1960) are absolutely emotionless, move as a group and understand each others' thoughts, and are all prodigious intellects. They are the wave of the future, man in his next stage of development.

These alien invaders practice a crime which is worse than murder. They do not simply kill the person. They obliterate him. In *The War of the Worlds*, the ray which issues from the rocket ship disintegrates all persons and objects in its path, leaving no trace of them but a light ash. In Honda's *The H-Man* (1959), the creeping blob melts all flesh with which it comes in contact. If the blob, which looks like a huge hunk of red Jello and can crawl across floors and up and down walls, so much as touches your bare foot, all that is left of you is a heap of clothes on the floor. (A more articulated, size-multiplying blob is the villain in the English film *The Creeping Unknown* [1956].) In another version of this fantasy, the body is preserved but the person is entirely reconstituted as the automatised servant or agent of the alien powers. This is, of course, the vampire fantasy in new dress. The person is really dead, but he doesn't know it. He is 'undead', he has become an 'unperson'. It happens to a whole California town in *The Invasion of the Body Snatchers*, to several Earth scientists in *This Island Earth*, and to assorted innocents in *It Came From Outer Space*, *Attack of the Puppet People* (1958) and *The Brain Eaters* (1958). As the victim always backs away from the vampire's horrifying embrace, so in science fiction films the person always fights being 'taken over'; he wants to retain his humanity. But once the deed has been done, the victim is eminently satisfied with his condition. He has not been converted from human amiability to monstrous 'animal' bloodlust (a metaphoric exaggeration of sexual desire), as in the old vampire fantasy. No, he has simply become far more efficient – the very model of technocratic man, purged of emotions, volitionless, tranquil, obedient to all orders. (The dark secret behind human nature used to be the upsurge of the animal – as in *King Kong*. The threat to man, his availability to dehumanisation, lay in his own animality. Now the danger is understood as residing in man's ability to be turned into a machine.)

The rule, of course, is that this horrible and irremediable form of murder can strike anyone in the film except the hero. The hero and his family, while greatly threatened, always escape this fate and by the end of the film the invaders have been repulsed or destroyed. I know of only one exception, *The Day That Mars Invaded Earth* (1963), in which after all the standard struggles the scientist-hero, his wife, and their two children are 'taken over' by the alien invaders – and that's that. (The last minutes of the film show them being incinerated by the Martians' rays and their ash silhouettes flushed down their empty swimming pool, while their simulacra drive off in the family car.) Another variant but upbeat switch on the rule occurs in *The Creation of the Humanoids* (1964), where the hero discovers at the end of the film that he, too, has been turned into a metal robot, complete with highly efficient and virtually indestructible mechanical insides, although he didn't know it and detected no difference in himself. He learns, however, that he will shortly be upgraded into a 'humanoid' having all the properties of a real man.

Of all the standard motifs of science fiction films, this theme of dehumanisation is perhaps the most fascinating. For, as I have indicated, it is scarcely a black-and-white situation, as in the old vampire films. The attitude of the science fiction films toward depersonalisation is mixed. On the one hand, they deplore it

as the ultimate horror. On the other hand, certain characteristics of the dehumanised invaders, modulated and disguised – such as the ascendancy of reason over feelings, the idealisation of teamwork and the consensus-creating activities of science, a marked degree of moral simplification – are precisely traits of the saviour-scientist. It is interesting that when the scientist in these films is treated negatively, it is usually done through the portrayal of an individual scientist who holes up in his laboratory and neglects his fiancée or his loving wife and children, obsessed by his daring and dangerous experiments. The scientist as a loyal member of a team, and therefore considerably less individualised, is treated quite respectfully.

There is absolutely no social criticism, of even the most implicit kind, in science fiction films. No criticism, for example, of the conditions of our society which create the impersonality and dehumanisation which science fiction fantasies displace onto the influence of an alien 'It'. Also, the notion of science as a social activity, interlocking with social and political interests, is unacknowledged. Science is simply either adventure (for good or evil) or a technical response to danger. And, typically, when the fear of science is paramount – when science is conceived of as black magic rather than white – the evil has no attribution beyond that of the perverse will of an individual scientist. In science fiction films the antithesis of black magic and white is drawn as a split between technology, which is beneficent, and the errant individual will of a lone intellectual.

Thus, science fiction films can be looked at as thematically central allegory, replete with standard modern attitudes. The theme of depersonalisation (being 'taken over') which I have been talking about is a new allegory reflecting the age-old awareness of man that, sane, he is always perilously close to insanity and unreason. But there is something more here than just a recent, popular image which expresses man's perennial, but largely unconscious, anxiety about his sanity. The image derives most of its power from a supplementary and historical anxiety, also not experienced consciously by most people, about the depersonalising conditions of modern urban life. Similarly, it is not enough to note that science fiction allegories are one of the new myths about – that is, one of the ways of accommodating to and negating – the perennial human anxiety about death. (Myths of heaven and hell, and of ghosts, had the same function.) For, again, there is a historically specifiable twist which intensifies the anxiety. I mean, the trauma suffered by everyone in the middle of the twentieth century when it became clear that, from now on to the end of human history, every person would spend his individual life under the threat not only of individual death, which is certain, but of something almost insupportable psychologically – collective in-cineration and extinction which could come at any time, virtually without warning.

From a psychological point of view, the imagination of disaster does not greatly differ from one period in history to another. But from a political and moral point of view, it does. The expectation of the apocalypse may be the occasion for a radical disaffiliation from society, as when thousands of Eastern European Jews in the seventeenth century, hearing that Sabbatai Zevi had been proclaimed the Messiah and that the end of the world was imminent, gave up their homes and businesses and began the trek to Palestine. But people take the news of their doom in diverse ways. It is reported that in 1945 the populace of Berlin received without great agitation the news that Hitler had decided to kill them all, before the Allies arrived, because they had not been worthy enough to win the war. We are, alas, more in the position of the Berliners of 1945 than of the Jews of seventeenth-century Eastern Europe; and our response is closer to theirs, too. What I am suggesting is that the imagery of disaster in science fiction is above all the emblem of an *inadequate* response. I don't mean to bear down on the films for this. They themselves are only a sampling, stripped of sophistication, of the inadequacy of most people's response to the unassimilable terrors that infect their consciousness. The interest of the films, aside from their considerable amount of cinematic charm, consists in this intersection between a naïve and largely debased commercial art product and the most profound dilemmas of the contemporary situation.

Ours is indeed an age of extremity. For we live under continual threat of two equally fearful, but seemingly opposed, destinies: un-remitting banality and inconceivable terror. It is fantasy, served out in large rations by the popular arts, which allows most people to cope with these twin spectres. For one job that fantasy can do is to lift us out of the unbearably humdrum and to distract us from terrors – real or anticipated – by an escape into exotic, dangerous situations which have last-minute happy endings. But another of the things that fantasy can do is to normalise what is psychologically unbearable, thereby inuring us to it. In one case, fantasy beautifies the world. In the other, it neutralises it.

The fantasy in science fiction films does both jobs. The films reflect worldwide anx-ieties, and they serve to allay them. They inculcate a strange apathy concerning the processes of radiation, contamination and de-struction which I for one find haunting and depressing. The naïve level of the films neatly tempers the sense of otherness, of alien-ness, with the grossly familiar. In particular, the dialogue of most science fiction films, which is of a monumental but often touching banality, makes them wonderfully, unintentionally funny. Lines like 'Come quickly, there's a monster in my bathtub', 'We must do something about this', 'Wait, Professor. There's someone on the telephone', 'But that's incredible', and the old American stand-by, 'I hope it works!' are hilarious in the context of picturesque and deafening holocaust. Yet the films also contain something that is painful and in deadly earnest.

There is a sense in which all these movies are in complicity with the abhorrent. They neutralise it. It is no more, perhaps, than the way all art draws its audience into a circle of complicity with the thing represented. But in these films we have to do with things which are (quite literally) unthinkable. Here, 'thinking about the unthinkable' – not in the way of Herman Kahn, as a subject for calculation, but as a subject for fantasy – becomes, however inadvertently, itself a somewhat questionable act from a moral point of view. The films perpetuate clichés about identity, volition, power, knowledge, happiness, social consensus, guilt, responsibility which are, to say the least, not serviceable in our present extremity. But collective nightmares cannot be banished by demonstrating that they are, intellectually and morally, fallacious. This nightmare – the one reflected, in various registers, in the science fiction films – is too close to our reality.

Technophobia/Dystopia
Michael Ryan and
Douglas Kellner

The triumph of conservatism made itself particularly felt in the fantasy genre, in large part because the sorts of representational dynamics afforded by fantasy were peculiarly well suited to the psychological principles of the new conservatism. Nevertheless, fantasy was not an entirely uncontested terrain at this time. In such major fantasy genres of the period as technophobic films and dystopias, a struggle between right-wing and left-wing uses of the fantasy mode is evident. And the major fantasist of the period – Steven Spielberg – consistently promotes liberal ideals through his films. If conservative filmmakers used the motifs of technology and dystopia to project terrifying images of collectivisation and modernity, liberals and radicals used them to launch covert attacks against the conservative ideals of capitalism and patriarchy. The flight into the future in many fantasy films is often a flight into the past, toward a world of more traditional values. But it is also often a flight toward more radical alternatives than the constraints of 'realism' (both as an aesthetic principle and as a principle of social control) allow to be elaborated. Detachment from the constraints of realism allows fantasy to be more metaphoric in quality and consequently more potentially ideological. Fantasy replaces an accurate assessment of the world with images that substitute desired ideals or feared projections for such an assessment. But such detachment from realist reference also permits the development of alternative constructions of social reality which might otherwise be smothered under hardnosed conservative realist injunction against being 'utopian'. If fantasy is given to metaphor, it is also an open terrain which permits the deployment of more metonymic rhetorical forms. Indeed, it is in the future-fantasy genre that one finds some of the most radical critiques of American society during this period.

Moreover, the fantasy mode became a locus for projected idealisations of empathetic social relations of the sort more and more unavailable in a public sphere increasingly dominated by conservative principles of survivalism. The fantasy genre is especially revealing in this regard, since, as a result of the conservative occupation of the public sphere, the society's dominant institutions less and less satisfied people's sense of idealisation, their sense of being 'good'. Meanness and venality are not particularly cherishable traits. The rise of economic realism (the triumph of criteria of efficiency over criteria of welfare) in the public sphere in the 1980s put a burden on the private sphere (the family particularly) as a locus of idealisation. It should not be surprising, then, that Steven Spielberg's family fantasy films became tremendously popular during this era. Displaced from the public sphere, liberal ideals of empathy, tolerance, and care tended to retreat to the private sphere.

This shift is telling because it indicates that the new conservatism was not entirely in sync with what most Americans believed. Even if the Republicans succeeded in playing to resentment against taxation, welfare and affirmative action hiring in order to enlist support for a procapitalist economic programme, by the mid-1980s most Americans were expressing distrust of the Republican economic agenda. The majority correctly saw it as unfair. Moreover, Republicans were incapable of attaining hegemony in the social sphere of the sort they held in the political and economic spheres. Thus, as much as liberalism, conservatism found itself in a dilemma during this time. It could seize political power on the basis of economic doctrine, but it could not transform American culture in a way suitable to its social ideals. What one could call an American quandary developed in the 1980s. In the face of entrenched social liberalism, conservatives could not impose their values on the private domain, but liberals faced with entrenched conservative power in business were powerless to reform the economy and to make it more humane.

Technophobia

Fantasy films concerning fears of machines or of technology usually negatively affirm such social values as freedom, individualism and the family. In the 1970s technology was frequently a metaphor for everything that threatened 'natural' social arrangements, and conservative values associated with nature were generally mobilised as antidotes to that threat. But technophobic films were also the site where the metaphor of nature which sustains those values was most saliently deconstructed. From a conservative perspective technology represents artifice as opposed to nature, the mechanical as opposed to the spontaneous, the regulated as opposed to the free, an equaliser as opposed to a promoter of individual distinction, equality triumphant as opposed to liberty, democratic leveling as opposed to hierarchy derived from individual superiority. Most important for the conservative individualist critique, it represents modernity, the triumph of radical change over traditional social institutions. Those institutions are legitimated by being endowed with the aura of nature, and technology represents the possibility that nature might be reconstructable, not the bedrock of unchanging authority conservative discourse requires. Indeed, as the figure for artificial construction, technology represents the possibility that such discursive figures as 'nature' (and the ideal of free immediacy it connotes) might merely be constructs, artificial devices, metaphors designed to legitimate inequality by positing a false ground of authority for unjust social actions.

The significance of technology thus exceeds simple questions of mechanics. It is usually a crucial ideological figure. Indeed, as the possibility of reconstructing institutions conservatives declare to be part of nature, technology represents everything that threatens the grounding of conservative social authority and everything that ideology is designed to neutralise. It should not be surprising, then, that this era should witness the development of a strain of films that portray technology negatively, usually from a conservative perspective.

The technophobic theme is most visible in the early 1970s in Lucas's *THX 1138* (1970), a quest narrative set in a cybernetic society where all of life is regulated by the state. Individuals are forced to take drugs to regulate sexual desires; thoughts and individual action are monitored by electronic surveillance devices. A sense of mass, collectivist conformity is connoted by shaved heads, the assigning of numbers instead of names, and starkly-lit white environments. The lack of differentiation between individuals is suggested by the limitless quality of space; everything lacks boundaries, from the self to

the city. The libertarian basis of the film's value system cuts both ways politically – liberally, in that recorded messages allude to the McCarthyite repression of dissidents, and conservatively, in that they also refer negatively to socialism ('Blessings of the State, blessings of the masses. We are created in the image of the masses, by the masses, for the masses'). Against undifferentiated totalitarianism, the film valorizes the differentiated individual. THX flees the cybernetic society, and the last image depicts his emergence into freedom and nature. His liberation is associated with a bright orange sun that strikingly isolates him as he emerges. The bright sun is a metaphor for individual freedom, for the departure from a world of contrivance and artifice into nature. The sun literally singularises THX by giving him a distinguishing boundary. He is no longer one of the intersubstitutable mass. In addition, the sense the image imparts is of something literal, the thing itself, nature in its pure presence. Indeed, nature is supposed to be just that, something outside contrivance, artifice, technology, and the sort of substitution which rhetorical figures (the very opposite of what is literal) usually connote. The grounding of the ideology of liberty in nature is tantamount to grounding it in literality, since literality implies things as they are, unadulterated by the sort of artificial intersubstitution of people which prevails in the egalitarian city. Visual style connotes political attitudes, and given a choice between the deep white frieze of equality and the warm orange glow of liberty, one suspects what people are likely to choose.

The rhetorical strategy of many technophobic films, therefore, is to establish a strong opposition between terms (liberty vs. equality) that does not permit any intermediation. The elimination of the middle ground is an essential operation of this ideology. A major mid-1970s film that executes this strategy is *Logan's Run* (1976), in which a policeman named Logan is induced into fleeing a cybernetic city by a young female rebel against the city's totalitarian regime. The representation of the city evokes all the negative traits in the conservative vision assigned to the figure of technology – the destruction of the family, the interchangeability of sexual partners so that feeling is destroyed by rationality, enforced mass conformity that places the collective before the individual and effaces individual differences in an egalitarian leveling, the power of state control over the freedom to choose, and so on. The city is a mid-1970s liberal pleasure dome where one can summon sexual partners at the touch of a button or periodically receive a new identity. Population size is regulated, and no one has parents. This lack of self-identity is associated with hedonism and collectivity. Logan and the woman rebel get caught up in an orgy at one point, and the colours suggest hell. When the two are separated (divorced, one might say, to emphasise the ideological motif), they almost lose their identities in the teeming crowd. In such a sexually permissive, hedonistic world, clearly no social hierarchy or subjective boundary can be established or maintained. Collectivity is thus associated with a loss of self-identity and a lack of sexual discipline that breaks family bonds.

One of the first things that Logan says upon emerging into nature is, 'We're free.' In nature one knows who one's mother and father are, whereas in the city of collectivism and sexual hedonism no one knows his/her parents. Thus one can only be an individual, a self, within a society of monogamous marriage, in which sexuality primarily serves the 'natural' function of reproduction rather than pleasure. In the film's conservative ideology, the restoration of the traditional family, the preservation of individualism, and the curtailing of nonreproductive sexuality seem to be interdependent, and they all depend on the rejection of everything technology represents – mediation, equality, intersubstitutability, and so on. In this vision one catches a glimpse of the actual ingredients of the emerging conservative movement whose values the film transcodes.

Outside the technological city, the rebels discover nature as well as supposedly natural social institutions like patriarchy and political republicanism. The woman ceases to be an equal of the man, a structure of equivalence generated in the city by representations, primarily wide-angle long shots of crowds, that place everyone on the same plane in the same frame and imply their equality. In nature, she assumes a subordinate position, both socially and within the camera frame as they sit by a crude campfire. Close-ups connote an unmediated spontaneity of 'natural' feeling, a literality of social structure uncontaminated by liberal revision. This is the real thing once

again, not a technical substitute or an artificial contrivance. One senses why empiricism is often the best recourse of ideology. At the level of empirical literality, equivalences cannot be established of the sort that thrive in the technological city, where the possibility of infinite copies annuls individual differences. At the level of social literality, everything is radically individuated, incapable of comparison. Appropriately, then, Logan kills his police partner, who has followed the rebels out of the city. He is a double or copy who is Logan's functional equal, and his death individuates Logan. He renounces his identity as a cybernetic functionary precisely because his intersubstitutability means he has no identity as such. The death occurs at the moment in the narrative when the rebels have come to Washington and rediscovered the United States's republican political system. With it, they rediscover the predominance of liberty over equality, the individual over the collective.

The peculiar twist of this ideal of liberty, therefore, is that it is a social theory that rejects the social (being other than oneself, mediated by social relation, a copy or technological robot). The choice of nature, as an alternative to technological collectivity, is thus appropriate, since nature is what is entirely nonsocial. What conservatives ultimately want is a ground of authority that will make inequalities that are in fact socially constructed seem natural. This is tantamount to saying that such instituted inequalities must seem to embody the literal truth of nature, things as they are and should always be. For this reason, the strategy of ontologising, of making technology and technological constructs seem as if they possess a being or essence in themselves, independent of context and use, is crucial to the conservative ideological undertaking. Technology must seem to be intrinsically evil, and this is so if the natural alternatives to technological society – the family and the individual especially – are to seem inherently good, ontologically grounded in themselves and not subject to figural comparison or connection to something outside them that might possibly serve as a substitute or equivalent. What is literal cannot be transported, as in metaphor, out of itself and made to stand for something else. Thus, technology represents a threat not only to self-presence in the sense of individual freedom in the conservative frame, but also to presence as the criterion of the ontological ground, the nature and the literality that anchor conservative social institutions.

A deconstructive analysis would point out that what is posited in this ideology as an ontological and literal cause that gives rise to social institutions – as well as to derivative, secondary, and unauthorised deviations of the original intent of nature through technological simulation and figural substitutions – is in fact an effect of those very things. The nature of ideology is the product of technology; literality is an effect of rhetoric. One notices this at those moments when nature and the literal are shown forth in films like *THX* and *Logan*. Nature takes on meaning as such within the films only as the other of urban technology. Its immediacy is mediated by that against which it is posed, just as the individual is necessarily mediated by society. Moreover, the supposed literal ground of social institutions is the effect of the metaphoric comparison of those institutions to nature. In order to call them natural, one has to engage in precisely the sort of metaphoric or figural comparison, the sort of rhetorical 'technology' that is supposedly excluded by that ascription. It is a case of innocence by association, and as a result, those institutions are guilty of being something they must claim not to be, that is, rhetorical constructs, mere technology. Thus a deconstructive reading points out the extent to which representation plays a constitutive role in the making of social institutions, because the metaphors and representations that construct the ideal images of such institutions are also models for social action.

The ideological character of the conservative technophobia films stands in greater relief when they are compared to more liberal or radical films that depict technology not as in itself, by nature, or ontologically evil, but as being subject to changes in meaning according to context and use. For example, the figure of technology is given socially critical political inflections in *Silent Running* (1971), which opposes nature and individual freedom to corporate misuse of technology in an ecological vein, representing the corporation as putting profit before the preservation of the environment. In *Star Trek* (1979) a human actually mates with an astral body born of a space probe, proving that humans and machines can get along more intimately than

conservatives ever imagine. And in *Brainstorm* (1983), the story of a technological invention that can be used either for war or peace, the family is shown falling apart, then mending with the help of the invention. Through this narrative motif the family is depicted as a constructed institution, itself an invention reliant more on negotiation than on naturally given laws.

Perhaps the most significant film in regard to an alternative representation of technology that takes issue with the ideology deployed in conservative technophobia films is *Blade Runner* (1982), directed by Ridley Scott. The film, based on the novel by Philip K. Dick, concerns four androids ('replicants') who revolt against their 'maker', the Tyrell Corporation. A policeman, Deckard (Harrison Ford), is assigned to 'retire' them. Deckard falls in love with Rachael (Sean Young), one of Tyrell's most advanced replicants. With Rachael's help, he manages to kill three of the rebels and fights a final battle with the fourth, Roy (Rutger Hauer), who allows Deckard to live because he himself is about to die. At the end, a fellow policeman allows Deckard and Rachael to escape from the city and flee to nature. The film offers a mediation between technology and human values. 'Replicants are like any other machine. They can be a benefit or a hazard,' Deckard says. And the film concludes with a happy marriage of humans and machines.

Blade Runner deconstructs certain ideological oppositions at work in more conservative technology films. The marrying of human and replicant undercuts the posing of nature as an opposite to a negative technological civilisation. The film also deconstructs the conservative romantic opposition of reason and feeling. In the film, reason is represented by analytic machines that dissect human and objective reality. The police detect replicants with analytic instruments that observe emotional reactions in the eye. When Deckard analyses the photograph of a room, he breaks down the reality into small parts until he captures what he seeks. The analytic gaze is thus represented as an instrument of power. Posed against this power is feeling. But the film suggests that feeling is not the polar opposite of reason. Rather, feeling, especially in the replicants, is the product of technology. And these machine humans are shown to be in many ways more 'human' than their makers. Analytic rationality is depicted as irrational and anti-human when used instrumentally in a policed, exploitative society, but it is also the instrument for constructing a more communal ethic. Thus, the film deconstructs the oppositions – human/technology, reason/feeling, culture/nature – that underwrite the conservative fear of technology by refusing to privilege one pole of the dichotomy over another and by leaving their meaning undecidable.

Blade Runner also calls attention to the oppressive core of capitalism and advocates revolt against exploitation. The Tyrell Corporation invents replicants in order to have a more pliable labour force, and the film depicts how capitalism turns humans into machines, a motif that recalls Lang's *Metropolis*. Indeed, German Expressionist features are evident throughout. The bright pink and red colours of the huge electric billboards contrast with the dark underworld of the streets, and this contrast highlights the discrepancy between the realm of leisure consumption and the underclass realm of urban poverty and labour in capitalism. In addition, the neo-Mayan architecture of the corporate buildings suggests human sacrifice for the capitalist god, and Tyrell is indeed depicted as something of a divine patriarch.

Although the film contains several sexist moments (Deckard more or less rapes Rachael), it can also be read as depicting the construction of female subjectivity under patriarchy as something pliant and submissive as well as threatening and 'castratory'. (The female replicants are sex functionaries as well as killers.) Similarly, the flight to romance and to nature at the end of the film gives rise to at least a double reading. Romance is escape to an empathetic interior realm from the external realm of public callousness in a capitalist society. Although it promotes personalisation and atomisation, the final flight also creates a space of autonomy and compassion which can be the basis for collective and egalitarian social arrangements. If the film privileges privatism, it may be because in U.S. society of the time, it was possible to locate humane values only in the private sphere.

The film implies that even the supposedly grounding, ontologically authoritative categories of conservatism like the individual, nature, the family and sentiment are indeterminate. They have alternative political inflections that revalorise their meaning according to pragmatic criteria of context and use. It is important, then, that unlike the conservative films that end with a move toward (cinematic as well as ideological) literality that supposedly reduces constructed social institutions to a natural or ontological ground of meaning, this film ends in a way that foregrounds the construction of alternative meanings from the literal through the figural or rhetorical techniques of substitution and equivalence, especially the equivalence of human life and technology (of Rachael the machine and Deckard the human at the end, for example). Figurality is foregrounded through juxtapositions that are not justified by the literal logic of the narrative. For example, Roy suddenly carries a white dove that soon becomes a symbol of charity and forgiveness. He himself in fact becomes a figure for Christ as he lowers his head and dies. The dove he releases flies up into a blue sky that also appears out of nowhere for the first time in the film, for no literal reason. The figural or rhetorical quality of these images is thus underscored by their narratively illogical emergence. The same is true of the origami doll the other detective leaves for Deckard as he and Rachael flee; it signals that the detective allows them to escape and becomes a figure for charity. And the wry, ironic comments Deckard makes at the end about his new relationship with the android woman foreground a figural doubleness or undecidability of meaning.

All of these figures place literality in abeyance, and they underscore the fact that the metaphors conservatives employ to create a sense of a natural or literal ground are irredeemably figural. Indeed, the reconstituted family at the end is working on such a high level of constructedness and figurality, an open-ended relationship between a human and a machine, that it could never touch ground with any literal authority of a sort that the closing images of nature might have conveyed in a conservative or ideological film. What rhetoric, like technology, opens is the possibility of an ungrounded play with social institutions, simulating them, substituting for them, reconstructing them, removing them from any ground of literal meaning that would hold them responsible to its authority. Perhaps this is why technology is such an object of fear in conservative science fiction films of the current era. It is a metaphor for a possibility of reconstruction that would put the stability of conservative social institutions in question.

But the longing for literality and nature in conservative technophobic films might also be indicative of an antinomy of conservatism in the modern world. As conservative economic values became ascendent, increasingly technical criteria of efficiency came to be dominant. In addition, conservative economic development emphasises the displacement of excessively costly human labour by machines. The increasingly technical sophistication of the economic world and the shift away from industrialised manufacturing to tertiary sector 'information age' production creates a hypermodernisation that is at odds with the traditionalist impulse in conservatism, the desire that old forms and institutions be preserved. Yet the new technologies make possible alternative institutions and lifestyles, as well as the reconstruction of the social world. Perhaps this accounts for the desire for a more literal, natural world in conservative films. It is a reaction to the world they themselves help create through an ideal of efficient economic development. One antinomy of conservatism is that it requires technology for its economic program, yet it fears technological modernity on a social and cultural plane. This can be read as a sign of the dilemma conservatives faced in the 1980s. In control of political and economic life, they could not gain power in the private realm of social values that on the whole continued to be more liberal.

Although in the mid-1980s there was a marked decline in the number of conservative technophobic films, those fearful of technology do not give up easily, as might be suggested by a film like *The Terminator* (1984), in which androids continue to look and act like Arnold Schwarzenegger. Indeed, the film is about a punitive robot that just won't give up. It keeps coming on, not having seen *Blade Runner*, unaware that it is supposed to forgive and forget.

Dystopias

Films about the future might seem to be the most aloof from contemporary social problems. Yet they frequently are characterised by radical positions that are too extreme for Hollywood realism. In some respects, the genre that seems most distant from the contemporary world

is the one most free to execute accurate descriptions of its operations. Fantasies of the future may simply be ways of putting quotation marks around the present. They carry out a temporal displacement that short-circuits the implicit ideological censors operative in the reigning realist narrative regime of Hollywood.

Future films on the Right dramatise contemporary conservative fears of 'terrorism', or socialism, or liberalism as in *Logan's Run* or *Escape from New York*. Left films (*Outland*, *Blade Runner*) take advantage of the rhetorical mode of temporal displacement to criticise the current inequalities of capitalism. These films display what we have called the American quandary. Conservative films evidence fears of liberal modernity, while Left films advertise the tremendous power of conservatism in economic matters even as they criticise it. The films put on display the split that runs through American society between a civil sphere dominated by liberals and run on quasi-democratic, pluralist principles, and an economic sphere, dominated by conservatives and run in a feudal manner, in which workers are essentially slaves of capital. As such, however, these films delineate a salient antinomy of contemporary capitalism. The principles of political liberty and self-determination that informed the bourgeois revolutions from the seventeenth to the nineteenth century have been successfully blocked from making incursions into the economic sphere, which has continued to operate on two levels. The liberal principle of 'freedom' governs the intercourse between capitalists as the principle of marketplace competition, while the intercourse between capitalists and workers operates according to the preliberal principle of domination and exploitation. Freedom, in the liberal sense of self-determination, has yet to reach that level of society, and one function of capitalist ideology is to prevent it from doing so. But the strategy of defense, like all such strategies, indicates a danger and a potential even as it successfully deflects them. The capitalist civil sphere must adhere to 'democratic' principles of operation because by so doing the ideological illusion is fostered that the whole society, including the economy, operates according to such principles. It is not accidental that capitalists now refer to their national fiefdoms as 'industrial democracies'. But the capitalist attitude toward such liberalism will always be only tentatively supportive. To prevent the incursion of the principles of political liberty into the economic sphere, capitalists will reserve the right to impose the neofeudal principles of the economy on civil society as a whole, revoking liberalism entirely. The prevalence of capitalist 'states of siege' in the world, from Pakistan and Turkey to South Korea and Chile, is an indicator of this reality, as is indeed also the undeclared state of siege carried out against workers and poor people during the Reagan years. But they also point to a threat; a siege indicates an embattled position. And this is the progressive possibility embedded in the American quandary and in the antinomy between liberal civil society and neofeudal, conservative economic society that became strikingly clear in the 1980s. The threat is that the principles of liberty and self-determination will finally enter the economic sphere, and one could interpret the hypertropism of capitalist self-justifications at this period in film (the hero phenomenon) as an indicator of an increase in that threat.

Signs of the threat emerge clearly in the imaginarily liberated space of the future film, especially in what are called dystopias. Dystopias, or negative utopias, predominate in the future-film culture of the 1970s and 1980s, in part as a result of the era's crisis of confidence. Dystopias generally project into the future the fears of the present, and their themes often transcode the sorts of anxieties that characterised that crisis – uncontrolled corporations, untrustworthy leaders, a breakdown of legitimacy, rising crime, etc. They are vehicles for populist and radical critiques of the capitalist ethic and of capitalist institutions (evident particularly in the popular *Road Warrior* films, which pose an ecological vision of liberal hope against the brutal primitivism of competitive capitalism). The dystopia films can therefore be seen as indirect, displaced articulations of progressive forces and desires that constituted a resistance to conservative hegemony in the 1980s and that pointed forward, literally as well as figurally, to alternative futures.

In the mid-1970s, populist fears were directed at the power of large corporations in films like *Soylent Green* (1973) and *Rollerball* (1975). Values of nature, family, ecology and individuality are posed against statist

domination, characterised by massification, modernisation and the destruction of family life. The destruction of the family, a locus of personal attachments, is equated with the impersonality of corporations. *Rollerball* concerns a sports hero named Jonathan (James Caan) whose world is controlled by a cartel of corporations and characterised by the breakdown of the family. Jonathan's wife is taken away by a corporate executive. In keeping with the populist ethos of the film, he in the end engages in an individualist rebellion against the corporations that rallies the people to him in a kind of revolution. As in so many films, the choice of literal examples is relevant to metaphoric meaning structures. The team against which he has to contest in the end is Japanese, and of course at this time the Japanese were beginning to undercut American world economic power. The radical edge of populism is evident in the film's critique of capitalist domination. Yet a conservative potential emerges in the privileging of traditional male-dominated family life and of individualism conjoined with a leadership principle. *Rollerball* operates ideologically by dichotomising the world of social alternatives into two possibilities – either individual freedom (linked with male property right over women) or totalitarian domination. No middle ground is allowed in this equation, no middle term. And anything that departs from the ideal of pure individual freedom (corporations, but also socialism) is by implication lumped under domination. Audience sympathy is thus potentially channeled toward support for small-business individualist capitalism, since everything else – from socialism to corporate liberalism to the welfare state – is made to look bad by being subsumed under the polar opposite of individualism. The success of such representational strategies in popular culture helps account for the absence of a socialist alternative in the United States.

If the mid-1970s are characterised by populist dystopias that articulate the growing feelings of resentment against corporations in American culture, in the late 1970s and early 1980s, a number of left-liberal and radical dystopias (*Quintet*, *Blade Runner*, *Outland*) appear that negatively represent the basic tenets of capitalism (the right to exploit labour, competition, etc.). In Altman's *Quintet* (1979) post-holocaust life consists of playing a brutal game in which the goal is to kill the other players through a complex system of alliance and betrayal. It is a market world; no one can be trusted; and kisses frequently precede slit throats. This disturbing allegory of capitalism was too bleak for late-1970s audiences desirous of more romanticised visions, and the film flopped.

Peter Hyams' *Outland* (1981) was more successful, perhaps because it was an obvious pastiche of *High Noon*, the story of a sheriff betrayed by his fellow townspeople who must stand up to outlaws alone. But the film is also one of the most accurate representations of the reality of labour exploitation under capitalism that has appeared in Hollywood. At a space mine, workers are given drugs to make them more productive, but as a result they become psychotic and commit suicide. The drugs eliminate the boring and oppressive features of work. 'When the workers are happy, they dig more; when they dig more, the company is happy; when the company is happy, I'm happy,' the manager tells the sherriff of the mine town, who attempts to end the practice. The company sends killers to prevent him, and he defeats them with the help of a woman scientist.

The conservative ascendancy of the early 1980s seemed to invite more radical counterattacks than Hollywood had hitherto seen. What is striking about films like *Outland* and *Blade Runner* is that in a future fiction mode they depict the present reality of capitalist labour exploitation, a reality usually kept off the Hollywood screen. Indeed, the harshness of that reality in part accounts for that absence, since it makes it necessary for the leisure world of post-work entertainment to be something that alleviates the boredom, lack of fulfillment, and pain of wage-labour exploitation. It is a commonplace of radical cultural criticism to say that many Hollywood films can in fact be characterised as the real world equivalents of the drugs of *Outland*. But what this suggests as well is that such drugs are indicators of very real pain, potentially threatening diseases.

These radical future films point out the feudal character of the wage-labour system and attempt to mobilise traditional representational forms (the western, the hard-boiled detective), as well as traditional liberal humanist ideals (freedom, charity) as critical weapons against that exploitation. The use of traditional representational codes is especially significant for drawing out the contradiction between the political ideals of liberty and the feudal reality of the economy. For those codes – especially the detective and the western – are associated in the tradition with the principles of liberalism. Even if they do so in an individualist manner, they promote the liberal value of freedom or self-determination. And they frequently argue as well for community cooperation and social responsibility. The anti-wealth ethos of the detective is especially marked by this trait. However, the dominant procapitalist ideological system of American culture has succeeded in limiting the applicability of those ideals to capitalist entrepreneurs and, as we have seen, that ideology is refortified during this era.

Because the western and the detective genres usually serve the ends of that ideology, their very narrative form suggests the liberal value of self-determination. The detective acts alone; the cowboy usually rejects community (as in *Shane*) for the open road. It is part of the critical strategy of films like *Outland* and *Blade Runner*, then, to apply those forms to the critique of economic exploitation. The use of such forms dramatises more strikingly the discrepancy between the values of freedom and self-determination on the one hand and the realities of mass exploitation on the other. On a formal level, they draw out the antinomy between a capitalist ideological sphere that justifies itself with ideals of freedom and a capitalist economic sphere that belies those ideals. In so doing, the films suggest that the reason for this segregation is that a revolution of the sort *Blade Runner* enacts metaphorically would probably result were those ideals allowed entry into the world of labour.

The American quandary we have described is thus one that promises to be more threatening to the Right than to the Left. For one senses that the Right can only be on the defensive, given the distribution of forces and of possibilities. Our argument has suggested that their hold on economic power is not firm; it is defensive, and it probably cannot forever withstand the incursion of liberal principles of self-determination into the economic sphere that dystopian films either imagine or suggest. Indeed, the growing prevalence of liberal principles in the civil sphere would seem to indicate that the current tendency is for liberal values to spread and for conservative ones to contract. This seems confirmed by the dominant defensive and resentful attitude toward non-economic matters that is evident in conservative dystopian films. In John Carpenter's *Escape from New York* (1981), for example, the metaphor of the 'fallen city' covers a lot of modern liberal terrain, from punk subcultures to feminism to liberal politics. The city is a conservative nightmare of minorities and criminals rampant. It is a case once again when the literal vehicle of the metaphor is a direct representation of conservative fears. A pro-*détente* president is about to sell out the United States to the Soviets, but he is kidnapped by terrorists. Only a tough, conservative, martial arts, military hero named Snake can save the day. In the last scene, he walks away contemptuously from the buffoonish president and the press as an American flag looms behind. (Will the real Führer please step forward?)

The edgy, resentful mood of the film characterises conservatives faced with the increasing power of liberal modernity (in social relations, sexuality and politics) and the increasing threat (reflected in a negative mode in current life and in the film as underclass crime) that the liberal principles which conservatives cannot quell in the private sphere might spread to the public economic sphere. If, at this time, liberal ideals tend to be reclusive and sentimentalist, confined to the private sphere, conservative social ideals tend to be hostile and resentful, in part because they are so much at odds with a modernity they cannot turn back. If liberal dystopias are either tragic or whimsically metaphysical and ironic in the early to mid-1980s – modes appropriate to a value system out of power – conservative dystopias evidence the brutal and resentful edginess of those anxious to turn the dystopia of modernity into a utopia of brutality. Yet we see something progressive in this situation. When the Nazi said that whenever he heard the word culture he reached for his revolver, it was because the radical Jewish culture of Weimar Berlin was indeed a threat to the Right. If conservatives seemed to be reaching for their guns a lot in this period, it was probably for a similar reason.

Human Artifice and the Science Fiction Film
J. P. Telotte

The human artifice of the world separates human existence from all mere animal environment, but life itself is outside this artificial world, and through life man remains related to all other living organisms. For some time now, a great many scientific endeavours have been directed toward making life also 'artificial', toward cutting the last tie through which even man belongs among the children of nature … There is no reason to doubt our abilities to accomplish such an exchange, just as there is no reason to doubt our present ability to destroy all organic life on Earth.

– Hannah Arendt[1]

'I know I'm human', the protagonist of John Carpenter's film *The Thing* asserts, as he frantically searches for a threatening alien presence among his comrades. Taken out of context in this way, such a declaration sounds almost pointless, like an assurance of something that should be evident to the gaze of those around, as indeed it seems to the movie viewers. The very need for such an assertion, consequently, hints at an unexpected uncertainty here, even an uneasiness about one's identity and, more importantly, about what it is that makes one human. It is an uneasiness, moreover, which cannot be dispelled by a simple gaze, the means by which we typically evaluate our world, others and ourselves. I call attention to the character MacReady's predicament because it makes overt a spectre which has continually haunted the science fiction film genre. Periodically throughout its history, but increasingly so in recent years, this formula has taken as its focus the problematic nature of the human being and the difficult task of being human. And as Hannah Arendt makes clear, the former concern seems to pose an ever greater barrier for the latter.

In this context, we should note the number of recent films which take as their major concern or as an important motif the potential doubling of the human body and thus the literal creation of a human artifice. Among others, films like the remakes of *Invasion of the Body Snatchers* and *The Thing*, *Blade Runner*, *Alien*, and even *Star Trek* explore some aspect of this motif, but especially a welcome or threatening capacity which inheres in this cloning or copying of the self, cell for cell, and which promises to make man both more and less than he already is. Not simply a current development, though, this motif runs throughout the history of science fiction film. Viewed from the perspective of their 'mad scientist' themes, the numerous Frankenstein and Dr. Jekyll/ Mr. Hyde films represent paradigms of this tendency; in fact, the enduring confusion in the popular imagination that attributes the single name of Frankenstein to both a monster and its creator underscores the effect of this doubling pattern. One of its earliest and most characteristic treatments, however, occurs in a film that many see as the prototype for the genre, Fritz Lang's *Metropolis*. The modeling of the heroine Maria into a destructive android look-alike serves as the narrative's centerpiece and prompts its greatest display of scientific gadgetry – that which we have come to expect to be the very core of the science fiction film. Visually indistinguishable from the real Maria, the android threatens to unleash dangerous desires in the human community and thus bring about disaster. Because she is both alluring and potentially destructive, the artificial Maria well represents the disturbing implications of that capacity for doubling and artifice which man's science has attained.

Probably the landmark treatment of this doubling motif occurs in the original *Invasion of the Body Snatchers*, which focuses precisely upon a threatening possibility for perfectly duplicating the human body, 'cell, for cell, atom for atom', as one character explains. In this case, it is an alien life form that uses nature wrongly, to grow seed pods which will deprive man of his own true nature, as they duplicate his body, 'snatch' his intellect, but deprive him of all emotional capacity. While films had previously presented such duplication as a threat, the product of human aberrance or some misguided science, *Invasion* added a disconcerting note and also laid open a desire which has frequently moved just beneath the surface of these films, by pointing up a subtle attraction at the heart of the doubling process. The bloodless victory of the copy, of the pods, is actually lauded by those who have been subsumed into this emotionless community.

This reaction suggests an elemental desire in man for the security and tranquillity which the sameness of duplication promises; as another character notes, this transformation permits man to be 'born into an untroubled world' and to abdicate from the many problems of modern life's problems posed, it is implied, by the very advances of science, especially in the field of warfare, which, on the surface, usually seem a basic concern of these films.

Don Siegel, director of the original *Invasion*, admits that he sought to inject this challenge of attractiveness in response to a widespread desire he noted to abdicate from human responsibility in the face of an increasingly complex and confusing modern world. To this end he

> purposely had the prime spokesman for the pods be a pod psychiatrist. He speaks with authority, knowledge. He really believes that being a pod is preferable to being a frail, frightened human who cares. He has a strong case for being a pod. How marvelous it would be if you were a cow and all you had to do is munch a little grass and not worry about life, death and pain. There'a strong case for being a pod.[2]

It is this 'strong case' that has been repeatedly and increasingly stated in films since the time of *Invasion*. *The Stepford Wives*, for instance, plays not just upon the threat of a gradual, insidious replacement of the women in a small town by mindless, dispassionate androids – apparently the perfect housewife – but also on the terror implicit in their similarity to what is held up as a cultural ideal and in the fact that this duplication is obviously desirable to those closest to the women, their own husbands. Perhaps because of our increasing concern with the potential for cloning and genetic research, such possibilities no longer seem so far-fetched, hence the recent spate of films exploring this complex proposition. They all emphasise man's fascination with knowledge and science, as has always been typical of the genre, but they link a single-minded pursuit of knowledge with that disconcerting desire to duplicate the self – or unleash the unknown power of duplication, as in *The Thing* – and its consequent rendering of the self almost irrelevant. In sum, they suggest how the human penchant for artifice – that is, for analysing, understanding and synthesising all

things, even man himself – seems to promise a reduction of man to no more than artifice.

This paradox also sheds some light on a subtle distinction which the science fiction film has typically sought to make in its depiction of man's attitudes towards science. As critics have frequently noted, the genre often seems to juxtapose a good and a bad science, white and black magic, as it were, with the one working to serve man and the other to threaten his position in the world. We might recall the novel *Frankenstein*'s subtitle, *The Modern Prometheus*, for it can help us to discern an even more telling distinction at work in the film genre. In its recurring manifestations, the doubling motif denotes a Faustian drive for knowledge or power, a dangerous and even self-destructive impulse behind that fascination with the power of science or some select knowledge to enable man to duplicate himself artificially. This Faustian impulse, however, typically tries to go masked as a Promethean one, that is, as a desire to bestow significant boons upon man. Of course, it is in the nature of those boons – not light but likeness, and not the potential of fire but its destructive force – that we eventually perceive the Faustian persona beneath the Promethean seeming that science and the scientist usually bear in the genre.

Why this seeming, however, and why should its ultimate expression take the very shape of seeming, namely the doubling or copying of the self? The persistence of this theme hints at a certain hubris of the mind with which the genre is concerned: a pride in a science which is seen as seeking to accommodate all things to the self, ultimately even the self, which, because of a lingering Cartesian dualism between the mind and body, thinking and feeling, has become associated with both the internal life of the mind and an external world of otherness, the not-mind.[3] The fashioning of other bodies, other forms of the self, only reinforces that split between mind and body and reasserts the hegemony of the former over the latter. What I would like to suggest, following Arendt's lead, then, is that we might see in this doubling motif the indication of a science turned inside out, a drive for knowledge and control become a desire for oblivion, although it is a blind desire, of the self unwittingly turned upon itself, even while apparently engaged in a process of valorising the self through the ability for replication.

The full paradox and threat inherent in this artificing of life lurks just beneath the surface of a film like *Alien*. In fact, the film's central horror, a monstrous presence that thrives on man, yet is apparently invulnerable to his normal defenses, seems metaphoric of some flaw within man, perhaps the Faustian drive that increasingly seeks expression. The murderous alien is brought into the spaceship because the company sponsoring the flight has established a primary directive for the crew to gather any information on life forms that might prove valuable. Arguing for this directive, and thus directly precipitating the alien's murderous rampage among the crew, is an android, a replica of man so perfect that he fools his fellow crew members. A perfect example of the danger behind this doubling pattern, he has been programmed to ensure the mission's knowledge-gathering activities, regardless of any danger which might accrue to the human component of the expedition. In the film's most startling scene, the alien creature that has embedded itself within one of the crew members suddenly bursts through his chest, killing the human host. Born from within man, this creature metaphorically embodies the monstrous potential of the double which has made its life possible. In short, the alien represents the displaced terror and the frightening aspect of that desire for knowledge which, also arising from within man, has begun to produce life-threatening doubles. It is only through this perspective of displacement that the complex plotting of *Alien*, and especially the discomfiting relationship between android and monster, comes into proper focus. In his discussion of the nature of man's proclivity for doubles, René Girard predicts just such a link and connects the desire for doubling to man's most violent impulses; as he notes, there is 'no double who does not yield a monstrous aspect upon close scrutiny'.[4]

The new version of *The Thing* specifically emphasises this 'close scrutiny', that is, the visual problem posed by the double. When a scientific research team stumbles upon and accidentally unthaws an alien creature embedded in the polar ice for thousands of years, they unleash not simply a monstrous creature, one that threatens those discoverers, but a figure that seems to summarise the problems of doubling located in both *Invasion of the Body Snatchers* and *Alien*. As one character

notes, this creature 'wants to hide inside an imitation' and it possesses the power to 'shape its own cells to imitate' any other being in its environment. That this capacity for perfect mimesis is not simply a protective mechanism, like a chameleon's colour adaptation, but a very real threat to man is underscored by the gruesome scenes of possession and transformation for which the film has been scored on occasion. In fact, *The Thing* seems to draw on *Alien*'s 'chest-buster' sequence as a model for these scenes – a connection which underscores the importance I have here attached to that previous scene and one which hints at an internal component in this alien doubling. What *The Thing* particularly adds to the previous formulations of this doubling motif is an emphasis on the contagiousness of this tendency, and thus its more than individual menace. As the doctor among the group calculates, at its current rate of assimilation of man, the alien polymorph could take over all of humanity in '27,000 hours from first contact'. It thereby threatens rapidly to reduce man's world to a realm of imitations, to make everyone simply an extension of that alien presence.

With the awareness of this threatening possibility, an equally devastating potential also emerges, one which inheres in every act of doubling. Because man is possessed of an absolute desire for certainty or knowledge – at least, so the science fiction genre argues through its emphasis on the compulsion for knowledge – he can easily become prey to an almost debilitating anxiety in the face of whatever stubbornly resists his attempts at formulation. And when this enigma is his own double or potential double, the anxiety may take even deeper root. Almost frantically, therefore, the men at this isolated outpost reach out for some answer, some assurance, even 'some kind of test', as one of them puts it, which might detect this alien presence in their midst and thus assure them that they are all just what they appear to be, truly men. Significantly, however, this task of detection and inquiry into the visible world quickly transforms into a suspicion of the human society in which they are immersed, even an uneasiness about the self; as one man asks, 'How do we know who's human?' It is a question that betrays a deep-seated fear, normally kept hidden yet essentially commonplace, of all that is not the self. Calling attention to this rapid breakdown of human society which the alien visitation has precipitated, MacReady notes that 'Nobody trusts anybody now.' What such a comment also bears witness to is an alien potential which resides in man, ever ready to be triggered by circumstances and to raise a disturbing suspicion not only about one's fellow man, but even about the self and its relationship to that human world it must inhabit.

What *The Thing* locates, therefore, is a certain thing-ness within man, an absence or potential abdication from the human world whi ch can only be made present or visualized in the mirror furnished by the doubling process. The confrontation with which the film ends, as MacReady and a black man, the only other survivor of the group, eye each other suspiciously, each equally sure that the other is only a double fashioned by the alien, metaphorically points up the distrust and fear which already typically mark modern society, and particularly its race relations. Of course, the doubling process which the alien initiated promised to render everyone the same, each an extension of that single intruder, and in their mutual fear of the other MacReady and his comrade have already fulfilled that promise after a fashion. Moreover, that threat precipitates with both men a retreat into the private space of the mind, the one stable ground upon which they feel they can still stand. In effect, the mind is thus seen as the true repository of the self, protectively questioning all about, while asserting with ever decreasing conviction one's own humanity, as we have already seen MacReady doing. If that phrase, 'I know I'm human', seems to ring hollow, it is because the narrative, through its visitation of this disconcerting doubling, has managed to undercut all certainty, all dependable knowledge, certainly all reliance on appearance. Consequently, at the film's conclusion even we are unsure if one or neither of the survivors is indeed a copy, just waiting his chance to spread his mimetic reign into the outside world. Indeed, we are left to question the very future of man's life on Earth, just as Arendt does.

In another sort of investigation into the nature of our modern culture, Loren Eisely has attempted to trace out the process by which 'man becomes natural', that is, how he came to see himself as a part of nature and its historical processes, rather than as a strange occurrence and an intrusion into the natural world. 'Before life could be viewed as in any way natural', he explains, 'a rational explanation of change through the ages' was needed;[5] man had to acquire a thorough knowledge of the patterns of evolution. The recent film *Blade Runner* dramatises the logical consequences of this mastery of evolutionary principles. The development of this understanding, the film suggests, serves as the springboard for the current concern with the possibilities of genetic engineering, which, in its turn, has generated a potential for scientifically controlled evolution: the creation and programming of perfect replicas of man, gifted with unusual beauty, strength or intelligence, and made to serve their human creators. As a result of this original step in 'becoming natural', however, apparently something has also been lost. As Eisely points out, while 'man has, in scientific terms, become natural … the nature of his 'naturalness' escapes him. Perhaps his human freedom has left him the difficult choice of determining what it is in his nature to be.'[6] The problematic nature of human nature is precisely the topic on which *Blade Runner* with its formulation of the doubling motif attempts to shed some light.

As in *The Thing*, a sense of uncertainty and the anxiety which attends it seem to colour the very world of *Blade Runner* and to derive in large part from the fascination with doubling which it chronicles. The futuristic environment the film describes seems perpetually dark and rainy, as gloomy as that of film noir – the conventions of which *Blade Runner* does in fact draw on. In this bleak atmosphere we can see mirrored an interior darkness that afflicts the characters here and seems brought on by the problems arising from a culture practically predicated upon the possibilities of duplication. In this future world, man has progressed to such a point that he can genetically design and reproduce virtually anything that lives; thus we see mechanical birds, snakes, dogs, and especially people – or 'replicants', as they are here termed – all of which are virtually indistinguishable from the real thing. They have been fashioned by man's science in order to satisfy his various desires, to free him from labour and the dangers of combat, or simply to amuse him. And yet in spite of these benefits, no one seems truly happy in this society; in fact, those who can do so readily abandon this world in favour of one of the 'off-world colonies', doubles of the Earth itself which, like so many of the copies here, are apparently perceived as being better than their original. We thus see a vision of man not only no longer at home with himself, but no longer at home with his home; and the human doubles promise to increase the level of anxiety by refusing to remain in their servile roles and demanding instead a life like that of their creators and models.

As is typically the case in the science fiction genre, then, a kind of monstrous creation has transpired, but it has gone masked as scientific advance. In the place of Frankenstein are two geneticists – Dr. Tyrell, master designer of replicants, and J. F. Sebastian, his chief genetic engineer. Both appear to have given that Promethean impulse free reign, pushing the desire to fashion a copy of man to its extreme in their specially designed androids for every task and every distraction. The ostensible project of providing for human needs, however, has clearly been submerged by a pride in the process of doubling itself. Tyrell, it seems, is moved solely by his fascination with creating ever more perfect copies, replicants which can defy those tests for humanity which have developed in this future world – just as *The Thing* predicts. And with the girl Rachael, whom he addresses at one point as 'my child', he has nearly succeeded. Sebastian has turned his engineering skills to a no less subjective end, the task of filling his lonely life with manufactured 'friends', albeit small, misshapen, flawed figures – apparently various reflections of his own flawed body, which suffers from 'premature decrepitude'. In sum, these scientists have turned their capacities for creating copies to their own ends, and in the process have endowed their creations with a certain reflexive capacity, Tyrell's figures mirroring his own desire for perfection, beauty and transcendence of mechanical limitation, Sebastian's reflecting not only his own defects, but also his flawed view of himself.

In these projections of the self, moreover, both have already created the conditions that must eventually render them irrelevant. Because they have programmed their replicant creations with memories of a life that never was – even providing them with photographs of supposed relations and friends – and thus

tried to convince them of their humanity, these engineers have erected a potentially dangerous bridge between the human and android realms. In fact, they have succeeded too well, for they have unleashed a synthetic but powerful desire for real life, one which – as is the case in films like *Frankenstein*, *Invasion of the Body Snatchers* and *The Thing* – initially places itself in opposition to the possessors of normal life, mankind. In attempting to return to Earth from the off-world colonies, the group of replicants with whom the narrative is concerned have already killed 23 humans; and after finding their way back, they predictably turn their attention to their creators, particularly Tyrell and Sebastian. What they quest for is the secret of their programmed lives, and particularly, after the fashion of men through the ages, the means to a longer life. In effect, they have embarked on a Promethean search of sorts, seeking the archetypal fire of life itself, but in that murderous trail they leave behind, we see the clearest signs of that violence which, as René Girard has noted, usually goes masked by the doubling process.[7]

An even more telling measure of the ambiguity which attaches to this doubling process is found in the absence of a sure anchor for our own sympathies in this situation. That is, in the absence of the more typical monstrous presence and as a natural outgrowth of the desire for a nearly perfect mimesis which has produced these doubles, our concern shifts uneasily about between the world-weary, alienated bounty hunter Rick Deckard and those replicants whom it is his task to hunt down and destroy. Another and equally compelling reason for these shifting sympathies, of course, is that, as we quickly recognise, both man and android here essentially share the same – a doubled – fate. Like Sebastian, the replicants suffer from their own form of premature decrepitude, a programmed mortality which ensures their inevitable death after four years of service. As a consequence, these androids face the same sort of disconcerting knowledge that man has always had to abide with, that of an inescapable and onrushing death. Fed up with his work as a bounty killer, meanwhile, Deckard meditates on the nature of his quarry and, in turn, begins to wonder about his own place in this confusing welter of being wherein everything, perhaps even himself, seems to have its double or be itself a copy. Thus he comments at one point, 'Replicants weren't supposed to have feelings; neither were blade runners' like himself. It is a complex mirroring pattern which has resulted from the doubling process, as men and androids begin to see themselves in each other and, discomfitingly, prod the others into a questioning of their very nature.

In the character of Rachael, Tyrell's nearly perfect replicant, this increasingly blurred distinction between man and the copies with which he has become obsessed finds its clearest example. Accepting the testimony of his own experienced eye, Deckard is initially fooled into believing her human, and he finds himself mysteriously attracted to her. What is more unsettling is that his fascination continues even after he administers the Voight-Kampff Empathy Test, which reveals that she is a replicant. The precise meaning of those test results quickly seems to evaporate in light of Rachael's manifest 'humanity', however: her love of music, desire for affection, concern for others and apparently a love for Deckard. Her response to the test's conclusions, asking Deckard, 'Did you ever take that test yourself?' only compounds his quandary; it causes him to reflect on his own humanity, on the nature, that is, of a hired killer. As a result of this reflection, the subsequent order to kill Rachael along with the other replicants prompts a marked shift in the blade runner's attitude, a questioning of that which usually goes unquestioned, namely the humanity of those who create – and destroy – these artificial lives. He thus refuses the order and instead runs off with her to spend whatever little time her short, engineered life leaves them together in a different world, as a last shot indicates, a realm of light, greenery and life, rather than the dark, rainy cityscape which has produced them both. In effect, Deckard takes Arendt's warning to heart, abandoning 'the human artifice of the world' in favour of a natural environment in which man might regain his truly human nature.

If it seems ironic that a replicant or double should provide the stimulus for such an awakening to the self and a proper sense of humanity, it may be a telling indication of how far modern man has come in his fascination with artifice and how much he has lost in exchange for that knowledge of how to double the self. No longer viewed simply as the abnormal desire of aberrant types, as

in the numerous films which have focused on mad-scientist types, doubling has here become the very hallmark of society, something its members take for granted – but like many things we take for granted, it is also a pernicious influence. As *Blade Runner* suggests, when this abiding fascination with doubling becomes a dominant force in man's life, he clearly runs the risk of becoming little more than a copy himself, potentially less human than the very images he has fashioned in his likeness. Man's scientific advances, in sum, threaten to render him largely irrelevant, save as an empty pattern within which knowledge might be stored and through which it might extend its grasp, further increase its capacities, and expand the realm of artifice.

At another level we should find it most fitting that a double should spur an awakening to a sense of self. In essence, another form of the doppelgänger archetype, the replicant might be expected to serve the sort of salutary function that other archetypal patterns do. In explaining the effect of archetypal images on the psyche, psychologist James Hillman notes that 'reversion through likeness, resemblance', affords the mind 'a bridge … a method which connects an event to its image, a psychic process to its myth, a suffering of the soul to the imaginal mystery expressed therein'.[8] In such 'resemblance', he claims, there is located a path to a psychic truth which we have forgotten or lost sight of amid the welter of modern-day experience. Because of its reflective dimension, then, the image of the double, android, replicant or copy holds out a great promise, even as it seems rather threatening, for it carries the potential of bringing us back to ourselves, making us at home with the self and the natural world almost in spite of ourselves. We might view the combat between Deckard and the android Roy Batty in exactly this context. In the middle of their fight, Deckard slips from the top of a building and dangles precariously in the air; only the outstretched hand of Batty, grabbing Deckard at the last moment, stops his fall and brings him back from the brink of death to a possible life. It is precisely the sort of saving potential or 'reversion' which always inheres in the image of the double and which may ultimately best explain the continuing fascination it holds for us.

In attempting to map out the large territory of fantasy narratives, Tzvetan Todorov identifies a singular tension at work in the form which reflects the fundamental experience of its audience. Both reader (or viewer) and protagonist, he asserts, 'must decide if a certain event or phenomenon belongs to reality or to imagination, that is, must determine whether or not it is real. It is therefore the category of the real which has furnished a basis for our definition.'[9] As a result of this indeterminacy, we experience 'a certain hesitation' as we try to 'place' the events of the narrative within a known field of personal experience or reservoir of knowledge, just as the story's characters do. In this moment of hesitation, we should be able to discern the problem of representation which lies at the genre's very core, for we hesitate because of an immediate challenge to our usual system of referents, the stock of images which lived experience normally affords. At the same time, of course, that hesitation achieves a valuable purpose in prompting this stock-taking and thus starting a most subtle reflective experience.

In its recurrent concern with a doubling motif, the science fiction film thus draws on one of the fantastic's deepest structural patterns. In those images which fall outside of our normal lexicon, the film genre admits to a mystery or enigma that is at its centre; and in bracketing the image of man – through those copies or replicants – within this enigmatic category, it admits of a puzzle to which we too are a part. Even as it limns the progress or potential of science, reason and knowledge, therefore, the genre also acknowledges an underlying mystery and ambiguity, certainly in the approximations with which our mimetic impulse has always had to content itself. The fact that these disconcerting copies are in our own shape reminds us how little science has yet learned of substance about man, how little,

in essence, we know about the most alluring of models for mimesis. As Arendt noted – and as our accomplishments in genetic engineering every day point up – we already possess the potential which science fiction films have so frequently described, that for crafting artificial versions of man. What these films hope to forestall is the dark obverse of this capacity, that for making human nature artificial as well.

Notes

1 *The Human Condition* (Chicago: University of Chicago Press, 1958), p. 2.

2 Quoted by Stuart Kaminsky in *Don Siegel: Director* (New York: Curtis Books, 1974), p. 104.

3 For a more detailed discussion of this split between the rational and sensory or emotional aspects of man, see Vivian Sobchack's *The Limits of Infinity* (New York: A. S. Barnes, 1980), and Lane Roth's 'The Rejection of Rationalism in Recent Science Fiction Films', *Philosophy in Context*, 11, (1981), 42–55.

4 *Violence and the Sacred*, trans. Patrick Gregory (Baltimore: Johns Hopkins University Press, 1977), p. 160. As Girard notes elsewhere, 'mimetic desire cannot be let loose without breeding a midsummer night of jealousy and strife', 'Myth and Ritual in Shakespeare', in *Textual Strategies*, ed. Josue V. Harari (Ithaca: Cornell University Press, 1979), p. 192.

5 *The Firmament of Time* (New York: Atheneum, 1966), p. 72.

6 *The Firmament of Time*, p. 114.

7 In addition to *Violence and the Sacred*, see Girard's *Deceit, Desire, and the Novel*, trans. Yvonne Freccero (Baltimore: Johns Hopkins University Press, 1966).

8 *The Dream and the Underworld* (New York: Harper & Row, 1979), p. 4.

9 *The Fantastic: A Structural Approach to a Literary Genre*, trans. Richard Howard (Ithaca: Cornell University Press, 1975), p. 167.

Dream Girls and Mechanic Panic: Dystopia and its Others in *Brazil* and *Nineteen Eighty-Four*

Linda Ruth Williams

In 1983 a short Terry Gilliam film was released as a B-feature to Monty Python's *The Meaning of Life*, but *The Crimson Permanent Assurance* could also be seen as the companion text to *Brazil* (1985), Gilliam's next full-scale project. A group of slavishly downtrodden office lackeys (old guard refugees from a world when commerce was more gentlemanly) rise up and mutiny, overthrowing their free-market corporate oppressors, an act so miraculous that it transforms their building into a galleon, which sets sail on the Gilliamesque 'wide accountant-sea'. The complete defeat of the parent company, The Very Big Corporation of America, is next on their list. Opening, as the voice-over puts it, 'in the bleak days of 1983, as England languished in the doldrums of a ruinous monetarist policy', the fantasy of 'reasonably violent' office-pirates successfully trashing their erstwhile employers is hardly subtle. A utopian daydream of collective action, which, in the time-honoured tradition of using the bosses' ropes to hang them with, turns filing cabinets into cannons, coat-hooks into cutlasses and office minions into vigilante heroes. Unlike other filmic utopias, which focus on personal gain or map out brave new future-worlds, the mission of Gilliam's men is to overthrow corporate dominance. Part-way between an Ealingesque revenge-of-the-little-man and *Battleship Potemkin* (1925). (Gilliam also parodies the Odessa steps sequence in *Brazil*), *The Crimson Permanent Assurance* replaces proletarian sweat with bureaucratic drudgery, but the defeated enemy is still the same: 'A financial district swollen with multinationals, conglomerates and fat, bloated merchant banks.' Nothing can stop the victorious ship – except the fact that this is utopia (ou-topia – no-place) not Thatcher's Britain, and it happens to be cartoon-flat. The ship drops off the edge of the earth.

Then in 1985 came *Brazil* (one working title of which was *1984½*), a dark, surrealistically-witty dystopian vision of an unlocatable time in which bureaucracy manipulates people rather than the other way around, and the compliant hero/cog-in-the-wheel (Sam Lowry, played by Jonathan Pryce) is finally punished for his conformist complicity. *Brazil* is quintessentially Gilliamesque, in blurring the distinction between real and dream-states, sane and mad, inside and outside; in its fascination with the machine as body and the body in the machine; and in its obsession with systems. It is uneasily pitched somewhere between past and future, generally identifiable yet also quite specific: the opening text reads '8.49 pm: Somewhere in the twentieth century'.

Quite a different film was the previous year's *Nineteen Eighty-Four*. Directed by Michael Radford, this was the second cinematic reworking of George Orwell's 1949 novel (the first was Michael Anderson's rather dutiful 1956 version). Winston Smith (played by John Hurt) might be Sam Lowry's depressed brother, positioned against a canvas of a totalitarian but visibly mid-twentieth-century Britain (despite its renaming as Airstrip One, the centre of Oceana, now one of the world's three superpowers). Oceana is engaged in an ongoing war with Eurasia, and news reports give constant updates, broadcast incessantly, along with messages from Party leader Big Brother, through the omnipresent two-way telecast screens which are fixed into every room, breaking down the distinction between the public and the private. Propaganda infuses every scene; indeed, it is Winston's job at the Ministry of Truth to rewrite history according to the purposes of the Party, inscribed in Newspeak. Truth is a commodity, manipulable and entirely subject to power. As the film proceeds, and as Winston's distance from these 'truths' becomes more marked, the question of whether the war – and indeed Big Brother – are real, or just a fabrication used to manipulate the populace into compliance, is raised. The ultimate rule-breaking comes when Winston meets the free-spirited Julia. In a society which has outlawed not just private life but the orgasm itself, the pair become erotic dissidents by embarking on a sexual relationship. They are punished for it: arrested, tortured (Winston is taken to the dreaded Room 101 to confront his worst fears), brainwashed into compliance and mutual betrayal, the pair finally submit individual identity and will to the overarching vision of the Party and the world of 'doublethink'.

Brazil's strange future-past is altogether different, although the films have some uncanny similarities. *Nineteen Eighty-Four* fits quite neatly into a long tradition of filmically imaged worlds both better and worse, and *Brazil* too might be read alongside other black-humorous, parodic-postmodern dystopias of the 1980s and 1990s – *Delicatessen* (1990), *Prayer of the Rollerboys* (1991), even *Mad Max* (1979) – although it owes far more to Kafka or Lewis Carroll than to the visual stylistics of the pop video, and is infused with a dark eco-horror which echoes *Blade Runner* (1982) and looks towards *The Fifth Element* (1997). *Brazil* is a vertiginous urban nightmare – it is also very funny.

Bureaucracies are Gilliam's particular *bête noire*, and machines themselves, more than how they are used, become his prime signifiers. Gilliam's 'tech noir' is never 'high tech' – the grungy, Heath-Robinsonesque machines which are the externalisation of baroque bureaucracies and psyches are the most striking element of his *mise-en-scène* – think of the devil's machines in *Time Bandits* (1981), the time machines in *Twelve Monkeys* (1996). As Gilliam said with a shrug in a recent interview, 'It just seems that I have this German-Expressionistic-Destructivist-Russian-Constructivist view of the future' (Morgan 1996: 20). *Brazil* is set in an enclosed world when even outdoors feels like indoors, when social stratification is keen, but success is particularly marked both by the pleasures of conspicuous consumption and by the power to manipulate bureaucratic processes. But all inhabitants seem to be equal prisoners of their disastrous world: this is not *Metropolis* (1926), the golden palace built on the slavery of workers doomed to pay for others' excesses which benefits an elite strata. Here there are no winners.

Like Winston Smith, Sam Lowry is a lowly government pen-pusher, existing in a Hades of office procedure at the Ministry of Information. If Winston Smith collapses or subsumes his private, dissenting self into a flat faith in public 'truths', Sam retains a private self as a space of escape: his 'real' life exists in his dreams of a blonde damsel in distress, who gives him the chance to be a hero (the inane 1930s song 'Brazil', which gives the film its title, is about escape or return to a lost romantic idyll). Retreat into fantasy as interior dream-state

or as mass romance is crucial to the film's sense of darkness. The images of Hollywood icons which cram the walls of Sam's flat are little glimmers of light; his nocturnal heroics set the futile drudgery of daytime into relief. The sinister surveillance systems which, in *Nineteen Eighty-Four*, bear out the phrase 'Big Brother is Watching You', are subverted into a bizarre facility for fantasy-escape in *Brazil*: the 'surveyors' use their telescreens not to look out for illegalities but to hack into old movies.

However, Sam has connections in higher places. He is persuaded to take up a job at the leaner, meaner department of Information Retrieval, and so is able to trace this dream-girl, whom he has stumbled upon in real life. Jill (Kim Griest) is a suspected terrorist, and after Sam gets involved with her, he is arrested and tortured (by his best friend Jack Lint [Michael Palin], who is only doing his job). The film ends twice: first, in the 'happy' ending preferred by Universal Studios in America (who insisted on a more cheerful, shorter edit for US audiences), with the couple's heroic escape to an idyllic rural location; second, when this is revealed as a false ending, and we cut back to Sam's blank face in the torture chamber. Rural escape is then just Sam's mental act, a hallucination dreamed up to negate the horror of torture.

Brazil is infused with a machine-age panic, the keynote of its dystopianism, reminiscent of Chaplin's famous factory-floor pantomime in *Modern Times* (1936): the motors – actual or procedural – just keep running, sometimes to excess and always regardless of the bodies that are in the way. Flailing around the edges of the process are human beings – worried conformists (like Sam), exuberant vigilantes (like Robert De Niro's Tuttle), real victims (like Buttle's family), frustrated punters passed from desk to desk (like Jill, before she gets into her truck and takes action). Gilliam's machines act like fleshly and extrapolated bureaucratic systems. When Sam's air-conditioning system goes wrong it invades his flat and forces him to retreat into the fridge: the very fabric of the building revolts. He can do nothing without Form 27B/6 which jobsworth Central Services engineer Spoor (Bob Hoskins) demands before he will make Sam's life livable again. The film thus partly investigates the success of the totalitarian personality: how or whether Sam can become worker DZ/015 when he finally takes up the job at Information Retrieval. If *Nineteen Eighty-Four* shows the success a brutal system has in slotting its minions into their allotted roles given enough acts of 'persuasion', *Brazil* shows how hard it is to enforce absolute compliance. If its characters conform, it is only with great resistance and difficulty. Even Spoor's procedural arch-perfectionism is not an act of selfless submission, as it might be in *Nineteen Eighty-Four*, but a sadistic strategy: Hoskins's performance is more that of a cowboy builder who's taking you for a ride than a by-the-book drone. The stupidity of a baroque rule-system has become a way of inflicting psychological pain or flaunting petty power-gains.

The grotesque is also more interesting to Gilliam than the normal or the natural. In *Brazil* standardisation breeds weirdness; there are cracks and we get to glimpse what oozes out of them – even the storm-troopers are caught practising Christmas carols in the basement. In one of the film's most impressive performances, Kathryn Pogson plays repressed spinster Shirley as a twitchy, gauche bundle of neurosis, the animated sign of familial and social ill-health. Clearer walking examples of the system's failure to guarantee completely the response of its people are Gilliam's maverick heroes, who can't be bothered with form-filling and cannot be identified by Information Retrieval (these wild men are everywhere – De Niro here is echoed in Robin Williams's fallen yuppie in *The Fisher King* (1991); a darker escapee is Bruce Willis's character in *Twelve Monkeys*, split between two time zones and belonging in neither). But in actual fact it is hard to find any images of a fully and successfully mechanised self in *Brazil*, despite the film's obsession with processes of control. One exception might be the audio-typist who works for torturer Lint, cheerfully typing the screams and pleas she's hearing through her headphones, her powers of comprehension bypassed by a skill developed so perfectly that information can come in (through the ears) and go out (onto paper) without ever pausing in her conscience.

A dialogue of difference and similarity animates comparison between *Nineteen Eighty-Four* and *Brazil*, yet the closer they are scrutinised the more different they become. It is hard to find a contemporary review which doesn't mention the Orwellian nature of Gilliam's film, which he himself had tagged 'a post-Orwellian view of a pre-Orwellian world'

(Johnson 1993: 204). Philip French called *Brazil* 'pop-Orwell played for laughs' (*Observer* 24 February 1985), whilst Mat Snow saw it as a 'Pythonised' *Nineteen Eighty-Four* (*New Musical Express* 23 February 1985). Keith Nurse wrote that 'if [*Brazil*] is Orwellian in tone, it is also positively Pythonesque in form' (*Daily Telegraph* 22 February 1985), whilst George Perry's *Sunday Times* headline was 'Big Brother and the Python' (*Sunday Times* 27 January 1985). Both films are haunted by the spectre of 1984 as a real year as well as an Orwellian horror. *Nineteen Eighty-Four* is not just any 1980s film (it would have been perverse to have released it, say, in 1982 or 1985); it hangs on to the legend not just of its text but of its year. As the closing credits roll at the film's conclusion its claim to authenticity is sealed by the message, 'This film was photographed in and around London during the period April–June 1984, the exact time and setting imagined by the author.' Though it went into production later than *Brazil*, its producers ensured that it would nevertheless appear in its eponymous year. After Gilliam's protracted battle with Universal, his film finally premiered in the US in 1985. Although *Brazil* was backed by American finance and directed by a born-American, it was shot mostly in Britain (except for a couple of scenes shot in France) using a largely British cast and crew; Gilliam had lived and worked in Britain for close to twenty years prior to its release; and it was received as the product and representation of a very British sensibility. That both films work through peculiarly British dystopian visions is crucial to their tone, cult status and relationship to their moment.

But that both films retain traces of utopianism is also crucial to the tone of their darkness. It is hard to discuss dystopias without addressing their imaginative Other; utopia is implied by dystopia, in these films and in wider thought. Few theorists address one without reference to the other: study of dystopianism is sometimes understood as a sub-set of the much larger area of utopian studies, which has burgeoned since the 1960s. Indeed, the distinction between the two, the sense that dystopias and utopias are negative and positive definitions of each other, is further blurred by the frequent argument that one man's utopia is another man's dystopia. In her illuminating 1990 survey of utopian thought, Ruth Levitas discusses how both Aldous Huxley's *Brave New*

World (1932) and B. F. Skinner's *Walden Two* (1948) 'were received by some as utopias and by others as anti-utopias' (Levitas 1990: 22). '[T]he optimism of utopia and the pessimism of dystopia,' writes Levitas, 'represent opposite sides of the same coin – the hope of what the future could be at best, the fear of what it may be at worst' (Levitas 1990: 139, discussing Kumar 1987). In the films under discussion here, utopian moments are contained within a largely dystopian vision. True, almost every detail of *Nineteen Eighty-Four*'s *mise-en-scène* is discomforting and at times quite hard to watch, and the film's morbid 'message' is viscerally clear. The ending of *Brazil* is one of the bleakest in 1980s cinema. Fredric Jameson argues that 'anti-Utopianism constitutes a far more easily decodable and unambiguous political position' than its utopian Other (Jameson 1988: 76); dystopian images, like Orwell's, are for Jameson a version of utopian socialism rendered in negatives, and *Nineteen Eighty-Four*, film and novel, bears this out. However, I will argue here that at the heart of these bleak visions of totalitarian control lies a singular utopian image, the vision of a woman, the centre of both films' dystopic contradictions. Woman functions in *Brazil* and *Nineteen Eighty-Four* as a spectacle of interruption, an escape from the dark dystopic terrain – a sublime 'pause' which opens up a set of crucial issues about the inextricability of dream and despair in 1980s cinematic culture.

'The other side of now': Nineteen Eighty-Four as topical allusion

If in the 1960s 'the question of Utopia' was reinvented (Jameson 1988: 75), the 1970s and 1980s also saw its dystopian Other explored afresh. H. Bruce Franklin begins his survey of 'Visions of the future in science fiction films from 1970 to 1982' with the crashing generalisation, 'By the end of the 1960s, it seemed that we were experiencing the most profound crisis in human history … visions of decay and doom had become the normal Anglo-American cinematic view of our possible future' (Franklin 1990: 19). It may also be that by the time Terry Gilliam and Michael Radford came to make *Brazil* and *Nineteen Eighty-Four* respectively in the mid-1980s, dystopianism was not primarily a means of articulating a feared future or of fending off an alternative (socialist) social

structure (as was Orwell's original novel), but a shrewd engagement with Britain's present (Gilliam's 'bleak days of 1983').

Fredric Jameson's important 1977 discussion of cultural utopianism, 'Of islands and trenches: neutralisation and the production of utopian discourse' (in Jameson 1988), bears this out. Although Jameson is addressing how utopian thought functions as a critique of the conditions which bring it into being, much of what he has to say is relevant to this analysis. For Jameson, one of the 'distinctive traits' of the utopian text is contemporaneity: an element 'of topical allusion,' he writes, 'is structurally indispensable in the constitution of the Utopian text' (Jameson 1988: 82). Utopias operate dialectically by neutralising the (dystopian) world from which they sprung. This is in keeping with a wider tradition of utopian criticism, but dystopias function in a similar way. Ruth Levitas writes that dystopias have often been read 'as apologetics for the status quo', but she highlights Krishan Kumar's view that dystopianism is 'intimately connected to the utopian impulse itself and … may be deeply critical of the present' (Levitas 1990: 176). *Brazil*'s Preliminary Production Notes situated the film in a 'retro-future' which is defined as 'a way of looking at the future through the past, of revealing, so to speak, the other side of now'. If Orwell's novel addressed his present, Radford's and Gilliam's films address theirs.

Critics have found it hard to discuss *Nineteen Eighty-Four* outside of a debate about adaptation and the film's faithfulness to Orwell's original text. A narrative if not visionary ancestor is also George Lucas's *THX 1138* (1970), featuring a story-line of illicit love dragged straight out of Orwell, but worked through visionary *mise-en-scène* which is Lucas's own, focusing on star-crossed lovers who discover illicit desire in the shadow of a nebulous totalitarian regime. When read in terms of Anthony Burgess's point that *Nineteen Eighty-Four* is not future but past, not dystopian prediction but nihilistic analysis of Orwell's own 1948, the film's timely appearance in 1984 itself seems perhaps irrelevant. Clearly its tone and design evoke the grim postwar austerity of Orwell's anti-communist tract rather than conjuring up any dark scene of future shock – this is a future built from the past.

How, then, do we read the film through Jameson's observation, that 'The ultimate subject matter of Utopian discourse ... [is] ... its own conditions of possibility as discourse' (Jameson 1988: 101)? Is it necessary to read *Nineteen Eighty-Four* as itself a reading of 1984, not 1948, suspended as it is – in *mise-en-scène*, in its identity as film-of-novel, in its peculiar faithfulness to a postwar vision – between two times, and two different cultural forms? Or – in Krishan Kumar's words – 'How much is 1984 like *Nineteen Eighty-Four*?' (Kumar 1987: 292). Kumar (whose discussion is confined to analysis of Orwell's text and does not touch on Radford's film) is keen to retain the possibility that a novel ostensibly written about or for 1948 still addresses the real 1984 which Orwell did not live to see. For Kumar, its contemporaneity is bound up with its Englishness: '*Nineteen Eighty-Four* is about us,' he writes, 'it is about our own times. That, as Orwell points out, is one reason for the English setting of the novel: to show that it could happen here' (Kumar 1987: 295). The film's producer, however, preferred to see *Nineteen Eighty-Four* as a bizarre kind of feelgood film: Sheila Johnston quotes Simon Perry as saying 'Orwell's vision mercifully bears little resemblance to the real state of things in this year of 1984 ... When you come out of the theatre, it will be a lift to find the world as it actually is' (*Monthly Film Bulletin* December 1984). Some hope. Those who saw the whole of Thatcher's reign as a trial of totalitarianism may be tempted to schematically map film events onto real events (and Kumar's 'here' may even extend to 1997, when I noticed that a security and surveillance company employed by one Liverpool store was calling itself 'Big Brother Inc'). However, this is an extension of critical practice adopted in relation to Orwell's text itself. A whole area of Orwell studies is dominated by analysis of the novel as prophecy not fiction, with critics merrily 'ticking off' what Orwell got right and what he got wrong as history passes.

But given *Nineteen Eighty-Four*'s acute scrutiny of the problem of truth in the form of propaganda, reading its fictional history as an adjunct of real history seems strange. If anything, the film suggests that we can never know the truth of our moment behind the obfuscation of what 'they' would want us to know of it. It does, after all, begin with the lines:

Who controls the past controls the future.
Who controls the present controls the past.

This is a 'truth' which Radford, and maybe Orwell himself, would have us read across the film and back out to our own awareness of the conditions of our history and readings.

The film adds another layer to this quandary of the real and the fictive, of the fictive as a prophetic allegory of the real. In this it goes one visual stage better than its source-novel. One of its primary assaults on the senses is the incessant telescreen announcements which saturate all levels of the world of *Nineteen Eighty-Four*. Wherever Winston goes there is a telescreen, showing documentary war footage or the still image of Big Brother, accompanied by a flat, triumphal, dogmatic Voice orating the latest Newspeak of the war with Eurasia. The images are often real (the film uses 'found' documentary footage rather in the manner of Oliver Stone in *JFK* (1991) and *Nixon* (1995). *Nineteen Eighty-Four* thus in part takes in a history of real conflict which stands in, visually, for the perpetual war Oceana is fighting. Only three locations offer a brief escape from the Voice and the telescreen, which is obligatory in every room: the countryside visited on an illegal Sunday excursion, the bedroom which Winston and Julia rent for their liaisons, and – most significantly – O'Brien's (Richard Burton's) office. As a high-ranking Party official, O'Brien has the power to turn the Voice off (one of his privileges, he says – even though the telescreen is mouthing his truths), so turn it off he does.

But what the Voice speaks is lies; what the images tell us are both lies and truth: 'These are our people', says the announcement as we see soldiers going over the top, planes crashing, blitzed houses, tanks advancing, all apparently 'found' images from the major conflicts of the twentieth century, accompanied by the Voice telling us of Oceana's glorious victories. A vague composite of Nazi rallies, holocaust victims, fleeing refugees, is montaged in sync with an Oceana-specific spoken text. Later in the film, as Winston sinks into ideological scepticism, the same footage is repeated, this time accompanied by Winston's own gloss: 'War is not real,' he says 'or when it is victory is not possible. The war is not meant to be won, it is meant to be continuous.' Finally, in the film's last sequence when Winston has conformed, the same images recur for a third time, with a voice-over which returns to its triumphal mode. What we see and what we hear are then two different things. What we see is recognisably 'our' history. The images reach, if not to the war beyond the image, then at least to a history of news and newsreel images we know (or thought we knew) were images of the real. Even in the half-seen flashes of moments of conflict, surrender, defeat and execution which pervade the film on the omnipresent telescreens, the awful roll-call of twentieth-century warfare is all too clear, its malleable truth-value even clearer. But what we hear accompanying this is a pastiche of propaganda, a controlling fiction masked as news. We see our history, we hear someone else's fiction. Between real 'found' images and the Voice itself there is a gap which begs the question, if that is not an image of the defeat of Eurasia, which does not exist, what is it? Whose truth? The truth and not the truth: a sepia staccato history of war from the moment it could first be filmed, undermined, resignified, in its juxtaposition with words. The distrust of the visual is pervasive, even when what you see rightly 'belongs to' and speaks of a world outside of the film's fiction.

However, perhaps more important than *Nineteen Eighty-Four*'s deployment of historical footage to signify its Otherness is the way it uses images which are far more familiar – grassy fields, glamorous women, sexual excess – to signify utopian escape, offering a confrontation of difference which Jameson calls the 'utopian event'. I want to turn back to Jameson briefly to explain how this utopic Otherness is displayed rather than told.

The utopian event: spectacle and narrative

For Jameson, utopian texts are important not because of what they are but because of what they *do*, functioning as critique (like Thomas More's 'neutralisation' of Tudor England as the negative referent in *Utopia* [1516]) and as a kind of imaginative provocation, encouraging a contemplation both of what is and of what could be. The post-1960s moment is for Jameson not Bruce Franklin's dystopian backlash of decay and doom, but a space of positive reflection and theorising that is the logical follow-up to the action of May 1968, with the 1970s inaugurating 'the maturation of a whole new generation of literary Utopias': 'The transition from the 1960s to the 1970s was a passage from spontaneous practice to renewed theoretical reflection ... after the reawakening of the Utopian impulse of the

previous decade' (Jameson 1988: 76–7). For Jameson, cultural texts (and he is particularly interested in Ursula LeGuin's *The Dispossessed* [1974]) can enact that theoretical reflection, but they do so in a very specific way, privileging spectacle and exegesis rather than narrative explanation and dynamism. '[I]t is less revealing', writes Jameson,

> to consider Utopian discourse as a mode of narrative, comparable, say, with novel or epic, than it is to grasp it as an object of mediation, analogous to the riddles or koan of the various mystical traditions, or the aporias of classical philosophy, whose function is to provoke a fruitful bewilderment and to jar the mind into some heightened but uncon-ceptualisable consciousness of its own powers, functions, aims and structural limits. (Jameson 1988: 87–8)

Utopias thus work by instigating 'a concrete set of mental operations', rather than setting out 'someone's 'idea' of a 'perfect society'' (Jameson 1988: 81). The utopian moment is a kind of hesitation or hiatus, a shock or disjunctive interval when narrative action is subordinated in an act of showing.

Throughout 'Of Islands and Trenches' Jameson quotes (and heavily depends upon) Louis Marin's *Utopiques: Jeux d'espaces* (1973). Developing the notion of utopia as a 'break' which neutralises the conditions from which it springs, he writes that, 'the Utopian event itself' is a 'revolutionary fête [in which] ... historical time was suspended' (Marin quoted in Jameson 1988: 77). A moment outside of history – outside of narrative unfolding? – Jameson seems to edge closer to suggesting an almost deistic possibility of the suspension of time. But we might more positively see this as an activation of that etymological rendering of utopia as 'no place'. Utopia in Jameson is a suspension of *this* place which enables something else to be imagined. Thus by definition utopia cannot be ordinarily 'eventful':

> if things can really happen in Utopia, if real disorder, change, transgression, novelty, in brief if history is possible at all, then we begin to doubt whether it can really be a Utopia after all, its institutions ... slowly begin to turn around into their opposite, a more properly dystopian repression of the

unique existential experience of individual lives. (Jameson 1988: 95)

Jameson's balancing act here is subtle. I am reminded of that David Byrne line, 'Heaven is a place where nothing ever happens' – and Earth is a place where everything does. It is so tempting to read this within a theological framework which would deem earthly action – movement or drive – as the agent, if not of the devil, then of the dystopic, with the stillness and stasis of utopia as a reinvented heavenly, if revolutionary, space. Jameson's moment of *fête* is not empty, however, even if it is non-narrative. 'In Utopian discourse,' writes Jameson, 'it is the narrative itself that tends to be effaced by and assimilated to sheer description, as anyone knows who has ever nodded over the more garrulous explanatory passages in the classical Utopias' (Jameson 1988: 95). Utopia is spectacle more than story (or explanation); it is a kind of provocative *showing*. Although he is discussing literary texts, Jameson picks open a form of writing which might be likened to the cinematic spectacle, calling utopian writing a 'timeless maplike extension of the nonplace' (Jameson 1988: 95). There is, of course, a paradox here. With the suspension of history in that 'revolutionary fête' goes narrative too, particularly difficult since the texts Jameson is dealing with are utopian narratives. As the plethora of utopian titles indicates (William Morris's *News from Nowhere* [1890], Samuel Butler's *Erewhon* [1872], or Tom Moylan's survey of feminist utopias, *Demand the Impossible* [1896]), utopias are essentially impossible, and they address impossibility:

Utopia's deepest subject, and the source of all that is most vibrantly political about it is precisely our inability to conceive it, our incapacity to produce it as a vision, our failure to project the Other of what is, a failure that, as with fireworks dissolving back into the night sky, must once again leave us alone with this history. (Jameson 1988: 101)

Utopian narratives are then not only stories which enact a hesitation in the history from which they came, but narratives which ask to be read outside of the time they are formally and historically subject to, as *fête*, event, a literary form of *showing*. Utopian discourse is profoundly characterised by a tension, 'between

description and narrative, between the effort of the text to establish the co-ordinates of a stable geographical entity, and its other vocation as sheer movement and restless displacement, as itinerary and exploration and, ultimately, as event' (Jameson 1988: 95). This tension, this crisis between 'events' and 'display', shows the utopian hiatus, in Jameson's literary texts, to be remarkably like the kind of work in which our *dystopian* films are engaged. Dystopian as well as utopian texts are provocative rather than representational, important not because of what they *are* but because of what they *do*. The dystopias under discussion here are important not because of what they overtly *say* – their dark 'content', their narrative gloom and enveloping pessimism – but because of how they provoke the reflection and conceptual stimulus which Jameson identifies in the utopian. They also contain within them – bear out, as it were, in miniature – their own utopian moments, which 'suspend' the active sweep of the film. Though not classic examples of 'action cinema', both films expose a contradiction in its general aesthetic. For during the 1980s and 1990s the term 'action' came to mean not dynamic narrative movement but regular interruptions of the spectacular. Moments of spectacular interruption *are*, then, the action. 'Action' is thus, paradoxically, not narrative movement but visual event: shootouts, sex scenes, exploding helicopters. Such cinematically spectacular 'moments' do not necessarily 'provoke fruitful bewilderment', but there is still something particularly appropriate about Jameson's utopian argument deployed as a politicised film theory. Both *Brazil* and *Nineteen Eighty-Four* are dystopian narratives 'interrupted' by utopian spectacles. But these films' utopian images are arguably far more explicitly 'suspending' than conventional 'action' could be: they are dystopic visions which contain within them moments of explicitly utopian hesitation and contemplation – figured in each film as the spectacle of a woman's body. If we take utopia to mean not just (literally and etymologically) 'no place' but also as provocative critical vision, then the dark dreams of *Nineteen Eighty-Four* and *Brazil* must be read as uncomfortable forms of utopian cinema.

Utopia's female face

Both dystopia and utopia in *Nineteen Eighty-Four* are rendered through the human face. The film's blighted other-worldliness is presented not through the motifs of the futuristic (weapons, vehicles, the architecture of the strange so beloved of science fiction design), but through its attitude to human skin as the limit of the self. As the film proceeds, any notion of human three-dimensionality – an illusion crucial to our identification, pleasure, recognition – gradually breaks down. Its narrative charts the progressive suturing of skin to self: self becomes what the skin displays. Despite Winston's dreamscape flashbacks, briefly intruding into the linear 'now' of the film's plot-time, character in *Nineteen Eighty-Four* is increasingly written blankly on the face, there is nothing beneath what we see. The politics of depersonalisation which Orwell feared and loathed has resulted in a blanking out of the concept of 'inner self', flattening difference so that all the fragments of contradictory subjectivity are gathered and synthesised into a singular, chanting, un-questioning mask-like retro-future-self. It is as if the Party's attempt at eradicating all traces of private being – individual linguistic quirks, memory, desire itself – has resulted in the most cinematically simplistic human form – one in whom what you see is what you get, fusing surface and interior.

However, the film (as well as Orwell) judges this to be a bad thing. This synthesis of (democratic) difference into (totalitarian) sameness is rendered through a palette of grey and sepia, a 'rubble film' *mise-en-scène* of cluttered frames and mildewed walls. Escape brings a more expansive sense of space, more vibrant colours. Mentally releasing himself from the horrors of torture, Winston flashes back to the open downland location of his rendezvous with Julia: sunshine and an unbroken, undulating green hillside. Dystopia is quite characteristically viewed as urban containment and overpopulation, utopia as solitary rural escape. But this recognisable world is there only to make the mask-face of Winston as dystopic non-subject accepting his prison, all the more horrific in contrast. These flashbacks precede Winston's total submission under torture, referring back to one of the film's most significant moments, a utopic glimpse which is not only Winston's fantasy, but the whole film's. Jameson's utopian moment was a flashpoint of ecstatic disturbance, but the 'disturbance' of dystopian images is not the same as this. Dystopias disturb as an effect of

their displeasurable qualities, not because they interrupt. *The Oxford English Dictionary* defines disturbance as agitation, interruption, as a break or gap – displeasure only if what is being interrupted is equilibrium, calm or tranquillity. Developing Jameson's argument, we need to get away from the value-led understanding of disturbance as negative. That which 'disturbs' the dystopic terrain of *Nineteen Eight-Four* and *Brazil* is an image which offers a break from the negative.

I have read Jameson's 'hesitant' utopic mo-ment as the subordination of narrative to still spectacle, when action, events or even history are suspended. This is an event uncannily like the woman's face, 'freez[ing]' the flow of the action in moments of erotic contemplation' in Laura Mulvey's famous conception of sexual spectacle (Mulvey 1989: 14–26). Both *Nineteen Eighty-Four* and *Brazil* stunningly articulate the fusion of Jameson and Mulvey's frozen moments. In both films, the woman's face is the utopic image which does 'freeze the flow of the action'. Yet in *Nineteen Eighty-Four*'s case, that old adage that one man's utopia is another man's dystopia comes to mind again. The key 'hesitant' image is set up thus. Julia – the active party in the development of the relationship ('I'm corrupt to the core', she says as she seduces the passive Winston) – brings to their meetings trinkets and motifs of the lost past, commodities which have been all but rationed out of existence – jam, 'proper white bread' and coffee. These made a bleak enough picnic, but the couple are grateful. At their next meeting she betters this, in an extra-ordinary scene in which, like some grotesque parody of postfeminism, freedom becomes the power to use cosmetics and don a pretty dress. Here, her gift to them both is the repackaged commodity of herself, as first she withdraws behind a screen, and then emerges, a proper woman, in floral print and subtle make-up. For just a moment – a moment which echoes that 'timeless' scene of memory collapsing into the present in *Vertigo* (1958), when Kim Novak's Judy remakes herself as Madeleine and appears from the bathroom – the film's time stops, *Nineteen Eighty-Four*'s history is halted. Femininity in this conventional form is the agent of interruption.

Earlier I mentioned Jameson's argument, that dystopian images are often the dark ren-derings of anti-socialists:

from religious arguments about the sinful hubris of an anthropocentric social order all the way to the vivid 'totalitarian' dystopias of the contemporary counter-revolutionary tradition (Dostoyevsky, Orwell, etc.), Utopia is a transparent synonym for socialism itself, and the enemies of Utopia sooner or later turn out to be the enemies of socialism. (Jameson 1988: 76–7)

The enemies of utopia are then those who reread utopia as dystopia, by translating its key positive terms (the effacing of sexual difference, for instance) into negatives. This is nowhere clearer than in the moment when Julia masquerades as, and so becomes, a Real Woman, a refeminisation cast by the film as only the latest act in a long line of rebellions, following illegal daytrips, purloined sugar, orgasms and subversive notes passed to Winston. Her makeover may be read as parody or performance, an active self-shaping which self-consciously constructs femininity, controlling it as well as displaying just what a construction it is. That the made-up woman offers Winston a brief glimpse of something better suggests that the film might in part be striking a bold challenge to the normative dogma of natural beauty. When Julia dresses up and makes up, is she fighting the fiction that real beauty must be natural? That this is the couple's last liaison, and that their arrest soon follows, suggests otherwise. To see such a conventional image of femininity as a bold escape from the strictures of a pseudo-communist state is a little like complimenting Soviet youth on their rebellious desire for Levis and Big Macs. Julia's is a desperate act which binds forbidden eroticism to sexual nostalgia, sealing arousal in a memory of a more gender-sure time, when Oceana's grey minions were not consigned to the social and sartorial sameness which effaced sexual difference. Underpinning all this is an insidious gender paranoia, that the result of social egalitarianism is sexual non-difference: it is not the orgasm specifically but its gender in general which is in peril.

By contrast, Brazil's sexual discourse is both more outrageous and less compromising. Terry Gilliam's dream girls are rather different, although Kim Griest's Jill, glimpsed swathed in ethereal gauze in Sam's dreams, may at first glance seem to be another of the elements of overlap between the two films under discussion here, constituting Brazil's as well as Sam's utopic escape. Gilliam lays open a wide range of feminine images to question the mutability of fashion, the malleability of flesh, the demands made of femininity. If Nineteen Eighty-Four accepts the image of escape from 'oppression' figured first through Julia's nakedness, then through her act of dressing up, Brazil sets up femininity as an escape which becomes a trap, as both the best and the worst possible visions. But one act of dressing up has particular significance for how we read the film's dystopianism.

Nineteen Eighty-Four resists the awkward questions raised by its positive presentation of Julia's desire for frills and femininity, and perhaps Brazil fares no better in answering the real sexual problems it poses. But what it does do is show how every positive form and image is always grounded in desire, a desire which is itself subject to the strictures of context. Sam's dream girl is his fantasy – the marked difference between the Jill of his dreams and Jill as she emerges in the 'real' world of the narrative, as an overall-clad truck driver, exposes the terms under which Sam desires at all. At first, Jill is only the dream girl who activates and animates Sam's internal escape-valve. She then appears as a 'real' woman, doing an active macho job, refusing to do anything but push forward the narrative. Finally, in her romance with Sam, she succumbs to Sam's dream and swaps action for spectacle. As the doomed romance proceeds, the pair exchange their respective images of what a 'dream girl' is. Sam increasingly falls for the truck driver as long as, in the end, she will drive him to the countryside to escape his urban nightmare (this is his final fantasy). But Jill goes the other way. In an extraordinary scene at Sam's mother Ida's flat (Ida Lowry is played by Katherine Helmond), Jill realises his dream, posing for him swathed in gauze in Ida's blonde wig. The dream comes alive in Sam's mother's bed. Jill disappears – from the story itself soon after this, and at this moment when she turns into his mother – and Ida takes her place. Then a little later in the film Ida disappears under the cosmetic knife, and Jill takes her place. In the end, Sam's mother's surgery turns her into his lover: Ida reveals that her final reconstruction has turned her into Jill. Gilliam brings this off by switching actresses: we see Ida's back – recognisable as Sam's mother – and then she turns around. Dream-girl becomes mother-lover: briefly it is Griest not Helmond who plays Sam's mother.

If this is *Brazil*'s version of Julia's feminine masquerade, it twists the issue in a powerfully oedipal direction. The worst thing of all, Sam's final nightmare image, is that his mother is his dream girl. It is of course the best thing of all, too, as fulfilled oedipal fantasy briefly presents Sam's secret desire as the result of some of *Brazil*'s most dystopian reconstructive practices. Hitherto the film may have focused on the unnaturalness of the surgical manipulation itself as key sign of *Brazil*'s future-horror. In this final frieze, bodily manipulation becomes the process through which dystopia and utopia collapse into each other. The raw mechanism of the oedipal taboo, sharpening Sam's terminal panic as the film draws to a close, is laid bare in the wilful unfixity of the woman's face. That lover can become mother, mother lover, is the best and the worst of all possible desires. When Jill dons the wig, Sam's dreams take on flesh. When Ida turns around, he is confronted by the dream which can only bring punishment.

Bibliography

Franklin, H. Bruce (1990) 'Visions of the future in science fiction films from 1970 to 1982', in Annette Kuhn (ed.) *Alien Zone: Cultural Theory and Contemporary Science Fiction Cinema*, Verso: London.

Garrett, J. C. (1984) *Hope or Disillusion: Three Versions of Utopia: Nathaniel Hawthorne, Samuel Butler, George Orwell*, Christchurch, New Zealand: University of Canterbury Publications.

Jameson, Fredric (1986) *The Political Unconscious: Narrative as a Socially Symbolic Act*, London: Methuen.

_____ (1988) *The Ideologies of Theory: Essays 1971–1986, Volume 2: The Syntax of History*, London: Routledge.

Johnson, Kim 'Howard' (1993) *Life Before and After Monty Python: The Solo Flights of the Flying Circus*, London: Plexus.

Kumar, Krishan (1987) *Utopia and Anti-Utopia in Modern Times*, Oxford: Basil Blackwell.

Levitas, Ruth (1990) *The Concept of Utopia*, Hemel Hempstead: Philip Allan.

Mathews, Jack (1987) *The Battle of Brazil*, New York: Crown Publishing.

Morgan, David (1988) 'The mad adventures of Terry Gilliam', *Sight and Sound*, Autumn: 238–42

_____ (1996) 'Extremities', *Sight and Sound*, January 1996: 18–21.

Mulvey, Laura (1989) *Visual and Other Pleasures*, London: Macmillan.

SPATIAL ABYSS:
THE SCIENCE FICTION CITY

THREE | SPATIAL ABYSS: THE SCIENCE FICTION CITY

Science fiction is often at its most poetic and political when it uses and organises physical or real space and symbolic or psychological space to structure its utopian or dystopian stories. The science fiction city, the embodiment of such spatial organisation, is often a spectacular and/or horrifying environment, built out of special effects that render it omnipresent, fluid, foreboding and/or simultaneously awe-inspiring. Sitting in the modern cinema, one really knows that one is witnessing a possible world emerge when great edifices rise out of the dark skies and endless walkways, skywalks, hi-rises, low-rises, tunnels and bridges – made of shimmering steel, bright plastic and glass, or crumbling, dismal concrete – intersect like the clogged up arteries and veins of some gigantic organism.

In the science fiction city impression is everything. When the rain falls acid eats its way into the very fabric of people's everyday lives. When the sun shines people make

their way to the country or fly off-world. The garish neon exteriors and interiors promise sleaze, cheap booze, sex, or the latest drug or technological commodity, but ultimately all they often do is dazzle and disappoint the city's inhabitants. In these squalid hovels people are always in a rush, driven by an impossible, inhuman tempo. In these dismal inner-city re-imaginings, people are uprooted, disenfranchised and dislocated, cars and spacecraft fly overhead and underneath feet so that one has the impression that all space, public and private, has been dissolved or has no end point or beginning. One often walks alone in the dizzy science fiction city while being at the same time surrounded by people, pollution, traffic, endless signs, security and surveillance devices, and deafening noise.

By contrast, the shiny, spotless skyscrapers and sumptuous split-level homes that also populate science fiction promise a future where difference and inequality has been eradicated. In these heavenly spaces, people have been given the time to pursue leisure, the arts and scientific knowledge at their will. In these cultured spaces, people are happy and contented in the science fiction city.

In the science fiction city boundaries and borders are everything. Hierarchies of power and control are marshalled out of one's spatial positioning so that where you live – how high or low or whether you are on the 'inside' or the 'outside' of the metropolis grid – how you live – exotic, nostalgic, cheap, stylish – and who (if anybody) you live with or next to is a key determinant of your social position, racial and class background. If you live too low in the science fiction city, or in the wrong neighbourhood, or you live alone or with somebody you love desperately, or you live next to the meat shop and the late-night tech-noir, then you are ticketed and docketed as Other, and all narrative events emanate from this social 'fact'

Vivian Sobchack argues that 'the science fiction film's spatial articulations provide the literal premises for the possibilities and trajectory of narrative action'. The city space is considered to be a 'specific power' that can 'affect both people and materials – a power that modifies the relations between them'. Sobchack goes on to examine the changing nature of this specific power in science fiction film. In the 1930s 'utopian impulses represent the city as eternal ideal'. In the 1950s the city is about dissolution and destruction, and is either razed to the ground or encountered as empty or barren. In the 1960s and 1970s the city becomes a symbol for 'lowering oppressiveness and overcrowdedness', haunted by the then-contemporary fears about over-population, food shortages and an ageing population. And in the 1980s onwards, the city is totally exhausted, 'groundless in both time and space', and 'totally resigned to its ruination'.

Eric Avila also examines a particular period of what he calls urban science fiction cinema – the 1950s. But instead of seeing a collectivised sense of dissolution and destruction being represented in the structures and mise-en-scène of the city, he sees the expression of 'white flight' and the fear of the racialised Other. Avila argues that 'the urban science fiction film provided a cultural arena where suburban America could measure its whiteness against the image of alien Other'. Providing a close textual analysis of War of the Worlds and Them!, he goes on to suggest that 'mainstream white audiences may have viewed the movement of blacks and other racialised minorities into cities as not so much a migration, but rather an invasion of what had been previously white space'.

Wong Kin Yuen examines the importance of Hong Kong's cityscape to cyberpunk cinema, suggesting that it provides the model city 'for the sf genre of 'future noir''. Yuen takes two case studies in his essay – Blade Runner and Ghost in the Shell – and compares the architectural layout of the former with a shopping mall in Times Square, Hong Kong, drawing on post-modern arguments to understand the relationship. Yuen suggests that 'considering Hong Kong as among the cinematic models for the Future City may inspire not only a further look at Hong Kong at this present moment of political transition but also its potential for developing into a forerunner of what the contemporary Capitalist world city will eventually become'.

Cities on the Edge of Time: The Urban Science Fiction Film
Vivian Sobchack

In 1952, science fiction writer Clifford Simak published *City*, a loosely-related collection of short stories unified by their location in a metropolis that – over thousands of narrative years – radically changes its shape, its functions and its citizenry. This episodic and millennial history of urban transformation is framed by its narration as a 'bedtime story' – told by a golden robot to a pack of articulate young dogs gathered around a blazing hearth, wondering if it is really true that once, and very long ago, the nearby city (and the world) was populated by animate, two-legged beings called 'humans'.[1]

Like most of the cities in science fiction literature and film, Simak's city with its fabulous transformations over time is clearly a city of the imagination. Owing no necessary allegiance to representational verisimilitude, such a metropolis serves as a hypnogogic site where the anxieties, desires and fetishes of a culture's waking world and dream world converge and are resolved into a substantial and systemic architecture. This imaginary architecture – particularly as it is concretely hallucinated in American science fiction film images – is more than mere background. Indeed, the science fiction film city's spatial articulations provide the literal premises for the possibilities and trajectory of narrative action – inscribing, describing and circumscribing an extrapolative or speculative urban world and giving that fantasised world a significant and visibly signifying shape and temporal dimension. That is, enjoying particular representational freedom as a genre of the fantastic, the science fiction film concretely 'real-ises' the imaginary and the speculative in the visible spectacle of a concrete image. Thus, it could be argued that because it offers us the most explicitly poetic figuration of the literal grounds of contemporary urban existence, the science fiction city and its concrete realisation in US cinema also offers the most appropriate representational grounds for a phenomenological history of the spatial and temporal transformation of the city as it has been culturally experienced from the 1950s (when the American science fiction film first emerged as a genre) to the present (in which the genre enjoys unprecedented popularity). Indeed, although not as radical in its transformations as Simak's *City* (nor as long-lived), the imaginary city of the American science fiction film from the 1950s to the 1990s offers us a historically qualified and qualifying site that might be explored as both literal ground and metaphoric figure of the transformation of contemporary urban experience and its narratives in that period now associated with 'postmodernism'.[2] This, then, is a historical trajectory – one we pick up at a generic moment that marks the failure of modernism's aspirations in images that speak of urban destruction and emptiness and that leads to more contemporary moments marked by urban exhaustion, postmodern exhilaration, and millennial vertigo.

The following analysis of the cityscapes in American science fiction film refuses the perspective of classical urbanism, which looks at the city as an 'object' distinct from the subjects who inhabit it. My project is best summed up as a desire to 'let 'the city' emerge, in the complex and shifting fashion proper to it, as a specific power to affect both people and materials – a power that modifies the relations between them'.[3] Thus I wish to describe the nature of this affective power as it appears historically in a dominant set of poetic science fiction film images, and then to thematise these images as they emerge from and co-constitute a phenomenology of urban experience. That is, these historically shifting urban images express a lived structure of meanings and affects experienced by the embodied social subjects who inhabited, endured and dreamed them.

Given this historical as well as phenomenological project, it might seem strange to begin by focusing on a series of 'detached' images – images of the science fiction city described and given importance 'out of context' and not in relation to the specific texts and narratives in which they play a major or minor part. However, as Gaston Bachelard tells us in *The Poetics of Space*, the poetic image 'has touched the depths before it stirs the surface', and by its very novelty it 'sets in motion the entire linguistic mechanism'.[4] Thus the poetic image can be seen as *constitutive* of its narrative context. It generates, coalesces, condenses, embodies, 'troubles' and transforms the more elaborated text of which it is ultimately a part, and is itself open to transformation as it performs the semiotic and affective work of adjusting the systems of representation and narrative and the demands of the psyche and culture to each other.[5] The following 'detached' images of the American science fiction film city, then, are not to be seen as ahistorical or absolute and essential. They are not really taken 'out of context', abstracted from the 'text'. Rather, it could be said that their poetic reverberations generate and configure not only the discretion of their individual texts, but also a larger historical narrative – one that generally dramatises the transformational character of the American city and its shifting affective significance for us. It is that larger narrative which is of ultimate concern here. To *configure* that larger narrative, however, we must first grasp its *figures* and treat each of them phenomenologically – as Bachelard says, 'not as an object and even less as the substitute for an object', but rather in 'its specific reality'.[6] That is, prior to narrativising the poetic image, we should be receptive to its reverberations within us, to its compelling originality – understood not only as immediately significant but also as strangely familiar. Indeed, the poetic image is an image that we have already deeply lived but never before imaginatively projected.

As mentioned previously, the American science fiction film emerges as a genre with a marked corpus only in the 1950s. Yet to appreciate the poetic significance of this postwar and postmodern genre's various spatial and temporal transformations of the city from the 1950s to the present, we need briefly to evoke an image of the city as it was figured in American film fantasies before the 1950s. This fantasised city, one must remark, reverberates quite differently from the city figured as 'contemporary' in the popular genres of the musical or gangster films of the 1930s or in the urban melodramas and films noirs of the 1940s.

First, there is *Just Imagine* (1930), a bizarre wedding of science fiction futurism and musical comedy. Set in 1980, the film shows New York City as a high rise of skyscrapers intricately connected by a network of aerial thoroughfares and bridges. Here, one sees no base and pedestrian street level. The hero and heroine stop their little one-seater planes and hover in mid-air to rendezvous – the city around them busy with traffic that, however quotidian, is nonetheless emphatically and literally 'uplifted'. Although this rather loony film posits a repressive – if café – society, its concrete imagination reverberates as soaring aspiration. Indeed, finding its poetic source in Fritz Lang's *Metropolis* (1926), whose futuristic bi-level city was inspired by Bauhaus architecture and the German director's 1924 visit to New York, *Just Imagine* is selective in what it borrows. It does not visualise a New York whose architecture is as oppressive as it is also liberating and beautiful – a cityscape that, for Lang, also evoked confusion, exploitation and 'living in perpetual anxiety'.[7] Ignoring the baseness of Lang's lower city, and drawing only upon *Metropolis*'s most affirmative modernist architecture, the New York of *Just Imagine* seems – to quote Lang in a moment of positive description – 'a vertical veil, shimmering, almost weightless'.[8] In sum, *Just Imagine*'s New York poetically reverberates only with the vertical power, vast size and ethereal delicacy of Lang's upper city.

Three other fantastic images of the city dominate the 1930s, but they do not appear in science fiction films (although one is frequently associated with the genre). Each is so strong as to have gained lasting iconic status – and, indeed, one was explicitly acknowledged by the filmmaker as the generative force informing the narrative. Meriam C. Cooper, co-director of *King Kong* (1933), claims that his 'first idea was of the giant ape on top of a building battling a fleet of planes'.[9] In the image, the fifty-foot-tall great ape 'towers' over Manhattan, momentarily triumphant and forever poetically transcendent atop what once could be called 'New York's tallest phallus', the Empire State Building – officially opened on 1 May 1931, only two years before the film's release.[10] Despite Kong's fall and death on the street below the world's then tallest building, it is this *ascendant* image that we remember – Kong's anarchic and 'primitive' natural presence surrealistically at ease (as well as at odds) with Western culture's most modern and 'civilised' architectural presence by virtue of their shared transcendent scope, the imaginative monumentality and aspiration they so differently (but yet so similarly) embody.

The two other major fantasy images of the city in 1930s films neither signify *aspiration towards the future* (as in *Just Imagine*) nor celebrate *transcendence in the present* (as in *King Kong*). Instead, their utopian impulses represent the city as eternal ideal. Both cities are visualised in aspiring architecture and explicitly located in transcendent space – for one film, in the highest reaches of the Himalayas, and for the other, 'somewhere over the rainbow'. In each, however, the temporal nature of the 'eternal' is encoded differently. The Shangri-la of the aptly-titled *Lost Horizon* (1937) seems a mirage of aspiration, shimmering in an eternal nostalgia that has nothing to do with modernity – either present or future. This idealised and lofty city signifies a utopian reach always in excess of modern man's venal grasp, an eternal ideal always already ephemeral and lost. However, appearing in the same year as the microcosmic, utopian and modern city that was the 1939 New York World's Fair (marked by the idealist geometry of the Trylon and the Perisphere) was the emerald city of *The Wizard of Oz*. Given to our sight for the first time, Oz is set off in the distance, framed by a foreground field of poppies (the stuff of dreams). Standing as both eternal and modern, it is aspiring, atemporal, ethereal, and yet evergreen and contemporary, its softened skyscrapers giving the lie to the term since they have no sharp rectilinear edges and, belonging to the sky, have no need to assault it.

The dominant theme of these few fantastic images of the city stands apart from more contemporaneous, realist and 'grounded' visualisations of urban life in the 1930s. With the exception of Shangri-la (its perpetual evocation of loss prescient about the 'down' side of modernity, aspiration and urbanism), they concretely construct 'modernity' in an architecture of 'aspiration' that has commerce with the 'transcendent'. These images emphasise the vertical, lofty and aerial quality of the city rather than its pedestrian and base horizontality. Indeed, equating 'height' with the active reach of human aspiration, the 'loftiness' of the city stands concretely as its most aesthetically significant social value. Here, cultural geographer Yi-Fu Tuan is apposite:

The vertical versus the horizontal dimension? … common response is to see them symbolically as the antithesis between transcendence and immanence, between the ideal of the disembodied consciousness (a skyward spirituality) and the ideal of earthbound identification. Vertical elements … evoke a sense of striving, a defiance of gravity, while the horizontal elements call to mind acceptance and rest.[11]

As we shall see in science fiction films of the 1970s and 1980s, however, horizontal elements can call to mind less positive modes of passive being: resignation, stasis, asphyxiation and death – as well as more active modes of being: expansion, dispersion and play.

Traditionally, America's spatial mythology has privileged the non-urban and has been, indeed, anti-urban (the paradise of the New World symbolically located in the garden, the West, the frontier, the wilderness, and now – after Steven Spielberg – on the lawns of suburbia). Nonetheless, as we have seen in these few images from the 1930s, the fantasy of the imaginary city constitutes it in a positive image of highness and fullness, envisions it as the site of human aspiration – its vertical projection pointing towards spiritual transcendence and, perhaps, a better and fuller (that is, a materially expanded and more 'civilised') future. In an extremely popularised and 'softened' way, then, the positive image of the 1930s city has its roots in the earlier urban and technological visions of Futurism and Modernism.

Given that social events in the 1940s were not conducive to continuing this utopian fantasy of the city, it is not surprising that, but for the nightmarish and labyrinthine 'low' life hyperbolically figured in the urban introspections of film noir, most film images of the city during this period are neither extrapolative nor speculative. We must move into the 1950s for our next set of explicitly fantastic urban images. It is during this decade marked by nuclear fear and Cold War tensions, by a growing dependence upon electronic technology, by the emergence of new global information and communications systems, and by increasing consumerism and suburbanism, that the American science fiction film coalesces as a recognised genre that, more often than not, poeticises the city through what Susan Sontag has called the 'imagination of disaster'.[12] Two poetically powerful images reverberate through the 1950s – each spectacularly and concretely articulating a loss of faith in previous utopian and futurist visions of the modern city as the architectural and transcendent embodiment of human aspiration. Although quite differently, both address the failure of concrete verticality and 'highness' spiritually to sustain and uplift modern existence. And, as aspiration and 'highness' are lost or neutralised, so too is the sense of a future.

The first image is an angry, destructive one, and it appears in a great many films of the period – clearly generating its simple and repetitive narratives as a ritual context in which it serves as centre. The elements of the image are all the same, although their specific articulations may change. The *mise-en-scène* is urban and given to our sight in long shot. The city in this image is identifiable: New York, Washington DC, San Francisco. Culturally symbolic and discrete architectural features like the Statue of Liberty, the Coney Island rollercoaster, the Washington Monument and the Golden Gate Bridge place and 'name' the urban scene and give it a specificity that makes its imminent destruction seem an immediate, contemporaneous event. Into this scene comes a destructive force which may take any of three forms: an apocalyptic natural force like a tidal wave or comet; a primal Beast or Creature; or a technologically superior alien war machine. In each instance, however, the result is the same – the razing of the city and, most particularly, the bringing low of those monuments that stand as symbols of modern civilisation's aspiration and pride. In *When Worlds Collide* (1951), New York is inundated by a tidal wave and its buildings topple; in *The Beast from 20,000 Fathoms* (1953), an atomically-awakened prehistoric creature stomps cars and fleeing people, smashes the New York skyline, and tangles with the Coney Island rollercoaster as it mindlessly seeks its ancient breeding ground; in *Earth vs the Flying Saucers* (1956), the sleek and quick alien craft of technologically superior extraterrestrials castrate the Washington Monument and bring the nation's capitol low.

It might seem that the affective power of this image is similar to that of primal Kong atop the Empire State Building swatting planes as if they were flies. Yet fascination with the poetry of destruction is not quite what the image of Kong is about: rather, it touches us deeply with the visible – if brief – resolution of a monumental social and psychic desire, of both the building and Kong's impossibly epic aspirations. The 1950s science fiction image I am describing here is not about resolution, but about dissolution. Its poetic reverberations have nothing to do with aspiration and ascendancy and everything to do with, as

Sontag puts it, 'the fantasy of living through one's own death and more, the death of cities, the destruction of humanity itself'.[13] Thus the failure of modern and urban civilisation and its aspirations is poetically represented in appropriately monumental images which constitute an 'aesthetics of destruction' whose peculiar beauty is found in 'wreaking havoc, making a mess'.[14] The city's aspiring verticality, its lofty architecture, its positive 'highness' that thrusts civilisation towards transcendence and the future is – through privileged special effects – debased and brought low, in a *mise-en-scène* that is bustling with contemporary activity and traffic and emphatically temporalised as 'now'.

The second image of the failure of the aspiring city is equally powerful, yet quite different – retaining the city's highness, but temporising its value as 'past'. Here, the city's lofty architecture is not destroyed; rather, the originally positive and transcendent value of architectural 'highness' becomes dominated by the negative and nihilistic value of '*emptiness*'. Highness thus remains an ideal value but now has little to do with human beings. As Philip Strick reminds us: 'Science fiction writers like Simak, Bradbury and Kuttner, with varying degrees of irony, have frequently recognised … the ideal city contains no citizens whatever.'[15] Again, the basic elements of this poetic response to concrete human aspiration remain the same across a variety of science fiction elaborations. In *Five* (1951), we see two characters enter New York City – an empty concrete canyon whose walls are skyscrapers, whose floor is punctuated by static and forlorn automobiles distraughtly angled: nothing moves but the car in which they slowly ride, and a skeleton stares out at them from a window. In *On the Beach* (1959), trying to find the source of a signal from a radioactively-dead USA, submarine crewmen wander about an empty San Francisco. And in *The World, the Flesh, and the Devil* (1959), the image of deadly stillness and emptiness overwhelms one with a sense of irrevocable loss as a single character roams through New York, into a vacant Times Square, down an abandoned Wall Street, around an aseptic United Nations building. Cars eternally stalled on a bridge, newspaper blowing down a city street caught up in some ill-begotten wind, street lights and neon blinking on and off in a mockery of animate existence – this is the iconography of emptiness and stillness that marks the American cinematic imagination of the post-holocaust city in the 1950s until the mid 1970s. And this imagination is nostalgic – always already fixed on an irrecoverable past rather than on a future that has not yet occurred.

One of the elements of our lived experience of the modern city is its immediate vitality: its present-tense and up-to-the-minute activity, its busyness, its people and traffic always in motion. To see the city empty and still emphasises its concrete 'loftiness', but also temporally codes the value of such architectural aspiration as 'past'. Marking the death of the city as an actively functional structure, skyscrapers in these films stand as monumental gravestones. Although this image of urban emptiness lingers on into the 1980s – in films like *Dawn of the Dead* (1979) and *Night of the Comet* (1984) – it appears less as this nostalgic response to the city's original loftiness and the failure of its aspiration than as a positive opportunity to dramatise the ultimate consumer fantasy of having a shopping mall all to oneself (barring a few extremist shoppers in the form of ghouls and mutants).

The destruction of the city and its symbolic architecture and the city as empty graveyard – these two powerful poetic responses to the failure of the city's aspiration (and to the failure of 'modern' civilisation) mourn the out-moded value of loftiness, the ineffectual outcome of aspiration; but they still hold aspiration as a positive value and offer no alternative to its failure. Things get even worse in the 1960s and most of the 1970s. If the utopian vision of the imaginary city emphasises concrete loftiness and spiritual fullness as positive values, then 1950s science fiction film kept at least one of these values operative – even if only in a literal way. That is, in those films where the city's architecture is destroyed and brought low, its literal fullness is asserted in busy human activity and an emphasis on the 'masses' (whether they are screaming beneath the behemoth's scaly feet or 'cooperating' with the 'authorities'). And in those films in which the city's utopian plenitude is challenged by its literal emptiness, at least its concrete loftiness remains. However, from the late 1960s to 1977 (the year that marks the release of both *Close Encounters of the Third Kind* and *Star Wars*), the science fiction city poeticised neither highness nor fullness as positive values. Rather, both were imagined negatively – and turned in on themselves to become *lowering oppressiveness* and *overcrowdedness*. Indeed, if the utopian science fiction city is perceived as aspiring, then the science fiction city during this period is dystopian and perceived as *asphyxiating*.

Pointing to the despair of a country involved in both domestic and international contestation, Joan Dean describes the science fiction films of the late 1960s and most of the 1970s as articulating a 'diminishing fear of nuclear apocalypse' and 'a growing concern with domestic, terrestrial issues – most of which are related to totalitarian government control of people's lives or over-population, food shortages, pollution, and ecology'. Indeed, the 'single theme' that 'dominated the science fiction imagination between 1970 and 1977 was over-population and its concomitant problems of food shortage and old age'.[16] The image of the city that generates science fiction film narratives of this period emerges most forcefully in *Soylent Green* (1973), which visualises a New York City that no longer aspires but suffocates and expires. Emphasis is not on the height of buildings but on their baseness. Verticality is no longer significant – and the city's horizontal dimension stresses its limitations, not its openness. In 2022, New York is not seen in its positive fullness. Rather, it is impossibly overcrowded: its population is forty million. People overflow the streets and most live and huddle in dark masses and clots on the sidewalks, in the alleys, and stairwells of buildings that all look like slum tenements. Their whispering and overlapping cries and coughs and sobs sound like the sighing of some desolate wind. This New York City has no monumental centre, no moral centre. Indeed, it is all corrupted and base, all suddenly inner-city. The *mise-en-scène* is dark, claustrophobic, polluted and dirty; as Robert Cumbow points out, in 'its crumbling buildings and rotting cars were the beginnings of … junkyard futurism'.[17] But this is a futurist image that imagines no future. This New York is literally a *concentration* camp, and the temporality its constraining spaces construct cannot stretch and stream forward, has nothing to do with positive notions of spatial progression or expansion. All is decay and entropy. In the late 1960s to the mid-1970s, the science fiction city has no positive values to sustain it – and so it falls down and apart. Indeed, many of the period's films – from *Planet of the Apes* (1968) to *Logan's Run* (1978) – imagine cities such as New York and Washington DC in a fantasy of 'the body in pieces', monuments and buildings now fragments strewn on an abandoned landscape on a radically altered planet. The aspiring city, once the centre and architectural symbol of civilisation, has fallen in ruins, is no longer functional, no longer the centre of civilised human activity.

By the 1980s, the idealised and lofty science fiction city is imagined as completely decentred and marginalised. The citizens of dominant bourgeois culture are either 'offworld' in outer space or in the suburbs.[18] In 1977, with *Star Wars* and *Close Encounters*, George Lucas and Steven Spielberg provided the mainstream and nostalgic routes by which to *Escape From New York* – the entire city in that 1981 film imagined literally as a prison. *Star Wars* and *Close Encounters* rally a cinematic exodus from the constraints, pollution and crime of the failed city – and those who leave are all those upstanding and economically franchised folks who believed (and rightly so) that the 'Force' was with them, or (wrongly so) that 'when you wish upon a star, it makes no difference who you are'. What results from this mass bourgeois abandonment of the city, however, is a peculiar and hallucinatory screen liberation for those 'others' left behind. They are the dregs of bourgeois society: punks, winos, crazies, gays, druggies, Blacks, Latinos, new Asians, the homeless, the hipsters, the poor – in sum, everyone previously marginalised and disenfranchised in bourgeois urban culture. Let loose and left to their own devices in a city which now has no centre and no constraints, which has been 'junked' rather than urbanly 'renewed', this newly dominant and diverse population energises and reformulates the negative and nihilistic urban values of the 1960s and 1970s as sublimely positive. In a complete reversal, the imaginary science fiction city's lowness, baseness, horizontality; its over-crowdedness, over-populatedness and over-stuffedness, are celebrated and aestheticised. That is, the old imaginary and centred science fiction metropolis is totally resigned to its ruination, its displacement to its own edges, its concrete transformation from city as centre to city as inner, from aspiring city to city dump. But this total and concrete resignation to the city's debasement results in

a positive symbolic re-signing. The junkyard, the dump, the trashy edges of town are culturally reinscribed as a novel and exotic urban space that eroticises and fetishises material culture, that is valued for its marvellously unselective acquisitive power, its expansive capacity to accumulate, consume and contain 'things', *anything*, and its existential status as irrefutable testimony to the success of material production. The omnipresence of waste serves as a sign that the digestive tract of advanced capital's body politic must still be working, indeed working 'overtime' and at full capacity. The city is thus re-energised – finding both a new function and a new aesthetic. It is imagined explicitly as the most monumental and concrete *consumer* and, with its unselective juxtapositions and conservation of material artefacts, as the most eclectic 'pop' *collector*. Fredric Jameson writes of this re-signed city:

> The exhilaration of these new surfaces is … paradoxical in that their essential content – the city itself – has deteriorated or disintegrated to a degree surely still inconceivable in the early years of the twentieth century … How urban squalor can be a delight to the eyes, when expressed in commodification, and how an unparalleled quantum leap in the alienation of daily life in the city can now be experienced in the form of a strange new hallucinatory exhilaration – these are some of the questions that confront us.[19]

Within the context of this new urban exoticism and its erotics of commodification and consumerism, two new images of the science fiction city emerge. And, given that the postmodernist city is experienced as having no centre – being all centre or decentred, dispersing its activities in every direction – it is hardly surprising that the site of both of them is Los Angeles. The first and most aestheticised comes, of course, from *Blade Runner* (1982). Its Los Angeles of 2019 is a crowded and polyglot megalopolis filled with a multinational and marginal populace, additive architecture, sensuous 'clutter', and highly atmospheric pollution. This is a city experienced less as base and degraded than as dense, complex and heterogeneous: it stimulates and exhausts the eyes, for there is always – literally – more to see. (Indeed, the eye is a crucial narrative motif.) This imaginary Los Angeles is concretely constructed from 'layers of texture':

> visual information is imparted in every square inch of screen. Details proliferate. The umbrellas carried by extras have lighted tips because the streets are so murky. The television monitors that have replaced traffic signals provide deliberately poor pictures. Skyscrapers are built on top of existing structures – and are shown ... in their hundreds of stories.[20]

Despite the skyscrapers, the visual experience of this Los Angeles has little to do with verticality and lofty aspiration. Rather, the trajectory of our attention tends to stay grounded – fascinated by the city's retrofitted transformation of its ruins, its 'spaces and objects whose original purpose has been lost, due not to obsolescence but rather to an overinvestment brought about by constant recycling'.[21] It is not surprising that industrial pipes and ducts figure prominently in the *mise-en-scène* (as they would even more explicitly in 1985's *Brazil*). This Los Angeles is literally exhausted – generating that strange blend of hysteria and euphoria that comes with utter fatigue.

The emphasis of the second science fiction image of Los Angeles is less on design than on random, discontinuous and dispersed movement. It seems no accident that the company that made *Repo Man* (1984) refers to itself as Edge City Productions. The Los Angeles of *Blade Runner* is decentred by being all centre, whereas the Los Angeles of *Repo Man* is centred by being all margin. The Los Angeles of *Blade Runner* unifies its outmoded and vastly disparate material signifiers into new 'retrofitted' and eroticised architectural forms, whereas the Edge City of *Repo Man* celebrates convulsive spatial discontinuities in a constantly moving culture: its *mise-en-scène* is not cluttered, merely littered (occasional newspapers, strange people, garbage, drunks, dead derelicts and abandoned sofas punctuating otherwise empty and unwalked streets). Indeed, in *Repo Man* the city is perceived as a set of discrete and unconnected spatial rather than architectural fragments – framed by the windscreen of a moving car that, in this city of repossessions, is always changing hands and drivers and points of view.

This is the city in a schizophrenic representation – 'reduced to an experience of pure material Signifiers ... of a series of pure and unrelated presents in time'.[22] The city does not cohere, has no causal logic to unify it. Discussing Los Angeles as the 'automobile city', Yi-Fu Tuan points out: 'Driving on a freeway can be disorienting. A sign, for example, may direct one to the far left lane for an objective that is clearly visible to the right.'[23] But repo men find sublime pleasure in these discontinuities, automotively 'troping' the city's streets and freeways – that is, rhetorically swerving from expected trajectories to create new relations of meaning, or, as the film's philosopher Miller would say, new 'lattices of coincidence'. The Los Angeles of *Repo Man* is a city whose spatiality is not bound by architecture but rather by trajectories of movement which, no matter how seemingly random, will – like the freeway system – eventually intersect. Thus, no matter how they disperse themselves, repo men, vicious LA punks, a nuclear physicist, a pair of car thieves, and a Chevy Malibu with a trunk full of extraterrestrial weaponry keep meeting up again. Whereas in *Blade Runner* the pastiche of new and old genres, recycled aesthetic styles, and eclectic material objects constituted Los Angeles' temporal mode as literal and increasingly collective present, *Repo Man*'s Edge City is temporally encoded as an eternally recurrent present.

Thus the science fiction city of the 1980s, while not mourning the failed aspirations of its past, was not really capable of envisioning its future but, rather, was euphorically lost in erotic play with its material present. The imaginary Los Angeles of *Blade Runner* and *Repo Man*, the New York of *Liquid Sky* (1983), only dream their complete reversal of bourgeois utopian values, only hallucinate their liberation from the bourgeoisie who have gone off to live in Spielberg films or gone *Back to the Future* (1985). These cities, in visible fact, eroticise consumption and fetishise material culture in scenographic paeans to advanced capitalism. And, while these cities celebrate their counter-cultural funkiness, their heterogeneity, horizontality and cultural levelling, their alienated terrestrials and terrestrialised aliens whose differences supposedly make no difference in this dispersed and marginalised culture (1984's *Moscow on the Hudson* and *Brother from Another Planet* are, after all, the same movie), they function as virtual ghettoes – or, wishing upon that bourgeois star, effectively efface those differences that do make a difference who you are. Positing, on the one hand, a new and liberating model of the city and, on the other, buying back into its failed model by merely reversing (rather than altering) its terms and values, the imaginary postmodernist science fiction film city of the 1980s is truly a city on the edge, offering us a hallucinatory future we might want to visit, but a present in which – unless we just happen to be bourgeois cinemagoers and 'slumming' – we would not want to live.

Indeed, if the urban *mise-en-scène* of the 1980s science fiction film is both intensified and compacted as all 'inner' city, and diffused and dispersed as all 'marginal' city, future urban experience would hardly appear to accommodate normative 'middle class' life at all. Thus, looking at the 1990s, we might ask whether (and, if so, in what manner) the bourgeois cinematic imagination has effected some form of 'urban renewal'? What can the imagination construct in or beyond a city 'on the edge'? In the last decade of the twentieth century, the cinematic response to these questions has been cities imagined spatially (and tonally) in an urban experience of going 'over the top' or plunging 'over the edge'. That is, although manifest in two quite different modes, the current science fiction film city has been figured as *groundless*, lacking both logically secure and spatially stable premises for its – and our – existence. This is a city virtually 'bottomed out' and literally fathomless: its inhabitants suffer from giddiness or vertigo and, rootless, they 'free fall' in both space and time.

One contemporary mode of imagining this groundless or bottomed-out city is so cinematically reflexive as to be comic or 'safe' – and thus without much consequence or poetic resonance. This mode returns us in a fashion to 1950s science fiction: to the image of the city brought low, its identifiable architecture destroyed by catastrophic 'natural' disaster or 'alien' attack. Nevertheless, while *Independence Day* and *Mars Attacks!* (both 1996), *Godzilla*, *Deep Impact* and *Armageddon* (all 1998) draw upon older science fiction movie tropes, they seem themselves temporally rootless and spatially disaffected.

In *Independence Day*, alien flying saucers blow up the White House and the Empire State Building, visibly reducing the USA's major cities to rubble. Nonetheless, while there is panic in the streets, there is no Cold War fear and anxiety here to inform and historically ground it – merely cinematic nostalgia and the imperatives of the latest special effects. And, while one might want to link the urban destruction in *Independence Day* and the films that follow it with recent and explosive acts of urban terrorism in New York and Oklahoma City, there seems to be no human affect or real consequence attached to it. The cities in these films appear to have little meaning; they seem hardly to matter at all. As Roger Ebert notes of *Independence Day*: 'The news comes that New York, Washington and Los Angeles have been destroyed, and is there grief? Anguish? … Not a bit.'[24] Indeed, in the comedy *Mars Attacks!*, manic Martians decimate not only Washington but also Las Vegas in what is less an apocalypse than a wacky celebration. In *Godzilla*, taking on the functions of nearly every 1950s city-stomping giant reptile or insect, Godzilla tromps Manhattan – but lacks the affect generated by Atomic Age anxieties about nuclear annihilation, mutation, and a return to the world as 'primal sink'. And, in both *Deep Impact* and *Armageddon*, in which meteors and asteroids threaten Earth and tidal waves and flames engulf the urban cityscape, the cultural stakes seem remarkably low. What these films have in common (besides a penchant for de-capitating the Art-Deco Chrysler Building) is an astonishing – and itself historical – lack of care. Their cities, however familiar, are not 'grounded' or substantial: they seem to exist only for destruction. Reviewing *Mars Attacks!*, Jonathan Rosenbaum might well be summarising this mode of urban imagination when he writes of a

> postmodernist free fall through the iconography of 1950s and 1960s science fiction in relation to the present: a singular sense of giddy displacement that clearly locates the movie in the 1990s, but a 1990s largely made up of images and clichés from previous decades that are subtly turned against themselves, made into a form of camp, affectionately mocked, yet still revered as if they had a particular purchase on the truth.[25]

There is, however, a second and more affectively engaged mode of imagining the science fiction city in the 1990s. This urban imagination borrows heavily from the film noir roots and urban *mise-en-scène* of *Blade Runner*, but its poetic resonance is less eroticised and much bleaker; and, in at least one of its latest expressions, *Dark City* (1998), the entire narrative explicitly foregrounds and visually concretises the rootless, vertiginous and insecure sense that the city is groundless in both time and place. The cinematic experience of this city is not of the free fall or giddy displacement of going 'over the top', of campy exaggeration or nostalgic pastiche. No longer merely 'on the edge', this urban imagery takes us literally 'over the edge'. The city's inhabitants (if, indeed, they still can be called such) are increasingly dislocated in space – and, dislocated, their very identities shift and become displaced and ungrounded. Thus, it is not coincidental that this mode of urban science fiction film is as concerned with time and memory as it is with space and place. Its correlations between the ungrounding of urban space and the ungrounding of identity begin with *Blade Runner* and are followed by *The Terminator* (1984), *Robocop* (1987), *Total Recall* (1990), and more recently by *Strange Days* (1995) and *Twelve Monkeys* (1996). In these films, we see the city of the future as what Roger Ebert has succinctly described as 'a grunge pit'.[26] The word 'pit' here is telling.

Increasingly, urban science fiction space seems not only grungy but also bottomless and, in various ways, unfathomable. In the mid-twenty-third-century New York of *The Fifth Element* (1997), for example, the protagonist is literally located in mid-air: he is a cab driver in a vehicle vulnerable from above and below (the heroine, leaping from a building whose top and bottom recede into invisibility, falls through the roof into his back seat; later, he is chased by vehicles beneath him). Radically different from the ordered urban airways envisioned by both *Metropolis* and *Just Imagine*, this city is a dizzying and densely layered labyrinth of architecture and motion: it has neither skyscrapers (there is no visible sky as such) nor ground. This is a city that seems to have no boundaries and yet, at the same time, is peculiarly hermetic.[27]

These unstable, boundless, and yet hermetic qualities become the very stuff of narrative in the aptly named *Dark City*. Through the use of digital morphing and warping, the very ground of urban and cinematic space and time is destabilised by digital effects and the effects of the digital. Both literally and metaphorically, the city's premises no longer hold. *Dark City*

is some perpetually nocturnal and hermetic metropolis that combines the urban visions of German Expressionism, Edward Hopper and film noir; and its human inhabitants never seem to know where they are, where they are going, or how to get anywhere. The film's alien 'Strangers' are responsible: they literally and metaphorically keep both the city and its inhabitants 'in the dark'. Furthermore each midnight, through a communal act of will, they literally warp, expand, shrink, and shift buildings and streets to transform the entire cityscape architecturally and spatially – which is nonetheless bounded as a finite and hermetic world. Correctively, in secret experiments, the Strangers also literally remember and relocate the memories of the city's inhabitants. There is nothing in this city, then, that holds or is stable – except for a recurrent, if also suspect, postcard-like image of a 'perfect' (and decidedly non-urban) seaside town.

Ultimately, Shell Beach in *Dark City* is a postcard construction of the protagonist's wish and will – as unstable and hermetic as the city he escapes. It is at this point that the contemporary science fiction film departs from the unfathomable and ungrounded experience of urban life. But where cinematically does it go? Most recently, it has fled – in full awareness of its own desires and devices – to the allied genre of fantasy where variations on the Edenic small-town alternative to the groundless city only 'appear' more hospitable to human existence. In recent paranoid fantasies such as *The Truman Show* or *Pleasantville* (both 1998), the small town offers no satisfactory escape from science fiction's urban nightmares. Indeed, it offers merely a sunnier imagination of inhospitable space – replacing the science fiction film city's incoherence with an utterly scripted order, and containing its dizzying boundlessness in the small and hermetic frame of a television set.

Notes

1 This chapter is revised and expanded from its initial publication in *East-West Film Journal*, vol. 3, no. 1, 1988, pp. 4–19.

2 Since there have been many debates surrounding the concept and definition of 'post-modernism', for the purposes of this essay I refer the reader to Fredric Jameson, 'Post-modernism or The Cultural Logic of Late Capitalism,' *New Left Review*, no. 146, 1984, pp. 53–94;

and to my use of Jameson's work in *Screening Space: The American Science Fiction Film* (New Brunswick, NJ: Rutgers University Press, 1997), ch. 4.

3 'Forward', *Zone*, nos 1/2, 1987, p. 11.

4 Gaston Bachelard, *The Poetics of Space*, trans. Maria Jolas, (Boston, MA: Beacon Press, 1964), p. xix.

5 On this issue, see the chapter on 'Figuration' in Dudley Andrew, *Concepts in Film Theory* (New York: Oxford University Press, 1984).

6 Bachelard, *The Poetics of Space*, p. xv.

7 Michael Webb, 'The City in Film', *Design Quarterly*, no. 136, 1987, p. 9. Reading Lang's description of New York, one is reminded more of *Blade Runner*'s imaginative science fiction cityscape than of any other – including Lang's own *Metropolis*.

8 Ibid., p. 8.

9 John Brosnan, *Future Tense: The Cinema of Science Fiction* (New York: St. Martin's Press, 1978), p. 48.

10 Ibid., p. 47. See also Webb's description of the building's 'phallic crown, designed as a mooring for dirigibles' ('The City in Film', p. 11).

11 Yi-Fu Tuan, *Topophilia: A Study of Environmental Perception, Attitudes and Values* (Englewood Cliffs, NJ: Prentice-Hall, 1974), p. 28.

12 Susan Sontag, 'The Imagination of Disaster', *Commentary*, October 1965, pp. 42–8.

13 Ibid., p. 44.

14 Ibid.

15 Philip Strick, 'Metropolis Wars: The City as Character in Science Fiction Films', in Danny Peary, ed., *Omni's Screen Flights/Screen Fantasies: The Future According to Science Fiction Cinema* (Garden City, NY: Dolphin/Doubleday, 1984), p. 47.

16 Joan F. Dean, 'Between 2001 and Star Wars', *Journal of Popular Film and Television*, vol. 7, no. 1, 1978, pp. 36–7.

17 Robert Cumbow, 'Survivors: The Day After Doomsday', in Peary, ed., *Omni's Screen Flights/Screen Fantasies*, p. 41.

18 In relation to Steven Spielberg's oeuvre, see Yi-Fu Tuan's discussion of suburban values and ideals in *Topophilia*, pp. 236–40.

19 Jameson, 'Postmodernism', p. 76.

20 Bart Mills, 'The Brave New World of Production Design', *American Film*, vol. 7, no. 4, 1982, p. 45.

21 Eric Alliez and Michel Feher, 'Notes on the Sophisticated City', *Zone*, nos. 1/2, 1987, p. 44.

22 Jameson, 'Postmodernism', p. 72. Emphasis added.

23 Tuan, *Topophilia*, p. 190.

24 Roger Ebert, *Chicago Sun-Times* (online), n.d.

25 Jonathan Rosenbaum, *Chicago Reader* (online), n.d.

26 Roger Ebert, *Chicago-Sun Times*, 5 January 1996.

27 This image of the city to some degree draws upon contemporary Japanese anime and postmodern comics, but it also recalls a singular image from 1950s science fiction film: namely, the Krel city revealed in *Forbidden Planet* (1956). However, unlike the contemporary vision, and more in keeping with urban themes of its own period, that city was shown as empty and signified the hubris of technological aspiration.

Dark City: White Flight and the Urban Science Fiction Film in Postwar America
Eric Avila

> I am an invisible man. No, I am not a spook like those who haunted Edgar Allan Poe; nor am I one of your Hollywood movie ectoplasms. I am a man of substance, of flesh and bone, fiber and liquids – and I might even be said to possess a mind.
>
> – Ralph Ellison, *Invisible Man*

At the outset of *Invisible Man*, Ralph Ellison seeks to dispel white perceptions of black people. Such perceptions, he realised, often drew upon the vast array of images that saturated the cultural life of mid-twentieth-century white America. Writing in the early 1950s, a time when American movie audiences reveled in the spectacular images of alien invasions, Ellison took strides to deny his similarity to 'Hollywood movie ectoplasms'. Although he painfully recognised his invisibility as a black man in cold war America, he also protested his visibility in cultural productions like the urban science fiction film of the 1950s. Ellison, like other black intellectuals discouraged by the misrepresentation of black Americans in popular culture, recognised the ominous affinity between the alien Other of science fiction film and the racialised Other of American history. *Invisible Man* draws upon the painful awareness that racialised minorities in the United States are usually invisible as human beings and often visible only through the disfiguring lens of American popular culture.[1]

Ellison's commentary upon the cultural milieu of cold war America resonated within a material context in which the racial divide between black America and white America widened. Such disparities were most visible in the cities, where the force of suburbanisation furthered the distance between white and black. 'White flight' names the process by which American cities of the postwar period saw increasing racial segregation and socioeconomic fragmentation. As racialised minorities concentrated in American inner cities during the late 1940s and throughout the 1950s, millions of 'white' Americans took to new suburban communities to preserve their whiteness. Through the postwar collusion of federal policy, local land development strategies, and the popular desire to live in racially exclusive and homogenous neighborhoods, 'chocolate cities' and 'vanilla suburbs' became the spatial and racial paradigm of American life during the 1950s.[2]

Typically, white flight refers to political practices and economic processes that enforce the racial divide between the suburbs and the city.[3] However, there is a cultural dimension to this process that has been overlooked. As an ideology rooted both in a historical preference for private rather than public life and in contemporary anxieties about subversion and deviance, white flight penetrated the sphere of American popular culture and affirmed whiteness often at the expense of racialised minorities. The rise of Hollywood science fiction paralleled the acceleration of white flight in postwar America and not only recorded popular anxieties about political and sexual deviants, but also captured white preoccupations with the increasing visibility of the alien Other.

Historically, science fiction film and literature have posited the city as the object of both utopian and dystopian fantasies about modernity. The urban science fiction film of the 1950s, figuratively and literally, emphasised the darker side of urban life. Films such as *Them!* (1954) and *War of the Worlds* (1953) emerged at the height of postwar suburbanisation, a time when millions of white Americans reaped the privileges of affordable housing in the suburbs and rejected the city as a viable way of life. The perceived threat to the American city underlies both cultural constructions like the urban science fiction film and material processes such as white flight. Indeed, such films confirmed the suburban suspicion of city life through spectacular representations of the alien Other and its violent onslaught upon the city. Within the changing racial geography of the postwar, post-industrial metropolis, the urban science fiction film provided a cultural arena where suburban America could measure its whiteness against the image of the alien Other. In their representational emphasis, visual style, and promotion, films such as *Them!* and *War of the Worlds* recorded popular perceptions of racialised minorities in the age of white flight.

Conventional understandings of 1950s science fiction film have looked to the political climate of the cold war to explore the deeper meanings of science fiction cinema. Martians, monsters, giant insects, crawling eyes, fifty-foot women, blobs, pods, various 'its' and other 'things' were all commonly understood as cinematic apparitions of Communists and the 'Red Menace'. And rightly so. Science fiction film offers a window onto the political culture of postwar America, a time when Americans built bomb shelters in their backyards, practiced disaster drills with a religious devotion, and gazed fixedly upon the televised witch-hunts of the House Un-American Activities Committee (HUAC). Through films such as *Invasion of the Body Snatchers* (1956), *It Came From Outer Space* (1953) and *Invasion of the Saucer Men* (1957) Americans could work out their obsession with Communist subversion and catch a glimpse into the nexus between politics and culture in postwar America.[4]

Communists, however, were not the only subversives in postwar America. As it had throughout American history, the presence of racialised minorities continued to trouble white Americans. The 'race question', however, seemed all the more poignant in the age of *Brown v Board of Education*. Before, white Americans could confront their racial anxieties in a separate but equal world. During the 1950s, however, the lines between black space and white space increasingly blurred, particularly in the cities, where racialised minorities, blacks in particular, concentrated in unprecedented numbers. Although cities have historically functioned as points of contact between diverse social groups, the nature of sociodemographic upheaval and economic change proved so pronounced that it forced white Americans to confront the darker face of the city in postwar America.

The urban science fiction film emerged within this racial climate. Because this brand of cinematic science fiction took as its subject the plight of the city, its meaning is further illuminated by an understanding of the spatial transition from the industrial city of the nineteenth century to the post-industrial metropolis of the twentieth century. Implicit in this transition is the concentration of racialised minorities in the inner city and the subsequent racial polarisation of the city between its dark core and white suburbs. As black Americans secured housing and employment in the older, industrialised cores of such cities as Detroit, Philadelphia and Los Angeles during the postwar era, white Americans secured housing and employment in newly developed suburban communities. Within this context, the popularity of films about alien invasions suggests that mainstream white audiences may have viewed the movement of blacks and other racialised minorities into the cities as not so much a migration, but rather an invasion of what had previously been white space. 'Invasion' became a key metaphor, central to understanding larger social processes in postwar America, including the urbanisation of African-Americans.

The urban science fiction film coincided with the rise of the black ghetto as the dominant feature of urban life in postwar America. U.S. mobilisation for World War Two and the postwar economic boom initiated a dramatic spatial shift in the nation's black population. The urbanisation of African-Americans entailed the migration of blacks from the South to the Northeast and West. The largest decennial black migration occurred between 1940 and 1950. Overall, between 1940 and 1970, more than 4 million blacks left the South for Northern and Western cities. On the eve of World War Two, 70 percent of American blacks lived in the South, whereas only 53 percent lived there thirty years later.[5] The number of black urbanites, moreover, increased dramatically in the United States between 1945 and 1960. During that period, New York's black population increased two-and-a-half times, and the number of blacks tripled in Detroit. The West, however, experienced the greatest growth in its African-American population. Los Angeles, a city with a relatively small black population until 1940, saw an 800 percent increase in its black population, from 75,000 to 600,000.[6]

Given the white response to black urbanisation, the ghetto became the dominant experience of African-American life in postwar America. Many whites deployed violence against the encroachment of African-Americans upon white space. Throughout the postwar era, white aggression toward blacks and other non-whites increased, particularly in such public spaces as buses, schools, restaurants, and, to a larger extent, in private spaces such as the residential neighborhood. For example, in

Levittown, Pennsylvania, a planned community of 60,000, a Confederate flag-waving crowd threw stones at the one house that belonged to a black family in 1957.[7] In 1945, the Ku Klux Klan firebombed the Fontana, California, home of a black family that refused to move from a white neighborhood, killing the wife and only child of civil rights activist O'Day Short.[8] The Cicero Riots of 1951, similarly, demonstrated the extent to which white Chicagoans would go to protect the whiteness of their neighborhoods. There, a crowd of six thousand invaded and wrecked the home of a black war veteran, hauling his furniture into the street and setting his apartment on fire.[9] As blacks became more visible in postwar American cities, many white Americans fought, by any means necessary, to uphold the barriers between black space and white space.

Most whites, however, found a less violent yet more thorough means of enforcing the colour line. Although the suburbanisation of the United States began in the 1920s, it was not until the postwar era that the process gave way to white flight through the collusion of public policy and private practices.[10] Federal legislation during the Roosevelt administration established the means for postwar suburbanisation, particularly through the creation of the Home-owner's Loan Corporation (HOLC), the Federal Housing Authority (FHA) and the Veterans Administration (VA). The FHA and the VA adopted the underwriting practices of the HOLC, which devised a racially discriminatory system of financing home loans. The FHA and VA, in turn, influenced the lending policies of private financial institutions, which avoided investment in 'affected' areas. By severely limiting the flow of capital into the inner city, the FHA and VA significantly enhanced the impoverishment of those areas and encouraged the selective exodus of working-class and middle-class whites to the suburban periphery.[11]

Policy making at the local level bolstered these federal attempts to facilitate suburbanisation. The innovation of municipal incorporation strategies influenced the course of suburbanisation throughout the American Sun Belt and ensured the reproduction of white space. The infamous 'Lakewood Plan' shaped the socioeconomic geography of southern California and the American Sun Belt during the 1950s and 1960s. In 1950, developer Ben Weingart, along with two partners, purchased 3.375 acres of farmland in the southwestern portion of Los Angeles County. There they built Lakewood, a community of 17,000 homes, including the nation's largest shopping centre. Rather than incorporating into the county, the residents of Lakewood contracted county services for minimal costs, while remaining an independent municipality. Following Lakewood's example, 25 municipalities in southern California adopted the Lakewood Plan between 1945 and 1960.[12]

The invention of the 'contract city' ensured tighter control over the social composition of southern California suburban communities. Lakewood Plan cities could effectively direct the makeup of a local population to exclude service-demanding, low-income or renting populations, usually blacks and quite often Latinos as well. Judged by the sociospatial character of suburban southern California during the postwar period, the Lakewood Plan was an overwhelming success. In 1950, there were 38 cities in southern California with less than one percent black populations; these cities contained 24 percent of the metropolitan area's population. In 1970, by contrast, there were 58 cities with less than one percent black populations, containing 33 percent of the regional population. Both the number of segregated cities and the population living within those cities increased. Essentially a white political movement, the Lakewood Plan defined white resistance to black urbanisation during the postwar era. By enacting more privatised methods of city government, Lakewood Plan cities ensured the reproduction of white space in the suburban Sun Belt of postwar America.[13]

The Real Other

The racial character of the postwar suburban boom emerged from wartime anxieties about the 'alien invasion' of American cities. In Los Angeles, for example, the local media generated mass hysteria with its wartime rhetoric directed against the Japanese and Japanese-Americans. The 'Great Los Angeles Air Raid' demonstrated the level of anxiety in Los Angeles regarding such an invasion. At 2:25am on February 26, 1942, the US Army announced the approach of hostile aircraft, activating the city's air raid warning system for the first time. The February 27 issue of the *Los Angeles Times* reported:

Roaring out of a brilliant moonlit western sky, foreign aircraft flying both in large formation and singly flew over Southern California early today and drew heavy barrages of anti-aircraft fire – the first ever to sound over United States continental soil against an enemy invader.

Despite the fleeting moment of panic, no one reported the dropping of bombs or the sighting of enemy aircraft. In fact, the 'air raid' never occurred, but the incident revealed the extent to which the people of Los Angeles psychologically anticipated the kind of 'alien' invasion dramatised in films such as *Them!* and *War of the Worlds*.[14]

Popular anxieties about invasion did not subside with the end of the war, but rather increased as the influx of other racialised groups displaced the Japanese as the alien invaders. *U.S. News* and *World Report*, for example, alarmed its readers in 1956 with a report of a black invasion of Los Angeles. An article, entitled 'West Coast, Too, Has its Race Problem', labeled the influx of Southern blacks to Los Angeles as a 'race problem' to its white readership. As the mere presence of blacks in post-emancipation America constituted a 'race problem', their increasing visibility in postwar American cities illustrated the heightened poignancy of that 'problem'. This was especially the case in Los Angeles, which absorbed a greater number of African-Americans than any other city of the postwar era. 'At every hand', reported the magazine, 'in the factories, offices and schools of Los Angeles, you find growing numbers of the 'new negro' in America – ambitious and aggressive in his demands.'[15]

Certainly, *U.S. News* and *World Report* did not possess any special expertise about the changing racial demography of a city like Los Angeles. The magazine, however, recorded popular perceptions of urban life during the 1950s. Millions of Americans who identified as white looked upon the 'darkening' of the city as nothing less than a crisis. That crisis took shape in the national culture not only in such alarming reports of the growing numbers of 'ambitious and aggressive Negros', but also in science fiction thrillers about the alien invasion of American cities. At a time when blacks concentrated in inner cities in unprecedented numbers and when 'whites' fled older portions of the city for the suburban periphery, urban

science fiction thrillers such as *Them!* and *War of the Worlds* confirmed popular suspicions of American urban life.

The Reel Other

Hollywood faced its own crisis in the age of white flight. Suburbanisation shifted the locus of American popular culture during the postwar era and emptied downtown movie theaters in cities across the nation. Still reeling from the turmoil of the HUAC witch-hunt, Hollywood suffered another blow when movie attendance sharply declined during the late 1940s and continued to fall in the early years of the following decade. Among other factors, the postwar retreat from the public arena and the concurrent emphasis upon private life played no small part in that decline. One astute critic observed in 1950 that 'tall grass will be shortly growing amidst the ruins of Rialtos, Criterions, Granadas and other abandoned landmarks from coast to coast'.[16]

As the cultural component of suburbanisation, television also challenged the hegemony of Hollywood in the cultural landscape of postwar America. While white suburbanites retreated from the real world of increasing complexity and diversity, television offered a glimpse into an alternative world that reflected and reinforced a white suburban worldview. That world had little place for minorities, save the few stereotypical references to the jungle natives of Tarzan films and the manufactured Indians of TV westerns. Television, moreover, afforded the opportunity to 'go out', without compromising the privacy of the single-family home. The advent of this medium radically changed the spatial context of popular culture, underscoring the postwar retreat from public life. Manufacturers marketed television as a way of 'bringing the world to people's doorsteps', emphasising the security and convenience of home entertainment. As a privatised cultural experience, television pulled suburbanites away from older sites of public amusement and accelerated the fragmentation of what had once been the diverse multitudes of urban audiences.[17]

Unable to compete with the convenience and availability of television, Hollywood struggled to maintain its sovereignty in the cultural terrain of postwar America. Innovations in special effects became a strategy for luring spectators back to the movies, and science fiction film became a major venue for marketing these special effects technologies. Thus, a film like *War of the Worlds* could draw huge audiences without the names of major motion picture stars. 'What starring honours there are', wrote one film critic for *Variety* in a review of *War of the Worlds*, 'go strictly to special effects, which create an atmosphere of soul chilling apprehension so effectively audiences will take alarm at the danger posed in that picture.'[18]

Special effects alone, however, do not explain the immense popularity of science fiction thrillers like *Them!* and *War of the Worlds*. To spark an audience 'comeback' to the movies, Hollywood needed more than just technical innovations such as rear projection and miniature sets – it needed to connect, almost psychically, with its audience, recording its hopes and aspirations, as well as its despair and anxiety. Given the social, political, and cultural climate of postwar America, Hollywood emphasised the dark side of the collective conscious, projecting the concerns that dominated public discourse. Thus, anxieties about Communism surfaced in films such as *Double Indemnity* (1944), which exposed the 'evil within', and *Invasion of the Body Snatchers* (1956), which stressed the external threat from abroad. Similarly, films like *Mildred Pierce* (1945) and *Rebel Without a Cause* (1955) revealed American anxieties about powerful women and the sexual threat to domestic stability in postwar America. Such films articulated the concerns that preoccupied postwar Americans.

While sexual and class anxieties inform the meaning of these films, race was a dominant factor. Science fiction films like *Them!* and *War of the Worlds* named racial anxieties about 'alien' invasions that troubled suburban Americans of the 1950s. Of course, these films are open to multiple interpretations and clearly allude to other anxieties of the day, but it is their urban settings that complicate any facile interpretations of the Martians of *War of the Worlds* or the giant ants of *Them!* as exclusively Communists. Cold war anxieties, after all, were neither urban nor rural. Racial anxieties, however, emerged from a prevalent perception that American cities were really under 'attack' during the postwar period. In their narratives of alien invasion and their emphasis upon the difference between 'us' and 'them', the urban

science fiction film effectively reached the suburban audiences that had largely forsaken the city as a satisfying way of life.

Both *War of the Worlds* and *Them!* are narratives about alien invaders and the destruction they wrought upon American cities. Central to these narratives is a visual distinction between 'us', a homogenous citizenry, and 'them', the alien Other. *Them!* depicted the invasion of Los Angeles by giant ants, enlarged by overexposure to radiation from atom bomb testing sites in the desert. Although an allegory for the dangers of atomic energy, the film presents creatures as ordinary as ants transformed into hideous aliens who invade vulnerable cities and attack their innocent citizenry. The giant ants, with bulging eyes and deadly mandibles, recall historic stereotypes of racialised groups as animalistic and especially alien. Such stereotypes ran rampant in times of international or domestic crisis. Japanese-Americans, for example, became rats in the political cartoons of the early 1940s. In the late nineteenth century, similarly, when California suffered from economic depression and high unemployment, Chinese-Americans bore the brunt of racist stereotypes, depicted in visual and literary media as bats with sharp claws and gnarled fangs. African-Americans have suffered such vicious kinds of representation throughout their history, stereotyped in the national culture most often as simian creatures. At various points in American history, racialised groups have been likened to monkeys, bats, rats, ants, and other creatures, reinforcing the perceptual affinity between non-human and non-white.[19]

War of the Worlds takes such representation a step further, as Martians replace ants as the alien Other. The Martians of *War of the Worlds* land upon Earth in search of a more hospitable climate for procreation. Though we know the Martians only by their sleek metal saucers that hover above the ground, a few scenes reveal a grotesquely inhuman Other. In one sequence of images, the noted scientists, Dr. Clayton Forrester, and his companion, Sylvia Van Buren, take refuge inside an abandoned home. Although Sylvia is rarely seen apart from the company of men, she is momentarily separated from Forrester, distracted by a hunch that the invaders are nearby. As Van Buren searches the quarters alone, audience suspicion is heightened: the encounter with the Martians seems dreadfully imminent. With the camera behind her, Sylvia is unaware that an alien is watching her every move. The camera mimics the alien's predatory gaze, targeting the white woman as the object of the alien's (and by visual implication, the audience's) desire. As the bright, slimy green arm of the Martian reaches toward her, the whiteness of her skin contrasts sharply with the alien physiognomy. The *Los Angeles Herald Express* noted this graphic scene, remarking upon the 'skinny tentacles' of the Martians, with 'vacuum cups at the end of each finger' and 'flesh which looks like a piece of pulsating raw liver'.[20]

War of the Worlds draws upon a common trope of the urban science fiction film. The alien lust for the white woman is evident not only in the narrative content of the urban science fiction film, but also in its publicity materials. For example, the garish advertisement poster for 'Invasion of the Saucer Men' captures some of white America's deepest anxieties about the alien Other. In the central image of the advertisement, a scantily-clad white woman with heaving breasts flails in the clutches of a hideous green alien monster. In the background is the metropolis, under attack by flying saucers. Again, the alien bears a familiar resemblance to cultural stereotypes of racialised minorities, blacks in particular. With their bulging round eyes, enormous heads, and dark, almost black skin, the saucer men seem more familiar than alien, recalling lurid representations of 'coons', 'sambos' and 'pickaninnies' in American popular culture. The blackness of the aliens contrasts sharply with the milky whiteness of the woman's skin. She is helpless in the grips of an alien predatory sexuality, naming historical anxieties about black male lust for white women. Such anxieties, of course, are not unique to the urban science fiction genre, but draw upon the racist practices of early filmmaking.

The films of D. W. Griffith, for example, often emphasise non-white male lust for white women, a lust almost always motivated by an attempt to rape. The character of Gus in *Birth of a Nation* (1915) epitomises then-prevalent white perceptions of a ferocious black male sexuality and its threat to white women. His lust for Elsie Stoneman culminates in a famous chase scene in which she leaps to her death to avoid sacrificing her virtue to the mulatto sexual predator. Prior to the release of *Birth of a Nation*, *The Girls and Daddy* foreshadowed

Gus's behavior. The film narrates the story of two thieves, one white and one in blackface, who, unlike the white burglar, lustfully chases after two white women. Although Griffith did not invent the cinematic stereotype of black or mulatto men as lustful monsters preying upon the virtue of white women, he popularised those stereotypes, which, in turn, informed the work of subsequent generations of filmmakers.[21]

During the postwar period, a time when the national culture reemphasised the sanctity of the nuclear family, the urban science fiction film echoed the work of former generations of filmmakers like Griffith and reiterated the alien threat to white women. Some historians have illuminated the ways in which suburbanisation reasserted the nuclear family as the most fundamental unit of American society. The many threats that preoccupied post-war Americans – Communists, homosexuals, racialised minorities – were viewed as dangers not so much to the individual or to the society at large, but rather to the stability and coherence of the American family. The national culture, moreover, almost always coded the family as white. In the racialised climate of postwar America, white flight could be viewed therefore as a collective attempt to maintain the hegemony of the white nuclear family.

In their representations of the alien threat to white womanhood, urban science fiction films such as *Them!* and *War of the Worlds* also implied the vulnerability of the white family. As their narratives dramatised alien invasions of the city and their occupation of urban space, the films emphasised the direct threat to the dominance of the white American family. In *Them!* that threat is realised as the ants kill the white father of a family and take his two sons hostage, leaving their mother in despair. The whiteness of the two boys is visually enhanced when the ants hold their young captives in the darkness of the city's sewer system. The threat to the nuclear family in *Them!* again recalls an earlier discourse of the white family in the films of Griffith, where stories of the family usually involve a racial component that casts non-white males as a threat to the dominance of white patriarchy. The aim of such stories, of course, is to segregate the races and uphold the unity of the family, the purity of the white woman, and the power and divinity of the white family. *Them!* extends that message into the postwar era of U.S. history, emphasising once again the non-white/non-human threat to the stability of the American family.

War of the Worlds, similarly, asserts the divinity of the white family while exposing the potential threat to that institution. In the climactic scene of the film, as masses of Los Angelenos take refuge inside a church shortly before the imminent holocaust, a white family – mother, father, son and daughter – huddles together in prayer, gazing up toward the image of Christ at the altar. As the camera hones in upon their faces, the audience is reminded exactly who the victim is in this narrative of alien aggression. Lighting, thrown upon their faces at a 45° angle, highlights the fair skin, blonde hair and blue eyes of the family members. The sanctity of this image is reinforced through editing, which cuts from images of the white family to the image of a white Christ at the altar, the supreme embodiment of Western humanity. Such editing supports a visual association between Christ and the family within a racialised context of whiteness.[22]

Yet, while these films exalt the white woman and the white family, they simultaneously emphasise the deadly potential of alien motherhood. *Them!*, for example, is a film about alien motherhood run amok, depicting the nightmare of uncontrolled, mindless reproduction of the Other. The film's climax is loaded with sexual tension, as the 'queen' ant takes shelter in the 'egg chamber' deep within the sewers of Los Angeles. The queen ant represents the nativist's worst nightmare: alien procreation gone mad, uncontrollable and unstoppable. Such representations of endless reproduction do not simply resonate with postwar anxieties about maternal domination. Rather, they underscore popular fears about alien motherhood in particular. The antagonist, after all, is an insect. Ultimately, climactic tension is resolved as the phallic bazookas of the army incinerate the queen and her eggs, thereby securing the city for white supremacy and against the reproduction of the alien Other.[23]

Another way in which these films lend themselves to the construction of whiteness is through racial censorship. James Snead argues that 'omission', or exclusion, is the most common form of racial stereotyping, but also the most difficult to identify because its manifestation is absence itself. In other words, the absence of black characters in film is a form of stereotyping, one that reinforces the idea that blacks and other non-white groups are obscure, marginal and dependent. Both *Them!* and *War of the Worlds* feature white scientists, white generals, white presidents, white policemen, white pilots, white ministers, white nurses, white doctors, and other racialised figures of authority. Blacks, however, play neither major nor minor roles in either film, positing a polarised landscape in which the only Other is the alien Other.[24]

Racial images are coupled with urban images in such science fiction films, dramatising the political and cultural conditions of the United States in the age of white flight. Just as the term 'white flight' implies the movement of white masses away from the city, films such as *Them!* and *War of the Worlds* depict the flight of a homogenous white citizenry from the violent onslaught of the Other. In *Them!*, for example, 'UFO reports' confirm that 'flying saucers shaped like ants' are heading west toward Los Angeles. Subsequent images cut to urban crowds in frenzied preparation for the imminent arrival of 'them'. A state of emergency is declared and the National Guard is called upon to protect the white citizenry from the 'savage and ruthless' invaders. Panic ensues prior to their arrival as, with what must have been a startling similarity to the actual tests of the Emergency Broadcasting System, radio and television broadcasters announce:

> By direction of the President of the United States, in full agreement with the Governor of the State of California, and the Mayor of Los Angeles, the city of Los Angeles is, in the interests of public safety, hereby claimed to be under martial law ... curfew is at 1800 hours. Any persons on the street or outside their quarters after 6:00pm tonight will be subject to arrest.

Similarly, in *War of the Worlds*, the prospect as well as the reality of doomsday maintains the air of suspense. Though the aliens initially descend upon a small California town, it is their slow, yet steady approach toward the metropolis that constitutes the suspense of the narrative. The path of the Other from the small town to the metropolis recalls the great migration of blacks during the 1940s and 1950s, in which masses of black rural Southerners migrated to cities like Los Angeles. Migration becomes invasion in *War of the Worlds* as the Martians draw nearer to the city. The skies darken upon their arrival and panic descends upon the hoards of Angelenos, who flee in desperation. Police cars patrol the streets of downtown to maintain what little social order remains, their loudspeakers blaring, 'Everybody listen carefully! We must evacuate the city! All major highways have been marked to lead you to shelter and welfare centres in the hills'. The very anticipation of doomsday in the urban science film corresponded to the sense in the postwar American city that someone or something was about to bring crisis and destruction.

As panic ensues, the masses flee the city. The exodus is a significant part of *War of the Worlds*. As people jam the freeways with their possessions bundled atop their cars, others take flight on foot, seeking refuge in the hills above the city. A voice-over narrates the spectacle of catastrophe, implying the historical process of white flight itself:

> As the Martians burned fields and forests, and great cities fell before them, huge populations were driven from their homes. The stream of flight rose swiftly to a torrent. It became a giant stampede – without order and without goal. It was the beginning of the route of civilization – of the massacre of humanity.

Finally, the aliens arrive, and it is doomsday for the city. Special effects recreate the holocaust. 'See Los Angeles Crumble Before Your Very Eyes!' runs the headline of the *Los Angeles Herald Express* on November 11, 1953. The realism of such images of destruction are enhanced not only through innovations in special effects, but also through the use of real and recognisable buildings and landscapes, which promote audience identification with the crisis upon the screen. In *War of the Worlds*, for example, a spectacular scene depicts the obliteration of the Los Angeles City Hall, a symbol of municipal authority and civic order exploding in a brilliant burst of flames. In other science fiction films, the use of the Empire State Building, Times Square, the Washington Monument or the Golden Gate Bridge serves to name the urban scene and to deepen our familiarity with the events taking place in the film. In each instance, the result is the same: total eradication of the most poignant symbols of Western progress and American civilisation.

Susan Sontag identifies a certain kind of poetry in such images, which she describes as the 'aesthetics of destruction'. Images of aliens and their onslaught upon the city held an ambiguous fascination for postwar white suburban audiences, who not only recoiled in horror from such a vision of their own destruction, but also took a certain delight in that vision. Urban, industrial audiences have historically held mixed feelings toward the macabre, the alien and the exotic, drawing upon ambivalent feelings of shock, terror, curiosity and even delight. The urban science fiction film, with its emphasis upon disaster, disorder and the grotesque, inherits its appeal from carnival sideshows and dime museums, which drew thousands who paid admission fees to ogle at such curiosities as 'the Fee Jee Mermaid' and 'What is it?'[25]

The postwar popularity of films like *War of the Worlds* and *Them!* revealed the extent to which this fascination persisted, even among suburban, post-industrial audiences of the 1950s. Although suburban audiences found themselves increasingly regimented into racial, sexual and economic hierarchies, they maintained a lurid attraction to the baser elements of the culture. Through terrifying spectacles of disaster and horrific representations of the alien Other, the urban science fiction film may have offered an arena where American audiences could sublimate the attraction to, or even love of, the Other. Recalling the intense popularity of Orson Welles's 1939 radio broadcast of *War of the Worlds*, one film critic anticipated a similar reception of the film adaptation in 1953, 'just as listeners willingly mesmerised themselves into being scared half to death by the Welles broadcast, so will viewers take vicarious pleasure in the terror loosened in the film'.[26]

Conclusion: The Post-White Flight City

While films such as *War of the Worlds* and *Them!* represent the city in the age of white flight, other urban science fiction films portray the city after the exodus. In her study of the urban science fiction film, Vivian Sobchack identifies images of a 'dead' city, devoid of people, as another common trope of the genre. New York, for example, is an empty concrete canyon in *Five* (1951), where nothing moves save a slowly-moving car in which the two main characters ride. In *On the Beach* (1954), San Francisco is equally lifeless, as submarine crewmen search for the source of a mysterious radio signal. Similarly, in *The World, The Flesh and the Devil* (1959), a single character roams through the vacant cityscapes of Times Square and Wall Street. This is the post-white flight city: 'cars eternally stalled on a bridge, newspaper blowing down a city street caught up in some ill-begotten draft, street lights and neon often blinking on and off in a mockery of animate existence', writes Vivian Sobchack, 'this is the iconography of the post-holocaust city in the 1950s to the mid-1970s.'[27] As white suburbanites turned their backs upon the old downtowns and retreated to the suburbs, images of empty cities reflected and reinforced the symbolic 'death' of the city in postwar America.

The ultimate post-white flight city, however, emerged after the heyday of the urban science fiction film. Ridley Scott's *Blade Runner* returns the science fiction audience to Los Angeles in the year 2019, after the flight of ex-suburbanites to the 'off-world' colonies in outer space. Electronic advertisements hover above the noxious hypersprawl of twenty-first-century Los Angeles, promising the good life in the depths of outer space: 'a golden land of opportunity awaits you in the off-world colony!' Such campaigns recall the turn-of-the-century booster promotions of Los Angeles, in which people of adequate means fled the over-industrialised, immigrant-ridden cities of the eastern seaboard. Scott's Los Angeles is not far from that history. His city represents a negative melting pot, where non-white immigrant groups are left to scavenge over the scraps of a deindustrialised landscape. An ugly street language, a hybrid dialect of Spanish, Japanese, and German, has replaced English. This is Los Angeles after alien colonisation (most likely Japanese investors), where whiteness is a historical figment of an ancient civilisation.

Images of the post-white flight city projected the racial anxieties that surfaced in such postwar blockbusters as *Them!* and *War of the Worlds*. While these films are not exclusively about white anxieties, the spatial emphasis of *Them!* and *War of the Worlds*, that is, their use of the city as setting and subject, suggests that it is essential to understand the spatial transformation of post-war America in order

to grasp the multiple meanings of these films. Americans suburbanised in unprecedented numbers during the post-World War Two era, abandoning older portions of the inner city. By and large, that process was a privilege afforded to those who could identify themselves as white, while non-white, racialised minorities 'filled in' the decrepit spaces left behind, moving us toward Ridley Scott's ominous vision of the twenty-first-century city. As white flight and suburbanisation promoted the racial polarisation of postwar America between 'chocolate cities' and 'vanilla suburbs', cultural productions such as the urban science fiction film represented that polarisation in graphic images of alien invaders and the spectacular disintegration of American cities.

The racial politics of suburbanisation in postwar America drew not only upon material processes, such as the Lakewood Plan and the racially-biased lending policies of the FHA and VA, but also upon the production of cinematic spectacles such as the urban science fiction film. Although such films did not create white flight, they dramatised the anxieties that undergirded the racial politics of suburbanisation. The urban science fiction film created a space in which white Americans could imagine themselves and their predicament in the years following the conclusion of World War Two. The invasion and ultimate obliteration of the city so graphically represented through the advanced technology of special effects corresponded to the very real rejection of urban life by white America. The urban science fiction film conjured a realm of dreadful possibilities that heightened the sense of urgency with which white Americans abandoned the older portions of cities like Detroit and Los Angeles and sought refuge in homogenous communities like Lakewood. Just as it was not difficult for white suburban Americans to sympathise with the terrified masses of films such as *Them!* and *War of the Worlds*, so it was not difficult for black inner-city writers such as Ralph Ellison to suspect that they might have been the 'Hollywood movie ectoplasms' of 1950s science fiction.

Notes

1 My thanks to James Cook for pointing out this citation from *Invisible Man* to me.

2 These terms were introduced by Reynolds Farley, Howard Schuman, Diane Colasanto, and Shirley Hatchet,

'Chocolate City, Vanilla Suburbs: Will the Trend Towards Racially Separate Communities Continue?', *Social Science Research* 7 (1978), p. 330. George Clinton, with Parliament-Funkadelic, also recorded a song entitled 'Chocolate Cities, Vanilla Suburbs' in 1978.

3 The literature on the spatial and racial organisation of the post-industrial metropolis is extensive. See Thomas Sugrue, *The Origins of the Urban Crisis: Race and Inequality in Postwar Detroit* (Princeton, NJ: Princeton University Press, 1998) and Arnold Hirsch, *Making the Second Ghetto: Race and Housing in Chicago, 1940–1960* (Chicago: University of Chicago, 1998). See also Douglas S. Massey and Nancy A. Denton, *American Apartheid: Segregation and the Making of the Urban Underclass* (Cambridge, MA: Harvard University Press, 1993) and Reynolds Farley and Walter Allen, *The Color Line and the Quality of Life in America* (New York: Russell Sage, 1987).

4 Peter Biskind, *Seeing is Believing: How America Learned to Stop Worrying and Love the Fifties* (New York: Pantheon Books, 1983) and Michael Rogin, *Ronald Reagan, The Movie* (Berkeley: University of California, 1987).

5 Arnold Hirsch, 'Black Ghettos', in *The Reader's Companion to American History*, ed. Eric Foner and John A. Garrity (New York: Houghton Mifflin Company, 1991), p. 112.

6 Gordon de Marco, *A Short History of Los Angeles* (San Francisco: Lexikos, 1988), p. 164.

7 Richard Polenberg, *One Nation Divisible: Class, Race and Ethnicity in the United States Since 1938* (New York: Penguin, 1980), p. 162.

8 Mike Davis, *City of Quartz: Excavating the Future in Los Angeles* (London: Verso, 1990), p. 400.

9 Paul Gilje, *Rioting in America* (Bloomington: Indiana University Press, 1996), p. 165.

10 George Lipsitz, *The Possessive Investment in Whiteness: How White People Profit from Identity Politics* (Philadelphia: Temple University Press, 1998).

11 Kenneth T. Jackson, *Crabgrass Frontier: The Suburbanization of the United States* (New York: Oxford, 1985), 195–203.

12 Gary Miller, *Cities by Contract: The Politics of Municipal Incorporation* (Cambridge, MA: MIT Press, 1981).

13 Ibid., p. 22.

14 Jack Smith, 'The Great Los Angeles Air Raid', in *Los Angeles: Biography of a Metropolis*, eds John and LaRee Gaughey (Berkeley: University of California, 1976), p. 364.

15 'West Coast, Too, Has its Race Problem', *U.S. News and World Report*, July 14 (1956), p. 36.

16 John Houseman, 'Hollywood Faces the Fifties', *Harper's*, December 2, 1950, p. 50.

17 Lynn Spiegel, 'Installing the Television Set: Popular Discourses on Television and Domestic Space, 1948-1950', *Camera Obscura*, 16 (1988), pp. 14–20.

18 *Variety*, November 3 (1953), p. 6.

19 Marlon Riggs, *Ethnic Notions* (San Francisco: California Newsreel, 1986), videocassette.

20 *Los Angeles Herald Express*, November 26, 1953.

21 Daniel Bernardi, 'The Voice of Whiteness: D. W. Griffith's Biograph Films', in *The Birth of Whiteness: Race and the Emergence of U.S. Cinema*, ed. Daniel Bernardi (New Brunswick, NJ: Rutgers University, 1996), p. 122.

22 For a discussion of cinematic lighting and whiteness, see Richard Dyer, *White* (London: Routledge, 1997), pp. 116–42.

23 Charles Ramirez Berg, 'Immigrants, Aliens and Extra-terrestrials: Science Fiction's Alien 'Other' as (Among Other Things) New Hispanic Imagery', *CineAction!*, 18 (1989).

24 James Snead, Colin MacCabe and Cornel West, eds, *White Screens, Black Images: Hollywood From the Dark Side* (London: Routledge, 1994), pp. 6–7.

25 James Cook, 'Of Men, Missing Links and Nondescripts: The Strange Career of P. T. Barnum's 'What is it?' Exhibition', in *Freakery: Cultural Spectacles of Extraordinary Body*, ed. Rosemarie Garland Thompson (New York: New York University, 1996), pp. 139–57.

26 *Variety*, March 3, 1953.

27 Vivian Sobchack, 'Cities on the Edge of Time: The Urban Science Fiction Film', *East-West Film Journal* I, no. 3 (December 1988), p. II.

On the Edge of Spaces: *Blade Runner, Ghost in the Shell* and Hong Kong's Cityscape
Wong Kin Yuen

Colonial cities can be viewed as the *fore-runners* of what the contemporary capitalist world city would eventually become. For ... in the colonial and paracolonial societies and especially Asia, Africa and Latin America ... the representatives and institutions of industrial capitalism first confronted those of ethnically, racially, and culturally different pre-industrial and pre-capitalist societies at any significant scale.
— Antony King, *Global Cities* (38)

The gigantic mass is immobilised before the eyes. It is transformed into a text-urology in which extremes coincide — extremes of ambition and degradation, brutal oppositions of races and styles, contrasts between yesterday's buildings, already transformed into trash cans, and today's urban irruptions that block out its space ... Its present invents itself, from hour to hour, in the act of throwing away its previous accomplishments and challenging the future.
— Michel de Certeau, 'Walking in the City' (152)

It is now widely acknowledged that Ridley Scott's *Blade Runner* (1982/1992) initiated a whole tradition of cult movies later grouped under the label 'cyberpunk'. *Blade Runner*'s style draws its images from urban spaces all over the world, including such Asian cities as Tokyo and Hong Kong. Science fiction film critics are less aware, however, that when *anime* film director Mamoru Oshii was looking for a model of the city of the future in a computerised world, he turned for his primary inspiration to the cityscape of Hong Kong. Through his art designers, actual spots in the city of Hong Kong were transformed into the *mise-en-scène* of *Ghost in the Shell*, first released in the United States in March 1996.

Science fiction has not fared well in Hong Kong (either in terms of production or consumption), nor is there a cyberpunk culture among Hong Kong's young computer users. So the question arises: what elements in Hong Kong provided inspiration for this cinematic representation of a near-future city characterised by decadence, anarchy and fantasy on the one hand, and a mistrusted, high-tech hyper-reality on the other? Taking up this question, I will first suggest a reading of a shopping complex in Hong Kong that emphasises its fragmentation, disjunctiveness and ephemerality. Like *Blade Runner*'s 'Ridley-ville', this Hong Kong shopping complex intertwines past and future, memory and desire. Finally, I will analyse the setting of *Ghost in the Shell*, especially the parts that are clearly modeled on Hong Kong street scenes and architecture. I hope to validate Antony King's argument that colonial cities have the best chance of establishing a cityscape of the future that embraces racial and cultural differences.

Before going any further, let me address the politics of representation, especially in the visual media of cyberpunk art and films. Following the success of *Blade Runner*, such cyber-thrillers as *Johnny Mnemonic* (1995), *Hackers* (1995), *Lawnmower Man 2* (1996) and *Strange Days* (1995) have also selectively used motifs of 'Asian' design environments, together with their visual icons, to portray cultural difference and to create visual pleasure from postmodern pastiche. As in *Blade Runner*, the most popular model for artists' and filmmakers' dark and sprawling cities of the future is an Asian-dominated metropolis. Cyberpunk novels, including Gibson's *Neuromancer* (1984) and Stephenson's *Snow Crash* (1992), likewise emphasise Asian culture and urban style, suggesting (as John Christie has argued) 'the replacement of the hegemonic state apparatus by multinationals, its cultural pluralism' (173). Whereas *Snow Crash*'s 'Mr. Lee's Greater Hong Kong' is set in cyberspace, *Neuromancer*'s Night City, The Sprawl, coffin hotel and Ninsei are based on the Tokyo Bay area. In his recent novel, *Idoru* (1996), Gibson even presents organic buildings in a twenty-first-century Tokyo. (In this case, there must also be some connection to Hong Kong as well, since in his acknowledgment to a Japanese director, Gibson mentions 'Kowloon Walled City', which has 'continued to haunt him' [n.p.] ever since the latter told him about it.)

For sf illustrator Barclay Shaw, the merging of cyberspace with the sleazy, neon-lit visual passion in *Neuromancer* closely resembles a chaotic Hong Kong street. Commissioned as cover art for the 1986 Phantasia Press edition of the novel, the painting chooses some Chinese characters (presumably taken from Hong Kong shop signs) for the foreground, highlighting not only a sense of ethnic and cultural confusion and hybridity but also a continuous process of the destructions and reconstructions so characteristic of contemporary cityscapes. This is certainly in line with the cyberpunk convention of 'the run-down inner-city slum-cum-tent settlement, overcrowded, trashed and graffiti-ridden' (Bonner 194), reminding us at the same time of *Blade Runner*'s Ridleyville.

As Nigel Clark notes, '*Neuromancer* and its sequels feature a series of hyper-aestheticised urban spaces: terrains in which vibrant new signifying surfaces are layered over the detritus of obsolescent forms' (121). As a city hustler who understands 'the dynamics of street dealing' (*Neuromancer* 11), Case knows well 'that burgeoning technologies require outlaw zones', the kind of space provided by Chiba City, a 'magnet for the Sprawl's techno-criminal subcultures' and a place inhabited by Chinese experts in 'black medicine, implants, nerve-splicing and microbionics' (6). Looking at Shaw's cover art, one might assume that the dark alley to the right behind the drug store would be the sort of place where one of these black market clinics might be found.

We also find visual icons relating to Chinese characters, obviously within a 'Chinatown' setting, in cyberpunk films such as *Strange Days*. Set in Los Angeles a few days shy of the millennium, the film sustains film noir tradition through dark and explosive scenes of riots and chaos. In between these hybridised sites and battle zones on the streets, Chinatown's glittering lanterns (not the authentic kind with real candlelight, of course), together with the profusion of shops and commercial sign boards characteristic of a normal busy Hong Kong street, juxtapose visual alternatives and establish a tone somewhere between eroticism and dreariness. This kind of design, which marks the unmistakable miscellaneity of a metropolis, suggests a near future where centres and peripheries do not hold and where racial conflicts are at the point of explosion; it also provides an appropriate way to exhibit an 'inverted millennarianism' (Jameson 53). Scenes from a kitchen in a Chinese restaurant

depict violence and intrigues played out among individuals, while collective racial protests and riots are taking place in the streets. It is curious that such 'Chinese' vignettes have become a favorite among recent Hollywood filmmakers. Compared to the front of the restaurant in *Strange Days*, where decor and orderliness prevail, the kitchen is filmed as a clandestine negative space signifying hiddenness and disorder. In the restaurant kitchen, the flawed character Nero plays out his drama of fighting back against corporate crimes, providing a contrast with the public atrocities committed in front of millions of people during the New Year countdown celebration at the movie's conclusion.

In *Strange Days*, 'Chinese' spaces are re-presented as hidden within the context of the future urban setting. Is there any cultural or ideological significance in this – beyond the fact that a Chinese restaurant kitchen is an exotic spot? Does this added element of Chineseness (contrasted with the exploding warfare among races and social classes in *Strange Days*) help to bring out the theme of the intertwining relations between social space and media space? Finally, since Chinatown settings are spaces famous for being inhabited by illegal immigrants, we will need to follow Homi Bhabha's critique of the 'metropolitan histories' of the west, 'the anomalous and discriminatory legal and cultural status assigned to migrant, diasporic and refugee populations' who 'find themselves on the frontiers between cultures and nations, often on the other side of the law' (Bhabha 175).

We must be careful, however, in interpreting the ways the Hong Kong city-scape is appropriated by cyberpunk literature and films; we must remember that Hollywood has had a long history of misrepresenting Hong Kong, from white-male fantasies about oriental girls (*The World of Suzy Wong* [1961]) to exploitative soft-core pornographic eroticism (the *Emmanuelle* films). More recently, a quick shot in the low-budget *Lawnmower Man 2* shows a yellow rickshaw pulled by a Chinese man on the street of yet another Los Angeles of the future. An offensive example of 'non-equivalent sites of representation' (Bhabha 176), this rickshaw scene exemplifies a brutal seizure of a cultural sign by the west, a way of 'evoking ... savage colonial antecedents' for the sake of presumed 'ideals of civility' (Bhabha 175).[1] Whether cyberpunk film directors are themselves free from this mire of distortion in their renderings of Hong Kong's urban images is of course an important question to ask here.

Blade Runner's cultural references are indirect, yet I propose to compare the design of the film's city setting with an actual spot in Hong Kong that may provide a paradigm for future global cities. The incredibly detailed Los Angeles of 2019 in Blade Runner creates a futuristic noir atmosphere by heavily borrowing from Asian motifs, albeit vague and general ones, in its design of city icons and social spaces. With the artful 'retro-fitting' and 'layering' of the Japanese sushi bar, the gigantic media screen of the geisha girl ad, and a Chinese bio-engineer who 'only does eyes', the city, critics are quick to point out, looks like 'Chinatown in Tomorrowland' (Hunter 225); the sleazy cinematography results in a hybrid and fractal combination of 'Hong Kong, New York [and] Tokyo's Ginza district' (Sammon 101). I would argue that considering Hong Kong as among the cinematic models for the future city may inspire not only a further look at Hong Kong at this present moment of political transition but also its potential for developing into a 'forerunner of what the contemporary capitalist world city will eventually become' (King 38).

Perhaps because of its recent reabsorption by China, Hong Kong has drawn enormous interest from urban scholars and social critics. Struggling historically between traditional Chinese culture and British imperialism, and at this moment adjusting its full-fledged capitalism in order to be embraced by socialism, Hong Kong's postmodern identity has been singled out as a unique case in the world, characterised by 'disappearance' and 'hyphenation' (Abbas 1994; 1996) or dealt with in terms of 'discourses in collision under the volcano' (Cuthbert 1995).

As someone who grew up in Hong Kong, I am particularly fascinated by the dazzling visuals of Blade Runner's Ridleyville, its seamless weaving together of the futuristic and the traditional, as well as its paradoxical delighting of the eye through an emphasis on urban squalor. Other aspects – hybrid architectural spaces, crowdedness, the polyglot or mishmash city-speak, the chaotic proliferation of neon billboards above futuristic shopping arcades, the rain-soaked streets and dragon signs

– invite me to conclude that this Los Angeles of 2019 can indeed be read as 'Hong Kong on a bad day' (Salisbury 96; Doel and Clarke 163). The questions remain to be asked: what illumination does Blade Runner offer us for envisioning the twenty-first-century cityscape, and what role will Hong Kong play in shaping our expectations of the city of the future? This film's 'radical eclecticism or ad hoc-ism' (Bruno 66) catches my eye and inspires me to think about the evolving scenes of my own city, freeing me from clichés (Hong Kong is a dynamic and international city with post-industrial and postmodernist characteristics, etc.). Let me go right to a specific Hong Kong space for a detailed description, to demonstrate the value of placing Ridleyville and Hong Kong together.

The place is located at the juncture of Happy Valley and Causeway Bay around Russell Street and Sharp East Street, one of the most densely populated areas of Hong Kong. Perhaps no other place can demonstrate so well the strange mix of global and local in truly cosmopolitan downtown development. The space occupies half a square mile of streets, shops, flyovers and the recent addition of a mall, 'Times Square'. It is certainly an 'urban secret located at the intersection of postmodern and science fiction' (Bukatman 12).

Apparently no parody was intended by naming the place after New York's Times Square, but the name does reflect and even reaffirm its own historicity and timeliness – albeit the kind of schizophrenic temporality that Fredric Jameson uses in his famous reading of the Bonaventure Hotel (80–5). The complex itself, built on top of a busy metro station, stretches from several levels underground to skyscraper height, looking down on the adjacent, much older buildings, 'indifferent to its surrounding' (Abbas 1996, 221). For cityplanners, especially visitors, the awkward and abrupt sense of discrepancies on all levels is impossible to miss. The complex was built on a former tram-depot skirted by an old-style street market and the quarters for lower echelon tram-company employees. Thus an area once inhabited by comparatively low-income locals has been transformed by commercialism into a high-tech wonder, a bewildering collage of signs and patterns with enough anarchic elements remaining (a small part of the market and old-style shops) to create a sense of pastiche. Yet nothing unusual or uncanny is felt by the people who live there; and in general the logic of capitalism, in which 'shopping is an aesthetic experience' (Webster 212), works beautifully, since the spot has become (with its advantages of proximity and diversity, its availability and variety of consumer goods) one of the busiest and most prosperous places in Hong Kong.

But who are these inhabitants? They are shoppers, blue- and white-collar workers, tourists of all nationalities, and an ever-changing population of new immigrants (some of them illegal), working mostly in the old shops. The people of 'Times Square' are both rich and poor, young and old. More than Disneyland, this phoenix in the rubble is patronised by practically all walks of life; and this absolute accessibility to the fairyland of diversity and display accounts for its success. This is of course the exact opposite of the kind of cityscape deliberately designed 'to wall off the differences between people, assuming that these differences are more likely to be mutually threatening than mutually stimulating' (Sennet xii). To walk in this area is to float with, through, and against the crowd, always on one's way to somewhere else. This may well be an indication of a degree of pedestrian movement and flow unique to Hong Kong. Arjun Appadurai's comments on the landscape of people (as constituting this shifting world of ours) is particularly pertinent to description of Hong Kong's Times Square:

[T]ourists, immigrants, refugees, exiles, guestworkers and other moving groups and persons constitute an essential feature of the world and appear to affect the politics of (and between) nations to a hitherto un-precedented degree. This is not to say that there are no relatively stable communities and networks, of kinship, of friendship, of work and of leisure, as well as of birth, residence and other filiative forms. But it is to say that the warp of these stabilities is everywhere shot through with the woof of human motion, as more persons and groups deal with the realities of having to move or the fantasies of wanting to move. (7)

This postmodern architectural environment in Asian cities may have been the source of their fascination for cyberpunk film designers. I doubt that Ridley Scott knew of the existence of the Hong Kong Times Square when he was conjuring up his Los Angeles set in Blade Runner,

but I would like to juxtapose an early sketch of his with a couple of photos for comparison. What first catches the eye, besides striking resemblances in the busy streets, the futuristic shopping arcades, the neon-lit billboards, the garbage, the drunkards, and so on, is the huge 9x6 metre video screen acting almost as the backdrop, an immense icon of power. This gigantic screen hanging above busy streets in future cities has been a common and almost indispensable motif among cyberpunk films. From Running Man (1987) to Johnny Mnemonic and Hackers to Strange Days, this screen has become the hallmark of postmodern cities, a mirror of information networks, an entrance into cyberspace. Scott's screen is later changed into an even bigger one showing a close-up of an alluring Japanese geisha who is always trying to sell something, set in contrast with a flying blimp beaming with flashing lights to advertise off-world immigration. At Hong Kong's Times Square, however, the screen shows more than animated advertisements: since it is also connected to the cable TV channels, it broadcasts local and international news to passers-by. Indeed, for several months the cable TV channels have presented a live talk show on the square below the screen: hyperreality in its extreme comes into reality.

Much has been said about the relationship between cyberpunk culture and our so-called post-information age. Theoretical studies such as Debord's Society of the Spectacle and Bukat-man's Terminal Identity have illuminated the significance of such a gigantic screen as an alternative space of the visual. Starting from the Lacanian concept of subject-formation through the image in a mirror, critics have noticed that with the advent of optical technology, this mirror is turned into, say, the video camera, which does the work of at once creating, reflecting, and distorting the image of the self. All city dwellers, especially regular shoppers in modern malls, have had the experience of walking by a camera shop, leisurely looking, and then suddenly seeing their own image also walking by and looking on but from the opposite direction and angle. They then realise that this is the video camera set to automatic and placed behind the shop window, shooting outward.

Edward Soja has explained how some critics provide insights 'on how fragmentation, ruptures, deviation, displacements and discontinuities can be politically transformed from liability and weakness to a potential source of opportunity and strength'. He describes how the feminist critic Anne Friedberg, during her 'window shopping' in Paris, focuses on those 'machines of virtual transport [that] break us out of our constraining spatio-temporal con-trainers, starting with the panorama and the diorama and ending with the 'virtual tourism' provided by cinema and its extensions, most notably the television and the VCR' (Soja 117). In this context, the activities surrounding the screen on the square can be considered an extreme enlargement of the automatic video camera experience just mentioned.

Incidentally, there is at least one camera shop on one of the levels in the Times Square complex that does film the passers-by. I would suggest, following Baudrillard's assertion, that we are the first generation who actually live in science fiction: such experiences have become sf experiences, or even cyberpunk experiences.

At this point, a more careful reading of the differences in the architectural layout of *Blade Runner* and Times Square in Hong Kong is called for. Unlike Scott's near-future Los Angeles, Hong Kong is not disintegrating or in ruins. Yes, there is a lot of garbage on the streets; but it is not technological waste or post-industrial decay, at least not the 'height of exhibition and recycling' (Bruno 64). In addition, whereas the postmodern, hybridised, mismatched architectural styles in *Blade Runner* convey banality by an uneasy combination of pastiche quotations (Chinese-dragon characters and Egyptian decor in a Mayan pyramid), in Hong Kong's Times Square, the extravaganza of hybridity only reflects a grotesque piecing together of disparate times and styles – the temporality of architectural efforts. Instead of Sebastian's and Deckard's nearly empty 97th-floor apartments overlooking the deserted city, what we can see, through the glass-encased escalator from the mall, are shattered flats occupied by poor people. Yet although these are run-down buildings, they are not deserted and soon they will be pulled down to make space for new ones.

Besides, *Blade Runner* emphasises the likely explosion of the Asian population of Los Angeles in the twenty-first century. Such domination by Asian elements contributes to the film's emphasis on an 'explosion of urbanisation,

melting the futuristic high-tech look into an intercultural scenario, recreat[ing] the third world inside the first' (Bruno 66). How can this Los Angeles-becoming-Chinatown be put alongside the transformation of Hong Kong's urban spaces? While these discrepancies may discourage our attempt to juxtapose *Blade Runner's* future Los Angeles and Hong Kong's evolving urban topography, I would still like to argue that the 'fragmented temporality' or the Jamesonian 'perpetual present' as seen in the mixing of the old and the new for an effect of future noir in *Blade Runner* can be used to interpret postmodern Hong Kong, especially at this historical moment. Although most recent changes in architectural layout are express-ions of the logic of commercialism, it is also true that major construction projects such as the new airport and the surge in real-estate values are tinged with political intentions and discourses. By inspiring us to think through the future of urban development in terms of social space, *Blade Runner* reminds us to turn our attention to the importance of both spatialising history and historicising geography, as suggested by Soja.

Perhaps Hong Kong's citizens are replicants in a sense, lacking a history of identity. Maybe through art, film and architecture, we can become more equipped to take a closer look at our environment and our relation to it. Is our historical space, our evolving hybridity and urbanism, just an index of our looking for a genuine history of our own? In my subsequent use of Soja's theory of the 'thirdspace', I will work towards defining the radical possibilities inherent in Hong Kong's evolving city-scape.

Edward Soja, who started out as a geo-grapher, has been an important advocate of critical studies of social space. He is an appropriate figure to be enlisted in our 'tale of two cities', for he has been writing about the postmodernisation of Los Angeles for fifteen years. After his *Postmodern Geographies* (1989), he continued his research on cities and power in a major work entitled *Thirdspace* (1996). Expanding on Henri Lefebvre's concept of the 'trialectics' of spatiality in *The Production of Space* (i.e., perceived, conceived and lived space), Soja works out a similar 'trialectics of Being, of spatiality, historicality and sociality' (71) to delineate a way of interpreting urban space and its social significance beyond the traditional dualism (the same and 'other') in spatial thinking. By focusing on an act of 'thirding-as-othering', Soja is able to introduce into analysis of urban studies an emphasis on 'radical openness' or a 'multiplicity of space that difference makes' that joins forces with 'a polyvocal postmodernism that maintains a political commitment to radical change' (93). As 'spaces in the margins of hegemonic discourses' (111), they can then be reconceptualized to embrace Foucault's ideas of 'heterotopias', feminist geography and such post-colonial critiques as Homi Bhabha's *Politics of Location*. Soja's theory of the spatiality of human life emphasises the creative and artistic side of spatial discourse, especially when he describes the kind of thirdspace that is linked to the 'underground side of social life'. He also draws our attention to what feminists have done to create artful space in the city:

[T]he alternative spaces of the visual, kinetic and aesthetic imagination – in films, photography, advertising, fashion, museum exhibitions, murals, poems, novels, but also in shopping malls and beaches, factories and streets, motels and theme parks – are being creatively evoked by other spatial feminists as ways of seeing, hearing, feeling, interpreting and changing the city. (115)

For Vivian Sobchack, however, who traces the historical development of urban sf films, in the 1980s 'the idealised and lofty city of SF is imagined as completely decentered and marginalised' (13). She thinks that, seen from this 'new urban exorcism, the Los Angeles of *Blade Runner* unifies its outmoded and vastly disparate material signifiers into new retrofitted and eroticised architectural forms' (16). But this is as far as this imaginary city can go, since for her the film 'is not really capable of envisioning its future'. By celebrating visual heterogeneity, these cities:

function as virtual ghettos – or wishing upon the same bourgeois star, effectively effac[ing] those differences that do make a difference ... that is, gender, race, class. Positing, on the one hand, a new and liberating model of the city and, on the other, buying back into its failed model by merely reversing (rather than altering) its terms and values, the imaginary and postmodernist city of the American SF film is truly a city on the edge of time. (17)

Sobchack seems to be arguing that in emphasising the pleasure of viewing through an 'erotics of commodification and consumerism', the merely scenic is emphasised at the expense of history, since 'the pastiche of new and old and recycled material objects, aesthetic styles and even the narrative itself in *Blade Runner* constituted Los Angeles's temporal mode as neither past nor future but as literal and increasingly *collective present*' (16). If we look hard for possible 'thirdspace' elements in the city design of *Blade Runner*, however, there are suggestions of historicity in the decaying cosmopolitan urban spaces, no matter how gloomily the picture is painted on screen. If nothing else, *Blade Runner* at least 'posits questions of identity, identification and history in post-modernism' (Bruno 73).

To be sure, historical allusions in *Blade Runner* are eclectic, but 'pastiche is ultimately a redemption of history, which implies the transformation and reinterpretation in tension between loss and desire' (Bruno 74). This tension is expressed through the positing of so-called 'prosthetic memory', which seeks 'to rewrite history by means of architectural pastiched recycling' (Bruno 74). In the artistic rendering of a dystopic future in *Blade Runner*, a point is made about the thirdspace of 'the ramble city' (Bruno, Doel). We can also say that all the architectural motifs of hybridity and geographical displacement have been designed to provide an existential context for the plight of the replicants in the film. The cinematography, with its celebrated dominance of visual representations, functions to bring out 'fragmentary temporality' and 'schizophrenic vertigo' – the setting in which the replicants are destined to seek in vain for the meaning of their lives. Even Deckard is seen running for his life on the rooftop of a hundred-storey building, a place where one's being is lifted up from the firm ground and exposed to the destructive power of the machine. As a blade runner,[2] Deckard is supposed to be someone who 'runs on the knife's edge between humanity and inhumanity ... someone who scampers along the thin edge of life' (Sammon 379). *Blade Runner*, especially in the 1992 director's cut, ambiguously suggests that Deckard himself is a replicant who has dreams of the unicorn as symbol of purity. Through such 'knife's edge' images and hints, a radical space is opened up for the sort of counter-site Soja speaks of, a space created for 'oppositional practices', for 'critical exchange', and for 'new and radical happenings' (Soja 129).

Dreaming/constructing an identity while perched on a rooftop establishes one's past through memory, even if that memory be prosthetic. Refuting both Jameson's and Baudrillard's positing the existence of the 'real' as a result of 'a nostalgia for a prelapsarian moment', Alison Landsberg goes straight to the ability of cinema (mass media and photography included) to 'provide individuals with the collective opportunity of having an experiential relationship to a collective cultural past they either did or did not experience' (Landsberg 178). True, implanted memories could be used as a means of surveillance and control, as is demonstrated in *Blade Runner* by Tyrell, who explains to Deckard that 'If we give them a past we create a cushion for their emotions and consequently we can control them better.' But in Deckard's incredulous response – 'memories, you're talking about memories' – we glimpse the kind of significance the film attaches to this memory motif and its power to produce identity.

To support her argument for the 'porta-bility of cinematic images', Landsberg draws our attention to the scene in *Blade Runner* in which Rachael, after playing a few notes on the piano, says 'I don't know if it's me or Tyrell's niece, but I remember lessons.' When Deckard responds by saying 'you play beautifully', Landsberg notes that at this point Deckard, in effect, rejects the distinction between 'real' and prosthetic memories. 'Her *memory* of lessons allows her to play beautifully, so it means little whether she lived through the lessons or not' (185). With all this, and especially with Batty's 'tears in the rain' dying moment, viewers of the film are asked to identify themselves with the 'primary object of our spectatorial investment and engagement' (183) – in a word, with the replicants, Rachael and Deckard and all, who are, like Donna Haraway's cyborgs, subjects living at the edge of time.

The rooftop chase, the Bradbury ledge where the showdown between Batty and Deckard takes place, and the jump between the edges of buildings, all are examples in the film of what Lefebvre calls spaces of represent-ation or lived space. They are, as Soja explains, 'linked to the 'clandestine or underground' [high, high up above the ground in *Blade Run-*

ner] side of social life' (Soja 67). In this light, one might argue that the city dwellers of Hong Kong are all blade runners (notwithstanding that this is not a perfect analogy, since they're not required to retire any replicants), living not only on the edge of time but also on the edge of empires. Moreover, one might see, in the architectural pastiche in *Blade Runner*, that the Hong Kong Times Square demonstrates the very postmodern condition that denotes both a crisis of identity and, at the same time, an attempt to accommodate alterity.

Regarding the sort of future Hong Kong's people are facing, Abbas writes that 'The 'end of Hong Kong' is therefore in another sense its beginning, the beginning of an intense interest in its historical and cultural specificity, a change from the hitherto almost exclusive fascination with its economic success' ('Building' 444). But this mixing of the old and the new within the shocking rate of changes, this putting aside the sense of historical and cultural sequentiality, may well give Hong Kong's people the potential to develop a new sense of identity. For Abbas, Hong Kong's space is 'both autonomous and dependent at the same time, both separate from and connected to other space' ('Hyphenation' 215). Maybe, just maybe, this particular urban site, so unique in its social and economic hybridity and accessibility, could function as a global symbol (or model) for diaspora in post-colonial narratives. As with all big cities, 'ordinary shopping districts frequented by ordinary people,' Sharon Zukin believes, 'are important sites for negotiating the street-level practice of urban public culture' (191). In the midst of settlements and political flux, such complex issues as the 'brain drain' of the 1980s, the 'right of abode' in the early 1990s, and the present problem of displaced and repatriated families, Hong Kong's citizens may be able to transform themselves to become 'world-travelers' par excellence, positioning themselves flexibly 'on the edge of empires.'[3]

The big screen at Hong Kong's Times Square suggests the close relation between social space and identity; it illustrates how the place (as a postmodern city of information and hence with the profusion and confusion of images and icons that we mentioned earlier) also provides a public space for the construction of identity. As mentioned before, the most unique characteristic of this square is that, unlike anywhere else in Hong Kong, it is accessible to all. It is a work place, a festive space, a real location and a hyperreal site for information exchange – all at once. We can of course look at the place as part of Paul Virillo's 'overexposed city [where] the city has become a space of simultaneous dispersion, as public space loses it relevance' (quoted in Bukatman 132); and we can consider the screen as similar to those in *Blade Runner*, which become 'the proliferation of walls' or sites of projection and terminal inscription (Bukatman 132). On the other hand, the screen on the wall of Hong Kong's Times Square can also be made to realise its potential as a possible 'countersite' of a radical city-scape. In fact, the live TV talk-show can be viewed as a social forum where all political and cultural issues are brought up for open argument.[4] In a commercial depicting a gathering of 40,000 people on screen with lit candles in hand, a voice-over announces: 'On June 4 tens of thousands of people will gather at Victoria Park. They are students, businessmen, workers, housewives. They will come to remember the victims of the Tienanmen massacre as they have done for the past eight years, and cable TV will be there.'[5] A more radical side of the public sphere may possibly be opened up by an alternative practice of spatiality in Hong Kong.

I now turn to *Ghost in the Shell* to expand on my discussion of the relation between urban space, high-tech information and cyberpunk films. Mamoru Oshii's full-length animated feature is based on Masamune Shirow's popular *manga* series; it employed artists and designers who had great success in *Akira* (1987). The year is 2029 and the world is a vast net of electronic information data in which computer wars are fought. During the hot pursuit of a phantom criminal nicknamed the Puppet Master, our hero Major Kusanagi, a female cybernetic organism, discovers that she has been targeted by the Puppet Master, who wishes to merge with her as a unified life form 'on a higher consciousness'. Released in theatres worldwide late in 1995 and 1996, *Ghost in the Shell* soon became the topic of critical controversy. Some criticised the plot as too complicated and murky, or for its tendency to over-philosophise; others saw it as borrowing too much from *Blade Runner* and William Gibson. But in general, *Ghost in the Shell* has been welcomed by most fans as the most 'soulful' *anime* to date, with great visuals and a

central moral that asks what it is for a female cyborg to be human in the age of machines. As for myself, I am impressed with the seriousness of production, the hyperrealistic rendering, the soulful mood, and above all the uniquely dreamlike quality. But what actually riveted my eyes to the screen during my first viewing of the film was the Hong Kong cityscape featured as the setting.

So we are back to our initial question: what is so unique about Hong Kong's urban landscape that it has aroused the interest of cyberpunk filmmakers? In *The Analysis of Ghost in the Shell*, a beautiful Japanese picture book covering the film, the director, Mamoru Oshii, and his art designer, Takeuchi Atsushi, explain why the Hong Kong cityscape is significant in the film.[6] Note what the director has to say:

> As a model for the setting of *Ghost*, it is because Hong Kong, just like Singapore, is a unique city. It will, as it moves towards the twenty-first century, become a centre of world development and the model for cities in Asia. My prediction is that all the energies possessed by Asia will continue in the next century. When I was in search of an image of the future, the first thing that came to my mind was an Asian city. At first I did not think it was possible to create a perfect cityscape for the future; and what was done in the past seems unconvincing to me now … The only way, if one is to be true to the methodology of animation, is to use real streets as models, so I thought of Hong Kong. It is like the Los Angeles of *Blade Runner*; what has been achieved in that city set will be of use to later films. (Nozaki n.p.)

The designer Atsushi adds:

> *Ghost in the Shell* does not have a definite chosen set, but in terms of street scenes and general atmosphere, it is obvious that Hong Kong is the model. Such a choice has, of course, something to do with the theme: on the streets there flows an excess or a flood of information, along with everything this excess brings out. The modern city is swamped with billboards, neon lights and symbols … As people live [unaware?] in this information deluge, the streets will have to be depicted accordingly as being flooded … There is a sharp contrast between old streets

and new ones on which skyscrapers are built. My feeling is that these two, originally very different, are now in a situation where one is invading the other. Maybe it is the tension or pressure that is brought about by so-called modernisation! It's a situation in which two entities are kept in a strange neighboring relationship. Perhaps it is what the future is. (Nozaki n.p.)

Water imagery is used in *Ghost in the Shell* as a symbol for the flood or sea of data, its massive communication system in a new urban topography, with its complex electronically-controlled switchboard and fluorescent 3-D scanner images of road maps or grids. This, of course, seems to be an accurate projection of the political uniqueness of Hong Kong's mediascape, 'complicated in particular by the growing diaspora (both voluntary and involuntary) of Hong Kong intellectuals who continuously inject new meaning-streams into the discourse of democracy in different parts of the world' (Appadurai 11). This figuration of the city reminds us of Bukatman's 'fractal geography' interpretation of *Blade Runner*: a sense of aesthetic order can be drawn out from the de-centred and dispersed space that is seemingly confusing and even chaotic at first glance. Noting the play with scale and density by designers Syd Mead and Lawrence Paull, Bukatman adds together such elements as wall-like screens, 'multiple layers of traveling matter' (132), and 'a chaos of intersecting lines' from a high-angle view, concluding that fractal geometry may have been at the core of the visual aesthetics of *Blade Runner*.

The *Analysis* emphasises that *Ghost in the Shell*'s artists made meticulous sketches on location before actual shooting, sketches that emphasised chaotic crowdedness and a mad profusion of signs and icons. Hong Kong seems to be the only city in the world with such a degree of confusion – with gigantic signs and neon lights protruding into the space on and above the street and fighting for limited and precious visual space. The artist remarks on this phenomenon:

In the midst of the profusion of signs and the heat of the messy urban space, the streets are remarkably chaotic. Passers-by, shouts, cars, all kinds of mechanical noises and human 'sound pollution', all merging into one, forcing itself into humans' central nervous systems through their ears. But why do people succumb to this 'destructive' environment? Now that the artificial has replaced the natural, humans are like animals in the past, deprived of the characteristics of being human as a whole. Pulled directly into the whirlpool of information through the stimulation of visual and auditory senses, their feelings are henceforth numbed. On the other hand, countless mutually interfering and uncertain data pass through cables at light speed. This is the way informatics continues to expand its domain. Are people then like tiny insects caught in an enormous spider web? No, it cannot be. Humans are not tiny insects trying to escape from the web. It's not like that. In fact humans have willy-nilly become part and parcel of the spider web. Humans now have no idea of what their destination might be; they are like one of the silky-threads of the spider web. (Nozaki n.p.)

An imploded iconography as an aesthetics of scale can also be detected in the architectural design both within the Hong Kong Times Square and the surrounding streets outside. The traumas of de-territorialisation that Hong Kong's people are facing, as presented through their lived experience of the 'other spaces', will have to be dealt with by a general theory of global cultural processes. For Arjun Appadurai, chaos theory is the answer, since he considers 'the configuration of cultural forms in today's world as fundamentally fractal'. In order to 'compare fractally shaped cultural forms which are also polythetically overlapping in their coverage of terrestrial space ... we will need to ask how these complex, overlapping, fractal shapes constitute not a simple, stable (even if large-scale) system, but to ask what its dynamics are.' In other words, Appadurai proposes that 'in a world of disjunctive global flows, it is perhaps important to start asking ... [questions] in a way that relies on images of flow and uncertainty ... 'chaos,' rather than an older images of order, stability and systemacity' (Appadurai 20).

But it is not just on this large scale of global cultural flows (particularly of technoscape, mediascape and ideoscape) that fractal aesthetics are relevant to *Ghost in the Shell*. On a smaller level – namely, that of the body – the idea of the fractured body of the humanoid

liquid metal

hybrid has been popular in cyborg films; and it receives rather interesting if not controversial treatment in this Japanese *anime*. Corporeality, as we remember, is one of the four Cs listed by Frances Bonner to delineate a general pattern of plotting in cyberpunk films, which emphasise the *wetware* of mutable bodies. For Baudrillard, the body is now an infinite set of surfaces – *a fractal subject* – an object among objects (Baudrillard 40). In cyberpunk's hyper-techno culture, 'the centrality of body' is paradoxically represented by 'the fragmentation of the body into organs, fluids and 'bodily state' ... fractured body parts are taken up as elements in the constitution of cultural identities' (Balsamo 216). The cyborg woman warrior in *Ghost in the Shell*, following in this tradition, speaks also to the 'emergence of cyborg identities' that is predicated on 'the fractured, plural, decentered condition of contemporary subjectivity' (Robins 8). Yet because Major Kusanagi is presented in a 'perfect' female body (often sans clothes), she can be criticised, especially by feminist critics who interpret her as a commerical object for the male gaze. Indeed, if one looks through the original comic strip by Masamune Shirow, one will find more occasions for such an objection. Moreover, by simply nothing the bifurcation of the title, we may assume that the so-called 'theme' of the film remains confined to a Cartesian duality-of-body-and-mind paradigm, and by extension, the binarisms surrounding gender issues. As one of the reviewers notes, corporate work in Japan nowadays is 'so exhausting and dehumanising that many men (who form the largest part of the animation audience) project both freedom and power onto women, and identify with them as fictional characters' (Ebert). Whereas I have no quarrel with such an argument, the fact remains that a tough woman protagonist in sf action movies, especially in the Hollywood tradition, will stir up some kind of emotion marking masculine anxieties:

> Cinematic images of women who wield guns, and who take control of cars, computers and the other technologies that have symbolised both power and freedom within Hollywood's world, mobilise a symbolically transgressive iconography (Tasker 132).

The problem here is that despite its mode of presenting a perfect female body in the nude,

the film as a whole is strangely de-gendered in the sense that sexuality is minimised. Through images that 'speak of both bodily invincibility and vulnerability', the so-called *Angst* of the protagonist revolves around what it means to her, as a 90 percent cybernetic organism, to be a free human consciousness. One can of course complain in the vein of cyberfeminism, as Nicola Nixon has done, that we are here faced with a strong cyborg who is 'effectively depoliticised and sapped of any revolutionary energy' (Nixon 222, see also Silvio). But Major Kusanagi, for all her bravado, is not an avenger in the style of Gibson's Molly Millions in 'Johnny Mnemonic' (1981) and Sarah in Walter Jon William's *Hardwired* (1981). By representing her as a perfect female body, the film, in a peculiar way, avoids the complex problem of the 'masculinisation of the female body', (139) as Yvonne Tasker observes of Hollywood films.

The only scene in *Ghost* that dramatises the Major's bodily transformation into a muscular hulk soon exposes her mechanical interior with wires and steel, so that the issue of gender is pushed aside in favor of a militaristic/cyborg iconography. And throughout the film, from the opening ritual of birth (or manufacture) in a feast of visuals dominated by images of numerals and water or fluid, to the later horror of the mutilated torso and limbs registering the monstrosity of cybernetic organisms, corporeality is closely linked first to the sea of information and then to the human-machine interface, both of which are firmly grounded in and contrasted with the background of a future Hong Kong city-scape. Instead of dwelling on the gender politics of the body, the poetic rendering of the birth scene, which highlights both the hardness of the mechanical and the softness of cybernetics, gears itself towards a process of merging the born and the made in becoming one soft machine, as Kevin Kelly predicts (qtd. in Dry 20).

The monstrous, mutilated and deviant body, shattered by violence, comes close to Donna Haraway's notion of 'regeneration after injury' for salamanders, though the 'regrown limb can be monstrous, duplicated, potent' (Haraway 100). This production of horror, according to Judith Halberstam in her study of the gothic and the technology of monsters, makes strange 'the categories of beauty, humanity, and identity that we still cling to' (Halberstam 6). In a sense, the final scene of horror of mutation and the attempt by the 'Ghost' of Puppet Master to merge with the 'Shell' of our heroine is symbolic of the entanglement of 'self and other within monstrosity and the parasitical relationship between the two' (Halberstam 20).

As for the image of the shell, the great phenomenologist of space, Gaston Bachelard, meditated about the dream-like effect produced by its infinite spiral surfaces that form both house and body:

A creature that comes out of its shell suggests day dreams of a mixed creature that is not only 'half fish, half flesh', but also half dead, half alive, and in extreme cases, half stone, half man. (109)

Moreover, a 'creature that hides and 'withdraws into its shell', is preparing a 'way out' … by staying in the motionlessness of its shell, the creature is preparing temporal explosion, not to say whirlwinds of being' (Bachelard 111). Bachelard's poetics of this particular space of the shell suggests another interpretation of *Ghost in the Shell*: when the heroine spends her spare time diving into the 'ocean' (the ocean of information which Hong Kong urban space comes to symbolise), she tells us that 'I feel fear, cold, alone, sometimes down there I even feel hope.' Her philosophic probing into her very being as an individual seems congruent with Bachelard's ruminations on the poetics of the house:

And I feel sorry for myself. So there you are, unhappy philosopher, caught up again by the storm, by the storms of life! I dream an abstract-concrete daydream. My bed is a small boat lost at sea; that sudden whistling is the wind in the sails. (28)

For Mazzoleni, the body is a basic cultural imaginary beyond language, and the city is its shell-like extension outside itself. For her, the postmodern cosmopolis is a 'grotesque body':

In the metropolis there is something rather more similar to a shell: the spiral pattern. Absence of symmetries and segmentations, because there are no (for the moment, or forever?) *results, conclusions* of the growth processes. The metropolis reactivates modalities of organisation vital at a level deeper than what we call 'life': it is a struc-

ture of structures – but this even at the limits between organic and inorganic: it resembles, in its spiral nature, features such as gorges, galaxies and whirlwinds. (297)

Such a spiral pattern of the shell can well be placed alongside the idea of fractal geometry used earlier to describe the sense of order in the disorder of urban space as well as the hybrid form of the cyborg body. One artistic achievement of *Ghost in the Shell* is a deliberate juxtaposition of shots of electronic road maps on the computer and idle people wandering as we see these actual 'walkers' (in the sense de Certeau presents them): these *Wandersmänner* roam the city in 'the chorus of idle footsteps' (153, 157).

The spiral of Ridleyville in *Blade Runner* may be decaying, but the poetic negotiation of such a space belongs to the 'social practice' that exposes the fact that it is rather 'the concept-city' which 'is decaying' (de Certeau 156). By concept-city, de Certeau refers to the collective administrative side of city planning, as opposed to the lived space, the everyday practice of 'the disquieting familiarity of the city' (157). This dialectics of transparency and opacity can also be seen as parallel to the Enlightenment in its rational mapping of cities on the one side, and the Baudelairean *flâneur* wandering in labyrinthine urbanity on the other. For Walter Benjamin, especially in his *Passagen-Werk*, the 'new urban phantasmagoria' is a dream world of dazzling, crowd-pleasing total environments (Buck-Morss 6):[7] these oneiric figurations are best represented by the cinema with its ingenious special effects. These urban dream images in the 'irredeemable opacity of the social' become, according to James Donald, 'particularly evident in the anti-documentary representation of urban space that runs from *Metropolis* (1927) and *King Kong* (1933) to *Blade Runner, Brazil* (1985), *Batman Returns* (1992) and the *manga* animation to *Akira* (1988)' (Donald 90). Had Donald seen *Ghost in the Shell* before writing his article, no doubt he would have included it.

The voluptuous pleasure afforded by both city walking and cinema can finally be bought to bear on our discussion of both *Blade Runner* and the Hong Kong city-scape. For in the dream of Deckard, the ultimate replicant in *Blade Runner*, and the walkers who find Hong Kong a habitable space, a thirdspace of unassimilated otherness is created. Governed by 'another spatiality', Hong Kong citizens follow what de Certeau calls 'ways of going out and coming back in' on the edge of empires. In their 'travelings', which again in de Certeau's perambulatory rhetorics represent 'a substitute for the legends that used to open up space to something different' (de Certeau, 160), Hong Kong's city dwellers are crossing between worlds as they traverse their city-scape. As a postmodern city par excellence, a mega-pastiche, Hong Kong has the potential to transform itself into an *inter*national culture based not on the exoticism of multiculturalism or the *diversity* of cultures, but on 'the inscription and articulation of culture's *hybridity*'. Instead of being dissolved 'in a universal melting pot or a pluralist jumble of equals' (Soja 141) in the name of the international city, Homi Bhabha teaches that we should take it upon ourselves to choose 'the 'inter' – the cutting edge of translation and negotiation, the in-between space' (Bhabha 39).

Hong Kong's citizens might create narratives that reflect their 'subject's self-positioning and social agency in a cosmopolitan context' (Ong 755); they might make Hong Kong a model for the global megalopolis of the future. I think that it is Hong Kong's urbanity in embracing racial and cultural differences on the edge of empire that has caught the eye of cyberpunk writers and filmmakers. It may be true that everyone in Hong Kong lives, as it were, on a boat: they have been repeatedly warned against rocking it. But for Foucault a boat is the 'heterotopia *par excellence*, given over to the infinity of the sea'. It will float 'as far as the colonies in search of the most precious treasure they conceal in their gardens'. 'In civilizations without boats,' Foucault concludes in his 'Of Other Spaces', 'dreams dry up, espionage takes the place of adventure, and police take the place of pirates' (Foucault 27).

Notes

1 In Hong Kong the 'rickshaw' phenomenon has been vigorously preserved until very recently, perhaps for the sake of tourism. In delineating a theory that Hong Kong is a 'space of disappearance', Ackbar Abbas points to another long-enduring representation, 'a Chinese junk in Victoria Harbour against a backdrop of tall modernistic buildings', and notes that 'a stylised red junk is also the

logo of the Hong Kong Tourist Association'. According to him, the issue at stake is 'how an image of Hong Kong's architecture and urban space supports a narrative that implicitly attributes the colony's success to the smooth combination of British administration and Chinese entrepreneurship'. He calls this discourse 'decadent', since 'it manages to make complex space disappear into a one-dimensional image, structured on a facile binarism' ('Building', 445).

2 In an interview with Paul Sammon in 1995, Ridley Scott said that when he and his designers 'began to create the architecture of the film' he thought it was not futuristic enough to call Deckard a 'detective'; the term 'blade runner' was taken from William Burroughs' short novel (Sammon 379).

3 In 'On the Edge of Empires: Flexible Citizenship among Chinese in Diaspora', Aihwa Ong argues that, 'as postcolonial transnational subjects', Hong Kong's Chinese can turn their experience of having been 'caught between British disciplinary racism and Chinese opportunistic filial claims, between declining capitalism in Britain and surging capitalism in Asia' into an advantageously 'flexible position among the myriad possibilities (and problems) found in the global sphere' (752). Ong cites Los Angeles as a case in point, arguing for the existence of 'self-orientalising discourses' by Asian-Americans who have 'created an explosion of cultural codes' or a 'new hybrid role for Asian Americans'. Ong then uses Michael Woo, the first Asian mayor of Los Angeles, to illustrate the self-narratives of what Woo calls 'bridge-builders', a metaphor of 'corporate Chinese as they shift through multinational sites of operations'.

4 This hyperrealistic blending of screens and social space can be considered as an everyday practice of what Mark Poster calls the second media age. In his book of this title, Poster arrives at the conclusion that: 'as the second media age unfolds and permeates everyday practice, one political issue will be the construction of new combinations of technology with multiple genders and ethnicities. These technocultures will hopefully be no return to an origin, no new foundationalism or essentialism, but coming to terms with the process of identity constitution and doing so in ways that struggle against restrictions of systematic inequalities, hierarchies and asymmetries' (42).

5 This is impressive since other TV channels seem to have started a self-censorship process by toning down the incident. It should be mentioned here that despite the plea made by Tung Chee-hwa, the Chief Executive-designate, that Hong Kong people should put the 'baggage' of June 4 behind them, and in the midst of fears that this might be the last candlelight vigil allowed in the territory, over 70,000 (compared to the 50,000 last year) came to mark the tenth anniversary of China's pro-democracy movement. Yet it remains to be seen whether

the 'Pillar of Shame' sculpture by Dane Jans Gakchiot, which symbolises suffering from oppression (already refused by the municipal councils of some urban parks), will itself find a 'place' in Hong Kong.

6 Since I don't read Japanese, I would like to thank Ms. Doo Suen for her translation of the relevant parts of the commentaries. Please also note that my quotations from this book are general and rough and should not be considered as the official translation of the original.

7 This aspect of Benjamin's thought is summarised by Mike Savage. According to Savage, Benjamin's interest in the city was linked to its role as a labyrinth where dreams, hopes, artifacts, past, and present mingle together for the urban wanderer to explore.

Bibliography

Abbas, Ackbar 'Building on Disappearance: Hong Kong Architecture and the City', *Public Culture* 6.3 (1994), pp. 441–59.

_____ *Hong Kong: Culture and the Politics of Disappearance* (Hong Kong: Hong Kong University Press, 1997).

_____ 'Hyphenation: The Spatial Dimensions of Hong Kong Culture', in *Walter Benjamin and the Demands of History*, ed. Michael P. Steinberg (Ithaca: Cornell University Press, 1996), pp. 214–31.

Appadurai, Arjun 'Disjuncture and Difference in the Global Cultural Economy', *Public Culture* 2.2 (1990), pp. 1–24.

Bachelard, Gaston *The Poetics of Space*, trans. Maria Jolas. Boston: Beacon, 1958.

Balsamo, Anne 'Forms of Technological Embodiment: Reading the Body in Contemporary Culture', in *Cyberspace, Cyberbodies, Cyberpunk: Cultures of Technological Embodiment*, eds Mike Featherstone and Roger Burrows (London: Sage, 1995), pp. 215–37.

Baudrillard, Jean *The Ecstasy of Communication*, trans. Bernard Schutze and Caroline Schutze (New York: Semiotext(e), 1988).

Bhabha, Homi K. *The Location of Culture* (London: Routledge, 1994).

Bonner, Francis 'Separate Development: Cyberpunk in Film and TV', in *Fiction 2000: Cyberpunk and the Future of Narrative*, eds George Slusser and Tom Shippey. (Athens: University of Georgia Press, 1992), pp. 171–82.

Bruno, Giuliana 'Ramble City: Postmodernism and *Blade Runner*', *October* 41 (1987), pp. 61–74. Reprinted in *Alien Zone: Cultural Theory and Contemporary Science Fiction Cinema*, ed. Annette Kuhn (London: Verso, 1990).

Buck-Morss, Susan 'The City as Dreamworld and Catastrophe', *October* 73 (1995), pp. 3–26.

Bukatman, Scott. *Terminal Identity* (Durham: Duke University Press, 1993).

Christie, John 'Of AIs and Others: William Gibson's Transit', in *Fiction 2000. Cyberpunk and the Future of Narrative*, eds George Slusser and Tom Shippey (Athens: University of

Georgia Press, 1992), pp. 191–207.

Clark, Nigel 'Rear-View Mirrorshades: The Recursive Generation of the Cyberbody', in *Cyberspace, Cyberbodies, Cyberpunk: Cultures of Technological Embodiment*, eds Mike Featherstone and Roger Burrows (London: Sage, 1995), pp. 113–33.

Cuthbert, Alexander 'Under the Volcano: Postmodern Space in Hong Kong', in *Postmodern Cities and Spaces*, eds. Sophie Watson and Katherine Gibson (Cambridge: Blackwell, 1995), pp. 138–48.

de Certeau, Michel 'Walking in the City', in *The Cultural Studies Reader*, ed. Simon During (London: Routledge, 1993), pp. 151–60.

Doel, Marcus A. and Clarke, David B. From Ramble City to the Screening of the Eye: *Blade Runner*, Death and Symbolic Exchange', in *The Cinematic City*, ed. David B. Clarke (London: Routledge, 1997), pp. 140–67.

Donald, James 'The City, the Cinema: Modern Spaces', in *Visual Culture*, ed. Chris Jenks. London: Routledge, 1995, pp. 77–95.

Dry, Mark 'Soft Machines', *Magazine 21 C* 23 (1997), pp. 18–23.

Ebert, Roger Review of *Ghost in the Shell* in Chicago Sun-Times, April 30, 1997.

Foucault, Michel 'Of Other Spaces'. *Diacritics* 16.1 (1986), pp. 22–7.

Friedberg, Anne *Window Shopping: Cinema and the Postmodern* (Berkeley: University of California Press, 1993).

Gibson, William *Neuromancer*. New York: Ace, 1984.

_____ *Idoru*. London: Viking, 1996.

Halberstam, Judith *Skin Shows: Gothic Horror and the Technology of Monsters*. Durham: Duke University Press, 1995.

Haraway, Donna 'A Manifesto for Cyborgs: Science, Technology, and Socialist Feminism in the 1980s', *Socialist Review* 15 (1985), pp. 65–107.

Hunter, Stephen. *Violent Screen*. New York: Delta, 1995.

Jameson, Fredric 'Postmodernism, or The Cultural Logic of Late Capitalism', *New Left Review* 146 (July–August 1984), pp. 53–94.

Jencks, Charles *Heteropoli: Los Angeles: The Riots and the Strange Beauty of Hetero-Architecture* (London: Academy, 1993).

Kelly, Kevin *Out of Control: The New Biology of Machines, Social Systems, and the Economic World* (Reading, MA: Perseus, 1994).

King, Anthony *Global Cities* (London: Routledge, 1990).

Landsberg, Alison 'Prosthetic Memory: *Total Recall* and *Blade Runner*', in *Cyberspace, Cyberbodies, Cyberpunk*, eds Mike Featherstone and Roger Burrows (London: Sage, 1995), pp. 175–89.

Mazzoleni, Donatella 'The City and the Imaginary', In *Space and Place: Theories of Identity and Location*, ed. Erica Carter et al. (London: Lawrence, 1993), pp. 285–301.

Nixon, Nicola 'Cyberpunk: Preparing the Ground for Revolution or Keeping the Boys Satisfied?', *SFS* 19.2 (July

1992), pp. 219–35.

Nozaki, Tohru et al. The Analysis of GHOST IN THE SHELL, Tokyo: Kodansha Young Magazine, 1995.

Ong, Aihwa 'On the Edge of Empires: Flexible Citizenship among Chinese in Diaspora', Positions 1.3 (1993): pp. 745–78.

Poster, Mark The Second Media Age (Cambridge: Polity, 1995).

Robins, Kevin 'Cyberspace and the World We Live In', in Fractal Dreams: New Media in Social Context, ed. Jon Dovey (London: Lawrence, 1996), pp. 1–30.

Salisbury, M. 'Back to the Future', Empire 42 (1992), pp. 90–6.

Sammon, Paul M. Future Noir: The Making of Blade Runner. (New York: Harper, 1996).

Savage, Mike 'Walter Benjamin's Urban Thought: A Critical Analysis', Society and Space 13.2 (1995), pp. 201–16.

Sennett, Richard. The Uses of Disorder: Personal Identity and City Life (Harmondsworth: Penguin, 1973).

Silvio, Carl 'Refiguring the Radical Cyborg in Mamoru Oshii's Ghost in the Shell', SFS 26.1 (March 1999), pp. 54–72.

Sobchack, Vivian 'Cities on the Edge of Time: The Urban Science Fiction Film', East–West Film Journal 3.1 (1988), pp. 4–19, re-printed in this volume.

Soja, Edward. Thirdspace. Cambridge: Blackwell, 1996.

Tasker, Yvonne Spectacular Bodies: Gender, Genre and the Action Cinema. London: Routledge, 1993.

Webster, Frank Theories of the Information Society. London: Routledge, 1995.

Zukin, Sharon The Cultures of Cities. Cambridge: Blackwell, 1995.

THE ORIGIN OF SPECIES:
TIME TRAVEL AND THE PRIMAL SCENE

THE ORIGIN OF THE SPECIES: TIME TRAVEL AND THE PRIMAL SCENE

FOUR

Science fiction is in essence a time travel genre. Events either open in the altered past, the transformed present or the possible future, transporting the reader or viewer to another age, place, dimension or world. Or: events involve time travel devices and technologies that take people backwards and forwards across time, and through time and space, often at near unimaginable speeds, as the narrative progresses. When science fiction film time travels one truly knows that one is in a science fiction movie because time travel provides not only the futuristic narrative dynamic needed for the genre but the diegetic space for the use of astonishing special effects. In time travel scenarios, the sky splits open, clouds dissolve, and precision-engineered shimmering spacecrafts emerge, smothered in pyrotechnics and lights, from infinite space to engulf the screen, and the audience in turn.

But the time travel motif also has an ideological function because it literally provides the necessary distancing effect that science fiction needs to be able to metaphorically address the most pressing issues and themes that concern people in the present. If the modern world is one where the individual feels alienated and powerless in the face of bureaucratic structures and corporate monopolies, then time travel suggests that Everyman and Everybody is important to shaping history, to making a real and quantifiable difference to the way the world turns out. If the modern world is dislocated, chaotic and disenfranchises a large number of people then time travel allows the individual to (finally) bring order to the chaos of the cosmos. Time travel, then, becomes both a civilising process and one that is also built on the hero myth, because when one time travels one finds that history is made in one's own image. If the modern world produces a particularly acute identity crisis and existential schizophrenia, then time travel allows one to come face to face with one's own doppelgänger, alter ego, or mirror reflection.

When one time travels one is searching for wholeness, for metaphysical answers to the confusion at the core of the self and to the terrifying plight of the human condition. When one time travels one returns to the primal scene or to the origins of one's own conception in the vain hope that one can be whole again.

Andrew Gordon notes that since 1979 a greater number of time travel-based science fiction films have been made because there is 'a pervasive uneasiness about our present and uncertainty about our future, along with a concurrent nostalgia about our past'. What Gordon is suggesting here is that there is a close correspondence between the political and economic crises that shaped this decade and the flight or evacuation mentality that characterised a range of science fiction films of the time. However, Gordon also argues, focusing on *Back to the Future*, that the time travel film resonates in terms of the Oedipal scenario. *Back to the Future* is 'the first science fiction film to make explicit the incestuous possibilities that have always been at the heart of our fascination with time travel. Time travel is an unnatural act which is frequently used to allow the fulfilment of Oedipal fantasies or family romance.' In this scenario, the character Marty thus becomes a 'teenage Oedipus' and the DeLorean time machine the 'primary symbol of 'phallic' power'.

Constance Penley examines the time travel and time-loop paradox of *The Terminator* both in terms of its critical dystopia and its Oedipal trajectory. According to Penley, the film interrogates the ideological implications of the machine aesthetic in the contemporary age, suggesting that in terms of *The Terminator*'s diegesis 'if technology can

go wrong or be abused, it will'. In terms of the film's primal scene, Penley examines the way psychosexual crises produces a desire or yearning to return 'home'. In this context, *The Terminator*'s displaced John Connor 'is the child who orchestrates his own primal scene, one inflected by a family romance, because he is able to choose his own Father, singling out Kyle from the other soldiers. That such a fantasy is an end-run around Oedipus is also obvious: John Connor can identify with his Father, can even be his Father in the scene of parental intercourse, and also conveintly dispose of him in order to go off with (in) his Mother'.

Jonathan Bignell examines the 1960 film version of *The Time Machine* in terms of its relationship to modernity, subjectivity and the difference 'between the virtual and the real', a difference that he argues mirrors the machinery of cinema and the spatial transformations that occurred with industrialisation. Bignell argues that 'time travellers and cinema spectators are displaced from the reality of their own present and their own real location in order to be transported to an imaginary elsewhere and an imaginary elsewhen'.

Caron Schwartz Ellis looks at time travel in terms of the figure of the benevolent visiting alien who 'originate(s) in the sky, evoking the archetypal symbolism of the sky and the figure of the sky God'. Ellis argues that the Sky God is often humanoid in form and personifies 'our deepest fears about technology and answers spiritual questions about our destiny'. The Sky God film provides the audience with 'a mythic experience; through watching space alien films we are getting in touch with our roots, exploring the secret, sacred dimension of our scientific worldview'.

Back to the Future:
Oedipus as Time Traveller
Andrew Gordon

Back to the Future is a significant phenomenon of recent American popular culture. The movie, written by Robert Zemeckis and Bob Gale, directed by Zemeckis, and produced by Steven Spielberg, Frank Marshall and Kathleen Kennedy, was the biggest Hollywood moneymaker of 1985, surpassing even *Rambo*. Its first run at many theatres was an unprecedented six or seven months straight.

What is the secret of its appeal? On the surface it has all the necessary ingredients – comedy, action, suspense, romance, sentiment, fantasy, special effects and catchy music – integral to other recent blockbuster SF films such as *Star Wars* and *E.T.* But these elements alone, or in the wrong mixture, are not enough to guarantee success with a large audience. In addition, *Back to the Future* has a clever plot and the appeal of 1950s nostalgia. The teen hero attracts the young, and the theme of reconciliation between past and present, child and adults, attracts their parents as well. Even the critics loved it, taken in by its charm, sentiment, and an ingenious script which was nominated for an Academy Award – another unprecedented achievement for an SF film.[1]

Like *Star Wars*, *Back to the Future*'s success depends to a great degree upon its ritualistic, celebratory, therapeutic aspects: it is a 'clean' family film which attracts all ages, and encourages audience participation (spontaneous clapping and cheering) and repeat viewing (many fans return, bringing friends or family).[2]

It is this level of the film that most interests me: the paradox of a family comedy which flirts with incest. I would argue that the film succeeds because it deftly combines two current and oddly connected American pre-occupations – with time travel and with incest – and defuses our anxieties about both through comedy.

Since 1979, there has been a proliferation of time travel films, including *Time After Time* (1979), *Somewhere in Time* (1980), *The Final Countdown* (1980), *Time Bandits* (1981), *Timerider* (1983), *Twilight Zone: The Movie* (1983), *The Philadelphia Experiment* (1984), *The Terminator* (1984), *Trancers* (1985; an imitation of *The Terminator*), *Back to the Future* (1985), *My Science Project* (1985), the made-for-television movies *The Blue Yonder* (1986) and *Outlaws* (1986), and, most recently, *Peggy Sue Got Married* (1986), *Flight of the Navigator* (1986) and *Star Trek IV* (1987). According to Wyn Wachhorst, 'time travel has only recently become a frequent cinematic theme, having increased by more than fifty percent relative to the rise in total science fiction films during the past decade (340).

I believe that this recent explosion of time travel films represents a pervasive uneasiness about our present and uncertainty about our future, along with a concurrent nostalgia about our past. These time travel films rarely attempt a vision of the future, and when they do, as in *The Terminator*, the future is bleak and post-apocalyptic. And during the same period (1979–87), in other SF films without a time travel premise, the future is almost always a negative extrapolation from the present: overcrowded, decayed, bureaucratic and soulless, repressive, and either on the verge of destruction or post-apocalyptic. H. Bruce Franklin has summarised the negative Hollywood vision of the future from 1970–82 ('Don't Look Where We're Going'); the picture hasn't changed much in the past five years, and the *Star Trek* movies remain about the only optimistic cinematic vision of the future, which may account in large measure for their enormous popularity. It also helps to account for the success of *Back to the Future*, which attempts to reassure us that, in the words of the movie, 'the future is in your hands'.

The majority of recent time travel films do not, in fact, concern the future at all (*Back to the Future* does not, despite its title) but deal instead with an escape into an idealised past in a desperate attempt to alter the present and the future. They reflect a growing dissatisfaction with a present that is sensed as dehumanised, diseased, out of control, and perhaps doomed. Somewhere along the line, the unspoken feeling goes, something went drastically wrong; if we could only return to the appropriate crossroads in the past and correct things, we could mend history and return to a revised, glorious present or future, the time line we truly deserve. *Back to the Future*, *The Blue Yonder* (about a boy who travels back from 1986 to 1927 to help his grandfather), and *Peggy Sue Got Married* deal with the attempts of individuals to revise their personal time lines by a return to the past; *The Terminator* and *Star Trek IV* concern groups from the future attempting a rescue in our present so that humanity may have a future. A similar premise holds in Gregory Benford's novel *Timescape* (1980), where the ecologically poisoned, dying world of 1998 sends a warning back to the prelapsarian world of 1963. The effect of the message is to avert the catastrophe by creating an alternate time line.

Such, then, is the contemporary preoccupation with time to which *Back to the Future* appeals. But along with our anxieties about the future, the film also comically mirrors new, more accepting popular attitudes about time travel, or rather, 'time shifting', and a flattening out of our perspective of time. Thus Tom Shales notes that, from 1979–85, most time travel movies failed at the box office. 'The only one to hit it really big was *Back to the Future*, a phrase that almost sums the 1980s up, and that's partly because the movie made time travel a joke, a gag, a hoot. We are not amazed at the thought of time travel because we do it every day' (p. 67). Shales labels the 1980s 'The Re Decade', a decade of replays, reruns and recycling of popular culture, epitomised by videorecorders. 'Television is our national time machine (68).

Back to the Future demonstrates the reciprocity of contemporary image-making, which cuts across all time lines. In the course of the movie, we see video images of the present (Dr Brown's 1985 experiment) rerun in the past, as well as images of the past (*The Honeymooners*) rerun in the present. The self-reflexivity of *Back to the Future*'s use of video points to what Garrett Stewart calls 'the 'videology' of science fiction': movies about the technology of the image allow us to observe the ideologies 'by which we see and so lead our lives' (207). But this self-reflexivity also illustrates Vivian Sobchack's claim: '*Back to the Future* is a generic symptom of our collapsed sense of time and history' (274).

In fact, past and present are so collapsed in the plot of the movie that the young hero Marty's life threatens to become nothing more than a rerun, like the *Honeymooners* episode repeated during two separate family dinners. The audience gets the eerie comic effect of instant replay when we see gestures, lines or entire scenes from 1985 echoed almost word for word in 1955. The present reruns the past, or vice-versa. These characters seem subject

to a sort of repetition compulsion, doomed to neurotic closed loops until Marty intervenes to rewrite the script.

As SF comedy, *Back to the Future* is more successful than *Time Bandits* or *Peggy Sue Got Married* in playing the incongruities of time travel for laughs. *Time Bandits* is episodic in structure and only fitfully funny, and *Peggy Sue* shifts uncomfortably in tone between farce and melodrama. But *Back to the Future* is consistently funny because it is grounded in the broad humour of television sitcoms and classic Hollywood 'screwball comedy'.

Harlan Ellison despised *Back to the Future*, complaining that 'the lofty time paradox possibilities are reduced to the imbecile level of sitcom' (88). But it seems to me that the use of a sitcom framework was a deliberate strategy on the part of the filmmakers to tame the potentially touchy subject of incest. In the 1970s, sitcom, through such innovative series as *All in the Family* and *M.A.S.H.*, became a liberal forum for dealing with controversial social and political issues with a humorous touch. *Back to the Future* offers a popular audience familiarity and reassurance through its stock characters (the Nerd, the Bully, the Nutty Professor) and stock premise (time travel, the subject of so many movies and TV shows) and its star, Michael J. Fox, borrowed from a successful sitcom (*Family Ties*). And the small-town environment it presents is equally formulaic and reassuring to audiences. As Vivian Sobchack mentions, 'the *mise-en-scène* of *Back to the Future* spatialises neither 1955 nor 1985, but the television time of *Leave it to Beaver* and *Father Knows Best*' (274). The filmmakers are aware of the film's roots in television: thus producer Steven Spielberg called *Back to the Future* 'the greatest *Leave it to Beaver* episode ever produced' and writer-director Robert Zemeckis described it as 'a cross between Frank Capra and *The Twilight Zone*' (Stein: 41). And I have already noted the homage to Jackie Gleason's *The Honeymooners*.

But the film's comedy is not pure sitcom. Zemeckis, who has directed comedy before (*I Wanna Hold Your Hand*, *Used Cars*, *Romancing the Stone*), attributes his success partially to his reverence for 'comedy classics' and traditional methods of making comic films (Stein: 37). Jack Kroll called *Back to the Future* 'a true American comedy, with the sweet and benevolent bite of Preston Sturges and Frank Capra' (76). Indeed, with its smalltown hero, humour and time travel premise, it bears some comparison with Capra's *It's a Wonderful Life*. And Pauline Kael wrote that *Back to the Future* 'has the structure of a comedy classic' (58). I also noticed that the image of Dr Brown dangling perilously from the hands of a clock evokes Harold Lloyd. In other words, the film draws on the traditions of both sitcom and classic Hollywood comedy. It has a sure comic sense, employing a whole range of comic devices, including physical humour such as farce and slapstick, situational humour, irony, comedy of character and verbal wit. The movie exhilarates audiences because it glories in its own outrageousness and plays almost everything for laughs.

So *Back to the Future* makes us laugh at the incongruous possibilities of time travel. But it also makes us laugh at incest, or at least flirts with the possibility of a sexual relationship between mother and son. What is funny about that, especially for a family audience?

It has been thirty years since Vladimir Nabokov's *Lolita* made the violation of the incest taboo a possible subject for American popular culture. Since that time, sociologists and psychologists have been collecting data on incest, and newspaper stories have focused attention on the frequent violations of the taboo and the connections between incest, prostitution, child abuse and child molestation. Our uneasiness on the subject has not necessarily decreased as our knowledge has increased (cf. Twitchell). In fact, it might be argued that the publicity has perhaps enhanced social anxiety: people may fear that incest is all around them, like AIDS, and that they may be the next to catch it. In any event, in 1985 there was a television movie (*Something About Amelia*) and two feature films on the subject of incest: *The Color Purple* and *Back to the Future*. The most popular of these films, *Back to the Future* makes the (attempted) incest laughable, just as *Lolita* made the subject more palatable by dealing with it through black humour.

But although *Back to the Future* temporarily frees us from some of our anxiety by making incest laughable, it no more renders incest acceptable or guiltfree than Woody Allen's *Hannah and Her Sisters* condones adultery. Instead, *Back to the Future* distances us from the incest by making both the mother's brazenness and the son's terror laughable. And it teases our fear and desire by a last-minute avoidance of the physical act. The desire, guilt and fear are still attached to the incest taboo, but the audience is comfortable with those feelings because we get a momentary comic bonus from them.

On one level, the film is therapeutic comedy, filled with psychosexual anxiety that is aroused and then relieved. One critic (Hoberman) calls it 'teenage Woody Allen', and writes that 'Marty resolves his sexual crisis by working through his own family romance ... Marty is nothing less than an American Oedipus who learns to conquer his desire for his mother (projected, in the film's key scene, back onto her) and accede to the rule of the father.' And other critics assert that 'it is on the timeless plane of myth that *Back to the Future* has its finest moments ... In that timeless realm Marty can participate (or rather, almost participate) in that delightful parody of the Oedipus myth' (Barksdale & Pace: 57).

I would argue that *Back to the Future* is the first SF film to make explicit the incestuous possibilities that have always been at the heart of our fascination with time travel. Time travel is an unnatural act which is frequently used to allow the fulfillment of oedipal fantasies or family romance. By changing the relative ages of family members and turning the hero into a stranger to his own family, time travel permits the hero to freely romance his own mother or other ancestors or descendants.

Critics have noted that H. G. Wells's Time Traveller comes face to face with a Sphinx and walks with a limp, both of which connect him with Oedipus (cf. Scafella, Ketterer). And some twentieth-century American SF writers have openly explored the incestuous possibilities of time travel. For example, the hero of Robert Silverberg's *Up the Line* wipes himself out by meddling with the past: he defies the time traveller's code by making love to a woman who is his remote ancestor. Robert A. Heinlein is the American writer most fascinated with the possibility of violating the incest taboo through time travel. In *The Door into Summer*, the protagonist, through time travel, is able to marry a little girl who is his ward. In *Time Enough for Love*, Lazarus Long falls in love with several adopted daughters, including 'Llita' (suggesting 'Lolita') and 'Dora' (suggesting Freud's case study of a woman who loved her father too much), and finally goes back in time to physically consummate his love for his mother. In 'All You Zombies', the hero commits the ultimate incest; through time travel and a sex-change operation he is able to seduce himself and give birth to himself.[3]

Wyn Wachhorst explains the recent rise in popularity of time-travel films in psychological terms as 'an attempt to reenchant the world, to regain a sense of belongingness, to reinstate the magical, autocentric universe of the child and the primitive – while retaining the reality projected by rational, individualised consciousness' (350). For Wachhorst, the 'time-travel romance' is a disguised oedipal fantasy. He notes that in such recent movies as *Somewhere in Time*, *Timerider* and *The Final Countdown*, the omnipotent male time traveller returns to the past (symbolically, Paradise or the world of childhood) where he romances an innocent woman who stands in for the mother (in *Timerider*, she is his grandmother). The variations on this pattern, such as *Time After Time* and *The Philadelphia Experiment*, where the hero goes from the past into the future to find romance with the innocent woman, Wachhorst considers less successful. One could add to his list of time travel romances involving sublimated incest the recent film *The Terminator* (1984), in which a man sends his father into the past to ensure that his father will impregnate his mother.

Back to the Future represents the de-sublimated form of the time travel romance since the heroine and hero no longer stand in for mother and son but *are* mother and son. Marty McFly is the time traveller as a would-be teenage Oedipus. Like Oedipus, Marty attempts to flee his fate – not to another town but to another time. And like Oedipus, his flight leads him directly into the very predicament he dreaded (and Freud would claim, secretly desired): into his mother's bed. But this is comedy, not tragedy: whereas Oedipus kills his father at the crossroads, Marty rescues his; and whereas Oedipus marries his mother, Marty temporarily endures his mother's sexual attentions for the sake of reuniting his parents. Marty, in other words, is a reluctant Oedipus, an innocent and blameless, comic Oedipus who never consummates the act.

Back to the Future enacts a fantasy of innocent power: Marty is portrayed as an innocent victim of circumstances, yet as time traveller he has omnipotent powers. His return to the past enables him to resolve an oedipal crisis and reshape his life and the lives of his parents for the better. He acts out the 'family romance' to which Freud referred: the desire to replace unsatisfactory parents with idealised ones.

Marty as omnipotent time traveller goes from the degraded present of 1985 – with its graffiti, X-rated movies, homeless drunks sleeping on benches in littered parks, terrorists stalking the streets – to the prelapsarian 1955; spotless, pristine, virginal. But it is a virginity panting to be deflowered. Our innocent hero now finds himself subject to the sexual terrorism of his own mother, who sees him as the man of her dreams.

Back to the Future, like *It's a Wonderful Life*, is a film about dreams, dreams turned into nightmare and changed back into happy endings. 'It's all a dream', Marty tells himself when he arrives back in 1955, 'Just a very intense dream.' As he walks through the town square, the song that's playing is 'Mr Sandman, Bring Me a Dream'. When he first wakes up in his mother's bed, he still believes it is all a bad dream. But his mother, Lorraine, in 1955 considers Marty a 'dreamboat' and 'an absolute dream'.

What exactly is the content of this dream? In 'The Relation of the Poet to Day-Dreaming', Freud talks about the kind of 'time travelling which normally occurs in fantasy, dreams and daydreams:

> The relation of phantasies to time is altogether of great importance. One may say that a phantasy at one and the same moment hovers between three periods of time – the three periods of our ideation. The activity of phantasy in the mind is linked up with some current impression, occasioned by some event in the present, which had the power to rouse an intense desire. From there it wanders back to the memory of an earlier experience, generally belonging to infancy, in which this wish was fulfilled. Then it creates for itself a situation which is to emerge in the future, representing the fulfillment of the wish – this is the day-dream or phantasy, which now carries in it traces both of the occasion which engendered it and of some past memory. So past, present and future are threaded, as it were, on the string of the wish that runs through them all. (38)

Marty's experiences in 1955 and his return to an altered 1985 can be considered an elaborate daydream whose relationship to time corresponds to the pattern described by Freud. His daydream is occasioned by his frustration and failure in 1985, by his personal and sexual insecurity. He retreats to the past, to 1955 – but symbolically he is in the world of infancy, when the bond between himself and his mother was strongest. As Wachhorst says, the time travel romance reinstates 'the magical, autocentric universe of the child' (350). In 1955, Marty is both a child overpowered by his mother and, paradoxically, an omnipotent adult who can become the parent to his own parents. After he has indulged and overcome his oedipal fears and desires, and restructured his parents' lives to create the idealised family he desires, he returns to a revised 1985 in which his problems have magically disappeared. In truth, his past, present and future are threaded 'on the string of the wish that runs through them all'.

The structure of the film resembles that of the classic Hollywood fantasy, *The Wizard of Oz*: a 'realistic' opening sequence establishes a problem for the young protagonist which a 'fantastic' second sequence resolves. Characters and scenes from the first sequence recur in the second one, echoed but strangely reshaped by the wish-fulfilling distortions of the dream. The Wizard adheres to the conventions of fantasy: the transformation is apparently effected by means of a twister; only at the end is it revealed that the Oz sequence was a feverish dream induced by a blow on the head. Future instead uses the conventions of SF: the transformation is effected by machinery (the DeLorean car/time machine), and the second sequence is presented as real. But it may be significant that the first thing Marty encounters in 1955 is a scarecrow, reminding us of Dorothy in Oz!

Moreover, both Dorothy and Marty are presented as innocents, strangers in a strange land stranded there by accident, not by their own desires, and wishing only to go home. Marty depends upon the bumbling scientist, Dr Brown, to send him back to his own time, just as Dorothy relied upon the inept Wizard to return her to Kansas. Both films are fantasies of innocent power, in which the protagonist combines the helplessness of a child with the superpowers that the child perceives the adult as having: Dorothy's magical helpers and ruby slippers, or Marty's time machine and other advanced technology from 1985 (skateboard, videocamera, and Sony Walkman). Dorothy is acclaimed a powerful witch by the Munchkins, and Marty in 1955 is at first mistaken for an invader from another planet by the paranoid citizens, who have seen too many 1950s SF films and read too many comic books. Later, he takes advantage of their gullibility and happily assumes the role of an extraterrestrial with superpowers: 'Darth Vader from the planet Vulcan.'[4]

The opening sequence of *Back to the Future*, like the opening of *The Wizard of Oz*, is a catalogue of frustration and failure for the protagonist, failures which will all be rectified in the following 'dream' sequence. We are introduced to Marty McFly, a 17-year-old living in the California town of Hill Valley in 1985. The chronically tardy Marty first loses his race against time and is late for school the fourth day in a row. There he is put down by a hostile teacher, Mr Strickland, who accuses him of being a failure like his father George McFly. Then, as Mr Strickland predicts, Marty loses the school rock band competition. Next, he is frustrated in his attempts to neck with his girlfriend, Jennifer, and arrives home to find the family car wrecked by his father's supervisor, Biff, ruining Marty's hopes for a hot date on the weekend with Jennifer. He sees his father humiliated by Biff and sits down to dinner with a family of nerds and losers, among whom he seems hopelessly out of place. 'No McFly ever amounted to anything in the history of Hill Valley', the nasty Mr Strickland told him, to which McFly cockily replied, 'History is gonna change.' The second sequence, Hill Valley in 1955, functions as a wish-fulfillment fantasy in which history can be changed, this entire day of defeat cancelled and all of Marty's dreams realised.

Marty lacks confidence because he has a weakling for a father and an overpowering mother; thus, he has not yet successfully overcome the oedipal phase. He wishes for a strong father to dominate his threatening mother and help him earn his manhood. Marty's mother in the opening sequence is dissatisfied with her husband and her life: she smokes, eats and drinks to excess. Her sexual dissatisfaction has made her both repressed and repressing: she denies having any sexuality when she was a girl and disapproves of Jennifer for pursuing Marty. For Marty, this means that she is trying to prevent his sexual development and keep him bound to her.

The father image is split into three stock characters: George the wimp, Biff the bully, and Dr Brown the nutty professor and kindly 'uncle'. If George is impotent, then Biff is overly potent (and a rapist), and the celibate Brown is comfortingly asexual (but omnipotent). Biff humiliates the spineless father in front of Marty: in a sense he is as much a representation of Marty's hostility toward his father as he is a symbol of the avenging, sexual, castrating side of the father. Biff bosses the household like the 'real man' to whom George's wife and everything else George possesses (job, family, house, refrigerator and car) belongs. 'Say hi to your mom', Biff leeringly tells Marty. Biff's unhealthy intrusion into and destruction of the household, his overturning of the authority of the father, and his symbolic possession of the mother – all these, plus the exaggeration in his depiction, turn him into a symbol of the child's œdipal rebellion against the father. Biff is the unhealthy side of Marty; thus Biff's power must be tamed and restored to its rightful owner, the father, for the film to conclude successfully. Of course, Biff is a stock character, like the rest of the characters: that makes it that much easier for the audience to engage in the same kind of splitting of desires that the film is indulging as a defense. By providing a bully we can hoot at, the film also enables us to cheer for the hero without ambivalence.

As for Dr Brown the Wizard, he gives Marty the call to adventure and provides him with superscience, the magical tools and the wisdom and confidence he needs to undergo his initiation into manhood. As Zemeckis explains, 'The story is anchored in a sort of benevolent Merlin/Arthur kind of relationship between Dr. Brown and Marty' (Stein: 42). Their relationship also echoes that of Ben Kenobi and Luke in *Star Wars*. Just as Ben Kenobi provides Luke with a lightsaber and the power of 'The Force', so Brown provides Marty with a time machine. And Luke witnesses Ben's death and resurrection (as part of the Force), whereas Marty sees Brown murdered and then return to life; both sequences could be said to do and undo patricidal wishes. Brown also expresses the desires in the film for omnipotence, perhaps as a way to overcome fears of failure, castration or impotence. The audience roots for both Brown and Marty, for both triumph

after a long string of failures and return from near death or apparent death. Finally, since a kid has the power for much of the film, and we are distanced from the parents and other adults, who are made to seem either physically or sexually intimidating, pathetic or foolish, Dr Brown serves as a substitute, idealised parent who is wise but funny, and completely asexual.

The father image may be split into three, but the mother image is split into two, which are, roughly, mother-nun and virgin-whore. The repressive mother of the opening sequence in 1985 is transformed into the horny teenager Lorraine in 1955. When Marty rescues his father from an automobile accident, Marty is injured and takes his father's place in his mother's affections. Now he must undo all this, under threat of never being born. What we see here is a simple role reversal or projection of desires: horny Marty and the repressive mother simply switch places, and the mother's lustful pursuit of him expresses both oedipal fears and desires. Throughout, Marty is portrayed as purely innocent, acting only from the noblest of motives and merely the victim of circumstances. This, plus the mother's exaggerated lust and Marty's exaggerated sexual terror, enable us to enjoy it as comedy.

The best that Marty can do is to stage a rescue fantasy in which the father is to save the mother from the pawing of the son, thereby putting Oedipus to rest. Through an ironic (and appropriate) twist of fate, George ends up rescuing Lorraine instead from the molestations of Biff: that is, from innocent Marty's evil stand-in, a sexual beast.

The resolution the film offers is to transform George into a strong father by effectively castrating Biff and transferring his potency to George. Biff's loss of power also represents Marty's abandoning of the desire for the mother. But the desire for omnipotence (perhaps as a defense against the fear of castration) remain at the end: Marty has passed his initiation ritual but he is once again lured into adventure by Dr Brown. Having rewritten the past and the present, they will now presumably go on to reshape the future. In the exhilarating conclusion, Marty and Jennifer depart with the Professor in the DeLorean (now run by fusion and able to fly), off to the future to rescue their children. The audience leaves the movie on this exhilarating note, feeling a sense of infinite possibilities, feeling that, as a line from the movie goes, 'The future is in your hands.'

The struggle in the film, then, for Marty and Dr Brown and George, is to gain power and control over that power, to counter impotence and failure with omnipotence and success. To put it another way, there is a phallic struggle contained within the oedipal one. In the film's opening scene, Marty enters the lab, switches on a machine and turns it all the way up to 'Overdrive'. He plugs in an electric guitar and stands in front of a monstrously huge amplifier. The first chord he strums destroys the amp and blows him across the room. But Marty makes a soft landing in a chair and is unharmed, despite a bookcase tipping over and dumping its contents on him. The scene prefigures the later scenes when the DeLorean is revved up to Overdrive and blows Marty across time to a safe landing. The film shows the exhilaration of playing around with omnipotence. Marty is the sorcerer's apprentice whose dream comes true, who overcomes all the dangers inherent in possessing fantastic power.

Aside from the electric guitar, the time machine itself is the primary symbol of 'phallic' power. It is powerful and intrusive, building up energy and then releasing it in an orgasmic burst. Marty is constantly crashing the car into things. It is difficult for him to control and prone to embarrassing failures to start. The clock tower can be taken as another phallic symbol, particularly in the climactic scene, when it is struck by lightning. And the bazooka with which the Libyan terrorists threaten Marty is made to seem particularly phallic by the camera angle.

The movie also makes comedy out of the exaggerated contrasts between little Marty and the big guys who intimidate him, such as Lou (the owner of the diner) and Biff. These contrasts in size could also be interpreted as phallic. In scene after scene, the camera exaggerates Biff's size as he looms ominously over Marty. Repeatedly, the power balance is restored by cutting Biff down to size, tripping him or hitting him so that he falls down. Biff gets his final comeuppance after he has knocked Lorraine to the ground and forced George to his knees by twisting his arm. At this point, George's fist seems to act independently of him, and he fells Biff with one mighty blow. Afterwards, George pants ecstatically and admires his hand with astonishment and delight

before he helps Lorraine to her feet. Because this crucial scene is staged so melodramatically, the sexual symbolism becomes blatant.

Including this scene, I counted 14 instances in which characters tripped, fell, fainted, were knocked down, knocked out or gunned down. The climactic scenes for all five major characters – Marty, Dr Brown, George, Lorraine and Biff – involve their being forced down. We see all of them get up again, though, except for the villain Biff, who goes down and stays down. When Marty is with his mother in 1955, he is constantly backing away from her or falling over out of sexual terror. There are also six car crashes in the film. These many pratfalls and crashes provide both comedy and action, but they might also suggest an underlying concern with potency, with staying up and crashing through barriers.

Aside from its indulgence in oedipal and phallic fantasies, the film also involves a great deal of voyeurism and exhibitionism. At times, it even seems as if the main pleasure and the main sin is not in incest but in looking, watching, spying and being looked at. Young Lorraine gazes with longing at Marty, Dr Brown keeps rerunning the image of himself on videotape, Marty turns his head to gaze at the girls walking by in leotards (and his girlfriend Jennifer forcibly returns his gaze to her), Marty exhibits himself onstage in his guitar performances, Lorraine undresses with the blinds up as George, a 'peeping Tom', spies on her through binoculars, and Biff tells Marty repeatedly to stop staring at him ('What are you looking at, butthead?') and tells his buddies to stop staring as he is about to rape Lorraine: 'This ain't no peep show.' In one of the film's most memorable scenes, we see two Martys: One watches helplessly as Dr Brown is assassinated while the other, just returned from time travelling, helplessly watches himself watching helplessly.

So *Back to the Future* is indeed a fascinating 'peep show'. Of course, as critics have mentioned, voyeurism and exhibitionism may be an intrinsic feature of making and viewing films, and in most Hollywood films the primary object of the gaze is a woman.[5] This movie is no exception. But the particular emphasis in *Back to the Future* on voyeurism, aside from providing some incidental pleasure for viewers, may be a way of displacing our interest from the overt incest of the plot to the sublimated incest of spying on the parents.[6] In fact, *Back* to the Future might even be considered one extended 'primal scene'.

The most remarkable primal scene imagery in the film occurs when Marty plays his guitar at the high school dance in 1955. He has just witnessed his parents' first kiss, itself a symbolic primal scene. Marty, who had feared being wiped out of existence if they didn't kiss, has just been reborn, so he plays Chuck Berry's joyous rock anthem 'Johnny B. Goode' to celebrate his new lease on life. By a twist of history, his rebirth coincides with the birth of rock and roll. In one of the film's funniest scenes, Marty shows off before this hick 1955 crowd, exhibiting 1985 savvy, as he had done before with his skateboarding. But he overdoes it and embarrasses himself. Marty quickly recapitulates the history of rock and roll and winds up on the floor of the stage, producing heavy metal squeals as he practically copulates with his guitar. Like many rock and roll performances, it is a phallic celebration, with overtones of public masturbation. When Marty opens his eyes, he sees the 1955 audience staring in shocked silence. Shamefacedly, he apologises: 'I guess you guys aren't ready for that yet. But your kids are gonna love it!'

In the context of this film, 'it' could stand for either rock and roll or sex (which have always been closely connected in the popular imagination, anyway, as in 'drugs, sex and rock and roll'). Earlier, Marty's sexuality was repressed by his mother, and his music was repressed by the school. He lost the band contest because his brand of rock was deemed 'too darn loud' (read 'too sexual'). So when Marty undoes this failure by playing at the high school dance, he expresses a new confidence both in his music and in his sexuality. After all, he has just rejoiced in witnessing his parents' first kiss, which means that he has accepted their sexuality and so is better able to accept his own.

Thus it is possible to read his guitar playing not simply as masturbatory exhibitionism, which it is, but also as a recapitulation of the primal scene: Marty stands in for both father and mother in the act of conceiving him, and the silent, staring crowd, shocked and puzzled by this violent activity and the strange sounds accompanying it, stands in for the child witness.[7] The scene is pleasurable for an audience in part because it makes primal scene imagery not terrifying but *funny*: the performance is a

comic triumph for Marty, who easily shrugs off his embarrassment, showing a new mood of confidence and self-acceptance.

Back to the Future, as I have attempted to demonstrate, appeals on many different psychosexual levels to viewers: it makes comedy out of voyeurism, phallic exhibitionism, incest and the primal scene. But I should also mention one last level of its humour, which is excremental comedy, a delight in *mess*: the overflowing bowl of dog food, the overturned book-shelf, and the truckload of manure tipped over on Biff. In the final scene, Dr Brown maniacally rummages through the garbage cans for fuel to power his 'Mr Fusion' generator. It may also be significant that, in such a 'clean' comedy, the only vulgarities uttered are 'butthead', 'serious shit' and 'assholes'.

Moreover, it is a psychoanalytic commonplace that problems relating to the 'anal' phase of development revolve around autonomy and control, cleanliness and order, and time. Not surprisingly, the film concerns all these issues: a struggle for autonomy and control, a revolt against cleanliness and order, and an obsession with time. These conflicts are unconsciously connected, so that the central battle to overcome time also represents Marty's and Brown's struggle for autonomy and control. The opening shot is a long pan of the ticking clocks in Dr Brown's laboratory, including one with a man dangling from the hands of the clock, just as Dr Brown will do later. Marty is chronically tardy and, like the Professor, always racing against time. In other words, although an oedipal fantasy is at the heart of the movie, it is connected with and strongly coloured by concerns from the stage that Erik H. Erikson called 'autonomy vs. shame and doubt' (251–4).

It is easy enough to dissolve a film into relatively primitive psychosexual levels. But a fantasy of omnipotence will not work for an audience unless it has speed, energy and style. And *Back to the Future* has these in abundance: its infectious high spirits and restless camera movements catch the viewer up in the action from beginning to end.

The recent proliferation of time travel films speaks to our nostalgia for the past, our dissatisfaction with the present and our dread of the future. *Back to the Future* is a therapeutic comedy because it suggests that time and human character are malleable, which is what Americans have always wanted to believe.

Granted, it is possible to fault the film for its 'blandly positivist' notions of mental health (Hoberman), its antiseptic vision of the 1950s (Hoberman; Kael: 58), and its final conversion of Marty's family into yuppies (Kael: 58). Nevertheless, these are not fundamental flaws and they do not detract from the film's power to make us laugh and to reassure us.

The therapeutic nature of *Back to the Future* consists in rendering explicit the incestuous possibilities that have always been at the core of our fascination with time travel and exploiting those possibilities for the purposes of a comic resolution to an oedipal crisis. *Back to the Future* allows us to laugh at potentially dangerous material by placing it within the context of classic film comedy and situation comedy and by deliberately using stock character types. Moreover, it distances the oedipal crisis through the fantastic, displaces it from the present to the past and from the child to the parent. Through a fantasy of innocent power, it permits us to identify with an innocent hero, to retreat to the purity of childhood while retaining the power and control of adulthood. The sophistication of the 1980s meets the naïveté of the 1950s, and the film validates both. *Back to the Future* is an ingenious wish-fulfillment fantasy with an upbeat message, a therapeutic family comedy, allowing a rare, momentary reconciliation between past and present and between parent and child.

Notes

1 For some representative, largely positive, responses to *Back to the Future*, see the reviews by Hoberman, Kael, Kauffman and Kroll.

2 I conducted an informal survey of audience response to *Back to the Future*. I asked two undergraduate classes at the University of Florida to write their responses and I taped interviews with some audience members immediately after they viewed the film in a theatre. Some of the results were unexpected. First, entirely without prompting, many praised the film as scrupulously *clean*: 'the viewer does not feel dirty'; 'good, clean humour ... no sex, gore or profanity'; 'not at all offensive'; and 'one of the cleanest films, without any type of filth in it'. Either these comments are defensive denials, or else this is a sad commentary on the current state of Hollywood films, because *Back to the Future* deals with a peeping tom, attempted rape and attempted incest, and includes three (admittedly mild) vulgarities: 'butthead', 'shit' and 'assholes'. Second, based on my limited sampling, this film

is apparently very popular with 13-year-old boys, some of whom went first with friends and then returned with their families, including their mothers. You can make of this what you will, but to me it indicates that the film is a therapeutic family comedy.

3 I am indebted to H. Bruce Franklin's discussion of the incest theme in Heinlein in *Robert A. Heinlein*, pp. 120–4, 184–6, 191–7.

4 *Back to the Future*, like most SF films since 1977, is openly inter-textual, and our pleasure in the film to a degree depends upon our shared knowledge of twentieth-century American popular culture and the shock of recognition of seeing familiar material reworked in a new context. As Sobchack mentions, 'It is only recently that the SF film has so reflexively embraced its own former status as 'schlock' and 'kitsch' and/or embraced the whole 'degraded' landscape of schlock and kitsch that represents contemporary American popular culture' (249).

5 On two kinds of voyeurism in film, see Metz, pp. 89–98. On woman as image in film, see Mulvey.

6 Based on my survey, many viewers were fascinated by the idea of spying on the parents: 'when the boy finds himself in the past, he seeks the home of his parents' (this response is not strictly true to the plot); 'everyone would probably love to go back ... and see what it was like when their parents were young'; 'made me wonder about my parents at that age'; 'I really enjoyed seeing the main character with his parents as teenagers'.

7 For a thorough investigation of primal scene imagery in films, including science fiction films, see Dervin.

Bibliography

Barksdale, E. C. & David Paul Pace 'Back to the Future', *Cinefantastique* (March 1986), pp. 45, 56–7.

Dervin, Daniel *Through a Freudian Lens Deeply: A Psycho-analysis of Cinema* (Hillsdale, NJ: The Analytic Press, 1985).

Ellison, Harlan 'Harlan Ellison's Watching', *The Magazine of Fantasy and Science Fiction*, (Jan 1986), p. 88.

Erikson, Erik H. *Childhood and Society*, 2nd ed. NY, 1963.

Franklin, H. Bruce. 'Don't Look Where We're Going: Visions of the Future in Science Fiction Films, 1970–82', SFS, 10 (1983): pp. 70–80.

_____ *Robert A. Heinlein: America as Science Fiction*. New York: Oxford University Press, 1980.

Freud, Sigmund 'The Relation of the Poet to Day-Dreaming' (1908), in *Character and Culture*, ed. Philip Rieff (New York: Collier Books, 1972), pp. 34–43.

Hoberman, J. 'Spielbergism and Its Discontents', *The Village Voice*, 9 July 1985, p. 45.

Kael, Pauline 'Back to the Future', *The New Yorker*, 29 July 1985, pp. 57–8.

Kauffman, Stanley 'Travelling to the Past', *The New Republic*,

5 Aug. 1985, p. 24.

Ketterer, David 'Oedipus as Time Traveller', SFS, 9 (1982), pp. 340–1.

Kroll, Jack 'Having the Time of His Life', *Newsweek*, 8 July 1985, p. 76.

Metz, Christian *The Imaginary Signifier: Psychoanalysis and the Cinema*. 1977; Bloomington, IN: Indiana University Press, 1982.

Mulvey, Laura 'Visual Pleasure and Narrative Cinema', in *Movies and Methods*, vol. 2, ed. Bill Nichols (Berkeley: University of California Press, 1985), pp. 303–15.

Scafella, Frank 'The White Sphinx and The Time Machine', SFS, 8 (1981), pp. 255–65.

Shales, Tom 'The Re Decade', *Esquire* (March 1986), pp. 67–72.

Sobchack, Vivian *Screening Space: The American Science Fiction Film*, 2nd. ed. New York: Rutgers University Press, 1987.

Stein, Michael 'Director Bob Zemeckis' Tale of Teen Time Travel', *Fantastic Films* (Oct. 1985), pp. 37, 41–3.

Stewart, Garrett 'The 'Videology' of Science Fiction', in *Shadows of the Magic Lamp: Fantasy and Science Fiction in Film*, ed. George E. Slusser & Eric S. Rabkin (Carbondale, IL: Southern Illinois University Press, 1985), pp. 159–207.

Twitchell, James *Forbidden Partners: The Incest Taboo in Modern Culture*. New York: Columbia University Press, 1986.

Wachhorst, Wyn 'Time-Travel Romance on Film: Archetypes and Structures', *Extrapolation*, 25 (1984), pp. 340–59.

Time Travel, Primal Scene and the Critical Dystopia
Constance Penley

If the sure sign of postmodern success is the ability to inspire spin-offs, *The Terminator* was a prodigy. The film was quickly replicated by *Exterminator, Re-animator, Eliminators, The Annihilators* and the hardcore *The Sperminator*, all sound-alikes if not look-alikes. It then went on to garner one of popular culture's highest accolades when a West Coast band named itself *Terminators of Endearment*. And just to show that postmodernity knows no boundaries, national or otherwise, an oppressively large (2x3ft) and trendy new Canadian journal has appeared, calling itself *The Manipulator*.

For some science fiction critics, Fredric Jameson among them, *The Terminator*'s popular appeal would represent no more than American science fiction's continuing affinity for the dystopian rather than the utopian, with fantasies of cyclical regression or totalitarian empires of the future. Our love affair with apocalypse and Armageddon, according to Jameson, results from the atrophy of utopian imagination, in other words, our cultural incapacity to imagine the future.[1] Or, as Stanislaw Lem puts it, in describing the banality and constriction of most American science fiction, 'The task of the SF author today is as easy as that of the pornographer, and in the same way.'[2] But surely there are dystopias and dystopias, and not all such films (from *Rollerball* to *The Terminator*) deserve to be dismissed as trashy infatuations with an equally trashy future. While it is true that most recent dystopian films are content to revel in the sheer awfulness of *The Day After* (the *Mad Max* trilogy and *A Boy and His Dog* come readily to mind), there are others which try to point to present tendencies that seem likely to result in corporate totalitarianism, apocalypse, or both. Although *The Terminator* gives us one of the most horrifying post-apocalyptic visions of any recent film, it falls into the latter group because it locates the origins of future catastrophe in decisions about technology, warfare and social behavior that are being made today. For example, the new, powerful defense computer that in *The Terminator* is hooked into everything – missiles, the defense industry, weapons design – and trusted to make all the decisions, is clearly a fictionalised version of the burgeoning 'Star Wars' industry. This computer of the near future, forty years hence, gets smart – a new order of intelligence. It 'began to see all people as a threat', Reese tells Sarah as he tries to fill her in on the future, 'not just the ones on the other side. It decided our fate in a microsecond. Extermination.'

A film like *The Terminator* could be called a 'critical dystopia' inasmuch as it tends to suggest causes rather than merely reveal symptoms. But before saying more about how this film works as a critical dystopia, two qualifications need to be made. First, like most recent science fiction from *V* to *Star Wars*, *The Terminator* limits itself to solutions that are either individualist or bound to a romanticised notion of guerilla-like small-group resistance. The true atrophy of the utopian imagination is this: we *can* imagine the future but we *cannot* conceive the kind of collective political strategies necessary to change or ensure that future. Second, the film's politics, so to speak, cannot be simply equated with those of the 'author', James Cameron, the director of *The Terminator*, whose next job, after all, was writing *Rambo* (his disclaimers about Stallone's interference aside, he agreed to the project in the first place). Instead *The Terminator* can best be seen in relation to a set of cultural and psychical conflicts, anxieties and fantasies that are all at work in this film in a particularly insistent way.

Tech Noir

What are the elements, then, of *The Terminator*'s critical dystopian vision? Although the film is thought of as an exceptionally forward-thrusting action picture, it shares with other recent science fiction films, like *Blade Runner*, an emphasis on atmosphere or 'milieu', but not, however, at the price of any flattening of narrative space. (In this respect it is closest to *Alien*.) *The Terminator* is studded with everyday-life detail, all organised by an idea of 'tech noir'. Machines provide the texture and substance of this film: cars, trucks, motorcycles, radios, TVs, time clocks, phones, answering machines, beepers, hair dryers, Sony Walkmen, automated factory equipment. The defense network computer of the future which decided our fate in a microsecond had its humble origins here, in the rather more innocuous technology of the film's present. Today's machines are not, however, shown to be agents of destruction because they are themselves evil, but because they can break down, or because they can be used (often innocently) in ways they were not intended to be used. Stalked by a killer, Sarah Conner cannot get through to the police because the nearest phone is out of order. When she finally reaches the LAPD emergency line, on a phone in the Tech Noir nightclub, it is predictably to hear, 'All our lines are busy … please hold…'. Neither can she get through to her roommate, Ginger, to warn her because Ginger and her boyfriend have put on the answering machine while they make love. But Ginger wouldn't have been able to hear the phone, in any case, because she'd worn her Walkman to bed. Tech turns noir again when the Terminator, not Ginger, takes the answering machine message that gives away Sarah's location. Later Sarah will again reveal her whereabouts when the Terminator perfectly mimics her mother's voice over the phone. And in one of the film's most pointed gestures toward the unintentionally harmful effects of technology, the police psychiatrist fails to see the Terminator entering the station when his beeper goes off and distracts him just as their paths cross. Lacking any warning, scores of policemen are killed and the station destroyed. The film seems to suggest that if technology can go wrong or be abused, it will be. To illustrate this maxim further, Kyle Reese is shown having a nightmare of his future world where laser-armed, hunter-killer machines track down the few remaining humans; he wakes to hear a radio ad promoting laser-disk stereos. It comes as no surprise, finally, to see that his futuristic concentration camp number is the ubiquitous bar code stamped on today's consumer items.

That tech turns noir because of human decision-making and not something inherent in technology itself is presented even more forcefully in the 'novelisation' of The Terminator by Randall Frakes and Bill Wisher.[3] The novelisation adds a twist, perhaps one that originally appeared in the script but was discarded because it would have generated a complicated and digressive subplot. Or perhaps the authors of the book made it up on their own, unable to resist pointing out, once again, that it is humans, not machines, that will bring on the apocalypse. Near the end of the book,

after the Terminator has been destroyed, a man named Jack, a Steve Wozniak-like computer prodigy, discovers a microchip in the debris. His entrepreneur friend, Greg, decides that they will go into business for themselves, once they figure out how to exploit what they take to be a new kind of microprocessing unit. Sixteen months later, they incorporate under the name Cyberdyne Systems … the company that goes on to make the same defense network computer that will try to destroy humanity in Reese's day. Here the case is being made not so much against the tunnel vision of corporate greed, but against the supposedly more benign coupling of golly-gosh tech-nerd enthusiasm with all-American entrepreneurship.

The film, moreover, does not advance an 'us against them' argument, man versus machine, a Romantic opposition between the organic and the mechanical, for there is much that is hybrid about its constructed elements. The Terminator, after all, is part machine, part human – a cyborg. (Its chrome skeleton with its hydraulic muscles and tendons of flexible cable looks like the Nautilus machines Schwarzenegger uses to build his body.) And Kyle's skills as a guerilla fighter are dependent upon his tech abilities – hot-wiring cars, renovating weapons, making bombs. If Kyle has himself become a fighting machine in order to attack the oppressor machines, Sarah too becomes increasingly machine-like as she acquires the skills she needs to survive both the Terminator and the apocalypse to come. The concluding irony is that Kyle and Sarah use machines to distract and then destroy the Terminator when he corners them in a robot-automated factory. At the end of one of the most harrowing, and gruelingly paced, chase scenes on film, Sarah terminates the Terminator between two plates of a hydraulic press. This interpenetration of human and machine is seen most vividly, however, when Sarah is wounded in the thigh by a piece of exploding Terminator shrapnel. Leaving aside the rich history of sexual connotations of wounding in the thigh,[4] part of a machine is here literally incorporated into Sarah's body ('a kind of cold rape', the novelisation calls it). While the film addresses an ultimate battle between humans and machines, it nonetheless accepts the impossibility of clearly distinguishing between them. It focuses on the partial and ambiguous merging of the two, a more complex response, and one typical of the critical dystopia, than the Romantic triumph of the organic over the mechanical, or the nihilistic recognition that we have all become automata (even if those automata are better than we are, more human than human, as in *Blade Runner*).[5]

Time Travel

The Terminator, however, is as much about time as it is about machines. Because cinema itself has the properties of a time machine, it lends itself easily to time travel stories, one of the staples of science fiction literature. Surprisingly, however, there have been relatively few attempts in film to create stories around the idea of time travel. Hollywood, to be sure, has always been more drawn to conquering space and fighting off alien invaders than thinking through the heady paradoxes of voyaging through time. The exceptions have been very successful, however, and so it is curious that the industry has not made more effort to produce such stories. George Pal's *The Time Machine* (1960) was so exquisite (it brought the MGM look to science fiction film) that one even forgave the film's suppression of H. G. Wells's kooky class analysis of the Eloi and the Morlocks, which was, after all, the conceptual centre of the original tale. And the runaway success of the banal and clumsily made *Back to the Future* should have convinced Hollywood that there is something commercially attractive about the idea of time travel. Indeed, *The Terminator*'s appeal is due in large part to the way it is able to put to work this classical science fiction theme.

Compared to the complexity of many literary science fiction time travel plots, *The Terminator*'s story is simple: in 2010 a killer cyborg is sent back to the present day with the mission of exterminating Sarah Conner, a part-time waitress and student, the future mother of John Conner, the man who will lead the last remnants of humanity to victory over the machines which are trying to rid the world of humans. John Conner chooses Kyle Reese, a young and hardened fighter, to travel back in time to save Sarah from the Terminator. If the Terminator succeeds in his mission, John Conner, of course, will never be born, and the humans will never be able to fight back successfully against the machines. Kyle has fallen in love with Sarah through her photograph, given to him by John Conner. He says he always wondered what she was thinking

about when the photo was taken for she has a faraway look on her face and a sad smile. 'I came across time for you', he professes. 'I love you. I always have.' They make love, he is killed soon after, Sarah destroys the Terminator and leaves for the mountains to give birth to her son and wait out the holocaust to come. The film ends South of the Border with a Mexican boy taking a Polaroid of Sarah as she is thinking of Kyle. It is the photograph that John Conner will give to Kyle, forty years later, knowing that he is sending his own father to his death.

This sort of story is called a time-loop paradox because cause and effect are not only reversed but put into a circle: the later events are caused by the earlier events, and the earlier by the later.[6] If John Conner had not sent Kyle Reese back in time to be his father, he would never have been born. But he was born, so Kyle Reese must already have traveled back to the past to impregnate Sarah Conner. As another instance of paradox, John Conner's fighting skills were taught him by his mother. Sarah Conner, however, learned those skills from Kyle Reese, who had himself learned them while fighting at John Conner's side. (The novelisation adds another time-loop paradox in locating the origin of the defense network computer in the microchip found in the Terminator debris.) Small wonder then that Sarah looks slightly bewildered when Kyle says he has 'always loved' her. How could this be true when, from the perspective of her point in time, he hasn't been born yet?

What is the appeal of time-loop paradox stories? They are so fascinating that many people who used to read science fiction but have long since given it up will usually remember one story in particular, Ray Bradbury's 'A Sound of Thunder', even if they can no longer recall the author or the title (others have also noted this phenomenon). In this famous story, big-game hunters from the future travel back to the age of the dinosaurs. They don't have to fear that their shooting and bagging will affect the future, however, because dinosaurs will soon be extinct anyway. They are strictly warned, though, not to step off the walkway that has been prepared for them over the primeval jungle. One hunter disobeys and in doing so crushes a tiny butterfly under his boot. When the hunting party returns to the future, everything is ever so slightly different, the result of killing one small insect millions of years earlier.

Primal Scene

The essential elements of time travel and its consequences are witnessed in a very succinct way in 'A Sound of Thunder'. That is why the story is remembered. But when plots of this kind become more complex, one theme tends to predominate: what would it be like to go back in time and give birth to oneself? Or, what would it be like to be one's own mother and father? Robert Heinlein has given us the seminal treatment of this paradoxical situation in 'All You Zombies'. A time traveler who has undergone a sex-change operation not only encounters both earlier and later versions of himself but turns out to be his own mother and father. Similarly, in David Gerrold's *The Man Who Folded Himself*, each time the protagonist travels in time, he reduplicates himself. Eventually this results in a large group of identical men who find each other to be ideal lovers. One of them goes very far back in time and meets a lesbian version of himself. They fall in love, have children, and then break up, to return to their copy-lovers. (As the narrator says in 'All You Zombies', 'It's a shock to have it proved to you that you can't resist seducing yourself.') The appeal of *Back to the Future* should now be apparent – it is only a more vulgar version of the desire manifested in these stories. There is of course a name for this desire; it is called a primal scene fantasy, the name Freud gave to the fantasy of overhearing or observing parental intercourse, of being on the scene, so to speak, of one's own conception. The desire represented in the time travel story, of both witnessing one's own conception and being one's own mother and father, is similar to the primal scene fantasy, in which one can be both observer or one of the participants. (The possibility of getting pregnant and giving birth to oneself is echoed in *Back to the Future*'s TV ad: 'The first kid to get into trouble before he was ever born.') The reconstruction of a patient's primal scene assumes, in fact, a great deal of time travel. (Freud said the most extreme primal scene fantasy was that of observing parental intercourse while one is still an unborn baby in the womb.)[7] The Wolf-Man, supine on the analytic couch, is sent further and further back in time to 'remember' the moment

when, as a child, he saw his parents having sex. Although Freud's interpretation depends upon the Wolf-Man witnessing such a scene, he decides, finally, that it was not necessary for the event to have *actually occurred* for it to have had profound effects on the patient's psychical life. A patient can consciously fabricate such a scene only because it has been operative in his or her unconscious, and this construction has nothing to do with its actual occurrence or nonoccurrence. The idea of returning to the past to generate an event that has already made an impact on one's identity lies at the core of the time-loop paradox story.

What is *The Terminator*'s primal scene? The last words that Kyle Reese throws at the Terminator, along with a pipe bomb, are 'Come on, motherfucker!' But in the narrative logic of this film it is Kyle who is the mother-fucker. And within the structure of fantasy that shapes the film, John Conner is the child who orchestrates his own primal scene, one inflected by a family romance, moreover, be-cause he is able to choose his own father, singling out Kyle from the other soldiers. That such a fantasy is an attempted end-run around Oedipus is also obvious: John Conner can identify with his father, can even *be* his father in the scene of parental intercourse, and also conveniently dispose of him in order to go off with (in) his mother.

Recent film theory has taken up Freud's description of fantasy to give a more complete account of how identification works in film.[8] An important emphasis has been placed on the subject's ability to assume, successively, all the available positions in the fantasmatic scenario. Extending this idea to film has shown that spectatorial identification is more complex than has hitherto been understood because it shifts constantly in the course of the film's narrative, while crossing the lines of biological sex; in other words, unconscious identification with the characters or the scenario is not necessarily dependent upon gender. Another element of Freud's description of fantasy that also deserves attention, particularly in discussing fantasy in relation to popular film, is the self-serving or wish-fulfilling aspect of fantasy. In 'The Paths to the Formation of Symptoms', Freud constructs two analogies between the creation of fantasy and instances drawn from 'real life'. He begins by saying that a child uses fantasies to disguise the history of his childhood, 'just as every nation disguises its forgotten prehistory by constructing legends' (368). A fantasy is thus not 'just a fantasy' but a story *for* the subject. The fantasy of seduction, for example, serves to deny the subject's acts of auto-eroticism by projecting them onto another person. (Such fantasy constructions, Freud says, should be seen separately from those real acts of adult seduction of children that occur more frequently than is acknow-ledged.) Similarly, in the 'family romance' the subject creates another parent, an ideal one, to make up for the perceived shortcomings of the real mother or father. Thus a film like *The Terminator* that is so clearly working in relation to a primal fantasy, is also working in the service of pleasure (already a requirement for a mass audience film), a pleasure that depends upon suppressing conflicts or contradictions. (Because such suppression does not always work, and because desire does not always aim for pleasure – the death drive – much recent film analysis is devoted to examining those aspects of film that go distinctly 'beyond the pleasure principle'.[9])

Take, for example, the seemingly contra-dictory figure of Kyle Reese. The film 'cheats' with his image in the same way that *The Searchers* 'cheats' with Martin Pauley's image, which is, variously, wholly Indian, 'half-breed', 'quarter-blood' Cherokee, one-eighth Cherokee, or wholly white, depending upon the unconscious and ideological demands of the narrative at any given moment.[10] In *The Terminator* Kyle is the virile, hardened fighter barking orders to the terrified Sarah, but alternately he is presented as boyish, vulnerable and considerably younger in appearance than her. His childishness is underscored by Sarah's increasingly maternal affection for him (bandaging his wounds, touching his scars), and in the love scene, he is the young man being initiated by the more experienced, older woman. Kyle is thus both the father of John Conner and, in his youth and inexperience, Sarah's son, John Conner. The work of fantasy allows the fact of incest to be both stated and dissimulated. It is only in fantasy, finally, that we can have our cake and eat it too. Or as the French equivalent puts it, even more aptly, that we can be and have been – *peut être et avoir été*.

Freud also compared the mental realm of fantasy to a 'reservation' or 'nature reserve', a place set aside where 'the requirements of agriculture, communication and industry threaten to bring about changes in the original face of the earth which will quickly make it unrecognisable' (almost a description of a post-apocalyptic landscape). 'Everything, including what is useless and even what is noxious, can grow and proliferate there as it pleases. The mental realm of fantasy is just such a reservation withdrawn from the reality principle' (372). Can a film like *The Terminator* be similarly dismissed as merely escapist, appealing as it does to a realm of fantasy 'withdrawn from the reality principle', where even our incestuous desires can be realised? For one possible answer we can turn to the end of Freud's essay on symptom formation, where he tells us that there is 'a path that leads back from fantasy to reality – the path, that is, of art'. An artist, he says, has the ability to shape a faithful image of his fantasy, and then to depersonalise and generalise it so that it is made accessible to other people. Even if we do not have as much faith in 'art' or the 'artist' as Freud has, we can still draw some useful conclusions from what he says.

One could argue that *The Terminator* treads the path from fantasy back to reality precisely because it is able to generalise its vision, to offer something more than this fully, though paradoxically, resolved primal fantasy. This *generalising* of the fantasy is carried out through *The Terminator*'s use of the topical and everyday: as we have seen, the film's texture is woven from the technological litter of modern life. But this use of the topical is not, for example, like *E.T.*'s more superficial referencing of daily life through brand name kid-speak, that is, topicality for topicality's sake. Rather, it is a dialogue with Americana that bespeaks the inevitable consequences of our current technological addictions. To give another example, the shopping mall in George Romero's *Dawn of the Dead* is more than a kitsch ambience, it is a way of concretely demonstrating the zombification of consumer culture. By exposing every corner of the mall – stores, escalators, public walkways, basement, roof – the location becomes saturated with meaning, in a way that goes far beyond *E.T.*'s token gesturing toward the commodification of modern life. If *The Terminator*'s primal scene fantasy draws the spectator into the film's paradoxical circle of cause and effect and its equally paradoxical realisation of incestuous desire, its militant everydayness throws the spectator back out again, back to the technological future.

Science Fiction and Sexual Difference

In the realm of the unconscious and fantasy, the question of the subject's origin, 'Where do I come from?' is followed by the question of sexual difference, 'Who am I (What sex am I)?' It is by now well-known that the narrative logic of classical film is powered by the desire to establish, by the end of the film, the nature of masculinity, the nature of femininity, and the way in which those two can be complementary rather than antagonistic.[11] But in film and television, as elsewhere, it is becoming increasingly difficult to *tell the difference*. As men and women are less and less differentiated by a division of labour, what, in fact, makes them different? And how can classical film still construct the difference so crucial to its formula for narrative closure? Ironically, it is science fiction film – our hoariest and seemingly most sexless genre – that alone remains capable of supplying the configurations of sexual difference required by the classical cinema. If there is increasingly less practical difference between men and women, there is more than enough difference between a human and an alien (*The Man Who Fell to Earth*, *Starman*), a human and a cyborg/replicant (*Android*, *Blade Runner*) or a human from the present and one from the future (*The Terminator*). In these films the question of sexual difference – a question whose answer is no longer 'self-evident' – is displaced onto the more remarkable difference between the human and the other. That this questioning of the difference between human and other is sexual in nature, can also be seen in the way these films reactivate infantile sexual investigation. One of the big questions for the viewer of *Blade Runner*, for example, is 'How do replicants do it?' Or, of *The Man Who Fell to Earth*, 'What is the sex of this alien who possesses nothing that resembles human genitals (its sex organs are in its hands)?'

But if recent science fiction film provides the heightened sense of difference necessary to the classical narrative, it also offers the reassurance of difference *itself*. In describing one important aspect of the shift in the psychical economy from the nineteenth century to the twentieth century, Raymond Bellour maintains that in the nineteenth century men looked at women and

feared they were different, but in the twentieth century men look at women and fear they are the same.[12] The majority of science fiction films work to dissipate that fear of the same, to ensure that there is a difference. A very instructive example is the NBC miniseries *V*, broadcast during the 1983–84 season. A rare instance of science fiction on television (*Star Trek* to the contrary, the television industry insists that science fiction does not work on television), *V* tried to be as topical and up-to-date as possible, particularly in the roles it gave to women. The Commander of the alien force that takes over Earth's major cities, the Supreme commander of the aliens, the leader of the Earthling guerrillas, and the leader of the alien fifth column aiding the Earthlings, are all played by women. They are seen performing the same activities as the men (planning, fighting, counterattacking, infiltrating, etc.), thus removing the most important visible signs of difference. The only difference remaining in *V* is that between the aliens (scaly, green reptiles in human disguise) and the humans. That difference, however, comes to represent sexual difference, as if the alien/human difference were a projection of what can no longer be depicted otherwise.[13] The leader of the guerrillas is captured and brainwashed by the alien commander. Although she is eventually rescued by her comrades, it is feared that the brainwashing has turned her into an alien. She even begins using her left hand rather than her right one, a reptile-alien characteristic. Thus when she and her boyfriend, the second in command of the guerillas, are shown making love, we realise, as they do, that this could be interspecies sex – the blond, all-American Julie may be a lizard underneath it all, whether in fact or in mind. It gives the otherwise banal proceedings a powerful source of dramatic tension, while it reassures TV-viewing audiences everywhere that there is a difference. (Such a radical disposition of difference always risks, of course, tipping over into the horror of *too much* difference.)

Similarly, it is instructive to see how *Aliens*, directed by James Cameron following his success with *The Terminator*, cracks under the strain of trying to keep to the very original *lack* of sexual differentiation in its precursor, Ridley Scott's *Alien* (not counting, of course, the penultimate scene of Ripley in her bikini underwear). Dan O'Bannon's treatment for the first film was unique in writing each role to be played by either a man or a woman.[14] Ridley Scott's direction followed through on this idea, producing a film that is (for the most part) stunningly egalitarian. In attempting to repeat the equal-opportunity camaraderie of the first film, Cameron's sequel includes a mixed squad of marines, in which the women are shown to be as tough as the men, maybe tougher. And Ripley is, again, the bravest and smartest member of the team. But this time there is a difference, one that is both improbable and symptomatic. Ripley 'develops' a maternal instinct, risking her life to save the little girl who is the only survivor of a group of space colonists decimated by the aliens. Tenaciously protective, she takes on the mother alien, whose sublime capacity for destruction is shown nonetheless to result from the same kind of maternal love that Ripley exhibits. Ripley is thus marked by a difference that is automatically taken to be a sign of femininity. (We do not see Hicks, for example – played by Michael Biehn, who was Kyle Reese in The Terminator – acting irrationally in order to rescue a child who is probably already dead.) Aliens reintroduces the issue of sexual difference, but not in order to offer a newer, more modern configuration of that difference. Rather, by focusing on Ripley alone (Hicks is awkwardly 'disappeared' from the film in the closing moments), the question of the couple is supplanted by the problem of the woman as mother. What we get finally is a conservative moral lesson about maternity, futuristic or otherwise: mothers will be mothers, and they will always be women. We can conclude that even when there is not much sex in science fiction, there is nonetheless a great deal about sexuality, here reduced to phallic motherhood: Ripley in the robot-expediter is simply the Terminator turned inside out.

Just as it is ironic that science fiction film can give us the sharper notion of sexual difference lost from contemporary classical film, so too it is ironic that when this genre does depict sexual activity, it offers some of the most effective instances of eroticism in recent film. The dearth of eroticism in current filmmaking is pointed up by Woody Allen's success in providing the paradigm of the only kind of sexual difference we have left: the incompatibility of the man's neuroses with the woman's neuroses. Understandably, this is not very erotic. But science fiction film, in giving us an extreme

version of sexual difference, coincides with the requirements of the erotic formula, one which describes a fantasy of absolute difference and absolute complementarity (the quality of being complementary, of course, depending upon the establishment of difference). Unlike in classical cinema, the science fiction couple is often not the product of a long process of narrative differentiation; rather, the man and the woman are different from the very beginning. The narrative can then focus on them together and the exterior obstacles they must overcome to remain a couple. The erotic formula has, in fact, two parts: first, the two members of the couple must be marked as clearly different. (In non-science fiction film, for example, she is a nun, he is a priest; she is white, he is black, she is a middle-class widow, he is a young working-class man; she is French, he is German/Japanese, etc.) Second, one of the two must die or at least be threatened by death. If the man and the woman, in their absolute difference, are absolutely complementary, then there is nothing left to be desired. Something has to be taken away to regenerate desire and the narrative. Thus, although the lovemaking scene in The Terminator is not a very distinguished one in terms of the relatively perfunctory way that it was filmed, it nonetheless packs a strong erotic charge, in its narrative context because it is a kiss across time, a kiss between a man from the future and a woman from the present, an act of love pervaded by death. For Kyle has to die in order to justify the coda, in which Sarah ensures the continuity of the story, now a legend, of their love for each other.

Time Travel as Primal Scene: La Jetée

If time travel stories are fantasies of origins, they are also fantasies of endings. Mark Rose has pointed out that many of the narratives that deal with time travel tend to be fictions of apocalypse.[15] (As in The Terminator, however, these visions of endings may also be visions of new beginnings – in the Genesis version, after God destroys the world by flood, it is Sarah who is anointed 'mother of all nations'.) Rose cites Frank Kermode's The Sense of an Ending to show that we create fictions of endings to give meaning to time, to transform chronos – mere passing time – into kairos, time invested with the meaning derived from its goal. History is given shape, is made understandable by spatialising time, by seeing it as a line along which one can travel. Such spatialisation of time, however, introduces the paradox of time travel. 'Much of the fascination of the time loop is related to the fact that it represents the point at which the spatialisation of time breaks down' (Rose, 108). If I could travel back into the past, I could (theoretically) murder my own grandmother. But I would cease to exist. How then could I have murdered her?

If this example illustrates the collapse of time as we know it, it also shows that it is impossible to separate ourselves from time. (The time traveler who murders her grand-mother ceases to exist.) Thus time travel paradox narratives typically explore either the question of the end of time or the reciprocal relation between ourselves and time (Rose, 108). Although *The Terminator* is concerned with both apocalypse and the question of time in relation to personal identity, another film which preceded it by more than 20 years, Chris Marker's *La Jetée*, weaves the two together in a way that still haunts the spectator of this stunning film. *The Terminator*, in fact, bears such an uncanny resemblance to *La Jetée* that Cameron's film could almost be its mass-culture remake. Marker's film too is about a post-apocalyptic man who is chosen to be a time traveller because of his fixation on an image of the past. It too involves a love affair between a woman from the present and a man from the future, and an attempt to keep humanity from being wiped out.

A crucial difference between *The Terminator* and *La Jetée*, however, is that Marker's film explicitly addresses the paradox of time travel. After being sent on numerous journeys through time, *La Jetée*'s time traveller attempts to return to the scene from his childhood that had marked him so deeply. On that day, a Sunday afternoon before a third World War which will drive the few remaining survivors underground, his parents had brought him to Orly to watch the planes take off. He remembers seeing the sun fixed in the sky, a scene at the end of the jetty, and a woman's face. Then, a sudden noise, the woman's gesture, a crumbling body, the cries of the crowd. Later, the voice-over tells us, he knew that he had seen a man die. When he tries to return to that Sunday at Orly, he is killed by one of the scientists from the underground camp who had sent him voyaging through time; they no longer have any use for him. The moment, then,

that he had been privileged to see as a child and which had never stopped haunting him, was the moment of his own death. In the logic of this film he has to die, because such a logic acknowledges the temporal impossibility of being in the same place as both adult and child. In *La Jetée* one cannot be and have been.

The film goes even further when it insists on the similar paradox at work in the primal scene fantasy by depicting the psychical consequence of attempting to return to a scene from one's childhood: such a compulsion to repeat, and the regression that it implies, leads to the annihilation of the subject.[16] But the subject is also extinguished in another way, this time through a symbolic castration depicted as a very real death. The woman he is searching for is at the end of the jetty, but so is the man whose job it is to prevent him from possessing her, the man and the woman on the jetty mirroring the parental (Oedipal) couple that brought the little boy to the airport. (This film's version of the Terminator succeeds in its mission.) While *The Terminator* gives us a time travel story that depends upon a primal scene fantasy for its unconscious appeal, its fantasmatic force, *La Jetée* shows that the two are one and the same: the fantasy of time travel is no more nor less than the compulsion to repeat that which manifests itself in the primal scene fantasy. Moreover, since *La Jetée*'s circular narrative is wholly organised as a 'beginning toward which [one] is constantly moving',[17] it suggests that all film viewing is infantile sexual investigation.

The Terminator, in many respects, merely abstracts and reifies *La Jetée*'s major elements. Marker's film, for example, is composed almost entirely of still images, photographs that dissolve in and out of one another in a way that constantly edges toward the illusion of 'real' filmic movement. As Thierry Kuntzel has pointed out,[18] such a technique allows *La Jetée* to be a film about movement in film, and our desire for movement. Using still images to make a film is also a perfect way to tell a time travel story because it offers the possibility of mixing two different temporalities: the 'pastness' of the photographic image and the 'here-nowness' of the illusionistic (filmic) movement.[19]

Although I suggested that *The Terminator* could be seen as the industry remake of *La Jetée*, it should now be clear that Marker's film could not be remade because in its very structure it is unrepeatable. Inasmuch as it acknowledges the paradox of the time loop and rejects the rosy nostalgia of a wish-fulfilling version of the primal scene fantasy, it is not likely remake material with respect to popular film's demand for pleasure without (obvious) paradox. Similarly, one could not imagine a sequel to La Jetée because of the way the film collapses time in its rigorous observance of the fatalistic logic of time travel. But one can be sure that Terminators is already more than a gleam in a producer's eye. After all, what is to stop John Conner, in another possible future, from sending Kyle Reese back in time again, but at a later date, perhaps so that he could rendezvous with Sarah in her South of the Border hide-out?

Would it not be too easy, however, to conclude by pitting La Jetée against The Terminator? To end by falling back on less-than-useful dichotomies like the avant-garde versus Hollywood or even the Symbolic versus the Imaginary? It is true that La Jetée is governed by 'the laws of recollection and symbolic recognition' (in Lacan's terms) while The Terminator is ruled by 'the laws of imaginary reminiscence'.[20] But it is precisely the way The Terminator harnesses the power of 'imaginary reminiscence' (the primal scene fantasy of time travel) that allows it to present one of the most forceful of recent science fiction tales about the origins of techno-apocalypse. The film is able to do so, as I have argued, by generalising its core of fantasy through the systematic use of the topical and everyday, reminding us that the future is now. As a critical dystopia, The Terminator thus goes beyond the flashy nihilism of apocalypse-for-the-sake-of-apocalypse to expose a more mundane logic of technological modernity, even if it is one that is, finally, no less catastrophic.

Notes

1 Fredric Jameson, 'Progress Versus Utopia; or Can We Imagine the Future?', Science Fiction Studies 9 (1982).

2 Stanislaw Lem, 'Cosmology and Science Fiction', trans. Franz Rottenstein, Science Fiction Studies 4 (1977), p.109.

3 Randall Frakes and Bill Wisher, The Terminator (a novel based on the screenplay by James Cameron with Gale Anne Hurd) (New York: Bantam Books, 1984).

4 See Jessie L. Weston, From Ritual to Romance: An Account of the Holy Grail from Ancient Ritual to Christian Symbol (Cambridge: Cambridge University Press, 1920), pp. 42–8.

5 For a full and very interesting discussion of the political dimensions of the cyborg, see Donna Haraway, 'A Manifesto for Cyborgs: Science, Technology, and Socialist Feminism in the 1980s', Socialist Review, no. 80 (March–April, 1985) [reprinted in this volume].

6 Useful essays on time travel and its paradoxes include Stanislaw Lem, 'The Time-Travel Story and Related Matters of SF Structuring', Science Fiction Studies 1, 1974; Monte Cook, 'Tips for Time Travel', Philosophers Look at Science Fiction (Chicago: Nelson-Hall, 1982); and David Lewis, 'The Paradoxes of Time Travel', Thought Probes, eds. Fred D. Miller, Jr. and Nicholas D. Smith (New Jersey: Prentice Hall, 1981).

7 Sigmund Freud, 'The Paths to the Formation of Symptoms', The Standard Edition of the Complete Psychological Works of Sigmund Freud, ed. and trans. James Strachey (London: Hogarth Press, 1958), vol. 16, p. 370.

8 See, among others, Elisabeth Lyon, 'The Cinema of Lol V. Stein', Camera Obscura no. 6 (1980); Elizabeth Cowie, 'Fantasia', m/f no. 9 (1984); and Steve Neale, 'Sexual Difference in Cinema', Sexual Difference, special issue of The Oxford Literary Review 8, nos. 1–2 (1986).

9 For the best formulation of this idea, see Joan Copjec, 'India Song/Son nom de Venise dans Calcutta désert: The Compulsion to Repeat', October 17 (Summer 1981).

10 Brian Henderson, 'The Searchers: An American Dilemma', Film Quarterly 34, no. 2 (Winter 1980–81); reprinted in Movies and Methods Vol. II, ed. Bill Nichols (Berkeley: University of California Press, 1985).

11 There are, of course, important exceptions to this standard narrative logic, as Jacqueline Rose has shown, for example, in her analysis of The Birds, in which Mitch's 'successful' attainment of a masculine and paternal identity comes at the price of regression and catatonia for Melanie. 'Paranoia and the Film System', Screen 17, no. 4 (Winter 1976–77).

12 Raymond Bellour, 'Un jour, la castration', L'Arc, special issue on Alexandre Dumas, no. 71 (1978).

13 This wholly unremarkable series seems surprisingly capable of taking on a great deal of cultural resonance in its radical presentation of 'difference'. Andrew Kopkind (The Nation 243, no. 17, Nov. 22, 1986) reports that V is currently one of the most popular shows in South Africa. He speculates that the show's success lies in the unconsciously ironic, allegorical reading that it allows. Kopkind cites the newspaper description of the week's episode (broadcast on the state-controlled television channel): TV 4: 9:03, 'Visitor's Choice'. The Resistance Stages a daring attack at a convention of Visitor Commanders where Diana intends to show off the ultimate device in processing humans for food. Robit Hairman in The Voice (Jan. 13, 1987) also reports on the cult that has grown up around V in South Africa because of the allegorical readings that escaped the government

censors. Before the series was over, anti-government forces were spraying slogans from the series on walls in Johannesburg and Soweto, and T-shirts with a large *V* painted on front and back became a feature on the streets: '*V* joined the mythology of the resistance.' There are also at least two fanzines devoted to *V*, the newest of which, 'The Resistance Chronicles', describes its first issue in terms that evoke infantile sexual investigation: 'This volume will contain the answers to the following burning questions – Why is that blue Chevy with the fogged-up windows rocking back and forth??? How does Chris Farber feel about virtue … and boobs? What colour underwear does Ham Tyler wear? What do Ham and Chris keep in their medicine cabinet?' Plus a musical *V* parody, 'We're off to See the Lizard…'. Description taken from *Datazine*, no. 44 (Oct.–Nov. 1986).

14 Danny Peary reports this in his interview with Sigourney Weaver, 'Playing Ripley in *Alien*', *OMNI's Screen Flights/ Screen Fantasies: The Future According to Science Fiction Cinema*, ed. Danny Peary (Garden City, N.Y.: Doubleday, 1984), p. 162.

15 Mark Rose, *Alien Encounters: Anatomy of Science Fiction* (Cambridge, M.A..: Harvard University Press, 1981), p. 99.

16 My discussion of primal scene fantasy in *La Jetée* is indebted to Thierry Kuntzel's lectures on that topic in his 1975–76 seminar at the American University Center for Film Studies in Paris.

17 Ned Lukacher's formulation of the primal scene fantasy in *Primal Scenes: Literature, Philosophy, Psychoanalysis* (Ithaca: Cornell University Press, 1986), p. 42. This book contains the best recent discussion of the structure of the primal scene fantasy.

18 In his lectures on *La Jetée* at the American University Center for Film Studies.

19 The distinction is made by Roland Barthes in 'Rhetoric of the Image', trans. Stephen Heath (New York: Hill and Wang, 1977), p. 45.

20 Jacques Lacan, *Ecrits: A Selection* (New York: Norton, 1977), p. 141. A distinction cited by Lukacher, p. 43.

Another Time, Another Space: Modernity, Subjectivity and *The Time Machine*
Jonathan Bignell

H. G. Wells' science fiction novels have long been attractive to filmmakers. Film versions include *The Island of Dr Moreau* (Erle C. Kenton, 1932 [titled *The Island of Lost Souls*], Don Taylor, 1977, John Frankenheimer, 1996), *The Invisible Man* (James Whale, 1933, sequels Joe May, 1940, Ford Beebe, 1944), *Things to Come* (William Cameron Menzies, 1936), and *War of the Worlds* (Byron Haskin, 1953). I want to focus here on Wells's short novel *The Time Machine*, first published in 1895, and the film adaptation directed by George Pal (1960).[1] *The Time Machine* does feature strange creatures, but not aliens in the usual science fiction sense. The central character, unnamed in the novel but called George Wells in the film, is a late-nineteenth-century inventor who constructs a sled-like vehicle enabling him to travel into the future. In the year 802,701, the Time Traveller discovers two races of humanoids, the Eloi and the Morlocks. In the novel the frail and childlike Eloi are the passive and effete descendants of the elite of an advanced society, living in a sunlit paradise on the surface. The Morlocks are the ape-like cannibal descendants of the workers who operated the subterranean machines that kept this elite supplied with all its needs. This vision of the future counters the Victorian myth of progress, and explores the interdependence of workers and masters, perverted into the dependence of the Morlocks on the flesh of the Eloi who they formerly served. The Time Traveller realises that evolutionary development toward technical refinement and social order will lead to decadence (in the Eloi) and to savagery (in the Morlocks) at the same time.

In Pal's film version, a global war fought with nuclear weapons has exhausted the resources of this future society, and the remnants of the race have divided into those who continued to dwell on the irradiated surface (who became the Eloi) and those who stayed in underground shelters (and became the Morlocks). Clearly, the Cold War nuclear fears of 1960 have informed the future vision of Pal's film, just as anxieties around Darwinism and class conflict fuel the novel. The changes made to the narrative in the film version essentially involve the updating of the journey into the future so that the fears and fantasies of 1960 can be included.[2] Each version of *The Time Machine* explores future times which are by definition alien to the audience, but this alienness is necessarily consonant with familiar ideas.

My focus here is less on the alienness of the creatures in the future than on the alienness yet familiarity of the time travel experience and the futuristic settings of the story. The Time Traveller becomes a spectator who watches time move like a speeded-up film, and stops several times to explore the future scene. Like the cinema spectator, the Time Traveller sits on a red plush seat and watches a marvellous spectacle, and the journey into the future depends on a machine, a technological apparatus rather than magic or dream. The subjective experience being outlined in the novel is a subjectivity to be developed in cinema and in modern consumer culture in general, where technology transports the consumer to a virtual environment primarily experienced visually. Temporal mobility in *The Time Machine*, as in cinema, allows the subject to encounter what is alien, yet necessarily familiarises this as a consumable media experience. But time travel allows more than a cinematic visual spectacle. Since the hundreds of centuries traversed in the Time Traveller's fictional journey involve changes in buildings, people and even the geology of the landscape, the journey through time is in effect a tourist trip to alien spaces that he can leave his seat to explore. The Time Machine itself, as described in the novel and portrayed in Pal's film, looks like a sled with brass rails and over-decorated Victorian ornaments. It has a large revolving dish mounted vertically behind the inventor, and coloured lights and indicators on its control surface. The Time

Machine is envisioned on an analogy with a machine for travelling in space rather than time, signalling the association between temporal movement and spatial movement.

Both the novel and the film are predicated on what Anne Friedberg has called a 'mobilised virtual gaze', a characteristic aspect of modernity developing through the nineteenth century into the twentieth, whereby movement in space and time is simulated by visual apparatuses of representation: 'The virtual gaze is not a direct perception but a *received* perception mediated through representation. I introduce this compound term in order to describe a gaze that travels in an imaginary *flânerie* through an imaginary elsewhere and an imaginary elsewhen.'[3] Wells's fictional Time Traveller experiences the future directly, but the reader of the story and the viewer of the film experience a mediated version of this, mediated through language in the novel, and through the visual and aural resources of cinema in the film. The reader or spectator becomes a *flâneur* or stroller, led on an exploratory journey through alien worlds. Friedberg continues: 'The cinema developed as an apparatus that combined the 'mobile' with the 'virtual'. Hence, cinematic spectatorship changed, in unprecedented ways, the concepts of the *present* and the *real*.'[4] In both Wells's novel and Pal's film adaptation, travel in time is experienced predominantly as a visual experience. But one of the main attractions of the novel and the film is the ability to stop the headlong rush into the future, so that the Traveller can stop and stroll around in a realistically presented space. Time travel, like cinema, renders the moment virtual in order to allow a real-seeming experience of an alien space-time. Time travellers and cinema spectators are displaced from the reality of their own present and their own real location in order to be transported to 'an imaginary elsewhere and an imaginary elsewhen'.

The opening of Pal's film makes it clear that it is the cinema spectator who will be moved in virtual space and time and who will become the virtual subject of the time travel experience. It begins with a collection of brightly-lit timepieces, appearing in chronological order of their invention, moving out of the black and dimensionless space of the screen towards the spectator. It is as if the spectator is travelling through space, plunging headlong into black emptiness with the cinema screen functioning as a window onto the journey. The final clock is London's Big Ben, tilted at an angle, as the hour is heard to strike. Lightning flashes and thunder crashes as the shot changes to a rapidly rising sun over which the film's title is superimposed. Then leaves and snow blow across a blue sky, succeeding each other rapidly as the seasons rush past. The first scene establishes the interior of the inventor's house, and the camera pans over a large collection of watches, mantel clocks and grandfather clocks, continuing the time motif and associating the spectator's own plunge through time with the interests of the central character. Already we can see that there is a slippage between the spectating subject in the cinema and the central time-travelling character. Furthermore, travel in time is parallel to travel in space, as the rushing forward movement past a series of clocks makes rather literally evident.

George Pal was drawn to Wells' story in part because it provided opportunities for state-of-the-art visual effects. His film version of *The Time Machine* uses many techniques including accelerated motion, reverse motion, pixellation, model shots and mattes to render the experience of time travel, and the future worlds the Traveller encounters, with as much verisimilitude as was possible in 1960. Pal was a specialist in these technologies of illusion. He began his career as a puppeteer making short advertising films in the late 1930s. In 1940 he went to Hollywood and moved on to adventure films where he specialised in trick effects, receiving an Academy Award in 1943 for his development of innovative methods and techniques. The films he worked on included *Destination Moon* (Irving Pichel, 1950), *When Worlds Collide* (Rudolph Maté, 1951), *War of the Worlds*, *Tom Thumb*

(1958, which he also directed) and *The Time Machine*. All of these films won Oscars for their special effects. Pal's special skill, then, was to realise the incredible, to make the alien and strange comprehensible according to visual conventions we can accept. In this respect he was part of a long tradition in cinema where, since the emergence of the medium, film had been used as a support for wondrous spectacles, where what was absent, novel, distant or unfamiliar became vividly present as part of an entertainment for the paying consumer.

Science fiction, historiography and archaeology, which all blossomed in the later decades of the nineteenth century, share an interest in time: representing a future moment, a documented moment in the past, or an arrested time which we can uncover and see. Time travel in literature in the work of Wells or Jules Verne appears at the same period as stories about lost civilisations in Conan Doyle's *The Lost World*, and novels by Bulwer Lytton and Butler. It is in this period that Roman sites in Britain, the pyramids and Mycenae were excavated, and Arthur Evans recreated parts of the Bronze Age city of Knossos in Crete so that tourists could walk around it. The common feature in these different aspects of culture is the refinement of techniques of representation which can make what is past, absent or fantastic into something which can be recreated, simulated and rendered virtually present for an individual subject. Similarly, the beginning of cinema is associated with nineteenth-century science's quest for knowledge of the physical world, with that period's obsession with memory, death and preservation, with fairground trick effects, magic and the supernatural, and with the possibilities of exploiting mechanical inventions for a mass consumer public. All of these aspects of the culture of modernity are signalled near the beginning of *The Time Machine*. The story is told mainly in flashback in both the novel and in Pal's film, as a dishevelled inventor appears late to meet his houseguests, and tells the story of his time travels. The first flashback returns us to the day when his guests were

shown a model Time Machine vanishing, an experiment which all four of them believe may be a parlour trick, like the seances, magic lantern shows and short novelty films of the period. Like the spectators of the first films, the Time Traveller's audiences are thrown into doubt about the evidence of their own eyes. For them, the disappearance of the model Time Machine might be real, but more likely a trick, a simulation, a scientific demonstration or an optical illusion. *The Time Machine*, then, exploits the distinction between the virtual and the real, a distinction fundamental to the culture of modernity and to cinema.

Wells' novel was written amid a long-standing fascination with visually-based representational devices in the late nineteenth century, exemplified by the dioramas, panoramas and other proto-cinematic devices of the period. Dioramas and panoramas were buildings where groups of spectators were presented with large back-lit illuminated images painted on semi-transparent screens, and used highly realistic painted backdrops and carefully arranged effects of perspective and depth of field to seem to place the spectator in a remote landscape, or at the occurrence of a famous past event. They offered the viewer a highly realistic visual environment, representing places to which the great majority of people could never go. These devices were enthralling because they transported the spectator to alien places and alien times by means of visual technologies and supporting special effects. What was there to be seen might be alien, a vision of another place and another time, but the whole spectacle depended on the spectator's familiarity with how to look, and on some familiarity with the cultural significance of what was represented. Effects of perspective, of the play of light and shade, were carefully calculated to be as real-seeming as possible, to allow the spectator to immerse himself or herself in the sense of 'being there' in the scene. Although the spectator would never have visited the great cathedral of Chartres, the eve of the Battle of Waterloo or the Swiss Alps, these places and events had already to be culturally established as significant and recognisable, so that there was a peculiar thrill in seeing them in all their grandeur. Like any consumer technology or media experience, the new, the alien, the surprising, had to be balanced with the expected, the familiar and the conventional.

In the novel and the film, time travel is a curious mixture of scientific experiment and fairground thrills. The experience of time travel gives the inventor in the novel 'a feeling exactly like that one has upon a switchback – of a helpless headlong motion!'[5] The Doctor in Pal's film version, one of the inventor's guests, suggests that the Time Machine is of no use or commercial value. Instead, he recommends that the inventor should do something to help Britain in the ongoing Boer War. The inventor is presented as a scientist who resists the military or commercial potential of his work, and his trip into the future seems to be an escape from war and commerce. As if escaping into the virtual world of the cinema, to a film in which he is both spectator and central character, the Time Traveller quits the time and space of his quotidian present. As Walter Benjamin wrote:

> Our taverns and our metropolitan streets, our railroad stations and our factories appeared to have locked us up hopelessly. Then came the film and burst this prison-world asunder by the dynamite of the tenth of a second, so that now, in the midst of its far-flung ruins and debris, we calmly and adventurously go travelling.[6]

Like the newly invented cinema, time travel frees the subject from the present and the real, to replace these with a virtual present and a virtual reality which is novel, exciting and technological. Like cinema technology, time travel seems to offer opportunities for science as well as tourism and commercial entertainment, yet the appeal of both Wells's story and of Pal's film is based on the pleasures of fantasy and speculation which they offer, rather than the exploration of the

the science fiction film reader

geometric and physical principles which each version refers to in order to ground time travel in scientific fact.

While early pioneers used film to explore the science of animal movement and to record contemporary life, entertainment rapidly became the most commercially successful use for the new technology. In 1894 the first Edison Kinetoscope parlour opened in New York, offering films of less than a minute, viewed by individual spectators who peeked into the Kinetoscope cabinets to see vaudeville performers and famous personalities. The film historian Terry Ramsaye wrote to Wells in 1924 asking whether the idea for *The Time Machine* was born from Wells's experience of the Edison Kinetoscope.[7] Wells replied that he did not remember any connection between early motion pictures and the writing of the story, though the description of the Time Traveller's first jaunt into the future is highly suggestive of cinema. The Time Traveller is in his laboratory, and catches sight of his housekeeper just before he accelerates forward in time:

> Mrs. Watchett came in and walked, apparently without seeing me, towards the garden door. I suppose it took her a minute or so to traverse the place, but to me she seemed to shoot across the room like a rocket. I pressed the lever to its extreme position. The night came like the turning out of a lamp, and in another moment came tomorrow. The laboratory grew faint and hazy, then fainter and ever fainter. Tomorrow night came black, then day again, night again, day again, faster and faster still.[8]

The experience is entirely visual and places the Time Traveller in the role of filmmaker (controlling the machine) and spectator at the same time. As he speeds forward, the flickering motion of a film projector is suggested in the rapid alternation of day and night. The Kinetoscope allowed the novelty of seeing simple action speeded up or reversed, which was one of the most entertaining aspects of early films for their spectators. Films showed the acceleration of mechanical or natural processes (like the growth of plants), and this is mirrored when the Time Traveller sees 'great and splendid architecture rising about me, more massive than any buildings of our own time, and yet, as it seemed, built of glimmer and mist. I saw a richer green flow up the hillside, and remain there without any wintry intermission.'[9] When the Time Traveller returns to his original time, he sees accelerated reverse motion:

> I think I have told you that when I set out, before my velocity became very high, Mrs. Watchett had walked across the room, travelling, as it seemed to me, like a rocket. As I returned, I passed again across that minute when she traversed the laboratory. But now every motion appeared to be the exact inversion of her previous ones. The door at the lower end opened, and she glided quietly up the laboratory, back foremost, and disappeared behind the door by which she had previously entered.[10]

What both time travel and cinema can do is to make the familiar appear unfamiliar by changing the manner of its perception. What is rapid can be slowed down, what moves slowly can be speeded up, and forward motion can be reversed. Time travel and cinema seem to show the spectator the workings of the laws of nature, granting him or her a special perception, which makes the ordinary marvellous and strange.

In Pal's film, the first journey through time uses various cinematic trick effects, and the laboratory has a large glazed wall which enables it to function like a cinema screen, through which the inventor seated at the machine can see a panorama of the changing world outside. Special effects include fast-motion shots of the sun and clouds moving across the sky, a snail speeding across the floor, shadow and light flitting across the inventor and the machine, and people moving rapidly in the street across from the laboratory. While the sequence is anchored through shot/reverse-shots to George's point of view, many of the fast motion sequences are not from his spatial position, and function to make us share George's wonder and disorientation (noted in the voice-over narration) as he makes this short hop into the future. Time travel and cinema place the spectator in a privileged position, able to see movement in a way alien to normal experience. Because the Time Traveller is moving so rapidly through time, the people he sees cannot see him, and events unfold as if he were not present. One of the components of cinematic pleasure explored by Christian Metz[11] and other film theorists is exactly this transcendent vision, where the cinema spectator seems to master and control what is seen on the screen, while being excluded from the action and removed from responsibility for it. The Time Traveller at this point, and the cinema spectator, are both apparent masters of vision, and also voyeurs of a world which they cannot enter.

In 1895 the Lumière brothers showed the first publicly projected films in Paris, exhibited at the Empire Music Hall in London in 1896. Also in 1895, the year *The Time Machine* was published, Robert Paul, a scientific instrument-maker from London who had copied and improved the Kinetoscope, designed a motion picture camera with his collaborator the photographer Birt Acres. By 1896 Robert Paul was showing his own films at Olympia in London and the Alhambra music hall, and had made the first British fiction film, *The Soldier's Courtship*. Ramsaye reports that Robert Paul read *The Time Machine* soon after its publication, and it gave him an idea for a new way to use the film medium.[12] Paul wrote to Wells, who visited him at his London studio. After the meeting with Wells, Paul entered patent application no. 19984, dated 24 October 1895, for 'A Novel Form of Exhibition or Entertainment, Means for Presenting the Same'.[13] It begins:

> My invention consists of a novel form of exhibition whereby the spectators have presented to their view scenes which are supposed to occur in the future or the past, while they are given the sensation of voyaging upon a machine through time.[14]

Paul's invention was never built, due to lack of funds, and belonged among a rash of inventions at the turn of the century which were combinations of film with diorama-like attractions or fairground magic effects. In 1904, for instance, at the St Louis Exhibition, George C. Hale presented Hale's Tours, where travelogue films were shown to spectators seated in a railway carriage, with train sound effects and a wobbling floor to simulate movement. The similarities between the descriptions of time travel in Wells's novel and the experience of cinema seem to have triggered Paul's idea for a virtual time travel attraction exploiting aspects of several recently invented technologies.

The mechanism was to be a 'platform, or platforms' which could contain a group of spectators enclosed on three sides, facing a screen on which 'views' were to be projected. The platform would be moved by cranks to produce 'a gentle rocking motion'.[15] While the platform was moving, fans would blow air over the spectators, simulating the effect of motion, or the fans could be visibly attached to the platform as if they were a means of propulsion.

> After the starting of the mechanism, and a suitable period having elapsed, representing, say, a certain number of centuries, during which the platforms may be in darkness, or in alternations of darkness and dim light, the mechanism may be slowed and a pause made at a given epoch, on which the scene upon the screen will gradually come into view of the spectators, increasing in size and distinctness from a small vista, until the figures, etc., may appear lifelike if desired.[16]

Time travel would be simulated, as in Wells' novel, by a motion not unlike a fairground ride, and would involve passages from darkness to light reminiscent of Wells' description. It was important that the scene should be 'realistic', showing a 'hypothetical landscape, containing also the representations of the inanimate objects in the scene', and would use slides showing moving objects like a balloon which could 'traverse the scene'.[17] There would also

be 'slides or films, representing in successive instantaneous photographs, after the manner of the kinetoscope, the living persons or creatures in their natural motions'.[18] To produce dissolves and to enlarge or reduce the picture area, the projectors would be mounted on moveable tracks, which could bring them closer to or further from the screen. Paul's invention reproduces Wells's fictional time travel experience quite closely: putting the spectator into a conveyance like a switchback car, so that travel in time felt not unlike travel in space, and presenting the journey through time as a movement through light and darkness where the spectator stops to see a future epoch in the form of a film. While the alienness of the experience is what is attractive, it resembles familiar experiences like a fairground ride and a film show.

In some ways, Paul's invention looks forward to the experience of watching Pal's 1960 film. Pal's film can offer a modern cinematic experience, where trick effects, synchronous sound and music, and the use of cuts and camera movement have been developed to encourage the spectator's identification with the action, a sense of verisimilitude and dramatic pacing. Despite the futuristic settings of the film, and the alienness of the creatures in the future (especially the blue-skinned, shaggy-haired and sharp-toothed Morlocks), by 1960 cinema was calculated to produce an impression of reality. Paul's invention drew on the familiar technology of nineteenth-century amusement parks, such as the movement of the car and the blowing of air over the spectators, to produce similar effects. Following the practice at dioramas and panoramas, Paul also planned to use built sets which the spectators could physically explore:

> In order to increase the realistic effect I may arrange that after a number of scenes from a hypothetical future have been presented to the spectators, they may be allowed to step from the platforms, and be conducted through grounds or buildings arranged to

represent exactly one of the epochs through which the spectator is supposed to be travelling.[19]

Here physical movement and temporal movement appear together, and the spectating subject literally becomes a *flâneur* or stroller, on a tourist trip, complete with guide, through a three-dimensional simulation of the future. In Wells's novel and in Pal's film this experience has to be mediated through the spectator's identification with the Time Traveller himself, who narrates his journeys and describes his wonderment at what he sees, and whose point of view in the film is aligned with the camera as he enters buildings and explores new landscapes. In *The Time Machine* the Time Traveller is not only a voyeur but also a tourist having adventures in future locations, and Paul's invention clearly aimed to replicate this kind of experience.

In Pal's film the inventor stops to look around in 1917, 1940 and 1966. These interludes give the film the chance to create street scenes reminiscent of one of Robert Paul's future environments. The immediate space around the Time Traveller is a dressed set in each case, using glass shots for background, and different cars, costumes and shopfronts to establish location in time. In 1940 Pal departs from the Time Traveller's point of view and uses stock shots of blazing fighter planes, and a diorama model of London in the Blitz, but then from the Time Traveller's point of view the spectator witnesses post-war reconstruction. New concrete buildings rise and cranes and scaffolding grow up at high speed accompanied by jaunty music on the soundtrack. Accelerated motion is intended to be comic here, just as it was when the projector's ability to change the speed of natural movement was realised at the turn of the century. So far, the film has represented the known past in 1960, aiming for visual verisimilitude and focusing thematically on the immediate effects of war. In 1966, the projected future from the perspective of 1960 is like a sunny American suburb. The inventor's house (destroyed by a wartime bomb) has been replaced by a

park. The local shop, which had become a department store by 1917, is now a glass and concrete shopping mall, and shiny American cars are in the street. The film's thematic emphasis on the effects of war continues as extras rush past and an air-raid siren sounds. As well as continuing the precise simulation of a realistic location, the film presents the future by extrapolation from a relatively pessimistic vision of humankind's folly. This virtual future environment is alien but familiar, all too obviously determined by a 1960 anxiety (but also shared by Wells in the 1895 novel) that the future will be the same as the present, only more so. The 1966 scene ends as an atomic blast devastates the street, volcanoes erupt, seemingly the earth's vengeance against humankind's misuse of atomic power, and lava streams shunt burned-out cars across the set.

The Time Traveller speeds forward to a landscape seen first in a wide establishing shot featuring a futuristic domed hall and tower falling into decay. Like Robert Paul's walk-through simulations of the future, the settings are 'realistic' in terms of visible detail, dimension, props and set dressing. In 802,701 the buildings and sets in Pal's film draw on an eclectic mix of forms familiar to the audience of 1960. The domed pavilions and towers are reminiscent of the structures built for Disneyland (which opened in 1955), the 1951 Festival of Britain, and other realised versions of the future built for the tourist visitor of the period. Settings are to some extent matched with contemporary preconceptions of the relation between architectural form and function, so that the dome in which decayed books and museum exhibits are found has the wide steps and frontage of a European or American palace of culture. The dark caverns inhabited by the cannibal Morlocks contain the heavy-industrial machines of a dank nineteenth-century factory, while the Morlocks' gruesome deserted dining area, littered with the bones and skulls of their Eloi prey, seems like a reconstruction of an archaeological site. The costumes of the sylvan and vegetarian Eloi are toga-like, and they are most often seen in a wooded and verdant setting like an idealised recreation of the civilisation of ancient Greece. Pal's version of the future is not visualised as a consistent environment. It is neither solely utopian nor dystopian in terms of the signification of elements of *mise-en-scène*, but draws on the cultural currency of signs in the physical environment which were in circulation in the period when the film was made. This virtual future is necessarily unlike the present the spectator knows, but far from alien because of the use of a bricolage of elements with familiar connotations and resonances.

Cinema in general, as the film theorist Jean-Louis Baudry argued, proceeds from a 'wish to construct a simulation machine capable of offering the subject perceptions which are really representations mistaken for perceptions'.[20] As theories of spectatorship have shown, the principle of cinema and other audio-visual technologies is to offer what is recognisable and familiar, balanced against the pleasures of the new, the alien, of what cannot be seen or experienced in quotidian reality. The spectator is moved through represented space and time, offered an imaginary spatial and temporary mobility. The case of *The Time Machine*, novel and film, provides a strikingly literal illustration of the principles of pleasure in representation, which cinema became focused on from a very early period in its development. A brief consideration of Paul's time travel spectacle links Wells's novel with cinema historically, showing that the novel was read, at least by someone who knew of the technical possibilities of the new medium, as a proto-cinematic experience. At the same time, as a science fiction story, *The Time Machine* reminds us that science fiction is especially significant in an examination of the subjectivity of modernity. Works in this genre often focus on spatial and temporal mobility and on the realisation of imaginary alien scenarios. The principle of science fiction is the simulation of another world which is both alien yet representable through the conventions, competencies and technologies we already know. In 1902 in France, only a few years after Wells's novel was published and Paul had entered his patent for a time

travel entertainment, the first science fiction film, *A Trip to the Moon*, was first shown. It portrayed a journey through space by means of a gigantic projectile to an alien world where strange creatures are encountered, and used theatrical sets, backdrops and trick effects drawing on the capabilities of the film camera. The film's director, Georges Méliès, had formerly made his career as a stage magician. Just a few years after Paul's idea for a time travel attraction, movement in time and space were simulated on the cinema screen, rather than by elaborate combinations of film, static images, built sets, viewing platforms and tour guides. The modern notions of travel in space and time, which Wells's novel narrated in such visual form, began to become the stock in trade of film as commercial entertainment for the individual consumer, enjoying a mobile gaze but sitting still in the auditorium. The subject in modernity, strolling either literally or by means of a mobile gaze, through a virtual reality associated with commodity consumption and mass entertainment, is both necessary to and furthered by the pleasures of cinema, time travel, science fiction and tourism.

Notes

1 Earlier and shorter versions of *The Time Machine* were 'The Chronic Argonauts', serialised in the *Science Schools Journal*, April to June 1888, and an uncredited and unfinished serial 'The Time Machine', March to June 1894 in the *National Observer*. In January to May 1895 the *New Review* published a serial 'The Time Machine' similar to the first book editions published in 1895 by Heinemann, London, and Henry Holt & Co., New York. The 1960 film *The Time Machine* was directed by George Pal, with a screenplay by David Duncan, produced by MGM/Galaxy, and stars Rod Taylor and Yvette Mimieux. Other versions of Wells's story on film and television include a faithful rendition on BBC television adapted and directed by Robert Barr (screened 25 January 1949, revised and repeated 21 February 1949), a Canadian film version directed by Terence McCarthy in 1973, and an American 1978 TV movie adaptation directed by Henning Schellerup.

2 There is insufficient space here to discuss the many diff-

143

erences between the novel and the film. For example, the endings are very different: in the novel, the Time Traveller journeys to a time when the Earth is about to become lifeless, and, depressed, he returns to collect materials for gathering specimens from the future as evidence of his travels. In the film, he falls in love with Weena, an Eloi woman, and after returning briefly to his own time he sets off again to find her.

3 Anne Friedberg, *Window Shopping: Cinema and the Post-modern* (Berkeley, CA: University of California Press, 1993), pp. 2–3.

4 Ibid.

5 H. G. Wells, *The Time Machine*, in Harry M. Geduld (ed.), *The Definitive Time Machine: A Critical Edition of H. G. Wells's Scientific Romance with Introduction and Notes* (Bloomington and Indianapolis: Indiana University Press, 1987), p. 42. Geduld uses the text of Volume 1 of the Atlantic edition of Wells's work, H. G. Wells, *The Time Machine, The Wonderful Visit and Other Stories* (New York: Charles Scribner & Sons, 1924).

6 Walter Benjamin, 'The Work of Art in the Age of Mechanical Reproduction', in *Illuminations*, trans. Harry Zorn (New York: Schocken Books, 1969), p. 316.

7 Terry Ramsaye, 'Robert Paul and *The Time Machine*' from T. Ramsaye, *A Million and One Nights* (New York: Simon & Schuster, 1926), reprinted in Geduld, The Definitive Time Machine, p. 196.

8 Wells, *Time Machine*, pp. 41–2.

9 Ibid., p. 43.

10 Ibid., p. 87.

11 Christian Metz, *The Imaginary Signifier: Psychoanalysis and the Cinema* (Bloomington: Indiana University Press, 1982).

12 See Ramsaye 'Robert Paul and *The Time Machine*', p. 196.

13 The patent application is reprinted in full in Geduld, *The Definitive Time Machine*, pp. 198–9.

14 Ibid., p. 198.

15 Ibid.

16 Ibid.

17 Ibid.

18 Ibid.

19 Ibid., p. 199.

20 Jean-Louis Baudry, 'The Apparatus: Metapsychological Approaches to the Impression of Reality in Cinema', in P. Rosen (ed.) *Narrative, Apparatus, Ideology* (New York: Columbia University Press, 1986), p. 315.

With Eyes Uplifted:
Space Aliens as Sky Gods
Carol Schwartz Ellis

Keep watching the skies!
                        – from *The Thing*

From the alarming 'carnivorous carrot' in *The Thing* (Christian Nyby/Howard Hawks, 1951) to Steve McQueen's getting 'slimed' by *The Blob* (Irvin S. Yeaworth Jr., 1958) to Richard Dreyfuss's *Close Encounters of the Third Kind* (Steven Spielberg, 1977) to the downright cuddly *E.T.:The Extra-Terrestrial* (Steven Spielberg, 1982), science fiction films have been bringing alien life into American movie theatres, drive-ins, televisions and VCRs for nearly forty years.[1] This fascination with aliens reveals much about Americans' deepest fears. During the 1950s, cinematic aliens clearly reflected Cold War fear[2] of 'penetration, invasion and colonisation by an alien Other'.[3] One thinks of films such as the aptly named *Red Planet Mars* (Harry Horner, 1952) and the emotionless, faith-free pod people of *Invasion of the Body Snatchers* (Don Siegel, 1956), both representing what life under communism would be like. During the 1960s, space aliens descended less frequently to earthly screens. Film scholar Vivian Sobchack posits that this shift away from overt representation of otherness may be the result of a new focus on the domestic 'Other' in the form of the proud Black, the liberated woman, or the alienated and rebellious youth.[4] During the 1970s, real space aliens returned, this time, however, in much less threatening forms. In this essay I focus on these kinder, gentler aliens, arguing that their appearance addressed our deep fears about technology and answered spiritual questions about our destiny.

The space alien dramatically reentered Earth's atmosphere in 1976 with the release of Nicholas Roeg's *The Man Who Fell to Earth*. Importantly, Thomas Jerome Newton appears entirely human. He is neither a repulsive blob nor a mechanised robot nor a blank-faced automaton nor a horribly deformed creature. He is an entirely recognisable human being.

In the decade that followed, humanoid aliens, markedly different from the classic Cold War aliens, were frequent visitors. This is not to say that nonhuman aliens stopped dropping by as well. *Close Encounters*, *E.T.*, *The Terminator* (James Cameron, 1984), and *The Abyss* (James Cameron, 1989) are but a few of the popular movies that deal with extraterrestrial visitors that are not humanoid. The focus of this essay, however, is on aliens who are unmistakably humanoid. Why has Hollywood begun to make aliens in our own image?[5]

This essay examines, along with *The Man Who Fell to Earth*, three other spaceman movies of the 1970s and 1980s: *The Brother from Another Planet* (John Sayles, 1984), *Starman* (John Carpenter, 1984) and *Man Facing South-east* (Eliseo Subiela, 1986). Each of these films centres around an intentional visitation. Some visitors come for purely selfish reasons: Newton (David Bowie) is on a quest for water for his drought-ridden planet, and the Brother (Joe Morton) is seeking asylum from galactic slavery. Starman (Jeff Bridges) seems to have simply responded to the invitation broadcast by Voyager II. The visitor in *Man Facing South-east* claims pure altruism; Rantes (Hugo Soto) wants to alleviate the suffering of the poor and helpless.

Each visitor, despite his familiarly human, nonthreatening appearance, is regarded with awe and fear – as a holy person and a fiend, a highly evolved superman creature, and a charlatan. The Earth-person's reaction toward the alien seems ambiguous and confused. The spaceman, seeming to burst out of nowhere into the everyday world, may be regarded as a hierophany, a manifestation of the sacred.[6] And the ambivalent earthling response of attraction and dread, fascination and fear, love and disgust reflects the visitor's numinous, or sacred, quality.[7] The alien is, quite simply, Other, not one of us. He may resemble us, but he is different.

Why do the aliens seem so mysterious, awesome and extraordinarily powerful? Why are the visitors always described as more highly evolved, more civilised, more intelligent, more technologically advanced than the people who make and watch the films? The fact that we can identify a virtual genre of films depicting such aliens suggests that these visitors are important to us. As film scholars such as Stuart Kaminsky argue, 'The more popular a film (the more people who see it), the more attention it deserves as a genre manifestation. If a film is popular, it is a result of the fact that the film or series of films corresponds to an interest – perhaps even a need – of the viewing public.[8] He continues, 'Genre analysis can involve an attempt to understand the milieu and background of the work through its relationship with religion, mythology, the social sciences, psychology and anthropology. The roots of genre are … in the fabric of existence itself … The very persistence of genre films argues that they must be dealing with basic aspects of existence and social/psychological interaction, or they could not continue to be made.'[9] Since these basic aspects of existence are also the prime subject matter and concern of myth, I would argue that generic films can act as powerful purveyors of myth.[10] These films serve as repositories and reminders of our deepest concerns.

Many would argue that in the twentieth century our central concern is technology. We modern Westerners regard ourselves as rational beings who understand creation through science. Our cosmogony has nothing to with gods, not with the spoken word of the Hebrews' Yahweh nor the cosmic dismemberment of the Hindus' Purusha, but with a chemical reaction. We believe all matter was created initially by a 'primeval fireball'.[11] After the Big Bang, hydrogen and helium coalesced into stars. That is our creation story. We and everything we know are essentially 'stardust'.[12]

Although we understand our creation story rationally through the hard sciences – physics, chemistry, mathematics – we enjoy experiencing our science in the form of fiction, especially at the movies. Science fiction films project a world at once familiar and other. Space travel happens in NASA-like space ships, numbers and lights flash on computer screens just like our comfortable and convenient personal computers, characters wear shiny uniforms and use multisyllabic words. As scientifically oriented people, it is as if we want to act as though we are not involved in myth. We resist admitting that we are like all other human communities, in need of orienting myths and transcendent values. Science fiction enables us to have our cake and eat it too, to experience a world centered on technology that nonetheless allows for an encounter with cosmic otherness. Consider this: We are fascinated with space aliens, with familiar-looking men who *fall to Earth* because this

genre tells us of our beginnings. By coming into contact with people who are *closer to the stars* than we are, doing nothing other than participating in a mythic experience; through watching space alien films, we are getting in touch with our roots, exploring the secret, sacred dimension of our scientific worldview. And, as Vivian Sobchack points out, 'The great force of the genre film is that it depicts truth without contemplating it, that it dramatises our deepest conflicts in such a way that they are apprehended indirectly, painlessly.'[13] We receive the message in a nondidactic way, as entertainment. We are 'indirectly, painlessly' seeing the deeper meaning of our cosmogonic myth enacted on the screen.

In order to understand their innate Otherness, let us examine the numinous quality of each spaceman. Each alien is regarded with awe and fear, as a manifestation of *mysterium tremendum et fascinans*.[14] Ambiguity is the key. *The Man Who Fell to Earth*, Tommy Newton, is strangely androgynous. When he first meets Oliver Farnsworth (Buck Henry), Newton's dark hat is dipped over one eye, and he refuses (or does not know how) to shake hands. His physical features and actions are such that his gender is nearly underminable. The diminutive Mary-Lou (Candy Clark) carries him out of the elevator. In this context, the fact that she is more able-bodied than he underscores Newton's uncertain gender. Androgyny is an ancient attribute of the gods. 'Universal bisexuality' is revealed in cults of a bearded Aphrodite and a bald Venus, in the androgynous nature of many vegetation and fertility gods, and in the Talmudic *midrashim* (commentaries) depicting Adam and Eve as sharing one body.[15] The significance of this divine 'totalisation' is that it forms a simultaneity of cosmos and chaos, 'a reintegration of opposites, a regression to the primordial and homogeneous. It is a symbolic restoration of 'Chaos', of the undifferentiated unity that preceded the Creation.'[16] Newton's physical 'undifferentiated unity' is a manifestation of his numinosity.

In *The Brother from Another Planet*, everyone seems to like the Brother, but most are somewhat disturbed by him as well. This is revealed best in the early scene in Odell's bar. Each of the 'regulars' has his own territory: Odell (Steve James) is comfortably in charge behind the bar, Smokey (Leonard Jackson) is seated at the bar, Walter (Bill Cobbs) slouches at a table, Fly (Darryl Edwards) mans the video game. As a group of four, they seem to represent order and stability, even though they also seem to be in their own worlds. When the Brother wanders in, the fifth wheel, he disturbs the easy equilibrium. The normally aloof men are forced to interact, even though, like themselves, the Brother sits by himself. When unable to engage the Brother in conversation, the men are frustrated, but they do not shun him. Smokey pops a bag behind his head to test him for deafness and tempts him with whiskey 'to find out if he's crazy'. Later, Sam (Tom Wright) arrives, evening up the number of men in the bar and restoring a sense of order. He sits with the Brother, finds him a job and a place to live. The men acknowledge that he is a little strange, yet they are attracted to him as another, somewhat alienated Black man adrift in Harlem.

Jenny's (Karen Allen) reaction to the *Starman* is one of fear and attraction. When she awakens to find a clone of her dead husband in her living room, she approaches, calling him by her husband's name. She is attracted to him because of the uncanny resemblance yet faints of fright when he approaches her. She dresses him in her husband's clothes, which shows her attraction. But when he puts on his cap she is repulsed because it is too weirdly familiar. Jenny nearly abandons him at a truck stop but changes her mind when she witnesses him reviving a recently slaughtered deer. Her emotions flip back and forth throughout the film as she tries to respond to an inexplicable, ineffable situation. National Security is also of two minds toward the visitor. George Fox (Robert Jaeckel), the businesslike professional man in charge, feels he should be captured and investigated and calls the chase 'a combat mission'. In contrast, Mark Shermin (Charles Martin Smith), the informal freelance scientist, wants to get to know him as an individual.

Rantes, the *Man Facing Southeast*, remains an enigmatic character. He is loved by his fellow inmates in the asylum, who accompany him on his daily vigils when he faces southeast 'receiving and transmitting information'. Yet Dr. Julio Denis (Lorenzo Quintero), despite his obvious affection for the man, never believes his celestial origin and continues to try to cure his 'neurosis'. Rantes's ambiguity climaxes in the scene at an outdoor concert when he displaces the conductor and leads the orchestra in a rousing Beethoven's *Ninth Symphony*, stirring the patients to march to the park. The movements of the patients are choreographed to the music, as are the swinging billy clubs of the police, lending an air of strange other-worldliness to the situation. Although it is possible to believe that the patients could have found their way to the park, it seems improbable that they would march there in time to the music. The police ultimately lead Rantes away. Is he criminal or savior? Is he a troublemaker or a problemsolver? Is he extraterrestrial or insane? We are never quite sure where to place him. He remains the Other, characterised by Rudolf Otto as 'that which is quite beyond the sphere of the usual, the intelligible, and the familiar, which therefore falls quite outside the limits of the 'canny'. The contrast between the Other and the familiar fills the mind with blank wonder and astonishment'.[17]

Like all sacred beings, each alien has extraordinary power. Newton is an extremely gifted electronics engineer whose nine basic patents can, as his business partner Farnsworth exclaims, 'take on RCA, Eastman Kodak, and Dupont, for starters'. This power is revealed on the screen primarily through monetary accomplishments. His lover, Mary-Lou, is at first a uniformed housekeeper in a hotel, supporting him in a crowded studio apartment. Soon she is wearing designer outfits and extravagant wigs and enjoying the expensive toys he lavishes on her including, ironically, a telescope.[18] Newton does not seem particularly gifted, either physically or psychically. Driving forty-five miles per hour makes him dizzy, and he faints in elevators. Yet, his power is manifest in his agelessness. At the end of the movie Mary-Lou and Nathan Bryce (Rip Torn) are paunchy and gray, indicating the passage of many years, whereas Newton remains slim and redheaded. His only 'inexplicable' act is to appear to Bryce, before they have actually met, as a ghostly apparition, dressed in black with a hood over his head, his face a white spot in the darkness,[19] saying 'don't be suspicious'. The next day when they do meet, Newton self-consciously repeats his plea, revealing that Bryce did not imagine their encounter.

The Brother demonstrates his power in several ways. He can fix things. When he first arrives at Ellis Island, he heals his own mangled leg with his glowing hand. The video machines in Odell's bar and Hector's (Jaime Tirelli) 'video graveyard' all respond to the power in his hand, as do Little Earl's (Herbert Newsome) scraped knee and broken television. As he works his magic, his face shines with a beatific glow. The Brother is also supersensitive to the pain of others. In the immigration centre he can sense those who have arrived before him; when he touches a pillar or sits on a bench, cries and voices leap out at him. In Odell's bar he violently recoils from 'the death seat', because by simply approaching it he 'hears' the scream of the man who was shot there. He experiences a heroin high by injecting himself with the empty syringe of an overdosed junkie. Moreover, the Brother can see more than ordinary people, having the remarkable ability to remove an eyeball and have it 'film' things he is unable to witness himself. These out-of-body visions are in slow motion and are jerky, as if to emphasise their uncanny nature.

Except for his ability to start a car, rig a slot machine in Las Vegas with his fingertip, and impregnate the infertile Jenny, the Starman's main source of power seems to be small, mirrored marbles.[20] It is as if the energy of the stars has been solidified, to be used as needed. With the help of these marbles, the Starman sends an emergency transmission to his planet, prints a map of the United States on a car windshield, heats up a lug wrench, and survives a car crash. The Starman is also a miraculous healer, able to resuscitate the dead. First, we see him bring a deer back to life. The camera remains in the truck stop with Jenny, viewing him through a plate-glass window across a parking lot. He does not have to touch the deer, he merely stands before it holding a glowing marble aloft. Because the camera, and, thus, the audience, remains at a distance, we are reminded of the taboo in most religions that is associated with extraordinary power, the injunction to approach the holy with great care.[21] Also, with his back toward us we are unable to witness how he works his miracle; we see only its results, making it seem all the more mysterious and uncanny. Later, the Starman revives Jenny. He kneels beside her, holding his uncannily potent nugget. Again, we view him from behind and are not privy to his healing knowledge, as the glow from his power source lights up the entire mobile home in which they are travelling.

Rantes's power is demonstrated mainly by his intense stare. If the eyes are the seat of the soul, this metaphor is a striking indicator of the potentiality of Rantes's soul. With his eyes he can not only move items, such as plates of food to a poor family in a restaurant, he can also move his fellow inmates at the asylum. His healing power is subtle; no one is 'cured', but the men seem to get better. He touches the forehead of a catatonic man and places his jacket around his shoulders, to which the man warmly responds. Rantes claims to have no feelings, and his unblinking, luminous eyes rarely betray emotion. His blank face may seem to reveal feelings, but often it is simply the actions and looks of those around him that impart emotion to his face.[22] He says he is merely 'programmed' to respond to stimuli, explaining to Dr. Denis, 'I'm more rational than you. I respond rationally to stimulus. If someone suffers I console him. If someone needs my help I give it.' Rantes is also a brilliant organist, and Beatriz (Ines Vernengo) reveals that he can deliver babies and is building a computer out of discarded electronic components. Yet it is only in his eyes that his extraordinary intelligence and compassion are revealed.

The films under investigation all begin with descent from the sky: Newton plunges in a humanoid-shaped stream of white light, crashing into a lake in New Mexico; the Starman arrives in a beam of light that crashes into the Wisconsin wilderness; the Brother is portrayed in his spacecraft before he tumbles into New York Harbour. Rantes, however, describes rather than demonstrates his descent from above.[23] But there is no question that these beings originate in the sky, evoking the archetypal symbolism of the sky and the figure of the sky god.

As Mircea Eliade observed, 'Simple contemplation of the celestial vault already provokes a religious experience … The 'most high' is a dimension inaccessible to man as man; it belongs to superhuman forces and beings.'[24] These forces and beings include a wide range of spiritual beings, depending upon which religious tradition is consulted. Sky gods are characterised as those who have come to Earth to participate in the creation and then withdraw to become *dei otosi*, absent gods.[25] Unlike angels, who are not originally from Earth but return there frequently to help individuals, sky gods are mysterious and remote beings whose Earthly appearances are associated with times of cosmic creation or collective crisis. It is the archetypal pattern of the sky god that can be traced in the careers of our cinematic aliens. Each of these aliens, despite tarrying on Earth, remains remote. Unlike the angel Clarence in *It's a Wonderful Life* (Frank Capra, 1946), they cannot really relax and enjoy human company. Newton, for instance, dreams of his celestial home and family and begins to withdraw into television and alcohol addiction. But when he reveals his 'true nature' to Mary-Lou, perhaps in an effort to renew intimacy, this leads to an increased sense of alienation. In a spectacularly bizarre sequence, filmed in low light and with unusual camera angles, he emerges from the bathroom as a hairless, nippleless, cat-eyed creature. Mary-Lou shrieks and drops her glass, repulsed by the sight of her tender lover transformed into a 'monster'. She tries to make love with him, to accept him as he is, but Newton does not seem to be there. He daydreams: the scene is intercut with shots of coitus on his planet, two glowing creatures embracing and exuding a gleaming liquid. When he reaches out, leaving his luminous bodily fluid on Mary-Lou's skin, she runs from him, screaming and crouches trembling as a wide-angle lens distorts her almost beyond recognition. His innate distance combined with her knowledge of his ineffable otherness destroys their intimacy. The once inseparable couple must part.

The Brother's alienation is evident in his inability to speak. Although he is able to communicate using hand and body language, his distance is apparent because he is often spoken to without an expectation of a response. Randy Sue (Caroline Aaron), who gives him room and board, drones on and on about her absent husband. Hector gabbles at him in Spanish. Ace (Liane Curtis), the video junkie, never taking her eyes from the blips on the screen to even acknowledge his presence, complains in a monotone of her dissatisfaction with slow video games. A rookie, white police officer talks confidently of his delight at working in Harlem; his crouched, self-protective posture, however, reveals his actual discomfort. Malverne Davis (Dee Dee Bridgewater), removing her false eyelashes in another room, blithely reminisces about her past. Although he appears to be accepted by those around him, the Brother, in truth and in silence, remains apart.[26]

The Starman's separation is demonstrated primarily – and effectively – by plot device.

He simply must leave again. His comrades are returning for him in three days[27] regardless of whether he falls in love with Jenny. He cannot survive long on Earth even with the relationship.

Rantes's separation from humankind is manifest in his blank face and his claim to feel no emotions. Despite his exceptional compassion for others, he avoids getting involved. Even with his fellow 'agent' Beatriz, he remains aloof. They sit on opposite sides of the hard, wooden table when she visits him. The camera remains distant, thus making the viewer see them from afar and increasing the sense of Rantes's alienation. As they dance at the outdoor concert, they hold each other not as intimates but in response to the up-lifting music.[28] When Dr. Denis discovers a photograph of Rantes and Beatriz, it is torn, and the piece that should have shown another person standing next to Rantes is missing. The doctor speculates on whether that person was one of his parents. Dr. Denis sadly acknowledges Rantes's supreme aloneness, and so does the audience. Space aliens cannot make themselves too much at home on earth, for they are true to the archetype of the sky god.

It is typical of sky gods to leave a son or representative to complete their work,[29] and these filmic aliens all leave a legacy of some sort. Newton makes a record album that tells his story, hoping that one day his wife will hear it on the radio. The Brother eludes his evil slave-trading pursuers, and they, in embarrassment and frustration, self-destruct. He has, at least temporarily, vanquished evil. The Starman leaves Jenny pregnant with their son, who, he declares, 'will know everything I know and when he grows to manhood, he will be a teacher'. Rantes has forever changed the lives of the mental patients. Dr. Denis says, 'The patients didn't accept Rantes's death. They said he had gone but that he would return in a spaceship. They would be there, waiting.'[30]

What is the significance of our fascination with space aliens? I suggest that it is part of our pursuit of origins. We have faith in a cosmic Big Bang creation myth that explains natural and supernatural phenomena – how the world came to be, why things are the way they are, what will happen next. Our perfect beginning involves the fallout from exploding stars. Cinematic space aliens appear to irrupt *from the stars*, becoming literal, visual representations of our origins. This is where I see the significance of their *human* appearance. The ancient sky god of the West spoke his desire to 'make man in our own image' (Gen. 1: 26), and this statement has often been taken literally in our Sistine Chapelesque (which also requires uplifted eyes) imaginings of a white-bearded human, heavenly Father.[31] We are simply more comfortable with recognisably human-looking gods. In seeing the familiar-looking people of the stars, we witness our stardust beginnings.

Their significance does not end with creation: 'The cosmogony is the exemplary model for every creative situation: Whatever man does is in some way a repetition of the pre-eminent 'deed', the archetypal gesture of the Creator God, the Creation of the World'.[32] In the movies discussed here, each alien, in one way or another, is a model for correct action. Although the aliens recall sacred beginnings, they are acting in profane time and are actively demonstrating that moral perfection can extend into ordinary existence. In this way they point in the direction of positive social action.

The man who fell to Earth fell for one reason: to search for solutions to environmental problems on his home planet, where a severe drought rages. Although Newton does not warn Earth of impending doom if its environmental problems are not addressed, I think the implication is clear. He hires Bryce to work on fuel conservation. The conservation of nonrenewable resources is a problem we earthlings have been grappling with for some time. However, Newton's ultimate goal is to develop a fuel-efficient spaceship to enable him to return to his family. He has been forced to leave his wife and family in search of water; overuse of natural resources on Earth may eventually cause similar familial breakups. Many of the products of his company, World Enterprises, appeal to the family – for instance, superior sound equipment and a self-developing camera. In his concern with nonrenewable natural resources – water, fuel and family – Newton appears as a role model for correct living.

The Brother's plight as an escaped slave opens the possibility for commentary on bigotry of all sorts, manifested in a wide variety of prejudicial comments. Potshots are hurled relentlessly at many races and minorities. Walter, sitting alone at his table in Odell's bar, rambles on about Haitian and Polynesian 'diseases'.

When Bernice (Ren Woods) suggests Szechuan food to Odell, he proclaims he 'won't eat anything he can't pronounce'. Sam is ridiculed by his buddies because he comes from New Jersey. Mr. Lowe (Michael Albert Mantel), owner of the video parlor, comments, 'They're clever with their hands, the coloured, but they forget things', and 'They give you a good day's work, the Spanish, but they have no sense of time.' Smokey, after encountering the Men in Black (John Sayles and David Strathairn), mumbles in bewilderment, 'White people get stranger all the time.' These prejudicial attitudes are never resolved, but their unrelenting frequency during the film leads the viewer to an awareness of our casual intolerance.

The Starman makes it clear that he comes from a more 'humane' civilisation. He protests the needless slaughter of animals, asking when he sees the slain deer, 'Do deer eat people?' He describes his planet this way: 'There is only one language, one law, one people. And there is no war, no hunger. The strong do not victimise the helpless.' As he speaks he is driving through the Arizona desert with a golden sunrise haloing his head, as if to emphasise his purity. He seems a totally responsible, mature humanitarian – a good example for Earth people to emulate. The Starman has not written off the Earth race but is fascinated and troubled by it. When Shermin asks him why he has visited, he replies, 'We are interested in your species ... You are a strange species, unlike any other. Bright, intelligent, but savage ... You are at your very best when things are worst.' Humans may be unpredictable, he implies, but at least they are able to cope with reality. He goes on to admit that his is not a perfect world: 'We are very civilised but we have lost something. You are all so much alive, all so different.' The implication is that perhaps superior technology can lead to impersonalisation and mindless conformity.

Rantes states rather plainly that his mission is to assist the helpless, which is why he has lived contentedly in the asylum and worked with the poor in the surrounding area. When Dr. Denis asks about his collection of newspaper clippings of natural and manmade disasters, Rantes explains, 'We are preparing the rescue of those who cannot survive amidst the terror, those who are without hope ... here.' Rantes exhibits many characteristics of Christ, the Western sky god known for extraordinary compassion toward the meek. He sits quietly hearing 'confession', as a long line of dejected men wait to see him. A 'last supper' is played out as Rantes, surrounded by men at a long, wooden table, hands out food to them from his own plate. Indeed, Dr. Denis refers to Rantes as the 'Cybernetic Christ'. He says, 'Since Rantes was becoming more Christ-like, his end would be the same.' The doctor refers to himself as Pilate for following the institute director's order to forcibly sedate Rantes, which leads to his deterioration and death. Rantes's final words are the plaintive cry, 'Doctor, doctor, why have you forsaken me?'

What, finally, explains the recent movie trend toward beneficent heavenly Otherness? These beings from outer space, living where other mythological sky gods live, are our celestial divine beings. They are numinous and awesome, technologically advanced creator gods who attract those of us who are fascinated with the myth of science. They are the *dei otisi* of stardust who until now have seemed inaccessible and withdrawn. We go to space alien movies to look up and 'worship'. Although we would like to look to the sky for revelation and redemption, the sky today is not always pleasant to regard. Sometimes all we see are palpable clouds of air pollution. Poisonous acid rain pours down from above. The diminished ozone layer permits dangerous levels of ultraviolet rays to penetrate the atmosphere.

But even more dramatic a concern is the fact that the sky may also be regarded as a 'corridor for chaos',[33] the place from which nuclear weapons fall. G. Simon Harak posits that the Strategic Defense Initiative (SDI, or 'Star Wars') was an effort to reinstate the benevolence of the sky. Since historically the United States has considered itself invulnerable to attack because it is surrounded by two oceans, 'the most apt solution [to nuclear invasion] is … to treat *the sky* as a 'third *ocean*' and make it, by technology, impenetrable'.[34] SDI, in effect, was a modern, rationalistic, scientific prayer to the ancient sky gods, pleading with them to protect humanity from above. In a similar vein, Ira Chernus has written that our relationship with the bomb is marked by the ambiguity inherent in the numinous. Perhaps we look to the sky to actually call upon the ultimately destructive, yet somehow fascinating, nuclear weapons because they, *irrupting from the sky*, have come to represent our absent gods. This is no doubt

a horrifying thought – that the bomb, because of its heavenly realm, may actually be regarded as a saviour.[35]

Technologically superior modern sky gods have been returning to earth in the technologically advanced art form of the movies for around forty years. Beginning in the 1970s, kinder, gentler aliens began appearing. Perhaps their appearance coincides with years that seemed more fraught with technological peril. Because of the remarkably swift advancement of science (as evidenced by myriad nuclear capabilities), Americans sought compensatory fulfillment through human-looking, extra-ordinarily powerful and compassionate gods who understand and use technology in nonthreatening ways. In viewing our gods, in hearing our mythic stories, in sitting around the brightly-lit screen in the darkened room, in seeing actors depicting mystery and Otherness, we are participating in one of the oldest human activities – the telling of the stories of the gods. Film scholar Darrol Bryant articulates this well when he writes, 'Film [is] a response to the ambition of a technological civilisation to discover the alchemical formula that could wed the machine to the transmutation of nature and the deification of human culture. In a word, as we sit and watch a film, we are participating in a central ritual of our technological civilisation.'[36] Our spacemen are important to us: They give us hope in a world in which our vision of the stars is obscured by pollution and the potential for nuclear holocaust.

Notes

1   Science fiction films did not suddenly appear in 1950. Some of the earliest moviemakers experimented with notions of space travel, as seen in *A Trip to the Moon* (Georges Méliès, 1902). Nor have the past forty years neglected space exploration and exploitation on the part of earthlings, beginning with what is widely considered the progenitor of modern, 'sophisticated' space-travel movies, *Destination Moon* (Irving Pichel, 1950). *Forbidden Planet* (Fred McLeod Wilcox, 1956), *2001: A Space Odyssey* (Stanley Kubrick, 1968) and the *Star Trek* epics of the 1970s (Robert Wise) and 1980s (Nicholas Meyer, Leonard Nimoy) are some other notables.

2   For an interesting, book-length analysis of this trend, see Nora Sayre, *Running Time: Films of the Cold War* (New York: Dial Press, 1982).

3   Vivan Sobchack, 'Science Fiction', in *Handbook of American Film Genres*, ed. Wes D. Gehring (New York: Greenwood

Press, 1988), p. 232.

4 Ibid., p. 235. Sobchack's *Screening Space: The American Science Fiction Film*, 2nd enl. ed. (New York: Ungar, 1987) is an excellent introduction to and overview of the science fiction film genre.

5 It can be argued that Klaatu, the 'gnostic messenger' of *The Day the Earth Stood Still* (Robert Wise, 1951), who bears a grave warning for earthlings, also looks human. His 'normal' physical appearance and 'beneficent' role are very unusual for a space alien of the early 1950s, going against the expectations of an evil, ugly invader. I will not include Klaatu in this analysis, because I do not consider him part of the recent trend discussed here.

6 As Mircea Eliade refers to manifestations of the holy. See especially *Patterns in Comparative Religion*, trans. Rosemary Sheed (New York: New American Library, 1958), pp. 1–4.

7 As described by Rudolf Otto. See *The Idea of the Holy* (London: Oxford University Press, 1950), especially Chapters 2–6, pp. 5–40.

8 Stuart M. Kaminsky, *American Film Genres*, 2nd ed. (Chicago: Nelson-Hall, 1985), p. 3.

9 Ibid.

10 Here I am relying on Eliade's definition of myth as "true story' and, beyond that, a story that is a most precious possession because it is sacred, exemplary, significant'. *Myth and Reality*, trans. Willard R. Trask (New York: Harper Torchbooks, Harper and Row, 1963), p. 1. Myth, as interpreted this way, is truth, reality, the way things are.

11 Paul G. Hewitt, *Conceptual Physics*, 5th edn. (Boston: Little, Brown, 1985), p. 591.

12 Ibid., p. 151.

13 Vivian Sobchack, 'Genre Film: Myth Ritual, and Sociodrama', in *Film/Culture: Explorations of Cinema in Its Social Context*, ed. Sari Thomas (Metuchen, N.J.: Scarecrow Press, 1982), p. 151.

14 See Otto, *Idea of the Holy*, pp. 5–40.

15 Mircea Eliade, *The Two and the One*, trans. J. M. Cohen (Chicago: University of Chicago Press, 1962), pp. 101–11.

16 Ibid., p. 114.

17 Otto, *Idea of the Holy*, p. 26.

18 It seems likely that he really bought the telescope out of sadness and homesickness, to search the skies for his own planet. However, it also serves as a symbol, perhaps, of the human need to look beyond the limited horizons of humanness and to find Otherness, as is reflected in the character of Newton.

19 A noteworthy visual pun on Bergman's character of Death in *The Seventh Seal* (1957).

20 He also presents one to Jenny for their son because 'the baby will know' what to do with it.

21 As Gerardus van der Leeuw puts it, 'Tabu is thus a sort of warning: 'Danger! High voltage!" in *Religion in Essence and Manifestation*, trans. J. E. Turner (Princeton: Princeton

University Press, 1986), p. 44.

22 This appears to be a manifestation of the famous Mozhukhin Experiment. In the early 1920s Russian filmmaker Lev Kuleshov put together a short film by splicing together alternating shots of actor Ivan Mozhukhin with a neutral facial expression and clips of a child playing with a toy, a bowl of soup and an old woman in a coffin. Audiences felt he was a terrific actor, expressing affection, hunger and grief in a very subtle manner. Screen performance ever since has emphasised underacting. See Bruce F. Kawin, *How Movies Work* (New York: Macmillan, 1987), pp. 227–8.

23 That no one, including the film audience, witnesses his arrival leads to a greater ambiguity of Rantes's character. Indeed, some people in the film are never convinced of his extraterrestriality.

24 Mircea Eliade, *The Sacred and the Profane*, trans. Willard R. Trask (New York: Harcourt Brace Jovanovich, 195?), pp. 118–19.

25 Ibid., pp. 121–2. For more detail on 'absent gods', see Eliade, *Patterns*, pp. 46–50.

26 Because of his muteness he appears to embody the often-expressed feeling that the gods no longer speak to humankind, particularly the familiar Western biblical God, who some contend ceased communicating with humankind after the time of the prophets.

27 This time frame of three days will be familiar to Westerners used to Christian mythology: Jesus's trial with death lasts three days, after which he, like the Starman, returns to the heavens.

28 Here the smiling, joyful Rantes's claim to have no feelings does not really work. But it is a delightful scene nonetheless.

29 Eliade, *The Sacred and the Profane*, p. 122. In the West, the Word meant to explain creation, in the form of sacred scriptures, descends from the heavens and is revealed in high places: the Torah on Mt. Sinai and the Qu'ran on Mt. Hira. Yet the most obvious Western manifestation of the completer of creation can be found in the myth of Jesus. I do not mean to imply that every Westerner is Jewish, Christian or Muslim but merely to indicate how religious mythology suffuses culture.

30 Yet another allusion to Jesus in terms of his Parousia, his Second Coming.

31 Again, I recognise that not every Westerner has read the Bible. This notion of appearance is simply a part of the undeniable and inescapable undercurrent of our culture.

32 Eliade, *Myth and Reality*, p. 32.

33 G. Simon Harak, 'One Nation, Under God: The Soteriology of SDI', *Journal of the American Academy of Religion*, 56 (Fall 1988), p. 504.

34 Ibid.

35 See Ira Chernus, *Dr. Strangegod: On the Symbolic Meaning of Nuclear Weapons* (Columbia: University of South Caro-

lina Press, 1986).

36 Darrol M. Bryant, 'Cinema, Religion and Popular Culture', in *Religion in Film*, ed. John R. May and Michael Bird (Knoxville: University of Tennessee Press, 1982), p. 102.

References

Giannetti, Louis (1987) *Understanding Movies*, 4th edn. (Englewood Cliffs, NJ: Prentice-Hall).

Hillman, James (1975) *Re-Visioning Psychology*. New York: Perennial Library, Harper and Row.

Jarvie, I. C. (1970) *Movies and Society*. New York: Basic Books.

Filmography

The Man Who Fell to Earth. Screenplay by Paul Meyersberg from the novel by Walter Tevis. Directed by Nicholas Roeg. Released by British Lion Films, 1976.

The Brother from Another Planet. Written, directed, and edited by John Sayles. Released by A-Train Films, 1984.

Starman. Written by Bruce A. Evans and Raynold Gideon. Directed by John Carpenter. Released by Columbia Pictures, 1984.

Man Facing Southeast. Written and directed by Eliseo Subiela. Released by Film Dallas, 1986.

LIQUID METAL:
THE CYBORG IN SCIENCE FICTION

FIVE | LIQUID METAL: THE CYBORG IN SCIENCE FICTION

In contemporary science fiction the cyborg is often one of the key signifiers of futuristic transformations driven by the melding of the machine with the human. The cyborg so often made of soft (human) tissue on the outside is at same time all hi-tech circuitry and computer chips on the inside. However, two distinct types of cyborg emerge in science fiction. The *humanist* cyborg is driven by the logic of the machine aesthetic and longs for the human emotion and human attachment that will add existential meaning to its fragile outer shell. He/she works with and for other humans, in democratic teams, with an important job to fulfil (as a science officer or engineer, for example). The humanist cyborg is constantly involved in situations that involve him watching and commenting on their colleagues as they fall in love, get angry, regret, and pass away. At key narrative moments they are called upon or challenged to act and react in the same way as their human compatriots. And while they seem incapable of this, fired as they are by objectivity and rationalist principles, and while they seem unable to bridge the emotional gap that is required of them, what is given away each time, through the use of a dramatic close-up that catches a forlorn glance, or an enigmatic reply, is a deeply hidden wish to be the *same kind* of human being. The humanist cyborg holds out for the hope (desire) of uniting and unifying the corporeal to the technological.

The *pathological* cyborg, by contrast, wants to melt away its human simulacra to symbolically rid the Earth (past, present and future) of what they rationalise to be is their fleshy, useless skin material and the flabby emotions that are tied to it. The pathological cyborg is programmed to be relentless in its pursuit of those who champion humanity and who stand in their path to greater, technological glory. They will stop at nothing, will undertake any and every heinous act to secure their will to power. The pathological cyborg wants nothing more than the complete genocide of the human race. The cyborg, nonetheless, always carries a weight of signification beyond its programmed impulses. Because the cyborg is part machine, part human, it necessarily comes to question the borders and boundaries of identity formation and the essential notion that there is a fixed and rooted trans-historical human condition. The cyborg is by definition a transgessive creation that plays out the power struggles over gender and sexuality, race and national identity, opening up potential spaces of resistance and opposition to masculine and feminine norms, and notions of otherness that circulate in 'culture' more widely. But, finally, the cyborg also stands as a form of cultural prophecy about the potential relationship between human and machine. On the one hand, the cyborg articulates the terror of letting too much technology into everyday life. On the other hand, the cyborg lives out the dream of corporeal and technological fusion where the gendered, sexualised and racialised body is left behind in a new (romantic) dawn of machine: human inter-dependence.

Donna Haraway's feminist manifesto on the cyborg heralds its potential to transform identity from one being predicated on essentialised gender roles to one that swims in its own liminality. In what becomes a 'post-gender world', the cyborg is 'about transgressed boundaries, potent fusions and dangerous possibilities which progressive people might explore as one part of needed political work'. Haraway marks out three key ways in which the borders of human identity have been breached in the late twentieth century: through human and animal fusion; human and machine fusion; and through the dissolution between the physical and the non-physical. In this cyborg world 'people are not afraid of their joint kinship with animals and machines, not afraid of permanently partial identities and contradictory standpoints'.

Mary Anne Doane offers a critical account of the way the machine has been used in science fiction to re-confirm the essentialised relationship between women and 'natural' reproduction. Doane argues that because of a 'revolution in the development of technologies of reproduction' issues of conception, birth and the Oedipal scenario have been put into fundamental, cultural crisis. This crisis 'debiologise[s] the maternal' and, as a consequence, opens up the potential to destabilise the notion of Motherhood and the maternal. However, films such as *Alien*, *Aliens* and *Blade Runner*

conservatively 'strive to rework the connections between the maternal, history and representation in ways that will allow a taming of technologies of reproduction' and a simultaneous re-centring of the link between the natural and the maternal.

Doran Larson examines the figure of the cyborg in relation to the way the American body politic functioned during the 1980s and 1990s. Looking at the two *Terminator* films, Larson argues that one can track a cultural shift in not only how technology is imagined in terms of democracy and notions of difference, but how the machine becomes 'incorporated into the body politic' by the appearance of *T2* in 1991. This shift 'reveals a popular surrender to the realisation that democracy in mass, capitalist society is inescapably technodemocracy: a body politic at best as cyborg, at worst on life-support systems'. Focusing on the Liquid Metal Man of *T2*, Larson argues 'this figure epitomises – as no figure before morphing technology could have – the morphology of the oppositional logic in the body politic: it is the thing, now Indian, now Communist, which continually changes forms yet must survive if the body politic in democracy is to sustain its own morphology. And by presenting a threat that forces us to cling to the machine, we are forced back again ... to rethink the Arnold from *T1*'.

Susan J. Napier examines the ambivalent attitude to technology and the technological body in *mecha* (hard science fiction) anime – an ambivalence that she argues articulates deep-seated fears in Japanese society. According to Napier 'while the imagery in *mecha* anime is strongly technological and is often specifically focused on the machinery of the armoured body, the narratives themselves often focus to a surprising extent on the human inside the machinery. It is this contrast between the vulnerable, emotionally complex and often youthful human being inside the ominously faceless body armour or power suit and the awesome power she/he wields vicariously that makes for the most important tension in many mecha dramas.'

A Manifesto for Cyborgs: Science, Technology and Socialist Feminism in the 1980s
Donna J. Haraway

An Ironic Dream of a Common Language for Women in the Integrated Circuit

This essay is an effort to build an ironic political myth faithful to feminism, socialism and materialism. Perhaps more faithful as blasphemy is faithful, than as reverent worship and identification. Blasphemy has always seemed to require taking things very seriously. I know no better stance to adopt from within the secular-religious, evangelical traditions of United States politics, including the politics of socialist feminism. Blasphemy protects one from the moral majority within, while still insisting on the need for community. Blasphemy is not apostasy. Irony is about contradictions that do not resolve into larger wholes, even dialectically, about the tension of holding incompatible things together because both or all are necessary and true. Irony is about humour and serious play. It is also a rhetorical strategy and a political method, one I would like to see more honoured within socialist-feminism. At the centre of my ironic faith, my blasphemy, is the image of the cyborg.

A cyborg is a cybernetic organism, a hybrid of machine and organism, a creature of social reality as well as a creature of fiction. Social reality is lived social relations, our most important political construction, a world-changing fiction. The international women's movements have constructed 'women's experience', as well as uncovered or discovered this crucial collective object. This experience is a fiction and fact of the most crucial, political kind. Liberation rests on the construction of the consciousness, the imaginative apprehension, of oppression, and so of possibility. The cyborg is a matter of fiction and lived experience that changes what counts as women's experience in the late twentieth century. This is a struggle over life and death, but the boundary between science fiction and social reality is an optical illusion.

Contemporary science fiction is full of cyborgs – creatures simultaneously animal and machine, who populate worlds ambiguously natural and crafted. Modern medicine is also full of cyborgs, of couplings between organism and machine, each conceived as coded devices, in an intimacy and with a power that was not generated in the history of sexuality. Cyborg 'sex' restores some of the lovely replicative baroque of ferns and invertebrates (such nice organic prophylactics against heterosexism). Cyborg replication is uncoupled from organic reproduction. Modern production seems like a dream of cyborg colonisation work, a dream that makes the nightmare of Taylorism seem idyllic. And modern war is a cyborg orgy, coded by C^3I, command-control-communication-intelligence, an $84 billion item in 1984's US defence budget. I am making an argument for the cyborg as a fiction mapping our social and bodily reality and as an imaginative resource suggesting some very fruitful couplings. Michael Foucault's biopolitics is a flaccid premonition of cyborg politics, a very open field.

By the late twentieth century, our time, a mythic time, we are all chimeras, theorised and fabricated hybrids of machine and organism; in short, we are cyborgs. The cyborg is our ontology; it gives us our politics. The cyborg is a condensed image of both imagination and material reality, the two joined centres structuring any possibility of historical transformation. In the traditions of 'Western' science and politics – the tradition of racist, male-dominant capitalism; the tradition of progress; the tradition of the appropriation of nature as resource for the productions of culture; the tradition of reproduction of the self from the reflections of the other – the relation between organism and machine has been a border war. The stakes in the border war have been the territories of production, reproduction and imagination. This essay is an argument for *pleasure* in the confusion of boundaries and for *responsibility* in their construction. It is also an effort to contribute to socialist-feminist culture and theory in a postmodernist, non-naturalist mode and in the utopian tradition of imagining a world without gender, which is perhaps a world without genesis, but maybe also a world without end.

The cyborg incarnation is outside salvation history. Nor does it mark time on an oedipal calendar, attempting to heal the terrible cleavages of gender in an oral symbiotic utopia or post-oedipal apocalypse. As Zoe Sofoulis argues in her unpublished manuscript on Jacques Lacan, Melanie Klein and nuclear culture, *Lacklein*, the most terrible and perhaps the most promising monsters in cyborg worlds are embodied in non-oedipal narratives with a different logic of repression, which we need to understand for our survival.

The cyborg is a creature in a post-gender world; it has no truck with bisexuality, pre-oedipal symbiosis, unalienated labour or other seductions to organic wholeness through a final appropriation of all the powers of the parts into a higher unity. In a sense, the cyborg has no origin story in the Western sense – a 'final' irony since the cyborg is also the awful apocalyptic *telos* of the 'West's' escalating dominations of abstract individuation, an ultimate self united at last from all dependency, a man in space. An origin story in the 'Western', humanist sense depends on the myth of original unity, fullness, bliss and terror, represented by the phallic mother from whom all humans must separate, the task of individual development and of history, the twin potent myths inscribed most powerfully for us in psychoanalysis and Marxism. Hilary Klein has argued that both Marxism and psychoanalysis, in their concepts of labour and of individuation and gender formation, depend on the plot of original unity out of which difference must be produced and enlisted in a drama of escalating domination of woman/nature. The cyborg skips the step of original unity, of identification with nature in the Western sense. This is its illegitimate promise that might lead to subversion of its teleology as star wars.

The cyborg is resolutely committed to partiality, irony, intimacy and perversity. It is oppositional, utopian and completely without innocence. No longer structured by the polarity of public and private, the cyborg defines a technological polis based partly on a revolution of social relations in the *oikos*, the household. Nature and culture are reworked; the one can no longer be the resource for appropriation or incorporation by the other. The relationships for forming wholes from parts, including those of polarity and hierarchical domination, are at issue in the cyborg world. Unlike the hopes of Frankenstein's monster, the cyborg does not expect its father to save it through a restoration of the garden; that is, through the fabrication of a heterosexual mate, through its completion in a finished whole, a city and cosmos. The cyborg does not dream of community on the model of the organic family, this time without the oedipal project. The cyborg would not recognise the Garden of Eden; it is not made of mud and cannot dream of returning to dust. Perhaps that is why I want to see if cyborgs can subvert the apocalypse of returning to nuclear dust in the manic compulsion to name the Enemy. Cyborgs are not reverent; they do not remember the cosmos. They are wary of holism, but needy for connection – they seem to have a natural feel for united front politics, but without the vanguard party. The main trouble with cyborgs, of course, is that they are the illegitimate offspring of militarism and patriarchal capitalism, not to mention state socialism. But illegitimate offspring are often exceedingly unfaithful to their origins. Their fathers, after all, are inessential.

I will return to the science fiction of cyborgs at the end of this essay, but now I want to signal three crucial boundary breakdowns that make the following political-fictional (political-scientific) analysis possible. By the late twentieth century in United States scientific culture, the boundary between human and animal is thoroughly breached. The last beachheads of uniqueness have been polluted if not turned into amusement parks – language, tool use, social behaviour, mental events, nothing really convincingly settles the separation of human and animal. And many people no longer feel the need for such a separation; indeed, many branches of feminist culture affirm the pleasure of connection of human and other living creatures. Movements for animal rights are not irrational denials of human uniqueness; they are a clear-sighted recognition of connection across the discredited breach of nature and culture. Biology and evolutionary theory over the last two centuries have simultaneously produced modern organisms as objects of knowledge and reduced the line between humans and animals to a faint trace re-etched in ideological struggle or professional disputes between life and social science. Within this framework, teaching modern Christian creationism should be fought as a form of child abuse.

Biological-determinist ideology is only one position opened up in scientific culture for arguing the meanings of human animality. There is much room for radical political people to contest the meanings of the breached boundary.[2] The cyborg appears in myth precisely where the boundary between human and animal is transgressed. Far from signalling a walling off of people from other living beings, cyborgs signal disturbingly and pleasurably tight coupling. Bestiality has a new status in this cycle of marriage exchange.

The second leaky distinction is between animal-human (organism) and machine. Pre-cybernetic machines could be haunted; there was always the spectre of the ghost in the machine. This dualism structured the dialogue between materialism and idealism that was settled by a dialectical progeny, called spirit or history, according to taste. But basically machines were not self-moving, self-designing, autonomous. They could not achieve man's dream, only mock it. They were not man, an author to himself, but only a caricature of that masculinist reproductive dream. To think they were otherwise was paranoid. Now we are not so sure. Late twentieth-century machines have made thoroughly ambiguous the difference between natural and artificial, mind and body, self-developing and externally designed, and many other distinctions that used to apply to organisms and machines. Our machines are disturbingly lively, and we ourselves frighteningly inert.

Technological determination is only one ideological space opened up by the re-conceptions of machine and organism as coded texts through which we engage in the play of writing and reading the world.[3] 'Textualisation' of everything in poststructuralist, post-modernist theory has been damned by Marxists and socialist feminists for its utopian disregard for the lived relations of domination that ground the 'play' of arbitrary reading.[4] It is certainly true that postmodernist strategies, like my cyborg myth, subvert myriad organic wholes (for example, the poem, the primitive culture, the biological organism). In short, the certainty of what counts as nature – a source of insight and promise of innocence – is undermined, probably fatally. The transcendent authorisation of interpretation is lost, and with it the ontology grounding 'Western' epistemology. But the alternative is not cynicism or faithlessness, that is, some version of abstract existence, like the accounts of technological determinism destroying 'man' by the 'machine' or 'meaningful political action'

by the 'text'. Who cyborgs will be is a radical question; the answers are a matter of survival. Both chimpanzees and artefacts have politics, so why shouldn't we (de Waal 1982; Winner 1980)?

The third distinction is a subset of the second: the boundary between physical and non-physical is very imprecise for us. Pop physics books on the consequences of quantum theory and the indeterminacy principle are a kind of popular scientific equivalent to Harlequin romances as a marker of radical change in American white heterosexuality: they get it wrong, but they are on the right subject. Modern machines are quintessentially microelectronic devices: they are everywhere and they are invisible. Modern machinery is an irreverent upstart god, mocking the Father's ubiquity and spirituality. The silicon chip is a surface for writing; it is etched in molecular scales disturbed only by atomic noise, the ultimate interference for nuclear scores. Writing, power and technology are old partners in Western stories of the origin of civilisation, but miniaturisation has changed our experience of mechanism. Miniaturisation has turned out to be about power; small is not so much beautiful as pre-eminently dangerous, as in cruise missiles. Contrast the TV sets of the 1950s or the news cameras of the 1970s with the TV wrist bands or hand-sized video cameras now advertised. Our best machines are made of sunshine; they are all light and clean because they are nothing but signals, electromagnetic waves, a section of a spectrum, and these machines are eminently portable, mobile – a matter of immense human pain in Detroit and Singapore. People are nowhere near so fluid, being both material and opaque. Cyborgs are ether, quintessence.

The ubiquity and invisibility of cyborgs is precisely why these sunshine-belt machines are so deadly. They are as hard to see politically as materially. They are about consciousness – or its simulation.[5] They are floating signifiers moving in pick-up trucks across Europe, blocked more effectively by the witch-weavings of the displaced and so unnatural Greenham women, who read the cyborg webs of power so very well, than by the militant labour of older masculinist politics, whose natural constituency needs defence jobs. Ultimately the 'hardest' science is about the realm of greatest boundary confusion, the realm of pure number, pure spirit, C³I, cryptography and the preservation of potent secrets. The new machines are so clean and light. Their engineers are sun-worshippers mediating a new scientific revolution associated with the night dream of post-industrial society. The diseases evoked by these clean machines are 'no more' than the minuscule coding changes of an antigen in the immune system, 'no more' than the experience of stress. The nimble fingers of 'Oriental' women, the old fascination of little Anglo-Saxon Victorian girls with doll's houses, women's enforced attention to the small take on quite new dimensions in this world. There might be a cyborg Alice taking account of these new dimensions. Ironically, it might be the unnatural cyborg women making chips in Asia and spiral dancing in Santa Rita jail (a practice at once both spiritual and political that linked guards and arrested anti-nuclear demonstrators in the Alameda County jail in California in the early 1980s) whose constructed unities will guide effective oppositional strategies.

So my cyborg myth is about transgressed boundaries, potent fusions and dangerous possibilities which progressive people might explore as one part of needed political work. One of my premises is that most American socialists and feminists see deepened dualisms of mind and body, animal and machine, idealism and materialism in the social practices, symbolic formulations and physical artefacts associated with 'high technology' and scientific culture. From *One-Dimensional Man* (Marcuse 1964) to *The Death of Nature* (Merchant 1980), the analytic resources developed by progressives have insisted on the necessary domination of technics and recalled us to an imagined organic body to integrate our resistance. Another of my premises is that the need for unity of people trying to resist worldwide intensification of domination has never been more acute. But a slightly perverse shift of perspective might better enable us to contest for meanings, as well as for other forms of power and pleasure in technologically mediated societies.

From one perspective, a cyborg world is about the final imposition of a grid of control on the planet, about the final abstraction embodied in a Star Wars apocalypse waged in the name of defence, about the final appropriation of women's bodies in a masculinist orgy of war (Sofia 1984). From another perspective, a cyborg world might be about lived social and bodily realities in which people are not afraid of their joint kinship with animals and machines, not afraid of permanently partial identities and contradictory standpoints. The political struggle is to see from both perspectives at once because each reveals both dominations and possibilities unimaginable from the other vantage point. Single vision produces worse illusions than double vision or many-headed monsters. Cyborg unities are monstrous and illegitimate; in our present political circumstances, we could hardly hope for more potent myths for resistance and recoupling. I like to imagine LAG, the Livermore Action Group, as a kind of cyborg society, dedicated to realistically converting the laboratories that most fiercely embody and spew out the tools of technological apocalypse, and committed to building a political form that actually manages to hold together witches, engineers, elders, perverts, Christians, mothers and Leninists long enough to disarm the state. Fission Impossible is the name of the affinity group in my town. (Affinity: related not by blood but by choice, the appeal of one chemical nuclear group for another, avidity.)[6]

Fractured Identities

It has become difficult to name one's feminism by a single adjective – or even to insist in every circumstance upon the noun. Consciousness of exclusion through naming is acute. Identities seem contradictory, partial and strategic. With the hard-won recognition of their social and historical constitution, gender, race and class cannot provide the basis for belief in 'essential' unity. There is nothing about being 'female' that naturally binds women. There is not even such a state as 'being' female, itself a highly complex category constructed in contested sexual scientific discourses and other social practices. Gender, race or class consciousness is an achievement forced on us by the terrible historical experience of the contradictory social realities of patriarchy, colonialism and capitalism. And who counts as 'us' in my own rhetoric? Which identities are available to ground such a potent political myth called 'us', and what could motivate enlistment in this collectivity? Painful fragmentation among feminists (not to mention among women) along every possible fault line has made the concept of *woman* elusive, an excuse for the matrix of women's dominations of each other. For me – and for many who share a similar historical location in white, professional middle-class, female, radical, North American, mid-adult bodies – the sources of a crisis in political identity are legion. The recent history for much of the US left and US feminism has been a response to this kind of crisis by endless splitting and searches for a new essential unity. But there has also been a growing recognition of another response through coalition – affinity, not identity.[7]

Chela Sandoval (1984), from a consideration of specific historical moments in the formation of the new political voice called women of colour, has theorised a hopeful model of political identity called 'oppositional consciousness', born of the skills for reading webs of power by those refused stable membership in the social categories of race, sex or class. 'Women of colour', a name contested at its origins by those whom it would incorporate, as well as a historical consciousness marking systematic breakdown of all the signs of Man in 'Western' traditions, constructs a kind of postmodernist identity out of otherness, difference and specificity. This postmodernist identity is fully political, whatever might be said about other possible postmodernisms. Sandoval's oppositional consciousness is about contradictory locations and heterochronic calendars, not about relativisms and pluralisms.

Sandoval emphasises the lack of any essential criterion for identifying who is a woman of colour. She notes that the definition of the group has been by conscious appropriation of negation. For example, a Chicana or US black woman has not been able to speak as a woman or as a black person or as a Chicano. Thus, she was at the bottom of a cascade of negative identities, left out of even the privileged oppressed authorial categories called 'women and blacks', who claimed to make the important revolutions. The category 'woman' negated all non-white women; 'black' negated all non-black people, as well as all black women. But there was also no 'she', no singularity, but a sea of differences among US women who have affirmed their historical identity as US women of colour. This identity marks out a self-consciously constructed space that cannot affirm the capacity to act on the basis of natural identification, but only on the basis of conscious coalition, of affinity, of political kinship.[8] Unlike the 'woman' of some streams of the white women's movement in the United States, there is no naturalisation of the matrix, or at least this is what Sandoval argues is uniquely available through the power of oppositional consciousness.

Sandoval's argument has to be seen as one potent formulation for feminists out of the world-wide development of anti-colonialist discourse; that is to say, discourse dissolving the 'West' and its highest product – the one who is not animal, barbarian or woman; man, that is, the author of a cosmos called history. As orientalism is deconstructed politically and semiotically, the identities of the occident destabilise, including those of feminists.[9] Sandoval argues that 'women of colour' have a chance to build an effective unity that does not replicate the imperialising, totalising revolutionary subjects of previous Marxisms and feminisms which had not faced the consequences of the disorderly polyphony emerging from decolonisation.

Katie King has emphasised the limits of identification and the political/poetic mechanics of identification built into reading 'the poem', that generative core of cultural feminism. King criticises the persistent tendency among contemporary feminists from different 'moments' or 'conversations' in feminist practice to taxonomise the women's movement to make one's own political tendencies appear to be the *telos* of the whole. These taxonomies tend to remake feminist history so that it appears to be an ideological struggle among coherent types persisting over time, especially those typical units called radical, liberal and socialist-feminism. Literally, all other feminisms are either incorporated or marginalised, usually by building an explicit ontology and epistemology.[10] Taxonomies of feminism produce epistemologies to police deviation from official women's experience. And of course, 'women's culture', like women of colour, is consciously created by mechanisms inducing affinity. The rituals of poetry, music and certain forms of academic practice have been pre-eminent. The politics of race and culture in the US women's movements are intimately interwoven. The common achievement of King and Sandoval is learning how to craft a poetic/political unity without relying on a logic of appropriation, incorporation and taxonomic identification.

The theoretical and practical struggle against unity-through-domination or unity-through-incorporation ironically not only undermines the justifications for patriarchy, colonialism, humanism, positivism, essentialism, scientism and other unlamented -isms, but *all* claims for an organic or natural standpoint. I think that radical and socialist/Marxist-feminisms have also undermined their/our own epistemological strategies and that this is a crucially valuable step in imagining possible unities. It remains to be seen whether all 'epistemologies' as Western political people have known them fail us in the task to build effective affinities.

It is important to note that the effort to construct revolutionary standpoints, epistemologies as achievements of people committed to changing the world, has been part of the process showing the limits of identification. The acid tools of postmodernist theory and the constructive tools of ontological discourse about revolutionary subjects might be seen as ironic allies in dissolving Western selves in the interests of survival. We are excruciatingly conscious of what it means to have a historically constituted body. But with the loss of innocence in our origin, there is no expulsion from the Garden either. Our politics lose the indulgence of guilt with the *naïveté* of innocence. But what would another political myth for socialist-feminism look like? What kind of politics could embrace partial, contradictory, permanently unclosed constructions of personal and collective selves and still be faithful, effective – and, ironically, socialist-feminist?

I do not know of any other time in history when there was greater need for political unity to confront effectively the dominations of 'race', 'gender', 'sexuality' and 'class'. I also do not know of any other time when the kind of unity we might help build could have been possible. None of 'us' have any longer the symbolic or material capability of dictating the shape of reality to any of 'them'. Or at least 'we' cannot claim innocence from practising such dominations. White women, including socialist feminists, discovered (that is, were forced kicking and screaming to notice) the non-innocence of the category 'woman'. That consciousness changes the geography of all previous categories; it denatures them as heat denatures a fragile protein. Cyborg feminists have to argue that 'we' do not want any more natural matrix of unity and that no construction is whole. Innocence, and the corollary insistence on victimhood as the only ground for insight, has done enough damage. But the constructed revolutionary subject must give late twentieth-century people pause as well. In the fraying of identities and in the reflexive strategies for constructing them, the possibility opens up for weaving something other than a shroud for the day after the apocalypse that so prophetically ends salvation history.

Both Marxist/socialist-feminisms and radical feminisms have simultaneously naturalised and denatured the category 'woman' and consciousness of the social lives of 'women'. Perhaps a schematic caricature can highlight both kinds of moves. Marxian socialism is rooted in an analysis of wage labour which reveals class structure. The consequence of the wage relationship is systematic alienation, as the worker is dissociated from his (sic) product. Abstraction and illusion rule in knowledge, domination rules in practice. Labour is the pre-eminently privileged category enabling the Marxist to overcome illusion and find that point of view which is necessary for changing the world. Labour is the humanising activity that makes man; labour is an ontological category permitting the knowledge of a subject, and so the knowledge of subjugation and alienation.

In faithful filiation, socialist-feminism advanced by allying itself with the basic analytic strategies of Marxism. The main achievement of both Marxist feminists and socialist feminists was to expand the category of labour to accommodate what (some) women did, even when the wage relation was subordinated to a more comprehensive view of labour under capitalist patriarchy. In particular, women's labour in the household and women's activity as mothers generally (that is, reproduction in the socialist-feminist sense), entered theory on the authority of analogy to the Marxian concept of labour. The unity of women here rests on an epistemology based on the ontological structure of 'labour'. Marxist/socialist-feminism does not 'naturalise' unity; it is a possible achievement based on a possible standpoint rooted in social relations. The essentialising move is in the ontological structure of labour or of its analogue, women's activity.[11] The inheritance of Marxian humanism, with its pre-eminently Western self, is the difficulty for me. The contribution from these formulations has been the emphasis on the daily responsibility of real women to build unities, rather than to naturalise them.

Catherine MacKinnon's (1982, 1987) version of radical feminism is itself a caricature of the appropriating, incorporating, totalising tendencies of Western theories of identity grounding action.[12] It is factually and politically wrong to assimilate all of the diverse 'moments' or 'conversations' in recent women's politics named radical feminism to MacKinnon's version. But the teleological logic of her theory shows how an epistemology and ontology – including their negations – erase or police difference. Only one of the effects of MacKinnon's theory is the rewriting of the history of the polymorphous field called radical feminism. The major effect is the production of a theory of experience, of women's identity, that is a kind of apocalypse for all revolutionary standpoints. That is, the totalisation built into this tale of radical feminism achieves its end – the unity of women – by enforcing the experience of and testimony to radical non-being. As for the Marxist/socialist feminist, consciousness is an achievement, not a natural fact. And MacKinnon's theory eliminates some of the difficulties built into humanist revolutionary subjects, but at the cost of radical reductionism.

MacKinnon argues that feminism necessarily adopted a different analytical strategy from Marxism, looking first not at the structure of class, but at the structure of sex/gender and its generative relationship, men's constitution and appropriation of women sexually. Ironically, MacKinnon's 'ontology' constructs a non-subject, a non-being. Another's desire, not the self's labour, is the origin of 'woman'. She therefore develops a theory of consciousness that enforces what can count as 'women's' experience – anything that names sexual violation, indeed, sex itself as far as 'women' can be concerned. Feminist practice is the construction of this form of consciousness; that is, the self-knowledge of a self-who-is-not.

Perversely, sexual appropriation in this feminism still has the epistemological status of labour; that is to say, the point from which an analysis able to contribute to changing the world must flow. But sexual objectification, not alienation, is the consequence of the structure of sex/gender. In the realm of knowledge, the result of sexual objectification is illusion and abstraction. However, a woman is not simply alienated from her product, but in a deep

sense does not exist as a subject, or even potential subject, since she owes her existence as a woman to sexual appropriation. To be constituted by another's desire is not the same thing as to be alienated in the violent separation of the labourer from his product.

MacKinnon's radical theory of experience is totalising in the extreme; it does not so much marginalise as obliterate the authority of any other women's political speech and action. It is a totalisation producing what Western patriarchy itself never succeeded in doing – feminists' consciousness of the non-existence of women, except as products of men's desire. I think MacKinnon correctly argues that no Marxian version of identity can firmly ground women's unity. But in solving the problem of the contradictions of any Western revolutionary subject for feminist purposes, she develops an even more authoritarian doctrine of experience. If my complaint about socialist/Marxian standpoints is their unintended erasure of polyvocal, unassimilable, radical difference made visible in anti-colonial discourse and practice, MacKinnon's intentional erasure of all difference through the device of the 'essential' non-existence of women is not reassuring.

In my taxonomy, which like any other taxonomy is a re-inscription of history, radical feminism can accommodate all the activities of women named by socialist feminists as forms of labour only if the activity can somehow be sexualised. Reproduction had different tones of meanings for the two tendencies, one rooted in labour, one in sex, both calling the consequences of domination and ignorance of social and personal reality 'false consciousness'.

Beyond either the difficulties or the contributions in the argument of any one author, neither Marxist nor radical feminist points of view have tended to embrace the status of a partial explanation; both were regularly constituted as totalities. Western explanation has demanded as much; how else could the 'Western' author incorporate its others? Each tried to annex other forms of domination by expanding its basic categories through analogy, simple listing or addition. Embarrassed silence about race among white radical and socialist feminists was one major, devastating political consequence. History and polyvocality disappear into political taxonomies that try to establish genealogies. There was no structural room for race (or for much else) in theory claiming to reveal the construction of the category woman and social group women as a unified or totalisable whole. The structure of my caricature looks like this:

• socialist feminism – structure of class / wage labour / alienation
• labour, by analogy reproduction, by extension sex, by addition race
• radical feminism – structure of gender / sexual appropriation / objectification
• sex, by analogy labour, by extension reproduction, by addition race

In another context, the French theorist, Julia Kristeva, claimed women appeared as a historical group after the Second World War, along with groups like youth. Her dates are doubtful; but we are now accustomed to remembering that as objects of knowledge and as historical actors, 'race' did not always exist, 'class' has a historical genesis, and 'homosexuals' are quite junior. It is no accident that the symbolic system of the family of man – and so the essence of woman – breaks up at the same moment that networks of connection among people on the planet are unprecedentedly multiple, pregnant and complex. 'Advanced capitalism' is inadequate to convey the structure of this historical moment. In the 'Western' sense, the end of man is at stake. It is no accident that woman disintegrates into women in our time. Perhaps socialist feminists were not substantially guilty of producing essentialist theory that suppressed women's particularity and contradictory interests. I think we have been, at least through unreflective participation in the logics, languages and practices of white humanism and through searching for a single ground of domination to secure our revolutionary voice. Now we have less excuse. But in the consciousness of our failures, we risk lapsing into boundless difference and giving up on the confusing task of making partial, real connection. Some differences are playful; some are poles of world historical systems of domination. 'Epistemology' is about knowing the difference.

The Informatics of Domination

In this attempt at an epistemological and political position, I would like to sketch a picture of possible unity, a picture indebted to socialist and feminist principles of design. The frame for my sketch is set by the extent and importance of rearrangements in worldwide social relations tied to science and technology. I argue for a politics rooted in claims about fundamental changes in the nature of class, race, and gender in an emerging system of world order analogous in its novelty and scope to that created by industrial capitalism; we are living through a movement from an organic, industrial society to a polymorphous, information system – from all work to all play, a deadly game. Simultaneously material and ideological, the dichotomies may be expressed in the following chart of transitions from the comfortable old hierarchical dominations to the scary new networks I have called the informatics of domination:

Representation	Simulation
Bourgeois novel, realism	Science fiction, postmodernism
Organism	Biotic component
Depth, integrity	Surface, boundary
Heat	Noise
Biology as clinical practice	Biology as inscription
Physiology	Communications engineering
Small group	Subsystem
Perfection	Optimisation
Eugenics	Population Control
Decadence, *MagicMountain*	Obsolescence, *Future Shock*
Hygiene	Stress Management
Microbiology, tuberculosis	Immunology, AIDS
Organic division of labour	Ergonomics / cybernetics of labour
Functional specialisation	Modular construction
Reproduction	Replication

the science fiction film reader

Organic sex role specialisation	Optimal genetic strategies
Biological determinism	Evolutionary inertia, constraints
Community ecology	Ecosystem
Racial chain of being	Neo-imperialism, United Nations humanism
Scientific management in home / factory	Global factory / Electronic cottage
Family / Market / Factory	Women in the Integrated Circuit
Family wage	Comparable worth
Public / Private	Cyborg citizenship
Nature / Culture	Fields of difference
Co-operation	Communications enhancement
Freud	Lacan
Sex	Genetic engineering
Labour	Robotics
Mind	Artificial Intelligence
Second World War	Star Wars
White Capitalist Patriarchy	Informatics of Domination

This list suggests several interesting things.[13] First, the objects on the right-hand side cannot be coded as 'natural', a realisation that subverts naturalistic coding for the left-hand side as well. We cannot go back ideologically or materially. It's not just that 'god' is dead; so is the 'goddess'. Or both are revivified in the worlds charged with microelectronic and biotechnological politics. In relation to objects like biotic components, one must think not in terms of essential properties, but in terms of design, boundary constraints, rates of flows, systems logics, costs of lowering constraints. Sexual reproduction is one kind of reproductive strategy among many, with costs and benefits as a function of the system environment. Ideologies of sexual re-production can no longer reasonably call on

notions of sex and sex role as organic aspects in natural objects like organisms and families. Such reasoning will be unmasked as irrational, and ironically corporate executives reading *Playboy* and anti-porn radical feminists will make strange bedfellows in jointly unmasking the irrationalism.

Likewise for race, ideologies about human diversity have to be formulated in terms of frequencies of parameters, like blood groups or intelligence scores. It is 'irrational' to invoke concepts like primitive and civilised. For liberals and radicals, the search for integrated social systems gives way to a new practice called 'experimental ethnography' in which an organic object dissipates in attention to the play of writing. At the level of ideology, we see translations of racism and colonialism into languages of development and under-development, rates and constraints of modernisation. Any objects or persons can be reasonably thought of in terms of disassembly and reassembly; no 'natural' architectures constrain system design. The financial districts in all the world's cities, as well as the export-processing and free-trade zones, proclaim this elementary fact of 'late capitalism'. The entire universe of objects that can be known scientifically must be formulated as problems in communications engineering (for the managers) or theories of the text (for those who would resist). Both are cyborg semiologies.

One should expect control strategies to concentrate on boundary conditions and interfaces, on rates of flow across boundaries – and not on the integrity of natural objects. 'Integrity' or 'sincerity' of the Western self gives way to decision procedures and expert systems. For example, control strategies applied to women's capacities to give birth to new human beings will be developed in the languages of population control and maximisation of goal achievement for individual decision-makers. Control strategies will be formulated in terms of rates, costs of constraints, degrees of freedom. Human beings, like any other component or subsystem, must be localised in a system architecture whose basic modes of operation are probabilistic, statistical. No objects, spaces or bodies are sacred in themselves; any component can be interfaced with any other if the proper standard, the proper code, can be constructed for processing signals in a common language.

Exchange in this world transcends the universal translation effected by capitalist markets that Marx analysed so well. The privileged pathology affecting all kinds of components in this universe is stress – communications breakdown (Hogness 1983). The cyborg is not subject to Foucault's biopolitics; the cyborg simulates politics, a much more potent field of operations.

This kind of analysis of scientific and cultural objects of knowledge which have appeared historically since the Second World War prepares us to notice some important inadequacies in feminist analysis which has proceeded as if the organic, hierarchical dualisms ordering discourse in 'the West' since Aristotle still ruled. They have been cannibaliSed, or as Zoe Sofia (Sofoulis) might put it, they have been 'techno-digested'. The dichotomies between mind and body, animal and human, organism and machine, public and private, nature and culture, men and women, primitive and civilised are all in question ideologically. The actual situation of women is their integration/exploitation into a world system of production/reproduction and communication called the informatics of domination. The home, workplace, market, public arena, the body itself – all can be dispersed and interfaced in nearly infinite, polymorphous ways, with large consequences for women and others – consequences that themselves are very different for different people and which make potent oppositional international movements difficult to imagine and essential for survival. One important route for reconstructing socialist-feminist politics is through theory and practice addressed to the social relations of science and technology, including crucially the systems of myth and meanings structuring our imaginations. The cyborg is a kind of disassembled and re-assembled, postmodern collective and personal self. This is the self feminists must code.

Communications technologies and biotechnologies are the crucial tools recrafting our bodies. These tools embody and enforce new social relations for women worldwide. Technologies and scientific discourses can be partially understood as formalisations, i.e., as frozen moments, of the fluid social interactions constituting them, but they should also be viewed as instruments for enforcing meanings. The boundary is permeable between tool and myth, instrument and concept, historical systems of social relations and historical anatomies of possible bodies, including objects of knowledge. Indeed, myth and tool mutually constitute each other.

Furthermore, communications sciences and modern biologies are constructed by a common move – *the translation of the world into a problem of coding*, a search for a common language in which all resistance to instrumental control disappears and all heterogeneity can be submitted to disassembly, reassembly, investment and exchange.

In communications sciences, the translation of the world into a problem in coding can be illustrated by looking at cybernetic (feedback-controlled) systems theories applied to telephone technology, computer design, weapons deployment or database construction and maintenance. In each case, solution to the key questions rests on a theory of language and control; the key operation is determining the rates, directions and probabilities of flow of a quantity called information. The world is subdivided by boundaries differentially permeable to information. Information is just that kind of quantifiable element (unit, basis of unity) which allows universal translation, and so unhindered instrumental power (called effective communication). The biggest threat to such power is interruption of communication. Any system breakdown is a function of stress. The fundamentals of this technology can be condensed into the metaphor C^3I, command-control-communication-intelligence, the military's symbol for its operations theory.

In modern biologies, the translation of the world into a problem in coding can be illustrated by molecular genetics, ecology, sociobiological evolutionary theory and immunobiology. The organism has been translated into problems of genetic coding and read-out. Biotechnology, a writing technology, informs research broadly.[14] In a sense, organisms have ceased to exist as objects of knowledge, giving way to biotic components, i.e., special kinds of information-processing devices. The analogous moves in ecology could be examined by probing the history and utility of the concept of the ecosystem. Immunobiology and associated medical practices are rich exemplars of the privilege of coding and recognition systems as objects of knowledge, as constructions of bodily reality for us. Biology here is a kind of cryptography. Research is necessarily a kind of intelligence activity. Ironies abound. A stressed system goes awry; its communication processes break down; it fails to recognise the difference between self and other. Human babies with baboon hearts evoke national ethical perplexity – for animal rights activists at least as much as for the guardians of human purity. In the US gay men and intravenous drug users are the 'privileged' victims of an awful immune system disease that marks (inscribes on the body) confusion of boundaries and moral pollution (Treichler 1987).

But these excursions into communications sciences and biology have been at a rarefied level; there is a mundane, largely economic reality to support my claim that these sciences and technologies indicate fundamental transformations in the structure of the world for us. Communications technologies depend on electronics. Modern states, multinational corporations, military power, welfare state apparatuses, satellite systems, political processes, fabrication of our imaginations, labour-control systems, medical constructions of our bodies, commercial pornography, the international division of labour and religious evangelism depend intimately upon electronics. Microelectronics is the technical basis of simulacra; that is, of copies without originals.

Microelectronics mediates the translations of labour into robotics and word processing, sex into genetic engineering and reproductive technologies, and mind into artificial intelligence and decision procedures. The new biotechnologies concern more than human reproduction. Biology as a powerful engineering science for redesigning materials and processes has revolutionary implications for industry, perhaps most obvious today in areas of fermentation, agriculture, and energy. Communications sciences and biology are constructions of natural-technical objects of knowledge in which the difference between machine and organism is thoroughly blurred; mind, body and tool are on very intimate terms. The 'multinational' material organisation of the production and reproduction of daily life and the symbolic organisation of the production and reproduction of culture and imagination seem equally implicated. The boundary-maintaining images of base and superstructure, public and private, or material and ideal never seemed more feeble.

I have used Rachel Grossman's (1980) image of women in the integrated circuit to name the situation of women in a world so intimately restructured through the social relations of science and technology.[15] I used the odd circumlocution, 'the social relations of science and technology', to indicate that we are not dealing with a technological determinism, but with a historical system depending upon structured relations among people. But the phrase should also indicate that science and technology provide fresh sources of power, that we need fresh sources of analysis and political action (Latour 1984). Some of the rearrangements of race, sex and class rooted in high-tech-facilitated social relations can make socialist-feminism more relevant to effective progressive politics.

The 'Homework Economy' Outside 'the Home'

The 'New Industrial Revolution' is producing a new worldwide working class, as well as new sexualities and ethnicities. The extreme mobility of capital and the emerging international division of labour are intertwined with the emergence of new collectivities, and the weakening of familiar groupings. These developments are neither gender- nor race-neutral. White men in advanced industrial societies have become newly vulnerable to permanent job loss, and women are not disappearing from the job rolls at the same rates as men. It is not simply that women in Third World countries are the preferred labour force for the science-based multinationals in the export-processing sectors, particularly in electronics. The picture is more systematic and involves reproduction, sexuality, culture, consumption and production. In the prototypical Silicon Valley, many women's lives have been structured around employment in electronics-dependent jobs, and their intimate realities include serial heterosexual monogamy, negotiating childcare, distance from extended kin or most other forms of traditional community, a high likelihood of loneliness and extreme economic vulnerability as they age. The ethnic and racial diversity of women in Silicon Valley structures a microcosm of conflicting differences in culture, family, religion, education and language.

Richard Gordon has called this new situation the 'homework economy'.[16] Although he includes the phenomenon of literal homework emerging in connection with electronics assembly, Gordon intends 'homework economy' to name a restructuring of work that broadly has the characteristics formerly ascribed to female jobs, jobs literally done only by women. Work is being redefined as both literally female and feminised, whether performed by men or women. To be feminised means to be made extremely vulnerable; able to be disassembled, reassembled, exploited as a reserve labour force; seen less as workers than as servers; subjected to time arrangements on and off the paid job that make a mockery of a limited work day; leading an existence that always borders on being obscene, out of place and reducible to sex. Deskilling is an old strategy newly applicable to formerly privileged workers. However, the homework economy does not refer only to large-scale deskilling, nor does it deny that new areas of high skill are emerging, even for women and men previously excluded from skilled employment. Rather, the concept indicates that factory, home and market are integrated on a new scale and that the places of women are crucial – and need to be analysed for differences among women and for meanings for relations between men and women in various situations.

The homework economy as a world capitalist organisational structure is made possible by (not caused by) the new technologies. The success of the attack on relatively privileged, mostly white, men's unionised jobs is tied to the power of the new communications technologies to integrate and control labour despite extensive dispersion and decentralisation. The consequences of the new technologies are felt by women both in the loss of the family (male) wage (if they ever had access to this white privilege) and in the character of their own jobs, which are becoming capital-intensive; for example, office work and nursing.

The new economic and technological arrangements are also related to the collapsing welfare state and the ensuing intensification of demands on women to sustain daily life for themselves as well as for men, children and old people. The feminisation of poverty – generated by dismantling the welfare state, by the homework economy where stable jobs become the exception, and sustained by the expectation that women's wages will not be matched by a male income for the support of children – has become an urgent focus. The causes of various women-headed households are a function of race, class or sexuality; but their increasing generality is a ground for coalitions of women on many issues. That women regularly sustain daily life partly as a function of their enforced status as mothers is hardly new; the kind of integration with the overall capitalist and progressively war-based economy is new. The particular pressure, for example, on US black women, who have achieved an escape from (barely) paid domestic service and who now hold clerical and similar jobs in large numbers, has large implications for continued enforced black poverty *with* employment. Teenage women in industrialising areas of the Third World increasingly find themselves the sole or major source of a cash wage for their families, while access to land is ever more problematic. These developments must have major consequences in the psychodynamics and politics of gender and race.

Within the framework of three major stages of capitalism (commercial/early industrial, monopoly, multinational) – tied to nationalism, imperialism and multinationalism, and related to Jameson's three dominant aesthetic periods of realism, modernism and postmodernism – I would argue that specific forms of families dialectically relate to forms of capital and to its political and cultural concomitants. Although lived problematically and unequally, ideal forms of these families might be schematised as (i) the patriarchal nuclear family, structured by the dichotomy between public and private and accompanied by the white bourgeois ideology of separate spheres and nineteenth-century Anglo-American bourgeois feminism; (ii) the modern family mediated (or enforced) by the welfare state and institutions like the family wage, with a flowering of a-feminist heterosexual ideologies, including their radical versions represented in Greenwich Village around the First World War; and (iii) the 'family' of the homework economy with its oxymoronic structure of women-headed households and its explosion of feminisms and the paradoxical intensification and erosion of gender itself. This is the context in which the projections for worldwide structural unemployment stemming from the new technologies are part of the picture of the homework economy. As robotics and related technologies put men out of work in 'developed' countries and exacerbate failure to generate male jobs in Third World 'development', and as the automated office becomes the rule even in labour-surplus countries, the feminisation of work intensifies. Black women in the United States have long known what it looks like to face the structural underemployment ('feminisation') of black men, as well as their own highly vulnerable position in the wage economy. It is no longer a secret that sexuality, reproduction, family and community life are interwoven with this economic structure in myriad ways which have also differentiated the situations of white and black women. Many more women and men will contend with similar situations, which will make cross-gender and race alliances on issues of basic life support (with or without jobs) necessary, not just nice.

The new technologies also have a profound effect on hunger and on food production for subsistence worldwide. Rae Lessor Blumberg (1983) estimates that women produce about 50 per cent of the world's subsistence food.[17] Women are excluded generally from benefiting from the increased high-tech commodification of food and energy crops, their days are made more arduous because their responsibilities to provide food do not diminish, and their reproductive situations are made more complex. Green Revolution technologies interact with other high-tech industrial production to alter gender divisions of labour and differential gender migration patterns.

The new technologies seem deeply involved in the forms of 'privatisation' that Ros Petchesky (1981) has analysed, in which militarisation, right-wing family ideologies and policies, and intensified definitions of corporate (and state) property as private synergistically interact.[18] The new communications technologies are fundamental to the eradication of 'public life' for everyone. This facilitates the mushrooming of a permanent high-tech military establishment at the cultural and economic expense of most people, but especially of women. Technologies like video games and highly miniaturised televisions seem crucial to production of modern forms of 'private life'. The culture of video games is heavily orientated to individual competition and extraterrestrial warfare. High-tech, gendered imaginations are produced here, imaginations that can contemplate destruction of the planet and a sci-fi escape from its

consequences. More than our imaginations is militarised; and the other realities of electronic and nuclear warfare are inescapable. These are the technologies that promise ultimate mobility and perfect exchange — and incidentally enable tourism, that perfect practice of mobility and exchange, to emerge as one of the world's largest single industries.

The new technologies affect the social relations of both sexuality and of reproduction, and not always in the same ways. The close ties of sexuality and instrumentality, of views of the body as a kind of private satisfaction- and utility-maximising machine, are described nicely in sociobiological origin stories that stress a genetic calculus and explain the inevitable dialectic of domination of male and female gender roles.[19] These sociobiological stories depend on a high-tech view of the body as a biotic component or cybernetic communications system. Among the many transformations of reproductive situations is the medical one, where women's bodies have boundaries newly permeable to both 'visualisation' and 'intervention'. Of course, who controls the interpretation of bodily boundaries in medical hermeneutics is a major feminist issue. The speculum served as an icon of women's claiming their bodies in the 1970s; that handcraft tool is inadequate to express our needed body politics in the negotiation of reality in the practices of cyborg reproduction. Self-help is not enough. The technologies of visualisation recall the important cultural practice of hunting with the camera and the deeply predatory nature of a photographic consciousness.[20] Sex, sexuality and reproduction are central actors in high-tech myth systems structuring our imaginations of personal and social possibility.

Another critical aspect of the social relations of the new technologies is the re-formulation of expectations, culture, work and reproduction for the large scientific and technical workforce. A major social and political danger is the formation of a strongly bimodal social structure, with the masses of women and men of all ethnic groups, but especially people of colour, confined to a homework economy, illiteracy of several varieties and general redundancy and impotence, controlled by high-tech repressive apparatuses ranging from entertainment to surveillance and disappearance. An adequate socialist-feminist politics should address women in the privileged occupational categories, and particularly in the production of science and technology that constructs scientific-technical discourses, processes and objects.[21]

This issue is only one aspect of enquiry into the possibility of a feminist science, but it is important. What kind of constitutive role in the production of knowledge, imagination and practice can new groups doing science have? How can these groups be allied with progressive social and political movements? What kind of political accountability can be constructed to tie women together across the scientific-technical hierarchies separating us? Might there be ways of developing feminist science/technology politics in alliance with anti-military science facility conversion action groups? Many scientific and technical workers in Silicon Valley, the high-tech cowboys included, do not want to work on military science.[22] Can these personal preferences and cultural tendencies be welded into progressive politics among this professional middle class in which women, including women of colour, are coming to be fairly numerous?

Women in the Integrated Circuit

Let me summarise the picture of women's historical locations in advanced industrial societies, as these positions have been re-structured partly through the social relations of science and technology. If it was ever possible ideologically to characterise women's lives by the distinction of public and private domains – suggested by images of the division of working-class life into factory and home, of bourgeois life into market and home, and of gender existence into personal and political realms – it is now a totally misleading ideology, even to show how both terms of these dichotomies construct each other in practice and in theory. I prefer a network ideological image, suggesting the profusion of spaces and identities and the permeability of boundaries in the personal body and in the body politic. 'Networking' is both a feminist practice and a multinational corporate strategy – weaving is for oppositional cyborgs.

So let me return to the earlier image of the informatics of domination and trace one vision of women's 'place' in the integrated circuit, touching only a few idealised social locations seen primarily from the point of view

of advanced capitalist societies: Home, Market, Paid Work Place, State, School, Clinic-Hospital, and Church. Each of these idealised spaces is logically and practically implied in every other locus, perhaps analogous to a holographic photograph. I want to suggest the impact of the social relations mediated and enforced by the new technologies in order to help formulate needed analysis and practical work. However, there is no 'place' for women in these networks, only geometrics of difference and contradiction crucial to women's cyborg identities. If we learn how to read these webs of power and social life, we might learn new couplings, new coalitions. There is no way to read the following list from a standpoint of 'identification', of a unitary self. The issue is dispersion. The task is to survive in the diaspora.

Home: Women-headed households, serial monogamy, flight of men, old women alone, technology of domestic work, paid homework, re-emergence of home sweat-shops, home-based businesses and telecommuting, electronic cottage, urban homelessness, migration, module architecture, reinforced (simulated) nuclear family, intense domestic violence.

Market: Women's continuing consumption work, newly targeted to buy the profusion of new production from the new technologies (especially as the competitive race among industrialised and industrialising nations to avoid dangerous mass unemployment necessitates finding ever bigger new markets for ever less clearly needed commodities); bimodal buying power, coupled with advertising targeting of the numerous affluent groups and neglect of the previous mass markets; growing importance of informal markets in labour and commodities parallel to high-tech, affluent market structures; surveillance systems through electronic funds transfer; intensified market abstraction (commodification) of experience, resulting in ineffective utopian or equivalent cynical theories of community; extreme mobility (abstraction) of marketing/financing systems; interpenetration of sexual and labour markets; intensified sexualisation of abstracted and alienated consumption.

Paid Work Place: Continued intense sexual and racial division of labour, but considerable growth of membership in privileged occupational categories for many white women and people of colour; impact of new technologies on women's work in clerical, service, manufacturing (especially textiles), agriculture, electronics; international restructuring of the working classes; development of new time arrangements to facilitate the homework economy (flex time, part time, over time, no time); homework and out work; increased pressures for two-tiered wage structures; significant numbers of people in cash-dependent populations worldwide with no experience or no further hope of stable employment; most labour 'marginal' or 'feminised'.

State: Continued erosion of the welfare state; decentralisations with increased surveillance and control; citizenship by telematics; imperialism and political power broadly in the form of information rich/information poor differentiation; increased high-tech militariation increasingly opposed by many social groups; reduction of civil service jobs as a result of the growing capital intensification of office work, with implications for occupational mobility for women of colour; growing privatisation of material and ideological life and culture; close integration of privatisation and militarisation, the high-tech forms of bourgeois capitalist personal and public life; invisibility of different social groups to each other, linked to psychological mechanisms of belief in abstract enemies.

School: Deepening coupling of high-tech capital needs and public education at all levels, differentiated by race, class, and gender; managerial classes involved in educational reform and refunding at the cost of remaining progressive educational democratic structures for children and teachers; education for mass ignorance and repression in technocratic and militarised culture; growing anti-science mystery cults in dissenting and radical political movements; continued relative scientific illiteracy among white women and people of colour; growing industrial direction of education (especially higher education) by science-based multinationals (particularly in electronics- and biotechnology-dependent companies); highly educated, numerous élites in a progressively bimodal society.

Clinic-hospital: Intensified machinebody relations; renegotiations of public metaphors which channel personal experience of the body, particularly in relation to reproduction, immune system functions, and 'stress' phenomena; intensification of reproductive politics in response to world historical implications of women's unrealised, potential control of their relation to reproduction; emergence of new, historically specific diseases; struggles over meanings and means of health in environments pervaded by high technology products and processes; continuing feminisation of health work; intensified struggle over state responsibility for health; continued ideological role of popular health movements as a major form of American politics.

Church: Electronic fundamentalist 'super-saver' preachers solemnising the union of electronic capital and automated fetish gods; intensified importance of churches in resisting the militarised state; central struggle over women's meanings and authority in religion; continued relevance of spirituality, intertwined with sex and health, in political struggle.

The only way to characterise the informatics of domination is as a massive intensification of insecurity and cultural impoverishment, with common failure of subsistence networks for the most vulnerable. Since much of this picture interweaves with the social relations of science and technology, the urgency of a socialist-feminist politics addressed to science and technology is plain. There is much now being done, and the grounds for political work are rich. For example, the efforts to develop forms of collective struggle for women in paid work, like SEIU's District 925 (Service Employees International Union's office workers' organisation in the US) should be a high priority for all of us. These efforts are profoundly tied to technical restructuring of labour processes and reformations of working classes. These efforts also are providing understanding of a more comprehensive kind of labour organisation, involving community, sexuality and family issues never privileged in the largely white male industrial unions.

The structural rearrangements related to the social relations of science and technology evoke strong ambivalence. But it is not necessary to be ultimately depressed by the implications of late twentieth-century women's relation to all aspects of work, culture, production of knowledge, sexuality and reproduction. For excellent reasons, most Marxisms see domination best and have trouble understanding what can only look like false consciousness and people's complicity in their own domination in late capitalism. It is crucial to remember that what is lost, perhaps especially from women's points of view, is often virulent forms of oppression, nostalgically naturalised in the face of current violation. Ambivalence towards the disrupted unities mediated by high-tech culture requires not sorting consciousness into categories of 'clear-sighted critique grounding a solid political epistemology' versus 'manipulated false consciousness', but subtle understanding of emerging pleasures, experiences and powers with serious potential for changing the rules of the game.

There are grounds for hope in the emerging bases for new kinds of unity across race, gender and class, as these elementary units of socialist-feminist analysis themselves suffer protean transformations. Intensifications of hardship experienced world-wide in connection with the social relations of science and technology are severe. But what people are experiencing is not transparently clear, and we lack sufficiently subtle connections for collectively building effective theories of experience. Present efforts – Marxist, psychoanalytic, feminist, anthropological – to clarify even 'our' experience are rudimentary.

I am conscious of the odd perspective provided by my historical position – a PhD in biology for an Irish Catholic girl was made possible by Sputnik's impact on US national science-education policy. I have a body and mind as much constructed by the post-Second World War arms race and cold war as by the women's movements. There are more grounds for hope in focusing on the contradictory effects of politics designed to produce loyal American technocrats, which also produced large numbers of dissidents, than in focusing on the present defeats.

The permanent partiality of feminist points of view has consequences for our expectations of forms of political organisation and participation. We do not need a totality in order to work well. The feminist dream of a common language, like all dreams for a perfectly true language, of perfectly faithful naming of experience, is a totalising and imperialist one. In that sense, dialectics too is a dream language, longing to resolve contradiction. Perhaps, ironically, we can learn from our fusions with animals and machines how not to be Man, the embodiment of Western logos. From the point of view of pleasure in these potent and taboo fusions, made inevitable by the social relations of science and technology, there might indeed be a feminist science.

Cyborgs: A Myth of Political Identity

I want to conclude with a myth about identity and boundaries which might inform late twentieth-century political imaginations. I am indebted to writers like Joanna Russ, Samuel R. Delany, John Varley, James Tiptree Jr, Octavia Butler, Monique Wittig and Vonda McIntyre.[23] These are our story-tellers exploring what it means to be embodied in high-tech worlds. They are theorists for cyborgs. Exploring conceptions of bodily boundaries and social order, the anthropologist Mary Douglas (1966, 1970) should be credited with helping us to consciousness about how fundamental body imagery is to world view, and so to political language. French feminists like Luce Irigaray and Monique Wittig, for all their differences, know how to write the body; how to weave eroticism, cosmology and politics from imagery of embodiment, and especially for Wittig, from imagery of fragmentation and reconstitution of bodies.[24]

American radical feminists like Susan Griffin, Audre Lorde and Adrienne Rich have profoundly affected our political imaginations – and perhaps restricted too much what we allow as a friendly body and political language.[25] They insist on the organic, opposing it to the technological. But their symbolic systems and the related positions of ecofeminism and feminist paganism, replete with organicisms, can only be understood in Sandoval's terms as oppositional ideologies fitting the late twentieth century. They would simply bewilder anyone not preoccupied with the machines and consciousness of late capitalism. In that sense they are part of the cyborg world. But there are also great riches for feminists in explicitly embracing the possibilities inherent in the breakdown of clean distinctions between organism and machine and similar distinctions structuring the Western self. It is the simultaneity of breakdowns that cracks the matrices of domination and opens geometric possibilities. What might be learned from personal and political 'technological' pollution? I look briefly at two overlapping groups of texts for their insight into the construction of a potentially helpful cyborg myth: constructions of women of colour and monstrous selves in feminist science fiction.

Earlier I suggested that 'women of colour' might be understood as a cyborg identity, a potent subjectivity synthesised from fusions of outsider identities and in the complex political-historical layerings of her 'biomythography', *Zami* (Lorde 1982; King 1987a, 1987b). There are material and cultural grids mapping this potential, Audre Lorde (1984) captures the tone in the title of her *Sister Outsider*. In my political myth, Sister Outsider is the offshore woman, whom US workers, female and feminised, are supposed to regard as the enemy preventing their solidarity, threatening their security. Onshore, inside the boundary of the United States, Sister Outsider is a potential amidst the races and ethnic identities of women manipulated for division, competition and exploitation in the same industries. 'Women of colour' are the preferred labour force for the science-based industries, the real women for whom the worldwide sexual market, labour market and politics of repro-duction kaleidoscope into daily life. Young Korean women hired in the sex industry and in electronics assembly are recruited from high schools, educated for the integrated circuit. Literacy, especially in English, distinguishes the 'cheap' female labour so attractive to the multinationals.

Contrary to orientalist stereotypes of the 'oral primitive', literacy is a special mark of women of colour, acquired by US black women as well as men through a history of risking death to learn and to teach reading and writing. Writing has a special significance for all colonised groups. Writing has been crucial to the Western myth of the distinction between oral and written cultures, primitive and civilised mentalities, and more recently to the erosion of that distinction in 'postmodernist' theories attacking the phallogocentrism of the West, with its worship of the monotheistic, phallic, authoritative and singular work, the unique and perfect name.[26] Contests for the meanings of writing are a major form of contemporary political struggle. Releasing the play of writing is deadly serious. The poetry and stories of US women of colour are repeatedly about writing, about access to the power to signify; but this time that power must be neither phallic nor innocent. Cyborg writing must not be about the Fall, the imagination of a once-upon-a-time wholeness before language, before writing, before Man. Cyborg writing is about the

power to survive, not on the basis of original innocence, but on the basis of seizing the tools to mark the world that marked them as other.

The tools are often stories, retold stories, versions that reverse and displace the hier-archical dualisms of naturalised identities. In retelling origin stories, cyborg authors subvert the central myths of origin of Western culture. We have all been colonised by those origin myths, with their longing for fulfilment in apocalypse. The phallogocentric origin stories most crucial for feminist cyborgs are built into the literal technologies – technologies that write the world, biotechnology and microelectronics – that have recently textualised our bodies as code problems on the grid of C[3]I. Feminist cyborg stories have the task of recoding communication and intelligence to subvert command and control.

Figuratively and literally, language politics pervade the struggles of women of colour; and stories about language have a special power in the rich contemporary writing by US women of colour. For example, retellings of the story of the indigenous woman Malinche, mother of the mestizo 'bastard' race of the new world, master of languages and mistress of Cortés, carry special meaning for Chicana constructions of identity. Cherríe Moraga (1983) in *Loving in the War Years* explores the themes of identity when one never possessed the original language, never told the original story, never resided in the harmony of legitimate heterosexuality in the garden of culture, and so cannot base identity on a myth or a fall from innocence and right to natural names, mother's or father's.[27] Moraga's writing, her superb literacy, is presented in her poetry as the same kind of violation as Malinche's mastery of the conqueror's language – a violation, an illegitimate production, that allows survival. Moraga's language is not 'whole'; it is self-consciously spliced, a chimera of English and Spanish, both conqueror's languages. But it is this chimeric monster, without claim to an original language before violation, that crafts the erotic, competent, potent identities of women of colour. Sister Outsider hints at the possibility of world survival not because of her innocence, but because of her ability to live on the boundaries, to write without the founding myth of original wholeness, with its inescapable apocalypse of final return to a deathly oneness that Man has imagined to be the innocent and all-powerful Mother, freed at the End from another spiral of apporpriation by her son. Writing marks Moraga's body, affirms it as the body of a woman of colour, against the possibility of passing into the unmarked category of the Anglo father or into the orientalist myth of 'original illiteracy' of a mother that never was. Malinche was mother here, not Eve before eating the forbidden fruit. Writing affirms Sister Outsider, not the Woman-before-the-Fall-into-Writing needed by the phallogocentric Family of Man.

Writing is pre-eminently the technology of cyborgs, etched surfaces of the late twentieth century. Cyborg politics is the struggle for language and the struggle against perfect communication, against the one code that translates all meaning perfectly, the central dogma of phallogocentrism. That is why cyborg politics insist on noise and advocate pollution, rejoicing in the illegitimate fusions of animal and machine. These are the couplings which make Man and Woman so problematic, subverting the structure of desire, the force imagined to generate language and gender, and so subverting the structure and modes of reproduction of 'Western' identity, of nature and culture, of mirror and eye, slave and master, body and mind. 'We' did not originally choose to be cyborgs, but choice grounds a liberal politics and epistemology that imagines the reproduction of individuals before the wider replications of 'texts'.

From the perspective of cyborgs, freed of the need to ground politics in 'our' privileged position of the oppression that incorporates all other dominations, the innocence of the merely violated, the ground of those closer to nature, we can see powerful possibilities. Feminisms and Marxisms have run aground on Western epistemological imperatives to construct a revolutionary subject from the perspective of a hierarchy of oppressions and/or a latent position of moral superiority, innocence and greater closeness to nature. With no available original dream of a common language or original symbiosis promising protection from hostile 'masculine' separation, but written into the play of a text that has no finally privileged reading or salvation history, to recognise 'oneself' as fully implicated in the world, frees us of the need to root politics in identification, vanguard parties, purity and mothering. Stripped of identity, the

bastard race teaches about the power of the margins and the importance of a mother like Malinche. Women of colour have transformed her from the evil mother of masculinist fear into the originally literate mother who teaches survival.

This is not just literary deconstruction, but liminal transformation. Every story that begins with original innocence and privileges the return to wholeness imagines the drama of life to be individuation, separation, the birth of the self, the tragedy of autonomy, the fall into writing, alienation; that is, war, tempered by imaginary respite in the bosom of the Other. These plots are ruled by a reproductive politics – rebirth without flaw, perfection, abstraction. In this plot women are imagined either better or worse off, but all agree they have less selfhood, weaker individuation, more fusion to the oral, to Mother, less at stake in masculine autonomy. But there is another route to having less at stake in masculine autonomy, a route that does not passes through Women, Primitive, Zero, the Mirror Stage and its imaginary. It passes through women and other present-tense, illegitimate cyborgs, not of Woman born, who refuse the ideological resources of victimisation so as to have a real life. These cyborgs are the people who refuse to disappear on cue, no matter how many times a 'Western' commentator remarks on the sad passing of another primitive, another organic group done in by 'Western' technology, by writing.[28] These real-life cyborgs (for example, the Southeast Asian village women workers in Japanese and US electronics firms described by Aihwa Ong) are actively rewriting the texts of their bodies and societies. Survival is the stakes in this play of readings.

To recapitulate, certain dualisms have been persistent in Western traditions; they have all been systemic to the logics and practices of domination of women, people of colour, nature, workers, animals – in short, domination of all constituted as others, whose task is to mirror the self. Chief among these troubling dualisms are self/other, mind/body, culture/nature, male/female, civilised/primitive, reality/appearance, whole/part, agent/resource, maker/made, active/passive, right/wrong, truth/illusion, total/partial, God/man. The self is the One who is not dominated, who knows that by the service of the other, the other is the one who holds the future, who knows that by the experience of domination, which gives the lie to the autonomy of the self. To be One is to be autonomous, to be powerful, to be God; but to be One is to be an illusion, and so to be involved in a dialectic of apocalypse with the other. Yet to be other is to be multiple, without clear boundary, frayed, insubstantial. One is too few, but two are too many.

High-tech culture challenges these dualisms in intriguing ways. It is not clear who makes and who is made in the relation between human and machine. It is not clear what is mind and what body in machines that resolve into coding practices. In so far as we know ourselves in both formal discourse (for example, biology) and in daily practice (for example, the homework economy in the integrated circuit), we find ourselves to be cyborgs, hybrids, mosaics, chimeras. Biological organisms have become biotic systems, communications devices like others. There is no fundamental, ontological separation in our formal knowledge of machine and organism, of technical and organic. The replicant Rachael in the Ridley Scott film *Blade Runner* stands as the image of a cyborg culture's fear, love and confusion.

One consequence is that our sense of connection to our tools is heightened. The trance state experienced by many computer users has become a staple of science fiction film and cultural jokes. Perhaps paraplegics and other severely handicapped people can (and sometimes do) have the most intense experiences of complex hybridisation with other communication devices.[29] Anne McCaffrey's pre-feminist *The Ship Who Sang* (1969) explored the consciousness of a cyborg, hybrid of girl's brain and complex machinery, formed after the birth of a severely handicapped child. Gender, sexuality, embodiment, skill: all were reconstituted in the story. Why should our bodies end at the skin, or include at best other beings encapsulated by skin? From the seventeenth century until now, machines could be animated – given ghostly souls to make them speak or move or to account for their orderly development and mental capacities. Or organisms could be mechanised – reduced to body understood as resource of mind. These machine/organism relationships are obsolete, unnecessary. For us, in imagination and in other practice, machines can be prosthetic devices, intimate components, friendly selves. We don't

need organic holism to give impermeable wholeness, the total woman and her feminist variants (mutants?). Let me conclude this point by a very partial reading of the logic of the cyborg monsters of my second group of texts, feminist science fiction.

The cyborgs populating feminist science fiction make very problematic the statuses of man or woman, human, artefact, member of a race, individual entity or body. Katie King clarifies how pleasure in reading these fictions is not largely based on identification. Students facing Joanna Russ for the first time, students who have learned to take modernist writers like James Joyce or Virginia Woolf without flinching, do not know what to make of *The Adventures of Alyx* or *The Female Man*, where characters refuse the reader's search for innocent wholeness while granting the wish for heroic quests, exuberant eroticism and serious politics. *The Female Man* is the story of four versions of one genotype, all of whom meet, but even taken together do not make a whole, resolve the dilemmas of violent moral action, or remove the growing scandal of gender. The feminist science fiction of Samuel R. Delany, especially *Tales of Nevèrÿon*, mocks stories of origin by redoing the neolithic revolution, replaying the founding moves of Western civilisation to subvert their plausibility. James Tiptree Jr, an author whose fiction was regarded as particularly manly until her 'true' gender was revealed, tells tales of reproduction based on non-mammalian technologies like alternation of generations of male brood pouches and male nurturing. John Varley constructs a supreme cyborg in his arch-feminist exploration of Gaea, a mad goddess-planet-trickster-old woman-technological device on whose surface an extraordinary array of post-cyborg symbioses are spawned. Octavia Butler writes of an African sorceress pitting her powers of transformation against the genetic manipulations of her rival (*Wild Seed*), of time warps that bring a modern US black woman into slavery where her actions in relation to her white master-ancestor determine the possibility of her own birth (*Kindred*), and of the illegitimate insights into identity and community of an adopted cross-species child who came to know the enemy as self (*Survivor*). In *Dawn* (1987), the first instalment of a series called *Xenogenesis*, Butler tells the story of Lilith Iyapo, whose personal name recalls Adam's first and repudiated wife and whose family name marks her status as the widow of the son of Nigerian immigrants to the US. A black woman and a mother whose child is dead, Lilith mediates the transformation of humanity through genetic exchange with extra-terrestrial lovers/rescuers/destroyers/genetic engineers, who reform Earth's habitats after the nuclear holocaust and coerce surviving humans into intimate fusion with them. It is a novel that interrogates reproductive, linguistic and nuclear politics in a mythic field structured by late twentieth-century race and gender.

Because it is particularly rich in boundary transgressions, Vonda McIntyre's *Superluminal* can close this truncated catalogue of promising and dangerous monsters who help redefine the pleasures and politics of embodiment and feminist writing. In a fiction where no character is 'simply' human, human status is highly problematic. Orca, a genetically-altered diver, can speak with killer whales and survive deep ocean conditions, but she longs to explore space as a pilot, necessitating bionic implants jeopardising her kinship with the divers and cetaceans. Transformations are effected by virus vectors carrying a new developmental code, by transplant surgery, by implants of microelectronic devices, by analogue doubles, and other means. Laenea becomes a pilot by accepting a heart implant and a host of other alterations allowing survival in transit at speeds exceeding that of light. Radu Dracul survives a virus-caused plague in his outerworld planet to find himself with a time sense that changes the boundaries of spatial perception for the whole species. All the characters explore the limits of language; the dream of communicating experience; and the necessity of limitation, partiality, and intimacy even in this world of protean transformation and connection. *Superluminal* stands also for the defining contradictions of a cyborg world in another sense; it embodies textually the intersection of feminist theory and colonial discourse in the science fiction I have alluded to in this essay. This is a conjunction with a long history that many 'First World' feminists have tried to repress, including myself in my readings of *Superluminal* before being called to account by Zoe Sofoulis, whose different location in the world system's informatics of domination made her acutely alert to the imperialist moment of all science fiction cultures, including women's science fiction. From an Australian feminist sensitivity,

Sofoulis remembered more readily McIntyre's role as writer of the adventures of Captain Kirk and Spock in TV's *Star Trek* series than her rewriting the romance in *Superluminal*.

Monsters have always defined the limits of community in Western imaginations. The Centaurs and Amazons of ancient Greece established the limits of the centred polis of the Greek male human by their disruption of marriage and boundary pollutions of the warrior with animality and woman. Unseparated twins and hermaphrodites were the confused human material in early modern France who grounded discourse on the natural and supernatural, medical and legal, portents and diseases – all crucial to establishing modern identity.[30] The evolutionary and behavioural sciences of monkeys and apes have marked the multiple boundaries of late twentieth-century industrial identities. Cyborg monsters in feminist science fiction define quite different political possibilities and limits from those proposed by the mundane fiction of Man and Woman.

There are several consequences to taking seriously the imagery of cyborgs as other than our enemies. Our bodies, ourselves; bodies are maps of power and identity. Cyborgs are no exception. A cyborg body is not innocent; it was not born in a garden; it does not seek unitary identity and so generate antagonistic dualisms without end (or until the world ends); it takes irony for granted. One is too few, and two is only one possibility. Intense pleasure in skill, machine skill, ceases to be a sin, but an aspect of embodiment. The machine is not an *it* to be animated, worshipped and dominated. The machine is us, our processes, an aspect of our embodiment. We can be responsible for machines; *they* do not dominate or threaten us. We are responsible for boundaries; we are they. Up until now (once upon a time), female embodiment seemed to be given, organic, necessary; and female embodiment seemed to mean skill in mothering and its metaphoric extensions. Only by being out of place could we take intense pleasure in machines, and then with excuses that this was organic activity after all, appropriate to females. Cyborgs might consider more seriously the partial, fluid aspect of sex and sexual embodiment. Gender might not be global identity after all, even if it has profound historical breadth and depth.

The ideologically charged question of what counts as daily activity, as experience, can be approached by exploiting the cyborg image. Feminists have recently claimed that women are given to dailiness, that women more than men somehow sustain daily life, and so have a privileged epistemological position potentially. There is a compelling aspect to this claim, one that makes visible unvalued female activity and names it as the ground of life. But *the* ground of life? What about all the ignorance of women, all the exclusions and failures of knowledge and skill? What about men's access to daily competence, to knowing how to build things, to take them apart, to play? What about other embodiments? Cyborg gender is a local possibility taking a global vengeance. Race, gender and capital require a cyborg theory of wholes and parts. There is no drive in cyborgs to produce total theory, but there is an intimate experience of boundaries, their construction and deconstruction. There is a myth system waiting to become a political language to ground one way of looking at science and technology and challenging the informatics of domination – in order to act potently.

One last image: organisms and organismic, holistic politics depend on metaphors of rebirth and invariably call on the resources of reproductive sex. I would suggest that cyborgs have more to do with regeneration and are suspicious of the reproductive matrix and of most birthing. For salamanders, regeneration after injury, such as the loss of a limb, involves regrowth of structure and restoration of function with the constant possibility of twinning or other odd topographical productions at the site of former injury. The regrown limb can be monstrous, duplicated, potent. We have all been injured, profoundly. We require regeneration, not rebirth, and the possibilities for our reconstitution include the utopian dream of the hope for a monstrous world without gender.

Cyborg imagery can help express two crucial arguments in this essay: first, the production of universal, totalising theory is a major mistake that misses most of reality, probably always, but certainly now; and second, taking responsibility for the social relations of science and technology means refusing an anti-science metaphysics, a demonology of technology, and so means embracing the skilful task of reconstructing the boundaries of daily life, in partial connection with others, in communication with all of our parts. It is not just that science and technology are possible means of great human satisfaction, as well as a matrix of complex dominations. Cyborg imagery can suggest a way out of the maze of dualisms in which we have explained our bodies and our tools to ourselves. This is a dream not of a common language, but of a powerful infidel heteroglossia. It is an imagination of a feminist speaking in tongues to strike fear into the circuits of the supersavers of the new right. It means both building and destroying machines, identities, categories, relationships, space stories. Though both are bound in the spiral dance, I would rather be a cyborg than a goddess.

Notes

1 Research was funded by an Academic Senate Faculty Research Grant from the University of California, Santa Cruz. An earlier version of the paper on genetic engineering appeared as 'Lieber Kyborg als Göttin: für eine sozialistisch-feministische Unterwanderung der Gentechnologie', in Bernd-Peter Lange and Anna Marie Stuby, eds (Berlin: Argument-Sonderband 105, 1984), pp. 66–84. The cyborg manifesto grew from my 'New machines, new bodies, new communities: political dilemmas of a cyborg feminist', 'The Scholar and the Feminist X: The Question of Technology', Conference, Barnard College, April 1983.

The people associated with the History of Consciousness Board of UCSC have had an enormous influence on this paper, so that it feels collectively authored more than most, although those I cite may not recognise their ideas. In particular, members of graduate and undergraduate feminist theory, science and politics, and theory and methods courses contributed to the cyborg manifesto. Particular debts here are due Hilary Klein (1989), Paul Edwards (1985), Lisa Lowe (1986) and James Clifford (1985).

Parts of the paper were my contribution to a collectively developed session, 'Poetic Tools and Political Bodies: Feminist Approaches to High Technology Culture', 1984 California American Studies Association, with History of Consciousness graduate students Zoe Sofoulis, 'Jupiter space'; Katie King, 'The pleasures of repetition and the limits of identification in feminist science fiction: reimaginations of the body after the cyborg'; and Chela Sandoval, 'The construction of subjectivity and oppositional consciousness in feminist film and video'. Sandoval's theory of oppositional consciousness was published as 'Women respond to racism: A Report on the National Women's Studies Association Conference'. For Sofoulis' semiotic-psychoanalytic readings of nuclear culture, see Sofia (1984). King's unpublished papers ('Questioning trad-ition: canon formation and the veiling of power'; 'Gender and genre: reading the science fiction of Joanna Russ'; 'Varley's *Titan* and *Wizard*: feminist parodies of nature, culture, and hardware') deeply informed the cyborg manifesto.

Barbara Epstein, Jeff Escoffier, Rusten Hogness, and Jaye Miler gave extensive discussion and editorial help. Members of the Silicon Valley Research Project of UCSC and participants in SVRP conferences and workshops were very important, especially Rick Gordon, Linda Kimball, Nancy Snyder, Langdon Winner, Judith Stacey, Linda Lim, Patricia Fernandez-Kelly and Judith Gregory. Finally, I want to thank Nancy Hartsock for years of friendship and discussion on feminist theory and feminist science fiction. I also thank Elizabeth Bird for my favourite political button: 'Cyborgs for Earthly Survival'.

2 Useful references to left and/or feminist radical science movements and theory and to biological/biotechnical issues include: Bleier (1984, 1986), Harding (1986), Fausto-Sterling (1985), Gould (1981), Hubbard *et al.* (1982), Keller (1985), Lewontin *et al.* (1984), *Radical Science Journal* (became *Science as Culture* in 1987), 26 Freegrove Road, London N7 9RQ: *Science for the People*, 897 Main St, Cambridge, MA 02139.

3 Starting points for left and/or feminist approaches to technology and politics include: Cowan (1983), Rothschild (1983), Traweek (1988), Young and Levidow (1981, 1985), Weizenbaum (1976), Winner (1977, 1986), Zimmerman (1983), Athanasiou (1987), Cohn (1987a, 1987b), Winograd and Flores (1986), Edwards (1985). *Global Electronics Newsletter*, 867 West Dana St, #204, Mountain View, CA 94041; *Processed World*, 55 Sutter St, San Francisco, CA 94104; ISIS, Women's International Information and Communication Service, PO Box 50 (Cornavin), 1211 Geneva 2, Switzerland, and Via Santa Maria Dell'Anima 30, 00186 Rome, Italy. Fundamental approaches to modern social studies of science that do not continue the liberal mystification that it all started with Thomas Kuhn, include: Knorr-Cetina (1981), Knorr-Cetina and Mulkay (1983), Latour and Woolgar (1979), Young (1979). The 1984 Directory of the Network for the Ethnographic Study of Science, Technology, and Organizations lists a wide range of people and projects crucial to better radical analysis; available from NESSTO, PO Box 11442, Stanford, CA 94305.

4 A provocative, comprehensive argument about the politics and theories of 'postmodernism' is made by Fredric Jameson (1984), who argues that postmodernism is not an option, a style among others, but a cultural dominant requiring radical reinvention of left politics from within; there is no longer any place from without that gives meaning to the comforting fiction of critical distance. Jameson also makes clear why one cannot be for or against postmodernism, an essentially moralist move. My position is that feminists and others need continuous cultural reinvention, postmodernist critique, and historical materialism; only a cyborg would have a chance. The old dominations of white capitalist patriarchy seem nostalgically innocent now: they normalised heterogeneity, into man and woman, white and black, for example. 'Advanced capitalism' and postmodernism release heterogeneity without a norm, and we are flattened, without subjectivity, which requires depth, even unfriendly and drowning depths. It is time to write *The Death of the Clinic*. The clinic's methods required bodies and works; we have texts and surfaces. Our dominations don't work by medicalisation and normalisation any more; they work by networking, communications redesign, stress management. Normalisation gives way to automation, utter redundancy. Michel Foucault's *Birth of the Clinic* (1963), *History of Sexuality* (1976) and *Discipline and Punish* (1975) name a form of power at its moment of implosion. The discourse of biopolitics gives way to technobabble, the language of the spliced substantive; no noun is left whole by the multinationals. These are their names, listed from one issue of *Science*: Tech-Knowledge, Genentech, Allergen, Hybritech, Compupro, Genencor, Syntex, Allelix, Agrigenetics Corp., Syntro, Codon, Repligen, MicroAngelo from Scion Corp., Percom Data, Inter Systems, Cyborg Corp., Statcom Corp., Intertec. If we are imprisoned by language, then escape from that prison-house requires language poets, a kind of cultural restriction enzyme to cut the code; cyborg heteroglossia is one form of radical cultural politics. For cyborg poetry, see Perloff (1984); Fraser (1984). For feminist modernist/ postmodernist 'cyborg' writing, see HOW(ever), 871 Corbett Ave, San Francisco, CA 94131.

5 Baudrillard (1983). Jameson (1984, p. 66) points out that Plato's definition of the simulacrum is the copy for which there is no original, i.e., the world of advanced capitalism, of pure exchange. See *Discourse* 9 (Spring/Summer 1987) for a special issue on technology (cybernetics, ecology, and the postmodern imagination).

6 For ethnographic accounts and political evaluations, see Epstein (forthcoming), Sturgeon (1986). Without explicit irony, adopting the spaceship Earth/whole Earth logo of the planet photographed from space, set off by the slogan 'Love Your Mother', the May 1987 Mothers and Others Day action at the nuclear weapons testing facility in Nevada nonetheless took account of the tragic contradictions of views of the Earth. Demonstrators applied for official permits to be on the land from officers of the Western Shoshone tribe, whose territory was invaded by the US government when it built the nuclear weapons test ground in the 1950s. Arrested for trespassing, the demonstrators argued that the police and weapons facility personnel, without authorisation

from the proper officials, were the trespassers. One affinity group at the women's action called themselves the Surrogate Others; and in solidarity with the creatures forced to tunnel in the same ground with the bomb, they enacted a cyborgian emergence from the constructed body of a large, non-heterosexual desert worm.

7 Powerful developments of coalition politics emerge from 'Third World' speakers, speaking from nowhere, the displaced centre of the universe, earth: 'We live on the third planet from the sun' – *Sun Poem* by Jamaican writer, Edward Kamau Braithwaite, review by Mackey (1984). Contributors to Smith (1983) ironically subvert naturalised identities precisely while constructing a place from which to speak called home. See especially Reagon (in Smith, 1983, pp. 356–68). Trinh T. Minh-ha (1986–7).

8 hooks (1981, 1984); Hull et al. (1982). Bambara (1981) wrote an extraordinary novel in which the women of colour theatre group, The Seven Sisters, explores a form of unity. See analysis by Butler-Evans (1987).

9 On orientalism in feminist works and elsewhere, see Lowe (1986); Said (1978); Mohanty (1984); *Many Voices, One Chant: Black Feminist Perspectives* (1984).

10 Kate King has developed a theoretically sensitive treatment of the workings of feminist taxonomies as genealogies of power in feminist ideology and polemic. King examines Jaggar's (1983) problematic example of taxonomising feminisms to make a little machine producing the desired final position. My caricature here of socialist and radical feminism is also an example.

11 The central role of object relations versions of psycho-analysis and related strong universalising moves in discussing reproduction, caring work and mothering in many approaches to epistemology underline their authors' resistance to what I am calling postmodernism. For me, both the universalising moves and these versions of psychoanalysis make analysis of 'women's place in the integrated circuit' difficult and lead to systematic difficulties in accounting for or even seeing major aspects of the construction of gender and gendered social life. The feminist standpoint argument has been developed by: Flax (1983), Harding (1986), Harding and Hintikka (1983), Hartsock (1983a, b), O'Brien (1981), Rose (1983), Smith (1974, 1979). For rethinking theories of feminist materialism and feminist standpoints in response to criticism, see Harding (1986, pp. 163–96), Hartsock (1987), and H. Rose (1986).

12 I make an argumentative category error in 'modifying' MacKinnon's positions with the qualifier 'radical', thereby generating my own reductive critique of extremely heterogeneous writing, which does explicitly use that label, by my taxonomically interested argument about writing which does not use the modifier and which brooks no limits and thereby adds to the various dreams of a common, in the sense of univocal, language

for feminism. My category error was occasioned by an assignment to write from a particular taxonomic position which itself has a heterogeneous history, socialist-feminism, for *Socialist Review*. A critique indebted to MacKinnon, but without the reductionism and with an elegant feminist account of Foucault's paradoxical conservatism on sexual violence (rape), is de Lauretis (1985; see also 1986, pp. 1–19). A theoretically elegant feminist social-historical examination of family violence, that insists on women's, men's and children's complex agency without losing sight of the material structures of male domination, race and class, is Gordon (1988).

13 This chart was published in 1985. My previous efforts to understand biology as a cybernetic command-control discourse and organisms as 'natural-technical objects of knowledge' were Haraway (1979, 1983, 1984).

14 For progressive analyses and action on the biotechnology debates: *GeneWatch, a Bulletin of the Committee for Responsible Genetics*, 5 Doane St, 4th Floor, Boston, MA 02109; Genetic Screening Study Group (formerly the Sociobiology Study Group of Science for the People), Cambridge, MA; Wright (1982, 1986); Yoxen (1983).

15 Starting references for 'women in the integrated circuit': D'Onofrio-Flores and Pfafflin (1982), Fernandez-Kelly (1983), Fuentes and Ehrenreich (1983), Grossman (1980), Nash and Fernandez-Kelly (1983), Ong (1987), Science Policy Research Unit (1982).

16 For the 'homework economy outside the home' and related arguments: Gordon (1983); Gordon and Kimball (1985); Stacey (1987); Reskin and Hartmann (1986); *Women and Poverty* (1984); S. Rose (1986); Collins (1982); Burr (1982); Gregory and Nussbaum (1982); Piven and Coward (1982); Microelectronics Group (1980); Stallard et al. (1983) which includes a useful organisation and resource list.

17 The conjunction of the Green Revolution's social relations with biotechnologies like plant genetic engineering makes the pressures on land in the Third World increasingly intense. AID's estimates (*New York Times*, 14 October 1984) used at the 1984 World Food Day are that in Africa, women produce about 90 per cent of rural food supplies, about 60–80 per cent in Asia, and provide 40 per cent of agricultural labour in the Near East and Latin America. Blumberg charges that world organisations' agricultural politics, as well as those of multinationals and national governments in the Third World, generally ignore fundamental issues in the sexual division of labour. The present tragedy of famine in Africa might owe as much to male supremacy as to capitalism, colonialism and rain patterns. More accurately, capitalism and racism are usually structurally male dominant. See also Blumberg (1981); Hacker (1984); Hacker and Bovit (1981); Busch and Lacy (1983); Wilfred (1982); Sachs (1983); International Fund for Agricultural Development

(1985); Bird (1984).

18 See also Enloe (1983a, b).

19 For a feminist version of this logic, see Hrdy (1981).

20 For the moment of transition of hunting with guns to hunting with cameras in the construction of popular meanings of nature for an American urban immigrant public, see Haraway (1984–5, 1989b), Nash (1979), Sontag (1977), Preston (1984).

21 For guidance for thinking about the political/cultural/racial implications of the history of women doing science in the United States see: Haas and Perucci (1984); Hacker (1981); Keller (1983); National Science Foundation (1988); Rossiter (1982); Schiebinger (1987); Haraway (1989b).

22 Markoff and Siegel (1983). High Technology Professionals for Peace and Computer Professionals for Social Responsibility are promising organisations.

23 King (1984). An abbreviated list of feminist science fiction underlying themes of this essay: Octavia Butler, *Wild Seed, Mind of My Mind, Kindred, Survivor*; Suzy McKee Charnas, *Motherliness*; Samuel R. Delany, the Neverÿon series; Anne McCaffery, *The Ship Who Sang, Dinosaur Planet*; Vonda McIntyre, *Superluminal, Dreamsnake*; Joanna Russ, *Adventures of Alix, The Female Man*; James Tiptree Jr, *Star Songs of an Old Primate, Up the Walls of the World*; John Varley, *Titan, Wizard, Demon*.

24 French feminisms contribute to cyborg heteroglossia. Burke (1981); Irigaray (1977, 1979); Marks and de Courtivron (1980); *Signs* (Autumn 1981); Wittig (1973); Duchen (1986). For English translation of some currents of francophone feminism see *Feminist Issues: A Journal of Feminist Social and Political Theory*, 1980.

25 But all these poets are very complex, not least in their treatment of themes of lying and erotic, decentred collective and personal identities. Griffin (1978), Lorde (1984), Rich (1978).

26 Derrida (1976, especially part II); Lévi-Strauss (1961, especially 'The Writing Lesson'); Gates (1985); Kahn and Neumaier (1985); Ong (1982); Kramarae and Treichler (1985).

27 The sharp relation of women of colour to writing as theme and politics can be approached through: Program for 'The Black Woman and the Diaspora: Hidden Connections and Extended Acknowledgments', An International Literary Conference, Michigan State University, October 1985; Evans (1984); Christian (1985); Carby (1987); Fisher (1980); *Frontiers* (1980, 1983); Kingston (1977); Lerner (1973); Giddings (1985); Moraga and Anzaldúa (1981); Morgan (1984). Anglophone European and Euro-American women have also crafted special relations to their writing as a potent sign: Gilbert and Gubar (1979), Russ (1983).

28 The convention of ideologically taming militarised high technology by publicising its applications to speech and motion problems of the disabled/differently abled takes on a special irony in monotheistic, patriarchal and frequently anti-semitic culture when computer-generated speech allows a boy with no voice to chant the Haftorah at his barmitzvah. See Sussman (1986). Making the always context-relative social definitions of 'ableness' particularly clear, military high-tech has a way of making human beings disabled by definition, a perverse aspect of much automated battlefield and Star Wars R&D. See Welford (1 July 1986).

29 James Clifford (1985, 1988) argues persuasively for recognition of continuous cultural reinvention, the stubborn non-disappearance of those 'marked' by Western imperialising practices.

30 DuBois (1982), Daston and Park (n.d.), Park and Daston (1981). The noun *monster* shares its root with the verb *to demonstrate*.

Technophilia: Technology, Representation and the Feminine

Mary Ann Doane

The concept of the 'body' has traditionally denoted the finite, a material limit that is absolute – so much so that the juxtaposition of the terms 'concept' and 'body' seems oxymoronic. For the body is that which is situated as the precise opposite of the conceptual, the abstract. It represents the ultimate constraint on speculation or theo-risation, the place where the empirical finally and always makes itself felt. This notion of the body as a set of finite limitations is, perhaps, most fully in evidence in the face of technological developments associated with the Industrial Revolution. In 1858, the author of a book entitled *Paris* writes, 'Science; as it were, proposes that we should enter a new world that has not been made for us. We would like to venture into it; but it does not take us long to recognise that it requires a constitution we lack and organs we do not have.'[1] Science fiction, a genre specific to the era of rapid technological development, frequently envisages a new, revised body as a direct outcome of the advance of science. And when technology intersects with the body in the realm of representation, the question of sexual difference is inevitably involved.

Although it is certainly true that in the case of some contemporary science fiction writers – particularly feminist authors – technology makes possible the destabilisation of sexual identity as a category, there has also been a curious but fairly insistent history of representations of technology that work to fortify – sometimes desperately – conventional understandings of the feminine. A certain anxiety concerning the technological is often allayed by a displacement of this anxiety onto the figure of the woman or the idea of the feminine. This has certainly been the case in the cinema, particularly in the genre which most apparently privileges technophilia, science fiction. And despite the emphasis in discourses about technology upon the link between the machine and *production* (the machine as a labour-saving device, the notion of man as a complicated machine which Taylorism, as an early twentieth-century attempt to regulate the worker's bodily movements, endeavored to exploit), it is striking to note how often it is the woman who becomes the model of the perfect machine. Ultimately, what I hope to demonstrate is that it is not so much *production* that is at stake in these representations as *reproduction*.

The literary text that is cited most frequently as the exemplary forerunner of the cinematic representation of the mechanical woman is *L'Eve future* (*Tomorrow's Eve*), written by Villiers de l'Isle-Adam in 1886. In this novel, Thomas Edison, the master scientist and entrepreneur of mechanical reproduction – associated with both the phonograph and the cinema – is the inventor of the perfect mechanical woman, an android whose difference from the original human model is imperceptible. Far from investing in the type of materialism associated with scientific progress, Villiers is a metaphysician. Edison's creation embodies the Ideal (her name is Hadaly which is, so we are told, Arabic for 'the Ideal'). The very long introductory section of the novel is constituted by Edison's musings about all the voices in history that have been lost and that could have been captured had the phonograph been invented sooner. These include, among others, 'the first vibrations of the good tidings brought to Mary! The resonance of the Archangel saying Hail! a sound that has reverberated through the ages in the Angelus. The Sermon on the Mount! The 'Hail, master!' on the Mount of Olives, and the sound of the kiss of Iscariot.'[2] Almost simultaneously, however, Edison realises that the mechanical recordings of the sounds is not enough: 'To hear the sound is nothing, but the inner essence, which creates these mere vibrations, these veils – that's the crucial things.'[3] This 'inner essence' is what the human lover of Lord Ewald, Edison's friend, lacks. In Lord Ewald's report, although her body is magnificent, perfect in every detail, the human incarnation of the *Venus Victorious*, she lacks a *soul*. Or, more accurately, between the body and soul of Miss Alicia Clary there is an 'absolute disparity'. Since Lord Ewald is hopelessly in love with the soulless Alicia, Edison takes it upon himself to mold Hadaly to the form of Miss Clary.

A great deal of the novel consists of Edison's scientific explanations of the functioning of

Hadaly. As he opens Hadaly up to a dissecting inspection, Lord Ewald's final doubts about the mechanical nature of what seemed to him a living woman are dispelled in a horrible recognition of the compatibility of technology and desire.

> Now he found himself face to face with a marvel the obvious possibilities of which, as they transcend even the imaginary, dazzled his understanding and made him suddenly feel to what lengths a man who wishes can extend the courage of his desires.[4]

Hadaly's interior is a maze of electrical wizardry including coded metal discs that diffuse warmth, motion and energy throughout the body; wires that imitate nerves, arteries and veins; a basic electro-magnetic motor, the Cylinder, on which are recorded the 'gestures, the bearing, the facial expressions, and the attitudes of the adored being'; and two golden phonographs that replay Hadaly's only discourse, words 'invented by the greatest poets, the most subtle metaphysicians, the most profound novelists of this century'.[5] Hadaly has no past, no memories except those embodied in the words of 'great men'. As Annette Michelson remarks, in a provocative analysis of the novel,

> Hadaly's scenes, so to speak, are set in place. Hadaly becomes that palimpsest of inscription, that unreasoning and reasonable facsimile, generated by reason, whose inter-locutor, Lord Ewald, has only to submit to the range and nuance of mise-en-scène possible in what Edison calls the 'great kaleidoscope' of human speech and gesture in which signifiers will infinitely float.[6]

As Edison points out to Lord Ewald, the number of gestures or expressions in the human repertoire is extremely limited, clearly quantifiable, and hence reproducible. Yet, precisely because Villiers is a metaphysician, something more is needed to animate the machine – a spark, a touch of spirit.

This spark is provided, strangely enough, by an abandoned mother, Mrs. Anny Anderson (who, in the hypnotic state Edison maintains her in, takes on the name Miss Anny Sowana). Her husband, Howard, another of Edison's friends, had been seduced and ruined by a beautiful temptress, Miss Evelyn Habal, ultimately

committing suicide. Miss Evelyn Habal was in a way the inspiration for the *outer* form of Hadaly, for through his investigations, Edison discovered that her alleged beauty was completely *artificial*. He displays for Lord Ewald's sake a drawer containing her implements: a wig corroded by time, a makeup kit of greasepaint and patches, dentures, lotions, powders, creams, girdles and falsies, etc. Edison's cinema reveals that, without any of these aids, Evelyn Habal was a macabre figure. The display demonstrates to Ewald that mechanical reproduction suffices in the construction of the forms of femininity. But its spirit, at least, is not scientifically accessible. The abandoned Mrs. Anderson, mother of two children, suffers a breakdown after the suicide of her husband. Only Edison is able to communicate with her and eventually her spirit establishes a link with his android Hadaly, animating it, humanising it. The mother infuses the machine. Perhaps that is why, for Edison, science's most important contribution here is the validation of the dichotomy between woman as mother and woman as mistress:

> Far from being hostile to the love of men for their wives – who are so necessary to perpetuate the race (at least until a new order of things comes in), I propose to reinforce, ensure and guarantee that love. I will do so with the aid of thousands and thousands of marvellous and completely innocent facsimiles, who will render wholly superfluous all those beautiful but deceptive mistresses, ineffective henceforth forever.[7]

Reproduction is that which is, at least initially, unthinkable in the face of the woman-machine. Herself the product of a desire to reproduce, she blocks the very possibility of a future through her sterility. Motherhood acts as a limit to the conceptualisation of femininity as a scientific construction of mechanical and electrical parts. And yet it is also that which infuses the machine with the breath of a human spirit. The maternal and the mechanical/synthetic coexist in a relation that is a curious imbrication of dependence and antagonism.

L'Eve future is significant as an early signpost of the persistence of the maternal as a sub-theme accompanying these fantasies of artificial femininity. It is also, insofar as Edison (a figure closely associated with the prehistory of cinema) is the mastermind of Hadaly's invention, a text that points to a convergence of the articulation of this obsession and the cinema as a privileged site for its exploration. In Michelson's argument, Hadaly's existence demonstrates the way in which a compulsive movement between analysis and synthesis takes the female body as its support in a process of fetishisation fully consistent with that of the cinema:

> We will want once more to note that assiduous, relentless impulse which claims the female body as the site of an analytic, mapping upon its landscape a poetics and an epistemology with all the perverse detail and sombre ceremony of fetishism. And may we not then begin to think of that body in its cinematic relations somewhat differently? Not as the mere object of a cinematic *iconography* of repression and desire – as catalogued by now in the extensive literature on dominant narrative in its major genres of melodrama, *film noir*, and so on – but rather as the fantasmatic ground of cinema itself.[8]

Indeed, cinema has frequently been thought of as a prosthetic device, as a technological extension of the human body, particularly the senses of perception. Christian Metz, for instance, refers to the play 'of that *other mirror*, the cinema screen, in this respect a veritable psychical substitute, a prosthesis for our primally dislocated limbs'.[9] From this point of view it is not surprising that the articulation of the three terms – 'woman', 'machine', 'cinema'– and the corresponding fantasy of the artificial woman recur as the privileged content of a wide variety of cinematic narratives.

An early instance of this tendency in the science fiction mode is Fritz Lang's 1926 film, *Metropolis*, in which the patriarch of the future city surveys his workers through a complex audio-visual apparatus resembling television. In *Metropolis*, the bodies of the male workers become mechanised; their movements are rigid, mechanical and fully in sync with the machines they operate. The slightest divergence between bodily movement and the operation of the machine is disastrous, as evidenced when the patriarch's son, Freder, descends to the realm of the workers and witnesses the explosion of a machine not sufficiently controlled by a worker. Freder's resulting hallucination transforms the machine into a Moloch-figure to whom

the unfortunate workers are systematically sacrificed. When Freder relieves an overtired worker, the machine he must operate resembles a giant clock whose hands must be moved periodically – a movement that corresponds to no apparent logic. In a production routine reorganised by the demands of the machine, the human body's relation to temporality becomes inflexible, programmed. The body is tied to a time clock, a schedule, a routine, an assembly line. Time becomes oppression and mechanisation – the clock, a machine itself, is used to regulate bodies as machines. *Metropolis* represents a dystopic vision of a city run by underground machines whose instability and apparent capacity for vengeance are marked.

But where the men's bodies are analogous to machines, the woman's body literally becomes a machine. In order to forestall a threatened rebellion on the part of the workers, the patriarch Fredersen has a robot made in the likeness of Maria, the woman who leads and instigates them. Rotwang, who is a curious mixture of modern scientist and alchemist, has already fashioned a robot in the form of a woman when Fredersen makes the request. The fact that the robot is manifestly female is quite striking particularly in light of Rotwang's explanation of the purpose of the machine: 'I have created a machine in the image of man, that never tires or makes a mistake. Now we have no further use for living workers.' A robot which is apparently designed as the ultimate producer is transformed into a woman of excessive and even explosive sexuality (as manifested in the scene in which Rotwang demonstrates her seductive traits to an audience of men who mistake her for a 'real woman'). In Andreas Huyssen's analysis of *Metropolis*, the robot Maria is symptomatic of the fears associated with a technology perceived as threatening and demonic: 'The fears and perceptual anxieties emanating from ever more powerful machines are recast and reconstructed in terms of the male fear of female sexuality, reflecting, in the Freudian account, the male's castration anxiety.'[10]

Yet, the construction of the robot Maria is also, in Huyssen's account, the result of a desire to appropriate the maternal function, a kind of womb envy on the part of the male. This phenomenon is clearly not limited to *Metropolis* and has been extensively explored in relation to Mary Shelley's *Frankenstein*, in which the hero, immediately before awakening to perceive his frightful creation, the monster, standing next to his bed, dreams that he holds the corpse of his dead mother in his arms. The 'ultimate technological fantasy', according to Huyssen, is 'creation without the mother'.[11] Nevertheless, in *Metropolis*, the robot Maria is violently opposed to a real Maria who is characterised, first and foremost, as a mother. In the first shot of Maria, she is surrounded by a flock of children, and her entrance interrupts a kiss between Freder and another woman so that the maternal effectively disrupts the sexual. Toward the end of the film, Maria and Freder save the children from a flood unwittingly caused by the angry workers' disruption of the machinery. The film manages to salvage both the technological and the maternal (precisely by destroying the figure of the machine-woman) and to return the generations to their proper ordering (reconciling Freder and his father). The tension in these texts which holds in balance a desire on the part of the male to appropriate the maternal function and the conflicting desire to safeguard and honour the figure of the mother is resolved here in favour of the latter. The machine is returned to its rightful place in production, the woman hers in reproduction.

The maternal is understandably much more marginal in a more recent film, *The Stepford Wives* (1975), in which the machine-woman is not burned at the stake, as in *Metropolis*, but comfortably installed in the supermarket and the suburban home. In this film, a group of women are lured to the suburbs by their husbands who then systematically replace them with robots, indistinguishable from their originals. The robots have no desires beyond those of cooking, cleaning, caring for the children, and fulfilling their husbands' sexual needs. Even the main character, Joanna, who claims, 'I messed a little with Women's Lib in New York', finds that she cannot escape the process. As in *L'Eve future*, the husbands record the voices of their wives to perfect the illusion, but unlike that of Hadaly, the Ideal, the discourse of these robot-housewives consists of hackneyed commercial slogans about the advantages of products such as Easy On Spray Starch. Here the address is to women and the social context is that of a strong and successful feminist movement, which the film seems to suggest is unnecessary outside of the science

fiction nightmare in which husbands turn wives into robots. *The Stepford Wives* indicates a loss of the obsessive force of the signifying matrix of the machine-woman – as though its very banalisation could convince that there is no real threat involved, no reason for anxiety.

The contemporary films that strike me as much more interesting with respect to the machine-woman problematic are those in which questions of the maternal and technology are more deeply imbricated – films such as *Alien* (1979) and its sequel, *Aliens* (1986), and *Blade Runner* (1982). As technologies of reproduction seem to become a more immediate possibility (and are certainly the focus of media attention), the impact of the associative link between technology and the feminine on narrative representation becomes less localised – that is, it is no longer embodied solely in the figure of the female robot. *Alien* and *Aliens* contain no such machine-woman, yet the technological is insistently linked to the maternal. While *Blade Runner* does represent a number of female androids (the result of a sophisticated biogenetic engineering, they are called 'replicants' in the film), it also represents male replicants. Nevertheless, its narrative structure provocatively juxtaposes the question of biological reproduction and that of mechanical reproduction. Most importantly, perhaps, both *Alien* and *Blade Runner* contemplate the impact of drastic changes in reproductive processes on ideas of origins, narratives and histories.

Alien, together with its sequel, *Aliens*, and *Blade Runner* elaborate symbolic systems that correspond to a contemporary crisis in the realm of reproduction – the revolution in the development of technologies of reproduction (birth control, artificial insemination, *in vitro* fertilisation, surrogate mothering, etc.). These technologies threaten to put into crisis the very possibility of the question of origins, the Oedipal dilemma and the relation between subjectivity and knowledge that it supports. In the beginning of *Alien*, Dallas types into the keyboard of the ship's computer (significantly nicknamed 'Mother' by the crew) the question: 'What's the story, Mother?' The story is no longer one of transgression and conflict with the father but of the struggle with and against what seems to become an overwhelming extension of the category of the maternal, now assuming monstrous proportions. Furthermore, this concept of the maternal neglects or confuses the traditional attributes of sexual difference. The ship itself, *The Nostromo*, seems to mimic in the construction of its internal spaces the interior of the maternal body. In the first shots of the film, the camera explores in lingering fashion corridors and womblike spaces which exemplify a fusion of the organic and the technological.[12] The female merges with the environment and the mother-machine becomes *mise-en-scène*, the space within which the story plays itself out. The wrecked alien spaceship which the crew investigates is also characterised by its cavernous, womblike spaces; one of the crew even descends through a narrow tubelike structure to the 'tropical' underground of the ship where a field of large rubbery eggs are in the process of incubation. The maternal is not only the subject of the representation here, but also its ground.

The alien itself, in its horrifying otherness, also evokes the maternal. In the sequel, *Aliens*, the interpretation of the alien as a monstrous mother-machine, incessantly manufacturing eggs in an awesome excess of reproduction, confirms this view. Yet, in the first film the situation is somewhat more complex, for the narrative operates by confusing the tropes of femininity and masculinity in its delineation of the process of reproduction. The creature first emerges from an egg, attaches itself to a crew member's face, penetrating his throat and gastrointestinal system to deposit its seed. The alien gestates within the stomach of the *male* crew member who later 'gives birth' to it in a grotesque scene in which the alien literally gnaws its way through his stomach to emerge as what one critic has labeled a phallus dentatus.[13] The confusion of the semes of sexual difference indicates the fears attendant upon the development of technologies of reproduction that debiologise the maternal. In *Alien*, men have babies but it is a horrifying and deadly experience. When the alien or other invades the most private space – the inside of the body – the foundations of subjectivity are shaken. The horror here is that of a collapse between inside and outside or of what Julia Kristeva refers to, in *Powers of Horror*, as the abject. Kristeva associates the maternal with the abject – i.e., that which is the focus of a combined horror and fascination, hence subject to a range of taboos designed to control the culturally marginal.[14] In this analysis, the function of nostalgia for the mother-

origin is that of a veil which conceals the terror attached to nondifferentiation. The threat of the maternal space is that of the collapse of any distinction whatsoever between subject and object.

Kristeva elsewhere emphasises a particularly interesting corollary of this aspect of motherhood: The maternal space is 'a place both double and foreign'.[15] In its internalisation of heterogeneity, an otherness within the self, motherhood deconstructs certain conceptual boundaries. Kristeva delineates the maternal through the assertion, 'In a body there is grafted, unmasterable, an other.'[16] The confusion of identities threatens to collapse a signifying system based on the paternal law of differentiation. It would seem that the concept of motherhood automatically throws into question ideas concerning the self, boundaries between self and other, and hence identity.

According to Jean Baudrillard, 'Reproduction is diabolical in its very essence; it makes something fundamental vacillate.'[17] Technology promises more strictly to control, supervise, regulate the maternal – to put limits upon it. But somehow the fear lingers – perhaps the maternal will contaminate the technological. For aren't we now witnessing a displacement of the excessiveness and overproliferation previously associated with the maternal to the realm of technologies of representation, in the guise of the all-pervasive images and sounds of television, film, radio, the Walkman? One response to such anxiety is the recent spate of films that delineate the horror of the maternal – of that which harbours an otherness within, where the fear is always that of giving birth to the monstrous; films such as *It's Alive*, *The Brood*, *The Fly*, or the ecology horror film, *Prophecy*. *Alien*, in merging the genres of the horror film and science fiction, explicitly connects that horror to a technological scenario.

In *Blade Runner*, the signifying trajectory is more complex, and the relevant semes are more subtly inscribed. Here the terror of the motherless reproduction associated with technology is clearly located as an anxiety about the ensuing loss of history. One scene in *Blade Runner* acts as a condensation of a number of these critical terms: 'representation', 'the woman', 'the artificial', 'the technological', 'history', and 'memory'. It is initiated by the camera's pan over Deckard's apartment to the piano upon which a number of photos are arranged, most of them apparently belonging to Deckard, signifiers of a past (though not necessarily his own), marked as antique – pictures of someone's mother, perhaps a sister or grandmother. One of the photographs, however – a rather nondescript one of a room, an open door, a mirror – belongs to the replicant Leon, recovered by Deckard in a search of his hotel room. Deckard inserts this photograph in a piece of equipment that is ultimately revealed as a machine for analysing images. Uncannily responding to Deckard's voiced commands, the machine enlarges the image, isolates various sections, and enlarges them further. The resultant play of colours and grain, focus and its loss, is aesthetically provocative beyond the demonstration of technical prowess and control over the image. Deckard's motivation, the desire for knowledge that is fully consistent with his positioning in the film as the detective figure of *film noir*, is overwhelmed by the special effects which are the byproducts of this technology of vision – a scintillation of the technological image which exceeds his epistemophilia. Only gradually does the image resolve into a readable text. And in the measure to which the image becomes readable, it loses its allure. The sequence demonstrates how technology, the instrument of a certain knowledge-effect, becomes spectacle, fetish. But one gains ascendancy at the price of the other – pleasure pitted against knowledge.

Historically, this dilemma has been resolved in the cinema by conflating the two – making pleasure and knowledge compatible by projecting them onto the figure of the woman. The same resolution occurs here: as the image gradually stabilises, what emerges is the recognisable body of a woman (neglecting for a moment that this is not a 'real' woman), reclining on a couch, reflected in the mirror which Deckard systematically isolates. The mirror makes visible what is outside the confines of the photograph strictly speaking – the absent woman, object of the detective's quest. To know in *Blade Runner* is to be able to detect difference – not sexual difference, but the difference between human and replicant (the replicant here taking the place of the woman as marginal, as Other). Knowledge in psychoanalysis, on the other hand, is linked to the mother's body (knowledge of castration and hence of sexual difference, knowledge of where babies come from) – so many tantalising

secrets revolving around the idea of an origin and the figure of the mother. There are no literal – no embodied – mothers in *Blade Runner* (in fact, there are no 'real' women in the film beyond a few marginal characters – the old Chinese woman who identifies the snake scale, the women in the bar). Yet this does not mean that the concept of the maternal – its relation to knowledge of origins and subjective history – is inoperative in the text. As a story of replicants who look just like 'the real thing', *Blade Runner* has an affinity with Barthes's analysis of photography, *Camera Lucida*.[18] Barthes's essay is crucially organised around a photograph of his mother which is never shown, almost as though making it present would banalise his desire, or reduce it. Both film and essay are stories of reproduction – mechanical reproduction, reproduction as the application of biogenetic engineering. In the film, however, our capability of representing human life begins to pose a threat when the slight divergence that would betray mimetic activity disappears.

In *Blade Runner*, as in *Camera Lucida*, there are insistent references to the mother, but they are fleeting, tangential to the major axis of the narrative. In the opening scene, the replicant Leon is asked a question by the examiner whose task it is to ascertain whether Leon is human or inhuman: 'Describe in single words only the good things that come into your mind about – your mother.' Leon answers, 'Let me tell you about my mother' and proceeds violently to blow away the examiner with a twenty-first-century gun. The replicants collect photographs (already an archaic mode of representation in this future time) in order to reassure themselves of their own past, their own subjective history. At one point Leon is asked by Roy whether he managed to retrieve his 'precious photographs'. Later Rachael, still refusing to believe that she is a replicant, tries to prove to Deckard that she is as human as he is by thrusting forward a photograph and claiming, 'Look, it's me with my mother.' After Rachael leaves, having been told that these are 'not your memories' but 'somebody else's', Deckard looks down at the photo, his voice-over murmuring 'a mother she never had, a daughter she never was'. At this moment, the photograph briefly becomes 'live', animated, as sun and shadow play over the faces of the little girl and her mother. At the same moment at which the photograph loses its historical authenticity vis-à-vis Rachael, it also loses its status as a photograph, as dead time. In becoming 'present', it makes Rachael less 'real'. Deckard animates the photograph with his gaze, his desire, and it is ultimately his desire that constitutes Rachel's only subjectivity, in the present tense. In this sense Rachel, like Villiers's *L'Eve future*, becomes the perfect woman, born all at once, deprived of a past or authentic memories.

Reproduction is the guarantee of a history – both human biological reproduction (through the succession of generations) and mechanical reproduction (through the succession of memories). Knowledge is anchored to both. Something goes awry with respect to each in *Blade Runner*, for the replicants do not have mothers and their desperate invocation of the figure of the mother is symptomatic of their desire to place themselves within a history. Neither do they have fathers. In the scene in which Roy kills Tyrell he, in effect, *simulates* the Oedipal complex,[19] but gets it wrong. The father, rather than the son, is blinded. Psychoanalysis can only be invoked as a misunderstood, misplayed scenario. Similarly, the instances of mechanical reproduction which should ensure the preservation of a remembered history are delegitimised; Leon's photograph is broken down into its constituent units to become a clue in the detective's investigation, and Rachael's photograph is deprived of its photo-graphic status. The replicants are objects of fear because they present the humans with the specter of a motherless reproduction, and *Blade Runner* is at one level about the anxiety surrounding the loss of history. Deckard keeps old photos as well, and while they may not represent his own relatives, they nevertheless act as a guarantee of temporal continuity – of a coherent history which compensates for the pure presence of the replicants. This compensatory gesture is located at the level of the film's own discourse also insofar as it reinscribes an older cinematic mode – that of *film noir* – thus ensuring its own insertion within a tradition, a cinematic continuity.

Yet, science fiction strikes one as the cinematic genre that ought to be least concerned with origins since its 'proper' obsession is with the projection of a future rather than the reconstruction of a past. Nevertheless, a great deal of its projection of that future is bound up with issues of reproduction – whether in its constant emph-

asis upon the robot, android, automaton and anthropomorphically-conceived computer or its insistent return to the elaboration of high-tech, sophisticated audio-visual systems. When Deckard utilises the video analyser in *Blade Runner*, it is a demonstration of the power of future systems of imaging. Furthermore, the Voight-Kampf empathy test designed to differentiate between the replicant and the human being is heavily dependent upon a large video image of the eye. In both *Alien* and its sequel, *Aliens*, video mechanisms ensure that those in the stationary ship can see through the eyes of the investigating astronauts/soldiers outside. Danger is signaled by a difficulty in transmission or a loss of the image. Garrett Stewart remarks on the overabundance of viewing screens and viewing machines in science fiction in general – of 'banks of monitors, outsized video intercoms, x-ray display panels, hologram tubes, backlit photoscopes, aerial scanners, telescopic mirrors, illuminated computer consoles, overhead projectors, slide screens, radar scopes, whole curved walls of transmitted imagery, the retinal registers of unseen electronic eyes'.[20] And in his view, 'cinema becomes a synecdoche for the entire technics of an imagined society'.[21]

Since the guarantee of the real in the classical narrative cinema is generally the visible, the advanced visual devices here would seem, at least in part, to ensure the credibility of the 'hyperreal' of science fiction. And certainly insofar as it is necessary to imagine that the inhabitants of the future will need some means of representing to themselves their world (and other worlds), these visual devices serve the purpose, as Stewart points out, of a kind of documentary authentication.[22] Yet, the gesture of marking the real does not exhaust their function. Technology in cinema is the object of a quite precise form of fetishism, and science fiction would logically be a privileged genre for the technophile. Christian Metz describes the way in which this fetishism of technique works to conceal a lack:

A fetish, the cinema as a technical perfor-mance, as prowess, as an exploit, an exploit that underlines and denounces the lack on which the whole arrangement is based (the absence of the object, replaced by its reflection), an exploit which consists at the same time of making this absence forgotten.

The cinema fetishist is the person who is enchanted at what the machine is capable of, at the theatre of shadows as such. For the establishment of his full potency for cinematic enjoyment [*jouissance*] he must think at every moment (and above all simultaneously) of the force of presence the film has and of the absence on which this force is constructed. He must constantly compare the result with the means deployed (and hence pay attention to the technique), for his pleasure lodges in the gap between the two.[23]

Metz here finds it necessary to desexualise a scenario which in Freud's theory of fetishism is linked explicitly to the woman and the question of her 'lack' (more specifically to the question of whether or not the mother is phallic). Technological fetishism, through its alliance of technology with a process of concealing and revealing lack, is theoretically returned to the body of the mother. Claude Bailblé, from a somewhat different perspective, links the fascination with technology to its status as a kind of transitional object: 'For the technology plays the role of transitional object, loved with a regressive love still trying to exhaust the pain of foreclosure from the Other, endlessly trying to repair that initial separation, and as such it is very likely to be the target of displacements.'[24] In both cases, the theory understands the obsession with technology as a tension of movement toward and away from the mother.

It is not surprising, then, that the genre that highlights technological fetishism – science fiction – should be obsessed with the issues of the maternal, reproduction, representation, and history. From *L'Eve future* to *Blade Runner*, the conjunction of technology and the feminine is the object of fascination and desire but also of anxiety – a combination of affects that makes it the perfect field of play for the science fiction/ horror genre. If Hadaly is the first embodiment of the cinematic woman (this time outside of the cinema) – a machine that synchronises the image and sound of a 'real' woman, Rachael is in a sense her double in the contemporary cinema, the ideal woman who flies off with Deckard at the end of the film through a pastoral setting. Yet, Rachel can be conceived only as a figure drawn from an earlier cinematic scene – 1940s *film noir* – the dark and mysterious femme fatale with padded shoulders and 1940s hairdo, as though the reinscription of a historically-dated

genre could reconfirm the sense of history that is lost with technologies of representation. What is reproduced as ideal here is an earlier reproduction.

Again, according to Baudrillard: 'Reproduction … makes something fundamental vacillate.' What it makes vacillate are the very concepts of identity, origin and the original, as Benjamin has demonstrated so provocatively in 'The Work of Art in the Age of Mechanical Reproduction'.[25] There is always something uncanny about a photograph; in the freezing of the moment the real is lost through its doubling. The unique identity of a time and a place is rendered obsolete. This is undoubtedly why photographic reproduction is culturally coded and regulated by associating it closely with the construction of a family history, a stockpile of memories, forcing it to buttress that very notion of history that it threatens to annihilate along with the idea of the origin. In a somewhat different manner, but with crucial links to the whole problematic of the origin, technologies of reproduction work to regulate the excesses of the maternal. But in doing so these technologies also threaten to undermine what have been coded as its more positive and nostalgic aspects. For the idea of the maternal is not only terrifying – it also offers a certain amount of epistemological comfort. The mother's biological role in reproduction has been aligned with the social function of knowledge. For the mother is coded as certain, immediately knowable, while the father's role in reproduction is subject to doubt, not verifiable through the evidence of the senses (hence the necessity of the legal sanctioning of the paternal name). The mother is thus the figure who guarantees, at one level, the possibility of certitude in historical knowledge. Without her, the story of origins vacillates, narrative vacillates. It is as though the association with a body were the only way to stabilise reproduction. Hence the persistence of contradictions in these texts that manifest both a nostalgia for and a terror of the maternal function, both linking it to and divorcing it from the idea of the machine-woman. Clinging to the realm of narrative, these films strive to rework the connections between the maternal, history and representation in ways that will allow a taming of technologies of reproduction. The extent to which the affect of horror is attached to such filmic narratives, however, indicates the traumatic impact of these technologies – their potential to disrupt given symbolic systems that construct the maternal and the paternal as stable positions. It is a trauma around which the films obsessively circulate and which they simultaneously disavow.

Notes

1 G. Claudin, *Paris* (Paris, 1867), 71–2, quoted in Wolfgang Schivelbusch, *The Railway Journey: The Industrialization of Time and Space in the 19th Century* (Berkeley: The University of California Press, 1986), p. 159.

2 Villiers de l'Isle-Adam, *Tomorrow's Eve*, trans. Robert Martin Adams (Urbana, Chicago, and London: University of Illinois Press, 1982), p. 13.

3 Ibid., p. 14.

4 Ibid., p. 125.

5 Ibid., p. 131.

6 Annette Michelson, 'On the Eve of the Future: The Reasonable Facsimile and the Philosophical Toy', in *October: The First Decade, 1976–1986*, eds. Annette Michelson, et al. (Cambridge: MIT Press, 1987), p. 432. See also Raymond Bellour, 'Ideal Hadaly: on Villier's The Future Eve', *Camera Obscura* 15 (Fall 1986), p. 111–35.

7 Villiers de l'Isle-Adam, p. 164.

8 Michelson, p. 433.

9 Christian Metz, 'The Imaginary Signifier', *Screen* 16:2 (Summer 1975), p. 15.

10 Andreas Huyssen, *After the Great Divide: Modernism, Mass Culture, Postmodernism* (Bloomington: Indiana University Press, 1986), p. 70.

11 Ibid.

12 See Barbara Creed, 'Horror and the Monstrous-Feminine – An Imaginary Abjection', *Screen* 27: 1 (January–February 1986), p. 44–71; and James H. Kavanagh, "Son of a Bitch':

13 Kavanagh, p. 94.

14 Julia Kristeva, *Powers of Horror* (New York: Columbia University Press, 1983).

15 Julia Kristeva, 'Maternité selon Giovanni Bellini', *Polylogue* (Paris: Édition du Seuil, 1977), p. 409; my translation.

16 Ibid.

17 Jean Baudrillard, *Simulations*, trans. Paul Foss, Paul Patton, and Philip Beitchman (New York City: Semiotext(e), 1983), p. 153.

18 Roland Barthes, *Camera Lucida: Reflections on Photography*, trans. Richard Howard (New York: Hill and Wang, 1981). For a remarkably similar analysis of *Blade Runner*, although differently inflected, see Giuliana Bruno, 'Ramble City: Postmodernism and *Blade Runner*', *October* 41 (Summer 1987), p. 61–74. Bruno also invokes Barthes's *Camera Lucida* in her analysis of the role of photography in the film.

19 See Glenn Hendler, 'Simulation and Replication: The Question of *Blade Runner*', honours thesis, Brown University, Spring 1984.

20 Garrett Stewart, 'The 'Videology' of Science Fiction', in *Shadows of the Magic Lamp: Fantasy and Science Fiction in Film*, eds. George Slusser and Eric S. Rabkin (Carbondale and Edwardsville: Southern Illinois University Press, 1985), p. 161.

21 Ibid.

22 Ibid., p. 167.

23 Metz, p. 72.

24 Claude Bailblé, 'Programming the Look', *Screen Education* 32/33, p. 100.

25 Walter Benjamin, 'The Work of Art in the Age of Mechanical Reproduction', *Illuminations*, trans. Harry Zohn (New York: Schocken Books, 1969), 217–52.

Feminism, Humanism and Science in *Alien*', *October* 13 (1980), p. 91–100.

Machine as Messiah: Cyborgs, Morphs and the American Body Politic

Doran Larson

The Liquid Metal Man of Terminator 2 exposes ambiguities in the figure of the American body politic that have existed for over three hundred years; in contrast, the reprogrammed T101 suggests a body politic as cyborg and offers false assurances of popular control over mass democracy under late capitalism.

I consider it possible to convert men into republican machines. This must be done, if we expect them to perform their parts properly, in the great machine of the government of the state.

    – Benjamin Rush, 'Of the Mode of
      Education Proper to a Republic'

A technological rationale is the rationale of domination itself.

    – Max Horkheimer and Theodor
      W. Adorno, *Dialectic of Enlightenment*

On 22 September 1676, a Dr. Brakenbury conducted the first human dissection by Europeans in North America. Samuel Sewell's diary records that a Mr. Hooper, 'taking the [heart] in his hand, affirmed it to be the stomack'.[1] As James Schramer and Timothy Sweet have remarked, this misrepresentation of the internal organs of a geo-political enemy was necessary to that ideological apparatus whereby the Puritan community gained its sense of social cohesion. The community of saints had inherited from monarchical England a single image, the body politic, to legitimate coherence as a political organisation. But this image was deeply problematic in the absence of a monarch as head. It was thus necessary to demonstrate the community's coherence as a body in relative and oppositional terms. In essence, the corporeal integrity of the Puritan community was confirmed by demonstrating the tangibly inhuman, bodily disorganisation not only among but inside the 'savages'. By this means, moreover, figural violence in the battle between good and evil legitimated physical violence.[2]

This structural necessity haunts us today: that section of the American population which both conceives of itself self-consciously as democratic and unconsciously as healthy cells and organs in the body politic requires a nonhuman Other which it can eviscerate in order to confirm its own political and spiritual legitimacy.[3] Real change occurs only insofar as there is politically opportune evolution in this Other: Native Americans, Redcoats, urban immigrants, Communists, and, since the end of the Cold War, drug dealers, feminists, homosexuals, PC academics, black jurists and so on.[4]

The internal contradictions of this will to self-conception as both a fixed, organised body and as a mobile, democratic republic is revealed in the vehemence with which the enemy is demonised in popular culture. For intrinsic to this psychopolitics is the gnawing possibility that such surgery, while it may mutilate the Other, in fact anatomises the self: that, for example, a cry to execute entrepreneurial drug dealers covers middle-class frustration with an economy more and more class-bound, that the black youth is condemned for engaging in violence the Crime Watch member desires to wield. In Norman O. Brown's formulation, 'there is only one psyche, in relation to which all conflict is endopsychic, all war intestine. The external enemy is part of ourselves, projected, our own bodies, banished.'[5]

As evidenced from Dr. Brakenbury's surgery to *Nightline* attacks on Simpson jurists, demonisation is both swift and culturally familiar whenever any figure threatens to expose this unconscious will. A popular survival of patristic notions of Christ and Satan as symbiotic tricksters, sly foxes for good as well as for bad,[6] American literature is filled with shape-shifters: characters who terrify because, rather than appearing overtly on the side of evil, they flow back and forth, frustrating attempts to stabilise binary opposition, and thus exposing the ambivalence – the ressentiment – in our embrace of the good. We think of Brockden Brown's Carwin the biloquist, Poe's many self-projections, Hawthorne's villagers in 'Young Goodman Brown' or Arthur Dimsdale, Melville's Confidence Man, on through Oates's Arnold Friend in 'Where Are You Going, Where Have You Been', and variations on the 'Sleeping with the Enemy' plot. Except during crises in national identity, however, it is rare to see a figure express so graphically as Brakenbury's victim the intimate tie between this Puritan notion of the demonic and the tensions intrinsic to democracy's dependence upon the metaphor of the body politic. And it is this tie, just such an identic crisis, and the links between this demonisation and the body politic metaphor and postmodernism/late capitalism that I will argue is expressed in James Cameron's T1000 or Liquid Metal Man (LMM) of *Terminator 2: Judgment Day* (1991).[7]

In Cameron's *Terminator* films (as in *Blade Runner* and *Metropolis* and arguably all films preoccupied with distinguishing humans from machines and cyborgs), we see the same political agenda motivating Dr. Brakenbury's Mayan sacrifice to civil order, for we revisit here the troubling ambiguities involved in distinguishing heathens from Christians, loyalists from patriots, Communists from free-enterprise democrats, the damned from the elect.[8] Fundamental is not only the loaded tautology, best articulated by feminism, in which 'we' (in this case humans) are who we are because we are not like 'them' (machines) but the next necessary step: we have hearts, while they have only stomachs; while we have charity and empathy, they have only political appetite. Coherence as a healthy political body is confirmed by cutting difference into the very viscera of the Other.

I do not propose, however, simply to write a political gloss over a rich tradition of cyborg and android-film criticism that explores the ambiguous state of boundary wars between male and female,[9] machines and humans,[10] or human spontaneity and capitalist rationalisation.[11] Instead I want to suggest that with the introduction of the morphing LMM, we see not simply a rehearsal of older cultural or psychological dichotomies but a profound cultural shift. For in marked contrast to Jefferson's belief of the body politic, this shift reveals a popular surrender to the realisation that democracy in mass, capitalist society is inescapably technodemocracy: a body politic at best as cyborg, at worst on life-support systems.[12] At the same time, in *Terminator 2* we see the fulfillment of the ideal of the fascist body, according to Klaus Theweleit: the machine incorporated into the body politic facing an extratechnological and fluid enemy.[13] I will argue, finally, that at the moment of such incorporation, anxieties intrinsic to democracy

in consumer capitalism are tellingly exposed in the very body and vanquishing of the Liquid Metal Man. First, I offer a brief synopsis of *Terminators 1* and *2*, followed by a reading of *Terminator 1* in order later to demonstrate the depth and thoroughness of revision of human-machine relations in *Terminator 2*.

Retrofitting the Enemy

In 1997, advances in computer technology lead to the creation of an unmanned military defense system which begins to learn at a 'geometrical' rate. The system triggers a nuclear holocaust in order to save itself from human intervention, but after years of struggle, led by one John Connor, humans defeat the machines. To rewrite history, the machines send a Terminator cyborg model T101 (played by Arnold Schwarzenegger) back through time to kill John Connor's mother before John's conception. John Connor sends back Kyle Reese, apparently to protect but also to impregnate Sarah Connor. *T1* ends with the death of Kyle Reese, the destruction of the T101 terminator unit, and a pregnant Sarah headed into Mexico to await the coming storm. In *Terminator 2: Judgment Day*, the old terminator model T101 has been reprogrammed by John Connor as a protector for (and subject to the command of) the young John Connor, while a new T1000 terminator (composed of liquid metal and sent back by the machines from an even later moment in history) seeks to kill John Connor as a boy.

Consistent with the serial killer genre as described by Kim Newman, the terminator of *T1* is without human motivation. Yet it does have what amounts to appetite in the machine age – a programme, here directing it to kill every Sarah Connor in the Los Angeles phone book. Appropriately, Arnold takes on synthetic clothing from a trio of punks, one complete with tire tracks tattooed down his face, motiveless rebels without a cause (met at James Dean's last stand, the Griffith observatory). Thus viewed simply as a serial killer, the original T101 is literally run-of-the-mill, 'a creature beyond powers of understanding'.[14] Arnold becomes more complicated as a figure, however, when we see him as other to Kyle Reese.

In passing through time, Arnold arrives unscathed in the superhuman (and hyper-masculine) body of a former Mr. Universe and assumes flawless functioning, Kyle, in his slender, war-scarred body, is dashed to the street, in foetal position and steaming agony, as he will later tell Sarah, 'like being born'.[15] The coding is clear; by virtue of flesh and heart that can suffer, Kyle is to represent the good, while Arnold – to complete the oppositional logic which will read Kyle's body as the threatened body politic of the present and future – must be evil, an incomprehensible Other.[16] Binary oppositions thus proliferate: flesh versus machine, tennis shoes versus jackboots, human wit versus computer programming, masculinity-qua-fatherhood versus masculinity-qua-violence-against-women.[17] Moreover, in true dystopian tradition, reminders are constant of how woefully naive the present is about the potential deadliness of machines. Walkmans, answering machines, and so on repeatedly subvert human communication and facilitate murder.[18] And while Arnold is the alarm to this danger, Kyle is the reassurance that we can save ourselves if we are capable of strict discipline.

The sin of prizing the works of our own hands is facilitated by a lack of diligence, by the sinner's delusion that fate is given rather than earned. The question is the same one asked of Cotton Mather in the aftermath of King Philip's War, of the House Committee to Investigate Un-American Activities, of the characters in *Blade Runner*, *Alien*, *Robocop* and of a populace harried by HIV, the question of whether we can purge the evil within in time to avoid the wrath of the evil without.[19] If this is to be done, we must be able to identify our enemy and, in turn, ourselves. As was the case for Hooper and Brakenbury, for Brockden Brown, Hawthorne, and Melville, the difference between man and machine, between Christ-like human and satanic trickster, is incarnateness itself, particularly the presence or absence of an organ of mercy and empathy, the presence or absence of a heart.

The aesthetics of this distinction becomes manifest when Arnold enters the Tech Noir nightclub, where Sarah is waiting for the police to rescue her. In a slow-motion sequence, Arnold walks through the room, stiff and linear as though on tracks, surrounded by the wonderfully fluid movement of young men and woman dancing. Hyperrational directedness (the fascist body) cuts through and identifies itself as distinct from fluid, organic human motion. When the shootout ensues, Arnold,

clearly lacking any organ of empathy, simply blasts everything in sight. Without remorse or pity, and like the 'Indian Spirits' in a poem by Benjamin Thompson (who witnessed the Brakenbury dissection), such cyborgs 'need/No grounds but lust to make a Christian bleed'.[20] In contrast, Kyle dodges and leaps, sparing the innocent, selflessly bruising and scarring himself, and so modeling the flexible but also humanely disciplined body we want to fancy our own.

To survive his militarised, post-apocalypse youth, Kyle Reese has been trained to believe pain can be 'disconnected' as though he were a machine. Like Germany's Freikorps, this armoured body is achieved through a 'lengthy process of 'self-distancing', 'self-control', and 'self-scrutiny'.[21] But in truth Kyle is vulnerable; he is in fact scarred both in soul and body. And while his body becomes even more scarred throughout the film, demonstrating the authenticity of his incarnation, his soul is further and further healed by the modern curative equivalent to religious faith, by romantic love. Like the bodies of other saints, as described in Samuel Willard's 1684 essay, 'Saints Not Known by Externals', Kyle's body 'putrifie[s] and rot[s]' even as his soul heals and he falls into love's dissolution of boundaries.[22] Thus he learns, as will Arnold in *T2*, to accept what fascist militarism abhors: antimechanical flow – tears for Arnold, procreative semen for Kyle. In contrast, we watch the soulless Arnold of *T1* cut the flesh from his arm and around his eye to repair himself, revealing rods for bones and a camera shutter in place of an iris. In a politically charged reversal of the Brakenbury evisceration, we witness Arnold rip the heart from the chest of one of the punks; and when Kyle is apprehended by the police, he screams that the T101 will come after Sarah and 'tear her heart out' simply because 'that's what it does' – it eviscerates humans, removing what it cannot itself have, the human heart.

On grounds deeper than mere empathy, we see in Kyle a viable representation of the political body of the American 1980s. He is scarred in soul and body by a foreign war (if we read the future, like the past, as another country); it is also a war it is clear 'we' should by moral rights win (or have been allowed to have won); and it's war whose continuing legacy is evident in attempts literally to rewrite the past (making *T1* a subtle compliment to the gross revisionism of the *Rambo* films). And it is a body, literally neglecting its domestic health for expenditures on defense.[23]

David B. Morris has observed that in the postmodern world, utopia has 'fixed its new location in the solitary, private, individual body', and in turn a healthy body must indicate a healthy society as a 'summarising metaphor of an ideal state'.[24] The body politic as such has been reduced to the politicised body, in this case reflecting a threatened state in a body in pain. But it is precisely that state's moral viability that is claimed when we see Kyle become not less but more human in the course of his suffering. And in the classic wish fulfillment of horror, thriller and adventure genres, the heathen/machine is destroyed by manipulation of existing technology. Let the heathens invade, the moral goes; even using relatively primitive tools, wielded with strong hearts, we can take care of ourselves. And so ends the postindustrial, Cold War nightmare of 1984.

It will be impossible within this essay to argue conclusively that the changes evident in T2 result from real political events between the 1986 release of T1 and the 1991 premier of T2.[25] Yet in the reading to follow I want to suggest that key shifts in the mythos of technology from T1 to T2 imply real changes in the body politic's self-conception. As Will Wright has remarked in his discussion of westerns, 'within each period the structure of the myth corresponds to the conceptual needs of social and self understanding required by the dominant social institutions of that period; the historical changes in the structure of myth correspond to the changes in the structure of those dominant institutions'.[26] Assuming such correspondence. I want to explore how T2, as a product of a myth industry, implies the cultural and economic truth of its own narrative content: that the myths of later 'dominant social institutions' (technoculture) literally return in time to rewrite their own, more human prehistory. More concretely, T2 works to endear us to the very technology – including its incapacity for flow – demonised in T1.[27] In T2 we are taught to identify with the reprogrammed T101, or 'Uncle Bob', as the young John Connor will rename him in one of many gestures to incorporate Arnold, John and Sarah into a postmodern family. In essence, we are taught to see not a machine with flesh on the outside but an inchoate human being with

an alloy core, and this shift, set in contrast to the LMM, represents a shift in the conception of the body politic vis-à-vis the technological landscape.

Fashion signals the initial recuperation from the first film: where Arnold Sr. took the synthetic-based, chain-draped clothes of the dead-end punks, Uncle Bob takes the leather chaps and jacket of a biker, a type older and figurally familiar as a descendent of the wilderness-taming frontiersman and cowboy. A kind of Natty Bumpo with attitude, he is backed by George Thorogood and the Delaware Destroyers singing 'Bad to the Bone'. Unlike the depiction of Arnold Sr., we are to appreciate that Arnold Jr. has bones, even if they are of tungsten, as well as 'data' for pain. And like Kyle, Uncle Bob becomes more human throughout the film (as well as a better father, Sarah Connor reflects, than any man she has known). If a machine can learn humanity and search for the meaning of tears, Sarah says at the end of the film, perhaps there is hope for mankind as well. The machine becomes the trickster/messiah/frontiersman to lead us from an inhuman technological wilderness. He is thus in body and cultural mythos our perfect champion against postmodern, postindustrial society, 'against which we find ourselves pitted … as we did with forests and mountains'.[28] Arnold can do this because he has been reprogrammed; he has, in effect, gone through the experience central to the elect of Old New England – conversion by JC (John Connor), the saviour of mankind.

Strange Love; or, How We Are Taught to Love a Machine

Consistent with the oppositional logic discussed above, we are only made to identify with Arnold as our culture hero once we learn that traditional human/machine antitheses have achieved synthesis. This is clarified in Arnold's first face-off with the newer T1000, or Liquid Metal Man. In a high noon-style shootout, in a back alley of the Main Street of suburban America, a shopping mall, Arnold proves John Connor's protector as his shotgun blasts stun and throw the LMM backward. But the LMM's wounds suck back together, healing not only the flesh but the clothing outside the flesh. Further, when he is blasted backward, his arms flail with wild fluidity. Thus the binary imagery used in the Tech Noir disco of *T1* no longer differentiates hero and enemy. In fact, the significance of fluid versus mechanical has been reversed. We know and understand a blunt, brutal machine like Arnold, whose strength is 'predictably mechanical'[29] (he is stronger than us because he is bigger), but we are disoriented by this flexible and seemingly more human enemy who is slender, has no Austrian accent, and seems a clean-cut American boy.[30] Arnold fits our understanding of a correspondence between size and power, and he retains his wounds and so does not strike us as uncanny. Like the technical arts for nineteenth-century theologians, Arnold is restrained by 'obedience to God's physical laws ... [the] outward correlative to the moral law.'[31] But the LMM seems neither a product of human technology nor subject to physical law. He is a monster of some diabolically other Nature.

What we eventually recognise is that this other is not a manmade machine but a machine-conceived element, reaching back through the patristic trickster to Proteus as we watch it become other people and things. Where Arnold imitated voices in *T1* and in *T2* does so only once, and then only in order to 'beguile the beguiler',[32] the LMM can become a floor, a prison guard, John Connor's foster mother, even Sarah Connor herself. Like the Indians viewed by Edward Johnson in the seventeenth century, the LMM is diabolically impenetrable.[33] The menace is perhaps best described in Giambattista Vico's discussion of Greek ideas of chaos: 'they imagined it as Orcus, a misshapen monster which devoured all things ... the prime matter of natural things which, formless itself, is greedy for forms and devours all forms'.[34] Also conceived as Pan, according to Vico, this figure of chaos is associated with forests and wilderness. Like the Native Americans in the eyes of Sewell and Brakenbury, it is a being 'having the appearance of men but the habits of abominable beasts' whom Odysseus – like Arnold in the final scenes – is 'unable to ... grip ... who keeps assuming new forms'.[35] But as we will see, this is chaos with a rigid program.

Like the Devil for Mather and Seward, the morphing LMM never does putrefy and rot and takes on human shape only as a convenient disguise. Above all, this figure epitomises – as no figure before morphing technology could have – the morphology of the oppositional logic

in the body politic: it is the thing, now Indian, now Communist, which continually changes forms yet must survive if the body politic in democracy is to sustain its own morphology. And by presenting a threat that forces us to cling to the machine, we are forced back again (our critical *recherche* mirroring the films' own time loops) to rethink the Arnold from *T1*.

What we appreciate now is that, though he is a machine, Arnold's prototype is the human body. He cuts the flesh painlessly from his own arm, but at least, like us, he requires repairing, and the model for his camera-shutter eye is the human iris. Distinctly unlike the LMM, after incineration he is reduced in *T1* to a robotic framework just as Sarah's dream of nuclear holocaust in *T2* proves the human body just such a framework of bones. And, reflecting a body that figures the political nation, his command centre is where we would expect it, in the skull.[36] Above all, this modeling after human anatomy facilitates symbiosis with and subordination to humans: *T1*'s flesh versus machine is revised in *T2* as flesh as prototype for machine, Kyle's tennis shoes versus Arnold's jackboots becomes John's tennis shoes commanding a jackbooted Arnold, human wit now supplements comp-uter programming, masculinity-qua-fatherhood motivates masculinity-qua-violence-against-Other,[37] and sensitive human anatomy (John's, Sarah's, and Arnold's own) mourns the tragic lack in heartless mechanism. And it is this *moral* relationship, in which the machine envies and so selflessly follows human understanding, that makes incorporation of the machine into the body politic acceptable. It is just such moral subordination – hyperphallic, yet safeguarded by the machine's self-consciousness of lack, its heart-envy – that underwrites the political cyborg of postmodern nationalism.[38]

In contrast, the LMM, 'devouring all forms', has no anatomy, no organ-isation, no subordination of internal parts definitive of the very raison d'être of the body politic. A part broken from his hand is reabsorbed into his foot. His head is several times blown apart without loss of command. When Arnold punches through his head, this head simply becomes gripping hands. As a vision of the body politic, the LMM man is dissolution into anarchy, a nightmare image of continually overturned hierarchy. As such he is an icon of the popular fear of democracy itself in the electronic age. In the LMM we see a body whose parts have lost rational priority, precisely as is bewailed of the political disorganisation of the state. The complaint, whose manifesto is the 'Contract with America', is monotonous: social engineering in accord with New Deal/ Great Society/Politically Correct agendas is overturning meritocracy, mutilating the body politic, and replacing the hegemony of strong (i.e., white male) hearts with bottomless (i.e., minority female) stomachs.[39]

Arnold versus the T1000 thus reduces to democracy versus democracy: the myth of all citizens rising regularly and systematically upon the disciplined back of laissez-faire capitalism and its proudest expression in technological innovation versus democracy's potential for permanent class upheaval; the myth, in short, of economic democracy versus fear of the mythically chaotic power of the 'rabble'.[40] Yet, paradoxically, what is most threatening in this potential chaos is its very discipline; for the fascistic, mechanical body demonised in *T1* is not simply embraced in *T2*, it is reprogrammed as a protector seeking the sources of human fluidities, of emotion, tears and self-determining fate, while at the same time demonstrating that just such fluidity can be channeled into 'humane' violence. (Arnold is taught not to kill, but he does cripple.) The question here is whether the apparent valuation of life and emotional flow is simply ideological in Althusser's sense of an 'imaginary relationship … to … real conditions of existence' – those real conditions being violent (however nonlethal) defense of human control of technical capital.[41] In contrast, the LMM, however fluid in body, cannot bleed, ejaculate, weep or defecate, and such limitation is the sign of a choice between disciplined and uncontrolled flow: 'The mass that is celebrated [by fascism] is strictly formed, poured into systems of dams … To the despised mass, by contrast, is attributed all that is flowing, slimy, teeming.'[42] In contrast to the simpler oppositions claimed here by Claudia Springer, Scott Bukatman and Mark Dery (mechanical versus fluid, male versus female, industrial versus electronic technology),[43] *T2* sets up an opposition of mechanical man seeking human fluidity versus fluid man seeking fascist channeling. Within this battle of political bodies, democracy versus democracy becomes right-wing capitalist rigidity proving its ability to bend to human need versus left-wing (albeit nominal) pluralism programmed for

totalitarian rule. For *T2* to create an aesthetic of violence with propaganda value, it must deny the latent fascism in such aestheticisation itself; it must endear us to the callow sentimentalism vindicating violence from the right and so legitimate that violence as both moral and physical defense against the tearless violence from the left.[44]

Vox Populi, Vox ex Machina

That democracy in a nation of one quarter of a billion citizens is untenable without technical assistance hardly requires documentation. That the means of this national connection, the news media, are themselves further consolidated in the hands of corporate America has been made quite clear in the work of Herman and Chomsky.[45] What is less obvious is the manner in which particular products of the 'culture industry' not only replicate this dependence upon the status quo of corporate capitalism but present the loss of popular control of political institutions as itself desirable. To understand how this is manifest in the *Terminator* films, we must again revisit the gestures by which the films endear us to the cyborg, as well as how this endearment is vitally tied to the film as a market product.

In the opening sequences of *T2*, we see briefly the adult John Connor as post-apocalypse commando: a scarred fighting machine in defense of humanity against machines. Indeed, this face bears a striking resemblance in shape to the T101's metallic skeleton featured menacingly behind the flaming opening credits, complete with scars that reflect the T101's metallic subcomponents. In such images the *Terminator* films evolve a cliché of wanna-be-human robots and cyborgs from Baum's Tin Man to *Star Trek*'s Data, suggesting not only that humanisation of the machine is possible but that humanisation itself is perishable. In *T1*, Sarah humanises warrior Kyle, becomes a formidable fighter in the closing sequence of the film, and reappears a fighting machine herself in *T2*. Young John humanises not only Arnold but his mother, teaching both not to kill and reconnecting the mother to her apparently more 'authentic' maternal self; yet John too could become the scarred warrior of the opening sequence.[46]

Change in character is represented in the flesh: in his humanisation, Kyle earns and exposes more and more scars; Sarah loses the little fleshiness she had in *T1* (once her maternal duty is served) and appears a sleekly muscled, caged animal in *T2*; John grows from savvy, baby-fattish boy to scarred macho commander.

The literal loss of undisciplined flesh (as a result of conditioning, maturation or wounds) signifies the loss of flowing humanity. In such a vicious circle, it is only the machine, Arnold, who proves truly humanised, for only the literal machine has minimal flowing excess to lose. Naturally enough, then, whereas the T101 of the first film ends as a robotic skeleton, Arnold Jr. retains his covering of flesh to the end, except for that scarring and tearing required to represent how he has endured human suffering for our sakes. Arnold, like Kyle, Sarah and John but distinctly unlike the T1000, records history across his very body and so teaches us how to suffer the abuses of postindustrial life.[47] Arnold is not only the perfect man, he is the perfect postmodern, Puritan pilgrim: demonstratively humanoid and incarnate, and thus of this world, but retaining just enough of his Puritan/fascist discipline in order not to be corrupted by it. Ultimately, of course, Arnold will prove not only the perfect pilgrim but the perfect postmodern Christ: technological genius incarnate and ready to die to smelt away the sins of technological man. Yet, as was the case for Kyle, it is in the organic body as flesh that Arnold's real political import resides.

That the state of the body is the state of the state is a notion set deep in the American psyche; moreover, from the ship as church and church as body metaphors of Winthrop and the community of saints, to Benjamin Rush's machine-men in 'the machine of government', to Teddy Roosevelt, champion of the Panama canal, stating, 'As it is with the individual, so it is with the nation', the politicised body in America has framed itself in technological landscapes.[48] Add to this Madison's faith that 'that national unity which nature had intended … the technological arts would fulfill', and we begin to understand that perhaps wherever we witness American bodies in conflict (or combination) with technology, we witness figures of the body politic in an age when the 'technological arts' are not only a means of national unity but are the *only means* that make any conception of a unified political body viable.[49]

Understood as depictions of the state in postindustrial democracy, the *Terminator* films

(as well, perhaps, as an obsession with bloody mutilation on big and small screens) represent a crisis in national identity. 'Outsiders' to the healthy state (immigrants, academics, minorities, the poor) would mutilate the body politic, rearranging parts in an 'unnatural' order. What I want to suggest now is the political implication of *T2*'s path out of this morass, the direction of its 'Come with me if you want to live.'

Selling Submission

Both popular and academic presses have noted that the *Terminator* films constitute, in Richard Corliss's phrase, 'an annunciation story', as well, as that the time-loop plot leads to a paradoxical *mise-en-abyme* of its own logical unraveling.[50] What has not been noted is a parallel universe of inevitability in humanity's triumph in this loop, the resonances of Christian historiography in this inevitability, and the commodification of these features in what was, in 1991, the most expensive Hollywood film to date.

As Christ's flesh was conceived in the premodern world merely as a 'bait' to Satan, so is John Connor bait to the T1000, and with equal assurance of a mercurial Satan's downfall.[51] By the very act of returning to destroy John Connor in order to preserve technological dominance, the T1000 causes a battle that aborts development of the very technology it is trying to defend. Were John not born, no terminator would return to kill him and no recovered chip facilitate the development of 'Skynet'. The question is not, then, whether John's hope for human dominance (that is, traditional control of technical capital) will succeed, just as it is never a question for the faithful whether the messiah will triumph, or for the American movie viewer whether good will triumph. Whether Arnold, Sarah or Kyle learn to cry or not, whether their tears ever bless this violence, it is only a question of *when* technocapital will triumph. And the answer, as invariably as it has been for millennialists for millennia, is 'later'.

Ostensibly this 'later' is in the initial and later attempts on John's conception and boyhood; of course, the true later is the later of all Hollywood sequels: once the public is ready to pay to see another *Terminator* film. But there is a larger and overarching 'later' of popular anxiety: we are slipping later and later into labyrinthine technologisation of daily life, losing the thread of connection to the world we thought we had come, finally, to understand – the world of the machine. It is the embrace of the machine as machine that signals the desperation with which we appear to be trying to take the machine (in nostalgia for the obsolete) into a public consciousness of national identity.[52]

Not only do the terminator units grow more advanced and incomprehensible in each film, but the means of their destruction grow more primitive. Whereas the older T101 is crushed in a late twentieth-century robotics factory, T1000 is smelted in what could well be a nineteenth-century steel mill. As technology moves farther beyond our full understanding, so much more primitive do we need to believe are the necessary tools of combat. With each invasion of contemporary life from a more distant future, each technical disenfranchisement of the populace from the control of life, each evolution of technology into its own ecosystem, the farther back we need to search for where we went wrong, for the place where we can ourselves rewrite history by turning technology against itself. As Hugh Ruppersburg remarks, such science fiction films do for us what the biblical epics did for the 1950s and 1960s; reactionary and defeatist, they present fantasies of the patterns of the past vanquishing the possibilities of the future.[53] One can thus speculate that terminator units in a *Terminator 3*, *4*, and so on, while leaping in advance of mere morphing, would somehow be destroyed in a steam engine, spinning jenny, mill wheel, ultimately developing into pure electrical energy vanquished by a glowing, white-bearded Arnold descending with stone tablets from Mount Sinai.[54]

It is no mystery that we are witnessing the cynical populism of Hollywood: presenting Arnold Jr. as a champion of individualism set against the extension of precisely those global forces which could *afford* to create *T2*.[55] What endears such sleight of hand to an American audience is long-standing Yankee faith in progress and the benevolent teleology of all technical innovation. For even today, particularly in the advent of breakthroughs in medical technology (including robotic prostheses), Americans continue to want to believe that, in the words of John C. Kimball writing in 1869 (despite four recent years of evidence of what technology could do to human flesh), 'The great driving

wheel of all earthly machinery is far up in the heavens, has its force and direction supplied immediately from Omnipotence.'[56] Moreover, we are also offered the moral satisfaction of demonising precisely that cycle of consumerism (sequelisation) in which we are caught. We are allowed to feel triumphant over the global Skynet even as we watch films bounced from satellites, from the extant 'earthly machinery … far up in the heavens'. This, according to Horkheimer and Adorno, truly is a pleasure of late capitalism: a pleasure that 'promotes the resignation which it ought to help to forget', a pleasure that allows 'flight … from the last remaining thought of resistance', a pleasure that 'identifies [oneself] with the power which is belaboring [one].'[57]

I have noted that we identify with Arnold Jr. because, like Kyle, he is vulnerable to wear and damage, suffers (limited) blood flow and loss, and records this damage in his material body. What this record shows us above all is that, like us, and unlike the LMM, Arnold is subject to time and the existential status of his own history. In contrast, Thomas Andrae has demonstrated the striking timelessness in the lives of other popular superheros. Andrae notes, for example, that the paradox of time in Superman (he is fresh for a new adventure each week) is 'the commodity structure of mass culture in late capitalism'.[58] If this is indeed the case for Superman's (and Dick Tracy's, and Batman's) recovery week by week, we seem to witness in the LMM not only a new fear of (rather than messianic reliance upon) commodity structure but a nightmarish impatience even with weekly regeneration, for he is a figure that reflects commodity structure as instant, time-lapse recovery and wish fulfillment. Yet perhaps even more importantly, he is himself the popular face of consumerism. The LMM, now suburban housewife, now policeman, now shining cutlery, now checkered floor, now security guard, now mother, represents commodities, consumers, and the security apparatus that protects private property. In one morphing gestalt, he is the mass consumer/commodity nexus and a guard against its undisciplined indulgence; once again, this becomes clear when the LMM is seen as a revision of his coequal in *T1*.

In the final fight scene in *T1*, the T101, reduced to its robotic skeleton, seems to express a confused sense of self-recognition as it searches for Sarah among robotic factory units. This scene is echoed and updated when the LMM stares quizzically at a featureless silver mannequin head in a men's clothing store. The revision is striking: the original T101's threat is that of the military-industrial complex turned against its creators, a threat that nonetheless confirms technology's proper conception as servant to humanity as commodity producer, and ultimately proves beatable by a wage-earning, time-clocked laborer, Sarah Connor. The T1000 is, instead, the facelessness of retail consumerism, the Everyman who is generic Noman. Its antecedents are not in production but in retail consumption, in the culture of commodified desire rather than in commodity manufacture. As J. P. Telotte observes, the LMM 'seems to be all surface, with no real 'inside'';[59] the LMM is also the very ideal of the fascist body, a 'polished artwork'.[60] And as such polished surface, he is as surely the image of humanity generated by market research as he is a figure generated by computer graphics. He is a material sign that 'the more absolutely the body armour is mechanised, the more its product becomes … an expression of being … [disassociated from] machinery as means of production.'[61]

The LMM emerging from fire, the feature-less mannequin progressively transformed into a clothed individual, is thus a kind of time-lapse metamorphosis of a mass market profile into the false individuality of the commodity consumer. For his is an individuality betrayed in wearing a uniform. And in this costume, he is an apt figure of Homo consumer, or mass-produced humanity: desire-driven, yet policed by programmed appetites. He is also, emerging from homogenising flames, the faceless citizen of the public opinion poll, a thing of round percentages, the cipher of a citizen evoked in claims to speak for 'the average American'.

Just as the change in Superman, for Andrae, from monster to hero was a switch from suspicions about Horatio Alger individualism to a championing of the experimental collect-ivism of the New Deal,[62] so is this new collective illness, and its cures, marked by its era:[63] Arnold is our technosuperman against the fait accompli of corporate-media take-over of democracy; he fights for us, and destroys himself, as a protest against the transformation of national identity into another surrender to that neofascism which offers identity through the disciplined mass: commodity consumerism.

In the final scene, by literally melting the LMM down into abhorrent flow and the specter of a commodity-dissipated vox populi, and bearing witness to his own, linear slowdown in power, Arnold appears to reverse mass culture's 'substitution of mythic repetition for historical development'.[64] The cynicism in this image in a $90million Hollywood sequel hardly requires comment.

Here the tension Mark Seltzer has out-lined in an earlier era, between 'possessive individualism and market culture' versus 'disciplinary individualism and machine cul-ture', breaks down and flows into a chaos of interdependence and self-conditioning.[65] The disciplinary individualism and machine culture Arnold represents (with John Connor playing the role of Frederick Taylor, thrilled by his ability to command and calibrate the movements of the man-machine), is here seen as the margin of safety enjoyed by an audience addicted to possessive individualism and mar-ket culture; and that margin is set up against nothing other than mass culture's capacity for endlessly titillating desire, for protean transformations in self-conception as a body unified by nothing so vitally as its machinelike adherence to the lead of the market-driven media. As Sardar Ziauddin remarks, 'When everything carries a market value, then human beings and bits of their bodies too become subject to market forces.'[66] Thus we see here indeed a reflection of a nation of Benjamin Rush's 'republican machines', with the proviso that the name of the republic is Market.

Shadowing forth a pattern evident from Sewell's diary to Salem, from lynch mobs to HUAC minutes, what we witness in T2 is the assurance offered to an audience afraid of its own protean, tempted-and-never-satisfied desires, seeking protection from itself, an audience afraid of its own powers and wants and particularly horrified by its own role as the nominal leadership of democracy. In the LMM, we see a reflection of ourselves as a political body: unvarying in our programmed need for change yet also seeking machines to protect us from ourselves, to protect us from the very production-consumption machinery to which we feel ourselves appendages.

And yet, in figuring what we fear most in ourselves, the LMM also presents an ironically utopian vision. In this political body, each part, or person, can be head, arm, heart, fist.

The LMM is the theoretical amorphism of democracy as feared by antidemocrats since Plato, an amorphism which has always plagued the reality of exclusive, hierarchical civil and economic order. It is an awe-filled image and one which cannot be destroyed so much as it can be dissipated, melted down into each of the mass cherishing his or her belief that when he or she makes a choice as a consumer – as the Skynet of advertisers say he or she does – he or she defines rather than abandons personal integrity.

T2 demonstrates popular inheritance from the cosmology of early Christianity along with the political/spiritual agenda of Puritanism. But it also exhibits a fundamental tenet of the postmodern: that the historically prior is no longer the culturally fundamental. For the film demonstrates not simple appropriation but expropriation of such heritage into the workings of late capitalism. And this expropriation constitutes abandonment of democracy to the very conditions of democracy's possibility: corporate mass media. In identifying with Arnold as he battles the LMM, we assure ourselves that we still wield control by destroying the Liquid Metal body we have ourselves become. We say that, so long as the recognisable man-machine envies our humanity we have not sold it away. We say that we can manage all but one of the frightening possibilities that stand before us. All save the recognition that were we ever to reach out and turn off the TV or leave the mall and movie-plex and assemble in the light of day with other workers, citizens and consumers, we might begin to contemplate seriously the power we could wield.

Notes

1 Samuel Sewell *The Diary of Samuel Sewell*, 1674–1729, vol. I, ed. M. Halsey (New York: Farrar, Strauss, and Giroux, 1973), pp. 23–4.

2 James Schramer and Timothy Sweet, 'Violence and the Body Politic in Seventeenth-Cetury New England', *Arizona Quarterly* 48, no. 2 (Summer 1992), pp. 1–32. For the standard (and still best) history of the concept of the body politic, see Ernst H. Kantorowicz, *The King's Two Bodies: A Study in Mediaeval Political Theology* (Princeton: Princeton University Press, 1957).

3 Schramer and Sweet, 'Violence and the Body Politic', p. 5.

4 Roy Harvey Pearce, among others, has documented the dehumanising view of Native Americans throughout our history in *Savagism and Civilization: A Study of the Indian in the American Mind* (Baltimore: Johns Hopkins University Press, 1965). The evolution of these images, applied opportunely to varying subaltern groups, has been discussed by several authors. For example, in *Form and History in American Literary Naturalism* (Chapel Hill: University of North Carolina Press, 1985), June Howard quotes Henry George, in 1880, writing about urban immigrants: 'there are in the heart of our civilisation large classes with whom the veriest savage could not afford to exchange' (p. 78). Herbert G. Gutman cites nine-teenth-century authors who, looking at the urban scene, invoke the threat of 'extermination' already leveled against Native Americans (see *Work, Culture and Society Industrializing America: Essays in American Working-Class and Social History* [New York: Random House, 1977], pp. 71–2). More broadly, Hayden White notes the dialectical use ideas of 'wildness' and 'savagery' to prescribe normative notions of civilisation and the familiar (see 'The Forms of Wildness: Archaeology of an Idea', in *The Wild Man Within An Image in Western Thought from the Renaissance to Romanticism*, ed. Edward Dudley and Maximillian E. Novak [Pittsburgh: University of Pittsburgh Press, 1972], p. 4).

5 Norman O. Brown, *Love's Body* (New York: Random House, 1966), p. 162. Similarly, Jean-Paul Sartre writes in *Saint Genet*, trans. Bernard Frechtman (New York: Pantheon, 1963), p. 29: 'And whom does one strike in the person of the 'dirty, greedy, sensual, negating' Jew? One's self, one's own greed, one's own lechery. Whom does one lynch in the American South for raping a white woman? A Negro? No. Again one's self. Evil is a projection. I would go so far as to say that it is both the basis and the aim of all projective activity.'

6 See Kathleen M. Ashley, 'The Guiler Beguiled: Christ and Satan as Theological Tricksters in Medieval Religious Literature', *Criticism* 24, no. 2 (Spring 1982), pp. 127–8.

7 For the relations between 'postmodernism' and 'late capitalism', see Fredric Jameson, *Postmodernism; or, the Cultural Logic of Late Capitalism* (Durham, N.C.: Duke University Press, 1991), pp. i–xxii, 1–55.

8 For Constance Penley, 'it is by now well known' that classical Hollywood's attempts to demarcate proper gender relations, in a gender-ambiguous age, have retreated to apparently easier distinctions such as man versus machine (see 'Time Travel, Primal Scene and the Critical Dystopia', *Camera Obscura* 15 [Fall 1986], pp. 75–6 [reprinted in this volume]). I would only add that what stands deepest behind the manifest opposition in these films may be variable: gender certainly in many cases, but also race and class could be argued as more fundamental sites of struggle in certain works, historical periods, or genres.

9 For examples, see Margaret Goscilo, 'Deconstructing *The Terminator*', *Film Criticism* 12, no. 2 (Winter 1987-88), pp. 37–52; Penley, 'Time Travel'; Claudia Springer, 'Sex,

Memories and Angry Women', *South Atlantic Quarterly* 92 (Fall 1993), pp. 713–33, and *Electronic Eros: Bodies and Desire in the Postindustrial Age* (Austin: University of Texas Press, 1996); and Jeffrey A. Brown, 'Gender and the Action Heroine: Hardbodies and *The Point of No Return*', *Cinema Journal* 35, no. 3 (Spring 1996), pp. 52–71.

10 See J. P. Telotte, '*The Terminator, Terminator 2* and the Exposed Body', *Journal of Popular Film and Television* 20 (Summer 1992), pp. 26–34; Mark Dery, 'Cyberculture', *South Atlantic Quarterly* 91, no. 3 (Summer 1992), pp. 501–23, and 'Cyborging the Body Politic', *Mondo 2000* 6 (1992), pp. 101–5; Per Schelde, *Androids, Humanoids and Other Science Fiction Monsters: Science and Soul in Science Fiction Film* (New York: New York University Press, 1993).

11 See Mark Jancovich, 'Modernity and Subjectivity in *The Terminator*: The Machine as Monster in Contemporary American Culture', *Velvet Light Trap* 30 (Fall 1992), pp. 3–17.

12 For Jefferson's attitude toward technology and the state, see *The Life and Selected Writings of Thomas Jefferson*, ed. Adrienne Koch and William Peden (New York: Modern Library, 1944), p. 280.

13 Klaus Theweleit, *Male Fantasies, Volume 1: Women Floods Bodies History*, trans. Stephen Conway (Minneapolis: University of Minnesota Press, 1987), and *Male Fantasies, Volume 2: Male Bodies, Psychoanalyzing the White Terror*, trans. Eric Carter and Chris Turner (Minneapolis: University of Minnesota Press, 1989).

14 Kim Newman, 'Time after Time', *Fear* 12 (December 1989), p. 9.

15 This fall is due to the fact that the homuncular sphere in which Kyle arrives in the present – unlike Arnold's – materialises above the ground. He has, after all, jockeyed a machine never intended for him and which he did not build, as he tells Sarah. This apparently trivial point again underlines both Kyle's Yankee wit and the human struggle with contingency in fighting technoculture.

16 See Goscilo, 'Deconstructing *The Terminator*', pp. 42–3.

17 Readings of performances of masculinity in these films vary; see Springer, *Electronic Eros* pp. 106–7, and Vivian Sobchack, 'Child/Alien/Father: Patriarchal Crisis and Generic Exchange', in *Close Encounters: Film, Feminism, and Science Fiction*, ed. Constance Penley et al. (Minneapolis: University of Minnesota Press, 1991), p. 23.

18 Jancovich, 'Modernity and Subjectivity', p. 8.

19 Schramer and Sweet make this point about the Puritans ('Violence and the Body Politic', p. 21).

20 Benjamin Thompson, *Benjamin Thompson, Colonial Bard: A Critical Edition*, ed. Peter White (University Park: Pennsylvania State University Press, 1980), p. 86. (Also quoted in Schramer and Sweet, 'Violence and the Body Politic', p. 19.)

21 Theweleit, *Male Fantasies*, vol. 1, p. 302.

22 Samuel Willard, 'Saints Not Known by Externals', in *The Puritans*, vol. 1, ed. Perry Miller (New York: Harper, 1963), p. 369. Theweleit cites Freud in discussing the Freikorps's repulsion at love's tendency to dissolve boundaries (*Male Fantasies*, vol. 1, p. 252).

23 Hiding out in a motel, Kyle returns to Sarah after shopping. She assumes he's brought food, but he has only the makings for explosives. We recall Reagan-era schoolchildren told that catsup is a vegetable while Star Wars contracts ballooned. How Vietnam hangs over this and other man-versus-machine movies is not mysterious: the programmed minions of a machinelike totalitarian state take advantage of the self-reliant and human Americans who play by the rules imposed by constitutional democracy.

24 David B. Morris, 'Postmodern Pain', *Heterotopia: Postmodern Utopia and the Body Politic*, ed. Tobin Siebers (Ann Arbor: University of Michigan Press, 1994), pp. 152–4.

25 Such an argument might cite the end of the Cold War, the rise of AIDS, the Rodney King videotape and riots, the Willy Horton, Bush/Dukakis/Duke campaign of 1988, the transformation of the American people into a jury-cum-chorus of millions witnessing the Greek tragedy of Hill/Thomas, the rise of daytime TV and radio talk shows, the Internet, the World Wide Web and its local tributaries, the computer-driven stock market panic of 1987, and the closest thing yet to an unmanned war, Desert Storm (which, if it did not cure the Vietnam syndrome, certainly made less convenient the stigmatisation of technology as a metaphor for totalitarian states). These events carry two intertwined implications: first, technology alone binds together the national consciousness; second, while we have no viable external enemies (or at least none more threatening than the video arcade games John Connor trains on), we don't need such enemies because we have more formidable problems in our inner cities, in our homes and offices, indeed, in our very blood. Even if technology contributes to a confusion in which one really cannot sort out the elect from the damned, the infected from the uninfected, friendly from unfriendly targets, or the forces of civil order from the sources of anarchic brutality, it is also certain that without technology such a sorting is hopeless.

26 Will Wright, *Six Guns and Society: A Structural Study of the Western* (Berkeley: University of California Press, 1975), p. 14.

27 I am not suggesting that *T1* is a problematic text or that its own business was left unfinished (except insofar as was required for a sequel). Indeed, more significantly, *T2* proves that business apparently finished, within technoculture, is always open to upgrading. To emphasise this point. I will below call the new T101 Arnold Jr., for in the revisions outlined below, particularly the Christ-like self-sacrifice the reprogrammed T101 makes at the end of the film, the new T101 truly plays technical revision as

the downloading of the merciful mediator-son both to humankind and to the plaguelike wrath of the Jehovah-like Arnold Sr.

28 William Fisher, 'Of Living Machines and Living-Machines: *Blade Runner* and the Terminal Genre', *New Literary History* 20, no. 1 (Autumn 1988), p. 195.

29 Scott Bukatman, *Terminal Identity: The Virtual Subject in Postmodern Science Fiction* (Durham, N.C.: Duke University Press, 1993), p. 306.

30 Springer claims that the LMM, representing feminine fluidity, is less physically powerful than Arnold and succeeds simply by absorption of blows and projectiles (*Electronic Eros*, 112). It is significant for my reading that this is not the case; in all hand-to-hand combat scenes, the LMM is, disconcertingly, Arnold's match in raw power. The film also teases by making us at first assume the LMM is John's protector, dressing him as a Los Angeles policeman, the motto on whose patrol car is 'To Protect and to Serve'. (The irony is, of course, bitter for viewers of the Rodney King beating tape.) In contrast, Schwarzenegger's brilliance as an endearing cyborg is precisely that he cannot act, that he always exhibits 'machinelike awkwardness' (Schelde, *Androids, Humanoids*, 203) and so is never confused with humans (let alone with actors competent at nonmachine roles).

31 John F. Kasson, *Civilizing the Machine: Technology and Republican Values*, 1776–1900 (New York: Grossman, 1976), p. 152.

32 Ashley, 'The Guiler Beguiled', p. 126.

33 Edward Johnson, *Johnson's Wonder-Working Providence*, 1628–1651 (1652), ed. J. Franklin Jameson (New York: Scribner's, 1910), p. 168.

34 Giambattista Vico, *The New Science of Giambattista Vico*, trans. Thomas Goddard Bergin and Max Harold Frisch (Cornell: Cornell University Press, 1984), p. 260.

35 Ibid., 260–1. See also Telotte, 'The Terminator', p. 29.

36 Lines of speech are also revised in *T2*: Kyle says to Sarah, 'Come with me if you want to live', as they both stare up at the T101; in *T2*, we have a low point-of-view shot up at Arnold as he delivers the same line, again to Sarah, now with the sense of surrender to a higher power; where Arnold's famous 'I'll be back' in *T1* is promise of destructive violence against a police station in an attempt to kill Sarah, in *T2* the line is a paternalistic promise to come back to John and Sarah after wiping out the police who would kill them all; whereas Arnold Sr. emerges from the fiery tanker truck with a limp, the LMM man walks out of his truck explosion virtually unscathed; where Arnold as evil force tells a trucker to 'get out' of a semi and the man falls to the street, the LMM not only repeats this scene but later tells a pilot to 'get out' of a hovering helicopter. In all of these cases, the old phrases and actions are transformed either into more lethal threats or work to reidentify our saviour-figure,

or are fully inverted in their meaning, from promises of destruction into promises of help.

37 Arnold Jr. is also sexualised. Arnold Sr. kills Sarah's roommate, Ginger, shortly after she has had sex (figuring a kind of puritanical, postcoital wrath), whereas in *T2* a waitress in the bar where he finds the bikers sighs in the face of Arnold as icon of masculine sexuality. This is not to say, however, that the misogyny of *T1* is overturned. For the LMM is, in Mark Dery's words, 'androgyny, hermaphroditism, and, most often, the feminine' ('Cyberculture', p. 505); further, Kyle, the slender, suffering lover, is replaced in the role of mankind's champion by Arnold's hypermasculinity.

38 Sarah Connor too is brought to feel heart-envy at the moment her phallic power (an M-16) threatens a father. The film ostensibly condemns hot-lead phallocentrism. But, as we will see, this is simply a sales pitch for more discrete violence. This, of course, models an ideal far distant from Donna Haraway's utopian cyborgs imagined in 'A Manifesto for Cyborgs: Science, Technology, and Socialist Feminism in the 1980's', *Socialist Review* 80 (1985): pp. 65–105 [reprinted in this volume]. This distance is articulated by Springer even while she sees both cyborg types 'aris[ing] from dissatisfaction with current social and economic relations' ('Sex, Memories, and Angry Women', p. 719). Here the cyborg suggests neither revolution nor prognosis but is simply – and more hopelessly – prescriptive and normative: a celebratory surrender to the status quo.

39 The Left, of course, has its own version of this conspiracy theory – that corporations consciously scheme to disenfranchise the disenfranchised. But this view (itself absurd since capitalism requires no such conspiracy in order to fulfill its agenda) today is in such disrepute as to be significant to national discourse only as straw man.

40 On the American faith in a link between technocapital and social progress, see Kasson, *Civilizing the Machine*, *passim*, and Leo Marx, *The Machine in the Garden: Technology and the Pastoral Ideal in America* (New York: Oxford University Press, 1964), p. 187. The Right's corporeal fear of democratization is well expressed in the follow-ing: 'The left has torn apart the social and cultural membranes that protect a society from opportunistic diseases … We feel that we participated in a destructive movement, which has had deleterious consequences for society, and we'd like to make some kind of restitution' (qtd. in Vince Stehle, 'The Right's Aggressive 'Battle Tank'', in *Heterodoxy* 3, no. 5 [September 1995], p. 3). This statement from former *Ramparts* editor David Horowitz nicely combines the image of body politic as host to infection (from those forces not favored by a conservative agenda), the tone of religious sanctimony surrounding the healthy parts of that body, and, in the statement's location, the tie to late capitalism. These words appear in an insert soliciting

donations to a conservative 'battle tank', printed directly above the space for Visa, Mastercard, Discover, or Amex numbers of those sick and tired of 'the power of leftists in American institutions' (ibid., p. 2).

41 Louis Althusser, *On Lenin and Philosophy and Other Essays*, trans. Ben Brewster (New York: Monthly Review Press, 1972), p. 162.

42 Theweleit, *Male Fantasies*, vol. 2, p. 4.

43 See Springer, Electronic Eros, p. 112; Dery, 'Morphing the Body Politic', pp. 102–3; Bukatman, *Terminal Identity*, pp. 306–7.

44 Within this essay on more traditional politics, I cannot, regrettably, engage all of the gender politics evoked here. But I would note that such oppositions, insofar as they are founded upon existing gender divides, are most profoundly undermined by theories of gender as performance, as demonstrated in the work of Judith Butler, *Gender Trouble: Feminism and the Subversion of Identity* (New York: Routledge, 1990). In contradistinction from Jeffrey Brown's (passing) application of gender-performance theory to Sarah Connor in 'Gender and the Action Heroine', my point is that *T2* seems to elide a simple dichotomy only in order to demonstrate one side to be politically self-sufficient – a reactionary manoeuvre in defense of the brutality of the status quo. For example, Brown sees Sarah and Arnold performing masculine and femine gender stereotypes, respectively (murderous gun toting versus protective nurturing). My observation here is that while Sarah's traditional model is Arnold's maternalism, her intentional (though failed) ideal is the LMM – channeling fluidity into rigid, unfeeling discipline. Thus even within performance theory, she is not a woman performing masculinity (i.e., a virtual male) but a man trying to outperform the film's (conservative) attribution of 'deep-down' femininity (i.e., a typical man); her tensions, in essence, are caused by the old binary logic.

45 Edward S. Herman and Noam Chomsky, *Manufacturing Consent: The Political Economy of the Mass Media* (New York: Pantheon, 1988), pp. 1–35.

46 This is so, of course, only in one possible future: the one the film is intent to abort. Yet Cameron apparently decided to keep this cycle consistent. In an early scene cut from *T2*, Sarah dreams in the hospital that Kyle comes to her. (Stills of the scene are reprinted in the book cited below, indicating the scene was shot and later cut in editing footage rather than simply dropped from the script.)

> *They gaze into each other's eyes. And in that look we see that his death and the horror she has been through hasn't touched their love at all.*
> SARAH: Hold me.
> *She melts into Reese's arms. Pulls him to her.*

REESE: I love you. I always will.
SARAH: Oh, God … Kyle. I need you so much.
  – James Cameron and William Wisher,
    *Terminator 2: Judgment Day – The Book
    of the Film: An Illustrated Screenplay* (New
    York: Applause Books, 1991), p. 37

47 The observation that this is the lesson of culture industry films in general was made in 1944 by Max Horkheimer and Theodor W. Adorno, *Dialectic of Enlightenment*, trans. John Cumming (New York: Continuum, 1982), p. 138.

48 Benjamin Rush, 'Of the Mode of Education Proper to a Republic', in *Essays Literary, Moral and Philosophical*, 2nd edn. (Philadelphia, 1806), pp. 7–8; Theodore Roosevelt, *The Works of Theodore Roosevelt*, vol. 15 (New York: Scribners, 1924–26), p. 267.

49 For Madison's ideas, see Kasson, *Civilizing the Machine*, p. 35. Taking body-as-nation literalism to its extreme in 1900, Ernst Haeckel wrote: 'We can only arrive at a correct knowledge of the structure and life of the social body, the state, through scientific knowledge of the structure and life of the individuals who compose it, and the cells of which they are in turn composed' (*The Riddle of the Universe* [New York: Harper, 1900], p. 8).

50 Richard Corliss, *Time*, November 26, 1984, p. 105. See also Penley, 'Time Travel'; Karen B. Mann, 'Narrative Entanglements: *The Terminator*', *Film Quarterly* 43 (Winter 1989-90): pp. 17–27; Hugh Ruppersburg, 'The Alien Messiah in Recent Science Fiction Films', *Journal of Popular Film and Television* 14, no. 4 (Winter 1987), pp. 158–66. The loop works as follows: John cannot be conceived unless he is already the adult who sends back Kyle to become his own father. It is worth noting that this conundrum at once demands solution and precludes reason; that is, it demands a leap of faith.

51 On Christ as bait, see Ashley, 'The Guiler Beguiled', p. 129.

52 On the reactionism and nostalgia of such gestures, see Springer, *Electronic Eros*, p. 111.

53 Ruppersburg, 'The Alien Messiah', pp. 165–6; see also Bonnie Brain, 'Saviors and Scientists: Extraterrestrials in Recent Science Fiction Films', *Et Cetera: A Review of General Semantics* 40 (Summer 1983), p. 219.

54 The reactionary nature of popular unease with dependence upon technology is evidenced in the popular press's treatment of *T2*. The vital concern here is to demystify morphing as a technology and show its subordination to human desire as a mere marketing device (Cliff Gromer, 'Morphing', *Popular Mechanics* [October 1992], pp. 54–5) or highlight the dependency of the morphed figure upon human input (e.g., 'Artists tell the computer what to do every step of the way. Machines can't do it on their own' [Stuart Weiner, 'Morphing It,' TV Guide, August 1–7, 1992, pp. 19–20]), or mourning with bitter chagrin that 'the cyber-effects are more potent than the

live actors' (Christopher Sharett, 'The Cinema of Human Obsolescence', *USA Today* [January 1993]: p. 67).

55 The flippant side of this commercial cynicism was expressed by Louis Ruykeyser in his opening comments on *Wall Street Week* for September 1, 1995, following the ABC-Disney merger. He joked that a nagging question might soon be answered: whether 'media' is plural or singular. In the foreseeable future. Ruykeyser smirked, hinting at the emergence of a real Skynet, we could literally speak of 'The Medium'.

56 John C. Kimball, 'Machinery as a Gospel Worker', *Christian Examiner* 87 (November 1869): p. 327. The current form of this position is best seen in Speaker of the House Newt Gingrich if we add to his unconditional faith in futurist technofantasy (see Joan Didion, 'Newt Gingrich, Superstar', *New York Review of Books*, August 10, 1995, p. 8) his support for Christian Coalition values.

57 Horkheimer and Adorno, *The Dialectic of Enlightenment*, p. 142, 144, 153.

58 Thomas Andrae, 'From Menace to Messiah: The Prehistory of the Superman in Science Fiction Literature', *Discourse: Journal for Theoretical Studies in Media and Culture* 2 (Summer 1980): p. 108.

59 J. P. Telotte, 'The Terminator', p. 29.

60 Theweleit, *Male Fantasies*, vol. 2, p. 207.

61 Ibid., p. 202.

62 Andrae, 'From Menace to Messiah', p. 90.

63 See Susan Sontag, *Illness as Metaphor* (New York: Vintage, 1979), p. 31–5.

64 This is Martin Jay's characterisation of an idea common to the Frankfurt School, and specifically Adorno, as stated in *The Dialectical Imagination: A History of the Frankfurt School and the Institute for Social Research, 1923–1950* (New York: Little, Brown, 1973), p. 187.

65 Mark Seltzer, *Bodies and Machines* (New York: Routledge, 1992), p. 5.

66 Sardar Ziauddin, '*Terminator 2*: Modernity, Postmodernism and the 'Other'', *Futures* 24 (June 1992), p. 496.

Ghosts and Machines:
The Technological Body
Susan J. Napier

Man's insecurity stems from the advance of science. Never once has science, which never ceases to move forward, allowed us to pause. From walking to ricksha, from ricksha to carriage, from carriage to train, from train to automobile, from there on to the dirigible, further on to the airplane, and further on and on – no matter how far we may go, it won't let us take a breath.
> – Natsume Sōseki, *The Wayfarer*

This picture – [of a transformer] – man mounted on machine, a joystick gripped in each hand, was and is the epitome of Japan's technological dream.
> – Ron Tanner, 'Mr. Atomic, Mr. Mercury, and Chime Trooper: Japan's Answer to the American Dream'

Fusion with the technological ... is tanta-mount to stepping into a suit of armor.
> – Claudia Springer, *Electronic Eros*

The bodies discusses in the previous chapters have all been strongly linked with notions of identity, from the frighteningly unstable to the rigidly fixed. The fixed masculine body types displayed in pornography suggest a negative response to the transgressive potential that the female and adolescent body is shown to be capable of. This yearning for a contained or armoured body is not limited to pornography, however. The world of hard science fiction anime known as *mecha* revolves around a quest to contain the body, this time quite literally in the form of some kind of technological fusion. As with the phallic demon in pornography, this kind of 'containment' can also be read as 'empowerment', perhaps even more obviously than the demons, since the viewer sees the frail human body literally becoming stronger as it fuses with its technological armour.[1] Usually huge, with rippling metallic 'muscles' and armed with a variety of weapons to the extent that it almost parodies the male ideal,[2] the *mecha* body clearly plays to a wish-fulfilling fantasy of power, authority, and technological competence.

However, this kind of empowerment can be a double-edged sword. Although the most conventional *mecha*, along with certain Western science fiction films such as *Terminator*, seem to privilege the robotic or cyborg body, many other anime present the technologically armoured body with profound ambivalence. Not only do these anime partake in the contradictory 'double vision'[3] that science fiction scholar J. P. Telotte ascribes to many Western science fiction films (the simultaneous celebration of technology through its privileged presence in the narrative and an excoriation of its destructive and dehumanising potential), but many works in the *mecha* genre actually enact this double vision on a more profound and darker level through insistently presenting the fusion of human and technology as one of ambiguous value. This often negative view of technology may surprise audiences who tend to think of the Japanese as masters of technological wizardry. However, it is a view long held by many thoughtful Japanese, such as the writer Natsume Sōseki quoted above, or more recent writers such as Abe Kōbō, who vividly describe the human cost of technology in their novels.[4]

The *mecha* genre of anime carries on this tradition. Perhaps the most ubiquitous of all anime genres, *mecha*'s vision of what Alessandro Gomarasca terms the 'technologised body' is one that has only increased in importance since 1963, when Japanese television premiered *Astro Boy* (*Tetsuwan Atomu*). This was not only the first Japanese animated television series, but the first of a long line of anime involving robots with human souls. In that same year the first 'giant robot' series aired, *Iron Man # 28* (*Tetsujin 28 go*) based on the comic by Yokoyama Misuteru. *Iron Man # 28* already displayed characteristics important to the genre, the most significant being that, unlike *Astro Boy*, the robot was controlled by a separate human being. As the genre developed, human and robot often combined, with the human inside guiding the powerful robotic body.

While the imagery in *mecha* anime is strongly technological and is often specifically focused on the machinery of the armoured body, the narratives themselves often focus to a surprising extent on the human inside the machinery. It is this contrast between the vulnerable, emotionally complex and often youthful human being inside the ominously faceless body armour or power suit[5] and the awesome power he/she wields vicariously that makes for the most important tension in many *mecha* dramas.

The three anime we will examine in this section, the two OVA series *Bubblegum Crisis* and its sequel *Bubblegum Crash* (*Baburugamu kuraishisu* and *Baburugamu kurashu*, 1987–91), *Neon Genesis Evangelion* (*Shinseiki Ebuangerion*, 1997), and the video *Guyver: Out of Control* (*Kyshoku soko gaiba*, 1986), all explore this ambiguous process of body-technofusion with varying degrees of skepticism toward the empowering nature of body armor. Although the three differ considerably from each other in tone and style and from other, more optimistic *mecha* works such as *Gundam* or *Orguss*, they all contain certain tropes common to the *mecha* genre that make their darker tone particularly interesting.

In contrast to the abjected feminine worlds of the gothic and the occult, which privileged women's bodies and their terrifying potential to engulf the male inside dark, organic spaces, the worlds of *mecha* might be seen as stereotypically masculine in their emphasis on hardedged, thrusting, outward-oriented power, privileging what scholar Claudia Springer calls 'the violently masculinist figure'.[6] The futuristic settings of *mecha*, inevitably high-tech and/or urban, with immense skyscrapers, laboratories, elevators, space stations and huge corporations permeated with robotic equipment, also evoke a hard-edged technological world, far removed from the traditional settings of gothic anime.

Also in contrast to the gothic and occult pornography, the narrative climaxes of *mecha*, while also fast-paced and often accompanied by throbbing music, are climaxes of combat rather than sex. Virtually any *mecha* narrative will build up to a lengthy climactic fight between huge and powerful machines engaged in combat involving crushing, dismemberment and explosions. These climaxes evoke not so much fear as what Springer calls 'techno-eroticism', a euphoric state of power, excitement and violence often associated with war. Indeed, Klaus Theweleit's discussion of the imagery and tropes employed by the German Freikorps (elite troops created in the aftermath of World War One), which resulted in an ideology in which each young man became a machine and this 'machine' was both 'one of

war and sexuality',[7] seems appropriate to the many intense confrontations in *mecha*.

From this point of view, it seems fitting to call the mecha a conservative genre, one that has links with such Western science fiction tech noir or even 'technophobic' films as *Robocop*, *Terminator* and *Total Recall*. These films, although more complex than some of their critics give them credit for, certainly seem to both privilege and problematise the robotic or cyborg body as a frightening form of the 'technofascist celebration of invulnerability', to use Andrew Ross's evocative phrase.[8] The cyborg or robotic body is therefore simultaneously appealing and threatening, offering power and excitement at the expense of humanity.

Of the three works to be examined, two of them, *Guyver: Out of Control* and *Bubblegum Crash*, certainly have conservative and specifically technophobic aspects to them at the same time as they glory in the *mecha* on *mecha* confrontations that make up a large part of each work. The two series also clearly display a nostalgia for what might be called 'Japanesé family values' and the premodern pastoral world. *Evangelion* is harder to pigeonhole, refusing to give any easy solutions to the horrific world it presents. Although *Evangelion* clearly has both nostalgic aspects (as in an early episode when Shinji, the protagonist, runs off into the country) and technophobic ones, they take place within an acknowledgment of both the fragmentation and the complexity of the real world that the other film and series resist. Even more than most *mecha*, the *Evangelion* series problematises human interaction with technology from the simplest to the most complex level.

The Armored Body: Guyver, Bubblegum Crash and Evangelion

> By what means is a young boy made a soldier? ... How does body armour attain its final form, what are its functions? How does the 'whole' man who wears it function – and above all – what is the nature of his ego? ... This, I believe, is the ideal man of the conservative utopia: a man with machinelike periphery, whose interior has lost its meaning...
> – Klaus Theweleit, *Male Fantasies*

The quotation above, taken from Theweleit's book on the early twentieth century German

Freikorps, gives a sense of some of the conventional ways Western critics have looked at the technologically armoured body. In this view the armored body (be it robotic or cyborg) is spiritually empty, hypermasculine, implicitly associated with fascism, and conceived of only in terms of its ability to wreak violence. Or as Springer says of the armored creations in *Terminator* and *Robocop*, 'What these cyborgs do best is kill'.[9]

Springer and Theweleit are basing their conclusion on Western prototypes, but at first glance much of what they say seems to work well in relation to Japanese *mecha*. The *mecha* in all three works we are looking at are also excellent at killing. Indeed, many of *mecha* anime's narrative structures are built around at least one but often several long fight scenes of *mecha* on *mecha*, scenes that are not simply violent in terms of mechanical brutality but bloodily anthropomorphic as well. The fusion of human pilot inside armored machine leads to bizarre combinations of mechanical/organic violence in which huge machines combat each other in fantastic displays of mechanical agility while at the same time hinting at the organic bodies inside them with graphic glimpses of dismembered limbs flying around and blood seeping through mechanical armour. The power and exaltation of the augmented body noted by Springer and Theweleit[10] is clearly on display in mecha as well; indeed, it is the dominant trope around which *mecha* plots revolve.

The Japanese stories often reveal a much bleaker world view than such Western fantasies as *Star Wars* or even *Terminator*, in terms of how much an individual can actually accomplish. This is partly due to the greater emphasis on the interiority of the characters than would seem to be the case in most Western science fiction films. These characters are far more complicated than the action heroes privileged in conventional Western science fiction. Although many *mecha* series of course have relatively one-dimensional characters, the protagonists of the three works to be examined here show a notable amount of emotional complexity, from Sho's lonely suffering as the Guyver to Priss's attempt to change the world in *Bubblegum Crash* to the hypersensitivity of *Evangelion*'s antihero Shinji.

The very idea of 'body armour', as opposed to the conventional robotic type of Western science fiction film, emphasises the body instead of the armour. In much Western science fiction film even if there is a human body inside the machine, as in *Robocop*, the emphasis is much more on the protagonist's dehumanisation by the alienating powers of technology. Likewise, the robotic hero of the *Terminator* series, while gradually appearing to develop some human emotion in the second film, is still seen largely in terms of a robot with only flashes of humanity, almost the opposite of the *mecha* protagonists who are first and foremost humans in robotic armor.[11] Contrary to Theweleit's and Springer's visions of the armoured body as lacking interiority, therefore, the protagonists in *mecha* anime often have a surprising amount of interiority.

The first text, the 1986 video *Guyver: Out of Control* is based on a popular manga series by Takaya Yoshiki that also spawned an OVA series, although the single video is far darker than the series. Both works have similar plots concerning a young boy named Sho who, through a chance discovery, fuses with something called 'bio-booster armour' to become a hideous cyborglike entity known as a 'Guyver'. He must protect himself from equally hideous agents of the evil Chronos corporation known as 'Zoanoids' while attempting to protect/rescue his girlfriend and, in the OVA series, his father. While the *Guyver* OVA episodes are a relatively uncomplicated series of fights between good Guyver and evil Zoanoids in which good triumphs over evil, the film *Guyver: Out of Control* has a far less triumphal tone, displaying, in certain scenes at least, a fundamental fear of and repulsion from technology. It is also a notably conservative work. It harks back, especially in its women characters, to a peaceful, pretechnological world in which a mother's welcoming breast explicitly contrasts with the dark and hard-edged technological nightmare into which the main character is plunged.

Guyver: Out of Control begins with a traditional pastoral scene: a rainy night in the mountains. Into this scene speeds an earthy truck driver who picks up a seedy looking man with a mysterious bag. When the truck driver attempts to question him about the bag the man only responds that it contains 'spare parts', at which point the truck driver, incensed, kicks him out of the truck, keeping the bag. Seconds later a demonic face (bearing striking similarities to the monster in the Hollywood *Alien* series) appears in the windshield and two arms burst in to kill the driver and take the bag.

In this early scene technology seems both powerful and negative. The truck blasts through the bucolic landscape as the monster's hands blast through the windshield to pick up the 'spare parts'. Even the humans associated with technology, the coarse truck driver and his seedy passenger, are singularly unimpressive. In contrast, the next scene opens to a world of peace and order where Fukamachi Sho and his girlfriend Mizuki are walking home from school. Clearly the 97-pound weakling type, Sho is almost knocked over by a male classmate on a bicycle. Soon after, however, he and Mizuki find a mysterious mechanical object that, in classic male science fiction fashion, Sho decides is a 'great discovery' while Mizuki just wants to leave it and go home. Too late.

Sho begins to transform into a grotesque monster while Mizuki screams helplessly. Soon a group of similarly revolting monsters try to abduct Mizuki but the now-transformed Sho kills them all (in various bloody scenes) and saves her. Although Sho then transforms back into human form, this is only temporary. Sho has unknowingly activated a Guyver, a top secret new kind of 'bio-booster armour' that organically attaches itself to the body's musculature to give it tremendous strength and other powers such as the ability to fly.

Agents from the sinister Chronos Company try desperately to retrieve the Guyver. They kidnap Mizuki and follow Sho to his high school, where they murder all his friends. Now an outcast, Sho hides for a while but finally decides to change into Guyver form and rescue Mizuki. The rescue sequence involves an immensely destructive fight with a female Guyver named Valkyria, who is a former human like Sho but, unlike the innocent boy, an aggressively evil employee of the Chronos Company. Sho-as-Guyver destroys Valkyria and, in an impressive series of explosions and fires, the Chronos Company as well. Although he also rescues Mizuki, who recognises him despite his Guyver armour, he realises he can never return to normal life and sadly disappears (to return, of course, in a lengthy series).

Altogether bloodier, more violent, and containing much more nudity than an American superhero story, *Guyver: Out of Control* is still a recognisable version of the universal adolescent fantasy of a weakling's transformation into a superhero. This is a very dark fantasy, however. The actual transformation sequences seem agonising rather than empowering. Even more negatively, Sho's new powers only serve to bring about the death of his friends and isolate him from humanity permanently.

Unlike the female transformations we have discussed in the section on pornography, Sho's metamorphosis is seen as painful and alienating. In many ways it echoes, on a more simplistic level, Tetsuo's extraordinary metamorphosis scene in *Akira*. As in *Akira*, the transformation is intensely grotesque and the protagonists' agony comes across vividly. Unlike Tetsuo, however, Sho manifests no signs of exulting in his new strengths. The transformation scene itself is much shorter and quickly cuts to the fight scene with the female Guyver to which Sho seems more resigned than excited.

Furthermore, in radical contrast to Tetsuo, Sho remains vulnerably human both in his concern for his girlfriend and his memory of his mother. There is even a poignant scene in which Sho recalls himself as a child running to his mother and being cradled at her breasts. The contrast between the little Sho and the revolting monster he has become is something that would be quite unimaginable in an American tech noir film such as *The Terminator*. The final scene when Mizuki recognises him through his Guyver armour is also significant. Rather than appreciate his muscles and strength, Mizuki sees and wants the 'real' Sho.

Women are thus seen in their most traditional form as oases of comfort (the mother whose breasts enfold Sho) and spirituality (Mizuki, who is capable of seeing the 'real' Sho through his armour). As is typical for this kind of conservative fantasy, untraditional women come across as threatening and evil. Although the Chronos corporation contains various greedy old men, it is significant that Sho's final Guyver enemy, Valkyria, is a woman.

Even before she becomes a Guyver, Valkyria is consistently associated with technology. The viewer first encounters her in a weight room, where she is seen molding her voluptuous body with the use of various steely machines. This linkage of sexuality and machinery is even more pronounced in the scene where she metamorphoses into a Guyver. Unlike Sho, who retains his clothes during transformation, the Guyver's tentacles are seen entwining around her nude body in a clearly phallic fashion. When her final transformation into Guyver form is completed, however, the only real difference between her shape and that of Sho are her pointed, armour-plated breasts.

Distinctly different from the fluid and engulfing female body of anime porn, Valkyria's Guyver form is a rejecting and resisting entity, confronting rather than inviting the male protagonist. In the high tech world of *mecha*, both male hero and female enemy confront each other in armored isolation with no hope even for the sexual union achieved by Taki and Makie in *Wicked City*. Interestingly, Sho does not actually kill the female Guyver, as he did with the male monsters early on. Instead, her 'control meter' is damaged and she falls apart, moaning horribly and ultimately dissolving into a pinkish puddle-like entity, a final form that of course has more feminine connotations.

It is only in that final fluid image that Valkyria seems to reassert a feminine presence, but her dissolving body is horrifying rather than welcoming. In both forms, therefore, Valkyria's body is seen as essentially hideous. Sho is briefly able to turn for relief to the recumbent form of Mizuki, who is clad in her traditional school uniform. But this relief is attained only through the violent subjugation of the technologically empowered female Guyver and can only provide a transient respite from a violent and frightening world. In the long run the body offers neither comfort (since his union with Mizuki is temporary) nor protection (since Sho's own armored body is simply a means of torment).

As Springer says of the (often misogynistic) violence endemic in American cyborg films, 'Violent, forceful cyborg imagery participates in contemporary discourses that cling to nineteenth-century notions about technology, sexual difference and gender roles in order to resist the transformations brought about by the new postmodern social order'.[12] Whether Guyver's notions about technology are strictly 'nineteenth-century' is perhaps questionable, but clearly its values are traditional ones and the film resists any notion of a technologically wrought utopia. In its relentlessly bleak vision, *Guyver: Out of Control* seems very far from Ron Tanner's description of Japan's postwar culture as having 'been built on the unflagging belief in the benefit of all things high tech'.[13]

A somewhat more complex vision of technology – and of women in technology in

particular – may be found in the popular 1980s series *Bubblegum Crisis* and its sequel *Bubblegum Crash*. Set in a high-tech near future where machines known as 'boomers' do most of the work for humanity, the series features a group of attractive young women who occasionally leave their normal working lives to become the 'Knight Sabers' a technologically-armoured paramilitary group who help out when the (also armoured) police are unable to cope with various forms of high-tech banditry inevitably wrought by perpetrators in equally heavy *mecha* armour (or else the armoured machines themselves). Although the series contains many scenes of *mecha* mayhem, the emphasis is not entirely on action. The series contains a certain amount of psychological depth in its characters as well as some satirical flourishes that amusingly skewer the materialist society of contemporary Japan. In fact, *Bubblegum Crisis/ Crash* seems to suggest that the women are more fulfilled inside their battle armour than when they return to 'normal' materialistic life.

In *Bubblegum Crash* Episode 1 the Knight Sabers seem to be on the verge of breaking up. Priss, the most masculine one, appears poised to become a teen idol, while another colleague, Linna, has become a stockbroker and is euphorically making money. Only one of the characters seems disconsolate about the breakup of the group but is unable to circumvent her friends' yuppie-esque obsession with material success. Fortunately, for the future well-being of the group, a band of terrorists calling for a new world order threaten the city, and the Knight Sabers somewhat reluctantly reconstitute themselves. However, once they don their heavily armoured (but at the same time curvaceously feminine) mobile suits, they swing enthusiastically into battle and easily defeat the terrorists. At the end of this episode the two characters who seemed ready to quit the group now see the error of their ways. No longer obsessed by their shallow consumerist lifestyles, they are willing to dedicate themselves more fully to their careers as Knight Sabers.

Although the episode contains hints of female empowerment, with the women winning out over their enemies, it also shows a strongly conservative subtext. While hardly a paean to militarism, the series still implicitly positions the technological, armoured world of the Knight Sabers and the police against the shallow yuppie lifestyles that two of the characters initially embraced. The communal, self-sacrificing spirit of the Knight Sabers, underlined by their ability to coordinate with and support each other once they get into attack formation, stands in obvious contrast to their giggling and back-biting while still in the throes of materialist consumer culture.

Bubblegum Crisis/Crash is far from being entirely protechnology, however. Machines without human guidance are consistently shown as ineffective and often dangerous. Or, as anime scholar Antonia Levi concludes in regards to the 'boomer' machines in the series, 'they are forever going on the rampage, shooting up innocent civilians and destroying urban areas. They are the whole reason for the existence of the Knight Sabers and the A. D. Police. Pure *mecha* equals pure menace.'[14]

In *Bubblegum Crisis* Episode 3 both technology and modernity in general are shown as evil and destructive. In this episode Priss befriends a young boy whose working mother dreams of moving with her child to the country. The mother's dream is thwarted by the plans of the evil Genom corporation, which is taking over and destroying her housing area. Priss, in human form, tries to take on Genom's thugs but discovers, when she tries to hit one of them, that they are actually 'boomer' machines disguised as men, and the demolition continues. The mother is killed under a collapsing building and Priss again takes on Genom's thugs in vengeful fury. This time, wearing her Knight Saber power suit and aided by the other Knight Sabers, she is triumphant. But the final tone of the episode is far from exultant. In the last scene the viewer sees a long shot of Priss delivering the now orphaned boy to what is clearly an institution of some sort while a moody rock song plays on the soundtrack.

The episode's final message is an ambiguous one. Technology and the huge modern corporations are destructive of both the landscape and the land. Yet the only way the Knight Sabers can successfully attack is to fuse with technology themselves. This is most obvious in the scene where Priss, in nonaugmented form, attempts to take on the boomer thugs from Genom but is too weak. Once in her power suit, however, she and her friends easily deal with them.

Yet the overall theme of this episode seems to be one of nostalgia for a simpler world in which Knight Sabers, like some latter day band

of *ronin*, can combat modernity with weaponry that is as much spiritual as it is technological. In a voice-over, Priss recalls the young boy's mother's desire to go to the country, and this seems to fuel her anger even further.[15] But unlike more simplistic *mecha* series, which might have ended with Priss and her friends' celebration after having avenged the boy's mother, the episode concludes on a deeply pessimistic note, one that emphasises the powerlessness of the orphan boy in the face of institution. In the final analysis the individual can only do so much.

Both *Bubblegum Crisis/Crash* and *Guyver: Out of Control* limn worlds in which outside forces overwhelm individual action, especially on the part of young people. The only way they can resist these forces is to augment their bodies through technological means. This theme is taken to its greatest extreme in the ground-breaking television series *Neon Genesis Evangelion*. An extraordinarily complex work, and one that has spawned a small cottage industry of criticism about it, the immensely popular *Evangelion* can be seen as a deconstruction of the entire *mecha* genre. Although it showcases brilliant combat scenes of *mecha*-on-*mecha* confrontations, these scenes take place within a bleak context of seriously dysfunctional family, work and sexual relationships that is permeated with a mystical and apocalyptic philosophy and interwoven with surreal graphic imagery.

In its basic plot outlines, *Evangelion* is classic *mecha*. Set in the near future after a catastrophe called the 'Second Impact', the narrative follows the adventures of a young boy named Shinji who is summoned to NERV headquarters, a secret government organisation in the city of Tokyo III, by his mysterious and coldly distant scientist father. In Episode I Shinji learns why he has been summoned – to pilot an enormous robotic weapon known as an 'Evangelion' (EVA for short), which has been constructed to fight the 'Shito' (translated as 'angel' but actually meaning 'apostle'), huge grotesque-looking creatures presumably from outer space that are stalking the planet. While adult scientists made the EVAs, only young adolescents (described with the English word 'children') can actually 'synchronise' with the EVAs well enough to pilot them. Although initially protesting his inability to pilot the EVA, Shinji finally complies, partly due to his glimpse of the only other EVA pilot available, a girl named Ayanami Rei. Rei has already been so exhausted by previous combat that she has to be wheeled into the control centre on a stretcher. Despite his reluctance, Shinji synchronizes very well with the giant EVA ('49.9 percent synchronicity', a scientist crows), and, after some early problems when it appears he will be defeated, ultimately triumphs over what the viewer later learns is only the first of a series of 'angels'.

Recounted in this way, *Evangelion* would seem to adhere to all the most important *mecha* conventions, a near-future high-tech setting, a fast narrative pace, and above all a youthful hero who pilots his robotic machine to victory over an apparently evil and apparently mechanical enemy. The television series even has an inspiring pop theme song exhorting an unnamed youth to 'become a legend'. However, the series actually turns these conventions inside out to produce a text that is as fascinating or perhaps puzzling as it is almost unrelentingly grim.

This subversive tone is established early in the first and second episodes. Perhaps the most obvious difference that helps set the tone is Shinji's attitude toward his *mecha*. Unlike the Knight Sabers with their cheerful enthusiasm or even Sho, who grows more enthusiastic in his work once he realises he can rescue his girlfriend (and in the television series actually shows some real zeal for transforming into his 'bio-booster armour'), Shinji looks on his augmented self with absolute loathing. His very first encounter with the EVA is instructive. Guided by his superior, Misato, he walks into the EVA holding pad to find it pitch black. When the lights are switched on he finds himself confronting an enormous robotic face, bigger than his entire body, a sight that makes him recoil in horror. Shinji's continuing sense of unease is clearly telegraphed by his disturbed expression as he is loaded into his EVA and propelled out to the fight with the Angel. He seems agonisingly reluctant, a far cry from the willing body-metal fusion on the part of more conventional protagonists.

The actual encounter with the Angel, while certainly exciting, is much more grimly presented than the usual slam-bang extravaganzas of typical *mecha*-on-*mecha* confrontations.[16] The soundtrack music is foreboding and the encounter itself is limned in a shadowy chiaroscuro, quite different from the

brightly-coloured fight scenes of most *mecha*. Finally, the actual fight sequence ends up in a fascinatingly low-tech manner. Menaced by the seemingly victorious Angel, Shinji's EVA, which has suffered enormous damage, manages to right itself at the last moment to produce, not a high-tech weapon, but a huge knifelike piece of metal. The scene becomes even more shadowy and the viewer sees the dark silhouette of Shinji's EVA savagely attacking the Angel with the metal piece.

No doubt, part of this grim tone is due to the apocalyptic nature of the text. With the fate of the world riding on Shinji's shoulders, it is hardly surprising that this is not a light-hearted fight scene. The apocalyptic aspects will be explored later but for the purpose of this essay, it is enlightening to look at what these dark early episodes say about body and identity.

It is possible to see this opening encounter in more mythic and/or psychoanalytical terms as the beginning of Shinji's reluctant rite of passage into manhood, with the EVAs and the Angels as aspects of the Self and Other that Shinji needs to confront in order to form his own identity. Many critics have noted that the construction of the EVA has a feminine aspect, in that it encloses Shinji in a liquid-filled womblike space. It can be suggested that the machine has a masculine aspect as well, in that it is essentially an offensive weapon thrust out of NERV headquarters to take Shinji on his quest for selfhood.

The actual journey begins when Shinji enters the darkened room and, as the lights suddenly go on, sees the EVA for the first time. The scene of the small boy's face next to the gigantic face of the EVA is a memorable one. It is as if Shinji were looking into a distorting mirror and is horrified by the self that he finds there. Shinji is unable to escape from this repellent aspect of himself, however. In the next scene we see him, looking very frail and vulnerable, being enclosed by the mammoth machine while a clear liquid rises around him that, the technicians assure him, will make it easier for him to breathe. As the liquid covers him the EVA begins to move out to the launching pad, and, after a few more technical procedures, Shinji and the EVA are ejected out of NERV headquarters to fight with the Angel.

With its image of a small human encapsulated within a large liquid cylinder, Shinji's immersion (perhaps a more appropriate word than 'fusion') in the EVA strongly suggests a birth scene. To make the message even clearer, the technicians are shown unlocking the so-called umbilical bridge (the English words are used) as the EVA moves out into battle. Thus the EVA has both aspects of the maternal – Shinji is inside its protective capsule – and the self – Shinji is 'synchronising' with it, fusing with it to make it act under his volition. In fact, the critic Kōtani Mari points out the increasing feminisation of Shinji in later episodes, hinting at the affect that the EVA has on Shinji's personality.

Kōtani views the basic structure of the series – the combat between EVA and Angels – as one in which the patriarchal family, NERV, fights with the abjected feminine Other, the Angels.[17] Although I believe that this is an important and illuminating point, since NERV is indeed depicted in an explicitly patriarchal way and the angels have clear links with the abject, I would also suggest that, at least early in the series, the Angels could also be seen as father figures, whom Shinji must annihilate. Huge, brutishly grotesque, and coming down from above, they exhibit an authoritative presence. They are also explicitly associated with Shinji's real father, a man who seems to have rejected his own son in order to work on the mysteries of EVA and the Angels and who appears to be the only person to know the real meaning of the Angels. In this light, the savagery of Shinji's final response to the first Angel is highly suggestive. This is not simply one machine attacking another, but, as the surprisingly primitive knifelike weapon attests, a deeply primal and murderous confrontation. The phallic nature of the knife is also interesting, suggesting that Shinji is attempting to arrogate his father's masculine power.

It is important to realise, however, that just as the EVA is both mother and self, it is also possible to see the Angel as both father and self. After all, the closest equivalent to the gigantic, powerful and grotesque Angel is the gigantic, powerful and grotesque EVA with which Shinji is fused. In this light, Shinji's final victory over the Angel is reminiscent of George Lucas's science fiction epic *The Empire Strikes Back* (1980), in particular the scene in which Luke Skywalker engages in a sword-wielding confrontation with Darth Vader, whom he is not aware is actually his father. In a scene of mythic and psychoanalytical resonance, Luke

finally manages to cut off Vader's 'head' (his helmet), only to discover that the head is actually his own.

In the case of most of the more conventional *mecha*, the triumphant resolution of a fight is a prelude to further victories that will explicitly or implicitly celebrate the growing competence of the youthful protagonist and his maturation into an adult form of identity. In *Evangelion*'s darker vision, however, such a celebratory coming-of-age fantasy is largely undermined. The sexual transgressiveness and ambiguity that mark both EVA and Angel are embodied in a more psychosocial way in the general dysfunctionality of the human protagonists. This is clear throughout the series as the focus turns at least as much to the bickerings, sexual angst, and family secrets of the three young *mecha* pilots and their mentors as to the *mecha* action. Also, as has been shown with Shinji, the characters' attitude toward their high-tech body armour is often ambivalent at best. Rather than empowering them, their huge EVAs leave them wracked with pain and deeply vulnerable. Far from bringing victory, body armour in this series only leads to physical and emotional damage.

Indeed, the EVAs can be seen as outward manifestations of the characters' own defenses, not only against the world but against each other. Instead of enabling them to feel protected and potentially more capable of human interaction, the EVAs only add to the characters' alienation from each other. Thus, while Shinji and his roommate and fellow EVA pilot, the striking Asuka Langley, might be expected to develop a romantic attraction for each other, their sexual tension, although clearly evident in some episodes of mutual fumbling, is usually subsumed under Asuka's intense competitiveness as to who gets to lead in combat with the Angels. As in *Ranma 1/2* this theme of competition can be seen as having links with the heavy pressures that Japanese society places on its citizens, but unlike *Ranma 1/2*, the competition here is apocalyptic rather than festive. Shielded in their EVA armour, Asuka, Shinji and Rei are incapable of any meaningful interaction beyond competitiveness in combat and the occasional bleak foray into sexual experimentation.

The alienation of the characters, especially that of Shinji, is spectacularly apparent in the puzzling and genuinely subversive final episode, a grand finale in which, bizarrely for a work in the *mecha* genre, not a single *mecha* is shown. Episode 26 comes after a dizzying series of revelations concerning both family and institutional secrets interwoven in a highly technological framework in which, among many other things, the true function of NERV and the real identity of the first EVA pilot, Ayanami Rei (she is actually a clone of Shinji's dead mother), are revealed. In contrast to the technological revelations of the previous episodes, however, the final episode is fascinating and to many viewers disappointing in its virtual lack of any high-tech special effects or apocalyptic imagery.

Instead, the final episode is an almost classically psychoanalytic exploration of the personal identities of Shinji and his friends/colleagues at NERV, who, the viewer has by now discovered, are all deeply psychologically damaged. The surreal framework in which the exploration takes place is a series of questions flashed across the screen that Shinji and the others then try to answer, as if they were prisoners being interrogated. The question that occurs most often is 'What do you fear?', and Shinji's answers have nothing to do with high-tech weaponry or Earth-threatening Angels and everything to do with his deeply dysfunctional family life and profoundly introverted personality.

In answer to 'What do you fear?' Shinji first responds, 'I fear the hatred of my father' and adds 'My father abandoned me. He hates me.' As the question continues to be pressed, however, Shinji expands his circle of fear to reveal that his deepest fear is 'not being wanted [by anyone]'. This leads him to confess, in answer to another question, that he pilots the EVA because his 'life is pointless otherwise', and, 'Without the EVA, I had no value.' The others apparently have similar revelations concerning their own sense of worthlessness and their need for the EVA to give their lives meaning.

As the episode continues however, Shinji learns that all of this is taking place in his own mind and, as the outside voice repeatedly tells him, this is a vision of the world that he has come to through his own decisions. Continually being asked the question 'What am I?' Shinji finally sees himself as utterly alone in a blank white world, a lonely cartoon figure floating in a perimeterless space.

Having come to the ultimate in identity deconstruction, Shinji then has a surreal vision of an alternate anime universe, a self-reflexive version of an animated high-school sex comedy that proves to him that there are many possible directions his anime life could go in. With this knowledge he appears ready to begin rebuilding his life and states 'I see I can exist without being an EVA pilot'. The series ends with Shinji thanking his father and saying goodbye to his mother.

Looking at this final episode unironically, Shinji's story is in a sense a coming-of-age drama as much as that of Luke Skywalker or the protagonists of more conventional *mecha*. Indeed, critic Endo Toru sees the final episode as an explicitly sexual coming of age in which Shinji, through the interrogation of the personas of his fellow female combatants in his mind (his anima, perhaps), ultimately is able to separate from his dead mother and move on to a more adult sexuality.[18] At one point in the episode, for example, he is told in Lacanian fashion that 'the first person you see is your mother' and at the end of the episode, he says goodbye to his mother. Even if Shinji's 'maturation' is perceived in a straightforward manner (and, given the dark tone of the series this would be rather problematic), it still seems to be highly ambiguous. Indeed, in the film *The End of Evangelion*, Shinji's sexual coming of age is shown in the bleakest of terms as the opening sequence reveals him masturbating miserably over the wounded body of Asuka. In contrast to Luke's learning to use the 'Force' in the *Star Wars* series, it seems clear in both film and these final episodes that mastery of the EVAs leads only to alienation and despair.

The very ubiquitousness and popularity of the *mecha* genre makes *Evangelion* in general and this final episode in particular peculiarly jarring. Through Shinji's self-questioning, the viewer is insistently reminded of the fundamental worthlessness of the power derived from the mechanical armor, thus undermining the whole basis of the mecha genre. The final scenes in which the unarmored Shinji floats gently in a world without directions, boundaries, or human contact are in striking contrast to the scenes of armored bodies in combat that ended many of the previous episodes. In the solipsistic world of *Evangelion*, *mecha* are finally unimportant except as a means to know the self. Even the human body is less important than the mind that creates its own reality.

Notes

1 It is also true, as with pornography, that these bodily changes can have strongly erotic overtones. In the case of this 'technoeroticism' (to use Springer's phrase) however, the erotic is usually not between male and female but between the human and the technological, as the body-armoured human engages with his – or sometimes her – machine in what are usually intensely violent scenes of battle (Claudia Springer, *Electronic Eros: Bodies and Desire in the Postindustrial Age* [Austin, TX: University of Texas Press, 1996], p. 4).

2 Although there are female transformer robots as well, the preferred machine woman in anime seems to me to be an android type such as Gally in *Battle Angel Alita* or Honey in *Cutey Honey*, whose mechanical bodies are, if anything, usually more beautiful and voluptuous than those of 'real' women. As Springer suggests, 'Cyber-bodies, in fact, tend to appear masculine or feminine to an exaggerated degree', *Electronic Eros* (p. 64). She suspects that this insistence on difference has to do with the fact that science fiction as a genre inherently questions human identity. She goes on to quote Janet Bergstrom's assertion that '[in science fiction] the representation of sexual identity carries a potentially heightened significance, because it can be used as the primary marker of difference in a world otherwise beyond our norms' (Ibid., p. 67).

3 J. P. Telotte, *Replications: A Robotic History of the Science Fiction Film* (Urbana and Chicago: University of Illinois Press, 1995), p. 115.

4 See Abe Kōbō's 1980 fantasy *Secret Rendezvous* (Mikai) for an extraordinary depiction of sexuality's inter-connection with technology.

5 Ron Tanner's article on Japanese robotic toys suggests some intriguing historical and cultural influences in their facial design, from Kabuki and Noh masks to the 'uglike facial features derived from the insect motifs of traditional Japanese art' ('Mr. Atomic, Mr. Mercury and Chime Trooper: Japan's Answer to the American Dream', in *Asian Popular Culture*, edited by John Lent [Boulder, CO: Westview Press, 1995], p. 93).

6 Springer, *Electronic Eros*, p. 96.

7 Klaus Theweleit, *Male Fantasies* (Minneapolis: University of Minnesota Press, 1989), p. 154.

8 Constance Penley and Andrew Ross, 'Cyborgs at Large: Interview with Donna Haraway', in *Technoculture*, edited by Constance Penley and Andrew Ross (Minneapolis: University of Minnesota Press, 1991), p. 7.

9 Springer, *Electronic Eros*, p. 96.

10 Both Springer and Theweleit stress the ecstatic, sexual subtext to the armoured body. As Springer says, 'significantly, muscle-bound cyborgs in films are informed by a tradition of muscular comic-book superheroes; their erotic appeal is in the promise of power they embody. Their heightened physicality culminates not in sexual climax but in acts of violence. Violence substitutes for sexual release' (*Electronic Eros*, p. 99). Or, Theweleit describes the Freikorps troop 'machine' as being 'one of both war and sexuality' (*Male Fantasies*, p. 154). He later goes on to quote Ernst Junger, a contemporary commentator on the Freikorps, whose description strongly recalls scenes of mecha combat: 'This was a whole new race, energy incarnate, charged with supreme energy ... These were conquerors, men of steel tuned to the most grisly battle' (quoted in ibid., p. 159).

11 Ironically, perhaps the first example of a *mecha* series was Osamu Tezuka's early *Astro Boy* (*Tetsuwan Atomu*), in which the appealing eponymous protagonist really was a robot. In contrast to contemporary American comics in which the heroes, although 'super', were always human, *Astro Boy* suggests that even in this early period Japanese animation and comics were willing to see the human within the technological.

12 Springer, *Electronic Eros*, p. 100.

13 Tanner, 'Mr. Atomic', p. 90.

14 Antonia Levi, *Samurai from Outer Space: Understanding Japanese Animation* (Peru, IL: Open Court Publishing, 1997), p. 86.

15 In its privileging of an escape to the country, the episode recalls the cyberpunk masterpiece *Blade Runner*, which also pits spiritual and human values against the world of modern high-tech corporations and ends with its protagonists actually managing to escape into a bucolic landscape. This similarity is probably not entirely coincidental since both Priss and her rock band, The Replicants, have obviously been named in homage to *Blade Runner*'s androids, one of the main characters of which is a replicant called Priss.

16 It is also interesting that the fight scene is not actually shown in the first episode. While the beginning of the encounter is shown in Episode 1, the episode actually ends with the fights denouement still unclear. It is only in the second episode, which starts with Shinji in a hospital bed, that we are shown a flashback of his triumph against the Angel. This fracturing of the narrative structure confounds conventional anime-based expectations, in which a fight and victory would develop in linear form.

17 See Ktani Mari, *Seibo Ebuangerion* (Tokyo: Magajin Hausu, 1997), pp. 32–40.

18 Springer and Theweleit also see the fascination with technology as a means of escaping from sexuality. The Japanese critic Endō Toru, writing on *Evangelion*, also sees Shinji's story as an attempt to escape from both female sexuality and adult sexuality in general. Although, as Endō points out, it seems that Shinji simultaneously fears and desires a sexual relationship, until the final episode

his desires are boundaried by the many quasimaternal relationships that he engages in, from the womblike body of the EVA itself to the quasimaternal ministrations of Katsuragi and even his ambiguous relationship with Rei. Only Asuka is allowed to seem explicitly sexual. Endō equates the sexual qualities Shinji discovers in Asuka in the final episode as being part of the 'real world' that Shinji, by accepting the maternal ministrations of both the EVA and Katsuragi Misato, has been unable to escape ('Konna kitanai kirei na hi ni wa:fujori to iu sukui', *Pop Culture Critique* 0 [1997], pp. 92–3).

IMITATION OF LIFE: POSTMODERN SCIENCE FICTION

SIX | IMITATION OF LIFE: POSTMODERN SCIENCE FICTION

Contemporary science fiction is immersed in the symbols, signs and polymorphous impressions of postmodernity and postmodernism. The contemporary science fiction city often speaks to notions of spatial fluidity and anomie, and to a dehistoricised sense of the past, present and future. This is because its architecture often combines a mixing of old and new styles – such as the Mayan inspired pyramids adjacent to the neon billboards in *Blade Runner* and because social interaction and communication is increasingly mediated through the flat and instantaneous surfaces of the computer or television screen that mediates its landscape. Time, space and living memory, then, in 'classical' postmodern fashion, seems to get all confused and blurry in the contemporary science fiction city. Similarly, the humanist or pathological cyborg who gets to walk in this schizophrenic metropolis articulates a postmodern sense of identity in crisis where the fears around technology, reproduction and a loss of the self are played out in this futurebody figure.

The sense of a postmodern world in a state of flux is replayed again and again in contemporary science fiction. Borders and boundaries of all descriptions collapse and merge as the real collapses into the fantasy and the simulated environment or given as much or even more ontological truth. When people dream or have nightmares in contemporary science fiction they never really wake up because the dream/nightmare is their actual living and waking state. Commodities to be bought and sold are to be found everywhere, and shopping and consumption haunt the narratives of contemporary science fiction. Even Oxygen is up for sale in *Total Recall*, heralding in the imaginable worst excesses of the trans-global economy. Contemporary science fiction acknowledges the global (village) through corporate ownership, the (reverse) flow of people, and consumption habits such as the foods eaten, cars driven and languages spoken. In contemporary science fiction, people are desperately lonely, isolated and disenfranchised and consequently turn to simulated and hyperreal pleasures to survive the nothingness or surface level nature of their lives. Contemporary science fiction plays homage to other, earlier, 'better' science fiction texts, in exchanges of parody and meaningless pastiche that in turn suggest a genre worn out and exhausted with itself. The state of contemporary science fiction is the state of the nation – all flabby heart, all existential confusion, with little hope of unity or progression or real escape, to be found anywhere or anymore.

Vivian Sobchack looks at the ideological, cultural and textual impact of new media technologies on everyday life and on the spatial and temporal organisation of modern science fiction films. Media pervasive inventions such as the home computer, video games and the widespread use of digital representation has not only transformed real experiences so that they are increasingly based on simulacrum and mediation but 'depth of perception has become less dominant as a mode of representing and dealing with the world. To a degree it has been flattened by the superficial electronic 'dimensionality' of movement experienced as occurring on – not in – the screens of computer terminals, video games, music videos and movies like *Tron* and *The Last Starfighter*'.

Scott Bukatman begins his essay by exploring what he considers to be the determining elements of the postmodern condition, drawing on the arguments and ideas of Baudrillard and Debord, amongst others, to interrogate the slippy nature of the image. Bukatman then draws on these key ideas to examine the oeuvre of David Cronenburg and in particular the film *Videodrome*, which he considers to be an exemplary example of a postmodern text that wrestles with the ontological nature of display and spectacle. According to Bukatman, '*Videodrome* presents a destabilised

reality in which image, reality, hallucination and psychosis become indissolubly melded; and it is on this level that the film becomes a work of postmodernism, rather than simply a work about it'.

Alison Landsberg takes issue with the postmodern idea that media simulation and technological mediation are inauthentic realities that negate history and disrupt the memory narratives of the self. To the contrary, Landsberg suggests they 'offer strategies for making history into personal memories' and for intervening 'in the production of subjectivity'. Taking the idea of prosthetic memories or 'implanted memories' and relating it to the memory mechanisms of cinema, Landsberg argues that the distinctions between authentic and second-hand memories cannot hold because 'memories are always already public … And can never get back to an authentic owner, to a proper body…'. According to Landsberg films such as *Total Recall* and *Blade Runner* 'thematise prosthetic memories as an allegory for the power of the mass media to create experiences and to implant memories, the experience of which we have never lived'.

Isolde Standish examines the Japanese anime film *Akira* through both a sub-cultural and postmodern framework. Standish suggests that *Akira* 'uses the *bosozuka* style to reflect a youth culture of resistance which exists alongside mainstream Japanese society', implicitly addressing the deep social divisions and the impact of economic transformations that emerged post-war. In terms of postmodernism, *Akira* demonstrates 'an effacement of boundaries, for instance between previously defined stylistic norms (Eastern and Western) and between past and present, resulting in pastiche and parody; and a schizophrenic treatment of time as 'perpetual present''.

Postfuturism
Vivian Sobchack

This chapter was written nearly a decade after the previous ones. It seems quite appropriate, however, that there be such a gap, such a rupture, between previous chapters and this last one – for in the time and space between, both our lived experience and our cultural representations of time and space have visibly changed. Ten years ago the digital watch, the personal computer, the video game, and the video recorder were elite objects rather than popular commodities. Now they are an integral part of our everyday lives – consuming us as much as we consume them. In the most pervasive and personal way, these electronic artifacts (whose function is representation) both constitute and symbolise the radical alteration of our culture's temporal and spatial consciousness. Such a change in our contemporary 'sense' of time and space cannot be considered less than a change in our technology, but it also must be considered something more – for, as Heidegger says, 'the essence of technology is nothing technological'.[1] Technology never comes to its particular specificity in a neutral context for neutral purpose. Rather, it is always 'lived' – always historically informed by political, economic and social content, and always an expression of aesthetic value.

Altered States

Any understanding of the aesthetics of the contemporary SF film depends upon our understanding the ways in which the experience of time and space have changed for us and the cinema in this last and most popularly electronic decade of American culture. As a major capitalist industry and institution, American cinema has increasingly incorporated the new electronic technology into its very modes of production, distribution and exhibition. And, as a symbolic medium whose function is representation, the American cinema has also increasingly articulated the new 'sense' and 'sensibility' generated by this technology and its spatial and temporal transformation of contemporary experience. As might be expected, this articulation is nowhere more evident or given more emphasis than in the SF

film – for SF has always taken as its distinctive generic task the cognitive mapping and poetic figuration of social relations as they are constituted and changed by new technological modes of 'being-in-the-world'.

In sum, the SF films of the late 1970s and 1980s differ from their predecessors – the culture's technological transformations radically altering their technical and aesthetic character and, more importantly, their conception and representation of the lived world. These differences go much further than a simple transformation of the nature and manner of the genre's special effects or of its representation of visible technology. Whether 'mainstream' and big-budget or 'marginal' and low-budget, the existential attitude of the contemporary SF film is different – even if its basic material remained the same. Cinematic space travel of the 1950s had an aggressive and three-dimensional thrust – whether it was narrativised as optimistic, colonial and phallic penetration and conquest or as pessimistic and paranoid earthly and bodily invasion. Space in these films was semantically inscribed as 'deep' and time as accelerating and 'urgent'.[2] In the SF films released between 1968 and 1977 (during a period of great social upheaval and after the vast spatial and temporal Moebius strip of *2001: A Space Odyssey* had cinematically transformed progress into regress), space became semantically inscribed as inescapably domestic and crowded. Time lost its urgency – statically stretching forward toward an impoverished and unwelcome future worse than a bad present. Pointing to the dystopian despair of a country negatively involved in both domestic and international contestation and unable to avoid its representation in constant and pervasive media imagery, Joan Dean tells us:

The science fiction films of the early 1970s mirror a developing neoisolationism (perhaps a result of a costly involvement in Southeast Asia); a diminishing fear of nuclear apocalypse (partially a result of the thaw in the Cold War); and a growing concern with domestic, terrestrial issues – most of which are related to totalitarian government control of people's lives or to overpopulation, food shortages, pollution and ecology. Consequently space travel appeared only infrequently ... Likewise, extraterrestrial visitors to this planet diminished in number. The single theme ...

that dominated the science fiction imagination between 1970 and 1977 was overpopulation and its concomitant problems of food shortage and old age.[3]

Not successful box office, the films of this period are overtly despairing in their evocation of a future with no future. Traditional space has no further frontiers and appears as constraining and destructive of human existence as a concentration camp. Traditional time no longer comfortably or thrillingly promises progress as anything other than decay and entropy. The films dramatise, as well, disenchantment with a 'new' technology whose hope has been exhausted, which has become 'old' – no longer hyperbolised in particularly flamboyant or celebratory special effects or fearful displays.

Then, in 1977, George Lucas's Star Wars and Steven Spielberg's Close Encounters of the Third Kind were released, initiating what seemed a sudden and radical shift in generic attitude and a popular renaissance of the SF film. Both films could hardly be described as 'cool' and 'detached' in their vision, or 'cautionary' and 'pessimistic' in their tone. Through some strange new transformation, technological wonder had become synonymous with domestic hope; space and time seemed to expand again, their experience and representation becoming what can only be called 'youthful'. Mechanical and biological aliens were realised as cuddly, if powerful, innocents. These seminal films and the ones that followed shared little attitudinal similarity with their generic predecessors. Even the low-budget and marginal SF films that emerged in the mid-1980s as a kind of 'counter-cultural' response to the spatial simplicity and suburban cleanliness initiated by Lucas and Spielberg were hardly pessimistic or paranoid, representing instead a peculiar form of born-again 'heart'. Celebrating all existence as wondrously e-stranged and alien-ated, films like 1983's Liquid Sky (Slava Tsukerman) and Strange Invaders (Michael Laughlin), or 1984's Repo Man (Alex Cox), The Brother from Another Planet (John Sayles) and Night of the Comet (Thom Eberhardt) accept or embrace trashed-out, crowded and complex urban space, and appreciate the temporal closure of the future for all the surprising juxtapositions such closure allows and contains.

Although there are exceptions, unlike their predecessors most of today's SF films

(mainstream or marginal) construct a generic field in which space is semantically described as a surface for play and dispersal, a surface across which existence and objects kinetically displace and display their materiality. As well, the urgent or hopeless temporality of the earlier films has given way to a new and erotic leisureliness – even in 'action-packed' films. Time has decelerated, but is not represented as static. It is filled with curious things and dynamised as a series of concatenated events rather than linearly pressured to stream forward by the teleology of plot. Today's SF film evidences a structural and visual willingness to linger on 'random' details, takes a certain pleasure (or, as the French put it, 'jouissance') in holding the moment to sensually engage its surfaces, to embrace its material collections as 'happenings' and collage. Indeed, both playfulness and pleasure are cinematic qualities new to SF in the late 1970s and the 1980s, replacing the cool, detached and scientific vision authenticating the fictions of its generic predecessors.

The changed sense of space and time experienced in the last decade has also transformed SF's representation of the 'alien', the cultural 'Other'. (Ridley Scott's 1979 Alien, John Carpenter's 1982 remake of The Thing, and Tobe Hooper's unpopular 1985 Life Force stand as the few contemporary echoes of the earlier period in which space was inscribed as deep, and invasion still possible.) The title of Enemy Mine (Wolfgang Petersen, 1985) only emphasises this major shift in attitude toward the cultural (and biological/mechanical) Other. In part, of course, this shift owes much to the last decade's 'recovery' from the upheavals of the late 1960s. During the last decade, the representations of both American politics and popular culture have attempted to recuperate and re-vison the past (and televised) failure of bourgeois patriarchy – both in relation to its challenge by the Civil Rights, youth, and feminist movements of the late 1960s, and by its loss of face and imperialist power in Southeast Asia. Most recently (and coincident with SF's most loving treatment of the alien), this 'recovery' has been celebrated in self-congratulatory and electronically represented acts of 'redemption' – among them the 'Live Aid' concert and the media blitz surrounding the recording of 'We are the world, we are the children'.[4] It is no accident that two related cinematic coincidences serve to mark both the mid-1970s renaissance of SF and its mid-1980s popularity as somehow entailed with the revisioning of America's history of failure and guilt in Vietnam. It is just after the 1977 release of *Star Wars* and *Close Encounters* (the first with its inverted tale of an evil imperialism fought by 'underdog' rebel heroes, the second with its scrawny, little and powerful aliens and childlike human males) that the first films to directly address American involvement in Southeast Asia are released to wide popularity: *Coming Home*, *The Deer Hunter* and *Apocalypse Now*. All represent American men as the naïve and innocent victims of an incomprehensible and criminal war. It is just as telling to note that in 1984 (at the height of SF's new popularity), Academy Award consideration is given to two performers who represented two different but similarly sympathetic, sweet, forgiving, and loving 'aliens' – the one from 'outer space' in *Starman* (John Carpenter) and the other from Cambodia in *The Killing Fields*. In effect (and counter to the further revisions of *Rambo*), recent SF has figured the alien as a heartrendingly, emotionally empowered 'innocent' – and its human protagonists as striving less toward an assumption of power (with all its negative responsibility and potential for failure) than toward an assumption of Heideggerean 'care' (in the mainstream films) or a peculiar transformation of Heideggerean 'dread' (in the marginal films).[5]

In part, however, this shift in sensibility toward the alien and Other seems also a function of that new technology which has transformed the spatial and temporal shape of our world and our world view. The popularisation and pervasiveness of electronic technology in the last decade has reformulated the experience of space and time as expansive and inclusive. It has recast human being into a myriad of visible and active simulacra, and has generated a semantic equivalency among various formulations and representations of space, time and being. A space perceived and represented as superficial and shallow, as all surface, does not conceal things: it displays them. When space is no longer lived and represented as 'deep' and three-dimensional, the 1950s concept of 'invasion' loses much of its meaning and force. The new electronic space we live and figure cannot be invaded. It is open only to 'pervasion' – a condition of kinetic accommodation and dispersal associated with the experience and representations of television, video games and

computer terminals. Furthermore, in a culture where nearly everyone is regularly alien-ated from a direct sense of self (lived experience commonly mediated by an electronic technology that dominates both the domestic sphere and the 'private' or 'personal' realm of the Unconscious), when everyone is less conscious of existence than of its image, the once threatening SF 'alien' and Other become our familiars – our close relations, if not ourselves.

As in the 1950s, the contemporary SF film seems to divide into two groupings related, in great measure, to the conditions of their production. But the two groups are no longer divided as a function of their big-budget optimism or low-budget pessimism. Rather, 'mainstream' and 'marginal' films differ in the way they both celebrate a thoroughly domestic space and domesticated technology, embrace the alien Other, and realise a temporal reformulation of the genre's traditional 'futurism'.[6] The dominant attitude of most mainstream SF has been *nostalgia* – an attitude clearly evidenced by *Star Wars'* shiny evocation of the future as 'Long, long ago...' by *Close Encounters'* yearning for childhood rather than for its end, and by the blatant pronouncement of the very title of *Back to the Future* (Robert Zemeckis, 1985). More complimentary than contradictory, the dominant attitude of most marginal SF toward the genre's traditional 'futurism' has been a literal (rather than ideological) conservatism: an embrace of *pastiche* – a nonhierarchical collection of heterogeneous forms and styles from a variety of heretofore distinguishable spaces and times. Indeed, the marginal nature of these independent SF films goes far beyond their production budgets and distribution problems, for their playful erasure of the boundaries marked between past, present and future, between outer space and domestic space, between alien and human, locates them liminally – both 'within' and 'without' the genre. Their presence and claim upon SF questions the very temporal and spatial premises upon which the genre has traditionally based its identity.

Whatever their apparent differences, then, the generally sanguine attitudes and spatial and temporal realisations of both mainstream and marginal SF are surprisingly coincident. However significantly opposed in *mise-en-scène*, *Starman* and *The Brother from Another Planet* offer us the same protagonists – the same male human being born again in a state of wonderful and innocent 'alien-nation'. *D.A.R.Y.L.* (Simon Wincer, 1985) and *Android* (Aaron Lipstadt, 1982) are made of the same innocent and sweet machinery. And, although their modes of sublimity resonate quite differently, the transcendent endings of both *Cocoon* (Ron Howard, 1985) and *Repo Man* have much in common with each other. In sum, whether mainstream or marginal, the majority of contemporary (and popular) SF films celebrate rather than decry an existence and world so utterly familiar and yet so technologically transformed that traditional categories of space, time, being and 'science fiction' no longer quite apply.

At this point, we might look more specifically at how the last decade of 'popular electronics' has altered the spatial and temporal state of our lived and represented experience, how the decade's technological 'essence' is more than technological.[7] The pervasive experience of electronic technology in the last ten years has caused traditional orientational systems to lose much of their constancy and relevance for us. New spatial and temporal forms of 'being-in-the-world' have emerged (to find their most poetic figuration, if not their proper names, in the SF film). For example, previous mention was made of 1950s space perceived and represented as three-dimensional and 'deep'. Today, however, the traditional perception of 'depth' as a structure of possible bodily movement in a materially habitable space has been challenged by our current and very real kinetic responses to – but immaterial habitation of – various forms of 'simulated' space (from flight training to video games). As a function of this new 'sense' of space, our depth perception has become less dominant as a mode of representing and dealing with the world. To a great degree, it has become flattened by the superficial electronic 'dimensionality' of movement experienced as occurring on – not in – the screens of computer terminals, video games, music videos, and movies like *Tron* (Steven Lisberger, 1982) and *The Last Starfighter* (Nick Castle, 1984).

Our experience of spatial contiguity has also been radically altered by digital representation. Fragmented into discrete and contained units by both microchips and strobe lights, space has lost much of its contextual function as the ground for the continuities of time, movement and event. Space is now more often a 'text' than a context. Absorbing time, incorporating movement, figuring as its own discrete event, contemporary space has become experienced as self-contained, convulsive and discontiguous – a phenomenon most visibly articulated through the *mise-en-scène* and editorial practices of *Blade Runner* (Ridley Scott, 1982) and *Repo Man*, and most audibly announced in *The Adventures of Buckaroo Banzai: Across the 8th Dimension* (W. D. Richter, 1984) when the king-of-all-trades hero philosophises on this new sense of spatial fragmentation and equivalence to his rock concert audience: 'Remember, wherever you go, there you are.'[8]

If the digital 'bit' has fragmented our experience and representation of space, then the character of electronic dispersal has dislocated our experience and sense of 'place'. We are culturally producing and electronically disseminating a new world geography that politically and economically defies traditional notions of spatial 'location'. As a system of orientation, conventional geography has served to represent relative spatial boundaries predicated by differences not only of latitude and longitude and 'natural' geophysical punctuation, but also of national real estate. Conventional geography, however, cannot adequately describe where contemporary Palestine is located. Nor was it able to circumscribe the boundaries of a Vietnam that 'placed' itself both 'inside' and 'outside' the American living room. Our new electronic technology has also spatially dispersed capital while consolidating and expanding its power to an 'everywhere' that seems like 'nowhere'. Again, traditional orientational systems fail to describe our new economic and political experience. Rather, it is the 'political unconscious' of the new American SF film that most powerfully symbolises and brings to visibility this apparent paradox of the simultaneous spatial dispersal and yet 'nuclear' concentration of economic and political power (although, as the unconscious is wont to do, it elaborates and projects its negative self-imagery onto an evil 'Other').[9] The 'Empire' of the *Star Wars* trilogy literalises both the 'cosmic' technological expansion and dispersal of economic and political power and the most intense and implosive technological concentration of that power – in the 'black star' that is figured as the Death Star. It is *Tron*, however, that most visibly casts its similar narrative in electronic form – the evil 'Master Control Program' both concentrating and dispersing corporate electronic power and militarism across a video game culture in which even the 'good guys' are electronic simulacra, occupying a new sort of space that defies traditional geographical description.

In this respect, *Rollerball* (Norman Jewison, 1975) seems a somewhat prescient attempt to figure the conjunction of electronic and corporate power – although, as with other SF films between 1968 and 1977, its vision is bleak and hopeless rather than celebratory. Tyrannical corporations have replaced national identity and individual difference with a global and electronic consumer culture – one ambiguously 'located' in relation to the concentrated and dispersed display space of the television screen. The electronic and 'nuclear' proliferation of multinational capitalism has increasingly concentrated and centralised control over the world as marketplace, but that centre now appears decentered – occupying no one location, no easily discernible place. Where is OPEC? IBM? AT&T? In 1975 their power and pervasive presence both 'everywhere' and 'nowhere' was perceived and represented as threatening and disturbing, but ten years later that concentrated power and its decentered nature are seen as merely normal. One of the teenage Valley Girl heroines of 1984's *Night of the Comet* whines to comic effect: 'You're not going to blame me because the phone went dead. I'm not the phone company. Nobody's the phone company any more.' How, in fact, can traditional orientational systems help us to conceptualise, comprehend, describe or locate a corporation called National General? The 'multinationals' (as we have come to familiarly call them) seem to determine our lives from some sort of ethereal 'other' or 'outer' space. This is a space that finds its most explicit figuration in the impossible towering beauty of *Blade Runner's* Tyrell Corporation Building – an awesome megastructure whose intricate facade also resembles a microchip. It is a space that finds its most alienated and inhuman articulation as the 'Corporation' in *Alien*, and its most outlandish expansion in the mining complex on Jupiter's moon, Io, in *Outland* (Peter Hyams, 1981).

Our traditional orientation toward ourselves as singular and private 'individuals' has also been severely challenged by recent technological change. So has our certainty about what it means to shape time humanly through images supposedly generated in the privacy of subjective memory and desire. Today, privately experienced 'interiority' appears less and less a necessary condition of human being. Intrasubjective 'personal' vision once invisible to others has become publicly visible and commodified through media imagery. Our private 'memory' has been increasingly constituted from previously mediated 'spectacle' rather than from 'direct' experience. Indeed, both *Brainstorm* (Douglas Trumbull, 1983) and *Dreamscape* (Joe Rubin, 1984) merely figure what is, in fact, the ground of contemporary culture's production of subjective visual activity as objective and/or inter-subjective visible activity. Similarly, our temporal sense also has been electronically transformed and made visible. Challenging our conventional orientation toward social and personal history as a linear and progressive movement, the nonchronological Moebius strip of television allows us to see and recognise the complexity and thickness of temporal experience. Retension and protension are personal structures suddenly made publicly visible in 'instant replays', 'previews', and 'rerun' narratives that subvert the temporally linear notion of 'series' in their display of familiar actors, characters and events in nonchronological representations of their youth and age, of past, present and future. Pervasive and invasive, immediately mediating our spatial and temporal experience of the world, and then analysing, replaying, dramatising, rerunning and exhausting it in insatiable acts of consumption, television has produced a historically novel form and model of cultural visibility and reflexive consciousness – heightened in the last decade by the video recorder and the personal computer. Now, more than ever before, different strata in our society have converged in their passionate interest in the image, in representation, in the very processes of mediation and simulation.

In 'Postmodernism, or The Cultural Logic of Late Capitalism' (the essay that critically informs both the structure and emphasis of this present chapter), Fredric Jameson tells us that we are in the midst of

a prodigious expansion of culture throughout the social realm, to the point at which everything in our social life – from economic value and state power to practices and to the very structure of the psyche itself – can be said to have become 'cultural' in some original and as yet untheorised sense.[10]

Immersed in media experience, conscious of mediated experience, we no longer experience any realm of human existence as unmediated, immediate, 'natural'.[11] We can only imagine such an experience (now aware that imagination, too, is an 'imaging', a mode of mediated representation). This new sense we have that everything in our lives is mediated and cultural explains, perhaps, why Deckard and Rachael's escape into the 'natural' landscape at the end of *Blade Runner* seems so implausible and artificial. The landscape seems completely imaginary – unnatural in its 'naturalness', its lack of the 'real' social density we have previously experienced. Thus, the 'nature' cinematography strikes us an inauthentic 'special effect' compared to the technical special effects we have seen and accepted as authentically 'natural' – and we become reluctantly aware of both cinema and narrative straining in their work to produce a traditionally 'happy' ending.

Throughout the last decade, even our bodies have become pervasively re-cognised as cultural, commodified and technologised objects. This is a phenomenon women and advertising agencies have long been aware of, but it now more globally informs a society obsessed with physical fitness. In the last decade we have come to idealise the human organism as a 'lean machine' – sometimes murderously 'mean', sometimes aerobically 'perfect', and nearly (and yet never) impervious to that temporal bodily 'terminator': death. Re-cognising the body as machine transforms 1960s narcissism. A cultural sensuality emerges based on bodily production as the production of bodies, and an androgynous erotics is figured in sweat, work and the notion of the 'routine' rather than in sexual difference. Indeed, in a decade when organ transplants and remarkable prosthetic devices are commonplaces, we are (for better and worse) theorising our bodies, ourselves, as cyborgs.[12] We have become increasingly aware of ourselves as 'constructed' and 'replicated' – not only through our abstract knowledge of recombinant DNA, but also through our heightened reflexive experience of using an always acculturated (and, therefore, 'artificial') intelligence, and of being a 'self' always (re)produced and projected as an image available to others. As Jameson puts it, we have become 'a society of the image or the simulacrum', a society that transforms 'the 'real' into so many pseudoevents'.[13] In Walter Benjamin's 'age of mechanical reproduction', the unique status of the work of art was challenged by the technological transformation of the social world.[14] In an age of electronic reproduction and replication, however, it is the unique status of the human being that is challenged by technological transformation.

In the context of our newly exteriorised self-consciousness, the contemporary SF film has emphatically figured reflexive robots, computers, androids and replicants seeking emotional as well as functional fulfillment. They evidence doubt and desire, a sense of negation and loss, a self-consciousness and sentimentality new to the genre. They are (as *Blade Runner* suggests) 'more human than human'. However prideful, Robby – a distinctly 1950s robot – displays none of the comical anxiety and continual self-interrogation of CP30, or the tenderness of 'Val' and 'Alta' in the robotic family romance of *Heartbeeps* (Allan Arkush, 1981). However intellectually powerful, the computer of *Colossus: The Forbin Project* (Joseph Sargent, 1970) feels no need to seek the origins of its own existence and meaning as does V(oya)ger in *Star Trek: The Movie* (Robert Wise, 1979), nor 'watching' displays of human affection and sexuality does it experience the love and jealousy 'felt' by the small 'PC' of *Electric Dreams* (Steve Barron, 1984). There are no previous SF film counterparts to the prurient sexual curiosity and image-consciousness of Max in *Android* – who, completely aware of his own existential status as an imitation, still strives to further model himself after images of images: the personae of Jimmy Stewart and Humphrey Bogart he has seen in old movies. And nowhere before in the SF film (if in Mary Shelley) has such a fully self-conscious longing for life and eloquently ferocious challenge to humanity been articulated as in *Blade Runner*. Its 'replicants' not only have human 'memories' – given to them (as to ourselves) in 'imaginary' constructions documented and conserved as the referential 'reality' of photographic images. Supremely self-conscious and reflexive, 'more human than human', they are also capable of irony and poetry.

In the ten years that separate the first three chapters of this book from this last, our traditional systems for representing ourselves to ourselves have become no longer fully adequate to our experience. Hierarchical distinctions between surface/depth, here/there, centre/margin, organic/inorganic, and self/other are now commonly challenged in our daily lives.

Thus, in the last decade, new symbolic descriptions of contemporary experience have begun to emerge and dominate older ones. One such new description has been the theorisation of 'the cultural logic of late capitalism' (and its radical entailment of new technological modes of production) as 'postmodernism'. Another new description has been the practice of this cultural logic as figured in the transformed poetics of the contemporary American SF film.

Notes

1 Martin Heidegger, 'The Question Concerning Technology', trans. William Lovitt, in *Martin Heidegger: Basic Writings*, ed. David Farrell Krell (New York: Harper & Row, 1977), p. 317.

2 For an elaboration of the sexual 'dreamwork' of the traditional SF film, see my 'The Virginity of Astronauts: Sex and the Science Fiction Film' in *Shadows of the Magic Lamp*, eds. George Slusser and Eric S. Rabkin (Carbondale: University of Southern Illinois Press, 1985), pp. 41–57.

3 Joan F. Dean, 'Between *2001* and *Star Wars*', *Journal of Popular Film and Television*, 7, no. 1 (1978), pp. 36–7.

4 This recuperation of patriarchy as a response to feminism and the failure of American aggressivity in Southeast Asia is treated not only in relation to the contemporary SF film, but also to the family melodrama/comedy and horror film in my 'Child/Alien/Father: Patriarchal Crisis and Generic Transformation' in *camera obscura* #13 (1986). In that text, I also draw attention to *E.T.*'s physical resemblance to starving Ethiopian children.

5 'Care' here is a philosophical concept that entails a recognition of the meaning of all beings, of meaning as 'Being'. 'Dread' is also a philosophical concept not to be seen as synonymous with 'fear'; the latter is specific and connected to a meaningful particular, to something that matters, whereas 'dread' is a condition of the denial of particular meaning, a vertigo in which all being and action stand as equivalent and therefore meaningless. The mainstream *Close Encounters*, for example, could stand as a representation of the urge towards a condition of 'care' as could *Blade Runner* (Ridley Scott, 1982), whereas the marginal *Liquid Sky* and *Repo Man* manifest

the recognition of meaninglessness and equivalency associated with 'dread' (albeit in a transformed way yet to be discussed). For a summary of these Heideggerean concepts, see Karsten Harries, 'Martin Heidegger: The Search for Meaning', in *Existential Philosophers: Kierkegaard to Merleau-Ponty*, ed. George Alfred Schrader, Jr. (New York: McGraw Hill, 1967), pp. 183–7.

6 'Futurism' here has a double sense. The term evokes SF's general tendency to project temporally possible (if sometimes improbable) events, technologies and social relations. But it also is a technical term that describes a 'modernist' and 'Utopian' art movement of the early twentieth century that celebrated machinery and speed. As Fredric Jameson notes in 'Postmodernism, or the Cultural Logic of Late Capitalism', at that time, new technological objects like the machine gun and the motor car 'are still visible emblems, sculptural nodes of energy which gave tangibility and figuration to the motive energies of that earlier moment of modernisation'. (*New Left Review*, No. 146, July–August 1984, p. 78) The 'visibility' of such emblems, their existence as some sort of 'tangible' evidence and figuration of the dynamism ('the motive energies') that constituted the 'modern', are precisely what the new 'marginal' SF film both mocks and tries to reformulate. In its recognition that 'visibility', 'tangibility', and 'dynamism' are terms descriptive of a 'modern' technology outmoded by an electronic culture to which those terms seem irrelevant, in rejecting the visual celebration and visible display of technology dominating current 'mainstream' SF, 'marginal' SF films like *Repo Man* or *The Brother from Another Planet* can be seen as consciously embracing what shall be elaborated as a 'postmodern' aesthetic.

7 This question can only be briefly addressed here – and as it furthers my discussion of the contemporary SF film. I would direct the interested reader to a most provocative phenomenological exploration of this question: Don Ihde, *Existential Technics* (Albany, NY: State University of New York Press, 1983), and to Section I. 'Technology and American Culture' (pp. 11–75) in *The Technological Imagination: Theories and Fictions*, eds. Teresa De Lauretis, Andreas Huyssen and Kathleen Woodward (Madison, WI: Coda Press, 1980).

8 Interestingly, this phrase is repeated (and makes the same statement of spatial equivalency) in the Australian *Mad Max: Beyond Thunderdome* (George Miller/George Ogilve, 1985).

9 Fredric Jameson, *The Political Unconscious: Narrative as a Socially Symbolic Act* (Ithaca, NY: Cornell University Press, 1981). See particularly, pp. 9–102.

10 Jameson, 'Postmodernism, or The Cultural Logic of Late Capitalism', *New Left Review*, no. 146 (July–August 1984), p. 87.

11 This 'ultimate victory' of cultural totalisation is discussed

in its form as a technological totalisation of nature by Ihde in 'Technology and Human Self-Conception', the first chapter in the previously cited *Existential Technics*. See, particularly, pp. 19–23.

12 While the theorisation (and idealisation) of the 'cyborg' is apparent in recent SF, I would direct the reader's attention to the popularity of recent non-SF films that consciously project and display the human body as well-oiled machine, as construction: both *First Blood* (with Sylvester Stallone) and *Conan the Barbarian* (with Arnold Schwarzenegger) in 1982, *Staying Alive* (directed by Stallone and starring his prize 'pupil', John Travolta) in 1983, and *Rambo* (with Stallone even more mean and naked this time), *Perfect* (with Travolta and Jamie Lee Curtis), and *Pumping Iron II: The Women* in 1985. While androids and cyborgs have always been part of SF, we have not previously been so self-identified with them, so ready to incorporate them as ourselves, nor have films like *Blade Runner*, *Android* (both 1982) and *The Terminator* (1984) been so cinematically 'replicated' in non-SF cinema. For an excellent discussion of this changed cultural perception of the human body and its social implications, see Donna Haraway, 'A Manifesto for Cyborgs: Science, Technology and Socialist Feminism in the 1980s,' (1985): 65–107 [reprinted in this volume]. (Although Haraway is basically hopeful about this new theorisation of the body and the possibility for human description it opens up, such a theorisation may also be seen as a way for popular culture to respond to the feminist critique of voyeurism with a canny recuperation.)

13 Jameson, 'Postmodernism, or The Cultural Logic of Late Capitalism', p. 87. On this issue, see also Jean Baudrillard, *Simulations*, trans. Paul Foss, Paul Patton, and Philip Beichtman (New York: Semiotexte, 1983), and 'The Ecstasy of Communication', trans. John Johnston, in *The Anti-Aesthetic: Essays in Postmodern Culture*, ed. Hal Foster (Washington: Bay Press, 1983), pp. 126–34; and Guy Debord, *The Society of the Spectacle* (Detroit: Black and Red Press, 1983).

14 Walter Benjamin, 'The Work of Art in the Age of Mechanical Reproduction', in *Illuminations*, ed. Hannah Arendt, trans. Harry Zohn (New York: Harcourt Brace Jovanovich, 1968), pp. 219–26.

Who Programs You?
The Science Fiction of
the Spectacle
Scott Bukatman

We are living in the era of the blip, what Alvin Toffler has labelled *blip culture*.[1] Toffler has written of our bombardment by these 'short, modular blips of information',[2] but for others the blip is more pervasive and more crucial in its implications. Into the 1990s, the human subject has become a blip: ephemeral, electronically processed, unreal.[3] Numerous writers have noted this implosion, the passage of experiential reality into the grids, matrices and pulses of the electronic information age. Exploration outward has been superseded by the inward spiral of orbital circulation – in cybernetic terms, the feedback loop. The world has been reconstituted as a simulation within the mega-computer banks of the Information Society, and terminal identity exists as the mode of engagement with the imploded culture.

Jean Baudrillard writes of orbital circulation as the matrix of the implosive process,[4] which implies a constant *turning-in*, and Arthur Kroker adds the valuable metaphor of 'black hole', that massive gravitational anomaly which draws all into it, from which no information can reliably emerge. Below the event horizon lie only abstraction and hypothesis; direct experience is, by definition, impossible. Acknowledging the strength of McLuhan's axiom, 'the medium is the message' ('the key formula of the age of simulation'),[5] Baudrillard notes that it is not only this implosion of the message in the medium which is at stake, but also the concurrent 'implosion of the medium and the real in a sort of nebulous hyperreality…'.[6]

Television, still the axiomatic form of electronic simulation, due to its mass penetration and continually functioning national and global networks, is therefore not to be seen as presenting an image or mirror of reality (neutral or otherwise), but rather as a constituent portion of a new reality. Society, the arena of supposed 'real' existence, increasingly becomes 'the mirror of television'.[7] 'The result of this image bombardment', Toffler wrote in *Future Shock*, 'is the accelerated decay of old images, a faster intellectual through-put, and a new, profound sense of the impermanence of knowledge itself'.[8] In the science fiction horror film *Videodrome* (David Cronenberg, 1982), media prophet Brian O'Blivion informs us that 'Television is reality, and reality is less than television'. Soon, 'everyone will have special names … names designed to cause the cathode-ray tube to resonate'. A new subject is being constituted, one which begins its process of being through the act of viewership. 'The TV self is the electronic individual *par excellence* who gets everything there is to get from the simulacrum of the media', write Kroker and Cook.[9]

The technologies of the mass media have thus been crucial to the maintenance of instrumental reason as a form of rational (and hence natural, invisible and neutral) domination. 'Domination has its own aesthetics', wrote Marcuse, 'and democratic domination has its democratic aesthetics'.[10] The plurality of channel selections serves as a kind of guarantee of the freedom of the subject to choose, to position one's *self* within the culture, while the constant flow of images, sounds and narratives seemingly demonstrates a cultural abundance and promise. Yet the choice is illusory: to view is to surrender. Early on, Baudrillard wrote: 'It is useless to fantasise about state projection of police control through TV … TV, by virtue of its mere presence, is a social control in itself.'[11]

Guy Debord's 1967 manifesto, *Society of the Spectacle*, begins by acknowledging the passage into a new mode of phenomenological and commercial existence. 'In societies where modern conditions of production prevail, all of life presents itself as an immense accumulation of *spectacles*. Everything that was directly lived has moved away into a representation.'[12] The citizen/viewer, no longer engaged in the act of producing reality, exists now in a state of pervasive separation – cut off from the producers of the surrounding media culture by a unilateral communication and detached from the mass of fellow citizen/viewers as the new community of television families and workplaces arise invisibly to take their place.

The spectacle controls by atomising the population and reducing their capacity to function as an aggregate force, but also by displaying a surfeit of spectacular goods and lifestyles among which the viewer may electronically wander and experience a simulation of satisfaction. Within the conditions of late capitalism, 'the satisfaction of primary human needs is replaced by *an uninterrupted fabrication of pseudo-needs* which are reduced to the single pseudo-need of maintaining the reign of the autonomous economy' (thesis 51, my emphasis). 'The real consumer becomes a consumer of illusions' (thesis 47). Kroker and Cook describe the 1980s self as 'a blip with a lifestyle'.[13]

Science fiction (from the 1950s), like critical theory (from much earlier), has frequently portrayed the mass media as a pacifying force; an opiate. In Ray Bradbury's *Fahrenheit 451* (1953), for example, the wife of the book-burning fireman is addicted to both tranquillizers and television. This juncture of technology, control and addiction evokes the writings of William S. Burroughs, whose incantatory prose reveals a world – a galaxy – completely given over to the pervasiveness and vulnerability of addiction. Addiction is pervasive in that it transcends the use of narcotics: one can be addicted to money or to dope; there are orgasm addicts, control addicts and image addicts. Vulnerability exists because when the desperation of addiction is brought into being, the potential for manipulation escalates. 'The pusher always gets it all back. The addict needs more and more junk to maintain a human form ... buy off the Monkey. Junk is the mold of monopoly and possession.' Burroughs then analogises addiction and capitalist control: 'Junk is the ideal product ... the ultimate merchandise. No sales talk necessary. The client will crawl through a sewer and beg to buy ... the junk merchant does not sell his product to the consumer, he sells the consumer to his product.'[14]

The nexus commodity/addiction/control is replicated in Debord's post-Frankfurt School analysis. The spectacle is the ultimate commodity in that it makes all others possible: advertisements generate the conditions for consumption, and thus for production as well. The spectacle stimulates the desire to consume (the one permissible participation in the social process), a desire which is continually displaced onto the next product, and the next. It is infinitely self-generating. Ultimately, the spectacle takes on the totalising function of any addictive substance; it differs from dope only in that its addictive properties remain hidden within the rational economic structures of capitalist society. Contrast the metaphors of

Burroughs to these of Debord: 'The spectacle is the moment when the commodity has attained the *total occupation* of social life' (thesis 42). 'The spectacle is a permanent opium war which aims to make people identify goods with commodities and satisfaction with survival...' (thesis 44). '[T]he spectacle is the *main production* of present-day society' (thesis 15). 'The spectacle subjugates living men to the extent that the economy has totally subjugated them' (thesis 16).

The spectacle-addict recurs in science fiction, and the more sophisticated works begin with the premise of voluntarism. The addiction to the video-narcotic means that the control apparatus is already emplaced and invisibly operating to secure the false consciousness of cohesion, democratic order and freedom. Works such as *Fahrenheit 451* or Orwell's *1984* ignore the crucial postulate of Marcuse's democratic domination: an effective ideological state apparatus replaces the need for the overt exercise of power. As Burroughs observed, 'A *functioning* police state needs no police'.[15]

According to Marshall McLuhan, our (post)modern technological capabilities function as 'the extensions of man'.[16] 'During the mechanical ages we had extended our bodies in space', while today, 'we have extended our central nervous system in a global embrace, abolishing both time and space as far as our planet is concerned'.[17] The metaphor reassures by fostering an acceptance of media culture as a natural evolutionary state. To extend the nervous system outside the body further empowers the brain and further centralises the individual.

Other theorists are less sanguine. Debord clearly posits unilateral forms of communication as an intrusive force: 'Lived reality is materially invaded by the contemplation of the spectacle' (thesis 8). Technologies might hold the possibility of revolutionising society but, since 'freedom of the press is guaranteed only to those who own one',[18] the possibility also exists that it will serve to consolidate rather than disseminate power. Power is the operative lack in McLuhan's discourse, rendering his vision compelling but incomplete. Baudrillard's writings share McLuhan's fascination with technological change, but always accompanied by a massive awareness of power's reification. He differs from Debord in several ways which distance him from a traditional Marxist position.

First, technology replaces economics as the structuring force of the discourse on power. Second, there is Baudrillard's rejection of 'use-value' in favour of a position which guarantees no rigid site of meaning.[19] Finally, he argues that power has been subsumed by technological forces to such a degree that it is no longer the province of the state, much less the citizen.[20] In Baudrillard's imploded universe, human power has itself become a simulation.[21] Power now resides in a technology which holds humanity in its thrall. The media are invading; there will be no survivors.

This shift accounts for the changing style of Baudrillard's prose from a rationally argued Debordian resentment at the reifying deployment of spectacular power, to a hyper-technologised, jargon-ridden language which refuses the possibility of a critical position. Baudrillard's text aspires to the condition of science fiction, and ultimately becomes performative of the process he once merely described.

The usurpation of power by the new technologies of information control leads Baudrillard to reject the neural metaphors of McLuhan. In its place, another biological trope is employed. What exists now is 'a *viral*, endemic, chronic, alarming presence of the medium … dissolution of TV into life, the dissolution of life into TV'.[22] The media are no longer the extensions of man, man instead extends the media in becoming a 'terminal of multiple networks'.[23]

Burroughs has frequently deployed virus as a metaphor for all the infiltrating forces of control to which people are subject. *Junky*, *Naked Lunch* and *Cities of the Red Night* all incorporate viral figures, but it is in the Nova trilogy,[24] and especially in *Nova Express*, that the control virus appears as an image: a media-form controlled by invading alien forces. Biology and the media are linked through the node of the image. Images are tangible and material, neither ephemeral nor temporary. A death-dwarf is a literal image-addict ('images – millions of images – That's what I eat…' [*Nova Express* (*NE*), p. 68]).

As Burroughs demonstrates, science fiction becomes the discourse best equipped to contend with this new state of things. Samuel Delany and Teresa de Lauretis both argue that the genre is defined by rhetorical heightening and a continual linguistic play resistant to any totalisation of meaning.[25] Something further is added in what we may term the science fiction of the spectacle, a subgenre which includes works by Burroughs; J. G. Ballard; James Tiptree Jr (Alice Sheldon); Philip Dick; David Cronenberg; Norman Spinrad and others. Representation and textuality become the explicit subjects of the text; discourse will comprise the content as well as determine textual form. The inherent rhetoricity of the genre is extended as the text turns in upon its own production and status. The science fiction of the spectacle often demands the recognition of its own imbrication in the implosion of the real. These discursive strategies are dominant in contemporary critical writing as well: Baudrillard's essays, for example, bear rhetorical resemblances to the fictions of Dick and William Gibson, resemblances which are hardly coincidental.

Burroughs has generated his mythology for the space age around the nexus of junk, virus, addiction, control and surrender: 'Hell consists of falling into enemy hands, into the hands of the virus power, and heaven consists of freeing oneself from the power, of achieving inner freedom, freedom from conditioning.'[26] In the Nova trilogy, 'image is virus', and 'junk is concentrated image'. Baudrillard nearly quotes Burroughs when he writes about 'this viral contamination of things by images'.[27] The Nova Police reports: 'This virus released upon the world would infect the entire population and turn them into our replicas' (*NE*, p. 48).

The virus is a powerful metaphor for the power of the media, and Burroughs's hyperbolic Manicheism does not completely disguise the accuracy of his analysis. Whether the viral form is an actual living proto-cell or simply a carrier of genetic information, it clearly possesses an exponentially increasing power to take over and control its host organism. The injection of information leads to control, mutation, and passive replication: the host cell 'believes' that it is following its own biologically determined imperative; it mistakes the new genetic material for its own. The image/virus is posited as invasive and irresistible; a parasite with only self-replication as its function.

Compare this to Debord's economic analysis, where the pervasiveness of the spectacle serves the similar function of creating a deceptive cohesion for the purpose of infinite self-regeneration. The hegemony of the subject is illusory; indeed, imagistic; while control over these images is elusive; in fact impossible. The recurrent image of the virus (the virus of the image), biologises the rise of spectacle and the consequent waning of autonomous reason. The subject becomes a 'carrier' of spectacle, of image, of pseudo-reality. This is what Eric Mottram has called 'the virus transformation into undifferentiated man, the terminal image of man as patient-victim'.[28] Earth's fate is all too clear: 'The entire planet is being developed into *terminal identity* and complete surrender'. (*NE*, 19) Terminal identity: an unmistakably doubled articulation in which we find both the end of the subject and a new subjectivity constructed at the computer station or television screen. Again the human is configured as a 'terminal of multiple networks'.

McLuhan wrote that *Nova Express* takes place 'in a universe which seems to be someone else's insides',[29] recognising that Burroughs's work represents an inversion of his own. He further notes that: 'The human nervous system can be reprogrammed biologically as readily as any radio station can alter its fare.' In this statement, which anticipates *Videodrome*, there is an acknowledgement of political and social control which is rare in McLuhan, and which allows a perception of the unasked question which lurks behind a reading of his works: whose nervous system is this, anyway?

The similarities between Burroughs and filmmaker David Cronenberg are certainly extensive. The invasion and mutation of the body, the loss of control, and the transformation of the self into Other are as obsessively deployed in the works of the latter as in those of the former. Christopher Sharritt has written that the pervasive concern for both is 'the rise of the addictive personality cultivated by dominant culture and the changing structures of power ... [Neither] finds a solution in organised revolt since the new technological environment absorbs and dilutes ideological principles and abstract values'.[30] Similarly, Baudrillard has written that

All the movements which bet only on liberation, emancipation, the resurrection of the subject of history, of the group, of speech as a raising of consciousness ... do not see that they are acting in accordance with the system, whose imperative today is the overproduction and regeneration of meaning and speech.[31]

Language is, in multiple senses, the definition and controller of the self, the site of identity; and Baudrillard's pessimism and rhetorical surrender are commensurate with Burroughs's tactics. Like Baudrillard, Burroughs assimilates the linguistic excess of science fiction, but goes further than Baudrillard towards the demolition of communication. The appropriation of other authors and other texts wrecks the hegemony of both writer and novel, while the technique of the cut-up, in its explicit evocation of surgical procedure which links textual and corporeal bodies, obliterates the linear coherence which generally defines the identity of the text. Relations among signifiers are lost, each now exists in glittering isolation: the rational *telos* of the narrator is replaced by a rhetorical intensification which foregrounds and reveals the random bombardments of the spectacular society. Mutation becomes an act of sabotage, and the cut-up becomes a crucial *immunisation* against the invasive forces of the media-virus.

Cronenberg replaces this emphasis on the physicality of language with an attention to the image of the body. While he constructs an elaborate semiotics of the body in all his work, it is only in *Videodrome*, to date, that he fully addresses the construction of *the body of the text*: the cinematic signifier. In Cronenberg's films, the eruptive and incisive mutations which the body undergoes rival Burroughs's cut-ups for their violence, randomness and capacity to produce chaos. The penile organ emerging from Marilyn Chambers's armpit in *Rabid* (1976), the extruded 'children' of *The Brood* (1979) and the genetic cut-up represented by the human/fly melange in *The Fly* (1986) all enact the breakdown of human hegemony through the deployment of new technologies. Burroughs wrote: 'The realisation that something as familiar to you as the movement of your intestines the sound of your breathing the beating of your heart is also alien and hostile does make one feel a bit insecure at first.'[32]

These transformations cannot be completely subsumed within the mind/body dualism of Cartesianism, as one critic proposes to do.[33] Such a humanistic balance fails to account for the evident and pervasive antihumanism of Cronenberg's production, as demonstrated by the recurrent fears of human contact, sexuality or physicality in any form. David Cronenberg is the filmmaker of panic sex (Kroker's pungent phrase) with the body as the overdetermined site for the expression of profound social anxiety.[34] The subject of the Cronenberg film is hardly human action: it is instead, as Sharritt states, the structures of external power and control to which the individual (in body and soul) is subjected. The dissolution of identity into new forms is connected to the rise of new technologies, and this has become evident in three of his more recent films, *Scanners* (1980), *Videodrome* and *The Fly*, in which the apparent mind/body dichotomy is superseded by the trichotomy of mind/body/machine. Carrie Rickey is closer to the mark when she writes that Cronenberg is: 'a visionary architect of a chaotic biological tract where mind and body, ever fighting a Cartesian battle for integration, are so vulnerable as to be easily annexed by technology.'[35] The mind/body struggle is a blind for the larger Burroughsian issues of addiction, technological control and the malleability of reality and identity.

Videodrome presents a destabilised reality in which image, reality, hallucination and psychosis become indissolubly melded: the most estranging portrayal of image addiction and viral invasion since Burroughs. 'Videodrome', a TV programme, itself broadcasts brutal torture and sadism in a grotesque display which exerts a strong influence upon its viewers. Cable-station operator Max Wren desires 'Videodrome': as a businessman he needs it to rescue his foundering station; as an individual he finds himself drawn irresistibly to its horrors. Connected to Wren's quest for the source of 'Videodrome' is a profoundly ontological passage beyond spectacle to the ultimate dissolution of the boundaries which might serve to separate and guarantee definitions of 'spectacle', 'subject' and 'reality' itself.

At times *Videodrome* seems to be a film which hypostatises Baudrillard's own polemic. Here, with remarkable syntactic similarity, Baudrillard and a character from Cronenberg's film are both intent upon the usurpation of the real by its own representation; upon the imbrication of the real, the technologised and the simulated. The language is hyper-technologised but anti-rational; moebius-like in its evocation of a dissolute, spectacular reality:

Jean Baudrillard: 'We are here at the controls of a micro-satellite, in orbit, living no longer as an actor or dramaturge but as a terminal of

multiple networks. Television is still the most direct prefiguration of this. But today it is the very space of habitation that is conceived as both receiver and distributor, as the space of both reception and operations, the control screen and terminal which as such may be endowed with telematic power…'.[36]

Professor O'Blivion: 'The battle for the mind of North America will be fought in the video arena – the Videodrome. The television screen is the retina of the mind's eye. Therefore the television screen is part of the physical structure of the brain. Therefore whatever appears on the television screen emerges as raw experience for those who watch it. Therefore television is reality and reality is less than television.'

Both, in fact, seem to be following Debord's programme that 'When *analysing* the spectacle one speaks, to some extent, the language of the spectacular itself in the sense that one moves through the methodological terrain of the very society which expresses itself in spectacle' (thesis 11) – precisely why science fiction has obtained such a lately privileged position. Baudrillard embraces a high-tech, alienating and alienated science fictional rhetoric to explore the very paradigm of high-tech alienation, while Cronenberg's horror films about the failure of interpersonal communications are an integral part of an industry which privileges the spectacular over the intimate, and pseudo-satisfaction over genuine comprehension. Both construct discourses of anti-rationalism to expose and ridicule any process or history of enlightenment occurring through the exercise of a 'pure' reason.

Television pervades *Videodrome*. O'Blivion is the founder of the Cathode Ray Mission, a kind of TV soup kitchen for the city's derelicts: 'Watching TV will patch them back into the world's mixing board.' Television is often a medium of direct address. Wren is awakened by a videotaped message. O'Blivion refuses to appear on television 'except *on* television', his image appears on a monitor placed beside the programme's host (in a gesture reminiscent of Debord's own prerecorded lectures).[37] As Wren awaits his own talk show appearance, he chats with Nicki Brand, but an interposed monitor blocks our view. The image on the monitor is coextensive with its own background, however – Magritte-like – and consequently, the conversation is between a live Wren and a video Brand. Such examples offer a preliminary blurring of the distinction between real and televisual experiences.

This parody of McLuhan's global TV village serves as backdrop to the enigma of 'Videodrome', which is finally revealed to be a government project. The explanation for 'Videodrome', is at least as coherent as any from Burroughs: Spectacular Optical, a firm which specialises in defence contracts, has developed a signal which induces a tumour in the viewer. This tumour causes hallucinations which can be recorded, then revised, then fed back to the viewer: in effect, the individual is reprogrammed to serve the controller's ends. Burroughs offered a similar vision: 'you are a programmed tape recorder set to record and play back/who programs you/who decides what tapes play back in present time.'[38]

But as Barry Convex of Spectacular Optical asks Wren, 'Why would anyone watch a scum show like 'Videodrome'?' 'Business reasons', is Wren's fast response, but his interest transcends the commercial. Coincident with his exposure to the 'Videodrome' signal is his attraction to Nicki Brand, an outspoken, alluring personality for C-RAM radio.[39] Transgression thus enters Wren's life in at least three ways: socially, via his soft-porn, hard-violence cable TV station; sexually, through his forays into sadomasochism with Brand; and the political and sexual transgressions of 'Videodrome' itself. The three levels are linked in a spiralling escalation which culminates in Wren's own hallucinated appearance on 'Videodrome', whipping, first Brand, then her image on a television monitor. Brand is the guide who leads Wren on towards his final destiny; after her death, her image remains to spur him on. Her masochism might indicate a quest for sensation: this media figure admits that: 'We live in overstimulated times. We crave stimulation for its own sake.' Brand wants to 'audition' for 'Videodrome': 'I was made for that show', she brags, but it might be more accurate to say that she was made by that show. Wren is told that 'They used her image to seduce you'.

The 'Videodrome' programme is explicitly linked by both Wren and Convex to male sexual response (something 'tough' rather than 'soft') and penetration (something that will 'break through'). Wren takes on the 'tough' sadistic

role with Brand, and yet there is no doubt that it is she who controls the relationship, she who dominates.[40] Similarly, the power granted to the 'Videodrome' viewer to observe and relish its brutality masks the programme's actual function: to increase social control and establish a new means of dominance over the population. Wren is superficially the master of Brand and 'Videodrome', but ultimately master becomes slave. In a Baudrillardian revision of the Frankenstein myth, even Brian O'Blivion is condemned: the creator of 'Videodrome' is its first victim.

The Third World flavour of the *mise-en-scène* of the 'Videodrome' programme, found in its low-tech electrified clay walls and the neo-stormtrooper guise of the torturers, exists in distinct contrast to the 'Videodrome' technology, which is electronic and invisible, disseminated 'painlessly' through the mass media. 'In Central America', Wren tells Brand, 'making underground videos is a subversive act'. In North America too, it would seem, as the 'Videodrome' signal is subversive of experience, reality, and the very existence of the subject.

It is the voluntarism of the television experience which permits the incursion of controlling forces. A strictly political-economic reading of *Videodrome* would find little difficulty in situating the work within Debord's model, but *Videodrome* moves beyond the classically political through its relentless physicality. Following his exposure to the 'Videodrome' signal, Wren begins a series of hallucinations. Wren assaults Bridey, his assistant, and in a series of shot/reverse shot pairings, Bridey becomes Brand, then Bridey again. Disorien-ted, Max apologises for hitting her. Bridey answers, 'Max … you didn't hit me'. As O'Blivion tells him: 'Your reality is already half-video hallucination.'

A videotaped message from O'Blivion suddenly becomes more interactive. 'Max', he says, all trace of electronic filtering gone, 'I'm so happy you came to me'. O'Blivion explains the history of the 'Videodrome' phenomenon while being readied for execution: the executioner is Nicki Brand. 'I want *you*, Max', she breathes. 'Come to me. Come to Nicki.' Her lips fill the screen, and the set begins to pulsate, to breathe. Veins ripple the hardwood cabinet; a videogame joystick waggles obscenely. All boundaries are removed as the diegetic frame of the TV screen vanishes from view: the lips now fill the movie screen in a vast close-up. Wren approaches the set as the screen bulges outward to meet his touch, literalising the notion of the screen as breast. His face sinks in, his hands fondle the panels and knobs of the set as the lips continue their panting invitation.

Later, Wren's body literally opens up – his stomach develops a massive, vaginal slit – to accommodate a new videocassette 'programme'. Image addiction and image virus reduce the subject to the status of a videotape player/recorder; the human body mutates to become a part of the massive system of reproductive technology ('you are a programmed tape recorder'). The sexual implications of the imagery are thus significant and not at all gratuitous: video becomes visceral.[41]

Cronenberg moves the viewer in and out of Wren's hallucinations, creating a deep ambiguity regarding the status of the image. It is easy to accept his attack as real, although the transmigration of identities clearly marks Wren's demented subjectivity. Yet the attack was entirely hallucinated: the 'real' cinematic image is unreliable. In the extended hallucination of the eroticised, visceral television, the filmmaker gracefully dissolves the bonds which contain the spectacle. The TV screen is contained by its own frame, but Cronenberg's close-up permits the image to burst its boundaries and expand to the non-diegetic limits of the cinema screen. In a later hallucination, a video-Brand circles Wren with whip in hand, proferring it for him to wield. The image moves from video hallucination to cinematic reality within a single shot; the shift in visual register marks the spectacle's passage from visual phenomenon to new reality. Wren accepts the whip, but Brand is now no longer present in corporeal form; she only exists, shackled, on a TV screen. Wren attacks the bound(ed) image in another moment which recalls the visual punning of Margritte.

Cronenberg, then, does not reify the cinematic signifier as 'real', but continually mutates the real into the image, and the image into the hallucination. There is no difference in the cinematic techniques employed, no 'rational' textual system, which might distinguish reality from hallucination for the film viewer. Each moment is presented as 'real': that is, as corresponding to the conventions of realist film making. These unbounded hallucinations

jeopardise the very status of the image: we must believe everything or nothing. Through these textual mutations, these estrangements of cinematic language, the science fiction of the spectacle destabilises the field of representation by constructing a set of indefinite semantic constructs.[42]

Wren hallucinates his appearance on 'Videodrome', but is 'Videodrome' a programme composed entirely of recorded hallucinations? If so, then there is a progression from hallucination, through image, to reality: the scene is real because it is televised, it is televised because it is recorded, it is recorded because it is hallucinated. In its themes and structure, the film serves as a graphic example of Baudrillard's viral immixture of TV and life (which echoes Burroughs's injunction that 'image is virus'). Baudrillard adds that the media is a virus which 'controls the mutation of the real into the hyperreal'. The viral metaphor is strikingly apt when applied to Videodrome – the literalised invasion of the body by the image, and the production of tumours which produce images. Image is virus; virus virulently replicates itself; the subject is finished. We remain trapped within a universe which seems to be someone else's insides.

Body and image become one: a dissolution of real and representation, certainly, but also of the boundaries between internal and external, as the interiorised hallucination becomes the public spectacle of the 'Videodrome' programme. In the post-spectacle society all such boundaries dissolve: 'We will have to suffer this new state of things, this forced extroversion of all interiority, this forced injection of all exteriority … we are now in a new form of schizophrenia.' Our response changes: 'No more hysteria, no more projective paranoia, properly speaking, but this state of terror proper to the schizophrenic: too great a proximity of everything, the unclean promiscuity of everything which touches, invests and penetrates without resistance.'[43] The subject has 'no halo of private protection, *not even his own body,* to protect him anymore.'[44]

The slippage of reality which marks the textual operations of Videodrome can certainly be associated with the commensurate process in the writings of the saboteur Burroughs, who repeatedly declared that we must 'Storm the Reality Studio and retake the universe'.[45] Burroughs's cinematic metaphor reaches a kind of apotheosis in Videodrome, as the images flicker and fall, their authority ultimately denied, but there is no glimpse of a Reality Studio behind the levels of reality-production.

Reality-slippage, with its echoes from Plato's cave, is also the province of science fiction author Philip K. Dick, another obvious influence on Cronenberg. Dick's paranoid sensibility explores the alienation which results from seeing *through* the spectacle. The central characteristic of his protagonists involves their crises of subjectivity which begin when the real violently dissolves around them. Such a metaphysical dilemma does not represent a failure to map oneself onto the world, but is interwoven with ontological change and primarily with the rise of spectacle and the expansion of the technologies of reproduction.

Dick challenges the instrumental rationalism of spectacular society through estranging rhetorical structures which construct a maze of decentred ambivalence in which multiple characters interact in a futile quest to fix reality, and therefore themselves, in place. The reader is plunged into the neologistic excess which characterises the science fiction text. These terms cannot be read through, for the unfamiliarity they engender is precisely their purpose. The discursive ambiguities of *Videodrome* surely derive from Dick's, and Burroughs's, spectacular/structural deformations.

Dick's novel *UBIK* (1969) is dominated by telepaths and half-lifers, dead people who retain some residual brain function and exist in a cryogenic partial existence. Joe Chip (a blip culture name if ever there was one) is subjected to reality erosion, as temporality itself seems to reverse its valence. Only UBIK, a product packaged in historically appropriate forms (aerosol, ointment, elixir), can briefly restore the familiarity of the present day, and so the narrative propels its characters on a quest for answers and for UBIK. *UBIK* first seems to stand as a Platonic meditation on the rift between appearance and reality. Objects are shadows of an ideal form. Chip's refrigerator devolves from computerised servant to freon-based cooling system to icebox: a reversed succession of manifestations of the Idea of a Refrigerator. Appearance, image and spectacle are homologous terms when placed in dichotomous opposition to 'the real'. If *UBIK*

simply remained with this Platonic analysis, it would only be notable for its ultimate reification of a reality which underlies shifting levels of appearance. But *UBIK* undermines such idealism. A character's ability to alter the past implies the existence of myriad presents, none more real, finally, than any other.

The depressing truth is that Chip is trapped in half-life, his 'reality' subject to the whims of a deranged, but stronger, psyche. He might be privileged to look upon the final level, the Reality Studio where reality is staged: but reality is nothing more than the fantasies of a madman. A final shift moves the reader out from Chip's half-life experience to his employer's position in the 'real world'. The living human finds currency adorned with the image of Joe Chip, just as Chip had earlier found money bearing his employer's image. 'This was just the beginning.' Final reality is itself only a shadow; the reification of the real is replaced by a recursive structure of infinite regression. *UBIK* presents, not a dichotomy of appearance and reality, but an unresolved dialectic.

Further, *UBIK* gains its force and originality by examining the central importance of the idea of reality, while resisting its existence. UBIK is in demand because it fixes reality (in both senses of the word: it repairs the real and locks it in place). Appearance is not simply negated as a deception, but is posited as a necessary condition of existence.

Five years after *UBIK*'s publication, Dick reworked it as a screenplay for Jean-Pierre Gorin. In a manoeuvre recalling the cinematic mutations of Burroughs's screenplay-novel, *The Last Words of Dutch Schultz* (1975),[46] Dick wanted his work to end by regressing to black-and-white stock, silent footage, flickering effects, and by finally bubbling and burning to a halt. The screenplay retains some of this: a drive through a simulated landscape features the repeating backgrounds of inexpensive television cartoons; a character speaks with defective sound synchronisation; another scene is 'very dim, as if 'bulb' is weak in 'projector''.[47] Film becomes a physical substance which bears traces of reality, but which remains pure appearance. Dick's manipulations, like Cronenberg's, deny cinema's status as transparent conduit of truth.

UBIK performs an effective deconstruction through its very structures, but it is in that commodity of commodities, UBIK, that the work rejoins the analysis of the spectacle performed by Debord, Baudrillard, Burroughs and Cronenberg. UBIK is the product which permits the maintenance of appearance and, in the novel, each chapter begins with an advertisement for this mysterious and ubiquitous balm. In becoming a consumer, the subject overcomes perceived lack, fixes appearance, becomes an image. The commodity defined reification for Marx; labour's abstraction is contained in its inertia.[48] Commodities and spectacles reassure and threaten by confirming a relation to the world through a temporary pseudo-satisfaction lasting only until the can is empty or a new commercial is on. UBIK stands as the ultimate example: the ur-commodity. *UBIK* becomes the work of commodity fetishism, featuring a product whose function is only to sustain the illusion of coherence. 'I came to UBIK after trying weak, out-of-date reality supports', beams a happy and secure(d) housewife.

In the screenplay these commercials interrupt the action, but also serve as a super-imposition, a layering of images which blocks appearance. 'We understand that despite [the image's] fidelity to graphic representationalism, it is incomplete' (p. 31). The spectacle is displayed in spectacular fashion, faithful to reality but, through its apparent incompletion, not interchangeable with it. 'Something has come between us and what we have been watching, something in a sense more real or anyhow real in a visibly different sense.' Diegetic reality shatters in a gesture which reflects on the experience of the real through the experience of the cinematic, as in *Videodrome*.

Reprogrammed by Bianca O'Blivion in *Videodrome*, Max Wren prepares to take the next step. 'You've become the video word made flesh', she tells him. 'Death to 'Videodrome' – long live the new flesh.' The terror must be overcome, the attachment to the body surrendered. Wren makes his way to a rusted hulk – a 'condemned vessel' – in the harbour. The decaying walls match the colour of his jacket. Wren is another 'condemned vessel', trapped within the confines of the old flesh, an outmoded conception of the body and the self. Aboard the vessel, Max fires at his own temple and there the film concludes; ambiguously, unsatisfyingly. What is the new flesh?

One postulation might hold that Max has attained the paradoxical status of pure image – an image which no longer retains any connection with the 'real'. *Videodrome* comes strikingly close to moving through the four successive phases of the image characteristic of the era of simulation as described by Baudrillard.[49] First, the image functions as 'the reflection as a basic reality'. Clearly, until the hallucinations begin, the viewer trusts the cinematic image as the sign of truth. Doubts may be raised concerning the enigmatic image of the 'Videodrome' programme, its ostensible Third World aesthetic belied by its Pittsburgh transmission point. Here the image 'masks and perverts a basic reality'. In the third phase, the image 'masks the *absence* of a basic reality', which has, in fact, been the argument behind the works explored here. The film propels its audience along this trajectory, possibly achieving the status of Baudrillard's fourth phase, in which image 'bears no relation to any reality whatever: it is its own pure simulacrum'. Beyond representation itself, such an image could not be represented, and thus the film ends. *Videodrome*, then, enacts the death of the subject and the death of representation simultaneously, each the consequence of the other.

Videodrome presents a destabilised reality in which image, reality, hallucination and psychosis become indissolubly melded, and it is on this level that the film becomes a work *of* postmodernism, rather than simply a work *about* it. The subversion of conventional structures of filmic discourse here corresponds to the 'progressive' use of language in science fiction where a neologistic excess and literalisation of language foreground the reading process in a discursive play which resists the totalisation of meaning. The viewer of the film is analogous to the viewer of the TV show: trapped in a web of representations which infect and transform reality. Cronenberg evidences an extensive concern with this dissolution of boundaries in all of his films. Plague viruses and parasites demonstrate the vulnerability of the body to invasion from without; telepathy and physical projection break down the dichotomy between public and private; subjectivity and temporality collapse; man merges with machine; a teleporter is proclaimed to end all concepts of borders. A particular yearning cuts across Cronenberg's body of work (work of the body); a desire for dissolution which is always accompanied by a fear of the void.

The final stage of Baudrillard's four phases of the image, wherein the image no longer bears a relation to an unmediated reality, is the hallmark of the age of postmodernism. The potential trauma which might be expected to accompany this realisation is frequently elided by a regression to simple nostalgia, as both Jean Baudrillard and Fredric Jameson have noted.[50] Arthur Kroker has further written that 'The postmodern scene is a panic site, just for the fun of it'; an era of crises for their own sake, where the injunction of crisis now ironically serves to cover over the abyss of non-meaning.[51] Conversely, the insistent figurations of Baudrillard, Burroughs, Cronenberg and Dick represent a stunning hypostatisation of the concerns of postmodern culture, and constitute a discursive field which retains the power to unsettle, disorient and initiate the crucial action of questioning the status of the sign in sign culture: a spectacular immunisation against the invasive powers of the image virus.

Notes

1 Alvin Toffler, *The Third Wave* (New York: Bantam Books 1981), p. 165.

2 Ibid., p. 166.

3 Arthur Kroker and David Cook, *The Postmodern Scene: Excremental Culture and Hyper-Aesthetics* (New York: St Martin's Press, 1986), p. 279.

4 Jean Baudrillard, *In the Shadow of the Silent Majorities*, trans. Paul Foss (New York: Semiotext(e), 1983), p. 21.

5 Ibid., p. 101.

6 Ibid.

7 This variation on Oscar Wilde is to be found in Kroker and Cook, p. 268.

8 Alvin Toffler, *Future Shock*, New York: Bantam Books, 1971, p. 161.

9 Kroker and Cook, p. 274.

10 Herbert Marcuse, *One-Dimensional Man* (Boston: Beacon Press, 1964), p. 65.

11 Jean Baudrillard, 'Requiem for the Media', in *For a Critique of the Political Economy of the Sign*, trans. Charles Levin (St Louis: Telos Press, 1981), p. 172.

12 Guy Debord, *Society of the Spectacle* (Detroit: Black & Red, 1983), thesis 1. Henceforth, thesis numbers follow quotations in the body of the text.

13 Kroker and Cook, p. 279.

14 William S. Burroughs, *Naked Lunch* (New York: Grove Press, 1959), pp. xxxviii and xxxix.

15 Ibid., p. 36.

16 Marshall McLuhan, *Understanding Media* (New York: New American Library, 1964).

17 Ibid., p. 19.

18 A. J. Liebling, *The Press*, second revised edn. (New York: Ballantine Books, 1975), p. 32.

19 Jean Baudrillard, *The Mirror of Production*, trans. Mark Poster (St Louis: Telos Press, 1975).

20 Jean Baudrillard, *Forget Foucault*, trans. Nicole Dufresne (New York: Semiotext(e), 1987), p. 11.

21 Ibid.

22 Jean Baudrillard, 'The Precession of Simulacra', in *Simulations*, trans. Paul Foss, Paul Patton and Philip Beitchman (New York: Semiotext(e), 1983), pp. 54–5.

23 Jean Baudrillard, 'The Ecstasy of Communication', in Hal Foster, ed., *The Anti-Aesthetic: Essays in Postmodern Culture* (Port Townsend, WA: Bay Press, 1983), p. 128.

24 The trilogy includes *The Soft Machine*, revised edn (1966), *The Ticket that Exploded*, revised edn (1967) and *Nova Express* (1964). All titles published by Grove Press, New York.

25 See Samuel R. Delany, 'About 5,750 Words', in *The Jewel-Hinged Jaw: Notes on the Language of Science Fiction* (Elizabethtown, NY: Dragon Press, 1977) or Teresa de Lauretis, 'Signs of W[a/o]nder', in Teresa de Lauretis, Andreas Huyssen and Kathleen Woodward, eds, *The Technological Imagination: Theories and Fictions* (Madison, WI: Coda Press, 1980).

26 Cited in Eric Mottram, *William Burroughs: The Algebra of Need*, London: Marion Boyars, 1977, p. 40.

27 Jean Baudrillard, 'Rituals of Transparency', in Sylvere Lotringer, ed., *The Ecstasy of Communication*, trans. Bernard and Caroline Schutze, New York: Semiotext(e), 1988, p. 36.

28 Mottram, p. 56.

29 Marshall McLuhan, 'Notes on Burroughs', *The Nation*, 28 December 1964, pp. 517–19.

30 Christopher Sharritt, 'Myth and Ritual in the Post-Industrial Landscape: The Horror Films of David Cronenberg', *Persistence of Vision* nos. 3/4, 1986, p. 113.

31 Jean Baudrillard, 'The Implosion of Meaning in the Media', in *In the Shadow of the Silent Majorities*, p. 109.

32 *The Ticket that Exploded*, p. 50.

33 William Beard, 'The Visceral Mind: The Films of David Cronenberg', in Piers Handling, ed., *The Shape of Rage: The Films of David Cronenberg* (New York: New York Zoetrope, 1983).

34 See the articles in the disturbing and entertaining Arthur and Marilouise Kroker, eds, *Body Invaders: Panic Sex in America* (New York: St Martin's Press, 1988).

35 Carrie Rickey, 'Make Mine Cronenberg', *The Village Voice*, 1 February 1983, p. 64.

36 'The Ecstasy of Communication', p. 128.

37 One of these 'Perspectives for Conscious Alterations in Everyday Life' is reprinted in *Situationist International Anthology*, ed. and trans. Ken Knabb (Berkeley: Bureau of Public Secrets 1981), pp. 68–75.

38 Burroughs, 'The Invisible Generation', in *The Ticket that Exploded*, p. 213.

39 Perhaps it should be noted that the RAM acronym is one familiar to computer users, and stands for Random Access Memory.

40 This exploration of sexuality is granted considerably more weight in Cronenberg's recent *Dead Ringers* (1988).

41 For an important feminist analysis of the figuration of the body, see Tania Modleski, 'The Terror of Pleasure: The Contemporary Horror Film and Postmodern Theory', in Tania Modleski, ed., *Studies in Entertainment: Critical Approaches to Mass Culture*, Bloomington: Indiana University Press 1986.

42 The phrase is borrowed from de Lauretis, p. 160.

43 'The Ecstasy of Communication', p. 132.

44 Ibid. Emphasis mine.

45 *The Soft Machine*, p. 155.

46 William Burroughs, *The Last Words of Dutch Schultz* (New York: Seaver Books, 1975).

47 Philip K. Dick, *Ubik: The Screenplay*, Minneapolis: Corroboree Press, 1985, p. 120.

48 Karl Marx, *Capital* Volume 1, trans. Ben Fowkes, New York: Vintage Books, 1977, pp. 163–77.

49 Ibid., pp. 11–12.

50 See Baudrillard, 'The Precession of Simulacra', p. 12; and Jameson, 'Postmodernism, or the Cultural Logic of Late Capitalism', *New Left Review*, no. 146, 1984, pp. 66–8.

51 *The Postmodern Scene*, p. 27.

Prosthetic Memory:
Total Recall and *Blade Runner*
Alison Landsberg

In the 1908 Edison film *The Thieving Hand*, a wealthy passer-by takes pity on an armless beggar and buys him a prosthetic arm. As the beggar soon discovers, however, the arm has memories of its own. Because the arm remembers its own thieving, it snatches people's possessions as they walk by. Dismayed, the beggar sells his arm at a pawnshop. But the arm sidles out of the shop, finds the beggar out on the street, and reattaches itself to him. The beggar's victims, meanwhile, have contacted a police officer who finds the beggar and carts him off to jail. In the jail cell, the arm finds its rightful owner – the 'proper' thieving body – a one-armed criminal, and attaches itself to him.

This moment in early cinema anticipates dramatically a preoccupation in more contemporary science fiction with what I would like to call 'prosthetic memories'. By prosthetic memories I mean memories which do not come from a person's lived experience in any strict sense. These are implanted memories, and the unsettled boundaries between real and simulated ones are frequently accompanied by another disruption: of the human body, its flesh, its subjective autonomy, its difference from both the animal and the technological.

Furthermore, through the prosthetic arm the beggar's body manifests memories of actions that it, or he, never actually committed. In fact, his memories are radically divorced from lived experience and yet they motivate his actions. Because the hand's memories – which the beggar himself wears – prescribe actions in the present, they make a beggar into a thief. In other words, it is precisely the memories of thieving which construct an identity for him. We might say then that the film underscores the way in which memory is constitutive of identity. This in itself is not surprising. What is surprising is the position the film takes on the relationship between memory, experience and identity. What might the 'otherness' of prosthetic memory that *The Thieving Hand* displays tell us about how persons come ordinarily to feel that they possess, rather than are possessed by, their memories? We rely on our memories to validate our experiences. The experience of memory actually becomes the index of experience: if we have the memory, we must have had the experience it represents. But what about the armless beggar? He has the memory without having lived the experience. If memory is the precondition for identity or individuality – if what we claim as our memories defines who we are – then the idea of a prosthetic memory problematises any concept of memory that posits it as essential, stable or organically grounded. In addition, it makes impossible the wish that a person owns her/his memories as inalienable property.

As it happens, we don't know anything about the beggar's real past. Memories, it seems, are the domain of the present. The beggar's prosthetic memories offer him a course of action to live by. Surprisingly enough, memories are less about validating or authenticating the past than they are about organising the present and constructing strategies with which one might imagine a livable future. Memory, this essay will argue, is not a means for closure – is not a strategy for closing or finishing the past – but on the contrary, memory emerges as a generative force, a force which propels us not backward but forwards.

But in the case of *The Thieving Hand*, the slippage the film opens up with the prosthetic hand – the rupture between experience, memory and identity – gets sealed up at the end of the film, in jail, when the thieving hand reattaches itself to what we are meant to recognise as the real or authentic thieving body, the one-armed criminal. In other words, despite the film's flirtation with the idea that memories might be permanently transportable, *The Thieving Hand* ends by rejecting that possibility, in that the hand itself chooses to be with its proper owner.

I have begun with *The Thieving Hand* to demonstrate that, as with all mediated forms of knowledge, prosthetic memory has a history. Although memory might always have been prosthetic, the mass media – technologies which structure and circumscribe experience – bring the texture and contours of prosthetic memory into dramatic relief. Because the mass media fundamentally alter our notion of what counts as experience, they might be a privileged arena for the production and circulation of prosthetic memories. The cinema, in particular, as an institution which makes available images for mass consumption, has long been aware of its ability to generate experiences and to install memories of them – memories which become experiences that film consumers both possess and feel possessed by. We might then read these films which thematise prosthetic memories as an allegory for the power of the mass media to create experiences and to implant memories, the experience of which we have never lived. Because the mass media are a privileged site for the production of such memories, they might be an undertheorised force in the production of identities. If a film like *The Thieving Hand* eventually insists that bodily memories have rightful owners, more recent science fiction texts like *Blade Runner* and *Total Recall* have begun to imagine otherwise.

In Paul Verhoeven's film *Total Recall* (1990), Douglas Quade (Arnold Schwarzenegger) purchases a set of implanted memories of a trip to Mars. Not only might he buy the memories for a trip he has never taken, but he might elect to go on the trip as someone other than himself. Quade has an urge to go to Mars as a secret agent – or rather, to remember having gone as a secret agent. But the implant procedure does not go smoothly. While strapped in his seat memories begin to break through – memories, we learn, that have been layered over by 'the Agency'. As it turns out, Quade is not an 'authentic identity', but one based on memories implanted by the intelligence agency on Mars.

In Ridley Scott's *Blade Runner* (director's cut, 1993), Deckard (Harrison Ford) is a member of a special police squad – a blade runner unit – and has been called in to try to capture and 'retire' a group of replicants recently landed on earth. Replicants, advanced robots created by the Tyrell Corporation as slave labour for the off-world colonies, are 'being[s] virtually identical to human[s]'. The most advanced replicants, like Rachael (Sean Young), an employee at the Tyrell Corporation who eventually falls for Deckard, are designed so that they don't know they are replicants. As Mr Tyrell explains to Deckard, 'If we give them a past we create a cushion for their emotions and consequently we can control them better.' 'Memories', Deckard responds incredulously, 'you're talking about memories.' Both of these films, as we shall see, offer provocative examples of individuals who identify with memories which are not their own.

If the idea of prosthetic memory complicates the relationship between memory and experience, then we might use films that literalise prosthetic memory to disrupt some postmodernist assumptions about experience. With postmodernity, Fredric Jameson asserts, we see 'the waning of our historicity, of our lived possibility of experiencing history in some active way' (1991: 21). He claims that in post-modernity, experience is dead. 'Nostalgia films', he suggests, invoke a sense of 'pastness' instead of engaging with 'real history'. He therefore finds a fundamental 'incompatibility of a postmodernist nostalgia and language with genuine historicity' (1991: 19). Not only does his account participate in a nostalgia of its own – nostalgia for that prelapsarian moment when we all actually experienced history in some real way – but, as I will argue, it offers a rather narrow version of experience. The flipside of Jameson's point is Jean Baudrillard's (1983) claim that the proliferation of different media and mediations – simulations – which have permeated many aspects of contemporary society, have dissolved the dichotomy between the real and the simulacrum, between the authentic and the inauthentic. He argues that with the proliferation of different forms of media in the twentieth century, people's actual relationship to events – what we are to understand as authentic experience – has become so mediated, that we can no longer distinguish between the real – something mappable – and what he calls the hyperreal – 'the generation by models of a real without origin' (Baudrillard 1983: 2). For Baudrillard, we live in a world of simulation, a world hopelessly detached from the 'real'. Or, to put it another way, postmodern society is characterised by an absence of 'real' experience. But Baudrillard's argument clings tenaciously to a real; he desperately needs a real to recognise that we are in a land of simulation. Both assumptions unwittingly betray a nostalgia for a prelapsarian moment when there was a real. But the real has always been mediated through information cultures and through narrative. What does it mean for memories to be 'real'? Were they ever 'real'? This essay refuses such a categorisation, but also shows the costs of such a refusal.

I would like to set this notion of the death of the real – particularly the death of real experience – against what I perceive as a veritable explosion of, or popular obsession with, experience of the real. From the hugely attended D-Day reenactments of 1994 to what I would like to call 'experiential museums', like the United States Holocaust Memorial Museum, it seems to me that the experiential real is anything but dead. In fact, the popularity of these experiential events bespeaks a popular longing to experience history in a personal and even bodily way. They offer strategies for making history into personal memories. They provide individuals with the collective opportunity of having an experiential relationship to a collective or cultural past they either did or did not experience. I would like to suggest that what we have embarked upon in the postmodern is a new relationship to experience which relies less on categories like the authentic and sympathy than on categories like responsibility and empathy.

This postmodern relationship to experience has significant political ramifications. If this fascination with the experiential might be imagined as an act of prosthesis – of prosthetically appropriating memories of a cultural or collective past – then these particular histories or pasts might be available for consumption across existing stratifications of race, class and gender. These prosthetic memories, then, might become the grounds for political alliances. As Donna Haraway (1991) has powerfully argued with her articulation of cyborg identity, we need to construct political alliances that are not based on natural or essential affinities.[1] Cyborg identity recognises the complicated process of identity formation, that we are multiply hailed subjects, and thus embraces the idea of 'partial identities'. The pasts that we claim and 'use' are part of this process.

If the real has always been mediated through collectivised forms of identity, why then, does the sensual in the cinema – the experiential nature of the spectator's engagement with the image – differ from other aesthetic experiences which might also be the scene of the production of sensual memory, like reading (see Miller, 1988)? Concern about the power of the visual sensorium – specifically, an awareness of the cinema's ability to produce memories in its spectators – has a lengthy history of its own. In 1928, William H. Short, the Executive Director of the Motion Picture Research Council, asked a group of researchers – mostly university psychologists

and sociologists – to discuss the possibility of assessing the effects of motion pictures on children. These investigations he initiated – the Payne Studies – are significant not so much in their immediate findings, but rather in what they imply about the popular anxiety about the ways in which motion pictures actually affect – in an experiential way – individual bodies. In a set of studies conducted by Herbert Blumer, college-aged individuals were asked 'to relate or write as carefully as possible their experiences with motion pictures' (1933: xi). What Blumer finds is that 'imaginative identification' is quite common, and that 'while witnessing a picture one not infrequently projects oneself into the role of hero or heroine' (1933: 67). Superficially, this account sounds much like arguments made in contemporary film theory about spectatorship and about the power of the filmic apparatus and narrative to position the subject (see, for example, Baudry, 1974–5; Comolli, 1986). However, Blumer's claims – and their ramifications – are somewhat different. Blumer refers to identification as 'emotional possession' positing that 'the individual identifies himself so thoroughly with the plot or loses himself so much in the picture that he is carried away from the usual trend of conduct' (1933: 74). There is, in fact, no telling just how long this possession will last, for 'in certain individuals it may become fixed and last for a long time' (1933: 84). In fact,

> In a state of emotional possession impulses, motives and thoughts are likely to lose their fixed form and become malleable instead. There may emerge from this 'molten state' a new stable organisation directed towards a different line of conduct. The individual, as a result of witnessing a particularly emotional picture, may come to a decision to have certain kinds of experience and to live a kind of life different from his prior career (Blumer 1933: 116).

A woman explains that when she saw *The Sheik* for the first time she recalls 'coming home that night and dreaming the entire picture over again; myself as the heroine, being carried over the burning sands by an equally burning lover. I could feel myself being kissed in the way the Sheik had kissed the girl' (Blumer 1933: 70). What individuals see might affect them so significantly that the images actually become part of their own personal archive of experience.

Because the movie experience decentres lived experience, it, too, might alter or construct identity. Emotional possession has implications for both the future and the past of the individual under its sway. It has the potential to alter one's actions in the future in that under its hold an individual 'is transported out of his normal conduct and is completely subjugated by his impulses' (Blumer 1933: 94). A nineteen-year-old woman writes,

> After having seen a movie of pioneer days I am very unreconciled to the fact that I live today instead of the romantic days of fifty years ago. But to offset this poignant and useless longing I have dreamed of going to war. I stated previously that through the movies I have become aware of the awfulness, the futility of it, etc. But as this side has been impressed upon me, there has been awakened in me at the same time the desire to go to the 'front' during the next war. The excitement – shall I say glamour? – of the war has always appealed to me from the screen. Often I have pictured myself as a truck driver, nurse, HEROINE (Blumer, 1933: 63).

What this suggests is that the experience within the movie theatre and the memories that the cinema affords – despite the fact that the spectator did not live through them – might be as significant in constructing, or deconstructing, the spectator's identity as any experience that s/he actually lived through.

Many of the Payne Studies tests were designed to measure quantitatively the extent to which film affects the physical bodies of its spectators. The investigators used a galvanometer which, like a lie detector, 'measure galvanic responses', electrical impulses, in skin, and a pneumo-cardiograph 'to measure changes in the circulatory system' (Charters 1933: 25), like respiratory pulse and blood pressure. This sensitive technology might pick up physiological disturbances and changes that would go unseen by the naked eye. These studies thus presumed that the body might give evidence of physiological symptoms caused by a kind of technological intervention into subjectivity – an intervention which is part and parcel of the cinematic experience. The call for a technology of detection registers a fear that we might

no longer be able to distinguish prosthetic or 'unnatural' memories from 'real' ones.

At the same historical moment, European cultural critics of the 1920s – specifically Walter Benjamin and Siegfried Kracauer – began to theorise the experiential nature of the cinema. They attempted to theorise the way in which movies might actually extend the sensual memory of the human body. By 1940 Kracauer believed that film actually addresses its viewer as a "corporeal-material being'; it seizes the 'human being with skin and hair': 'The material elements that present themselves in film directly stimulate the material layers of the human being: his nerves, his senses, his entire physiological substance" (1993: 458). The cinematic experience has an individual, bodily component at the same time that it is circumscribed by its collectivity; the domain of the cinema is public and collective. Benjamin's notion of 'innervation' is an attempt to imagine an engaged experiential relationship with technology and the cinema.[2] It is precisely the interplay of individual bodily experience with the publicity of the cinema which might make possible new forms of collectivity – political and otherwise.

More recently, Steven Shaviro (1993) has emphasised the visceral, bodily component of film spectatorship. He argues that psychoanalytic film theory studiously ignores the experiential component of spectatorship. In his account, psychoanalytic film theory has attempted 'to destroy the power of images' (1993: 16),[3] and that what those theorists fear is not the lack, 'not the emptiness of the image, but its weird fullness; not its impotence so much as its power' (1993: 17). We might say that the portability of cinematic images – the way we are invited to wear them prosthetically, the way we might experience them in a bodily fashion – is both the crisis and the allure. As if to emphasise this experiential, bodily aspect of spectatorship, Shaviro sets forth as his guiding principle that 'cinematic images are not representations, but events' (1993: 24).

I would like to turn to a scene in *Total Recall* which dramatically illustrates the way in which mass mediated images intervene in the production of subjectivity. The notion of authenticity – and our desire to privilege it – is constantly undermined by *Total Recall*'s obsessive rendering of mediated images. In many instances we see, simultaneously, a person and their mediated representation on a video screen. When Quade first goes to Rekal to meet with Mr McClane, the sales representative, we see McClane simultaneously through a window over his secretary's shoulder, and as an image on her video phone as she calls him to let him know that Quade has arrived. In *Total Recall* the proliferation of mediated images – and of video screens – forces us to question the very notion of an authentic or an originary presence. Video monitors appear on subway cars with advertisements (like the one for Rekal), and all telephones are video phones; even the walls of Quade's house are enormous television screens. Quade's identity, too, as we will see, is mediated by video images. When he learns from his wife that she's not his wife, that she 'never saw him before six weeks ago', that their 'marriage is just a memory implant', that the Agency 'erased his identity and implanted a new one' – basically that 'his whole life is just a dream' – any sense he has of a unified self, of a stable subjectivity, is shattered. When memories might be separable from lived experience, issues of identity – and upon what identity is constructed – take on radical importance.

The question of his identity – and how his identity is predicated upon a particular set of memories which may or may not be properly his own – surfaces most dramatically when he confronts his own face in a video monitor. That he sees his face on a portable video screen – one that he has been carrying around in a suitcase which was handed to him by a 'buddy from the Agency' – literalises the film's account of the portability of memory and identity. Quade confronts his own face in a video screen, but finds there a different person. The face on the screen says, 'Howdy stranger, this is Hauser ... Get ready for the big surprise. ... You are not you. You are me.' We might be tempted to read this scene as an instance of Freud's (1959) notion of the 'uncanny'. The sensation of the 'uncanny', as Freud articulates it, is produced by an encounter with something which is simultaneously familiar and unfamiliar; the sensation of the uncanny comes from the 'return of the repressed'. The experience of seeing one's double is therefore the height of uncanny.[4] But Quade's experience is not that way at all. The face he confronts is explicitly not his face; it does not correspond to his identity.

Since the film rejects the idea that there is an authentic, or more authentic, self underneath the layers of identity, there is no place for the uncanny. For Quade, the memories of Hauser seem never to have existed. In fact, he encounters Hauser with a kind of disinterest, not as someone he once knew or was, but rather as a total stranger.

In this way, the encounter seems to disrupt the Lacanian notion of the 'mirror stage'. According to Jacques Lacan, the mirror stage is initiated when a child first sees himself reflected as an autonomous individual, as a unified and bounded subject. As Lacan describes, the 'jubilant assumption of his specular image' (1977: 2) gives the child an illusion of wholeness, which is vastly different from the child's own sense of himself as a fragmentary bundle of undifferentiated drives. For Quade, the experience is exactly the opposite. In fact, we might say that the encounter with the face in the monitor, which looks like his face but is not the one he owns, disrupts any sense of a unified, stable and bounded subjectivity. Instead of consolidating his identity, the video screen further fragments it. This encounter undermines as well the assumption that a particular memory has a rightful owner, a proper body to adhere to.

This encounter with Hauser – who professes to be the real possessor of the body – becomes a microcosm for the film's larger critique of the preeminence of the 'real'. That we meet Quade first – and identify with him – makes us question whether Hauser is the true or more worthy identity for the body. If we are to believe that Hauser's identity is in some ways more 'real' than Quade's – because his memories are based on lived experience rather than memory implants – the question then becomes is realer necessarily better? At the climax of the film, Quade claims his own identity instead of going back to being Hauser. In his final exchange with Cohagen, Cohagen says, 'I wanted Hauser back. You had to be Quade.' 'I am Quade', he responds. Although Quade is an identity based on implanted memories, it is no less viable than Hauser – and arguably more so. Quade remains the primary object of our spectatorial investment and engagement throughout the film. His simulated identity is more responsible, compassionate and productive than the 'real' one. That Quade experiences himself as 'real' gives the lie to the

Baudrillardian and Jamesonian assumption that the real and the authentic are synonymous.

Part of what claiming this identity means is saving the Mutants on Mars from oxygen deprivation. The Mutants are the socio-economic group on Mars who are most opp-ressed by the tyrannical Cohagen; Cohagen regulates their access to oxygen. Quade refuses to go back to being Hauser because he feels that he has a mission to carry out. His sense of moral responsibility outweighs any claims on his actions exerted by the pull of an 'authentic' identity. By choosing to start the reactor at the pyramid mines – and thereby produce enough oxygen to make the atmosphere on Mars habitable – Quade is able to liberate the Mutants from Cohagen's grip.

Surprisingly enough, memories are less about authenticating the past, than about generating possible courses of action in the present. The Mutant resistance leader, Quato, tells Quade that 'A man is defined by his actions, not his memories.' We might revise his statement to say that a man is defined by his actions, but whether those actions are made possible by prosthetic memories or memories based on lived experience makes little diff-erence. Any kind of distinction between 'real' memories and prosthetic memories – memories which might be technologically disseminated by the mass media and worn by its consumers – might ultimately be unintel-ligible. *Total Recall* underscores the way in which memories are always already public, the way in which memories always circulate and interpellate individuals, but can never get back to an authentic owner, to a proper body – or as we will see in the case of *Blade Runner*, to a proper photograph.

Although *Blade Runner* is based on the 1968 Philip K. Dick novel *Do Androids Dream of Electric Sheep?*, its points of departure from the novel are instructive. In Dick's novel, the presence of empathy is what allows the bounty hunters to distinguish the androids from the humans. In fact, empathy is imagined to be the uniquely human trait. Deckard wonders 'precisely why an android bounced so helplessly about when confronted by an empathy measuring test. Empathy, evidently, existed only within the human community...' (Dick 1968: 26).

What exposes the replicants in the film, however, is not the lack of empathy as much as the lack of a past – the lack of memories.

Ridley Scott's film foregrounds this point in the opening sequence. The film begins with a Voight-Kampf test. This test is designed to identify a replicant by measuring physical, bodily responses to a series of questions which are designed to provoke an emotional response. Technological instruments are used to measure pupil dilation and the blush reflex to determine the effect the questions have on the subject. In this opening scene, Mr Holden, a 'blade runner', questions Leon, his subject. As Mr Holden explains, the questions are 'designed to provoke an emotional response' and that 'reaction time is important'. Leon, however, slows down the test by interrupting with questions. When Mr Holden says, 'You're in a desert walking along the sand. You see a tortoise', Leon asks, 'What's a tortoise?' Seeing that his line of enquiry is going nowhere, Mr Holden says, 'Describe in single words the good things about your mother'. Leon stands up, pulls out a gun, says, 'Let me tell you about my mother' and then shoots Holden. In this primal scene, what 'catches' the replicant is not the absence of empathy, but rather the absence of a past, the absence of memories. Leon cannot describe his mother, cannot produce a genealogy, because he has no past, no memories.

This scene, then, attempts to establish memory as the locus of humanity. Critics of the film have tended to focus on the fact that replicants lack a past in order to underscore the lack of 'real history' in postmodernity. David Harvey, for example, argues that 'history for everyone has become reduced to the evidence of a photograph' (1989: 313). In Harvey's account, that replicants lack a past illustrates the lack of depth – and the emphasis on surface – which characterises postmodernity. Giuliana Bruno claims that the photograph 'represents the trace of an origin and thus a personal identity, the proof of having existed and therefore having the right to exist' (1987: 71). Certainly the relationship between photography and memory is central to this film. However, both Bruno and Harvey presume that photography has the ability to anchor a referent; they presume that the photograph maintains an indexical link to 'reality'. The film, I would argue, claims just the opposite. After Deckard has determined that Rachel is a replicant she shows up at his appartment with photographs – in particular a photograph depicting her and her mother.

'You think I'm a replicant, don't you?', she asks. 'Look, it's me with my mother.' The photograph, she hopes, will both validate her memory and authenticate her past. Instead of reasserting the referent, however, the photograph further confounds it. Instead of accepting Rachael's photograph as truth, Deckard begins to recall for her one of her memories: 'You remember the spider that lived in the bush outside your window … watched her work, building a web all summer. Then one day there was a big egg in it.' Rachael continues, 'The egg hatched and 100 baby spiders came out and they ate her…' Deckard looks at her. 'Implants', he says. 'Those aren't your memories, they're someone else's. They're Tyrell's niece's.' The photograph in *Blade Runner*, like the photograph of the grandmother in Kracauer's 1927 essay 'Photography', is 'reduced to the sum of its details' (1993: 430). With the passage of time the image 'necessarily disintegrates into its particulars' (Kracauer, 1993: 429). The photograph can no more be a fixed locus of memory than the body can in *Total Recall*. The photograph, it seems has proved nothing.

We must not, however, lose sight of the fact that Rachael's photograph does correspond to the memories she has. And those memories are what allow her to go on, exist as she does, and eventually fall in love with Deckard. We might say that while the photograph has no relationship to 'reality', it helps her to produce her own narrative. While it fails to authenticate her past, it does authenticate her present. The power of photography, in Kracauer's account, is its ability to 'disclose this previously unexamined foundation of nature' (1993: 435–6) and derives not from its ability to fix, but rather from its ability to reconfigure. Photography, for Kracauer, precisely because it loses its indexical link to the world, has 'The capacity to stir up the elements of nature' (1993: 436). For Rachael, the photograph does not correspond to a lived experience and yet it provides her with a springboard for her own memories. In a particularly powerful scene Rachael sits down at the piano in Deckard's apartment, takes her hair down, and begins to play. Deckard joins her at the piano. 'I remember lessons', she says. 'I don't know if it's me or Tyrell's niece.' Instead of focusing on that ambiguity, Deckard says, 'You play beautifully'. At this point Deckard, in effect, rejects the distinction between 'real' and prosthetic memories. Her memory of lessons allows her to play beautifully, so it matters little whether she lived through the lessons or not.

Because the director's cut raises the possibility that Deckard himself is a replicant, it takes a giant step toward erasing the intelligibility of the distinction between the real and the simulated, the human and the replicant. Early on in the film Deckard sits down at his piano and glances at the old photographs that he has displayed upon it. Then there is cut to a unicorn racing through a field, which we are to take as a daydream – or a memory. Obviously it cannot be a 'real' memory, a memory of a lived experience. Later, at the very end of the film, when Deckard is about to flee with Rachael, he sees an origami unicorn lying on the floor outside of his door. When Deckard picks up the unicorn, which we recognise as the work of a plainclothes officer who has been making origami figures throughout the film, we hear an echo of his earlier statement to Deckard about Rachael – 'It's too bad she won't live, but then again who does?' The ending suggests that the cop knows about Deckard's memory of a unicorn, in the same way that Deckard knows about Rachel's memory of the spider. It suggests that his memories, too, are implants – that they are prosthetic. At this moment we do not know whether Deckard is a replicant or not. Unlike the earlier version of the film, the director's cut refuses to make a clear distinction for us between replicant and human, between real and prosthetic memory. There is no safe position, like the one Baudrillard implicitly supposes, from which we might recognise such a distinction. The ending of *Blade Runner*, then, registers the pleasure and the threat of portability – that we might not be able to distinguish between our own memories and prosthetic ones. Deckard is an empathic person who is even able to have compassion for a replicant. More importantly, he is a character 'real enough' to gain our spectatorial identification. Ultimately the film makes us call into question our own relationship to memory, and to recognise the way in which we always assume that our memories are real. Memories are central to our identity – to our sense of who we are and what we might become – but as this film suggests, whether those memories come from lived experience or whether they are prosthetic seems to make very little difference. Either way, we use them to construct narratives for ourselves, visions for our future.

***

Wes Craven's New Nightmare (1994) begins with an uncanny allusion to *The Thieving Hand*. The film opens on a movie set, where an electrical version of the Freddie Kruger hand – a hand with razor blades in the place of fingers – comes to life, as it were, remembering its prior activity of killing. While this hand is not the hand from the old movie, but rather an electrical prosthesis, it nevertheless possesses the Kruger hand's memories. After this prosthetic hand slices open several people on the movie set, we realise that this scene is 'just' a dream based on the main character's memories of working on the *Nightmare on Elm Street* films. Gradually, however, the film begins to undermine or question that notion of 'just'. What might it mean to say that those memories are 'just' from a movie? Does it mean, for example, that they are not real? Does it mean that those memories are less real? No, would be Wes Craven's answer. In fact, memories of the earlier *Nightmare on Elm Street* movies – and from the movies – become her memories. And as the film radically demonstrates, this is a life and death matter. In the course of the movie, memories from the earlier movies begin to break through. Those memories are not from events she lived, but rather from events she lived cinematically. The film actually thematises the way in which film memories become prosthetic memories. Her memories, prosthetic or not, she experiences as real, for they affect her in a life and death way, profoundly informing the decisions she has to make.

All three of these films gradually undermine the value of the distinction between real and simulation, between authentic and prosthetic memory – and in *Blade Runner,* the value of the distinction between human and replicant. In *Blade Runner*, even empathy ultimately fails as a litmus test for humanity. In fact, the replicants – Rachael and Roy (Rutger Hauer), not to mention Deckard – become increasingly empathic in the course of the film. The word empathy, unlike sympathy which has been in use since the sixteenth century, makes its first appearance at the beginning of this century. While sympathy presupposes an initial likeness between subjects ('Sympathy', OED, 1989),[5] empathy presupposes an initial difference between subjects. Empathy, then, is 'The power of projecting one's personality into ... the object of contemplation' (OED, 1989). We might say that empathy depends less on 'natural' affinity than sympathy, less on some kind of essential underlying connection between the two subjects. While sympathy, therefore, relies upon an essentialism of identification, empathy recognises the alterity of identification. Empathy, then, is about the lack of identity between subjects, about negotiating distances. It might be the case that it is precisely this distance which is constitutive of the desire and passion to remember. That the distinction between 'real' and prosthetic memory is virtually undecidable makes the call for an ethics of personhood both frightening and necessary – an ethics based not on a pluralistic form of humanism or essentialism of identification, but rather on a recognition of difference.[6] An ethics of personhood might be constructed upon a practice of empathy and would take seriously its goal of respecting the fragmentary, the hybrid, the different.

Both *Blade Runner* and *Total Recall* – and even *Wes Craven's New Nightmare* – are about characters who understand themselves through a variety of alienated experiences and narratives which they take to be their own, and which they subsequently make their own through use. My narrative is thus a counter-argument to the 'consciousness industry', or 'culture industry' (Horkheimer and Adorno, 1991) one. What I hope to have demonstrated is that it is not appropriate to dismiss as merely prosthetic these experiences that define personhood and identity. At the same time, however, memories cannot be counted on to provide narratives of self-continuity – as *Total Recall* clearly points out. I would like to end by leaving open the possibility of what I would like to call 'breakthrough memories'. When Quade is at Rekal Incorporated planning his memory package, he has an urge to go as a secret agent. In other words, memories from an earlier identity – not in any way his true or essential identity, but one of the many layers that have constructed him – seem to break through. It thus might be the case that identity is palimpsestic, that the layers of identity that came before are never successfully erased. It would be all too easy to dismiss such an identity as merely a relation of surfaces, as many theorists of the postmodern have done, but to do so would be to ignore what emerges in both texts as an insistent drive to remember. What both films seem to suggest is not that we should never forget, but rather that we should never stop generating memory. The particular desire to place oneself in history through a narrative of memories is a desire to be a social, historical being. We might say that it is precisely such a 'surface' experience of history which gives people personhood, which brings them into the public. What the drive to remember expresses, then, is a pressing desire to reexperience history – not to unquestioningly validate the past, but to put into play the vital, indigestible material of history, reminding us of the uninevitability of the present tense.

Notes

1 See Donna J. Haraway (1991). A cyborg world, she suggests, 'might be about lived social and bodily realities in which people are not afraid of their joint kinship with animals and machines, not afraid of permanent partial identities and contradictory standpoints' (1991: 154).

2 As Hansen (1993: 460) notes, 'the term innervation was used by Benjamin for conceptualising historical transformation as a process of converting images into somatic and collective reality'.

3 Shaviro (1993) offers a clear articulation of a shifting emphasis in film theory from a psychoanalytic paradigm to one that attempts to account for the power of the image to engage the spectator's body. Also see Linda Williams (1991); Murray Smith (1994).

4 In his famous footnote, Freud describes the following scene: 'I was sitting alone in my wagon-lit compartment when a more than usually violent jerk of the train swung back the door in the adjoining washing-cabinet, and an elderly gentleman in a dressing-gown and traveling cap came in. I assumed that he had been about to leave the washing-cabinet which divides the two compartments, and had taken the wrong direction and had come into my compartment by mistake. Jumping up with the intention of putting him right, I at once realised to my dismay that the intruder was nothing but my own reflection in the looking-glass of the open door, I can still recollect that I thoroughly disliked his appearance' (1959: 403).

5 According to the OED, sympathy is 'A (real or supposed) affinity between certain things, by virtue of which they are similarly or correspondingly affected by the same influence.'

6 Such an ethics would borrow insights from Subaltern and Post-Colonial Studies. See Jonathan Rutherford and Homi Bhabha (1990); Stuart Hall (1990); Iris Marion Young (1990).

References

Baudrillard, Jean (1983) *Simulations*. New York: Semio-text(e).

Baudry, Jean-Louis (1974-5) 'Ideological Effects of the Basic Cinematographic Apparatus', *Film Quarterly* 28 (2), p. 39–47.

Blumer, Herbert (1933) *Movies and Conduct*. New York: Macmillan.

Bruno, Giuliana (1987) 'Rumble City: Postmodernism and Blade Runner', *October* 41, p. 61–74.

Charters, W. W. (1933) *Motion Pictures and Youth: A Summary*. New York: Macmillan.

Comolli, Jean-Louis (1986) 'Technique and Ideology: Camera, Perspective, Depth of Field', pp. 421–33 in Philip Rosen (ed.) *Narrative, Apparatus, Ideology*. New York: Columbia University Press.

Dick, Philip K. (1968) *Do Androids Dream of Electric Sheep?* New York: Ballantine Books.

Freud, Sigmund (1959) 'The 'Uncanny'', pp. 368–407 in *Collected Papers, vol. IV*. New York: Basic Books.

Hall, Stuart (1990) 'Cultural Identity and Diaspora', in Jonathan Rutherford (ed.) *Identity: Community, Culture, Difference*. London: Lawrence and Wishart, pp. 222–37.

Hansen, Miriam (1993) ''With Skin and Hair': Kracauer's Theory of Film, Marseilles 1940', *Critical Inquiry* 19 (3), p. 437–69.

Haraway, Donna J. (1991) 'A Cyborg Manifesto: Science, Technology and Socialist-Feminism in the Late Twentieth Century', pp. 149-81 in *Simians, Cyborgs, and Women: The Reinvention of Nature*. New York: Routledge [reprinted in this volume].

Harvey, David (1989) *The Condition of Postmodernity*. Cambridge: Blackwell.

Horkheimer, Max and Theodor W. Adorno (1991) 'The Culture Industry: Enlightenment as Mass Deception', pp. 120–67 in *The Dialectic of Englightenment*. New York: Continuum.

Jameson, Fredric (1991) *Postmodernism, or, the Cultural Logic of Late Capitalism*. Durham, NC: Duke University Press.

Kracauer, Siegfried (1993) 'Photography', *Critical Inquiry* 19 (3), p. 421–37.

Lacan, Jacques (1977) 'The Mirror-Stage', in *Écrits: A Selection*. New York: W. W. Norton, pp. 1–7.

Miller, D. A. (1988) *The Novel and the Police*. Berkeley and Los Angeles: University of California Press. Oxford English Dictionary (1989) Oxford: Oxford University Press.

Rutherford, Jonathan and Homi Bhabha (1990) 'The Third Space: Interview with Homi Bhabha', in Jonathan Rutherford (ed.) *Identity: Community, Culture, Difference*. London: Lawrence and Wishart, pp. 207–21.

Shaviro, Steven (1993) *The Cinematic Body*. Minneapolis: University of Minnesota Press.

Smith, Murray (1994) 'Altered States: Character and

Emotional Response in the Cinema', *Cinema Journal* 33 (4), p. 34–56.

Williams, Linda (1991) 'Film Bodies: Gender, Genre, and Excess', *Film Quarterly* 44 (4), p. 2–13.

Young, Iris Marion (1990) *Justice and the Politics of Difference.* Princeton, NJ: Princeton University Press.

Akira, Postermodernism and Resistance
Isolde Standish

Contemporary urban style is empowering to the subordinate for it asserts their right to manipulate the signifiers of the dominant ideology in a way that frees them from that ideological practice and opens them up to the subcultural and oppositional uses.
— John Fiske (1991: 253)

This essay is concerned with a textual analysis of *Akira* (1988),[1] the highly successful cyberpunk film created by Otomo Katsuhiro. This analysis is an exploration of the complex systems of codes and practices employed by the film and the spectator[2] in the creation of meaning; however its main emphasis will be on the perspective of the spectator. As with most commercial films produced by the Japanese studio system, *Akira* (Tôhô Studios) is aimed at a specific audience: adolescent males who are fully conversant with the codes and cultural systems employed in the film.[3] Therefore, to reach an understanding of how a Japanese adolescent male creates meaning (and so derives pleasure) from *Akira* involves not only an understanding of the uses the film makes of other textual systems, but also an understanding of the position occupied by some adolescent males in Japanese society.

The aim of this essay; then, is twofold: first, to come to an understanding of *Akira* from the point of view of its intertextuality; and second, to present an interpretation of the film as a point of convergence of the spectator-film-culture nexus. To this end, I intend to discuss two categories of textual systems developed by Allen and Gomery (1985): first, the 'nonfilmic intertexts' which involve the film's use of conventions and codes from other systems of representations, such as the *bôsôzoku*[4] subculture and the *Akira* manga (comic) series; and second, the 'filmic intertext', that is, the film's use of conventions drawn from the *nagaremono* or 'drifter' films of the 1950s and 1960s, the science fiction/horror genre and other films, in particular the American film *Blade Runner* (Ridley Scott 1982).[5]

Through an examination of the *bôsôzoku* sub-culture as a cultural expression of a section of Japanese youth, the first part of this essay will demonstrate how Akira uses *bôsôzoku* style to reflect a youth culture of resistance which exists alongside mainstream contemporary Japanese society. This raises many questions in relation to the myths of Japanese social and cultural homogeneity and the supposed classless nature of Japanese society.[6] For ethnographic detail I shall be largely drawing on Satô's (1991) study of the *bôsôzoku* and *yankî* (punk) youths. I shall then proceed with a structural analysis of *Akira* as a text which draws on a postmodernist pastiche of conventions to create a *mise-en-scène* which denotes chaos and corruption.

It should be noted that while Satô provides a useful ethnographic account of *bôsôzoku*, he fails to present the sub-culture adequately within its larger social, political and economic contexts and as a result he fails to answer the following questions which are crucial to understanding the underlying causes of the development and attraction of the subculture. First, why is the membership of *bôsôzoku* gangs predominantly made up of youths from manual working-class backgrounds? Second, why is their behavior in opposition to the norms and standards of Japanese society? On the other hand, Satô does refute the psychological 'strain theory' which he states was the most common explanation cited by Japanese academics and the media during the 1970s for the occurrence of *bôsôzoku* activities and which he defines as

a behavioral expression of frustrated wants and needs, resulting from an incongruity between culturally induced aspirations and socially distributed legitimate means (1991: 3).

Satô argues instead that *bôsôzoku* behavior is an expression of *asobi* (play) which forms part of a rite of passage marking the change from childhood to maturity.

Asobi is an important factor, but it is only one in a multiplicity of factors which are related to the occurrence of *bôsôzoku* activities. By emphasising *asobi*, Satô fails to explain adequately the social and historical causes which lie behind the manifestation of this particular form of delinquent behavior. Therefore I intend to broaden the discussion by taking up these issues and by suggesting that at the social level, the factors listed below have contributed to the emergence of a generational consciousness which, despite myths of the classless nature of Japanese society, is linked to a post-war polarisation based on occupational status. The development of the youth sub-cultures in the post-war period should be viewed as one of the expressions of this generational consciousness through its manifestation of style and behavior. The factors we need to consider are: (i) post-war changes in the Japanese systems of education and work, part of which was a shift to a meritocracy and achievement-oriented social status; (ii) changes in the structure of the family, especially the gradual decline of the extended family; (iii) the proliferation of the mass media. Television was first broadcast in Japan in 1953. At that time there were 866 television sets, but by 1959 this number had jumped to two million and was increasing at a rate of 150,000 a month (Anderson and Richie 1959: 254); (iv) the changes in the comparative ranking of work and leisure. Material affluence has also increased the importance of leisure and recreation in the lives of all Japanese. Technological innovations in industrial production and the demands of unions for fewer working hours have, since the early 1970s, reduced working time (Satô 1991: 184); (v) the emergence of adolescence as a socially constructed category which accompanied the increase in the spending power of Japanese youth and the growth of a market designed to exploit this surplus spending power.

Bôsôzoku sub-culture, seen as an outward manifestation of a new generational consciousness poses a direct challenge to the traditional 'work ethic' and achievement-oriented ideology of the previous generation. *Bôsôzoku* have adapted and inverted images, styles and ideologies to construct an alternative identity, an otherness, which challenges the ideals of Japanese social and cultural homogeneity. Hence, the moral panic[7] which followed media reports of *bôsôzoku* activities in the mid-1980s may be explained in part as the fear of difference, 'otherness'.

Satô states that 'the majority of those who participate in gang activities are from middle-class families' (1991: 2). There is a problem here as most Japanese define themselves as middle-class, despite economic and occupational differences. Thus Satô goes on to state that the majority of *bôsôzoku* youths come from 'blue-collar' backgrounds, a point

supported by DeVos in his psycho-cultural study of deviancy in Japanese society (1973).[8] Therefore, it would perhaps be more accurate to say that most *bôsôzoku* youths do not come from economically disadvantaged backgrounds, such as in the UK and the USA where academic studies have made the link between delinquency and economic deprivation, but from lower status groups who do not fit in with the Japanese ideal of the white-collar salaryman and his family. So despite the fact that the majority of Japanese consider themselves to be middle-class, it is clear that there is a polarity of occupational status in society which can be said to be divided along the lines of blue-collar/low status workers, and the salaryman/white-collar/high status workers. The polarity of occupation is determined by education and is reflected in the emergence of distinct youth cultures divided along these lines.

Traditional explanations of the classless nature of Japanese society are by and large dependent on the linking of income to class and do not take into account the status attached to certain occupations and denied to others.[9] They also tend to ignore the fact that social standards and norms are determined by dominant elites, filtering down through society to become the consensual view. A person's ability to achieve status depends upon the criteria of status applied by other people in the society (*seken*) in accordance with the consensual view (*seken-nami*), that is, the standards and norms individuals use in evaluating other people (Cohen 1955: 140).[10] This raises 'status problems' for those who fail to achieve in a highly competitive education and employment system. Hence, the desire of the *bôsôzoku* youths to establish a set of status criteria outside the consensual view, in terms of which they can more easily succeed. *Bôsôzoku* discontent with mainstream society reflects the polarisation between blue-collar and white-collar status groups whose position is determined by their children's access to education. The emergence of two distinct youth cultures divided along these same lines, the manual working-class youth, *bôsôzoku*, and the college students' *dokushin kizoku* (literally, unmarried aristocrats) youth culture reflects this contraposition. It is also evident in the geographical division of Tokyo into the Yamanote region, mostly populated by salarymen, and the Shitamachi area where blue-collar workers tend to congregate.[11]

From this perspective of occupation-determined status divisions, the reason for the emergence of *bôsôzoku* can be explained in Cohen's (1955) terms of 'the compensatory function of juvenile gangs'. He suggests that working-class youths who under-achieve at school and who are unable to conform to 'respectable' society, often resort to deviant behavior as a solution to their problems:

> It is a plausible assumption ... that the working-class boy whose status is low in middle-class terms cares about that status [and] that this status confronts him with a genuine problem of adjustment. To this problem of adjustment there are a variety of conceivable responses, of which participation in the creation and maintenance of the delinquent subculture is one. Each mode of response entails costs and yields gratifications of its own ... The hallmark of the delinquent subculture is the explicit and wholesale repudiation of middle-class standards and the adoption of their very antithesis (Cohen 1955: 128–9).

This point is further supported by Satô when he states that

> while they may be faceless unskilled labourers or not very promising high school students in their everyday lives, they can become 'somebody' with definite status through their universe of discourse (1991: 69).

This 'compensatory function' is crucial to an understanding of *Akira* and the *bôsôzoku* sub-culture as a whole. In the analysis of *Akira* which follows, it will be demonstrated how, by drawing on the imagery of *kôha* (hard type) as a defining feature of masculinity, the narrative performs Cohen's 'compensatory function' which, I believe, is one of the reasons for *Akira*'s huge box-office success.

The meaning of bôsôzoku style

Having placed the occurrence of *bôsôzoku* behavior within the context of the emergence of a generational consciousness and the status divisions of labour in Japanese society, and linked this to Cohen's 'compensatory function', it is possible to argue that *bôsôzoku* style is a

form of resistance, which Fiske defines as 'the refusal to accept the social identity proposed by the dominant ideology and the social control that goes with it' (1991: 241). From a reading of the imagery and symbols which make up the *bôsôzoku* style, it becomes evident that the *bôsôzoku* members are attempting to negotiate a 'meaningful intermediate space' within the dominant work ethic and achievement-oriented ideology of modern Japanese society. This they have achieved through their particular behavior, such as the outright challenging of police authority, and through the creation of a unique style.

Bôsôzoku youths have appropriated historical and cultural objects and signs which are made to carry new, covert meanings. This violation of taken-for-granted meanings became a form of resistance to the dominant order: for example, the *bôsôzoku* phonetic use of Chinese characters, which are often complex, to express the names of their gangs. These work at two levels, the meanings created by the phonetic usage and the meanings inherent in the Chinese characters. For their clothing, they often wear *tokkôfuku*, the uniforms worn by the *kamikaze* pilots of World War Two, or *sentôfuku*, military combat uniforms. They often wear *hachimaki* (head bands) with the rising sun or the imperial chrysanthemum crest in the centre. These are all symbols usually associated with extreme right-wing political movements, including the *yakuza* (gangsters). Satô states that there is no real evidence to suggest that *bôsôzoku* youths are affiliated in any way with these organizations.[12]

I would suggest that the right-wing symbols employed by the *bôsôzoku* have been inverted into threatening symbols of group solidarity as well as referring to the traditional 'tragic hero' who has dominated Japanese popular culture since the *Chûshingura* (*Forty-seven Rônin*) story. These objects and symbols had already been imbued with new post-war meanings in war-retro films.[13] They have been re-positioned further within a *bôsôzoku* subcultural context, and part of their appeal and value is derived from their potential to shock. As Hebdige states, 'violations of the authorised codes through which the social world is organised and experienced have considerable power to provoke and disturb' (1991: 91).

Fiske has argued that the pleasure 'style' affords is its ability to empower the creator. He tells us that:

...it is a pleasure of control or empowerment, a carnivalesque concentration on the materiality of the signifiers and the consequent evasion of the subjectivity constructed by the more ideologically determined signifieds (1991: 250).

He then goes on to demonstrtate how Madonna, through style, 'turns herself into a spectacle' (253) and in so doing denies the spectator the position of voyeur. She does this by 'controlling the look', thereby inverting the normal power relations of looking just as in a carnival. It is interesting that in a questionnaire on pleasure and *bôsô* (mass vehicle rallies) activities, Satô found that '*medatsu koto* (being seen) was ranked as important as the 'activity itself' among the reasons of one's enjoyment' (27).

This pleasure in *medatsu koto* is further evidenced by *bôsôzoku*'s deliberate courting of the media, the staging of *bôsô* drives for the cameras and the writing of articles for magazines. Through the desire for *medalsu koto*, whether it is media coverage or inadvertent pedestrian spectators, it is the *bôsôzoku* youth who is in control of the look. A journalist clearly stated his sense of powerlessness when confronted by *bôsôzoku* youths:

> *Bôsôzoku* from all of Japan cooperate with our efforts to gather data. It is more than cooperation. They are almost aggressive. They phone the publisher night and day and demand to be interviewed. Some even come to the publisher's office driving motorbikes ... I am so overwhelmed by their *medachilagari seishin* [*medatsu*, spirit: desire to show off] that I feel like a subcontractor who is working under orders for a magazine which might be called, say, *Monthly Bôsôzoku* (quoted in Satô 1991: 93).

By creating a spectacle, in Fiske's 'carnivalesque' sense of the word,[14] they are inverting the 'look' as an expression of control and it is from this process of control that their pleasure derives, hence, the centrality of *medatsu koto* to that pleasure.

In summation, *bôsôzoku* youths have, through their style, sought control over their social identity in contemporary Japanese culture where, in a post-industrial consumer society, image and identity are no longer fixed, but open to be played with.[15] They have

taken right-wing political symbolism out of its traditional political and historical discourse (the rise of ultra nationalistic right-wing movements and World War Two), and have asserted their right to use it as a signifier of group identity and for the 'tragic hero' of the *Chûshingura* tradition. They have created a 'spectacular construction' of their own image which defines their 'otherness' and, by extension, their resistance to the dominant culture. How did the film *Akira* fit into *bôsôzoku* culture?

Akira and postmodernism

Having discussed the *bôsôzoku* as a sub-culture apart from, and in opposition to, mainstream Japanese society, I shall now analyse the role of *Akira* as part of the *patois* of *bôsôzoku* sub-cultural language. *Akira* is a film which legitimates and mythologises the position of *bôsôzoku* youth on the periphery of Japanese society and so becomes a sharp critique of contemporary corporate Japanese society.[16]

Akira is a text which simultaneously displays the two distinct characteristics of the postmodern which Fredric Jameson (1983) discussed: an effacement of boundaries, for instance between previously defined stylistic norms (Eastern and Western) and between past and present, resulting in pastiche and parody; and a schizophrenic treatment of time as 'perpetual present'. In *Akira*, this effacement of the boundaries between stylistic norms and between past and present does not manifest in an appeal to 'nostalgia' as Jameson has argued it does in Western postmodernist films. For example, Scott's *Blade Runner* (1982), although set in a futuristic Los Angeles/Tokyo[17] cityscape in the year 2019, simultaneously plays on 1950s' conventions of *film noir*. The Raymond Chandler image of the hero detective (Harrison Ford), the emphasis on faded sepia family photographs and memories, establish a nostalgic humanness which is contrasted with the alien cyborgs who also inhabit the film's space. *Akira* similarly draws on the 1950s and 1960s conventions of a specific male genre based on the drifter film (*nagare-mono*)[18] in the construction of the character called Kaneda. Kaneda displays all the positive attributes of the outsider as represented by the actors Ishihara Yujirô and Takakura Ken, all of whose films are still widely available. The outsider is physically strong, but, above all else, he remains loyal to the code of brotherhood, regardless of personal cost. He is thus brought into direct opposition with the establishment, represented in the films by the scheming, self-interested politicians and the moguls of the military-industrial complex. As an archetypal outsider, Kaneda is not bound by any of the conventions of the 'legitimate' society which, as the following discussion makes clear, is portrayed as corrupt and degenerate. Akira thus conforms to a central theme that runs through the films of the *nagare-mono* and the *yakuza* genres, that is, the clash between male codes of brotherhood and the constraints imposed on male freedom by the law and social institutions, such as the family. Hence the *nagare-mono* always exists on the margins of society, for it is only there that he can remain true to his moral code.[19]

Akira, while set in a futuristic present, takes four historical signifiers which are juxtaposed to underscore the corruption and degeneration of contemporary Japanese society, creating an historical 'pastiche'. The first historical signifier derives from the *kurai tani* (dark valley) period (1931–41) of pre-war Japan when right-wing military factions combined with *zaibatsu* (industrialists) and vied with politicians for political control of the country. In *Akira*, the Colonel is symbolic of this sort of military faction. The film's representation of the Colonel is so constructed that he is easily identified with the portrayal of General Anami, the War Minister in Prime Minister Suzuki's cabinet of 1945, in the highly successful film *Japan's Longest Day* (*Nihon no ichiban nagai hi*, directed by Okamoto Kihachi, 1967).[20] The industrialists, with whom the Colonel is in collusion, are shown to have connections with the terrorists, while the politicians are depicted as weakened through internal conflicts.

The second historical signifier relates to the dropping of the atomic bombs on Hiroshima and Nagasaki. The opening credit sequence of the film is dominated by a silent white flash which destroys the cityscape leaving only the impact crater over which the title *Akira* appears in red letters. When they lose control of their power, Akira, the most powerful of the mutant children, and Tetsuo become metaphorical nuclear weapons. Takeshi, Kyoko and Masaru, the spectral children, are haunting images of post-nuclear mutants. They are the result of the obsession of the military scientists' research into the psyche and, at the end of the film, they

will destroy the corrupt world as it is depicted in the first part of the film.

The third signifier relates to the Tokyo Olympics (1964) and the fourth to the political unrest and student demonstrations against the revision of the US-Japan Security Treaty (Anpo) in the 1960s. Kaneda and his *bôsôzoku* friends exist in a quintessential postmodern city, Neo Tokyo 2019, where the 'evils' of each modern historical period coalesce into a post-atomic world-war futuristic present. The havoc and destruction of the past is being simultaneously criticised and contrasted with a future utopian society that will come about after the film.

Akira is, above all else, concerned with the esthetics of movement and destruction, subordinating any sense of narrative sequence to images of the spectacular; a point which was partially determined by the serial nature of the *manga* (comic) series from which *Akira* the film was derived. *Akira* the comic first appeared in *Young Magazine* in December 1982. The long-running serial structure of the *manga* narrative directly influenced the structure of the film version. Serial forms are influenced by several factors; first, serials are resistant to narrative closure and they have an extended middle. Traditional Hollywood realist narratives are generally constructed in the Todorovian sense, that is, the narrative begins with a stable situation which is disturbed by some force and, finally, there is a re-establishment of a second, but different equilibrium. The serial structure of a long-running *manga* is naturally resistant to the re-establishment of a final equilibrium.

Secondly, the serial form has multiple characters and sub-plots. Hence, the compression of this long-running *manga* serial into a feature-length film curtailed the development of the multiplicity of sub-plots which developed individual characterisations, enhancing the film's sense of fragmentation and disruption of narrative flow. For in Akira, there is no one central character; there are multiple characters who interact within a given set of circumstances, reducing the film to a montage of multiple patterns of action. The *bôsôzoku* youths, Tetsuo and Kaneda, form the catalyst around which these multiple patterns of action coalesce.

The fast editing, the dislocation of narrative sequence and the disruption of the diegesis produce the sensation of fragmentation of images where meanings are disjointed and referential. This emphasises the sense of movement and the physical experience of 'flow' and the sensuality of destruction. Satô links the concept of 'flow' which refers to the 'holistic sensation that people feel when they act with total involvement', to the physical sense of pleasure that *bôsôzoku* experience when they hold mass bike and car rallies. Satô quotes from Mihaly Csikszentmihalyi:

> In the flow state, action follows upon action according to an internal logic that seems to need no conscious intervention by the actor. He experiences it as a unified flowing from one movement to the next, in which he is in control of actions, and in which there is little distinction between self and environment, between stimulus and response, or between past, present and future (1991: 18).

In fact, the whole structure of *Akira* is similar to that of a *bôsô* drive where there are periods of dare-devil driving which involve extreme concentration followed by rest periods at pre-arranged meeting places. These rest periods allow for stragglers to catch up with the main group and for the release of tension. In the film, there are periods of intense violence, destruction and physical movement punctuated by quiet periods when, for example, Kaneda is involved with his terrorist girlfriend Kei, or when the three mutant children converse. These quiet periods in the film allow the spectator to relax before the next sequence of violent and destructive images.

Through the techniques of fast editing and others listed above, the film reproduces the sense of 'flow' in, for example, the bike chase at the beginning of the film when Kaneda and his gang have cornered the Clown gang on the freeway and are in pursuit. The animation is that of a camera following the chase, sometimes from aerial shots which highlight the bike's headlamps as they pierce the empty night sky, and at others from low-angle shots which emphasise the size and power of the bikes as the wheels rotate with a whirring sound. When the gang members do engage in combat, the camera speed changes to slow motion as a biker is thrown over the handle-bars, and as soon as he hits the tarmac, the camera reverts to normal speed, maximising the sensation of the bike's movement as it speeds away leaving the victim instantly miles behind. These images, by emphasising the sensual experience of

movement, are not in any sense representations of the 'real'; they are images of what Baudrillard (1988) has called the 'hyperreal'. The 'hyperreal' effaces the 'contradictions between the real and the imaginary'; the 'sensuous imperative' of these images becomes our experience of the event depicted and our site of pleasure (Baudrillard 1988: 143–7). The sequence of the bike chase replicates, in the sensation of hallucinatory and hyperreal images, the 'flow' as experienced by actual *bôsôzoku* and described by Satô. The soundtrack further enhances the 'sensual imperative' of the images as the low key mechanical 'post-rock' music pulsates in time with the bike engines throughout the chase, complementing the metallic sparks that fly forth as bike hits tarmac and bodies fall to the ground with a thud. Satô noted the elaborate modifications *bôsôzoku* made to their vehicle exhaust systems and the importance of massed engine sounds to their pleasure in a *bôsô* drive. This pleasure is reproduced in the film through the soundtrack.

Baudrillard's concept of the 'hyperreal' also applies to the historical signifiers listed above. As stated earlier, *Akira* was targeted at a particular audience: adolescent males, who could relate to the *bôsôzoku* sub-cultural images and styles which pervade the film. These targeted spectators are at least one generation removed from the actual experiences of the historical events and so their knowledge of the 'dark valley' period and the political unrest of the 1960s is already indirect and fragmentary, a point the film exploits in its structuring of the images of demonstrations and the violence and degeneration of this cybernatised society.

The film reproduces futuristic images of a city in the age of simulation, where signs now bear no relationship to reality and the definition of the real becomes, in Baudrillard's words, 'that *for which it is possible to provide an equivalent representation* ... the real becomes not only that which can be reproduced, but that which is always already reproduced: the hyperreal' (his emphasis; 1988: 145–6). As already noted, the Neo Tokyo cityscapes that punctuate the film are drawing on the iconography of *Blade Runner*'s Los Angeles/Tokyo in the year 2019, which has become a metaphor for urban decay. The warm orange colours which Otomo uses in the night scenes are taken directly from the polluted haze of *Blade Runner*. *Akira*'s Neo Tokyo is a 'critical dystopia' in that it projects images of a futuristic city which perpetuates the worst features of advanced corporate capitalism: urban decay, commodification and authoritarian policing. High-rise buildings representing corporate wealth exist alongside the dark decaying streets of the old town, highlighting the divisive nature of the society. Colored neon signs and holographs dominate the skyline, signifying commercialisation. They also provide the dominant source of light for the night scenes, complementing the motor-cycle headlights of the *bôsôzoku*.

The cityscapes thus represent an aesthetic of postmodern decay, as well as revealing the dark side of scientific experimentation and technology. The uniqueness of architecture to a specific place, culture and time has been lost in Neo Tokyo. These images of a cityscape could be taken from any late capitalist city, such as New York, London. There is nothing in the scenes to link these images specifically to Tokyo.

As also has been noted, the film makes no attempt to place the images of violence and destruction within any logical form of cause-and-effect narrative. The images exist alone, relying on the shared cultural knowledge of the audience to produce meaning. The only assistance the audience is given is through a double mediation of news reports, which are either distorted background voice-over, as in the opening sequence, or television news flashes, complete with commercials, that echo forth from multiple video monitors in shop windows during riot scenes. The effect of this technique is to encourage the spectator to identify with Kaneda whose knowledge of the causes of the chaotic world in which he exists is at best fragmentary. It also works to foreground Kaneda and the Colonel who are, apart from Tetsuo and the three mutant children, the only characters given a semblance of a narrative flow in the film.

Both Kaneda and the Colonel are *kôha* types, the embodiment of a hard masculinity to which actual *bôsôzoku* youths aspire. Satô defines *kôha* as 'the hard type [that] is a traditional image of adolescent masculinity which combines violence, valour and bravado with stoicism and chivalry' (1991: 86). The *kôha* type of masculinity is contrasted with the *nanpa*, or soft type: 'a skirt chaser or ladies' man' (Satô 1991: 86). The college student/ *dokushin kizoku* belong to this latter group. The

kôha school of masculinity also carries with it connotations of *makoto* (purity of motive) which is very much evident in the characters of Kaneda and the Colonel. Neither have been taken in by the corruption that characterises the degenerate society in which they live. Their use of violence is legitimized by their purity of motive and so, despite his extremely violent behavior, Kaneda is the real hero of the film.[21]

In Japanese popular culture, *makoto* takes precedence over efficiency as an esteemed cultural value, hence the Japanese predilection for the 'tragic hero' who proves his purity of spirit in death. However, Kaneda is also 'efficient'. He is loyal as well, another highly valued characteristic in Japanese Confucian-based society. The flashbacks to the orphanage, where he first met Tetsuo, reinforce these characteristics while simultaneously exposing Tetsuo's deepening dependence on him. These flashbacks have two functions: first, they are constructed to arouse a sense of sympathy in the spectator for Kaneda and Tetsuo; and thereby they reinforce the simplistic media-perpetuated view that the breakdown of the traditional family is to blame for adolescent delinquent behavior. But more importantly for their young audience, the flashbacks are liberating, picking up on the conventions of the *nagare-mono*[22] and reflecting a trend in recent films targeted at the young, for example *Kitchin* and *Kimi wa boku o suki ni naru* (*You Are Going to Fall in Love with Me*), in which young adults (*dokushin kizoku*) are portrayed as being without the emotional clutter of the traditional extended family.

Kaneda's qualities of *makoto*, efficiency and loyalty are continually compared to the bumbling of the other 'bad' characters in the film, particularly with Tetsuo, his one-time friend who, through his own personal weakness and as a result of experiments carried out on him by a scientist, metamorphoses into a destructive mass of protoplasm and metal.[23] Tetsuo's character is carefully structured in one of the multiple character sub-plots (fully developed in the *manga* series, but only hinted at in the film through flashbacks) to provide a foil for Kaneda. As children they lived in the same orphanage and Tetsuo came to rely on Kaneda's superior strength. But Tetsuo's envy of Kaneda was the weakness which inadvertently led him to become a test case for scientific experiments, after which his nascent psychic powers make him go on the rampage, killing the barman from the gang's local haunt and Yamagata, another gang member. These incidents provide Kaneda with the legitimation necessary to confront the power that Tetsuo has become in the final climactic half of the film, for Tetsuo is no longer himself. As Yamagata asks just before his death, 'Are you really Tetsuo?'

Kaneda, a *bôsôzoku* youth, through his academic failure, has been placed on the margins of this corrupt and emotionally empty society. His qualities of efficiency and loyalty, combined with his failure at school and his ignorance, make him the film's embodiment of innocence and purity. Therefore he is qualified to become the founder of a new utopian society that will be formed after the old society has been purged through cataclysmic destruction.[24] In the final scenes, Akira and the other three mutant children, the gods of the post-atomic war age, sacrifice themselves (as would have the traditional 'tragic hero') so that a new society can come into being with Kaneda as its progenitor. Apart from Kaneda, his girlfriend Kei and one other junior gang member, the Colonel is the only other survivor. He has also shown attributes of efficiency and sincerity of purpose, but more importantly, he is in control of artifacts, such as helicopters, advanced scientific weapons, etc. As Sontag states, in science fiction films things

> are the locus of values because we experience them, rather than people, as the sources of power. According to science fiction films, man is naked without his artifacts (1979: 494).

Since the Colonel and Kaneda are both representations of the *kôha* school and are shown to be efficient, loyal and competent in their use and control of artifacts, they are obvious survivors in a film which seeks to promote this image of masculinity.

The core values of *makoto* and loyalty which the film promotes give the characters (particularly Kaneda and the Colonel) a sense of historical continuity, as these are themes which, as I have already argued, go back through *yakuza*, *nagare-mono* and war-retro films to the *jidai-geki* (period/historical films) and *Chûshingura* story. This historical continuity is brought into sharp contrast with the fragmented time-frame and postmodernist *mise-en-scène* of the film. These values of the *kôha* hero are seen

to override the postmodern social conditions which, according to the film, will self-destruct. Only those few, the *bôsôzoku*, who refuse to conform to the values of the corrupt world and who were forced to live on the margins of society, will survive to form a new and – by definition – a better world. The characters in *Akira* are spared the psychological struggle that Deckard experiences in Blade Runner over questions of how humanness is defined in a world of 'simulacrum'. It is the *bôsôzoku*'s ignorance which shields them. Kaneda has no doubt about his basic humanness, his core values of makoto and loyalty, his 'morality', are never questioned in the film. As Harvey explains:

> The depressing side of the film [*Blade Runner*] is precisely that, in the end, the difference between the replicant [cyborgs] and the human becomes so unrecognisable that they indeed fall in love ... The power of the simulacrum is everywhere (1992: 313).

Akira, on the other hand, becomes a reaffirmation of recognised core values of traditional Confucian society and so provides a continuity of 'morality' which is felt to be lacking in the outside 'de-industrialising' world where traditional values are threatening to disintegrate.

Conclusion

Through an analysis of the meanings of the *bôsôzoku* sub-culture of style, the conventions of the *nagare-mono* film, and an examination of the determining role of the *manga* series on the narrative structure of the film, as well as a discussion of the adoption of images of a postmodern society inspired by *Blade Runner*, this chapter has attempted to demonstrate the importance of intertextual signifying systems in the creation of meaning in *Akira*. It has also sought to demonstrate how *Akira*, as a science fiction/horror film, 'is [primarily] concerned with the aesthetics of destruction, with the peculiar beauties to be found in wreaking havoc, making a mess' (Sontag 1979: 491). Moreover, through the fragmentation of images and lack of narrative flow, the film makes disjointed references to politically unstable historical periods to create a view of a dystopic future.

Existing on the margins of this society are the *bôsôzoku* youths whose self-esteem is enhanced through the mythologising of their role in opposition to mainstream society, which is portrayed as corrupt and degenerate. This aspect of the film brings us back full circle to Cohen's 'compensatory function' and explains in part the tremendous success in Japan, first of the *manga* series and subsequently of the film. Yet what of its popularity with youths from high occupational status groups who presumably do not need this emotional 'compensation'? I would suggest that the film's appeal lies in part in its 'nostalgic' portrayal of the outsider, free from the social constraints which force individuals to compromise. This is certainly the case with the *nagare-mono* films of the 1950s and 1960s, whose principal audiences were salarymen, those Japanese who Tayama describes as 'being enmeshed in society' and 'living secure lives' (1966).

Notes

1 The film, *Akira*, grew out of a best-selling *manga* (comic) series of the mid-1980s.

2 This essay will attempt to explore the culturally specific codes and practices which a Japanese spectator employs to create meaning and derive pleasure from *Akira*. (Obviously, Western audiences will apply different – non-Japanese – codes and practices in their construction of meaning, thus leading to a different interpretation of the film, an issue not dealt with here.)

3 In Japan, *manga* and animation films tend to be gender-specific. There is very little cross-readership and cross-spectatorship. In bookshops signs clearly indicate which comics are for girls and which for boys, as does the colour-coding of the comic jackets: dark hard colors, blacks and blues, for boys and soft pastel shades of pink for girls. I suspect that at home siblings might engage in a degree of cross-gender readership; however, the industry itself appears to be structured so as to discourage this, despite the fact that thematically gender-specific *manga* and *anime* are often similar. At the time of writing (1996) the two top-rated series for boys and girls, *Dragon Ball Z* and *Sailor Moon* are, despite plot differences, thematically similar. In 1988, at about the same time that *Akira* was released, *Hana no Asukagumi* (*The Flower of the Asuka Gang*) was also released. This film is also set in a post-World War Three dystopic society where gangs rule the streets, the principal differences being that the main gang members and leaders are adolescent girls.

4 *Bôsôzoku* literally means 'tribe of running violently' (*bô* is violent, *sô* is to run, *zoku* is tribe); *bôsô* is more commonly defined as 'reckless driving', so the term might best be translated as 'gang of reckless drivers'; it is used to refer to members of motorcycle and car gangs. This term is perhaps best rendered in English as 'speed tribes' (Greenfeld 1994). In the late 1970s and 1980s, members of these gangs formed a socially cohesive section of Japanese youth.

5 *Blade Runner* was ranked 25th in Japan's *Kinema Junpo* Best Foreign Films for 1982. This film had an obvious influence on *Akira*, as is made clear by the fact that both films are set in the year 2019. However, it could be said that this is a superficial similarity as the sub-texts of the films are quite different.

6 For a detailed exposition of the myths surrounding Japanese cultural and social homogeneity see Dale (1988), Mouer and Sugimoto (1990) and Weiner (1997).

7 A film that plays on this 'moral panic' is *Sono otoko kyôbô ni tsuki* (*Because that Guy is Tough*, released in the UK as *Violent Cop*) 1988, starring Kitano (Beat) Takeshi in which he plays a tough policeman fighting corruption inside the police force on the one hand, and drug pushers on the other. The film feeds on fears of the degeneration of Japanese youth and of wanton violence. For example, the film opens with a group of relatively young high school boys beating up a tramp in a park. This is closely followed by a scene in which a group of young primary school boys (wearing yellow caps) are seen throwing cans from a bridge at a boatman passing below.

8 Mouer and Sugimoto also cite Japanese studies which confirm that 'juvenile delinquency … occurs more frequently among young people whose parents are in blue-collar occupations and self-employed' and that 'education is not unrelated to the occupational hierarchy. Those with higher levels of education are much less likely to commit crimes, particularly those of a violent nature. Juvenile delinquency is tied to the parents' level of education. Delinquency is lowest among those whose parents have had a university education, regardless of their occupation' (1990: 352–3).

9 The ideal is also based on how Japanese answer questions about their class position – not a very reliable way of assessing status evaluations.

10 For a more detailed discussion of the role of *seken* and its relationship to the formation of subjectivity, see Sugiyama-Lebra (1992).

11 This division is also seen in the film industry which targets films to specific youth audiences: for example, *Bîbappu Haisukûru* (*Bebop High School*) is a classic example of the *yankî*-style animation film which glorifies the school under-achiever in much the same way as the more complex *Akira* elevates the *bôsôzoku*. At the other end of the scale are the more sophisticated films such as *Kitchin* (based on the novel by Banana Yoshimoto) which are targeted at the *dokushin kizoku* end of the market.

12 However, there is some debate about this; Greenfeld (1994) suggests that this is not the case, as in fact *yakuza*

do draw on the *bôsôzoku* gangs for recruits.

13 Here I am referring to films such as *Kumo nagaruru hateni* (*Beyond the Clouds*, 1953), *Ningen gyorai kaiten* (*The Sacrifice of the Human Torpedoes*, 1955) and *Ningen gyorai shutsugeki su* (*The Human Torpedoes' Sortie*, 1956).

14 It is interesting to note that Satô's informants frequently used the words *matsuri* (festival) and *kânibaru* (carnival) to describe the atmosphere of a *bôsô* drive.

15 In contemporary capitalist societies, there has been a marked shift in the role of commodities – a move from use-value to sign-value. This has resulted in the fragmentation of the traditional (in the Western sense of the word) working classes, where people now choose their identity through commodities and style: in both the cases of architecture and clothing, the shift has not just been one from mass-ness to specialisation, but also from focus on function to a concern with style. In clothing, these characteristics in conjunction with the newer aesthetics of the shocking (and even the ugly) have justified the label of postmodern (Lash 1991: 39).

16 *Akira* does not have a narrative structure in the traditional Hollywood style, therefore, a plot summary is not very practical. However, the Collectors' Edition Double Pack Video released in Britain provides a file on the principal characters to assist non-Japanese viewers. Here is a brief summary from the tape:

Introduction

Akira ... awakened to his hidden powers, powers that he could not control; powers that swept the megalopolis of Tokyo and the world in the maelstrom of World War Three. Our stage is Neo Tokyo, the super techno city of 2019, thirty years after the holocaust – a ravaged city and one totally unaware of the cause of its misery...

Characters – Data File

KANEDA: AGE 16.

An outsider who is far from obedient and cooperative. He is known to act before thinking things out. The leader and organiser of a bike gang, he is perceived by his fellow students as more than a little egotistical.

TETSUO: AGE 15.

The youngest member of Kaneda's gang. Known to have an inferiority complex because he is thought to be weak and immature. He is also thought to be extremely introverted.

KAY: AGE 16.

Government-assigned code name, her real name remains classified. Joined and became active in a terrorist group shortly after her brother died in prison. Strong-willed yet sensitive.

THE COLONEL: AGE 42.

Career military, on special assignment in Neo Tokyo. Father was a member of the Self-Defence Forces and participated in the original Akira Project prior to the start of World War Three. The Colonel knows the secret of Akira.

KYOKO.

Sequestered by government. Realised extra-sensory powers at age 9; adept at telepathy and clairvoyance. Number 25 in the top secret Akira Project.

TAKESHI.

Sequestered by government. Realised extra-sensory powers at age 8. Especially adept at psycho-kinesis. Number 26 in the top secret Akira experiment.

MASARU.

Sequestered by government. Paralysed from the waist down by polio age 6. Realised extra-sensory powers at age 8. Especially adept at second sight and psycho-kinesis.

AKIRA.

28th and most successful ESP experiment.

File access restricted.

17 The designer of *Blade Runner* was inspired by the Californian designer Syd Mead who works for Bandai, a Japanese games company, where he designs futuristic images for Japanese computer games. It is more than a little ironic that *Blade Runner*'s cityscape was influenced by Tokyo and then that Otomo Katsuhiro should reproduce it once again, drawing on *Blade Runner*'s 2019 Los Angeles to create his 2019 Tokyo.

18 The *nagare-mono* film has its antecedents in the *matatabi-mono* (the wandering *samurai/yakuza*) genre. In the post-war period the actor Ishihara Yujirô came to prominence as an archetypal outsider in films such as *Ore wa matteruzo* (*I'll Wait*, 1957), and *Arashi o yobu otoko* (*The Man Who Calls the Storm*, 1957). However, Tayama, a Japanese critic writing in 1966, argued that by the early 1960s Ishihara had become entrenched in the establishment by appearing on television variety and talk shows. According to Tayama, this destroyed his *nagare-mono* persona, at which time the actor Takakura Ken took over the persona with his success in the highly popular *Abashiri bangaichi* (*Abashiri Wastelands*) series.

19 In the *nagare-mono* films of the 1960s, this code is referred to as *jingi*, which translates as 'humanity and justice'. However, in this case, 'justice' is not to be confused with the Western juridical-based definitions, but forms part of a nativist Confucian ethic. This term is also used extensively in *yakuza* films from the 1970s on, for example, the *Jingi naki tatakai* (*War Without Morality*) series. *Akira*, as a cybernatised version of the *nagare-mono* film, is primarily concerned with male/male relationships and the strains imposed on those relations by modern society. Female characters are marginalised, their principal function being to shore up the heterosexual imperative of the film.

20 This was ranked third in the *Kinema Junpô* Top Ten Films for 1967 and is still widely available on video.

21 As television studies on police dramas have shown in the

West, the 'main difference between heroes and villains is the greater efficiency of the heroes and the sympathy with which they are presented. Otherwise, there are few clear-cut distinctions, particularly in morality or method' (Fiske and Hartley 1989: 29).

22 In the first film of the *Abashiri bangaichi* series (1965), Tachibana's (the main character, played by Takakura Ken) unhappy childhood is depicted in flashbacks that show him and his mother being abused by his stepfather. This leads to a climactic clash and with Tachibana being thrown out of the house. The earlier films of Ishihara Yujirô are all similarly structured around generational conflict.

23 Tetsuo's very name is a play on his changing status in the film, as it means 'iron man'.

24 Here we have a re-working of a dominant theme of the war-retro genre of the early post-war period in which, through World War Two, Japan is purified by destruction only to emerge stronger in the post-war period. This theme is evident in films such as *Daitôyô Sensô to Kokusai Saiban* (*The Pacific War and the International Tribunal*, 1959), and *Japan's Longest Day*, 1967.

References

Allen, R. C. and Douglas Gomery (1985) *Film History, Theory and Practice*. London: McGraw-Hill.

Anderson, J. T. and D. Richie (1959) *The Japanese Film, Art and Industry*. Tokyo: Charles Tuttle.

Baudrillard, Jean (1988) 'Symbolic Exchange and Death', in *Jean Baudrillard, selected writings* (ed.) Mark Poster. Cambridge: Polity Press.

Cohen, A. K. (1955) *Deliquent Boys: The Culture of the Gang*. Glencoe, IL: The Free Press.

Dale, P. (1988) *The Myth of Japanese Uniqueness*. London: Nissan Institute/Routledge Japanese Studies Series.

DeVos, George (1973) *Socialization for Achievement, Essays on the Cultural Psychology of the Japanese*. Berkeley and Los Angeles: University of California Press.

Fiske, John (1991) *Television*. London: Routledge.

Fiske, John and John Hartley (1989) *Reading Television*. London: Routledge.

Greenfeld, Karl Taro (1994) *Speed Tribes: Children of the Japanese Bubble*. London: Boxtree.

Harvey, David (1989) *The Condition of Postmodernity, an Enquiry into the Origins of Cultural Change*. Oxford: Basil Blackwell.

Hebdige, Dick (1991) *Subculture: The Meaning of Style*. London: Routledge.

Jameson, Fredric (1983) 'Postmodernism and the Consumer Society', in *The Anti-Aesthetic: Essays on Postmodern Culture* (ed.) Hal Foster. Port Townsend, W.A.: Bay Press.

Lash, Scott (1991) *Sociology of Postmodernism*. London: Routledge.

Mouer, R. and Sugimoto Yoshio (1990) *Images of Japanese Society: A Study in the Social Construction of Reality*. London: Kegan Paul International.

Otomo, Katsuhiro (n.d.) *Akira* (orginal screenplay in Japanese).

Satô Ikuya (1991) *Kamikaze Biker, Parody and Anomy in Affluent Japan*. London and Chicago: University of Chicago Press.

Sontag, Susan (1979) 'The Imagination of Disaster', in *Film Theory and Criticism, Introductory Readings* (eds) Gerald Mast and Marshall Cohen. Oxford: Oxford University Press.

Sugiyama-Lebra, E. (1992) 'Self in Japanese Culture', in *The Japanese Sense of Self* (ed.) Nancy R. Rosenberger. Cambridge: Cambridge University Press.

Tayama R. (1966) 'Abishiri Bangaichi: Nagare-mono no Erejii', in *Shinario* (October), pp. 134–7.

Weiner, M. (ed.) (1997) *Japan's Minorities: The Illusion of Homogeneity*. London: Routledge.

POACHING THE UNIVERSE:
SCIENCE FICTION FANDOM

| # POACHING THE UNIVERSE: SCIENCE FICTION FANDOM

Science fiction is a genre that produces and promotes some of the most serious and long-term fan devotion to come out of the 'entertainment' media. Corporate and global merchandising, conventions and conferences, official and unofficial websites and chatrooms, memorabilia, collectibles, and personal shrines and temples of devotion, bare witness to the fact that the media machines sell fandom to world audiences. Audiences – people of all classes, races and sexual preferences across the globe – find something deeply meaningful and necessary (to the maintenance of their everyday lives) in the sci-fi text. Sci-fi fans pay homage to individual films, books and magazines, to whole film, TV and literary franchises, to auteurs and authors, to box-office and 'marginal' stars, to cult flops and to rarely seen or read sci-fi texts. Sci-fi devotees name their children after their favourite sci-fi characters, get married (and divorced) in sci-fi costume, and will re-enact episodes or key scenes in real life and digital scenarios. Sci-fi aficionados will argue and contest relentlessly about the allegorical or metaphorical meaning of a sci-fi text(s),

will recant dialogue from one/any episode (in a franchise of hundreds), or will be able to trace the lineage of a distant race or the origins of inter-galactic war in the time it takes to ask the question. Sci-fi fans will build models, websites, chatrooms and organise gatherings of fans to secure the continuing appreciation of their favourite sci-fi text. Sci-fi fans will also appropriate the meaning of sci-fi texts, inflecting, challenging and re-writing what might be considered the dominant reading. Sci-fi fans are, as a consequence, amazing people because they are simultaneous consumers and producers of cultural meaning in dynamic and empowered exchanges and articulations. One can argue, in fact, that science fiction doesn't have real 'meaning' until it is consumed and appropriated and adopted and adored by the science fiction fan community.

Science fiction draws the fan in because it is so openly polysemic and textually excessive in its imaginings: and it is this polysemy and richness in exploration of futuristic and possible themes and ideas that produces an instantaneous extra-textual dialogue with its audiences. Through time travel and the time-loop paradox, through invention and exploration, through special effect and spectacle, and through myth and allegory the science fiction text literally calls for the work of deconstruction and reconstruction to be carried out by the sci-fi viewer/reader as they watch/read, and in the communication and conversation spaces and places that follow reception. Science fiction is not meant to be left in the theatre or 'reading' room, but is meant to be enjoyed and examined again and again in other leisure and social contexts.

Henry Jenkins III adopts this empowering notion of fan as 'textual poacher', taking on what he considers to be reductionist models of audience behaviour that have sought to label (Star Trek) fans as mindless dupes. Jenkins argues that 'fans reclaim works that others regard as worthless and trashy, finding them a rewarding source of popular capital. Like rebellious children, fans refuse to read by the rules imposed on them … For fans, reading becomes a type of play responsive only to its own loosely structured rules and generating its own types of pleasure'. Jenkins examines the way 'women who write fiction based in the Star Trek universe … force the primary text to accommodate alternative interests … in order to make it a better producer of personal meanings and pleasures'.

John Tulloch examines the way the fans of Doctor Who assert their 'power to gloss, and to write the aesthetic history of the show – dividing its twenty-five years into a series of 'golden ages' and 'all-time lows''. This textual power occurs in a context where real transformative power – such as the power to affect production changes

on the show or motivate non-fans to watch more regularly, is largely absent. Society fans are 'situated as a privileged group with few powers – a powerless elite with little control over the floating voter on one side, the producers of the show on the other'. Tulloch, then, establishes a series of constraints on the fans' ability to seize or hold power over the outcome of a sci-fi text.

Will Brooker, in contrast, examines the way the fan reception of a postmodern text such as Star Wars can be 'part of a progressive narrative of change'. Re-released and newly marketed at the time the essay was originally written, Brooker examines the way the textures of nostalgia and the suggested fascistic politics within the film fuel the fan culture's response, appreciation and appropriation of its meaning(s) across a range of media sites and cultural contexts. For this Reader, Brooker also supplies a 'new' introduction outlining developments within fan culture, the Star Wars franchise, and recent political transformations in Britain and America, since the essay was written.

Kurt Lancaster examines what he argues to be are the highly creative online 'fanfic' responses to Babylon 5. By writing fan fiction and publishing web pages 'fans immerse themselves in the Babylon 5 universe … on their own terms outside the original creator's authorial presence'. Performing as 'textual nomads staking individual authorial claims' fans write their own characters and give narrative events new inflections and outcomes. By producing these new texts online and circulating them in cyberspace fans avoid 'the dominant social structure's conventional route for circulating creative production'.

Star Trek Rerun, Reread, Rewritten: Fan Writing as Textual Poaching

Henry Jenkins III

This essay rejects media-fostered stereotypes of *Star Trek* fans as cultural dupes, social misfits or mindless consumers, perceiving them, in Michel de Certeau's term, as 'poachers' of textual meanings who appropriate popular texts and reread them in a fashion that serves different interests. Specifically, the essay considers women who write fiction based in the *Star Trek* universe. First, it outlines how these fans force the primary text to accommodate alternate interests. Second, it considers the issue of literary property in light of the moral economy of the fan community that shapes the range of permissible retellings of the program materials.

In late December 1986, *Newsweek* (Leerhsen, 1986, p. 66) marked the twentieth anniversary of *Star Trek* with a cover story on the program's fans, 'the Trekkies, who love nothing more than to watch the same 79 episodes over and over'. The *Newsweek* article, with its relentless focus on conspicuous consumption and 'infantile' behaviour and its patronising language and smug superiority to all fan activity, is a textbook example of the stereotyped representation of fans found in both popular writing and academic criticism, 'Hang on: You are being beamed to one of those *Star Trek* conventions, where grown-ups greet each other with the Vulcan salute and offer in reverent tones to pay $100 for the autobiography of Leonard Nimoy' (p. 66). Fans are characterised as 'kooks' obsessed with trivia, celebrities and collectibles; as misfits and crazies; as 'a lot of overweight women, a lot of divorced and single women' (p. 68). Borrowing heavily from pop Freud, ersatz Adorno and pulp sociology, *Newsweek* explains the 'Trekkie phenomenon' in terms of repetition compulsion, infantile regression, commodity fetishism, nostalgic complacency and future shock. Perhaps most telling, *Newsweek* consistently treats *Trek* fans as a problem to be solved, a mystery to be understood, rather than as a type of cultural activity that many find satisfying and pleasurable.[1]

Academic writers depict fans in many of the same terms. For Robin Wood (1986, p. 164), the fantasy film fan is 'reconstructed as a child, surrendering to the reactivation of a set of values and structures [the] adult self has long since repudiated'. The fan is trapped within a repetition compulsion similar to that which an infant experiences through the fort/da game. A return to such 'banal' texts could not possibly be warranted by their intellectual content but can only be motivated by a return to 'the lost breast' (p. 169), by the need for reassurance provided by the passive reexperience of familiar pleasures. 'The pleasure offered by the *Star Wars* films corresponds very closely to our basic conditioning; it is extremely reactionary, as all mindless and automatic pleasure tends to be. The finer pleasures are those we have to work for' (p. 164). Wood valorises academically respectable texts and reading practices at the expense of popular works and their fans. Academic rereading produces new insights; fan rereading rehashes old experiences.[2]

As these two articles illustrate, the fan constitutes a scandalous category in contemporary American culture, one that provokes an excessive response from those committed to the interests of textual producers and institutionalised interpreters and calls into question the logic by which others order their aesthetic experiences. Fans appear to be frighteningly out of control, undisciplined and unrepentant, rogue readers. Rejecting aesthetic distance, fans passionately embrace favored texts and attempt to integrate media representations within their own social experience. Like cultural scavengers, fans reclaim works that others regard as worthless and trash, finding them a rewarding source of popular capital. Like rebellious children, fans refuse to read by the rules imposed upon them by the schoolmasters. For fans, reading becomes a type of play, responsive only to its own loosely structured rules and generating its own types of pleasure.

Michel de Certeau (1984) has characterised this type of reading as 'poaching', an impertinent raid on the literary preserve that takes away only those things that seem useful or pleasurable to the reader. 'Far from being writers ... readers are travellers; they move across lands belonging to someone else, like nomads poaching their way across fields they did not write, despoiling the wealth of Egypt to enjoy it themselves' (p. 174). De Certeau perceives popular reading as a series of 'advances and retreats, tactics and games played with the text' (p. 175), as a type of cultural bricolage through which readers fragment texts and reassemble the broken shards according to their own blueprint, salvaging bits and pieces of found material in making sense of their own social experience. Far from viewing consumption as imposing meanings upon the public, de Certeau suggests, consumption involves reclaiming textual material, 'making it one's own, appropriating or reappropriating it' (p. 166).

Yet such wanton conduct cannot be sanctioned; it must be contained, through ridicule if necessary, since it challenges the very notion of literature as a type of private property to be controlled by textual producers and their academic interpreters. Public attacks on media fans keep other viewers in line, making it uncomfortable for readers to adopt such inappropriate strategies. One woman recalled the negative impact popular representations of the fan had on her early cultural life:

> Journalists and photographers always went for the people furthest out of mainstream humanity … showing the reader the handicapped, the very obese, the strange and the childish in order to 'entertain' the 'average reader'. Of course, a teenager very unsure of herself and already labeled 'weird' would run in panic (Ludlow 1987, p. 17).

Such representations isolate potential fans from others who share common interests and reading practices and marginalise fan-related activities as outside the mainstream and beneath dignity. These same stereotypes reassure academic writers of the validity of their own interpretations of the program content, readings made in conformity with established critical protocols, and free them from any need to come into direct contact with the program's crazed followers.[3]

In this essay, I propose an alternative approach to fan experience, one that perceives 'Trekkers' (as they prefer to be called) not as cultural dupes, social misfits or mindless consumers but rather as, in de Certeau's term, 'poachers' of textual meanings. Behind the exotic stereotypes fostered by the media lies a largely unexplored terrain of cultural

activity, a subterranean network of readers and writers who remake programs in their own image. 'Fandom' is a vehicle for marginalised subcultural groups (women, the young, gays, etc.) to pry open space for their cultural concerns within dominant representations; it is a way of appropriating media texts and rereading them in a fashion that serves different interests, a way of transforming mass culture into a popular culture.

I do not believe this essay represents the last word on *Star Trek* fans, a cultural community that is far too multivocal to be open to easy description. Rather, I explore some aspects of current fan activity that seem particularly relevant to cultural studies. My primary concern is with what happens when these fans produce their own texts, texts that inflect program content with their own social experience and displace commercially produced commodities for a kind of popular economy. For these fans, *Star Trek* is not simply something that can be reread; it is something that can and must be rewritten in order to make it more responsive to their needs, in order to make it a better producer of personal meanings and pleasures.

No legalistic notion of literary property can adequately constrain the rapid proliferation of meanings surrounding a popular text. Yet, there are other constraints, ethical constraints and self-imposed rules, that are enacted by the fans, either individually or as part of a larger community, in response to their felt need to legitimate their unorthodox appropriation of mass media texts. E. P. Thompson (1971) suggests that eighteenth and nineteenth century peasant leaders, the historical poachers behind de Certeau's apt metaphor, responded to a kind of 'moral economy', an informal set of consensual norms that justified their uprisings against the landowners and tax collectors in order to restore a preexisting order being corrupted by its avowed protectors. Similarly, the fans often cast themselves not as poachers but as loyalists, rescuing essential elements of the primary text misused by those who maintain copyright control over the program materials. Respecting literary property even as they seek to appropriate it for their own uses, these fans become reluctant poachers, hesitant about their relationship to the program text, uneasy about the degree of manipulation they can legitimately perform on its materials, and policing each other for the abuses of their interpretive licence. They wander across a terrain pockmarked with confusions and contradictions. These ambiguities become transparent when fan writing is examined as a particular type of reader-text interaction. My discussion consequently has a double focus: first, I discuss how the fans force the primary text to accomodate their own interests, and then I reconsider the issue of literary property rights in light of the moral economy of the fan community.

Fans: from reading to writing

The popularity of *Star Trek* has motivated a wide range of cultural productions and creative reworkings of program materials: from children's backyard play to adult inter-action games, from needle-work to elaborate costumes, from private fantasies to computer programming. This abilty to transform personal reaction into social interaction, spectator culture into participatory culture, is one of the central characteristics of fandom. One becomes a fan not by being a regular viewer of a particular program but by translating that viewing into some type of cultural activity, by sharing feelings and thoughts about the program content with friends, by joining a community of other fans who share common interests. For fans, consumption sparks pro-duction, reading generates writing, until the terms seem logically inseperable. In fan writer Jean Lorrah's words (1984, p. 1)

> Trekfandom ... is friends and letters and crafts and fanzines and trivia and costumes and artwork and filksongs [fan parodies] and buttons and film clips and conventions – something for everybody who has in common the inspiration of a television show which grew far beyond its TV and film incarnations to become a living part of world culture.

Lorrah's description blurs all boundaries bet-ween producers and consumers, spectators and participants, the commercial and the home crafted, to construct an image of fandom as a cultural and social network that spans the globe.

Many fans characterise their entry into fandom in terms of a movement from social and cultural isolation, doubly imposed upon them as women within a patriarchal society and as seekers after alternative pleasures within dominant media representations, toward more and more active participation in a community receptive to their cultural productions, a community where they may feel a sense of belonging. One fan recalls:

> I met one girl who liked some of the TV shows I liked ... but I was otherwise a bookworm, no friends, working in the school library. Then my friend and I met some other girls a grade ahead of us but ga-ga over ST. From the beginning, we met each Friday night at one of the two homes that had a colour TV to watch *Star Trek* together ... Silence was mandatory except during commercials, and, afterwards, we 'discussed' each episode. We re-wrote each story and corrected the wrongs done to 'Our Guys' by the writers. We memorised bits of dialogue. We even started to write our own adventures. (Caruthers-Montgomery 1987, p. 8)

Some fans are drawn gradually from intimate interactions with others who live near them toward participation in a broader network of fans who attend regional, national and even international science fiction conventions. One fan writes of her first convention: 'I have been to so many conventions since those days, but this one was the ultimate experience. I walked into that Lunacon and felt like I had come home without ever realising I had been lost' (Deneroff 1987, p. 3). Another remarks simply, 'I met folks who were just as nuts as I was, I had a wonderful time' (Lay 1987, p. 15).

For some women, trapped within low-paying jobs or within the socially isolated sphere of the homemaker, participation with-in a national, or international, network of fans grants a degree of dignity and respect otherwise lacking. For others, fandom offers a training ground for the development of professional skills and an outlet for creative impulses constrained by their workday lives. Fan slang draws a sharp contrast between the mundane, the realm of everyday experience and those who dwell exclusively within that space, and fandom, an alternative sphere of cultural experience that restores the excitement and freedom that must be repressed to function in ordinary life. One fan writes, 'Not only does 'mundane' mean 'everyday life,' it is also a term used to describe narrow-minded, pettiness, judgemental, conformity, and a shallow and silly nature. It is used by people who feel very alienated from society' (Osborne 1987, p. 4). To enter fandom is to escape from the mundane into the marvelous.

The need to maintain contact with these new friends, often scattered over a broad geographic area, can require that speculations and fantasies about the program content take written form, first as personal letters and later as more public newsletters, 'letterzines' or fan fiction magazines. Fan viewers become fan writers.

Over the 20 years since *Star Trek* was first aired, fan writing has achieved a semi-institutional status. Fan magazines, sometimes hand typed, photo-copied and stapled, other times offset printed and commercially bound, are distributed through the mails and sold at conventions, frequently reaching an international readership. *Writer's Digest* (Cooper 1987) recently estimated that there were more than 300 amateur press publications that regularly allowed fans to explore aspects of their favorite films and television programs. Although a wide variety of different media texts have sparked some fan writing, including *Star Wars*, *Blake's Seven*, *Battlestar Galactica*, *Doctor Who*, *Miami Vice*, *Road Warrior*, *Remington Steele*, *The Man From U.N.C.L.E.*, *Simon and Simon*, *The A-Team* and *Hill Street Blues*, *Star Trek* continues to play the central role within fan writing. *Datazine*, one of several magazines that serve as central clearing houses for information about fanzines, lists some 120 different *Star Trek*-centred publications in distribution. Although fanzines may take a variety of forms, fans generally divide them into two major categories: 'letterzines' that publish short articles and letters from fans on issues surrounding their favorite shows and 'fictionzines' that publish short stories, poems, and novels concerning the program characters and concepts.[4] Some fan-produced novels, notably the works of Jean Lorrah (1976a, 1978) and Jacqueline Lichtenberg (1976), have achieved a canonised status in the fan community, remaining more or less in constant demand for more than a decade.[5]

It is important to be careful in distinguishing between these fan-generated materials and commercially produced works, such as the series of *Star Trek* novels released by Pocket Books under the official supervision of Para-

mount, the studio that owns the rights to the *Star Trek* characters. Fanzines are totally unauthorised by the program producers and face the constant threat of legal action for their open violation of the producer's copyright authority over the show's characters and concepts. Paramount has tended to treat fan magazines with benign neglect as long as they are handled on an exclusively nonprofit basis. Producer Gene Roddenberry and many of the cast members have contributed to such magazines. Bantam Books even released several anthologies showcasing the work of *Star Trek* fan writers (Marshak & Culbreath 1978).

Other producers have not been as kind. Lucasfilm initially sought to control *Star Wars* fan publications, seeing them as a rival to its officially sponsored fan organisation, and later threatened to prosecute editors who published works that violated the 'family values' associated with the original films. Such a scheme has met considerable resistance from the fan community that generally regards Lucas' actions as unwarranted interference in its own creative activity. Several fanzine editors have continued to distribute adult-oriented *Star Wars* stories through an underground network of special friends, even though such works are no longer publicly advertised through *Datazine* or sold openly at conventions. A heated editorial in *Slaysu*, a fanzine that routinely published feminist-inflected erotica set in various media universes, reflects these writers' opinions:

Lucasfilm is saying, 'you must enjoy the characters of the *Star Wars* universe for male reasons. Your sexuality must be correct and proper by my (male) definition.' I am not male. I do not want to be. I refuse to be a poor imitation, or worse, someone's idiotic ideal of feminity. Lucasfilm has said, in essence, 'this is what we see in the *Star Wars* films and we are telling you that this is what you will see. (Siebert 1982, p. 44)

C. A. Siebert's editorial asserts the rights of fanzine writers to consciously revise the character of the original texts, to draw elements from dominant culture in order to produce underground art that explicitly challenges patriarchal assumptions. Siebert and the other editors deny the traditional property rights of textual producers in favour of a right of free play with the program materials, a right of readers to use media texts in their own ways and of writers to reconstruct characters in their own terms. Once characters are inserted into popular discourse, regardless of their source of origin, they become the property of the fans who fantasise about them, not the copyright holders who merchandise them. Yet the relationship between fan texts and primary texts is often more complex than Siebert's defiant stance might suggest, and some fans do feel bound by a degree of fidelity to the original series' conceptions of those characters and their interactions.

Gender and writing

Fan writing is an almost exclusively feminine response to mass media texts. Men actively participate in a wide range of fan-related activities, notably interactive games and conference-planning committees, roles consistent with patriarchal norms that typically relegate combat – even combat fantasies – and organisational authority to the masculine sphere. Fan writers and fanzine readers, however, are almost always female. Camille Bacon-Smith (1986) has estimated that more than 90 percent of all fan writers are female. The greatest percentage of male participation is found in the 'letterzines,' like *Comlink* and *Treklink*, and in 'nonfiction' magazines, like *Trek* that publish speculative essays on aspects of the program universe. Men may feel comfortable joining discussions of future technologies or military lifestyle but not in pondering Vulcan sexuality, McCoy's childhood, or Kirk's love life.

Why this predominance of women within the fan writing community? Research suggests that men and women have been socialised to read for different purposes and in different ways. David Bleich (1986) asked a mixed group of college students to comment, in a free association fashion, on a body of canonised literary works. His analysis of their responses suggests that men focused primarily on narrative organisation and authorial intent while women devoted more energy to reconstructing the textual world and understanding the characters. He writes, 'Women enter the world of the novel, take it as something 'there' for that purpose; men see the novel as a result of someone's action and construe its meaning or logic in those terms' (p. 239). In a related study,

Bleich asked some 120 University of Indiana freshmen to 'retell as fully and as accurately as you can [William] Faulkner's 'Barn Burning'' (p. 255) and, again, notes substantial differences between men and women:

The men retold the story as if the purpose was to deliver a clear simple structure or chain of information: these are the main characters, this is the main action, this is how it turned out ... The women present the narrative as if it were an atmosphere or an experience (p. 256).

Bleich finds that women were more willing to enjoy free play with the story content, making inferences about character relationships that took them well beyond the information explicitly contained within the text. Such data strongly suggest that the practice of fan writing, the compulsion to expand speculations about characters and story events beyond textual boundaries, draws heavily upon the types of interpretive strategies more common to the feminine than to the masculine.

Bleich's observations provide only a partial explanation, since they do not fully account for why many women find it necessary to go beyond the narrative information while most men do not. As Teresa de Lauretis (1982, p. 106) points out, female characters often exist only in the margins of male-centered narratives:

Medusa and the Sphinx, like the other ancient monsters, have survived inscribed in hero narratives, in someone else's story, not their own; so they are figures or markers of positions – places and topoi – through which the hero and his story move to their destination and to accomplish meaning.

Texts written by and for men yield easy pleasures to their male readers, yet may resist feminine pleasure. To fully enjoy the text, women are often forced to perform a type of intellectual transvesticism, identifying with male characters in opposition to their own cultural experiences or to construct unwritten counter-texts through their daydreams or through their oral interaction with other women that allow them to explore their own narrative concerns. This need to reclaim feminine interests from the margins of masculine texts produces endless speculation, speculation that draws the reader well beyond textual boundaries into the domain of the intertextual. Mary Ellen Brown and Linda Barwick (1987) show how women's gossip about soap opera inserts program content into an existing feminine oral culture. Fan writing represents the logical next step in this cultural process: the transformation of oral countertexts into a more tangible form, the translation of verbal speculations into written works that can be shared with a broader circle of women. In order to do so, the women's status must change; no longer simply spectators, these women become textual producers.

Just as women's gossip about soap operas assumes a place within a preexisting feminine oral culture, fan writing adopts forms and functions traditional to women's literary culture. Cheris Kramarae (1981, pp. 3–4) traces the history of women's efforts to 'find ways to express themselves outside the dominant modes of expression used by men', to circumvent the ideologically constructed interpretive strategies of masculine literary genres. Kramarae concludes that women have found the greatest room to explore their feelings and ideas within privately circulated letters and diaries and through collective writing projects. Similarly, Carroll Smith-Rosenberg (1985) discusses the ways that the exchange of letters allowed nineteenth century women to maintain close ties with other women, even when separated by great geographic distances and isolated within the narrow confines of Victorian marriage. Such letters provided a covert vehicle for women to explore common concerns and even ridicule the men in their lives. Smith-Rosenberg (p. 45) concludes:

Nineteenth-century women were, as Nathaniel Hawthorne reminds us, 'damned scribblers'. They spoke endlessly to one another in private letters and journals … about religion, gender roles, their sexuality and men's, about prostitution, seduction and intemperance, about unwanted pregnancies and desired education, about their relation to the family and the family's to the world.

Fan writing, with its circulation conducted largely through the mails, with its marketing mostly a matter of word of mouth, with the often collective construction of fantasy universes, and with its highly confessional tone, clearly follows within that same tradition and serves some of

the same functions. The readymade characters of popular culture provide these women with a set of common references for discussing their similar experiences and feelings with others with whom they may never have enjoyed face-to-face contact. They draw upon these shared points of reference to confront many of the same issues that concerned nineteenth-century women: religion, gender roles, sexuality, family and professional ambition.

Why Star Trek?

While most texts within a male-dominated culture presumably have the capacity to spark some sort of feminine countertext, only certain programs have generated the type of extended written responses characteristic of fandom. Why, then, has the bulk of fan writing centred around science fiction, a genre that Judith Spector (1986, p. 163) argues until recently has been hostile toward women, a genre 'by, for and about men of action'? Why has it also engaged other genres like science fiction (the cop show, the detective drama or the western) that have represented the traditional domain of male readers? Why do these women struggle to reclaim such seemingly unfertile soil when there are so many other texts that more traditionally reflect feminine interests and that feminist media critics are now trying to reclaim for their cause? In short, why *Star Trek*?

Obviously, no single factor can adequately account for all fanzines, a literary form that necessarily involves the translation of homogeneous media texts into a plurality of personal and subcultural responses. One partial explanation, however, might be that traditionally feminine texts (the soap opera, the popular romance, the 'women's picture', etc.) do not need as much reworking as science fiction and westerns in order to accommodate the social experience of women. The resistance of such texts to feminist reconstruction may require a greater expenditure of creative effort and therefore may push women toward a more thorough reworking of program materials than so-called feminine texts that can be more easily assimilated or negated.

Another explanation might be that these so-called feminine texts satisfy, at least partially, the desires of traditional women yet fail to meet the needs of more professionally-oriented women. A particular fascination of *Star Trek* for

the science fiction film reader

these women appears to be rooted in the way that the program seems to hold out a suggestion of nontraditional feminine pleasures, of greater and more active involvement for women within the adventure of professional space travel, while finally reneging on those promises. Sexual equality was an essential component of producer Roddenberry's optimistic vision of the future; a woman, Number One (Majel Barrett), was originally slated to be the Enterprise's second in command. Network executives, however, consistently fought efforts to break with traditional feminine stereotypes, fearing the alienation of more conservative audience members (Whitfield & Roddenberry 1968). Number One was scratched after the program pilot, but throughout the run of the series women were often cast in nontraditional jobs, everything from Romulan commanders to weapon specialists. The networks, however reluctantly, were offering women a future, a 'final frontier' that included them.

Fan writers, though, frequently express dissatisfaction with these women's characterisations within the episodes. In the words of fan writer Pamela Rose (1977, p. 48), 'When a woman is a guest star on Star Trek, nine out of ten times there is something wrong with her.' Rose notes that these female characters have been granted positions of power within the program, only to demonstrate through their erratic emotion-driven conduct that women are unfit to fill such roles. Another fan writer, Toni Lay (1986, p. 15), expresses mixed feelings about Star Trek's social vision:

It was ahead of its time in some ways, like showing that a Caucasian, all-American, all-male crew was not the only possibility for space travel. Still, the show was sadly deficient in other ways, in particular, its treatment of women. Most of the time, women were referred to as 'girls'. And women were never shown in a position of authority unless they were aliens, i.e., Deela, T'Pau, Natira, Sylvia, etc. It was like the show was saying 'equal opportunity is OK for their women but not for our girls'.

Lay states that she felt 'devastated' over the repeated failure of the series and the later feature films to give Lieutenant Penda Uhura command duties commensurate with her rank: 'When the going gets tough, the tough leave the

women-folk behind' (p. 15). She contends that Uhura and the other women characters should have been given a chance to demonstrate what they could do when confronted by the same types of problems that their male counterparts so heroically overcome. The constant availability of the original episodes through reruns and shifts in the status of women within American society throughout the past two decades have only made these unfulfilled promises more difficult to accept, requiring progressively greater efforts to restructure the program in order to allow it to produce pleasures appropriate to the current reception context.

Indeed, many fan writers characterise themselves as 'repairing the damage' caused by the program's inconsistent and often demeaning treatment of its female characters. Jane Land (1986, p. 1), for instance, characterises her fan novel, Kista, as 'an attempt to rescue one of Star Trek's female characters [Christine-Chapel] from an artificially imposed case of foolishness'. Promising to show 'the way the future never was', The Woman's List, a recently established fanzine with an explicitly feminist orientation, has called for 'material dealing with all range of possibilities for women, including: women of colour, lesbians, women of alien cultures, and women of all ages and backgrounds'. Its editors acknowledge that their publication's project necessarily involves telling the types of stories that network policy blocked from airing when the series was originally produced. A recent flier for that publication explains:

We hope to raise and explore those questions which the network censors, the television genre, and the prevailing norms of the time made it difficult to address. We believe that both the nature of human interaction and sexual mores and the structure of both families and relationships will have changed by the twenty-third century and we are interested in exploring those changes.

Telling such stories requires the stripping away of stereotypically feminine traits. The series characters must be reconceptualised in ways that suggest hidden motivations and interests heretofore unsuspected. They must be reshaped into full-blooded feminist role models. While, in the series, Chapel is defined almost exclusively in terms of her unrequited passion for Spock and her professional sub-servience to Dr. McCoy, Land represents her as a fiercely independent woman, capable of accepting love only on her own terms, ready to pursue her own ambitions wherever they take her, and outspoken in response to the patronising attitudes of the command crew. Siebert (1980, p. 33) has performed a similar operation on the character of Lieutenant Uhura, as this passage from one of her stories suggests:

> There were too few men like Spock who saw her as a person. Even Captain Kirk, she smiled, especially Captain Kirk, saw her as a woman first. He let her do certain things but only because military discipline required it. Whenever there was any danger, he tried to protect her ... Uhura smiled sadly, she would go on as she had been, outwardly a feminine toy, inwardly a woman who was capable and human.

Here, Siebert attempts to resolve the apparent contradiction created within the series text by Uhura's official status as a command officer and her constant displays of 'feminine frailty'. Uhura's situation, Siebert suggests, is characteristic of the way that women must mask their actual competency behind traditionally feminine mannerisms within a world dominated by patriarchal assumptions and masculine authority. By rehabilitating Uhura's character in this fashion, Siebert has constructed a vehicle through which she can document the overt and subtle forms of sexual discrimination that an ambitious and determined woman faces as she struggles for a command post in Star Fleet (or for that matter, within a twentieth-century corporate board room).

Fan writers like Siebert, Land and Karen Bates (1982; 1983; 1984), whose novels explore the progression of a Chapel-Spock marriage through many of the problems encountered by contemporary couples trying to juggle the conflicting demands of career and family, speak directly to the concerns of professional women in a way that more traditionally feminine works fail to do.[6] These writers create situations where Chapel and Uhura must heroically overcome the same types of obstacles that challenge their male counterparts within the primary texts and often discuss directly the types of personal and professional problems particular to working women. Land's recent fan novel, *Demeter* (1987), is exemplary in its

treatment of the professional life of its central character, Nurse Chapel. Land deftly melds action sequences with debates about gender relations and professional discrimination, images of command decisions with intimate glimpses of a Spock-Chapel marriage. An all-woman crew, headed by Uhura and Chapel, are dispatched on a mission to a feminist separatist space colony under siege from a pack of intergalactic drug smugglers who regard rape as a manly sport. In helping the colonists to overpower their would-be assailants, the women are at last given a chance to demonstrate their professional competence under fire and force Captain Kirk to reevaluate some of his command policies. *Demeter* raises significant questions about the possibilities of male-female interaction outside of patriarchal dominance. The meeting of a variety of different planetary cultures that represent alternative social philosophies and organisations, alternative ways of coping with the same essential debates surrounding sexual difference, allows for a far-reaching exploration of contemporary gender relations.

From space opera to soap opera

If works like *Demeter* constitute intriguing prototypes for a new breed of feminist popular literature, they frequently do so within conventions borrowed as much from more traditionally feminine forms of mass culture as from *Star Trek* itself. For one thing, the female fans perceive the individual episodes as contributing to one great program text. As a result, fan stories often follow the format of a continuous serial rather than operating as a series of self-enclosed works. Tania Modleski (1982) demonstrates the ways that the serial format of much women's fiction, particularly of soap operas, responds to the rhythms of women's social experience. The shaky financing characteristic of the fanzine mode of production, the writers' predilections to engage in endless speculations about the program content and to continually revise their understanding of the textual world, amplifies the tendency of women's fiction to postpone resolution, transforming *Star Trek* into a never-ending story. Fan fiction marches forward through a series of digressions as new speculations cause the writers to halt the advance of their chronicles, to introduce events that must have occurred prior to the start of their stories, or to introduce secondary plot lines that pull them from the main movement of the event chain. This type of writing activity has been labeled a 'story tree'. Bacon-Smith (1986, p. 26) explains:

> The most characteristic feature of the story tree is that the stories do not fall in a linear sequence. A root story may offer unresolved situations, secondary characters whose actions during the main events are not described or a resolution is unsatisfactory to some readers. Writers then branch out from that story, completing dropped subplots, exploring the reactions of minor characters to major events.

This approach, characteristic of women's writing in a number of cultures, stems from a sense of life as continuous rather than fragmented into a series of discrete events, from an outlook that is experience centred and not goal oriented: 'Closure doesn't make sense to them. At the end of the story, characters go on living in the nebulous world of the not yet written. They develop, modify their relationships over time, age, raise families' (p. 28).

Moreover, as Bacon-Smith's comments suggest, this type of reading and writing strategy focuses greater attention on ongoing character relationships than on more temporally concentrated plot elements. Long-time fan writer Lichtenberg (personal communication, August 1987) summarises the difference: 'Men want a physical problem with physical action leading to a physical resolution. Women want a psychological problem with psychological action leading to a psychological resolution'. These women express a desire for narratives that concentrate on the character relationships and explore them in a 'realistic' or 'mature' fashion rather than in purely formulaic terms, stories that are 'true' and 'believable' and not 'syrupy' or 'sweet'. Fan writers seek to satisfy these demands through their own *Star Trek* fiction, to write the type of stories that they and other fans desire to read.

The result is a type of genre switching, the rereading and rewriting of 'space opera' as an exotic type of romance (and, often, the reconceptualisation of romance itself as feminist fiction). Fanzines rarely publish exclusively action-oriented stories glorifying the Enterprise's victories over the Klingon-Romulan Alliance, its conquest of alien creatures, its restructuring of planetary governments, or its repair of potential flaws in new technologies, despite the prevalence of such plots in the original episodes. When such elements do appear, they are usually evoked as a background against which the more typical romance or relationship-centred stories are played or as a test through which female protagonists can demonstrate their professional skills. In doing so, these fan writers draw inspiration from feminist science fiction writers, including Johanna Russ, Marion Zimmer Bradley, Zenna Henderson, Marge Piercy, Andre Norton and Ursula Leguin. These writers' entry into the genre in the late 1960s and early 1970s helped to redefine reader expectations about what constituted science fiction, pushing the genre toward greater and greater interest in soft science and sociological concerns and increased attention on interpersonal relationships and gender roles.[7] *Star Trek*, produced in a period when masculine concerns still dominated science fiction, is reconsidered in light of the newer, more feminist orientation of the genre, becoming less a program about the Enterprise's struggles against the Klingon-Romulan Alliance and more an examination of a character's efforts to come to grips with conflicting emotional needs and professional responsibilities.

Women, confronting a traditionally masculine space opera, choose to read it instead as a type of women's fiction. In constructing their own stories about the series characters, they turn frequently to the more familiar and comfortable formulas of the soap, the romance, and the feminist coming-of-age novel for models of storytelling technique. While the fans themselves often dismiss such genres as too focused upon mundane concerns to be of great interest, the influence of such materials may be harder to escape. As Elizabeth Segel (1986) suggests, our initial introduction to reading, the gender-based designation of certain books as suitable for young girls and others for young boys, can be a powerful determinant of our later reading and writing strategies, determining, in part, the relative accessibility of basic genre models for use in making sense of ready-made texts and for constructing personal fantasies. As fans attempt to reconstruct the feminine countertexts that exist on the margins of the original series episodes, they, in the process, refocus the series around traditional feminine and contemporary feminist concerns, around sexuality and gender politics, around religion, family, marriage and romance.

Many fans' first stories take the form of romantic fantasies about the series characters and frequently involve inserting glorified versions of themselves into the world of Star Fleet. The Bethann (1976, p. 54) story, 'The Measure of Love', for instance, deals with a young woman, recently transferred to the Enterprise, who has a love affair with Kirk:

We went to dinner that evening. Till that time, I was sure he'd never really noticed me. Sitting across the table from him, I realised just what a vital alive person this man was. I had dreamed of him, but never imagined my hopes might become a reality. But, this was real – not a dream. His eyes were intense, yet they twinkled in an amused sort of way.
'Captain…'
'Call me Jim.'

Her romance with Kirk comes to an abrupt end when the young woman transfers to another ship without telling the Captain that she carries his child because she does not want her love to interfere with his career.

Fans are often harshly critical of these so-called 'Lieutenant Mary Sue' stories, which one writer labels 'groupie fantasies' (Hunter 1977, p. 78), because of their self-indulgence, their often hackneyed writing styles, their formulaic plots, and their violations of the established characterisations. In reconstituting *Star Trek* as a popular romance, these young women reshape the series characters into traditional romantic heroes, into 'someone who is intensely and exclusively interested in her and in her needs' (Radway 1984, p. 149). Yet, many fan writers are more interested in what happens when this romantic ideal confronts a world that places professional duty over personal needs, when men and women must somehow reconcile careers and marriage in a confusing period of shifting gender relationships. Veteran fan writer Kendra Hunter (1977, p. 78) writes, 'Kirk is not going to go off into the sunset with anyone because he is owned body and soul by the Enterprise.' *Treklink* editor Joan Verba (1986, p. 2) comments, 'No believable character is gushed over by so many normally level-headed characters such as Kirk and Spock as a typical

Mary Sue.' Nor are the women of tomorrow apt to place any man, even Jim Kirk, totally above all other concerns.

Some, though by no means all, of the most sophisticated fan fiction also takes the form of the romance. Both Radway (1984) and Modleski (1982) note popular romances' obsession with a semiotics of masculinity, with the need to read men's often repressed emotional states from the subtle signs of outward gesture and expression. The cold logic of Vulcan, the desire to suppress all signs of emotion, make Spock and Sarek especially rich for such interpretations as in the following passage from Lorrah's *Full Moon Rising* (1976b, pp. 9–10):

The intense sensuality she saw in him [Sarek] in other ways suggested a hidden sexuality. She had noticed everything from the way he appreciated the beauty of a moonlit night or a finely-cut sapphire to the way his strongly-molded hands caressed the mellowed leather binding of the book she had given him … That incredible control which she could not penetrate. Sometimes he deliberately let her see beyond it, as he had done earlier this evening, but if she succeeded in making him lose control he would never be able to forgive her.

In Lorrah's writings, the alienness of Vulcan culture becomes a metaphor for the many things that separate men and women, for the factors that prevent intimacy within marriage. She describes her fiction as the story of 'two people who are different physically, mentally and emotionally, but who nonetheless manage to make a pretty good marriage' (p. 2). While Vulcan restraint suggests the emotional sterility of traditional masculinity, their alien sexuality allows Lorrah to propose alternatives. Her Vulcans find sexual inequality to be illogical and allow for very little difference in the treatment of men and women. (This is an assumption shared by many fan writers.) Moreover, the Vulcan mindmeld grants a degree of sexual and emotional intimacy unknown on earth; Vulcan men even employ this power to relieve women of labour pains and to share the experience of childbirth. Her lengthy writings on the decades-long romance between Amanda and Sarek represent a painstaking effort to construct a feminist utopia, to propose how traditional marriage might be reworked to allow it to satisfy the personal and professional needs of both men and women.

Frequently, the fictional formulas of popular romance are tempered by women's common social experiences as lovers, wives and mothers under patriarchy. In Bates' novels, Nurse Chapel must confront and overcome her feelings of abandonment and jealousy during those long periods of time when her husband, Spock, is deeply absorbed in his work. *Starweaver Two* (1982, p. 10) describes this pattern:

> The pattern had been repeated so often, it was ingrained ... Days would pass without a word between them because of the hours he laboured and pored over his computers. Their shifts rarely matched and the few hours they could be together disappeared for one reason or another.

Far from an idyllic romance, Bates' characters struggle to make their marriage work in a world where professionalism is everything and the personal counts for relatively little. Land's version of a Chapel/Spock marriage is complicated by the existence of children who must remain at home under the care of Sarek and Amanda while their parents pursue their space adventures. In one scene, Chapel confesses her confused feelings about this situation to a young Andorian friend: 'I spend my life weighing the children's needs against my needs against Spock's needs, and at any given time I know I'm shortchanging someone' (1987, p. 27).

While some male fans denigrate these types of fan fiction as 'soap operas with Kirk and Spock' (Blaes 1986, p. 6), these women see themselves as constructing soap operas with a difference, soap operas that reflect a feminist vision. In Siebert's words (1982, pp. 44–5), 'I write erotic stories for myself and for other women who will not settle for being less than human'. Siebert suggests that her stories about Uhura and her struggle for recognition and romance in a male-dominated Star Fleet have helped her to resolve her own conflicting feelings within a world of changing gender relations and to explore hidden aspects of her own sexuality. Through her erotica, she hopes to increase other women's awareness of the need to struggle against entrenched patriarchal norms. Unlike their counterparts in Harlequin romances, these women refuse to accept marriage and the love of a man as their primary goal. Their stories push toward resolutions that allow Chapel or Uhura to achieve both professional advancement and personal satisfaction. Unlike almost every other form of popular fiction, fanzine stories frequently explore the maturing of relationships beyond the nuptial vows, seeing marriage as continually open to new adventures, new conflicts and new discoveries.

The point of contact between feminism and the popular romance is largely a product of these writers' particular brand of feminism, one that, for the most part, is closer to the views of Betty Friedan than to those of Andrea Dworkin. It is a feminism that urges a sharing of feelings and lifestyles between men and women rather than radical separation or unresolvable differences. It is a literature of reform, not of revolt. The women still acknowledge their need for the companionship of men, for men who care for them and make them feel special, even as they are asking for those relationships to be conducted in different terms. Land's Nurse Chapel, who in *Demeter* is both fascinated and repelled by the feminist separatist colony, reflects these women's ambiguous and sometimes contradictory responses toward more radical forms of feminism. In the end, Chapel recognises the potential need for such a place, for a 'room of one's own', yet sees greater potential in achieving a more liberated relationship between men and women. She learns to develop self-sufficiency, yet chooses to share her life with her husband, Spock, and to achieve a deeper understanding of their differing expectations about their relationship. Each writer grapples with these concerns in her own terms, yet most achieve some compromise between the needs of women for independence and self-sufficiency on the one hand and their needs for romance and companionship on the other. If this does not constitute a radical break with the romance formula, it does represent a progressive re-formulation of that formula which pushes toward a gradual redefinition of existing gender roles within marriage and the work place.

The moral economy of fan fiction

Their underground status allows fan writers the creative freedom to promote a range of different interpretations of the basic program material and a variety of reconstructions of marginalised characters and interests, to explore a diversity of different solutions to the dilemma of contemporary gender relations. Fandom's IDIC philosophy (Infinite Diversity in Infinite Combinations, a cornerstone of Vulcan thought) actively encourages its participants to explore and find pleasure within their different and often contradictory responses to the program text. It should not be forgotten, however, that fan writing involves a translation of personal response into a social expression and that fans, like any other interpretive community, generate their own norms that work to insure a reasonable degree of conformity between readings of the primary text. The economic risk of fanzine publishing and the desire for personal popularity insures some responsiveness to audience demand, discouraging totally idiosyncratic versions of the program content. Fans try to write stories to please other fans; lines of development that do not find popular support usually cannot achieve financial viability.

Moreover, the strange mixture of fascination and frustration characteristic of fan response means that fans continue to respect the creators of the original series, even as they wish to rework some program materials to better satisfy their personal interests. Their desire to revise the program material is often counter-balanced by their desire to remain faithful to those aspects of the show that first captured their interests. E. P. Thompson (1971, p. 78) has employed the term 'moral economy' to describe the way that eighteenth-century peasant leaders and street rioters legitimised their revolts through an appeal to 'traditional rights and customs' and 'the wider consensus of the community', asserting that their actions worked to protect existing property rights against those who sought to abuse them for their own gain. The peasants' conception of a moral economy allowed them to claim for themselves the right to judge the legitimacy both of their own actions and those of the landowners and property holders: 'Consensus was so strong that it overrode motives of fear or deference' (pp. 78–9).

An analogous situation exists in fandom: the fans respect the original texts, yet fear that their conceptions of the characters and concepts may be jeopardised by those who wish to exploit them for easy profits, a

category that typically includes Paramount and the network but excludes Roddenberry and many of the show's writers. The ideology of fandom involves both a commitment to some degree of conformity to the original program materials as well as a perceived right to evaluate the legitimacy of any use of those materials, either by textual producers or by textual consumers. The fans perceive themselves as rescuing the show from its producers who have manhandled its characters and then allowed it to die. In one fan's words, 'I think we have made ST uniquely our own, so we do have all the right in the world (universe) to try to change it for the better when the gang at Paramount starts worshipping the almighty dollar, as they are wont to do' (Schnuelle, 1987, p. 9). Rather than rewriting the series content, the fans claim to be keeping *Star Trek* alive in the face of network indifference and studio incompetence, of remaining true to the text that first captured their interest some 20 years before: 'This relationship came into being because the fan writers loved the characters and cared about the ideas that are *Star Trek* and they refused to let it fade away into oblivion' (Hunter 1977, p. 77).

Such a relationship obligates fans to preserve a certain degree of fidelity to program materials, even as they seek to rework them toward their own ends. *Trek* magazine contributor Kendra Hunter (1977, p. 83) writes, '*Trek* is a format for expressing rights, opinions and ideals. Most every imaginable idea can be expressed through *Trek* ... But there is a right way.' Gross infidelity to the series concepts constitutes what fans call 'character rape' and falls outside of the community's norms. In Hunter's words (p. 75):

A writer, either professional or amateur, must realise that she ... is not omnipotent. She cannot force her characters to do as she pleases ... The writer must have respect for her characters or those created by others that she is using, and have a full working knowledge of each before committing her words to paper.

Hunter's conception of character rape, one widely shared within the fan community, rejects abuses by the original series writers as well as by the most novice fan. It implies that the fans themselves, not the program producers, are best qualified to arbitrate conflicting claims about character psychology because they care about the characters in a way that more commercially motivated parties frequently do not. In practice, the concept of character rape frees fans to reject large chunks of the aired material, including entire episodes, and even to radically restructure the concerns of the show in the name of defending the purity of the original series concept. What determines the range of permissible fan narratives is finally not fidelity to the original texts but consensus within the fan community itself. The text that they so lovingly preserve is the *Star Trek* that they created through their own speculations, not the one that Roddenberry produced for network air play.

Consequently, the fan community continually debates what constitutes a legitimate reworking of program materials and what represents a violation of the special reader-text relationship that the fans hope to foster. The earliest *Star Trek* fan writers were careful to work within the framework of the information explicitly included within the broadcast episodes and to minimise their breaks with series conventions. In fan writer Jean Lorrah's words (1976a, p.1), 'Anyone creating a Star Trek universe is bound by what was seen in the aired episodes; however, he is free to extrapolate from those episodes to explain what was seen in them.' Leslie Thompson (1974, p. 208) explains, 'If the reasoning [of fan speculations] doesn't fit into the framework of the events as given [on the program], then it cannot apply no matter how logical or detailed it may be.' As *Star Trek* fan writing has come to assume an institutional status in its own right and therefore to require less legitimisation through appeals to textual fidelity, a new conception of fan fiction has emerged, one that perceives the stories not as a necessary expansion of the original series text but rather as chronicles of alternate universes, similar to the program world in some ways and different in others:

The 'alternate universe' is a handy concept wherein you take the basic *Star Trek* concept and spin it off into all kinds of ideas that could never be aired. One reason Paramount may be so liberal about fanzines is that by their very nature most fanzine stories could never be sold professionally. (L. Slusher, personal communication, August 1987)

Such an approach frees the writers to engage in much broader play with the program concepts and characterisations, to produce stories that reflect more diverse visions of human interrelationships and future worlds, to rewrite elements within the primary texts that hinder fan interests. Yet, even alternate universe stories struggle to maintain some consistency with the original broadcast material and to establish some point of contact with existing fan interests, just as more faithful fan writers feel compelled to rewrite and revise the program material in order to keep it alive in a new cultural context.

Borrowed terms: Kirk/Spock stories

The debate in fan circles surrounding Kirk/Spock (K/S) fiction, stories that posit a homoerotic relationship between the show's two primary characters and frequently offer detailed accounts of their sexual couplings, illustrates these differing conceptions of the relationship between fan fiction and the primary series text.[8] Over the past decade, K/S stories have emerged from the margins of fandom toward numerical dominance over *Star Trek* fan fiction, a movement that has been met with considerable opposition from more traditional fans. For many, such stories constitute the worst form of character rape, a total violation of the established characterisations. Kendra Hunter (1977, p. 81) argues that 'it is out of character for both men, and as such comes across in the stories as bad writing ... A relationship as complex and deep as Kirk/Spock does not climax with a sexual relationship.' Other fans agree but for other reasons. 'I do not accept the K/S homosexual precept as plausible', writes one fan. 'The notion that two men that are as close as Kirk and Spock and cannot be 'just friends' is indefensible to me' (Landers 1986, p. 10). Others struggle to reconcile the information provided on the show with their own assumptions about the nature of human sexuality: 'It is just as possible for their friendship to progress into a love-affair, for that is what it is, than to remain status quo ... Most of us see Kirk and Spock simply as two people who love each other and just happen to be of the same gender' (Snaider 1987, p. 10).

Some K/S fans frankly acknowledge the gap between the series characterisations and their own representations yet refuse to allow their fantasy life to be governed by the limitations of what was actually aired. One fan writes, 'While I read K/S and enjoy it, when you stop to review the two main characters of *Star Trek* as extrapolated from the TV series, a sexual relationship between them is absurd' (Chandler, 1987, p. 10). Another argues somewhat differently:

> We actually saw a very small portion of the lives of the Enterprise crew through 79 episodes and some six hours of movies … How can we possibly define the entire personalities of Kirk, Spock, etc., if we only go by what we've seen on screen? Surely there is more to them than that! … Since I doubt any two of us would agree on a definition of what is 'in character', I leave it to the skill of the writer to make the reader believe in the story she is trying to tell. There isn't any limit to what could be depicted as accurate behaviour for our heroes. (Moore 1986, p. 7)

Many fans find this bold rejection of program limitations on creative activity, this open appropriation of characters, to be unacceptable since it violates the moral economy of fan writing and threatens fan fiction's privileged relationship to the primary text:

> [If] 'there isn't any limit to what could be depicted as accurate behaviour of our heroes', we might well have been treated to the sight of Spock shooting up heroin or Kirk raping a yeoman on the bridge (or vice-versa) … The writer whose characters don't have clearly defined personalities, thus limits and idiosyncrasies and definite characteristics, is the writer who is either very inexperienced or who doesn't have any respect for his characters, not to mention his audience. (Slusher 1986, p. 11)

Yet, I have shown, all fan writing necessarily involves an appropriation of series characters and a reworking of program concepts as the text is forced to respond to the fan's own social agenda and interpretive strategies. What K/S does openly, all fans do covertly. In constructing the feminine countertext that lurks in the margins of the primary text, these readers necessarily redefine the text in the process of rereading and rewriting it.

As one fan acknowledges, 'If K/S has 'created new characters and called them by old names', then all of fandom is guilty of the same' (Moore 1986, p. 7). Jane Land (1987, p. ii) agrees: 'All writers alter and transform the basic *Trek* universe to some extent, choosing some things to emphasise and others to play down, filtering the characters and the concepts through their own perceptions.'

If these fans have rewritten *Star Trek* in their own terms, however, many of them are reluctant to break all ties to the primary text that sparked their creative activity and, hence, feel the necessity to legitimate their activity through appeals to textual fidelity. The fans are uncertain how far they can push against the limitations of the original material without violating and finally destroying a relationship that has given them great pleasure. Some feel stifled by those constraints; others find comfort within them. Some claim the program as their personal property, 'treating the series episodes like silly putty', as one fan put it (Blaes 1987, p. 6). Others seek compromises with the textual producers, treating the original program as something shared between them.

What should be remembered is that whether they cast themselves as rebels or loyalists, it is the fans themselves who are determining what aspects of the original series concept are binding on their play with the program material and to what degree. The fans have embraced *Star Trek* because they found its vision somehow compatible with their own, and they have assimilated only those textual materials that feel comfortable to them. Whenever a choice must be made between fidelity to their program and fidelity to their own social norms, it is almost inevitably made in favour of lived experience. The women's conception of the *Star Trek* realm as inhabited by psychologically rounded and realistic characters insures that no characterisation that violated their own social perceptions could be satisfactory. The reason some fans reject K/S fiction has, in the end, less to do with the stated reason that it violates established characterisation than with unstated beliefs about the nature of human sexuality that determine what types of character conduct can be viewed as plausible. When push comes to shove, as Hodge and Tripp (1986, p. 144) recently suggested, 'Non-televisual meanings can swamp televisual meanings' and usually do.

the science fiction film reader

Conclusion

The fans are reluctant poachers who steal only those things that they truly love, who seize televisual property only to protect it against abuse by those who created it and who have claimed ownership over it. In embracing popular texts, the fans claim those works as their own, remaking them in their own image, forcing them to respond to their needs and to gratify their desires. Female fans transform *Star Trek* into women's culture, shifting it from space opera into feminist romance, bringing to the surface the unwritten feminine countertext that hides in the margins of the written masculine text. Kirk's story becomes Uhura's story and Chapel's and Amanda's as well as the story of the women who weave their own personal experiences into the lives of the characters. Consumption becomes production; reading becomes writing; spectator culture becomes participatory culture.

Neither the popular stereotype of the crazed Trekkie nor academic notions of commodity fetishism or repetition compulsion are adequate to explain the complexity of fan culture. Rather, fan writers suggest the need to redefine the politics of reading, to view textual property not as the exclusive domain of textual producers but as open to repossession by textual consumers. Fans continuously debate the etiquette of this relationship, yet all take for granted the fact that they are finally free to do with the text as they please. The world of *Star Trek* is what they choose to make it: 'If there were no fandom, the aired episodes would stand as they are, and yet they would be just old reruns of some old series with no more meaning than old reruns of *I Love Lucy*' (Hunter 1977, p. 77). The one text shatters and becomes many texts as it is fit into the lives of the people who use it, each in her or his own way, each for her or his own purposes.

Modleski (1986) recently, and I believe mistakenly, criticised what she understands to be the thrust of the cultural studies tradition: the claim that somehow mass culture texts empower readers. Fans are not empowered by mass culture; fans are empowered over mass culture. Like de Certeau's poachers, the fans harvest fields that they did not cultivate and draw upon materials not of their making, materials already at hand in their cultural environment; yet, they make those raw materials work for them. They employ images and concepts drawn from mass culture texts to explore their subordinate status, to envision alternatives, to voice their frustrations and anger, and to share their new understandings with others. Resistance comes from the uses they make of these popular texts, from what they add to them and what they do with them, not from subversive meanings that are somehow embedded within them.

Ethnographic research has uncovered numerous instances where this occurs. Australian schoolchildren turn to *Prisoner* in search of insight into their own institutional experience, even translating schoolyard play into an act of open subordination against the teachers' authority (Hodge & Tripp 1986; Palmer 1986). American kindergartners find in the otherness of *Pee-Wee Herman* a clue to their own insecure status as semisocialised beings (Jenkins, in press). British gay clubs host *Dynasty* and *Dallas* drag balls, relishing the bitchiness and trashiness of nighttime soap operas as a negation of traditional middle-class taste and decorum (Finch 1986). European leftists express their hostility to Western capitalism through their love-hate relationship with *Dallas* (Ang 1986). Nobody regards these fan activities as a magical cure for the social ills of post-industrial capitalism. They are no substitution for meaningful change, but they can be used effectively to build popular support for such change, to challenge the power of the culture industry to construct the common sense of a mass society, and to restore a much-needed excitement to the struggle against subordination.

Alert to the challenge such uses pose to their cultural hegemony, textual producers openly protest this uncontrollable proliferation of meanings from their texts, this popular rewriting of their stories, this trespass upon their literary properties. Actor William Shatner (Kirk), for instance, has said of *Star Trek* fan fiction: 'People read into it things that were not intended. In *Star Trek*'s case, in many instances, things were done just for entertainment purposes' (Spelling, Lofficier & Lofficier 1987, p. 40). Producers insist upon their right to regulate what their texts may mean and what types of pleasure they can produce. Yet, such remarks carry little weight. Undaunted by the barking dogs, the 'no trespassing' signs and the threats of prosecution, the fans already have poached those texts from under the proprietors' noses.

Notes

1 An earlier draft of this essay was presented at the 1985 Iowa Symposium and Conference on *Television Criticism: Public and Academic Responsibility*. I am indebted to Cathy Schwichtenberg, John Fiske, David Bordwell and Janice Radway for their helpful suggestions as I was rewriting it for CSMC. I am particularly indebted to Signe Hovde and Cynthia Benson Jenkins for introducing me to the world of fan writing; without them my research could not have been completed. I have tried to contact all of the fans quoted in this text and to gain their permission to discuss their work. I appreciate their cooperation and helpful suggestions.

2 For representative examples of other scholarly treat- ments of *Star Trek* and its fans, see Blair (1983), Greenberg (1984), Jewett and Lawrence (1977) and Tyre (1977). Attitudes range from the generally sympathetic Blair to the openly hostile Jewett and Lawrence.

3 No scholarly treatment of *Star Trek* fan culture can avoid these pitfalls, if only because making such a work accessible to an academic audience requires a translation of fan discourse into other terms, terms that may never be fully adequate to the original. I come to both *Star Trek* and fan fiction as a fan first and a scholar second. My participation as a fan long precedes my academic interest in it. I have sought, where possible, to employ fan terms and to quote fans directly in discussing their goals and orientations toward the program and their own writing. I have shared drafts of this essay with fans and have incorporated their comments into the revision process. I have allowed them the dignity of being quoted from their carefully crafted, well-considered published works rather than from a spontaneous interview that would be more controlled by the researcher than by the informant. I leave it to my readers to determine whether this approach allows for a less mediated reflection of fan culture than previous academic treatments of this subject.

4 The terms 'letterzine' and 'fictionzine' are derived from fan discourse. The two types of fanzines relate to each other in complex ways. Although there are undoubtedly some fans who read only one type of publication, many read both. Some letterzines, *Treklink* for instance, function as consumer guides and sounding boards for debates about the fictionzines.

5 Both Lorrah and Lichtenberg have achieved some success as professional science fiction writers. For an interesting discussion of the relationship between fan writing and professional science fiction writing, see Randall (1985).

6 Although a wide range of fanzines were considered in researching this essay, I have decided, for the purposes of clarity, to draw my examples largely from the work of a limited number of fan writers. While no selection could accurately reflect the full range of fan writing, I felt that

Bates, Land, Lorrah and Siebert had all achieved some success within the fan community, suggesting that they exemplified, at least to some fans, the types of writing that were desirable and reflected basic tendencies within the form. Further, these writers have produced a large enough body of work to allow some commentary about their overall project rather than localised discussions of individual stories. I have also, wherever possible, focused my discussion around works still currently in circulation and therefore available to other researchers interested in exploring this topic. No slight is intended to the large number of other fan writers who also met these criteria and who, in some cases, are even better known within the fan community.

7 I am indebted to K. C. D'alessandro and Mary Carbine for probing questions that refined my thoughts on this particular issue.

8 The area of Kirk/Spock fiction falls beyond the project of this particular paper. My reason for discussing it here is because of the light its controversial reception sheds on the norms of fan fiction and the various ways fan writers situate themselves toward the primary text. For a more detailed discussion of this particular type of fan writing, see Lamb and Veith (1986) who argue that K/S stories, far from representing a cultural expression of the gay community, constitute another way of feminising the concerns of the original series text and of addressing feminist concern within the domain of a popular culture that offers little space for heroic action by women.

References

Ang, I. (1986) *Watching Dallas*. London: Methuen.

Bacon-Smith, C. (1986) 'Spock among the women'. *The New York Times Book Review*, November 16, pp. 1, 26, 28.

Bates, K. A. (1982) *Starweaver Two*. Missouri Valley, IA: Ankar Press.

_____ (1983) *Nuages One*. Tucson, AZ: Checkmate Press.

_____ (1984) *Nuages Two*. Tucson, AZ: Checkmate Press.

Bethann (1976) 'The Measure of Love', *Grup*, 5, pp. 53–62.

Blaes, T. (1986) 'Letter', *Treklink*, 5, p. 6.

_____ (1987) 'Letter', *Treklink*, 9, pp. 6–7.

Blair, K. (1983) 'Sex and Star Trek', *Science Fiction Studies*, 10, pp. 292–7.

Bleich, D. (1986) 'Gender interests in reading and language', in E. A. Flynn & P. P. Schweickart (eds.), *Gender and Reading: Essays on Readers, Texts and Contexts*. Baltimore: Johns Hopkins University Press, pp. 234–66.

Brown, M. E., & Barwick, L. (1987) 'Fables and endless gen- erations: Soap opera and women's culture'. Paper presented at a meeting of the Society of Cinema Studies, Montreal.

Caruthers-Montgomery, P. L. (1987) 'Letter', *Comlink*, 28, p. 8.

Chandler, M. (1987) 'Letter', *Trekink*, 8, p. 10.

Cooper, C. (1987) 'Opportunities in the 'media fanzine'

the science fiction film reader

market', *Writer's Digest* (February), p. 45.

de Certeau, M. (1984) *The Practice of Everyday Life*. Berkeley: University of California Press.

de Lauretis, T. (1982) *Alice Doesn't: Feminism, Semiotics, Cinema*. Bloomington: Indiana University Press.

Deneroff, L. (1987) 'A reflection on the early days of *Star Trek* fandom', *Comlink*, 28, pp. 3–4.

Finch, M. (1986) 'Sex and address in *Dynasty*', *Screen*, 27, 24–42.

Greenberg, H. (1984) 'In search of Spock: A psychoanalytic inquiry', *Journal of Popular Film and Television*, 12, pp. 53–65.

Hodge, R. & Tripp, D. (1986) *Children and Television: A Semiotic Approach*. Cambridge: Polity Press.

Hunter, K. (1977) *Characterization Rape*. In W. Irwin & G. B. Love (eds.), *The Best of Trek 2*. New York: New American Library, pp. 74–85.

Jenkins, H. (in press) "Going bonkers!' Children, play and Pee-Wee', *Camera Obscura*, 18.

Jewett, R. & Lawrence, J. S. (1977) *The American monomyth*, Garden City, NY: Anchor Press.

Kramarae, C. (1981) *Women and Men Speaking*. Rowley, MS: Newburry House.

Lamb, P. F. & Veith, D. L. (1986) 'Romantic Myth, Transcendence and *Star Trek* Zines', in D. Palumbo (ed.), *Erotic Universe: Sexuality and Fantastic Literature*. New York: Greenwood Press, pp. 235–56.

Land, J. (1986) *Kista*. Larchmont, NY: Author.

_____ (1987) *Demeter*. Larchmont, NY: Author.

Landers, R. (1986) 'Letter'. *Treklink*, 7, p. 10.

Lay, T. (1986) 'Letter', *Comlink*, 28, pp. 14–16.

Leerhsen, C. (1986) '*Star Trek*'s nine lives', *Newsweek*, (December 22), pp. 66–73.

Lichtenberg, J. (1976) *Kraith collected*. Grosse Point Park, MI: Ceiling Press.

Lorrah, J. (1976a) *The Night of Twin Moons*. Murray: Author.

_____ (1976b) *Full Moon Rising*. Bronx, NY: Author.

_____ (1978) 'The Vulcan character in the NTM universe', in J. Lorrah (eds.), *NTM collected*, vol. 1, Murray, KY: Author, pp. 1–3.

_____ (1984) *The Vulcan Academy Murders*. New York: Pocket.

Ludlow, J. (1987) 'Letter', *Comlink*, 28, pp. 17–18.

Marshak, S. & Culbreath, M. (1978) *Star Trek: The New Voyages*. New York: Bantam Books.

Modleski, T. (1982) *Loving With a Vengeance: Mass-Produced Fantasies for Women*. Hamden, CT: Archon Books.

Modleski, T. (1986) *Studies in Entertainment: Critical Approaches to Mass Culture*. Bloomington: Indiana Univ-ersity Press.

Moore, R. (1986) 'Letter', *Treklink*, 4, pp. 7–8.

Osborne, E. (1987) 'Letter', *Treklink*, 9, pp. 3–4.

Palmer, P. (1986) *The Lively Audience*. Sidney, Australia: Unwyn & Allen.

Radway, J. (1984) *Reading the Romance: Women, Patriarchy and Popular Literature*. Chapel Hill: University of North Carolina Press.

Randall, M. (1985) 'Conquering the galaxy for fun and profit', in C. West (eds.), *Words in our Pockets*. Paradise, CA: Dustbooks, pp. 233–41.

Rose, P. (1977) 'Women in the Federation', in W. Irwin & G. B. Love (eds.), *The best of Trek 2*. New York: New American Library, pp. 46–52.

Schnuelle, S. (1987) 'Letter', *Sociotrek*, 4, pp. 8–9.

Segel, E. (1986) 'Gender and childhood reading', in E.A. Flynn & P. P. Schweickart (eds.), *Gender and Reading: Essays on Readers, Texts and Contexts*. Baltimore: Johns Hopkins University Press, pp. 164–85.

Siebert, C.A. (1980) 'Journey's end at lover's meeting', *Slaysu*, 1, pp. 28–34.

_____ (1982) 'By any other name', *Slaysu*, 4, 44–5.

Smith-Rosenberg, C. (1985) *Disorderly Conduct: Gender in Victorian America*. New York: Alfred A. Knopf.

Snaider, T. (1987) 'Letter', *Treklink*, 8, p. 10.

Spector, J. (1986) 'Science fiction and the sex war: A womb of one's own', in J. Spector (ed.), *Gender Studies: New Directions in Feminist Criticism*. Bowling Green, OH: Bowling Green State University Press, pp. 161–83.

Spelling, I., Lofficier, R. & Lofficier, J-M. (1987) 'William Shatner, captain's log: *Star Trek V*', *Starlog* (May), pp. 37–41.

Thompson, E. P. (1971) 'The moral economy of the English crowd in the 18th century', *Past and Present*, 50, 76–136.

Thompson, L. (1974) '*Star Trek* mysteries – Solved!', in W. Irwin & G. B. Love (eds.), *The Best of Trek*. New York: New American Library, pp. 207–14.

Tyre, W. B. (1977) '*Star Trek* as myth and television as myth maker', *Journal of Popular Culture*, 10, pp. 711–19.

Verba, J. (1986) 'Editor's corner', *Treklink*, 6, pp. 1–4.

Whitfield, S. E. & Roddenberry, G. (1968) *The Making of Star Trek*. New York: Ballantine Books.

Wood, R. (1986) *Hollywood from Vietnam to Reagan*. New York: Columbia University Press.

'We're Only a Speck in the Ocean': The Fan as Powerless Elite
John Tulloch

Golden Ages and the 'Unforgivable'

What, then, constitutes a 'good' episode that would keep the 'floating voter' (and the fan) switched on? This question plays a central role in the fans' reading of individual texts.

Doctor Who fans' sense of a good epi-sode is constructed in terms of quite a precise aesthetic: it should not 'leave things unexplained' (in order not to lose the wider audience); and it should adhere to the history and continuity of the series (in order not to lose the fans). 'Society' fans are, in effect, situated as a privileged group with few powers – a powerless elite with little control over the floating voter on one side, the producers of the show on the other. Consequently their explanation and evaluation of any one episode is strongly determined by this positioning as experts who have little control over either the conditions of production or reception of 'their' show.

In the absence of this, their power is the power to gloss, and to write the aesthetic history of the show – dividing its twenty-five years into a series of 'golden ages' and 'all-time lows'. They, thus, establish an officially constituted reading formation, which supervises reading of the show. Ian Levine, for many years a very senior British fan (and at one time unofficial continuity historian to the producers) had this to say:

> The series had a mood, and a charisma and atmosphere and a sort of gripping drama to it during Philip Hinchcliffe's era. The stories were meticulously made. A TV play or TV series like *Doctor Who* can turn out to be a work of art if everything comes together in the end which a lot of Hinchcliffe's were and a lot of John Nathan-Turner's are. Hardly any of Graham Williams's were, and if they were it was by accident.[1]

'Unforgivable' was a word that sprang easily to the lips of fans when they were being critical,

and it is a word used especially often by *Doctor Who* fans about 'the Graham Williams era' (1977–80). For instance, Ian Levine noted that

> facts they have given in one story clash grossly in the next ... We are told in one story that only the Doctor can fly the Tardis and in the next story he has got the savage Leela, who has no grasp of electronics at all, asking the Doctor what the co-ordinates are and flying the Tardis herself. That was unforgivable, that really was unforgivable.

Similarly another senior English fan Jeremy Bentham (author of *Doctor Who: The Early Years*) observed, 'I can't forgive Williams for the line he gave to the Sontarans in 'Invasion of Time' [1978], 'primitive rubbish'';[2] Levine adding, 'We know the Sontarans aren't as advanced as the Time Lords, so how could a Sontaran walk into the Tardis and say, 'This machine is a load of obsolete rubbish'? – that is the exact line.' The producer behind both of these 'unforgivable' examples was Graham Williams.

'Errors in continuity' (which Levine spotted throughout the series) entered, in his view, a qualitatively new stage as they became systematic under producer Graham Williams. Under Williams, 'errors in continuity' com-bined with a 'send-up' style which most fans disliked intensely.

> Under Graham Williams the decline set in as a rot ... The three stories in a row, 'The Creature from the Pit' (1979), 'The Nightmare of Eden' (1979) and 'The Horns of Nimon' (1979–80), *Doctor Who* reached an all-time low then and the ratings plummeted.

Despite Levine's error of fact here (current fans note that the ratings were very high for these stories, 'Horns of Nimon' rating eleven million), we should nevertheless recognise the integral link in fan consciousness between programme aesthetics and ratings 'outside the Society'. Fans quite generally agree with Levine that Williams's 'seventeenth season' was the worst in the show's history. Australian fan, Pat Fenech, writes in the fanzine *Zerinza* about their 'worst stories' survey results.

The most notable feature here is the placing of 4 out of the 5 stories broadcast in the seventeenth season as amongst the worst stories ever. This season is reputed to be the worst in *Doctor Who* history. These results certainly suggest ADWFC members consider it so.[3]

Of those four stories, Australian fans rated 'The Horns of Nimon' the worst story ever, 'Destiny of the Daleks' (1979) second worst, 'Nightmare of Eden' (1979) fifteenth and 'Creature from the Pit' (1979) sixteenth worst.

Fans are thus far from being uncritical or sycophantic about their show. Rather, they establish an aesthetic history of 'classics' and 'worst ever' episodes which they circulate through the fanzines. This aesthetic is articulated quite self-consciously in their discourse about 'continuity' and 'programme structure'.

Continuity: textual exegesis and the fans' power to gloss

The fans' particular competence is their intimate and detailed knowledge of the show; consequently any producer or script editor who needlessly breaches the continuity and coherence of that knowledge is 'insulting their intelligence'. Many fans particularly enjoy episodes which call up that knowledge and so address them directly as fans. Levine, for instance, 'loved 'Logopolis'' (produced by Nathan-Turner) because

> events in 'Logopolis' revolved around the myth itself of *Doctor Who*. In other words, the whole story started because the Doctor wanted to change his broken chameleon circuit which has been broken since the very first story – and even the reference back to Totters Yard which was in the first story, to explain it ... Bring in anything from the series' past and you get my vote anyway.

The 1981 DWAS president, David Saunders, and secretary, Garry Russell described 'Logopolis' as 'a nice fannish story' and 'all fandom and padding'.

> Saunders: It started off with a policeman looking around which is supposed to be reminiscent of the very first episode.
> Russell: The reintroduction of the Master and the fight at the end on top of a radio telescope which was completely taken from

the original Master's very first story where there was a fight on top of a telescope...
> Saunders: The Tardis, within a Tardis, within a Tardis is straight out of 'Time Monster' (1972).
> Russell: It's a fan story.
> Saunders: We love it. But it's made for our thousand [DWAS members] instead of made for the BBC's millions.[4]

As Levine put it, 'Logopolis' was especially enjoyed by fans because 'the entire plot of 'Logopolis' arose inside the myth of *Doctor Who* rather than taking the myth of *Doctor Who* to an outside planet'.

Fans on the other hand do not usually enjoy episodes which overtly undercut that myth. One of the 'most hated' *Doctor Who* stories in the ADWFC poll was Douglas Adams's first as script editor under Graham Williams, 'Destiny of the Daleks'. Mary Tamm, who played the companion Romana, had unexpectedly quit the show, leaving the producer with a number of scripts featuring her. As Romana was, fortuitously, the first companion who was also a Time Lord, the decision was taken to make Romana 1 regenerate as Romana 2, and thus plausibly explain a new actress playing the part. The way in which this was done infuriated many fans.

> Levine: I could never forgive Graham Williams for the regeneration scene ... It has been clearly established that a Time Lord can only have twelve regenerations, clearly established. In many stories that fact has been stated. So how can they have some supposedly responsible female Time Lord in the Tardis trying on about six different faces before she decides which one she wants? – which is obviously wasting six regenerations. It is just ludicrous. It is that sort of non-attention to the detail of the series that gives me no regard for Graham Williams at all.

Jeremy Bentham agreed:

> It was something that was done purely for a laugh – there is no other justification for it. If he knew that Mary Tamm wanted to leave, well at least you could have written something a bit more doom-laden – there is an outlet for it in 'The Armageddon Factor' (1979) where the Shadow is torturing her

very severely. The idea of that could have triggered off an involuntary regeneration.

And in Australia, fan Stephen Collins wrote:

There is no good reason for this regeneration. The body of Romana I is functioning perfectly at the end of 'Armageddon Factor', there is no hint of a decay in the bodily functions. Neither is Romana I very old – 'City of Death' (1979) establishes her as only 120. This is not a natural regeneration, Romana has forced it upon herself in a display of extravagance (considering she only has twelve to fool around with).[5]

Rather desperately, Collins looks for reasonable explanations within the history and myth of *Doctor Who* to explain this 'extravagance'.

There appear to be three valid approaches to the question. One stems from Baker's comment in 'Robot' about the stability of his regeneration. If you assume from that there is a period of instability around every Time Lord regeneration, during which the new physical appearance may change, and clearly that is what Baker is suggesting in 'Robot', then the changes Romana makes as she searches for the correct body can be construed as occurring during that period.

The second concerns 'The Key to Time' (1978–79). The White Guardian, having utilised the power of the key whilst it was assembled in the Tardis, decided to relocate the Sixth segment. He decided to rest the segment in Romana, triggering her regeneration cycle. Romana then utilises the ability of the segment to 'try on' the other bodies – 'Stones of Blood' (1978) established the ability of individual segments to allow transmutation of the possessor of the segment.

Finally, it is possible that the ability displayed by K'anpo Rinpoche in 'Planet of the Spiders' (1974) provides the solution. After regenerating into her new form, Romana shows the Doctor the finished result. He is not pleased, but she has no intention of changing her appearance to make him happy. So she retires from the control room and summons up possible future projections of herself, sending them to the Doctor to receive his appraisal. After she thinks the Doctor has had enough, Romana returns to

the control room in her Princess Astra form – the only one she regenerated into.[6]

Whichever the right answer might be, Collins insists that

Romana was not utilising normal powers of regeneration when she 'tried on' the three bodies to please the Doctor. Romana is far too intelligent to waste valuable regenerations on such a frivolous enterprise.[7]

This degree of exegesis of the 'holy writ' of *Doctor Who* may seem humourless to some, positively medieval to others. However, Collins is reading the episode inter-textually; the only difference being the degree to which fans call up series history in their quest for meaning. What Collins's analysis indicates is that the power of *Doctor Who*'s executive fans (i.e. fans who are executives of the fan club and its magazines) is discursive rather than institutional. In this aspect of series continuity, the fans are clearly in the hands of the producers, who responded to the situation differently. John Nathan-Turner, according to Levine, was 'careful to consult the facts to make sure that he is not clashing with anything'[8] – and during this period Levine 'helped out the *Doctor Who* office with continuity errors and continuity problems' (which is one reason for Levine's initial view that Nathan-Turner had 'restored *Doctor Who* to a golden age again'). Other producers, like Graham Williams, kept the 'Society' fans (who, numbering not more than 1,000 in the UK, constituted a tiny part of his audience) in their place. Williams told us that, as regards influence on the programme, fans had 'none whatsoever' even though 'they would rather like to think they have'.[9] We also asked DWAS executives David Saunders and Garry Russell whether they had an influence on the production of the show:

Russell: I think there is a straight answer – one has to take in the BBC's approach which … is 'fob them off with a few stories'. No, they don't take a great deal of notice … The fans don't make up the complete viewing public of *Doctor Who*.
Saunders: When all is said and done we hop around the thousand mark, and *Doctor Who*'s audience is millions. We are in some respects only a speck in the ocean.

But in the absence of power over either production of the series or over the wider viewing public, these senior fans do have discursive power in establishing the 'informed' exegesis for their subculture of fans. Thus they establish and control an important reading formation. Stephen Collins, for instance, as letters editor of the Australian fanzine *Zerinza*, specialised for a while in 'regeneration theory'. In this way, editors of fanzines can have an important agenda-setting function. Thus *Zerinza* editor, Tony Howe, noted after the latest skirmish between a correspondent and Stephen Collins: 'as *Zerinza* editor I think it is time that more attention be given to discussing other topics such as the new stories soon to be seen, the Survey results, the Season Reviews; Regeneration has been well covered for the present'.[10]

So executive fans' opinions matter within the subculture – on, for instance, which issues are controversial at any one time as well as the way in which these issues are interpreted and closed off. It is in the pages of the fanzines that the unfolding myth of *Doctor Who* is articulated, positioned and circulated – the view, for instance, that Tom Baker polarised the fans between, as Collins put it, 'the ones who are fans of *Doctor Who*' (who hated Baker for 'sending up' the show) and 'the ones who are fans of Tom Baker'; or the view that Sarah-Jane Smith and Tegan Jovanka were the 'all-time favourite companions' because of their 'strong, well-defined characters' (whereas, in Australia, Tegan was much less popular because of her 'pseudo-Australian character'); or the view (especially strong in Australia) that *Doctor Who* – far from being in a new 'golden age' under producer John Nathan-Turner – was 'going down the drain'. For instance, discussing the lack of cultural background in 'Kinda', Tony Howe commented: 'I think that's because *Doctor Who* is beginning to follow *Star Trek* down the drain in becoming too limiting. They were obsessed with making sure that every pepper shaker was the same colour as in the episode before, and that sort of thing.' Was Howe here breaching the fundamental fan aesthetic value of continuity? Not at all:

In *Doctor Who* they've got an almost strident disregard for continuity. If there's an established thing like the Daleks in one story, they'll have them doing this, and in another story … they'll have attitudes and reactions

to things which are totally different, which is completely unbelievable.[11]

Was Howe, then, being inconsistent between his comments on *Star Trek* and *Doctor Who*? Not that either:

Basic aliens, like the Cybermen are not supposed to be emotional, and then in the last story, 'Earthshock' (1982), they're positively hysterical, they're ranting and raving, they're very violently emotional … It's often trotted out that the breaches of continuity enable the series to be more flexible and to respond to changing audience demand and so on, with which I concur to a point – that the pepper shakers don't matter, that you can have a pink pepper shaker in one episode and a purple one in the next and you can say it's the same one. That's what *Star Trek* got worried about, that sort of trivia. But when you say that a basic character or an entire civilisation is like X and then you say the same civilisation two years later is like Y and is totally different from X … it's impossible, you can't reconcile it … Given that kind of thing is ignored over the years, it undermines its credibility.

However, it was not bad continuity in *Doctor Who* that was sending it 'down the drain' in the post-Hinchcliffe period. It was not this which was 'too limiting' in Howe's opinion. Howe's discussion of Cyber 'character' and 'civilisation' introduces another major aspect of the fans' aesthetic: concern for structure, coherence and character.

Programme structure: 'arguing with the producer'

Elaborating on why he thought 'Logopolis' was 'all fandom and padding', David Saunders complained about it being only a four-parter.

I said to John Nathan-Turner, it could have been a six-parter, because not a lot of attention was paid to the possible subplot with Nyssa thinking that the Master was her father. I felt at least another episode could be made out of her betraying the Doctor, not realising that it wasn't her father, whereas in fact it was all covered in half an episode.

For Saunders, all the self-referencing 'continuity' of 'Logopolis' could not make up for the weakness of the lack of development in a four-part story. And this in fact was the 'limitation' which ADWFC president Tony Howe saw as taking *Doctor Who* 'down the drain'.

> What I think they've done is deliberately un-limit themselves on that side by totally devaluing all of what went before in *Doctor Who* in terms of continuity, but completely impose a structure on themselves with this four-episode thing. If somebody … wrote a story considering all of the characters and stereotypes and thought about the civilisation of the Kinda – which was that this could become the case on Earth, that we could get so civilised that the entire civilisation would just disintegrate – that could have been done in a six-episode story. But now they've got themselves into a totally rigid thing. Every producer, script editor and person connected with *Doctor Who* says it has to be four episodes in every interview I've ever seen, and whenever a fan tries to argue with them … they get quite hot under the collar about it … If they limit the structure of the programme as they're doing, they're just going to stifle it.

The other Australian fans present at the 'Kinda' discussion agreed with Howe. ADWFC secretary Kerry Dougherty commented:

> In earlier times they had much greater flexibility. If a programme needed seven episodes, or five episodes, or two, or three … or even one episode, it got what it needed … And that's why the stories were complete or much more complete. It was not so often that you'd find something like 'Kinda' left hanging in mid-air, as you get so often with the modern *Doctor Whos*'.

It was, as we saw, things 'being unexplained', 'left hanging in mid-air' which the fans felt was turning the 'floating voter' off the show.

Again, we notice how the history of *Doctor Who* is called up to position and interpret 'Kinda'; and how 'classics' of *Doctor Who* are drawn on as a point of comparison to enforce the argument.

> Howe: 'The Talons of Weng Chiang' (1977) easily justified six episodes. You couldn't have cut that down to four.

Dougherty: You couldn't have made it in four. That would have destroyed it.

Howe: That would have been absolutely impossible. But today they wouldn't allow a story like that to be made. They say it has to be four episodes, so it wouldn't be half the story. It needed that development of the characters and the relationships which *Doctor Who* isn't allowed by its format any more.

Dougherty: Yes, it's become so limited. I mean there's no development of the Doctor's companions really in the way there used to be … In the earlier times you really got to see a lot about the characters – they developed as people in front of your eyes while they were there.

From this point a 'golden age of *Doctor Who*' discussion readily developed. These golden days were particularly those of the first three doctors and the first period of the fourth doctor under producer Philip Hinchcliffe (before Tom Baker 'sent the part up'). These were times, the fans noted, when companions like Susan and Jamie and Zoe had whole episodes or parts of episodes to themselves, or when (under Pertwee) there would be the Doctor in one place, Sarah in another, and UNIT (the United Nations 'alien-spotting' task force) operating in yet another, providing 'depth' and 'development' to the narratives of *Doctor Who*. These were the kinds of narrative, the fans believed, which made the show widely popular. As Ian Levine put it, the continuity is mainly important for the 'fans' point of view'. To attract the wider audience 'good plots' are needed, and these rely on (a) naturalistic and 'believable' characters, (b) a narrative closure which ties all the loose threads together, and (c) a recognition that *Doctor Who* is not about 'media hype' and 'star' actors, but about 'relationships and aliens and a whole plethora of different concepts and strands'. Among other things, it is what the producers see as the 'soapy' element of the series ('relationships') which the fans think is important to the wider public.

While (as always) concerned about what would keep the 'floating voter' watching, the underlying aesthetic assumptions here are of a very particular kind. They belong to what Ebert calls the 'mimetic conventions of the bourgeois novel with its preoccupation with socio-psychological realism'. The elaboration of believable characters is what, in the view of many *Doctor Who* fans, distinguishes it from US 'sci-fi' (Ebert's 'para science fiction') and from 'media hype' generally.

Believable chartacters: 'identification itself'

Bentham described his pleasure in the first *Doctor Who* episode, 'The Unearthly Child' (1963):

> That ultimate loneliness when you see London fading away when the Tardis takes off for the first time. Because you become so established with those characters and feel comfortable with them you can feel as well the sense of growing loneliness as you open the doors, again for the first time, nowhere near where you were – it is a fantastic jump to try and imagine literally waking up somewhere you couldn't believe in a million years could exist.

He explained the 'incredible peak' in the ratings for Philip Hinchcliffe's 'Ark in Space' (1975) in these identificatory terms:

> I think *Doctor Who* works best when you start inside the ship, the Tardis, and then your first sight of what is beyond it comes as the travellers start to explore ... In 'Ark in Space' everything was gradually developing as new, as you see it through the eyes of the three people, two of whom it was totally new to in the form of the Doctor's companions. It's internal, if you like, identification itself.

It was primarily because fans felt that Graham Williams betrayed this naturalistic quality of encountering 'new experiences' (by way of the senses of the regular characters) that he was especially disliked for 'pantomimic send-up'. Pantomime has a reflexive quality which draws attention to itself, becomes 'a little too obvious' in its inter-textuality, and so weakens the suspension of disbelief. For Ian Levine:

> If you watch 'The Horns of Nimon' you see a pretty abysmal story ... It was like a pantomime ... Graham Williams just sent the series up and turned it into mock comedy ... instead of depending on good plots.

For Jeremy Bentham, Williams's notorious 'seventeenth season', 'suffered tremendously

because of very poor execution of what could have been very, very good ideas ... What let it down was this almost pantomime-like execution that the production crew gave it for that story.'

So, whereas university students who followed (but were not fans of) *Doctor Who* told us they liked 'The Horns of Nimon' because of 'its pantomime quality', for many fans it was 'the worst story ever'. David Saunders noted that he was 'in a very, very small minority in actually liking 'The Horns of Nimon'. He pointed to ways in which an unfolding series like *Doctor Who* can appropriately have many signatures for the sophisticated fan provided that continuity is maintained on essentials.

> In 'The Horns of Nimon' everybody is hamming. It's the equivalent of the old Batman. Everybody is going over the top, therefore it works. To go back to one that I think is even worse, which is 'Nightmare of Eden', that is so bad because ... there are supporting cast being serious while Baker and Ward laughing and joking and all the rest of it. In 'Horns of Nimon' everybody is laughing and joking and therefore it works ... But there were elements in it that I can't approve of, like the Tardis making those horrible, stupid wheezing and groaning sounds at the beginning and the Doctor giving K-9 the kiss of life ... Graham Crowden walking along the corridor, twice, saying (in a falsetto) 'Lord Nimon', I can take because it is within the context of that particular story. But K-9 and the Tardis are ongoing elements, and you know that the Tardis has never made that noise before and we hope never will make it again.

For some executive fans, then, 'one-off' pantomime (provided that it is coherent within its genre and does not send up such basic elements of the *Doctor Who* myth as the Tardis) might be acceptable. But other senior fans like Jeremy Bentham worry about the effect of this on the general viewer, particularly the new, young viewer.

> Williams's ... style was camp, but it was without the very necessary ingredient with camp where it is done totally seriously. You can do camp, you can do it with things like 'The Image of the Fendahl' (1977) and do it well. But if you take it too

far, too excessively, then you send it up, and the easiest way you can find that out is by asking a youngster. If he is suddenly conscious that he is watching something that is making fun of his enthusiasm he will go off it fast.

Narrative closure: 'what sort of audience are they aiming for?'

We note, then, that fans regularly reference the 'wider audience' as the focus of their concern for naturalistically 'complex' (as against 'pantomimic') plots and characterisation. The same is true of their concern that different ('metaphysical' and 'scientific') strands of the storyline be brought together by the end of the narrative. As we have seen, the 'metaphysical' and 'scientific' contrasts in 'Kinda' were a 'postmodernist' trace from the episode's origins in Ursula Le Guin. But the *Doctor Who* fans were concerned with a much more materialistic problem than postmodernism.

At the time of the Liverpool 'Kinda' discussion mentioned earlier, it was well known among fans that *Doctor Who* might be living on borrowed time. The other BBC science fiction series, *Blake's 7*, had recently been taken off air after a couple of seasons' poor ratings. In its seventeenth and eighteenth seasons *Doctor Who* had recently had two poor-rating seasons, and it was widely thought that producer Nathan-Turner had to restore lost ratings or go off air. Hence the particularly ebullient emphasis of fans like Ian Levine that Nathan-Turner was 'restoring the series to a golden age again', with 'dazzling drama' as well as impeccable continuity.

The Liverpool fans were therefore well aware that more 'floating voters' were needed to save their show, and they discussed animatedly the new, twice-a-week evening time-slot which had just replaced the twenty-year-old convention of *Doctor Who* once-a-week (at somewhere between 5.00 and 6.15pm) on Saturdays. They anxiously discussed the problem of attracting new adult viewers without losing the traditional children's audience.

Graham: It's 7 o'clock or around 7 o'clock theoretically – it is an adult show and 'Kinda' should have been a lot more frightening because it was a frightening story. But it wasn't frightening. Hindle ... was the best character

for me. Some of the scenes where he was obviously disturbed – you wouldn't have got away with that at 5 o'clock on Saturday afternoon ... It's still hovering in between not knowing whether it's a children's series or adults.

Tony: It's sort of got to stick within children's limitations. They can't make it too frightening. And yet most children watching 'Kinda' wouldn't be able to follow it because it was high up enough intellectually for adults to follow ... I think they are really not sure what sort of audience they are aiming for ... If you try and move to a more adult slot then you have got to attract your adult audience before you can throw away your child audience, which is why moving a slot of any programme is really a bit of a risk.

As we have seen, this group (like the Sydney group) was particularly concerned that 'Kinda' (and the nineteenth season in general) was 'not tying the threads together' and 'leaving the audience up in the air'. 'Not giving explanations well enough is stupid. OK, looking back on a story that has got explanations you might find them laboured. But your average viewer does not look back on a story.' These fans make a very clear distinction between their relationship to the texts of *Doctor Who* and that of the 'average viewer'. Fans 'look back' at a story via video recordings and/or fanzine discussions. The 'average viewers' see the episode once only; and it is for them above all that a clear narrative closure is needed.

'Tom Baker is Doctor Who': the fans and 'media hype'

The Australian fans discussing 'Kinda' had very precise notions of what was 'wrong' with *Doctor Who* – the writing in particular was criticised for its failure to conclude strands it had begun; for its inability to 'meld' together the 'psychic' and 'technological' strands (other *Doctor Who* stories like 'The Stones of Blood' [1978] and 'Image of the Fendahl' were drawn on here to make the point); for the underlying inability of *Doctor Who* to blend into one whole the 'intuitive, metaphysical' side of the Doctor with his 'rational, scientific' side; and for the episode's failure to provide cultural background and perspective. Lacking completely feminist science fiction's emphasis on playing-off the 'magical' with the 'rational, scientific', these fans felt 'Kinda' failed too often to situate complex human characters coherently in their cultural context.

The Sydney fans' reference to the failure of *Doctor Who* as 'anthropological or sociological' texts reminds us that these are the modern generation of SF fans that Klein and Mellor describe – many with Arts or Social Science degrees (one Sydney fan drew briefly, for instance, on Fraser's *The Golden Bough* to discuss 'Kinda'). Yet despite this, they drew much more readily, in discussing 'Kinda', on their cultural competence in the history of *Doctor Who* than on these other, broader histories. No one followed up the *Golden Bough* reference; they knew (via the fanzines) that there were Buddhist references in 'Kinda', but they didn't know how these related to the text (had they done so, they might have understood better the relationship between the 'metaphysical' and the linear/scientific in the text[12]); and though they were able to recognise its 'Garden of Eden' references, these did not make sense of the plot for them. For the fans this 'making sense' was a major criterion of 'good' plot. It was important to them that the inter-textual analogies which abound in *Doctor Who* ('going back to the classics') must 'have a point' within a believable storyline.

In this area of narrative coherence and closure, too, it became clear as the discussion proceeded that the fans were not so much criticising *Doctor Who* as a whole, but a particular period of the show, for which nearly all their critical comments were reserved. Again, this was the Graham Williams era, with the addition (in the case of the Australian fans) of the Nathan-Turner period. In these two 'worst ever' eras, 'complex', 'believable' stories ('good drama') were replaced by the idiolects of 'stars'. It was this 'star gazing' which led, they felt, to the 'mannered' self-reference and pantomime.

> Howe: Tom Baker and Peter Davison both babble on a lot. They're very mannered too. You notice they'll point and gesture in very mannered ways, while the earlier Doctors were much more relaxed about being 'the Doctor'. They now think they've got to have all sorts of affectations, which turn me right off.'

Tom Baker, in particular, was associated by many fans with this 'face-pulling affectation' which,

Levine and Bentham argued, tended to draw attention to the star rather than the series.

> The thing about Graham Williams was that he was under very strict constraints to remove the violent element in the programme that Philip Hinchcliffe had introduced, and he did that by concentrating the programme towards the character of the Doctor himself, this charismatic figure which in essence gave Tom Baker a lot more control over the programme than perhaps he should have had – to the extent where the actor was dictating what the director would show on screen.

In his role as president of ADWFC, Tony Howe encountered another aspect of the star-making procedure surrounding Tom Baker.

> When I interviewed Baker for an hour ... it came across quite strongly that if Tom Baker wanted to present something ... he would bloody well do so whether the director or writer wanted to or not. I know people who have been on the set watching Tom Baker acting, and he will tell directors how to film it and how he's got to come across ... *Doctor Who* is not one person. *Doctor Who* is relationships and is aliens and is the Tardis and a whole plethora of different concepts and strands that come together. But you get the advertising people and the merchandising people whom I've had to deal with again and again with this fan club, and all they can see is Tom Baker, or whoever the new Doctor is ... We get great media hype – "Destiny of the Daleks' is a great Dalek story, we should all be pleased the Daleks are coming back' – and it's a disaster!

This view of Baker was one widely shared by senior fans in England and Australia, and was consistently circulated via the fanzines. Stephen Collins, for instance, replied in *Zerinza* to a fan's letter which compared Baker favourably with his replacement, fifth Doctor Peter Davison:

> Tom Baker is not the Doctor. He was a Doctor ... There is no question of Baker being better at doing what Davison is doing – Baker never tried. His Doctor was utterly and totally different, lacking in compassion, sincerity and depth of feeling. If Peter Davison is terrible because he

is incapable of rampaging through the scripts in the manner of Baker then I for one am glad that he is terrible.[13]

Underlying the fans' comments that Tom Baker was 'a bad actor', 'sent the part up', 'was too much of a lunatic', 'outstayed his welcome and wore out the inventiveness of the part', there are two distinct parameters of fan concern. On the one hand, there is the fans' general inability to control the TV industry which produces their show – indeed, which denies in important ways that it is their show by replacing the fans' complex history (of companions and aliens and Doctors and Tardis) with the present of 'advertising hype' and 'star charisma'. Jenkins quotes one fan as saying, 'I think we have made *Star Trek* uniquely our own, so we have all the right in the world (universe) to try and change it for the better when the gang at Paramount starts worshipping the almighty dollar'.[14] As Jenkins says, the 'fans respect the original text and their creators, yet fear that their conceptions of the character and other programme materials may be jeopardised by those who wish to exploit them for easy profits'.[15]

On the other hand, there is the perception that Baker led to 'TV sets being turned on all over the world to watch *Doctor Who*' – especially in the USA, where Tom Baker was the first Doctor screened, and so did become 'the Doctor' there. Constantly the fans have to tread this institutional space between two bodies they are relatively powerless to control: the BBC 'who don't accord *Doctor Who* a very high priority at all' and the fickle 'average audience' of 'floating voters'.

Australian fans like Howe came to regard producer Nathan-Turner himself as even worse than Tom Baker at merchandising himself as the 'star' of the show. '*Doctor Who* has degenerated into a vehicle for the self-aggrandisement of Nathan-Turner who regards himself as the show's greatest asset and publicity tool.'

Howe: It's a bit medieval the producer's relationship to the fans that's developed under Nathan-Turner. He controls all the patronage. He controls access to the news, access to the stars, access to the sets ... When I launched my attack on Nathan-Turner in 1985 ... I criticized the fan groups in England for being so uncritical on the grounds that they were

in Nathan-Turner's pocket because they were getting a lot of favours and goodies from him, but that these were benefiting the elite in England and America and not filtering down to the membership ... I think that raffling-off props, even if it's a good cause, is nothing compared to trying to save the programme from Nathan-Turner.[16]

By 1987 Ian Levine himself was well into his own campaign against 'a totally sterile and disinterested producer who stubbornly refuses to face the fact of the pantomime edge he has tarnished the series with'.[17] Levine provided a 'JN-T Must Go Now' cover article for the *Doctor Who Monthly Bulletin*, at the end of which there was a cartoon of Tony Howe kicking Nathan-Turner out of his producer's chair:

to 99.999% of the population, John Nathan-Turner (*Doctor Who*'s producer for the last eight years, in which time the show has been cancelled, halved in episode count, ridiculed in public by Grade, and has had its script editor quit in disgust at the producer's antics ...) is a total non-entity ... On the other hand because of the knowledge we have as fans we are more than aware of the rot that has been silently corroding away the magical essence of a once, quite simple, brilliant concept.[18]

Underlying the urgency of Howe's and Levine's attacks on Nathan-Turner is the fear that *Doctor Who* will lose the 'floating voter' and be taken off air (a very real possibility by 1985). For Howe,

The style of 'Romantic' Gothic Horror used by Philip Hinchcliffe for Tom Baker's early years was very successful and achieved the series' highest ratings ever, with some of the best stories ever, so that attacks in the Press then caused little danger to the series ... Nathan-Turner's 1985 season with Colin Baker is NOT the scary, stylised horror of the mid-1970's *Doctor Who*. The new style is sick, shock violence like Andy Warhol's: the Cyber-leader crushes a prisoner's hand until it oozes blood; two men die in a vat of acid in 'Vengeance on Varos' (... the Doctor jokes at the men's suffering and walks off ...); there is an attack with a kitchen knife in 'Two Doctors'; and in the new Dalek story someone is stabbed in the chest with a hypodermic needle. These incidents occur unexpectedly, they are not part of a total atmosphere for the whole story, they do not make the stories interesting, they are for cheap shock value only and intended to provoke criticism in the Press to get free publicity – Nathan-Turner made this clear while in Sydney during 1984. But that is a dangerous publicity gimmick, because this time the show has very low ratings, unlike the mid-1970s – attacks in the Press weaken an already vulnerable show ... Nathan-Turner's poor style lowered the ratings, his actions have ensured the show would be attacked while it was weak.[19]

Though there were clearly attacks on Nathan-Turner in England, Tony Howe felt that Australian fans responded more systematically to the need to 'save the programme' from its producer, and this was for very particular cultural reasons. First, there were the different cultures of the different national fan clubs which Tony Howe and Dallas Jones talked about; second, there was the decline, as Howe saw it, of British culture itself – which we will look at in the final section.

Howe: A point I want to make about fandom which I touched on in commenting on the English fan club, DWAS's obsession with trinkets is that, in a sense, you are setting yourself up as a representative on the audience's behalf for the programme, and I see that part of that is to lobby either for the programme's improvement or its continuation or, in the case of the ABC, to get it back on air and to get, as Dallas has been doing, good time slots and good scheduling arrangements ... The fan clubs shouldn't just exist for the self-gratification of just a bunch of fans. The fans' total membership will only amount to about half a per cent of the audience at the absolute maximum, and, only a tenth of those would be the active ones receiving benefit from these video screenings, trinket selling, etc., at conventions. So fan clubs should have a public orientation as well, getting things out for the viewers who are not members of a fan club and may not want to join but are keen on the programme.
Tulloch: So you feel that the Australian club is more active in that respect than DWAS?

Howe: Yes, I think so. The point is that the origins of the two clubs are different. You were talking about the 'powerless elite'. If the people that run the clubs are these elites, the cultures they come from are different. We started out in combat with the ABC, trying to get the programme back on air ... whereas when DWAS began Doctor Who was getting higher and higher ratings under Philip Hinchcliffe and everything was sweetness and light in England ... So they never had to battle to get any crumb off the table as we had to – even to get a photograph took years for us.
Tulloch: You seem to have had a much more continuous executive than DWAS – you two guys have been around for a long time.
Jones: DWAS's executive has been changing, but those people who move out of DWAS are still there, most of them, in fandom doing other things ... fan involvement with the professional side, the whole industry of Doctor Who ... You've got Jeremy Bentham writing books about the programme, John Peel novelising books, some of the people now actually work on the programme doing models and special effects, John McIllroy selling BBC photographs, some groups have gone into production of videos, producing video interviews, and they even produced a half-hour story called 'Wartime' about the character John Benton...
Howe: Because they have got a bigger population and a bigger concentration of fandom, they are able to make some money out of it ... So it's a much more comfortable situation for fans. They can really justify as adults devoting a lot of time to the programme, through into their 20s and 30s, whereas when you leave university here you can't be an adviser to a publisher, you can't be an adviser to the BBC and there's no role for a fan outside the fan club in Australia...
Jones: The USA is a bit different again ... They're not fans – or 75/25 percent not fans – they are people who say, 'This is important, people are interested in this.' People like Norman Rubinstein from Spirit of Light – he's the biggest one, who more or less took over Doctor Who fandom in America and produced the two huge conventions for the twentieth and twenty-first anniversaries, the mega conventions in Chicago where 8,000 people attended, with twenty-one guests

for the twenty-first anniversary, and the twentieth anniversary had all four of the living Doctors. ... Secondly, you have the Doctor Who Fan Club of America which was started by two 'fans' – in inverted commas – who started the fan club based on similar ideas to professional fan clubs in America and proceeded to get guests and tour them over say ten cities, which is where they made their money ... Then, thirdly, there was the Barbara Elder corporation – she was from a group called the North American Doctor Who Appreciation Society, which was related to the English DWAS until she got more commercial and called herself a corporation and got an exclusive contract to use Tom Baker at conventions, where they also sold merchandise they were producing. So America went beyond the cottage industry in England to being big business...

Tulloch: So you see yourselves in a sense as much more pure fans because you are interested in getting the programme out to a much wider audience? Whereas you feel that particularly the US, but to some extent also in England, the whole merchandising thing is kind of...?

Howe: Solipsistic, to use one of the words from your book.

Jones: 'And also, because we don't have the guests at our conventions out here, all we have is the programme to watch. In America it was all about guests, and now also in England ... We haven't got the actors to talk to, we've just got the programme to look at, and I think that Doctor Who in Australia is more involved with the programme rather than the people.[20]

While agreeing that the fan elite 'are setting the agenda for the other fans who don't make it to the conventions' by reviews of new material in their fanzines, Howe and Jones also emphasised the power of the producer via the commercial fan magazine in England, Doctor Who Monthly.

Jones: Once a year, once the season is in production, you will start getting hints in Doctor Who Monthly 'this is going to be the dud of the season'. So even before an episode goes to air, you will have a preview in the magazine, and this is usually coming from the production team – it's really strange.

Howe: If you are going to talk about a powerless elite, in this sort of context it's not even an elite at all because it's been captured by the producer who is already determining the agenda himself and they just lock step in line ... In so far as the Doctor Who Monthly has got a vastly bigger circulation than all the fanzines in the world put together, Nathan-Turner's influence there in setting the agenda through reviews and previews ... is quite dominant.

For these Australian executive fans it was the media hype of merchandising stars, rather than caring for the programme itself that most distinguished US and British fandom from their own. But for Tony Howe there were broader cultural reasons for the decline into 'Doctor Whooligan' during the Nathan-Turner years. Under the sixth Doctor, Colin Baker, the series had sunk, Howe argued, to the level of 'soccer hooligan ethics'. Seeking to explain the series' lurch into the 'cruel and needlessly violent', Howe began to see an entire culture in decline, emblematised by the decline of Doctor Who.[21] He began to talk about the politics of the show.

'The Monster of Peladon' and politics

The features of expertise and intimacy with the 'ongoing odyssey' of Doctor Who which we have looked at so far bear a close resemblance to Bernard Sharratt's discussion of the constituent features of contemporary popular culture.[22] Many of Sharratt's observations about fans of horror series and other popular TV genres seem to hold good for Doctor Who fans: the 'pseudo-knowledge' of individualism, intimacy and expertise (at the expense of socio-economic and structural knowledge) which lies at the basis of their aesthetic; the understanding of history (of the show) primarily in terms of individuals (Tom Baker, Colin Baker, John Nathan-Turner); the critical yet close (first name) relationship with the show's personalities. Yet, of course, most of the fans – especially the fan club executives – are middle class (often tertiary-trained, professional middle-class), not the oppressed working-class viewers of Sharratt's analysis.

These science fiction fans are highly articulate, sometimes philosophical in their comments about the show. Consider, for example, this discussion of aliens by Australian fans:

> Roach: I would be more concerned with the function of the monster than with its appearance ... I mean, as a representative of evil, I think evil would shun some of these monsters (general laughter).
>
> Howe: That's something I find a bit tedious about the aliens in *Doctor Who*. Almost without exception – and there are some notable exceptions – they are all evil. They are totally, irredeemably evil.
>
> Int: Quite often, though, there's two groups – there's the baddies...
>
> Roach: And the oppressed!
>
> Dougherty: And they're always stupid oppressed, they're never very intelligent.
>
> Int: Do you think this aspect of aliens reflects any view of society?
>
> Howe: Yeah, I think it's racism.
>
> Dougherty: It's xenophobic.
>
> Roach: It's obvious xenophobia, yeah.

As we have seen, these Australian fans do have a very precise sense of their situation as a 'powerless elite' between industry and audience; and, as the above quotation illustrates, they can, when prompted, relate the show beyond personalities to structures of oppression, rather than to Sharratt's history of individuals. When Tony Howe was asked whether the 'decline' in the morality of the Doctor during the Tom Baker period reflected anything more general, he elaborated at some length:

> The standards in *Doctor Who* are declining because they are showing that violence is an acceptable answer to situations ... It reflects what's happening in England, the decline in the effectiveness of institutions to deal with problems, and a breakdown in society ... The generality is that crimes of passion and violence have gone up and hence become more acceptable. Terrorism is acceptable, and that is a decline. Innocent individuals are to be punished for what the system does. I find that morally repugnant; and in *Doctor Who* that is gradually coming in, that innocent parts of a system can be destroyed for the supposed good of some other part of the system.

Howe's views were hotly contested by other fans in the group, however, on the grounds that

'There is no one standard of morality. The point is that we are shifting from one set of morals to another.' This kind of contentious debate was typical wherever the 'political' was introduced into discussion by fans. Ian Levine, for instance, argued strongly against Jeremy Bentham's contention that 'there is a strong chauvinist element in *Doctor Who* – there don't appear to be very many women actresses appearing in it apart from the screaming companions'.[23] Or, alternatively, where there was some consensus (as among the Sydney fans) about the sexism of the show's use of female companions or its xenophobic representation of aliens, these were responses to the interviewer's leading questions: 'Do you object to the portrayal of women as being so dependent?', or, 'Does this representation of aliens reflect any view of society?' Whether one speaks with *Doctor Who* fans, or goes to their conventions, or reads their fanzines, one gets the very strong impression that 'politics' is – most of the time, and at best – no more than an auxiliary discourse which is summoned up to explain that other, and much more central, 'decline' – in *Doctor Who* itself.

The point, then, is that 'displacement of knowledge' (as 'expertise' and 'intimacy') among fans does not deprive them of political awareness (as primarily middle-class feminists, conservatives, or whatever), but rather is what determines their cultural constitution and reading position as fans. As fans they achieve remarkable consensus (spanning different continents and parts of the world); but as individuals inhabiting different class, gender and ethnic subject positions, they quite clearly differ in their political readings.

Speaking as fans

The response of the Sydney fans to the question 'How does *Doctor Who* compare with other science fiction shows?' was quite uniformly pro-British, and not at all simply as 'consumers of gadgetry and action', as Ebert would predict of TV science fiction fans. Indeed, the English fans Levine and Bentham emphasized *Doctor Who*'s 'cerebral' quality as against the 'high gloss' and 'macho' action of US science fiction shows.

> Bentham: The Doctor is entirely different from the conventional mould of hero. He

doesn't go in for the three things that you find in all American heroes: (a) they are very, very macho, (b) they are usually interested in women and gambling, and (c) they all have a slant towards hardware and action. The Doctor breaks all of those boundaries, and he rarely resorts to violence. His personal interests he virtually keeps shielded and in fact he almost seems to enjoy them from a child-like level...

Levine: Personally, I would rather see a BBC science fiction production than an American one, because those 'cardboard sets', as people call it in *Doctor Who*, have more character than all the American 35mm film gloss.

The Australian fans were as convinced as English fans Bentham and Levine of the superiority of *Doctor Who* (and British SF products generally) over anything from the USA.

Howe: I think *Doctor Who*'s much better than *Star Trek*, because it's more original.

Dougherty: Oh yes, the script is better.

Howe: And as I said before, the format of *Doctor Who* is more flexible because they haven't got worried about whether the Tardis's nuts and bolts are the same from one episode to another.

Dougherty: The thing is, too, *Doctor Who* doesn't worry about offending minorities or anything like that, whereas *Star Trek* has always been.

Howe: That's English television compared to American television.

Dougherty: Yes, that's right, but it's something that's important in comparing them. And the other thing is, I know you were saying that they always meet evil aliens (in *Doctor Who*), but in *Star Trek* it didn't matter whether the aliens were evil, friendly, non-compos mentis, half-and-half, or whatever, their immediate reaction was 'Aliens! Ugh! Horror! Horror! Horror!'

Roach: Ugly, horrible aliens!

Dougherty: Yes, for a show that's been glorified by its fans on its liberal attitude, aliens took a terrible beating in *Star Trek*.

Roach: It's been glorified by its American fans for its liberal attitude simply because it conveys immediately and completely in condensed fashion the American ideal.

Dougherty: That's right.

Roach: I mean, at least you don't have Doctor

Who waving the British flag everywhere ... Saying 'England stands for the Westminster system'.

Dougherty: You know, there have been a few times when he's made lots of derisive comments about English institutions and the English military.

Howe: That's a strong tendency in *Doctor Who* ... All authority figures are automatically suspect in *Doctor Who*. In a way it's a socialist type of view of the thing. Whereas in *Star Trek* authority was shown as good and benevolent and you bring benefits from being part of a team.

Roach: And all weaknesses were based on individuals.

Howe: That's true – individuals were always the weak points ... The system wasn't wrong ... In *Doctor Who* there isn't really such a system because he's not part of a chain of command. But whenever he lands somewhere there's always a bad president, or a bad dictator, or a bad boss or someone in authority over people.

Roach: Bosses are bad.

Howe: Well, that is a message in *Doctor Who*, that bosses are bad, always *per se*, because they're bosses. There are very few stories you can think of where anyone in authority is shown as good or sympathetic.

Int: In 'The Monster of Peladon', say, there was situation where they portrayed a bureaucracy or whatever that had gone wrong because it wasn't able to relate to its public, and all it needed was *Doctor Who* to come in and fix it up and show them how they could have 'responsible government'.

Dougherty: Sarah showed the Queen how to get into Women's Lib (laughs).

Roach: But you'll notice that the Doctor saw nothing wrong with the monarchy. I mean, it is just a monarchy that's gone slightly wrong!

Howe: Because of bad advisers.

Int: And, I mean, the whole solution of that problem was mediation, so that the workers got better conditions, but there was never any...

Howe: That's an exceptional story because of the political overtones.

Roach: And it should be noted that when it was shown in Britain there was the background of the miners' strike.

Dougherty: Yes, that was topical at the time.

Howe: That was the time of the Heath

government and the coal strike. But in other stories, all authority is forcibly overthrown. Frequently in *Doctor Who* any attempt at mediation automatically fails and it has to be overthrown by force. That happens in a lot of stories, from Dalek stories down to less obvious stories – it's force that has to be used to replace the people in charge … You never have to look at the fact that running a planet may be a bloody difficult job.

Doctor Who fans, whether in Britain or Australia, achieve maximum consensus (like many other followers of the show that we have analysed) in accepting the 'high culture' superiority of a 'British' imagined community. *Doctor Who* is 'inventive' and 'ingenious' in its scripts, while *Buck Rogers* and *Battlestar Galactica* are 'plastic' and 'glossy' in their action. *Doctor Who* is 'flexible' and 'liberal' in its politics, whereas *Star Trek* is inflexibly 'moralistic' in presenting the 'American ideal'.

What is interesting about this discussion among Australian fans, however, is the way in which total fan consensus gives way to individual dispute over what *Doctor Who*'s 'anti-authority' position signifies.

Speaking as individuals

As well as being president of the Australian fan club, Tony Howe was a Sydney University-based postgraduate, doing an MA thesis in history. In this thesis, Howe was critiquing Marxist historiography. It was perhaps this particular cultural competence which began to provide inter-textual references as the discussion continued.

Howe: What I'm pointing up is the fact that it's automatically assumed that the authority figures are always the evil ones – and that's not necessarily so…
Roach: It's developing the Westminster system.
Howe: No, it's not…
Int: Isn't it the liberal tradition?
Howe: But it's more the left-wing liberal tradition, this tendency.
Dougherty: Have you been watching *The Omega Factor*? – again the figures in authority are evil.
Howe: Well, I think that shows the socialist bias in the BBC.

It was from this point in the discussion (about all authority being represented as bad, and about Tom Baker's Doctor tending towards 'means-to-end' violence rather than responsible leadership) that Howe launched into his view about the 'moral decline' of both *Doctor Who* as series and British society in general – and into territory hotly contested by the other fans present. Indeed, the debate became quite angry before finishing.

M: In the past even working-class people that didn't want ruling-class people to have palaces and things didn't want innocent people to be blown up for political slogans, and that's what's happening today.
F: That's why there was a Paris Commune?
M: What about the Paris Commune? The Paris Commune was much more complicated because it was besieged by the Prussians for several months beforehand – the situation was quite complicated. Yeah, and I've read a book on it too!
F: I hate to tell you…
M: Oh, forget about it.

They had, by then, stopped talking as 'fans'. Their self-concept as a unified subculture of fans could easily embrace a 'British' imaginary. But it broke down into hostility and silence when it began to encounter discussion about what 'the British way' actually meant in terms of power and class.

Conclusion

Our view is that fans are not 'fan-atics'. They are not simply the mindless, middle-class 'consumers whose passion for gadgetry is inexhaustible' of Ebert's analysis. Indeed, they are often closer to Ebert's 'serious' SF fans, with their assumptions of 'bourgeois realism'. Still less are they the psychologically 'deviant' personalities that the media like to construct. Indeed 'fans' are best understood not as unified individuals at all (whether 'deviant' or 'normal') but rather as a subculture with sets of discourses appropriate to a 'powerless elite', positioned in relations of expertise and intimacy with 'their' show. They are necessarily positioned, structurally positioned, in an immediate context of industry ('producers') and audience ('the floating voter'). Reliant on both these areas of culture industry – for the 'quality' of their show and for its very continuance – the fans' discourses readily refer to 'golden ages' and 'eras of the unforgivable'. Golden ages are times – usually in the fans' past, often transmitted before they were fans – when communication between producers, fans and audiences is perceived as transparent and true. As the 'fan' in the Nathan-Turner *Doctor Who* story, 'The Greatest Show in the Galaxy' (1989) puts it, 'Although I never got to see the early days, I know it's not as good as it used to be, but I'm still terribly interested.'

Golden ages are, Raymond Williams points out, partly a feature of nostalgia:'we notice their location in the childhoods of their authors, and this must be relevant.'[24] This clearly seems true of *Doctor Who* fans – for most of them the 'golden ages' of the show are set prior to 1977 which, given the average age of ADWFC members (in 1982, when first interviewed) of 'about eighteen or nineteen', means that their first valuation of Hartnell, Troughton and Pertwee eras was as children.

Golden ages, Williams also points out, have very precise social and historical constituents as well as personal and psychological ones. For instance, in *The Country and the City*, Williams analyses the 'structure of feeling' based on a 'temporary stability' in the process from feudalism to capitalism, a particular 'golden age' perspective of idealisation based on 'a deep desire for stability, served to cover and to evade the actual and bitter contradictions of the time'.[25] The themes of science fiction are frequently about just this historical transition – from feudalism to capitalism – but Williams's example is most interesting analogously, as a model for considering the audiences of science fiction.

Williams speaks of 'golden ages' constructed by both the lordly and the landless in this early-modern period, but the 'most interesting' construction depended on the social experience of the 'shifting and intermediate groups'.

An upper peasantry, which had established itself in the break-up of the strict feudal order, and which had ideas and illusions about freedom and independence from the experience of a few generations, was being pressed and expropriated by the great landowners, the most successful of just these new men ... A moral protest

was then based on a temporary stability. ... Such men, who had risen by change, were quick to be bitter about renewed or continuing change.[26]

The interest of this as analogy for the analysis of SF fans relates to the Klein/Mellor thesis of the SF audience as the exploited fraction (with 'ideas and illusions about freedom and independence') of the exploiting capitalist class (including 'the most successful of just these new men'). Perhaps the 'politics of decline' so deeply felt by Tony Howe is a late expression of what Mellor describes – the 'tragic vision' of a temporarily optimistic middle-class fraction.

But here we have preferred to examine the discourses of fandom, as it were synchronically – as a kind of perennial system (though with different national/cultural variations) in which the stable points of reference have been 'the producers', 'the floating voters' and the fans' own cultural competences in 'intimacy' and 'expertise'. It is in that communication system of industry, audience and fans that what fans call 'polarising debate' (for instance, over Tom Baker as Doctor) becomes meaningful. Positions are clearly ascribed ('fans of Tom Baker', 'fans of *Doctor Who*') and discourse relevances (to the show's 'unfolding odyssey', or to 'television sets switched on all over the world') equally clearly understood.

In contrast, polarising debates about wider histories, about Britain's 'contemporary decline', about the 'socialist bias' of the BBC, have much less relevance in this fan discourse, and are ascribed to 'personal opinion' in an indefinable moral order which is in 'shift not decline'. The 'political' representations of British or US values in *Doctor Who* are most easily accommodated by the fans (as fans) in terms of national imaginaries – 'the British way', 'the American ideal' – and these in turn are related to 'cerebral' versus 'high gloss' science fiction styles. Any political analysis beyond this was uncomfortable, personalised, contentious – and finally closed-off, 'forgotten' as not relevant to fan debate.

In this sense, the Australian and British fans of *Doctor Who* seem quite different from the more politicised fans that Henry Jenkins describes for *Star Trek* and other programmes within US fandom. Yet, although the weight of emphasis in Jenkins's book is certainly on fans whose pleasure comes in resisting the preferred meanings of the texts and ascribing to them oppositional meanings, if we look carefully, we find in Jenkins's science fiction fans quite the opposite as well.

To say that fans promote their own meanings over those of producers is not to suggest that the meanings fans produce are always oppositional ones or that those meanings are made in isolation from other social factors. Fans have chosen these media products from the total range of available texts precisely because they seem to hold special potential as vehicles for expressing the fans' pre-existing social commitments and cultural interests; there is always some degree of compatibility between the ideological construction of the text and the ideological commitments of fans.[27]

Fans, as Jenkins notes, are not ideologues; rather, they define their relationship to the text in terms of pleasure rather than politics, and cobble together their own culture from fragments of pre-existing media content: 'A poached culture, a nomadic culture, is also a patchwork culture, an impure culture, where much that is taken in remains semi-digested and ill-considered.'[28]

Interestingly, Jenkins points to the fact that Star Trek fans feel happier discussing 'politics' via the series rather than outside it:

Star Trek fans found the discussion of abortion appropriate as long as it was centred on the fictional characters and their on-screen adventures. Objections were raised to the introduction of 'politics' into this fan form as soon as the debate shifted onto a direct focus on the real-world implications of this issue.[29]

Jenkins argues that in particular situations – such as the role of women in science fiction – this helps to 'make the abstract concrete, to transform issues of public concern into topics of personal significance'.[30] Consequently, far from being apolitical, such discussions allow women who have traditionally felt excluded from political discourse to examine 'issues central to feminist debate and analysis', such as the 'marginalisation' of women in the workplace (through Uhura and Chapel) or traditional masculine authority (through Kirk). Fans, Jenkins argues, 'are drawn to specific programs in part because they provide the resources for discussing issues of central concern to them or

because they pose questions they would like to more fully explore'.[31]

In the case of the Doctor Who discussion quoted above, however, something different is happening. Here a female fan is explicitly laying claim to a competence in abstract political dialogue, and her 'That's why there was a Paris Commune?' directly challenges what has been an almost entirely male-dominated theorisation about ideology and Doctor Who up to this point. One fan's dismissive 'I've read a book too' works to reposition this 'extravagant' female gesture; and it is this potential male/female argument that other fans (including female fans) quickly move to cut off. It may well be for reasons of fan consensus (as in this case) that 'female fans are often uncomfortable identifying themselves as feminists and adopting its terms within their own discourse'.[32]

Fandom provides, as Jenkins says, an 'institutional filter' which adds to and mediates other sets of social identities which fans have. In the Doctor Who argument over politics discussed above, that institutional filter operated consensually through its own, familiar reading protocols, until the 'Commune' intervention threatened the series text with quite an 'other' text. The fan's claim to have 'read a book on it too' accesses this 'other' field of reading competence, ones where other fans compete or have nothing to say. As with Jenkins's Star Trek fans, it was not 'politics' as such which fans objected to, but 'politics' attached to another reading formation. It was on the edge of that arcane 'other' that the fans protected their community consensus with silence.

Notes

1 Interview with Ian Levine, November 1981.
2 Interview with Jeremy Bentham, November 1981.
3 P. Fenech (1985) Zerinza, 33/4, Supplement, p. 2.
4 Interview with David Saunders, Garry Russell and Deanne Holding, January 1982.
5 S. Collins (1982) 'Regeneration: A Time Lord Mystery', Zerinza, 23, p. 7.
6 Ibid.
7 Ibid., p. 10.
8 Interview with Ian Levine, November 1981.
9 Interview with Graham Williams, November 1981.
10 T. Howe (1982) Zerinza, 25/26, Supplement, p. 2.
11 Focus group interview with Sydney Doctor Who fan club members, November 1982.
12 J. Tulloch and M. Alvarado (1983) Doctor Who: The Unfolding

Text. London: Routledge, ch. 6.

13 S. Collins (1982) *Zerinza*, 24, Supplement, pp. 3-4.

14 H. Jenkins (1991), 'Star Trek Rerun, Reread, Rewritten: Fanwriting as Textual Poaching', in C. Penley, E. Lyon, and J. Bergstrom (eds), *Close Encounters: Film, Feminism and Science Fiction.* Minneapolis: University of Minnesota Press, p. 192 [reprinted in this volume].

15 Ibid.

16 Interview with Dallas Jones and Tony Howe, 23 November 1989.

17 I. Levine (1987) 'JN-T Must Go Now', *DW Bulletin*, 49, p. 1.

18 Ibid.

19 T. Howe (1985) *Doctor Who Newsletter*, December, p.2.

20 Interview with Tony Howe and Dallas Jones.

21 Tony Howe emphasised some years later that he had changed his views on this issue of cultural decline: his earlier views are only used here to indicate a particular reading in the early Thatcher period, not to represent any timeless and 'authentic' picture of a particular fan.

22 B. Sharratt (1981) 'The Politics of the Popular – From Melodrama to Television', in D. Bradby, L. James, and B. Sharratt (eds), *Performance and Politics in Popular Drama.* Cambridge: Cambridge University Press, pp. 275–95.

23 Interview with Ian Levine and Jeremy Bentham, 1981.

24 R. Williams (1975) *The Country and the City.* St Albans: Paladin, p. 60.

25 Ibid.

26 Ibid., pp. 58–9.

27 H. Jenkins (1992) *Textual Poachers: Television Fans and Participatory Culture.* New York: Routledge, Chapman and Hall, p. 35.

28 Ibid., p. 283.

29 Ibid., p. 84.

30 Ibid.

31 Ibid., p. 85.

32 Ibid.

New Hope: The Postmodern Project of *Star Wars*
Will Brooker

I wrote this chapter when I was twenty-five. For me, of course, the piece almost counts as juvenilia – I read it as I would a diary entry from that period, half-impressed and half-embarrassed. It is striking how long ago it all feels, and how we can already feel nostalgic for the mid-1990s; how a period that thought it was knowingly ironic can already feel like a time of naïve innocence.

A great deal has changed, and I wanted to note a few of those changes, just to suggest the ways in which this essay is, to some extent, a period piece and how some of its ideas could be reconsidered in the light of subsequent developments. Jake Lloyd, who plays Anakin in *The Phantom Menace*, was only six at the time of writing; Hayden Christensen, who plays the same character in *Attack of the Clones*, was fourteen with only TV credits to his name. The *Star Wars Special Editions* had not yet been released, and so crucial details of the canonical text remained unaltered. To take just one example, the 1997 version of *A New Hope*, regarded by Lucas as the definitive rewrite, tweaked Han Solo's character from cynical crook to honourable nice-guy by showing that he only killed Greedo after the bounty hunter shot first and missed; prior to this digital addition, Han had murdered his opponent in cold blood.

Trivial as it may sound, this retroactive nudging of character – which undermines Han's development from selfish loner to team player in *Return of the Jedi* – is of great significance to fans, and has prompted considerable debate across online discussion boards and websites dedicated to the *Special Edition* changes. But then, online discussion itself has only come into its own since 1995; the World Wide Web was still young when I wrote this essay, as demonstrated by my ponderous quotation marks around 'home pages' and the fact that I relegate internet fandom to a footnote below print zines and small press comics. The Web of the time was grindingly slow – with pages sometimes taking a full five minutes to load – relatively unpopulated, and incredibly amateurish compared to its current state – amateurish in the good sense, implying labours of love and the kind of home-grown talent that this essay identifies as a key strand in contemporary readings of the *Star Wars* saga.

With Lucasfilm currently policing online fandom, sending cease and desist letters to sites that present unwelcome interpretations – often gay readings – of its characters, recruiting promising film directors from online digital theatres and luring fans onto its official territory where it can control their homepage content, what we used to call 'cyberspace' is now far more fenced-off, far more corporately-controlled. Of course, there is still a wealth of creativity and constant ongoing debate across TheForce.net, Echostation.com and thousands of other *Star Wars* sites, but Lucasfilm has reclaimed the saga now after some fifteen years of inactivity from 1983–97, and the fans are no longer the main curators of an almost-abandoned mythos, as they were in the mid-1990s.

The political situation in both the US and UK has changed, and so has the political situation in the *Star Wars* galaxy; the prequels took us back in time to the Old Republic, which seems increasingly to be a state on its last legs, with a diminishing band of Jedi Knights, Jedi Masters who fail to see the corrupt senator in their own chambers and a rising force of opposition in the form of Darth Sidious. *Episode I* and *II* both tell a story of a system with a rotten core, with the golden boy Anakin Skywalker failed by his Jedi mentors and about to fall to darkness; perhaps the most potent achievement of these films is that they invite us, as an audience who cheered the Rebels in the original trilogy, not just to sympathise with Darth Vader, but to actually see the rise of the nascent Empire as a much-needed change to a tired and redundant Republic.

It would take another essay to consider the shifting parallels between Lucas' world and our own, but it might be worthwhile. Today's British youth are clearly not in the position I described in 1995, where a new government seemed unthinkable and the overthrow of the Conservative party was a fantasy; for many *Star Wars* fans, New Labour's landslide in 1997 may have brought a euphoria comparable to the end of the Death Star and destruction of the Empire. In turn, while the good guys of the original *Star Wars* trilogy were identifiable as *bricoleurs*, a rag-tag mish-mash making do within the totalitarian system, the Jedi of the prequels are in power and making a hash of it, showing themselves to be short-sighted and blinkered, interfering in the affairs of other planetary governments and lending military aid to one side of conflicts as it suits them; a case, arguably, of meet the new boss, same as the old, and a disappointment that some would see as a potential allegory for the Blair era.

That the Jedi triumph in *Episode II* with a clone army bred by their enemy – an army that will soon become the stormtroopers of the Empire – further problematises the divisions between 'good' and 'bad' that were fairly clear-cut in *A New Hope* and were only complicated by the revelation that the hero of the original trilogy is the arch-villain's son, with the potential to start a new dynasty along his lines. This theme of evil within, credited to Robin Wood within the essay, is developed to interesting effect in the prequels; the core of the Imperial military lies entirely within the Republic, not just allowed to grow through ignorance but authorised by Obi-Wan Kenobi and marshalled by Yoda. There are parallels, for those who want to take them further, with the US funding of Osama bin Laden and Saddam Hussein.

As a further sidenote, it would be surely difficult for George W. Bush to map his campaigns against Afghanistan or Iraq onto the *Star Wars* mythos of the plucky cowboy nation against the coldly oppressive Evil Empire – as Reagan successfully managed in the 1980s – when Al Qaeda's methods resemble the hit-and-run terrorism of the *New Hope* rebels, when the enemy nations are economically more similar to Luke Skywalker's home planet of Tatooine than to the Death Star, and when the US has become the only world superpower. As I point out below, though, the politics of *Star Wars* are vague enough to be fitted to a range of historical conflicts and international contexts, and my research into actual responses showed that even fans in the US military totally failed to make any connection between *Star Wars* and the Strategic Defense Initiative – a link that this essay treats as obvious.

Star Wars: A New Hope was a nostalgia film on its first release, and its postmodern pastiche was itself copied and echoed in the science fiction of the 1980s and 1990s. In a particularly curious couple of twists, the 'clones' subplot of *Judge Dredd*, which I accuse below of being an empty simulation of the original *Star Wars* trilogy, now seems to prefigure the 'clones' subplot of *Episode II*, just as Ian McKellen's Gandalf in Peter Jackson's *Lord of the Rings* films seems to pay tribute to Alec Guinness' Obi-Wan Kenobi – when the homage was, of course, originally the other way around. Watching the aged Obi-Wan and Vader duelling in *A New Hope* is a slightly melancholy experience now, rather than a rousing, Saturday-morning-pictures episode: we remember the young Obi-Wan, defying his master and losing his padawan, and we remember, even more unnervingly, the child Darth Vader, saying goodbye to his mother and shaking hands precociously with a spiky-haired Obi-Wan Kenobi. The prequels are meant to be the past, but it's the original trilogy, set decades later, that now feels like history.

Will Brooker, January 2003

Shopping in London; it's early 1996 but it feels, as the slogan had it, like a long time ago. It feels like 1977. There are life-size cardboard models of Darth Vader and C-3PO in the local Our Price, advertising the *Star Wars* trilogy on video for the last time this century. Further down the high street, W. H. Smiths has mounted a display of *Star Wars* paperbacks, the sheer range of which would surprise all but the most diehard fan: the Jedi Academy trilogy, the Corellian trilogy, the further adventures of Lando Calrissian and Han Solo. Next to the bulky volumes in their set groups of three are the flimsier illustrated teenage novels about the Junior Jedi Knights, and below those the Young Jedi Knights range, published in 1995 and clearly aimed at readers born long after the 1983 release of the most recent *Star Wars* film, *Return of the Jedi*.[1]

This is to suggest merely the films' new visibility in the populist mainstream of book and video stores; it is to neglect the role-playing department of the Virgin megastore, with its Star Wars New Republic Sourcebook, its Technical Companions, its Planets Collection and Twin Stars of Kira modules.[2] This is to ignore the upper floor of Forbidden Planet and its shelf of five monthly comics from Star Wars: Tales of the Jedi to Star Wars: X-Wing Rogue Squadron,[3] and the display downstairs of 1996 calendars, 'audio-book' cassettes and a recording of the 'original radio drama' retailing at over £80. Two conclusions can be drawn from this trawl; that this is a recent, on-going industry rather than a resale of old spin-offs dragged from the back of stockrooms, and that the nature of the merchandise has undergone a change since the mid-1980s, when *Star Wars* last generated any significant commercial interest.

In 1977, when *Star Wars – Episode IV: A New Hope*, to give it the subtitle purists prefer – was first released, its influence on the market included Walls Star Wars skinless pork sausages, Trebor Star Wars chews and Letraset notebooks with new covers hastily added proclaiming them as 'Stormtrooper's Manual' and 'Princess Leia's Rebel Jotter'. This year, apart from the videos and the apparently endless series of novels, the predominant line of merchandise lies in games for the Sega and Nintendo of which Dark Forces, at £49.99, is a typical example. The mini-action figures and model spacecraft so eagerly hunted out by ten-year-olds in 1980 have been hoarded for fifteen years and now fetch up to £60 on collectors' markets. Clearly, the target audience has shifted; put simply, it has grown up. Though the £80 boxed-set of the trilogy on video may have been bought by the indulgent parents of some under-tens, anecdotal evidence suggests that a great many young men in their late teens and twenties cajoled it from girlfriends as a Christmas present, and the traditional market for console games and science fiction novels suggests a similar group in terms of both age and gender.

This boom in consumer interest fits very neatly, of course, with the theatrical re-release of *A New Hope* – with revamped effects and some reinstated scenes cut from the original – scheduled for April 1997, and the first in a new trilogy promised in 1998; as such, the merchandise phenomenon can easily be traced back to efficient, long-term marketing strategies at Lucasfilm or 20th Century Fox, and would hardly bear further examination were it not for other, scattered signs of nostalgic reference to the original trilogy which suggest a wider, less quantifiable resurgence of interest and give an indication of the films' continuing cultural resonance among young men in particular.

Any list of these sources is bound to be both subjective and incomplete. It might include, however, the proliferation of *Star Wars* 'home pages' on the Internet and their print-based equivalents in amateur fanzines,

of which at least seven, with titles such as *Bounty Hunter, Moons of Yavin* and *Holocron*, are currently available in England alone.[4] Similarly, the English cottage industry of 'small-press' comic books, with a readership predominantly of twentysomething male graduates, makes strikingly frequent reference to the *Star Wars* trilogy as a site of shared cultural knowledge: a character asks, for example, 'who did you want to get off with Princess Leia? Han or Luke? Farm-boy or pirate?' and in another title the protagonist mourns a dead friend with 'he was my Chewbacca'.[5]

This sense of the films as the formative cultural influence on a particular generation, to be celebrated a decade later in low-budget, 'independent' media forms, is echoed in a *New Musical Express* interview with the band Ash, whose second single of 1995, 'Girl from Mars', was backed with a manic reworking of John Williams' 'Cantina Band' theme from *Star Wars*; the trilogy is cited as 'an immense influence', and the band linked with Oasis and Menswear as 'part of that *Star Wars* generation' in a re-emphasis of the films' central location within the cultural capital of young British males.[6] A similar quotation and reference can be seen in American sources, both in the range of fanzines like *Star Wars Insider*, largely equivalent to their British counterparts, and in more mainstream texts which speak of the slacker or 'Generation-Y' experience, again with a striking gender-specificity. Douglas Coupland's most recent novel *Microserfs*, for instance, has its disillusioned, 26-year-old narrator Daniel filling a computer file, and pages of text, with his own random patterns of thought: buried in the outpourings are the names Han Solo and R2-D2.[7] With a comparable project and audience, the no-budget film *Clerks* – directed by 23-year-old Kevin Smith in 1994 – involves its young male protagonists in a heated discussion about the contractors who built *Return of the Jedi*'s Death Star.[8]

An unsystematic and unscientific body of evidence, to be sure; but it suggests, I hope, that the resonance and meaning of the *Star Wars* films goes beyond a nostalgia imposed from 'above'. What I propose to do here is to examine the possible meanings of the films to the audience sketched in my account – that is, to the young men in their late-teens to mid-twenties who conceivably saw *A New Hope* on its first theatrical release – and, bearing in mind the right-wing connotations which the trilogy has been accused of carrying, and which have irreparably come to be borne by the term 'Star Wars' itself, the implications of this resurgence of interest and investment of nostalgia in a supposedly reactionary text.

Star Wars is, of course, a nostalgic text in itself and is famously cited as one of Fredric Jameson's examples of *la mode rétro*. In its pastiche of 'the Saturday afternoon serial of the *Buck Rogers* type' it satisfies

> a deep (might I even say repressed?) longing to experience them again: it is a complex object in which on some first level children and adolescents can take the adventures straight, while the adult public is able to gratify a deeper and more properly nostalgic desire to return to that older period and to live its strange old aesthetic artifacts through once again.[9]

The film's aesthetic of mythic recycling was noted by many reviewers at the time of its first release, who spotted allusions to 'everything from *The Searchers* to *Triumph of the Will*'[10] and either dismissed it as 'a ploddingly self-conscious pastiche' – this from a review which rather pompously traced the film's plot to *The Alamo*, its robots to *The Wizard of Oz* and its sentiment to *Lassie Come Home*[11] – or approved its project to synthesise 'a whole body of the most potent myths on which we have been raised'.[12]

As Jameson notes, though, the 'we' of this last observation was the adult public of 1977, not its children. Those seeing the film at age seven had no shared memory of *Buck Rogers*, *The Searchers* or *The Wizard of Oz*; *Star Wars* was no doubt, for many of its young viewers, the occasion of their first visit to the cinema, and its myths were of the first order rather than a self-conscious recycling. Here were Merlin, Ricky Nelson, the Tin Man, *The Seven Samurai* and *The Dam Busters*[13] crammed into one potent, electrifying folk story; a rush of concentrated iconography, of distilled myth. That young audience left the cinema having swallowed all the popular narratives that had thrilled their parents in one gulp; and the unprecedented, across-the-board marketing meant that for the first time children's lives were invaded by the film at every level of consumption from crisps to pyjamas to toys to

lampshades. As a review in the *Evening Standard* perceptively noted, Lucas had 'manufactured a sort of 'group memory' for kids who never knew the fantasies and myths that films dealt in when he was young'.[14]

Some eighteen years on, that group memory remains; and in 1995 the *Star Wars* generation began, like Lucas, to make films which recycled their own childhood myths. *Star Wars*, to 27-year-old Danny Cannon's generation, is the original; *Judge Dredd* is the nostalgia film. But something has changed; something has been lost which suggests that the continuing power of the *Star Wars* trilogy lies not simply in its 'best of' aesthetic of mythic compilation, but in its underlying ideological structure. It is in this project of the over-arching struggle, seen in terms of a 'grand narrative', that the film's reactionary political programme has been located, and which I shall consider after a brief comparison of *Star Wars* with its reworking in 1995's *Judge Dredd*.

If *Star Wars* embodies Jameson's nostalgia cinema, *Judge Dredd* works within a Baudrillardian aesthetic of pure surface, a 'dizzying collage of everybody else's ideas',[15] a lifting of images from *Demolition Man*, *Terminator 2* and *Robocop* which themselves borrowed freely from cinema's iconographic stockroom; in a final irony, the grimy, drizzled Mega-City One which Dredd patrols virtually replicates the Los Angeles of *Blade Runner*, a text analysed to within an inch of its life for its notorious plundering of noir and Victoriana, Egyptian architecture and Japanese neon. That city's reappearance in *Judge Dredd* was described by one reviewer as 'a museum-display composite seen too many times before ... Now That's What I Call A Dystopia Vol 27'.[16] Dredd himself, along with the genetically-bred soldiers he fights at the film's climax, is a clone, one of several copies from a prototype lawman.

Judge Dredd opens with a text crawl giving background to the film's scenario, voiced by Darth Vader actor James Earl Jones; a device which, aimed at precisely the audience of young men for whom the black actor's distinctive tones and the text scrolling slowly upscreen will immediately recall *A New Hope*, is clearly intended to self-consciously reference *Star Wars* for its nostalgic function. The pastiche goes on to incorporate from the earlier film 'the illuminating sojourn into the desert, the doomed but wise old mentor, the overbearing martial soundtrack that John Williams himself stole from Gustav Holst, and the ham-fisted whack of the computer equipment to get it to operate properly'.[17] This latter telling detail occurs during an airborne chase on jet-powered Lawmaster bikes which could, in its similarity to *Return of the Jedi*'s speeder-bike sequence, virtually have been shot from the same storyboards. The only difference is the inevitable loss of *Jedi*'s thrilling audacity, and a surprising paucity in the later film's special effects. *Judge Dredd*'s reworking-by-numbers is simulation in Baudrillard's sense of an endlessly self-mirroring, self-reflexive collection of images for which the 'original', if there was one, is lost in the 'uninterrupted circuit' of exchange and duplication;[18] but it also, in the more popular sense of the word, brings to mind the aimless pleasure of a *Star Wars* flight simulator – Disney's 'Star Tours', or perhaps the 'Skywalker Park' of William Gibson's novel *Virtual Light*.[19]

Aimless, for *Judge Dredd* has no aim, no point, no progression. The film's triumphant finale centres around Dredd's refusal to be anything but a 'street judge', and his return to duty. The judicial system, shown from the film's beginning to be brutal, militaristic and totalitarian, is reinstated, and we as audience, like the Mega-City citizens, are encouraged to celebrate the restoration of the old status quo. We are shown no possibility for social change; rather, the film suggests that change is unwise, and that the devil we know, however fascistic it may seem in its jackboots, epaulettes and blank-eyed helmet, is preferable to the chaos presented as the only alternative.[20] Significantly, the youth of Mega-City One are seen in only two roles and given two options; turning to crime and being policed as a juvenile delinquent, or to the law and becoming Judge Dredd. Compare this with the opportunity given to Luke Skywalker, and the key difference between the two films begins to emerge. Luke is initially a disaffected teenager living on an isolated homestead, a gentler James Dean held back by his uncle's unambitious vision of a lifetime in farming and small business – 'you can waste time with your friends when your chores are done'. Through his accidental discovery of a distress call from the diplomat Princess Leia, he is offered entry into a project spanning far beyond his own limited sphere. Luke, of course, becomes a Rebel, and he is given a cause.

In growing up, I kept hearing from all sides that we couldn't do anything, that we were helpless. The only positive thing I feel I can put across in the film is to generate a sort of vague I-can-do-anything feeling. Once you get that feeling, it comes true. Be positive – you can do it.[21]

This was the project of *Star Wars* as put forward by Lucas in a *Guardian* interview some ten months before the film opened in Britain. His hopes for the film were echoed by a review later that year, which saw *Star Wars* as the 'triumph of faith and innocence over cynicism and despair'.[22] To claim the same for *Judge Dredd* would be inconceivable. *Star Wars* entertains a vision of optimistic possibility of the kind which the 'slacker' mentality – and in Britain, the apathetic nihilism of youth portrayed in Danny Cannon's first film, *The Young Americans*, and Paul Anderson's *Shopping*[23] – made deeply unfashionable. However, this sense of the potential for change, the gaining of purpose and the validity of a struggle based on principles – of new hope, to put it at its simplest – is perhaps exactly why *Star Wars* has retained, or regained, such poignancy among the generation now in their twenties. The representations of youth culture over recent years, as suggested above, are depressingly bleak narratives of joyriders, shoplifters, ravers and dealers; as a review of *Shopping* had it, 'dull approximations of a lost generation, moving towards a self-ordained bad end like slightly disinterested lemmings. There is practically nothing to measure their rebellion against.'[24]

Star Wars, by contrast, is built around a trajectory towards liberation, emancipation and the overthrow of the tyrannical state; a narrative with understandable resonance for a generation which has seen a single government in office for seventeen years, and for whom political change may well seem the stuff of fairytales. This trajectory, however, also seems to constitute one of those equally unfashionable *grands récits* of social transformation against which Lyotard warned in 'What Is Postmodernism?';[25] and Lyotard's suspicion of the grand narrative's 'totality' can perhaps be seen as well-founded when we consider the wholesale appropriation of *Star Wars*' project by the Reagan administration.

Lucas went to court in 1985 in a vain attempt to sever the link between his film title and Reagan's Strategic Defense Initiative,[26] but the words 'Star Wars' would almost certainly have retained their secondary connotations in the popular mind even had he won. Like Lucas, Reagan drew on the cinema of previous decades for his own myth-making, and effectively hijacked them to his own ends. Susan Aronstein has argued that

> Apart from his freely acknowledged employment of the rhetoric and imagery of *Star Wars* ('the Strategic Defense Initiative has been labelled Star Wars. But it isn't about war. It is about peace. If you will pardon my stealing a film line … the Force is with us') most of Reagan's best lines and certainly his policies can be traced back to films, usually the countersubversive B movie of his own career, the same films that Lucas and Spielberg looked to in their revitalisation of early Hollywood genres.[27]

Yet it was not just Reagan who saw a right-wing project within the film's ideological premise. Years before the term 'Evil Empire' had been used to describe the Soviet Union, a newspaper editorial cartoon of 1978 showed Vader at the debating table on the side of the USSR, telling a sceptical United States team 've vant to assure you that ve have no thoughts or intentions of using space for military purposes'.[28]

Indeed, it is not hard to see some textual elements from which a reactionary reading, or reading of the film as reactionary, can be drawn. Luke Skywalker and Han Solo, for instance, embody the cowboy archetypes which Reagan so liked to evoke as the quick-shooting, frontier-taming West. J. G. Ballard's interpretation of the film as a 'parable of the US involvement in Vietnam, with the plucky hero from the backward planet … fighting bravely against the evil and all-destructive super-technology of the Galactic Empire'[29] falls within these parameters. Moreover, on Luke's home planet, the desert world Tatooine, the enemies are not just stormtroopers but the scavenging, scrap-dealing Jawas who attempt to cheat his uncle and the savage, alien Sandpeople; both can readily be seen as racist stereotypes of Arab culture. However, the Rebellion's struggle of opposition, couched in the vaguest terms of 'Republic' versus totalitarian Imperial state, is simply open to any and all political allegory, including Britain in India or England in Northern Ireland, and it is a tribute to Reagan's manipulation of the text that his preferred meaning has stuck so firmly to the film's key terms.

Perhaps the most extended discussion yet of the trilogy's ideological concerns can be credited to Robin Wood.[30] While Wood's inexcusably thoughtless errors – for C-3PO read 'CP-30'; for Obi-Wan 'Obi One'[31] – hardly inspire confidence in his 'close reading', he perceptively notes the dangers inherent in the Rebels' long-term project of liberation. The films' 'unease', Wood argues, lies in 'the problem of lineage: what will the rebels against the Empire create if not another empire?'[32] This dilemma, which Wood contextualises as an American fear of Fascism from 'within' – the fear that the American democracy, founded by a nation itself revolting against British oppression, 'may carry within itself the potential to become Fascist, totalitarian, a police state'[33] – is enacted also in the ongoing question as to Luke's 'lineage'; the revelation that he is the son of 'prototypal Fascist beast' Darth Vader.

In Wood's view, symbolic resolution comes with the redemption of Vader and a celebration of 'fathericity' which restores traditional structures and excludes or suppresses women (Princess Leia), blacks (Lando Calrissian) and gays (in a bizarre reading, Wood sees C-3PO, apparently because of his 'affected British accent', as engaged in a homosexual 'pedophile relationship' with R2-D2).[34] To an extent, Wood's interpretation simply demonstrates again the readiness of the trilogy's vague terminology and stylised iconography to fit a wide variety of 'symbolic' socio-historical meanings.[35] His discussion of the oppressive and totalitarian project contained within the Rebel struggle is, though, valuable for its analysis of a dilemma clearly at the heart of the conflict between Reagan's and Lucas' 'readings'.

It is not my intention to claim that the reactionary/Republican narratives drawn from the films by Wood, Ballard and Reagan are unfounded, or based on 'misreading'. Instead, I will argue that these are not the meanings at the heart of the films' current significance in the culture of fanzines, indie bands, comics and net sites. In effect, the producers and audience behind these texts are performing a reappropriation which places different stresses and privileges different textual elements from those which were foregrounded by the previous readings and which came to constitute the films' dominant ideological connotations. I want ultimately to suggest that this alternative reading, rather than harking back to a legitimating narrative of modernity with all its attendant dilemmas, implies instead a politically-directed postmodernism.

The project of the Rebellion in the *Star Wars* trilogy is marked from that of the Empire precisely in its aim to 'activate the differences'[36] rather than to shape the world in its own likeness. The Empire is a colonising force, imposing martial law on the communities within its net – we see roadblocks and armed troopers patrolling the town of Mos Eisley, for instance – and allowing no dissent within its own ranks. Significantly, there are suggestions in *A New Hope* of an internal conflict between the Empire's military/bureaucratic faction and its religious/feudal figurehead, Darth Vader, whose given title is Jedi Knight and Lord of the Sith. Any threat of disagreement is suppressed early in the film, however, as Vader throttles the official who scorns his 'sorcerer's ways' declaring 'I find your lack of faith disturbing.'[37] By the start of *The Empire Strikes Back* the Imperials' military leader, Tarkin, has been killed and Vader, with the Emperor above him, takes full control. It is only when a rift occurs between Vader and his master, at the end of the third film, that the Empire begins to crumble.

The Rebellion, by contrast, thrives on difference, and builds on small pockets of resistance from transitory, temporary outposts such as the ice planet Hoth which the Rebels are forced to flee at the start of *The Empire Strikes Back*. These are micro-narratives of rebellion, hit-and-run raids. Leia is able to give Vader the information that her colleagues are on Dantooine, knowing that the Empire will find only deserted buildings and footprints. The Rebellion's strength is primarily in its fragmentation, the fact of its being everywhere and nowhere; its aesthetic, in effect, of the postmodern sublime.

These differences are emphasised through the costume and *mise-en-scène* attached to the two opposing sides. The Empire's ranks are clearly marked through uniform and military insignia; its stormtroopers, snowtroopers and biker-scouts are encased in black and white armour with their faces hidden, much like the Judges we applaud in Cannon's film. Vader, of course, wears a dark cloak and a casque-like helmet which both conceals his face and distorts his voice; again, the break-up of the Empire is signalled by the removal of this concealing apparatus at the end of *Jedi*. The Imperial warships are sleek daggers, all built around the same sharp-edged design.

The Rebellion's design aesthetic is, as Ian Saunders has suggested, one of bricolage; a mish-mash of patched-together X-Wings with Y-Wings, A-Wings and B-Wings thrown in, aided by individually-owned craft like Han Solo's smuggling vessel the Millenium Falcon. Saunders sees Solo as 'the archetypal *bricoleur-poet*', and Vader as his dialectical counterpoint:

> As Solo's career is unplanned, Vader's ambitions, like his visage, are rigidly fixed. His 'world' is the regimented artificial nation-state, the 'Death Star'; while Solo's ship is its apolitical bricolage opposite. 'What a piece of junk', says Luke Skywalker when he first sees it. To which Solo, the ever-confident *bricoleur*, replies: 'She'll make .5 past light speed. She may not look like much but she's got it where it counts, kid. I've made a lot of special modifications myself.' Assembled from bits and pieces, poorly-resourced but somehow kept going by dint of ingenuity and know-how, the ship out-manoeuvres its vastly more powerful competitor through imagination and sheer cheek.[38]

Sheer cheek: this is the language not of the legitimating master narrative but of experiment and localised creativity.

Finally, the Rebellion fosters difference in its own organisation and direction. Its ranks, we see in *Return of the Jedi*, are made up of both humans and alien life forms from a bewildering variety of cultures; Chewbacca the towering, hair-covered Wookiee, of course, but also the lobster-headed Ackbar who holds the position of Admiral, and the jowled, mouse-like Nien Nunb who co-pilots the Millennium Falcon on its last raid. This is a political opposition which embraces the fantastic and the grotesque, encouraging others to its cause through an understanding of their culture and a broadening of its own; the Ewok tribe is drawn in through the droid C-3PO's relating of the Rebellion's narrative as a folk-tale complete with sound effects and actions, and in their own language. It would be possible to claim for the Ewok sequences, with their emphasis on the supernatural and the uncanny – the golden-plated C-3PO is worshipped as a god, and levitated through Luke's control of the Force – shades of the magic realism which Jameson suggests as a progressive alternative to both the ahistorical *mode rétro* and the blunted edge of avant-garde experimental cinema.[39] Significantly, the trilogy ends with songs, tribal music and joyful dance: a closure built around carnival.

The Rebellion's political meetings – before the final attacks in *A New Hope* and *Return of the Jedi* – take the form of conference-room debate rather than the formal ceremony of Vader and his master; authorities in a specific field take the floor, but those in attendance are seen to chip in with disagreement and suggestion. As such its project is similar to that described by James Donald in his discussion of the magic realist mode mentioned above; an alternative to 'one old avant-garde's death-or-glory resistance' and the other's 'utopian search for the 'progressive text' that would hasten the revolution'[40]

> The emphasis … seems to be on experimentation, the multiplication of different narratives, and the narration of differences. The aim is no longer the silence of negation, but the noise of negotiation and dialogue. This implies neither a predisposition to compromise and quiescence, nor the pluralist assumption that 'anything goes'. Dialogue, in this view, equals conflict. Such conflict is neither an embarassment nor a sign that the process is not working. On the contrary, the discord is essential. It demonstrates the aspiration to community, a community whose form and direction cannot be determined in advance, but only in the process of the dialogue.[41]

It is this sense of a progressive community based on debate and experiment, on small-scale projects and creativity within a postmodern mode of difference and fragmentation, which I believe is currently being 'read' from the trilogy into fan culture. It can be seen in the diplomatic open spaces of the Internet with its web of *Star Wars* home pages linked across states and oceans, and their invitations to leave e-mail comments or post up subjects for discussion opening them in turn to still wider networks of debate.[42] It is at the heart of the *Star Wars*

fanzine community, each promoting the others' titles and cramming pages produced on desktop publishing packages with short stories, comic strips, board games, 'filk' songs,[43] even fairytales,[44] and can even be located in the self-belief and playful experiment of indie bands like Ash, or the one-man, shoestring filmmaking of *Clerks*, a flourishing of the 'I-can-do-anything feeling' which Lucas hoped to instil.

This is the spirit behind the full-length *Star Wars* 'novels' by amateur writers,[45] advertised in fanzine columns and offered not for money but in exchange for other writing, and behind the small-press comic books written, drawn and handbound by a miniscule production team and circulated on subscription to a hundred readers; the belief that it is possible and worthwhile to work outside or in opposition to the dominant mainstream – the Boxtree and Bantam publishing houses responsible for the commercial *Star Wars* novelisations, and the 'Big Two' comic organisations, Marvel and DC – and to create a support network for small-scale creativity. This is the legacy of *Star Wars* to some of those who saw it as children, and the most optimistic reason for the trilogy's current nostalgic resonance; its suggestion that diversity, debate and the exchange of voices can be central to a community, its validation of struggle on the smallest level, and its implication that fragmentation, pastiche and bricolage, rather than leading inevitably to a superficial culture of surface, can be part of a progressive narrative of change.

Notes

1 Most significant and critically acclaimed is Timothy Zahn's trilogy, following directly on from the events in *Return of the Jedi*: *Heir to the Empire*, *Dark Force Rising* and *The Last Command* (New York, Bantam). Others include Kevin J. Anderson's 'Jedi Academy' trilogy, Roger MacBride Allen's 'Corellian Trilogy' and the most recent bestsellers, Dave Wolverton's *The Courtship of Princess Leia* and Kevin Anderson's *Darksaber*.

2 Produced by West End Games, most of these modules and sourcebooks were published in 1994 and 1995.

3 Apart from comic adaptations of the film – invariably renamed 'Classic Star Wars' – Boxtree (London) publish, in 'graphic novel' format, volumes including *Dark Lords of the Sith*, *Dark Empire* and *Tales of the Jedi*. These were all originally published monthly by Dark Horse comics, whose range currently includes an adaptation of Zahn's novel *Heir to the Empire*.

4 Other fanzines currently available in Britain include *Luminous Beings Are We* (Essex), also linked to an Internet site, *I Have A Bad Feeling About This* (Scotland), *Telesponder* and *Force Sensitive* (London).

5 Quotations from *The Jock*, edited by Rol Hirst (Huddersfield, privately published) and *Fell, Dr L.*, edited by Andrew Pack (Lincoln: privately published).

6 Interview with Ash, *New Musical Express*, 14 October 1995, p. 34. The title of Ash's 1996 debut album, *1977*, pays further tribute to the formative influence of *A New Hope*. The album opens with the distinctive screech of a TIE Fighter, and closes with 'Darkside Lightside', a reference to the twin aspects of the Force.

7 Douglas Coupland, *Microserfs* (London, Flamingo, 1995).

8 The film also features a track by Supernova called 'Chewbacca', celebrating Han Solo's co-pilot in its chorus 'what a Wookiee'.

9 Fredric Jameson, 'Postmodernism and Consumer Society', in E. Ann Kaplan, *Postmodernism and its Discontents* (London, Verso, 1988), p. 18.

10 Derek Malcolm, *Guardian*, 13 December 1977.

11 *Glasgow Herald*, 27 January 1978.

12 David Robinson, *The Times*, 16 February 1977.

13 Although the tracing of elements in *Star Wars* to their 'source' is bound to be subjective, many commentators have been in agreement about these particular aspects. Ben Kenobi is clearly a Gandalf or Merlin figure, while Mark Hamill's performance as Luke Skywalker has been compared (notably by Pauline Kael) to Ricky Nelson's style of acting. C-3PO has frequently been linked to the Tin Man, and Chewbacca to the Cowardly Lion. Finally, Darth Vader's costume, and the clash of opposing Jedi schools in his duel with Obi-Wan Kenobi, seem heavily indebted to samurai iconography, and the final dogfights in the Death Star trench to films of the Second World War.

14 Alexander Walker, *Evening Standard*, 10 November 1977.

15 Joe Queenan, *The Guardian Guide*, 15–21 July 1995.

16 Jonathan Romney, *Guardian*, 20 July 1995.

17 Queenan, *The Guardian Guide*, 15–21 July 1995.

18 Jean Baudrillard, 'Simulacra and Simulations', in *Selected Writings* (Oxford, Polity Press, 1988), p. 170

19 William Gibson, *Virtual Light* (London, Viking, 1993). In the same novel, the police satellite monitoring the protagonist, Rydell, is nicknamed the Death Star.

20 This is in direct contrast with the original 'Judge Dredd' strip in *2000AD*, which was intended to satirise Dredd's unbending adherence to his absurd and brutal Law; the strip's writers have spoken in interview of their despair that a young audience began to take the character at face value.

21 George Lucas, quoted in the *Guardian*, 1 March 1977.

22 David Levin, *Daily Mail*, 1 August 1977.

23 *The Young Americans*, directed by Danny Cannon, 1993; *Shopping*, directed by Paul Anderson, 1994. The latter film also involves a nostalgic discussion of *Star Wars* toy figures; as such it parallels *Clerks* in its portrayal of a disenfranchised youth for whom the trilogy is an important cultural reference.

24 Derek Malcolm, *Guardian*, 23 June 1994.

25 Jean-Francois Lyotard, *The Postmodern Condition. A Report on Knowledge* (Manchester, Manchester University Press, 1984). Lyotard concludes 'We have paid a high enough price for the nostalgia of the whole and the one ... let us wage a war on totality...' (pp. 81–2).

26 As documented in *Variety*, 3 June 1987.

27 Susan Aronstein, '"Not Exactly a Knight": Arthurian Narrative and Recuperative Politics in the Indiana Jones Trilogy', *Cinema Journal*, 34, (4) (Summer 1995).

28 Cartoon by 'Stayskal', published by the *Chicago Tribune/New York Times* syndicate, 1978.

29 J. G. Ballard, 'Hobbits in Space?', in *A User's Guide to the Millennium* (London, HarperCollins, 1996).

30 Robin Wood, *Hollywood from Vietnam to Reagan* (New York, Columbia University Press, 1986).

31 While not wishing to labour the point, it is ironic that Wood lambasts a Roger Ebert review for the same carelessness – 'Ebert's plot synopsis sets a new record in critical inaccuracy...' – earlier in the same volume (p. 123). Given that the character names are listed in the on-screen credits of *Star Wars*, Wood's errors suggest a contempt for his subject; he would surely not permit an article on Hawks's films to misspell the name of a protagonist.

32 Wood, *Hollywood*, p. 170.

33 Wood, *Hollywood*, p. 169. It is perhaps the culmination of this American nightmare which *Judge Dredd* depicts with its characteristic lack of irony or critique.

34 Wood argues that Leia is reduced to a position of 'helplessness and dependency ... there is never any suggestion that she might inherit the Force, or have the privilege of being trained by Obi One [sic] and Yoda' (p. 173). An attentive viewer would soon disprove this claim: Leia alone is able to hear Luke's mental plea for help at the end of *The Empire Strikes Back*, and knows, when Han does not, that Luke has escaped the Death Star at the close of *Return of the Jedi*. Indeed, Obi-Wan and Yoda note her potential as a replacement for Luke – 'there is another' – in *The Empire Strikes Back*, and her subsequent Jedi training is foregrounded in Timothy Zahn's novels.

35 Wood's complaints are echoed to an extent by the author Joanna Russ in her condemnation of *Star Wars* for its pleasures grounded in 'sexism, racism, heterosexism, competition and macho privilege'. Russ is quoted in John Tulloch and Henry Jenkins, *Science Fiction Audiences* (London, Routledge, 1995), p. 36. Tulloch argues, contra Russ, that a 'fan reading' of the film would 'stress the film's heroic treatment of resistance to totalitarian

authority and the need to form alliances across multiple planetary cultures, races and genders ... the utopianism of science fiction may emerge as much from the audience as from the producers' (p. 39). Although I think this is a simplification of the relationship between audience and text, the 'readings' which I have suggested as currently foregrounded in fan culture are indeed partly grounded in ideas of community and the embracing of difference.

36 Lyotard, *The Postmodern Condition*, p. 82.

37 The exchange is perhaps worth transcribing further as an instance of the rare conflict between Imperial characters, and of the speed with which such discourse is suppressed:

> Vader: The ability to destroy a planet is insignificant next to the power of the Force.
>
> General Tagge: Don't try to frighten us with your sorcerer's ways, Lord Vader. Your sad devotion to that ancient religion has not helped you conjure up the stolen data tapes. Or given you clairvoyance enough to find the Rebels' hidden... [He breaks off as Vader begins to choke him]
>
> Vader: I find your lack of faith disturbing.
>
> Tarkin: This bickering is pointless.

38 Ian Saunders, 'Richard Rorty and *Star Wars*. On the Nature of Pragmatism's Narrative', *Textual Practice*, 8, (3) (Winter 1994), pp. 438–9.

39 Fredric Jameson, 'On Magic Realism in Film', *Critical Enquiry*, 12, (2) (Winter 1986), p. 303.

40 James Donald, *Fantasy and the Cinema* (London, British Film Institute, 1989), p. 230.

41 Ibid.

42 A single net site on the trilogy will invariably promote others' sites, sometimes suggesting fifty or more. On the recommendation of one home page, I visited 'Star Wars Central', 'Boba Fett's Home Page', 'The New Republic Central Database', 'The Ultimate Site for the Dark Side of the Force', 'Guess What ... a Star Wars Page' and 'Ray-Traced Art by Anthony Yu'. Lists of 'bloopers' and memorable quotations from the trilogy on these pages are compiled by hundreds of fans e-mailing their own contributions to the collective work, and all are credited as authors, the list sometimes filling pages of text. Significantly, one *Star Wars* chat room is at the time of writing organising its own rebellion against the censorship inherent in Lucasfilm's official web site. Participants take an obvious pleasure in recruiting 'newbies' to their cause and signalling their loyalty through a 'Star of Alderaan' icon attached to their messages. This is a particularly ironic case of the impulse towards resistance-from-below rebounding against Lucasfilm, which now finds itself in the position of tyrannical authority.

43 Filk songs, a phenomenon apparently unique to science fiction fandom, involve new – occasionally, it has to be said, banal – lyrics put to traditional music. One example will suffice, to the tune of 'Clementine': 'Captain Solo, Captain Solo / Party to the Rebel band / Though you don't know you're a hero / Others help you understand.'

44 'Jedi Bedtime Stories. Traditional Star Wars Folk and Fairy Tales', a feature in *Holocron*, December 1995.

45 For example: *The Ormand Factor* by Louise Turner, advertised in fanzines as 'a *Star Wars* novel set post-ROTJ and featuring Wedge Antilles and Luke Skywalker. 116 pages of text, laser printed, photocopied and comb-bound with card cover.'

I would like to thank my student at West Kent College, Phil Edmunds, for introducing me to the *Star Wars* novels and for some productive discussions about the trilogy. May the Force...

Web of Bablyon
Kurt Lancaster

*Rewriting Unrequited Love and the Performance
of Fanfic*

In the episode 'Endgame', Straczynski wrote a
classical romantic death scene for his character
Marcus Cole. This Ranger was a virgin who
sacrificed his life in order to save Susan Ivanova,
the woman he was in love with; he had been too
proud to admit this to her. The unconsummated
love is a part of Straczynski's canon. However, in
'unsanctioned' fan fiction found online, this love
becomes requited. The 'Unicorn's I&M Storybook'
Web page contains a list of dozens of stories fans
have written based on these two characters; the
page was designed by Sarah Zelechoski when she
was fifteen years old. She is currently a physics
major at the University of California, San Diego
(Zelechoski 1999).

In the short story 'The First Time', an anonymous fan-writer references a scene already
viewed by fans in 'The Summoning' (Straczynski
1996c). In that scene Straczynski reveals that
Marcus is a virgin and had decided to save his first
sexual experience for the right woman. In the
fan's story, Ivanova speaks to Marcus:

> 'About waiting to do things properly. I've
> been thinking about what you said on the
> White Star a while back about having found
> the right person and not letting her know it
> yet' [in 'The Summoning']. Ivanova's face was
> stern and thoughtful.
> 'You have?' The ranger looked at her in
> sudden horror. Maybe he had talked in his
> sleep after all and she'd only been waiting to
> rip his lungs out in private.
> 'I usually don't volunteer advice to my
> friends, especially not advice of a personal
> nature, but in the last few years a lot of
> people have come to me looking for it, and
> I don't think I've been responsible for any
> major catastrophes to date.' Susan's voice
> was hesitant.
> 'Meaning what?'
> 'I think you should let this woman know
> how you feel, Marcus. Life's too short. If you
> wait too long, we're going to find ourselves
> in the middle of some kind of deviltry again
> and then you might miss your chance.' She

> punctuated her pronouncement with little
> affirmative shakes of her head, as though she
> was trying to convince both of them at the
> same time.
> 'Do you really think so?' the ranger asked
> her in a strangled voice.
> 'Yes, and I'm ready to help you in any way I
> can. It's the least I can do after all we've been
> through together.'
> Marcus Cole nodded mutely in shock.
> The woman of his dreams was offering to
> help him win the woman of his dreams. He
> suddenly found himself wishing he'd talked in
> his sleep.

The writer uses a narrative set-up that references
the scene written by Straczynski and previously
viewed by fans. This restores the behaviour of the
original scene and draws the fan-reader into the
plausible possibilities of the scenario. The reader
can imagine the scene as performed by actors
Claudia Christian and Jason Carter. Later, the
writer has the characters perform their first kiss
– a scene that never took place on the television
series *Babylon 5*, and is therefore unsanctioned
and outside the saga's canon:

> Susan's mouth was on his. He'd dreamt about
> this for so long. Well, maybe he hadn't dreamt
> about this exact sequence of events in this
> exact setting, but it was still Susan, it was still
> her lips covering his, and it was incredible. It
> might also be his only chance, he might as
> well do it right.
> Marcus took control of the kiss, bringing
> one hand up to cup her head as he curled
> the other arm around her shoulders and
> shifted his mouth. He traced her lips with
> the tip of his tongue, willing them to open,
> and groaning in bliss when they eased apart.
> She was sweet, so sweet. The heat of her
> blasted straight into his soul as he explored
> her warm willing mouth. He possessed
> her thoroughly, until the contours and the
> taste of her were seared into his memory
> and both their breaths came in little ragged
> gasps. They sagged against each other in the
> aftermath.
> Her knuckles were white from her grip on
> his shoulders. She was breathless, warm and
> wobbly. 'Marcus?' she breathed softly.
> The ranger bent his mouth to hers again.
> It was a gentler kiss this time. He lingered
> against her, tenderly brushing the spots

he'd plundered the minute before and then reluctantly retreating.

'Oh.' He'd never thought to hear such a small, surprised voice coming out of Ivanova's mouth.

Straczynski might say that the story of unrequited love made Marcus' death that much more tragic, especially when it took a profound sense of love to willingly sacrifice his life in order to save the woman he loves.

It is not enough for fans just to wonder what it would be like if Marcus were not killed. Some fans want to know what Marcus and Ivanova's love would have been like, how they would have performed their first kiss if Straczynski hadn't killed the character. Within the canon, fans have to rely wholly on Straczynski to provide this scene, and if it is not forthcoming (which it will not be, since the character is dead), fans create their own personal texts in order to perform, enact, share in, and see scenes that the canonical author never created. Fanfic, as these fictional stories written by fans are known, revolves around such issues. The 'forbidden kiss' between Marcus and Ivanova becomes the site where fans enter Straczynski's universe and shape it in their own image. 'The idea is to change the object while preserving it', cultural scholar Constance Penley says about fan writing (1997: 3). It allows them to perform Straczynski's characters in an 'alternative universe.' 'This story is just a short speculation about what might happen', the author writes, 'if Susan Ivanova decided to help Marcus Cole get his love life straightened out'. The author even makes sure to give the original creator and copyright holders their due: 'These wonderful people and places belong to JMS [Straczynski] and Warner Bros. I make no claim to them and have derived no profit whatsoever from their use (other than having a whole lot of fun!).' Fans are not necessarily looking for money and may not care where the stories end up – they want to have their works read. And it seems that with over 33,000 hits (as of January 2000), this Web site and these writers have gained an audience allowing them to approach 'best-seller' status.

Not entirely wanting to just view someone else's story, Babylon 5 fans write their own narratives based on characters created by Joe Straczynski. This does not necessarily reflect a lack of satisfaction with the story of Babylon 5, but as with other categories of the imaginary entertainment environment, fans want to part-icipate in that universe. If fans can't live in the imaginary fantasy, they can at least participate in the culture of creation. By writing fan fiction and publishing Web pages, fans immerse themselves in the Babylon 5 universe. One way they do this is to take favorite characters and put them into new stories. The writers become reconfigured through the stories they write and publish. Sometimes these stories go beyond the canon of Straczynski's one-hundred-and-ten-episode saga. Yet the fan writer's creations intersect with and become absorbed in Straczynski's universe.

'Fandom here', media scholar Henry Jenkins tells us, 'becomes a participatory culture which transforms the experience of media consumption into the production of new texts, indeed of a new culture and a new community' (1992: 46). Fans may create new cultural texts, but they do not necessarily build a new full-sized community. If anything, what evolves out of their creative productions are micro-communities. Straczynski's original narrative provides the spark for fans to create these micro-communities in which fan-created narratives circulate. Fans write new fictions and post them on Web pages, and they also create fan clubs online, which usually revolve around particular characters and the actors who perform them. Entire Web sites with multiple pages and links may be devoted to one character or theme. ('The Lurker's Guide to Babylon 5' lists over two hundred Web pages dedicated to the show; these range from pages about particular actors to trivia.) Web pages and fan fiction allow fans to explore the universe of Babylon 5 on their own terms outside the original creator's authorial presence.

Fans who perform such acts, Jenkins says, enter a 'realm of the fiction as if it were a tangible place they can inhabit and explore' (1992: 18), and where they are 'active producers and manipulators of meanings' (23). The very act of producing new texts and posting them online reconfigures the fan into the imaginary universe of Babylon 5. As fans restore memories of watching episodes of Babylon 5 – by writing and reading fan fiction – they become reconfigured. To a neophyte, these texts do not mean much. In original stories, readers must delineate the characters and environment in their minds. In media tie-in stories the world and characters are already stored in participants' memory. Fans write these stories in order to immerse themselves in someone else's premade universe, previously visited vicariously when they watched episodes of, for example, Babylon

5 on television. Now, however, they can tangibly enter this imaginary environment, inhabiting and exploring it by placing preexisting characters in new scenes. Many of the characters are already familiar. Memories of the actors' performances of these characters reside within the fan texts, and writers as well as readers restore these performances through this work.

Fans shape their texts with Schechnerian strips of behaviour, applying them in new ways. The process of restoring this performance leads the reader into the act of imagining the actors performing in new scenes built from these stored strips of performance behaviour. Mackay, writing about performances occurring in fantasy role-playing games, describes how players use 'fictive blocks' – fictional tropes culled from popular culture images – as an 'interface to the immaterial material from which a player assembles an imaginary character' (1998: 90). These 'fictive blocks', Mackay contends, 'are stored by the potential role-player as strips of imaginary behaviour – non-real behaviour that takes place in an imaginary environment' (90). The performance is not seen. Rather, it takes place in the 'imagination: not only the liminal stage, but the stages of decontextualisation (of the fictive block) and of recontextualisation (the strips of imaginary behaviour culled from the fictive block) take place in the player's mind' (91). Mackay calls these strips immaterial, because, as opposed to a fully realised, concrete performance, role-players have to imagine the *mise-en-scène* of their performance. Through a similar process (but executed differently from the role-player), a fanfic author places strips of behaviour garnered from watching episodes of *Babylon 5* into new contexts. The reader of the fanfic imagines the immaterial behaviours occurring in the story as being con-crete, or performed. Part of this imagination is realised through the recontextualisation of actors' performances from episodes of *Babylon 5*.

So, in this sense, performance scholar Peggy Phelan's contention that 'Performance's only life is in the present' is wrong. 'Performance cannot be saved, recorded, documented, or otherwise participate in the circulation of representations of representations', she contends: 'once it does so, it becomes something other than performance' (1993: 146). Furthermore, Phelan argues, if 'performance attempts to enter the economy of reproduction it betrays and lessens the promise of its own ontology' (146). However, performances occurring within fandom – the

sites that comprise the imaginary entertainment environment – rely on the circulation of the performance's originating production. Only by relying on the representation of the original – the circulation of reproduction – can fans 'play' with it: reperform it (apply the strip of performance behaviour) and make it into a new kind of performance. Phelan agrees that performance can be 'performed again, but this repetition marks it as 'different'' (146). Yes, it is something other than the original performance – but it is a performance nonetheless, despite how much it enters the 'economy of reproduction', deviates, or is applied differently. In the Schechnerian sense, a recorded, documented performance – such as a media image of *Babylon 5* – can be performed again. Fans take strips of recorded performance behaviour and reperform them in the present, embodied in new concrete performances.

Performing as textual nomads staking individual authorial claims, fans poach the primary text of *Babylon 5* in order to enter its universe. They do not betray and lessen the original performance's 'promise of its own ontology' – they heighten it. These writers create their own characters and then place them within already familiar scenes and/or with preexisting characters. Some of these scenes may be extensions of existing histories occurring 'off-screen' in episodes of *Babylon 5* that were never depicted on-screen. Fans can write new histories in Straczynski's imaginary universe. They circulate their own objects of preference in the *Babylon 5* universe and place them in an already familiar imaginary environment, like the author who wrote about Marcus and Susan's first kiss.

Rather than these stories being circulated in the traditional outlets of fanzines, magazines or novels, online technologies allow fans to publish them with no additional cost beyond the original purchase of a computer and modem. Those who do not know how to publish their own Web sites or lack the means to build and post pages can send stories and images to already existing sites by using regular email. Users can log on and view these different Web page performances. As fans publish their own *Babylon 5* sites, they provide 'a foundation for future encounters with the fiction, shaping how it will be perceived, defining how it will be used' (Jenkins 1992: 45). Through a confluence of high-tech capabilities, designers of Web sites have embedded these pages with preexisting images and sounds, creating their own new texts from them.

Fans who create these kinds of sites reconfigure the master narrative of *Babylon 5* into their own vision. This is different from CD-ROMs, where official producers create official texts (or products), usually in the desire to sell as many as possible. Fanfic also contrasts with *Babylon 5*'s official canon as created by executive producer Straczynski. Scholar Michel de Certeau has argued that 'official' canonical texts interpose 'a frontier between the text and its readers that can be crossed only if one has a passport delivered by these official interpreters' (1984: 171). The official interpretation of texts causes other readings of texts to be considered 'either heretical (not 'in conformity' with the meaning of the text) or insignificant (to be forgotten)', he argues (171). And so, he continues, the 'literal', correct interpretation of texts becomes a 'cultural weapon' wielded by 'an elite' – the 'socially authorized professionals and intellectuals' (171). In the case of material media culture, producers want to keep control over their own creations. Profits belong to a corporate franchise. From this point of view, fandom is okay, as long as people purchase and circulate 'official' products and texts created and sold by licensed manufacturers.

Due to the litigious nature of Hollywood, producers are afraid of fan-created fiction and Web pages, the belief being that a producer could be blamed for stealing a fan-writer's idea or scene and then placing it 'accidentally' in a television episode – opening themselves up to a potential lawsuit. Executives also become concerned when fans take images from their copyrighted material and place it on Web pages without paying proper (and often expensive) licensing fees. Studios want to create their own sites in order to maintain tight copyright control over their images.

Yet Straczynski maintains a 'don't see, don't tell' approach when it comes to fan fiction. He can't officially sanction it, but he says that the material should not be 'put it in a place where I can see it or stumble over it … I'm not here to be [the studio's] eyes and ears' (1994b). Executives at Paramount and Fox, for example, have been less gracious toward fandom, threatening and forcing the shut-down of many fan-created Web sites for *Star Trek* and *X-Files*. Yet, when asked outright about sanctioning such stories, Straczynski is more reluctant to side with the fans, stating that it is a 'form of copyright infringement'; if he did sanction such stories, then he would be 'at legal odds with [Warner Bros.], which owns the copyright' (1999b). Straczynski's ambivalent attitude is different from the attitudes of other studio executives, probably because he himself is a science fiction fan, attends science fiction conventions regularly (now as a guest speaker), and certainly understands fan culture intimately. And yet as the creator of the characters that appear on *Babylon 5*, he probably is not thrilled to see other people writing stories about his characters. He has even created sanctioned story outlines for the professional authors who write *Babylon 5* novels for Del Rey. However, fans continue to create texts and 'borrow' images from copyrighted material as a way both to challenge the establishment and to circumvent its attempts to control how they participate in fictional universes.

The anonymous Critical Art Ensemble, writing in *The Electronic Disturbance* (1994), believes that plagiarism is a necessary and healthy consequence of the electronic age. (In fact, their book 'may be freely pirated and quoted', the copyright page states.) Their definition of plagiarism widens the conventional definition of theft, where one takes another's work as one's own. It comes closer to what fans do with fanfic and Web pages: 'Readymades, collage, found art or found text, intertexts, combines, detournment and appropriation – all these terms represent explorations in plagiarism' (85). They believe that 'no structure within a given text provides a universal and necessary meaning' (86). The Critical Art Ensemble challenges what de Certeau defines as the 'official', literal or canonical meaning of texts coming from a social elite – where the dominant interpretation is the only correct reading.

With online Web pages, fans circulate their own poached products throughout cyberspace, avoiding the dominant social structure's conventional route for circulating creative production:

author » text » agent » editor » contract » publisher » printer » distributor » sales rep » bookstore » book » bookstore » consumer

In this sense, fan web designers and fanfic writers are plagiarists, for they not only disrupt the conventional process of getting an author's text to a reader, but they give readers texts that would be considered unacceptable in the conventional bureaucratic process of publishing 'official' texts. 'One of the main goals of the plagiarist', the Critical Art Ensemble contends, 'is to restore the dynamic and unstable drift of meaning, by appropriating and recombining fragments of culture' (1994: 86). By placing strips of *Babylon 5* behaviour within new contexts online, fans circumvent the cultural elite's power structure and publish their texts much more easily and quickly:

author » text » Web » story » web » reader.

Bibliography

Certeau, Michel de (1984) *The Practice of Everyday Life*. Translated by Steven Rendall. Berkeley: University of California Press.

Critical Art Ensemble (1994) *The Electronic Disturbance*. New York: Autonomedia.

Jenkins, Henry (1992) *Textual Poachers: Television Fans and Participatory Culture*. New York: Routledge.

Mackay, Daniel (1998) *The Dolorous Role: Towards an Aesthetics of the Role-Playing Game*. Master's thesis, New York University, Department of Performance Studies.

Penley, Constance (1997) *NASA/Trek: Popular Science and Sex in America*. London and New York: Verso.

Phelan, Peggy (1993) *Unmarked: The Politics of Performance*. London and New York: Routledge.

Straczynski, J. Michael (1999b) 'JMS Usenet messages', www.midwinter.com/b5/Usenet/latest.

_____ (1994b) 'JMS Usenet messages', www.midwinter.com/b5/Usenet/jms94-02-usenet.

Zelechoski, Sarah (1999) 'Unicorn's I&M Storybook', www.geocities.com/Area51/Dimension/2444/admin.html.

LOOK TO THE SKIES:
1950s SCIENCE FICTION
INVASION NARRATIVES

EIGHT | LOOK TO THE SKIES! 1950s SCIENCE FICTION INVASION NARRATIVES

Taken as a whole, 1950s US and British science fiction films are often argued to represent a collective paranoia that existed in American and British society during this time. These seemingly flimsy, low-budget B-movie texts, with hysterical titles such as *I Married A Monster From Outer Space*, are meant to be both a product of a post-war crisis in confidence and the amplifying agent for such cultural psychosis as it manifested itself in wider discourses and discursive practices of the time. One is able to read these films, then, through the filter of myth, metaphor and allegory, and by so doing one gets close(r) to being able to read the malaise at the core of society. The question that academics have wrestled with and contested is what this paranoia is centrally about. A number of distinct and sometimes contradictory answers have been given.

First, the Invasion Narratives are argued to be conduits for playing out the ideological battle that emerges from the Cold War between American and other Western Nation States, including Britain, during this period. In this reading alien invasion is seen as merely a code for soviet aggression and the imagined threat of nuclear, territorial and geographical domination. The in-(non-)human aliens are cold, pathological and demonstrate a crowd/herd instinct

as they seek and destroy all human life in their wake. These murderous clones or simulacra, without individual personal freedoms to speak of, are here seen to embody the Soviet political system, and it is this embodiment that gets narratively transposed onto a vulnerable/weak Western society precisely because ordinary people fail to recognise or resist the alien threat – until it is nearly too late, that is. The message that ordinary people must be ever vigilant and ever conscious of the communist Other is ever present in these Invasion Narrative texts.

Second, the Invasion Narratives are argued to symbolically foreground the importance of the new power elites to post-war decision making. At a time when the power bases in Western society were being reformulated to privilege the military, scientists and a new breed of technical experts, science fiction is credited with placing them in crises scenarios that required them to work together. In fact, it is argued that the defeat of the aliens is only achieved through military-scientific 'co-operation' and through military-scientific, rationalist means – often with the development of new weaponry or a new invention that requires the input of both agencies. However, it is also argued that the Invasion Narratives also highlighted the contest between these power elites with science/scientists often placed in direct opposition to the might of the military machine.

Third, Invasion Narratives are argued to be fundamentally about dislocating transformations in Western society brought about by the rise of these new power elites. In this critical reading Invasion Narratives become a critique of a modern world increasingly regulated, routinised and controlled by rationalist and technological procedures and 'mass produced' leisure practices. This is played out in the science fiction film through conformity and cloning and the emptying out of human emotions, rendering people docile and automaton-like. In this representational framework, science and scientists are particularly represented as Frankenstein like, creating things (monsters, bacteria, radiation, the atom etc.) that they cannot control, things that are destructive, and things that they ultimately come to admire more than humanity itself. Here science is imagined to be a destructive force and one that needs to be reigned in.

Finally, Invasion Narratives are argued to be texts where a growing post-war crisis of masculinity and femininity is played out. Those monsters and aliens that are marked by rationality and linked to the purest of scientific forms are often encoded as hyper-masculine and it is this rationalised and hard masculinity that poses a threat to the natural order of things. Women, by contrast, often personify those values and actions which are under threat from such regulatory masculinity – they show emotion, demonstrate intuition, and are totally family centred. In short, in these 1950s Invasion Narratives an ideological battle takes place over what it means to be masculine and feminine in an increasingly rationalised and pluralized 1950s Western world.

Peter Biskind examines *Them!* and *The Thing* through a number of the tropes outlined above. While Biskind argues that *Them!* 'reflects the new prestige of science by placing scientists at the centre of world-shaking events' it also locates the fear of invasion in terms of Soviet metaphors and imagery. Biskind suggests that the drone-like giant ants who wreak havoc in the film fit within a general discourse about Soviet people because 'those humans that Americans regarded as antlike … were, of course, Communists … Reds, in other words, were monsters from the id'. However, Biskind also suggests that the ants in the film work as an 'attack on women in a man's world … the ant society is, after all, a matriarchy presided over by a despotic queen'.

Mark Jancovich's re-examination of the 1950s Invasion Narratives takes issue, in part, with Biskind's position. Jancovich argues that these films often demonstrate a profound unease about science, masculinity, the rise of the new power elites within American (Western) society, and an increasing sense that everyday life was becoming more routinised, standardised and bureaucratic. In this context the co-operation that takes place to defeat the alien aggressor is often 'the co-operation of an interactive community threatened by Fordist rationalisation and domination'.

Peter Hutchings examination of British Invasion Narratives from the 1950s and 1960s locates the trappings of paranoia to a set of distinctly British fears and concerns that emerged post-war. Hutchings suggests that these films produce a rather despairing mood of the nation as national identity and national unity, elements of tradition, and normative gender roles are all shown to be fragmented and unstable in these films. As Hutchings argues, 'it seems from these films that Britain has lost its centre and become fragmented, its population scattered in isolated groups and its institutions and hierarchies no longer as efficacious as they once were … It is as if Britain, displaced from an imperial history and the glories of the Second World War and caught up in a series of bewildering changes, is more open to self-doubts and an accompanying acknowledgement of its own limits.'

The Russians Are Coming, Aren't They?: *Them!* and *The Thing*
Peter Biskind

When Ben Peterson (James Whitmore), a New Mexico state trooper, comes across a little girl wandering around in the desert, clutching a doll to her chest in Gordon Douglas's *Them!* (1954), he knows there's something amiss. 'Look, she's in shock', he says, and sure enough, she is. Her dad has just been killed and their trailer squashed like a beer can. The sides are caved in, the interior is a mess, and curiouser and curiouser, there are sugar cubes strewn about the ground, not to mention strange tracks in the sand. Pretty soon the scene of the crime is crawling with fingerprinters and police photographers, but no one can make head or tail of the sugar cubes, tracks, and above all, the peculiar high-pitched ringing sound that fills the air with a maddening throb. No money has been taken, and the whole thing 'doesn't make sense', as one cop says to another. Indeed, the police procedure seems completely inappropriate. As in *Twelve Angry Men* and *Panic in the Streets*, reality defies common sense; this is clearly a job for experts, not professionals; docs, not cops.

Later, we find out that the culprits were oversized ants who have a correspondingly lusty appetite for sweets, and that the destruction of the trailer was incidental; it happened while they were rummaging around for sugar, which they love more than life itself. But what may not have been so incidental is the identity of the little girl's dad, the ants' first victim: he was an FBI agent on vacation. The ants, in other words, spawned in the desert of the Southwest, have struck at J. Edgar Hoover's G-men, agents of the federal authority from the East.

Them! goes on to build this whisper of regional rivalry into a structural contrast by cutting between shots of desert locales, with the ants wreaking havoc and spilling sugar every which way, and shots of Washington, D.C. When the dry, dusty landscape of the Southwest fades away and the U.S. Capitol Building, lit up like a Christmas tree on a dark Washington night, fades in, we breathe a sigh of relief. We know that once the authorities in Washington are alerted to the danger, everything will be under control. In other words, if the threat arises in New Mexico, strikes at Washington through the death of the FBI agent, and then against Los Angeles, a major urban centre, the solution moves from the national to local. When the time comes to declare martial law, and the words we have been waiting for boom out over the loudspeakers – 'Your personal safety and the safety of the entire city depend on your full cooperation with the military authorities' – we know it's true. People in the street after the curfew are subject to arrest by the MPs, but we don't care. After all, it's a national emergency. *Them!* has effectively established the legitimacy of state power.

The federal government in Washington responds to the crisis by dispatching Dr. and Pat Medford (Edmund Gwenn and Joan Weldon), a father/daughter team of 'myrmecologists' from the U.S. Department of Agriculture (remember the U.S. Department of Health in *Panic?*), a general, and an FBI agent named Robert Graham (James Arness) bringing up the rear. Although the national elite, the coalition of the centre, runs the show, it does not sweep aside local authority, but works through it, forming an alliance with Ben Peterson, the state trooper. He becomes the agent of the federal government within the local community. Federal interests are administered, mediated by local officials.

It is the scientists who have pride of place. Dr. Medford is a benign, avuncular fellow, a far cry from the demented Thorkels of yesteryear. Although he wonders what God hath wrought ('We may be witnessing a biblical prophecy come true ... The beasts will reign over the earth'), he also knows that the test tube is mightier than the cross, and that once again, if it was science (in this case nuclear testing) that had caused the problem, science would solve it too.

Them! reflects the new prestige of science by placing scientists at the centre of world-shaking events. Dr. Medford meets with the president, lectures top public officials, and is able to command the full resources of the state. In the same way that the mayor in *Panic* had to take orders from Dr. Reed, so here the general has to take orders from Dr. Medford. In fact, he flies Medford around in his Air Force plane like a chauffeur, and Pat Medford observes, 'It's like a scientist's dream.' Poor agent Graham complains that the scientists are keeping him in the dark and won't tell him their theory. 'We're on this case, too', he says plaintively. The cachet of science is so great that it even seems to upset the traditional hierarchy of sex roles. When the men get ready to climb down into the ants' nest, Pat Medford wants to go along. 'It's no place for you or any other woman', says agent Graham manfully, but she puts up a fight. 'Somebody with scientific knowledge, a trained observer, has to go', she says, and not only does she have her way, she takes over, ordering the men to torch the queen's chamber. Far from resisting her power, agent Graham falls in love with her, raising the prospect that the alliance between science and the military, or, in this case, the law, will be ratified by marriage.

Often, in films like *Them!*, the military was not able to use its big guns because it was fighting on its own turf. Even the army, eager to bomb the ants in the desert, hesitated to nuke Los Angeles, so that the search for the appropriate weapon, more discriminating and selective than the H-bomb, became a major theme in corporate-liberal sci-fi, a distant echo of the fight within the defense establishment over big bombs or tactical nuclear weapons. The search for a flexible, limited response to the alien threat reflected corporate liberals' uneasiness with the all-or-nothing strategy of massive retaliation championed by conservatives like Dulles. In *Them!*, the appropriate weapon is gas, not guns; in *The Beginning of the End*, it is sound, not bombs, a sonar imitation of the grasshoppers' mating call, that lures them to a watery death in Lake Michigan.

While the scientists and soldiers were quarreling among themselves over the appropriate weapon, another group of scientists and soldiers was having its own troubles up north, in Howard Hawks's *The Thing* (1951). This film was based on a 1938 novella called *Who Goes There?* by John W. Campbell. Like *Them!*, *The Thing* is not only preoccupied with hierarchies of authority, the authority of groups, and groups in conflict, but also with the struggle between science and the military, and the nature of aliens. *The Thing*, however, is a conservative film, and so the outcome of these conflicts is somewhat different.

When Air Force Capt. Pat Hendry (Kenneth Tobey) arrives in a remote Arctic outpost of scientists to help them investigate a strange item buried in the ice, he finds an enormous object apparently shaped like a frying pan. His men fan out around it and quickly find that they have made a circle. 'We found a flying saucer', someone shouts, and indeed they have. 'This isn't any metal I know', says another, examining a fin protruding from the ice.

But Hendry's problems are just beginning, because it seems that the passenger aboard the saucer has survived; it is the Thing-from-Another-World, as the ads put it, and it lives on blood. As if this weren't bad enough, Hendry discovers that the head scientist at the base, Nobel Prize-winner Dr. Carrington (Robert Cornthwaite), is almost as dangerous as the Thing, much as Wyatt Earp in *Clementine* discovers that he has to deal with Doc Holliday before he can face the Clantons. We're tipped off right away by his goatee (facial hair in the 1950s was about as popular as bad breath) and his Russian-style fur hat. When he's not wearing that, he's attired in a dressing gown and ascot, a thinking man's David Niven, out of place among the rough-and-tumble soldiers.

Carrington is no Medford. He's a border-line-mad scientist, and in *The Thing* the tension between science and the military that was latent in *Them!* not only becomes much more pronounced, it is resolved in favour of the military. FBI agent Bob Graham complained in *Them!* that he couldn't understand the Medfords because they used too many big words ('Why don't we all talk English?' he says testily), but Graham was something of a clod anyway, and if he couldn't make out their technical lingo, it was probably his own fault. But when Captain Hendry asks a question and gets only mumbo jumbo in return, it's another matter. 'You lost me', he says, and this time it's the scientists' fault, a symptom of technocratic arrogance. In *Them!*, Medford's admiration for the 'wonderful and intricate engineering' of the ants' nest is reasonable, not unseemly or unpatriotic. But in *The Thing*, Dr. Carrington's scientific curiosity is given a sinister twist. He develops an altogether unhealthy interest in the Thing. 'It's wiser than we are', he says. 'If only we could communicate with it, we could learn secrets hidden from mankind.' Whereas Medford merely restrains the military because he wants to find out if the queen is dead, Carrington betrays it, defecting to the Other side. He helps the Thing reproduce itself, finds a nice warm spot in the greenhouse for it to lay its spores, and even sabotages Hendry's attempts to kill it.

Carrington's scientific disinterest, which reflects the value-free pragmatism of the corporate liberals, is regarded as appeasement. 'There are no enemies in science, only phenomena to be studied', he says, but he's wrong. There are no neutrals. When he rushes up to the Thing, alien groupie that he is, crying, 'I'm your friend', it swats him aside like a fly. The enemy is remorseless and cruel; negotiations with it are useless, and those who try are self-deceiving at best. Carrington is an unreliable element – private, moody, reclusive. He's soft on aliens, a Thing-symp, the J. Robert Oppenheimer of the Arctic base. The genial scientist and expert of *Them!* is transformed into an extremist 'egghead', a head-over-heart zealot, a man who can't be trusted because 'he doesn't think like we do', a man who has contempt for the average and is therefore dangerous. Unlike Dr. Medford, Carrington is derided as a genius or superman. 'These geniuses', says Hendry with contempt. 'They're just like nine-year-olds playing with a new fire engine.' Carrington's behaviour justifies the soldiers' mistrust of science, even turns them against the Bomb itself. 'Knowledge is more important than life. We split the atom', Carrington shouts in a transport of enthusiasm. 'That sure made everybody happy', comes the sour reply from one of Hendry's men.

But even here, science is by no means rejected wholesale. There are good scientists as well as bad, Tellers as well as Oppenheimers, and the difference between them is that the good scientists side with and defer to Hendry, instead of Carrington. Carrington's real crime, that is to say, worse than consorting with the enemy, is setting his own authority against that of the military. As in *Panic*, it is a question of turf. Hendry's appearance at the base signals a change in command like the ones in *Twelve O'Clock High* and *Flying Leathernecks*, and the figurative one in *Clementine*. When he first arrives, he is warned that he is treading on alien territory. 'Dr. Carrington is in charge here', says one of the scientists. Hendry's job is to seize control of the base and assert the authority of the soldiers over the scientists. Eventually confined to his quarters, Carrington shouts, echoing the mayor and reporter in *Panic*, 'You have no authority here', but when

one of Hendry's men pokes a revolver in his face, Carrington learns that power grows out of the barrel of a gun.

And what about the people, the average Joes and plain Janes who are neither scientists nor soldiers? In *Them!*, it seems that they are almost as much of a problem as the ants themselves. They spend most of their time in films like this fleeing for their lives, obstructing the best efforts of the government to save them from themselves. Occasionally they pause long enough to riot, destroying valuable scientific equipment or medical supplies. Since the people are helpless to help themselves, the war against the ants has to be carried on by experts behind closed doors. In one scene, pilot Fess Parker, who has seen a queen in flight winging her way west to Los Angeles, has been thrown into a loony bin. The doctors and the local authorities, who have been kept in the dark by the scientists and soldiers, think he's crazy. When agent Graham questions him, it becomes clear that he isn't nuts – the pilot did see the flying queen – but nevertheless, he is not vindicated, as he would be in a radical film. On the contrary, Graham tells the doctors to keep him locked up in the hospital, his therapeutic prison: 'Your government would appreciate it if you kept him here.' Reporters, as in *Panic*, threaten official secrecy. Like their readers, they have to be kept in the dark. 'Do you think all this hush-hush is necessary?' someone asks Dr. Medford. 'I certainly do', he replies. 'I don't think there's a police force in the world that could handle the panic of the people if they found out what the situation is.' When it's no longer possible to cover up the facts, and the ants are strolling down Sunset Boulevard, the mayor of Los Angeles finally calls a press conference, but 'there is no time for questions'.

There is bad blood between the authorities and the press in *The Thing* too, but this conflict is resolved differently than it is in *Them!* A nosy reporter named Scotty (Douglas Spencer) realises there's a big story afoot, and he wants to tag along. 'This is Air Force information', says Hendry, refusing to let Scotty near the saucer. 'The whole world wants to know', replies Scotty, sketching in the Big Picture for Hendry. But here, Big Picture-ism fails. 'I work for the Air Force, not the world', snaps Hendry, voicing the conservative preference for the concrete and local over the abstract and general. But instead of the reporter being thrown in jail, an amiable arrangement is reached. Scotty is allowed to accompany Hendry to the Arctic base in exchange for agreeing to withhold the story until he gets permission from the authorities to release it. And at the end of the film, when he does tell part of the story in a broadcast to the world, he is allowed to speak for everyone, Hendry and Carrington, the soldiers and the scientists. As the voice of the centre, he goes out of his way to pay special tribute to Carrington (who by this time has learned his lesson), papering over the differences that factionalised the group, as Fonda does in *Twelve Angry Men* and York does in *Fort Apache*. Once again, the centre closes ranks before the world.

Scotty can be accommodated more easily than the reporters in *Panic* and *Them!*, because *The Thing* is more populist. Within the community of soldiers and scientists at the base, relationships are more egalitarian than they are in similar communities in corporate-liberal films. When Tex, one of Hendry's men, enters a room and sees the group mobilising against the Thing, he quips, 'What's up? It looks like a lynching party.' In corporate-liberal films that regard people acting on their own as mobs or would-be vigilantes, it would be; here, it's not. Hendry may give the orders, but a number of ideas bearing on the disposal of the Thing originate with others, are adopted by Hendry, and ultimately work. Even the best lines of what for sci-fi is an unusually talky script (by Charles Lederer) are democratically distributed among the officers, noncoms, civilians, and (one) woman alike. There is a good deal of overlapping dialogue; people continually interrupt one another with wisecracks and good-natured insults. There is a real sense of community, of people engaged in a common effort, which nevertheless doesn't prevent them from expressing their individuality.

If people in *Them!* obstruct authority, authority in *The Thing* frustrates people. The conflict between soldiers and scientists is complemented by another, this one between Hendry, his superior officer General Fogarty in Anchorage, and the brass back in Washington. Hendry begins his odyssey as the perfect Air Force organisation man. He can't blow his nose without clearing it first with headquarters. Not only won't he allow Scotty to wire his paper without authorisation from Fogarty, but Fogarty

himself has to refer back to Washington. 'That's what I like about the Air Force', quips Scotty, 'smart all the way to the top.'

The critique of bureaucracy, an obligatory preoccupation of conservative films, is given some new twists in science fiction. The absurdity of 'going by the book', the limitations of 'standard operating procedure', are never more apparent than when you're dealing with flying saucers and little green men. When Hendry goes by the book, it's a recipe for disaster. Using standard operating procedure to free the saucer from the ice, he accidentally blows it up with thermite. The film is filled with jokes about military bureaucracy. As the men stare at the frozen saucer, someone recalls that the Air Force dismissed UFOs as 'a mild form of mass hysteria', but in *The Thing*, the masses aren't hysterical. On the contrary, the problem is the brass. Red tape, finally, immobilises Hendry altogether. 'Until I receive my instructions from my superior officers about what to do', he says, 'we'll have to mark time.'

When the orders finally do come, they are worthless. Although the Thing has been making Bloody Marys out of the boys at the base, Fogarty instructs Hendry to 'avoid harming the alien at all costs'. Like York in *Fort Apache* and Sergeant Warden in *From Here to Eternity*, Hendry is forced to disobey orders, even at the risk of court-martial. He can't go too far, like Carrington, but he has to do something, because the organisation is out of touch with reality. And reality here is not national and abstract, but local and concrete. The problem has to be resolved on the spot. Like most conservative films, *The Thing* ultimately deals with the problem without calling in the federal government. The Thing is dispatched by means of a do-it-yourself electric chair, improvised out of the materials at hand. But what keeps this from being a right-wing execution is that although the men at the base do it themselves, they are still soldiers employed by the government, working ultimately in its interests. By this kind of sleight of hand, conservative films avoided having to make the either/or choice Whyte presented to his organisation man. For all the ambivalence *The Thing* expresses toward the Air Force, Hendry's rebellion, like York's in *Fort Apache* and Warden's in *From Here to Eternity*, is confined to the parameters of the organisation. He remains an Air Force man to the last.

What about the Thing itself, and the ants? What do they 'represent'? First, on a level so obvious that it is usually ignored, the ants represent an attack by nature on culture. Nature, for all mankind's technological expertise, is still a threat, red in tooth and claw. But the anthropomorphic gravity of American films is so strong that they have difficulty dramatising genuine otherness. Aliens, no matter how seemingly strange and exotic, end up resembling humans in one way or another. It would be hard to imagine anything more Other than, say, giant ants, until Dr. Medford explains that 'ants are savage, ruthless and courageous fighters. They are the only creatures on Earth aside from man who make war. Ants campaign, they are chronic aggressors, they make slaves of those they can't kill.' In other words, the humans of *Them!* find that their adversaries are very much like Us.

If the ants are like humans, which humans are they like? In 1954, when *Them!* was made, those humans that Americans regarded as antlike, which is to say, behaved like a mass, loved war, and made slaves, were, of course, Communists, both the Yellow Hordes that had just swamped GIs with their human waves in Korea, and the Soviets, with their notorious slave-labour camps. Sci-fi films that presented Communists directly, like *Invasion U.S.A.* and *Red Planet Mars*, were rare. The analogy was usually oblique, but so close to the surface (in *The Naked Jungle*, also released in 1954, the ants that climbed all over Charlton Heston were actually red, and attacked private property to boot) as to be just below the level of consciousness. Presenting Reds as ants or aliens served to establish their Otherness. As Gerhart Niemeyer of Notre Dame put it, the Red mind 'shares neither truth nor logic nor morality with the rest of mankind'. They were not just like Us.

To corporate liberals, Russians in turn stood for the eruption of primitive aggressive behavior. Reds, in other words, were monsters from the id. If we press *Them!* a little further, it quickly becomes apparent that the ants are not only Reds, they're females. *Them!* has as much to do with the sex war as it does the cold war. The film's attack on extremism becomes an attack on women in a man's world.

Centrist films feared the eruption of nature within culture and were therefore afraid of sex and mistrusted women, particularly sexual women. In *Forbidden Planet*, we recall that the Skipper made Alta exchange her skimpy tennis dress for a long gown and put an end to her promiscuous kissing. The monster from the id, nature within, was provoked by Alta's burgeoning sexuality. Like Natalie Wood in *Bombers B-52*, she had become 'restless'.

Them! balances somewhat contradictory attitudes toward sex and sex roles. On the one hand, as we have seen, it explicitly presents an independent woman scientist, whose strong will prevails over agent Graham's this-is-no-place-for-a-woman conservatism. On the other hand, it implicitly presents, in slightly disguised form, a paranoid fantasy of a world dominated by predatory females. The ant society is, after all, a matriarchy presided over by a despotic queen. The queen, it seems, strikes only at patriarchy. Not only does she kill the male drones, but all her human victims are male (one man's phallic shotgun is bent like a paper clip), including two fathers. When the ants are finally cornered, they take cover in Los Angeles's womblike storm drains that conceal the queen's 'egg chamber'. 'Burn 'em out', is the verdict of the male scientists and soldiers at the end of the film, as they perform a hysterectomy by flamethrower.

Them! examines on a fantasy level and on an apocalyptic scale what it leaves unexamined on the 'realistic' level: the conflict between Pat Medford's independence and the chauvinism of the men. It conveys two complementary cautionary messages. To men the moral is: Better give an inch than lose a mile, better let Pat Medford assert herself, or face a far more serious challenge to male power in the future. To women: Don't be too assertive or you'll be punished for it. Centrist films often defined and negated the extremes, the limits of behavior, leaving it to the audience to negotiate an acceptable compromise within those limits.

Like *Them!*, *The Thing* in its most abstract aspect depicts nature's inhuman assault on civilisation. The vast, bleak Arctic wastes play the same role here that the desert plays in *Them!* The film's final lines, the celebrated injunction to 'watch the skies', ask us not only to fear that which comes from space, but space itself, absence, emptiness, the negation of culture. Like the expanse of ice, the sky is an image of Otherness, and that which is not-culture is dystopian. By contrast, enclosures, manufactured spaces, mean safety. The tiny

Arctic base does not feel claustrophobic, nor is it experienced as a prison; rather it becomes a fortress of human warmth, albeit a fragile one, easily destroyed, like the trailer in *Them!*

Like the ants, the Thing bears multiple meanings. The Russians immediately come to mind. Hendry actually speculates early on that the puzzling occurrences in the Arctic 'could be the Russians – they're all over the pole like flies'. But Hendry finds out that the problem is not the Russians, but the Thing – or does he? What is the Thing? Despite the fact that it is apparently part of the natural world, more vegetable than mineral, the Thing is a robot. Some films rendered the distinction between nature and culture as one between animals and vegetables, where vegetables take on the characteristics usually associated with machines: they don't feel pain, have no emotions, and aren't retarded by moral scruples. In *Invasion of the Brain Eaters* (1958), for example, once the plantlike parasites have taken over, people become 'like robots – machines taking orders'. But the Thing, like the ants in *Them!* – like most film symbols – 'depends on associations, not a consistent code' as critic Raymond Durgnat puts it. It slips and slides from one meaning to another. Although the Thing is supposed to be an entirely alien form of life, it looks like nothing more unusual than a large man. Which man is it like? Carrington, of course, the Thing's pal, the cold, unfeeling genius who is as superior to his colleagues as the Thing is smarter than garden-variety humans, and whose development has not been, as someone says of the Thing, 'handicapped by emotional or sexual factors'. (In one version of the script, Carrington is actually killed by the Thing, and Scotty says, 'Both monsters are dead.') Carrington, as we have seen, is a pluralist mad scientist, but with his beard and Soviet-style fur hat, he is also a Russian, so we have come full circle. This film attacks pluralists by equating them with Reds. And if a film like *Them!*, through its linkage of nature, ants, women and Russians, imagines Reds as monsters from the id, conservatives imagined them as emotionless veggies or robots, repressive, not eruptive. They represented reason run amok; they were monsters from the superego.

Finally, however, conservative films fell in line behind their corporate-liberal allies in time for the final fade-out. In *The Thing*, this means that although the blood-sucking carrot from another world is a head-over-heart veggie robot Red monster from the superego one minute, it is an extremist heart-over-head monster from the id the next.

When Hendry arrives at the Arctic base, before introducing himself to Carrington or investigating the strange 'disturbances', he makes straight for the only woman, Nikki Nicholson (Margaret Sheridan). First things first. It seems that the two are romantically involved, although Nikki is piqued because, on their last date, Hendry got drunk and took liberties. 'You had moments of making like an octopus', she tells him. 'I've never seen so many hands in all my life.' If the head can get out of hand, hands can lose their heads, and Hendry has to learn to keep his to himself. 'You can tie my hands, if you want to', he suggests, and in a bizarre scene, she does just that. As he sits in a chair, his hands safely tied behind his back, she pours a drink down his throat and then kisses him on the lips. In other words, she has to emasculate and infantilise him before he can become a safe and acceptable suitor. But the joke is on her. His hands aren't tied after all; he's just pretending, and at the end of the scene, he flings off the ropes and grabs her. Cut directly to a large block of ice bound with rope, just like Hendry. Inside the ice is the Thing, just as inside Hendry is the id. The ice accidentally melts, and the Thing gets loose, in the same way that Hendry escapes Nikki's bonds. At the end of the film, when the Thing is destroyed, the monster from Hendry's id is symbolically subdued, clearing the way for the union of Hendry and Nikki. The extremes of head (Carrington) and heart (Hendry's id), culture and nature, both represented by the Thing, have given way, once again, to the golden mean. But the dénouement is a characteristically conservative one. As in *Forbidden Planet*, force, not therapy, is the solution to the problems of the self.

This confusing plurality of meanings is at least in part an expression of the centre's inclination to reconcile contradictions, to be all things to all people. Conservative films, as we have seen, were torn between extremists on their right and corporate liberals on their left. They fought against and borrowed from both in an attempt to achieve their own distinctive equilibrium. Both *Them!* and *The Thing* want soldiers and scientists to work together. The differences between the two films are those of emphasis. Each, in a slightly different way, equated the cold war with the sex war, politics with personality, the Russians with the id or superego on both. Each implied that not only did the Soviets pose an external threat and, worse, an internal one through unreliable, wrong-thinking elements like Carrington, but worst of all, they penetrated our very selves. We were all potentially extremists inside. As Schlesinger put it, 'There is a Hitler, a Stalin in every breast.'

Re-examining the 1950s Invasion Narratives

Mark Jancovich

Rather than legitimating Fordism and its application of scientific-technical rationality to the management of American life, 1950s invasion narratives often criticised this system by directly associating the alien with it. It has often been pointed out that the qualities which identify the aliens with the Soviet Union is their lack of feelings and the absence of individual characteristics. It was certainly the case that during the 1950s, many American critics claimed that in the Soviet Union people were all the same; that they were forced to deny personal feeling and characteristics, and to become mere functionaries of the social whole. It should also be noted, however, that, as has been illustrated, it was common in the 1950s for Americans to claim that the effects of scientific-technical rationality upon their own society was producing the same features within America itself.

If the alien was at times identified with Soviet communism, it was also implied that this was only the logical conclusion of certain developments within American society itself. The system of scientific-technical rationality was impersonal, and it oppressed human feelings and emotions. It did not value individual qualities, but attempted to convert people into undifferentiated functionaries of the social whole, functionaries who did not think or act for themselves but were ordered and controlled from without by experts. It is for this reason that even in the most pro-scientific of the 1950s invasion narratives, the scientists often display a respect for, and a fascination with, the aliens which, it is stressed, represent their 'ideal' of a society ordered by scientific-technical rationality. Indeed, the aliens are often directly associated with technology. They either threaten the Earth with it, or are produced by it. Science may at times be necessary to destroy the aliens, but these texts often highlight the uselessness of scientific experts in favour of spontaneity, practicality and even domestic knowledge. As a result, even the most positive accounts of science within these texts suggest a sense of ambivalence with regard to technology.

The aliens are also often represented as the 'ideal' image of a scientifically-ordered military. Lucanio challenges Murphy and others by claiming that these films are not celebrations of militarism, but that the military simply offers an image of community.[1] Such a claim is ultimately unconvincing in itself, but it is significant that in those cases where military personnel are presented positively, they are usually distinguished from the scientific-rationality of the military high command. They are usually acting on their own and often directly disobeying orders from above. Co-operation may be necessary within these films, but it is not the co-operation required by the Fordist system. It is the co-operation of an interactive community threatened by Fordist rationalisation and domination.

For these reasons, it is difficult to argue that nature itself is the problem within these films. As Biskind himself claims in the case of *The Thing from Another World* (1951): 'Despite the fact that it is part of the natural world, more vegetable than mineral, the Thing is a robot.'[2] If the invaders are presented as natural, they are carefully distinguished from associations with 'human nature'. They are vegetables, insects or reptiles. They are cold-blooded beings which lack what are generally understood to be human feelings or thought processes. They resist anthropomorphism, and are usually presented as little more than biological machines.

As a result, the fact that many of these monsters are the products of science is significant. These texts often display an anxiety about humanity's role within the cosmos. The familiar world becomes unstable and potentially dangerous. Science may save us at times, but it also creates a world which we can no longer recognise, a world in which giant ants or man-eating plants threaten to overwhelm us. As Clarens claims, these texts represent a world in which 'humanity has slipped from its position at the centre of the cosmos'[3] and is now under threat from monsters which are often of its own making. In the case of the 1950s alien invasion narratives, this situation could be associated with the end of American isolationism and the nation's growing awareness of its place within a complex and often hostile world order. But even this context can only be seen as the result of more general anxieties about whether one can trust one's world, or whether one's life is subject to forces over which one has less and less control. In a world where people have faith in the rightness of their way of life, involvement in the international sphere would not provoke the anxieties which one finds in the 1950s invasion narratives.

It is also difficult to argue that these texts are patriarchal in the way that critics such as Biskind claim. The monsters' association with rationality and science usually means that they are associated with masculinity and not femininity. Furthermore, those qualities which are usually associated with femininity are highly valued within these texts. It is not rationality, but those qualities such as emotion, feeling, intuition, interaction and imagination – qualities that are usually defined as feminine and 'irrational' – that are identified as distinctly 'human'. Indeed, within these texts, women often occupy central positions within the action, as subjects rather than objects of the narrative. Lucanio argues that this is simply a ploy used by the texts in order to get women near the action where they can then be saved by the male hero,[4] but it is usually a key index of the ideological problems with which these texts are engaged. Rather than being merely a ploy, these texts often present women's active involvement in the struggle as absolutely essential to the victory over the menace, and it is the men who fail to appreciate their contribution who are usually portrayed as a 'problem'. It is these men who must learn to acknowledge the error of their ways, or else be punished for their failure to do so.[5]

Biskind himself acknowledges the active role which Pat Medford assumes in *Them!*, but he argues that the film's message is simple: 'Better to give them [women] an inch than lose a mile, better to let Pat Medford assert herself, or face a more serious challenge to male power in the future.'[6] To some extent, this may actually be the way in which gender issues operate within these films, but, even if this is the case, it seriously challenges many of the claims about the sexual politics of 1950s culture, including those of Biskind himself.

Many critics, drawing on Betty Friedan's *The Feminine Mystique*, argue that the message of 1950s popular culture was that women who assumed or even desired positions of power had failed to adjust to their rightful role within the family, and that the only roles within which women can be truly fulfilled were those of

wife and mother.[7] As a result, 1950s popular culture is often accused of having actively directed women away from public activities and towards the privacy of the domestic sphere. Even if Biskind is right about the way in which Pat Medford is used within *Them!*, the film is therefore not functioning in the way in which it is generally assumed that films of the period operated. Indeed, rather than confining women to the domestic sphere, many if not most of these texts actually challenge the separation of the public and the private, the masculine and the feminine, the rational and the irrational. It is only when these distinctions are rejected, these texts suggest, that the problems which threaten humanity can be overcome.

Nor is it the case that sexuality is the problem within these texts as Biskind and others have argued. Instead sexuality is usually defined as the ultimate expression of human feelings, emotions and interaction, and it is therefore opposed to the monstrousness of the aliens' asexual reproductive activities. Asexuality rather than sexuality is the problem, and this is related to a long history in horror fiction that dates back at least as far as Mary Shelley's *Frankenstein* (1818).[8] Furthermore, asexuality is a problem exactly because of its association with masculinity and science. As in *Frankenstein*, asexual reproduction is associated with the male fantasy of producing life without recourse to women, and it is this fantasy which is defined as monstrous specifically because it is founded on a male fear of female sexuality in particular, and sexuality in general.[9]

If these films do emphasise the need to 'pull together', they do not endorse the kinds of conformist consensus which Biskind, Tudor and others suggest. They are actually deeply critical of conformity, and clearly distinguish their positive groups from the centrally-organised systems of Fordism. Rather than a rational structure of domination and control, these groups are interactive communities which are trying to defend themselves against rationally-organised hierarchies.[10] Their 'xenophobia' is therefore less problematic than is often implied. It is not just a fear of strangers, but an altogether more admirable attempt to defend the human against the inhuman; to privilege certain communal values in opposition to the 'dehumanising' domination of scientific-technical rationality.

Indeed, it is worth noting that most critics of these texts attack them for being non-intellectual or even anti-intellectual. They are often accused of provoking anti-communist 'hysteria', and exploiting 'irrational' or 'primitive' emotions such as xenophobia. But these criticisms actually reproduce the very values and positions which these texts challenge and reject. These criticisms accept a clear distinction between the rational and the irrational in which the former is privileged over the latter. They fail to acknowledge the legitimacy of the 'irrational', and ultimately share the same values as the systems of power which these texts attack.

As a result, not only do these texts contradict the claims of most mass culture theories, they are also frequently more sophisticated and complex than those theories. First, they indicate that mass culture critics, such as Dwight MacDonald, were simply wrong when they claimed that mass culture is incapable of producing critical texts, and that it ultimately endorses an elite of experts and adherence to conformity. Second, these texts actually offer an advance over mass culture theory to the extent that they present the solution to mass culture as being social rather than individual. They emphasise not only the need for group interaction, activity and resistance, but also that the simple opposition between society and the individual is a myth. In many texts, the individual not only needs the support of a communal group, but also needs stable social patterns. The conflict in these texts is between different social orders, not simply between society and the individual. This situation also enables these texts to give a more satisfying account of the seductions of conformity and routine than is available in most mass culture theory. They are able to give some sense of why people might be willing to surrender to such systems and pressures.

Finally, these texts also raise an issue which is absent from mass culture theory, at least until *The Feminine Mystique* nearly ten years later,[11] and that is the relationship of mass culture and society to the construction of gender relations. While much mass culture theory was based on the implicit and even explicit concern that mass culture 'feminised' men by encouraging conformity and passivity,[12] the 1950s invasion narratives often challenged not only the ways in which masculinity was constructed within

1950s America, but also the ways in which femininity was constructed.

It is also worth noting that those critics who discuss these films in relation to the context of Cold War America often fail to examine their relationship to the science fiction literature of the period. In science fiction literature, the alien invader (or Bug-Eyed Monster [BEM] as it is often described) was not a product of the Cold War, but had been popular in the 1930s and 1940s. John Campbell's 'Who Goes There?', on which *The Thing from Another World* was based, was originally published in 1938.[13] Indeed, by the late 1940s, the subgenre had become so familiar that it was already the object of parodies such as Ray Bradbury's 'The Concrete Mixer' (1949).[14] By the 1950s, much science fiction literature was desperately trying to distance itself from an association with this subgenre. This is partly responsible for the derision with which 1950s science fiction/horror is often regarded by those with an investment in contemporary science fiction. They were seen as 'out of date' in relation to the science fiction literature of their period. On the other hand, not all advocates of science fiction have been negative about them. Indeed, Arthur C. Clarke and Michael Crichton, both of whom write more legitimate or 'serious' science fiction, claim that *The Thing from Another World* is one of the best science fiction films of all time. As a result, the relationship between this subgenre and the period of the 1950s is much more complex than is often implied. The alien invader predates the Cold War.

It is also dangerous to see the subgenre as a unitary object. Many texts use elements of this subgenre while remaining very different types of texts, and even the films which can easily be discussed as part of the subgenre use its elements in very different ways, and develop the subgenre in very different directions. They may deal with a common series of issues and problems, but they deal with them in different ways and frequently take different ideological positions. The subgenre not only develops historically, but within any particular stage of development, different films may contradict or conflict with one another.

1951: the year the aliens arrived!

One of the clearest examples of the ideological differences between films with in this subgenre can be found in comparisons between *The Thing from Another World*, the first significant example of the 1950s invasion narratives, and *The Day the Earth Stood Still*, which was released in the same year, 1951. These two films are frequently compared because they share common themes and issues, but while *The Thing from Another World* is usually seen as an authoritarian text, *The Day the Earth Stood Still* is often praised as liberal or even left-wing in its politics. This distinction can be seen in Bruce Kawin's discussion of the two films. Like Lucanio and Sobchack, Kawin is attempting to identify the features which distinguish science fiction and horror, but he argues that genre distinctions 'are determined not by plot-elements so much as by attitudes towards plot-elements'.[15] Indeed he shares Lucanio and Sobchack's claim that the difference lies in the two genres' respective attitudes towards science. If, as Kawin claims, these two genres are 'comparable in that both tend to organise themselves around some confrontation between an unknown and a would-be knower',[16] horror is claimed to present the unknown as threatening and works to defend and re-establish the status quo, while science fiction is not supposed to present the confrontation with the unknown as dangerous, but as potentially liberating. It allows for the possibility of change and development. If these differences are discussed in terms of genre distinctions, Kawin also implies a political judgement. Horror is identified as implicitly conservative, while science fiction is presented as implicitly progressive (as either liberal or radical).

Kawin's comparison of *The Thing from Another World* and *The Day the Earth Stood Still* is meant to draw out these distinctions. Both films, he points out, share similar issues and plot-elements. They both concern an alien being which comes to Earth, and they revolve around a similar series of distinctions. But he argues that they take very different positions in relation to these distinctions. For example, he notes that while the alien provokes a conflict between science and the military in both these films, *The Thing from Another World* presents the military as right to regard the alien as a threat which must be destroyed, while in *The Day the Earth Stood Still*, the scientists are presented as right to regard 'the alien as a visitor with superior knowledge, to be learned from, and if possible, joined'.[17] As a result, it is argued that these films have different ways of presenting the distinction between the human and the inhuman. In *The Day the Earth Stood Still*, the inhuman has value, while the inhuman is simply destructive in *The Thing from Another World*. The central opposition in these films is therefore claimed to be one between violence and intelligence. *The Thing from Another World* is supposed to value violence, while *The Day the Earth Stood Still* is supposed to value intellect. In the former, the creature is simply a threat and can only be dealt with through violence, while in the latter, the alien is highly intelligent and violence is an inappropriate response to it. Communication is the way of dealing with the alien in *The Day the Earth Stood Still*. A meeting of minds is possible, and rational discussion is the positive value.

Biskind comes to similar conclusions. He claims that *The Thing from Another World* associates the alien with Soviet aggression and so stresses the necessity of supporting the American state. But he also acknowledges that the alien's presence provokes a conflict between the military and the scientists. The former recognise the alien as a threat and want to destroy it, while the latter, led by Professor Carrington, want to communicate with it and learn from it. This latter goal is clearly presented as absurd within the film but, for Biskind, the film suggests that the scientists' real problem is not their use of reason, or even their attempt to consort with the enemy, but rather their refusal to accept the authority of the military, and by extension, the state. Biskind does acknowledge that the film presents rational, bureaucratic procedures as inadequate, and that the alien is presented as 'reason run amok',[18] but he still argues that the soldiers are 'employed by government, [and are] working ultimately in its interests'.[19] Indeed, Biskind claims that the film also associates the alien with the military leader's id (his irrational sexual desire), a force which must be 'symbolically subdued' in order to clear the way for socially sanctioned heterosexual behaviour (marriage). As a result, the film is read as a conservative one in which force is used to destroy anything that threatens or challenges the status quo. It is a film which cannot accept the validity of anything which departs from its limited notions of 'normality'.

In contrast, *The Day the Earth Stood Still* is seen as a radical critique of American society. Biskind argues that it uses the figure of the lone alien to challenge society for its inability to accept him, or the wisdom which he offers. In this film, the alien is good, and society is 'dystopian'.[20] Like *The Thing from Another World*, the alien is associated with science, and threatened by the military, but in this case, science is not only presented positively, but also as justifiably subversive in relation to the dystopian order. For example, Professor Barnhardt, the brilliant scientist who is able to recognise the alien's wisdom, is claimed to bear 'a striking resemblance to Albert Einstein'.[21] According to Biskind, 'Einstein was never a favourite of the authorities', and in 'making an Einstein figure the hero of sorts, *The Day the Earth Stood Still* was crawling far out on a very thin limb'.[22] Barnhardt also calls a meeting of scientists from all over the world to come and hear the alien's wisdom, and for Biskind, the meeting 'bears a passing resemblance to the Cultural and Scientific Conference for World Peace held at the Waldorf-Astoria Hotel in New York amid a storm of protest in 1949'.[23] People who attended this conference were criticised for being either naïve or subversive, but in *The Day the Earth Stood Still*, it is presented as the only hope for humanity.

Biskind does recognise that by making 'heroes of professors and aliens', the film 'creates a top-down hierarchy' in which ordinary people 'are not rational enough' and need to be controlled by experts.[24] But this situation does not seem to trouble him unduly. Nor does he seem particularly worried by the alien's mission. Klattu, the alien, has been sent to Earth to inform humanity that its 'irrationality' threatens the universal order and that it must accept the rule of a robot police force or else face annihilation. Gort, the robot which Klattu brings with him, has the power to destroy Earth if it does not put its 'irrational' squabbles and petty interests aside. But again Biskind does not seem particularly alarmed by this solution, which is presented as entirely just and benevolent – even utopian. Instead he argues that

> where Klattu comes from, the robot cop is trusted. It is only on Earth (and here, Earth stands for society, as society stands for centre) that Gort is dangerous, only on Earth, the world of disharmony and intolerance, that Gort would menace Helen Benson, that technology and humanity, head and heart, are

at odds. Where Klattu comes from, Gort is either an obedient servant or benevolent master...[25]

As a result, Biskind interprets *The Day the Earth Stood Still* as a positive, enlightened and even radical film, and claims that as a critique 'of the witch-hunt and the cold war, [it] skated close to the edge of permissible dissent'.[26]

The Thing from Another World

However, these films can be seen quite differently. Indeed, Biskind's interpretation of them contradicts his own claims about the dominance of scientific and therapeutic forms of control. Both he and Kawin also end up ultimately defending the very values of rationality and conformity on which the dominance of scientific-technical rationality is supposed to depend. In the process, they ignore or distort aspects of these films. For example, in *The Thing from Another World*, it is not the military personnel who are associated with the authority of the state, but the scientist. While he is associated with the highest levels of state authority and is given the full support of the military hierarchy, the military heroes have little authority and even have to disobey orders to defeat the alien. They are not the representatives of state authority, but its subjects.

The scientist, Carrington, is clearly presented as one of the experts of the new Fordist order. He has been involved in the Bikini atom-bomb tests, and both the government and the military elites look to him for advice. Indeed, so established is his authority that even the military superiors back at base camp complain that they are told nothing about what he is doing at the North Pole. The military heroes, on the other hand, are far from experts. They are not only required to refer back to their superiors at every available opportunity, but do not even understand the principles of scientific-technical rationality. Hendry, the hero, is constantly telling the scientists that they have 'lost' him as they try to explain scientific details and procedures, and the orders from his superiors are forever telling him to defer to Carrington.

As a result, the conflict is not simply between the military and the scientists, as Biskind suggests, but one between ordinary working people and the authority of experts. The military itself is not presented positively, but only the soldiers on the ground. The military authorities, and particularly the high command, are presented as not only inadequate, but as an actual problem. They are presented as cumbersome and out of touch. They install doorways which are inappropriate to the arctic environment and send pith helmets to the North Pole. They publish bulletins in *Stars and Stripes* which contradict the evidence, and lay down standard operating procedures which do not take account of the context of their use and so have destructive results. When the soldiers use these standard operating procedures to uncover the alien spaceship which they have found buried in the ice, they only succeed in blowing it up. Indeed, whenever orders do come from above, they are either too late or else completely misguided. As the battle against the alien intensifies, the soldiers keep getting messages which tell them to protect the creature at all costs.

In this context, Carrington's interest in the Thing is significant. After one confrontation with the alien, it is attacked by the camp dogs which tear off one of its arms. As the scientists inspect this arm, they find that the alien is a vegetable and that it has seed pods under its skin. From this information, Carrington deduces that the alien's reproductive system is asexual, and he proceeds to give a speech which indicates not only why he considers this discovery so important, but also the values which the creature embodies for him:

Yes, the neat and unconfused reproductive technique of vegetation. No pain or pleasure as we know it. No emotions. No heart. Our superior in every way. Gentlemen, do you realise what we've found? A being from another world, as different from us as one pole from the other. If we can only communicate with it, we could learn secrets that have hidden from man since the beginning.

For Carrington, the alien is the 'ideal' of the system of scientific-technical rationality. It is a creature which has no personal or irrational features. As Lukacs argues in relation to the labour process, scientific-technical rationality is not concerned with the individual qualities of its workers' labour, but only with the quantity of their labour, their output. Indeed, he claims

that as scientific-technical rationality is used by management to create greater efficiency, the individual qualities of a worker's labour are redefined 'as mere sources of error when contrasted with those special laws functioning according to rational principles'.[27] In this process of production, and by extension, in a society ordered according to the principles of scientific-technical rationality, individuals must deny their individual qualities in order to become interchangeable components within a system which is ordered and controlled by experts.

Carrington admires the alien because it lacks the very features which he defines as an impediment to efficiency. The alien race is not made up of individuals with individual features or qualities. Each is a replica of its parent and is produced through a system of reproduction which is not only seen as more efficient by Carrington, but is also associated with the standardisation of mass production. Not only does this system of reproduction define the alien race as little more than biological machines, it also means that they lack the features which Carrington sees as the ultimate form of 'irrationality', sexual desire. It is sexual desire which is seen as the ultimate expression of all human emotions and feelings, but it is this very feature which Carrington's scientific-technical rationality seeks to control or erase. It is not only seen as an impediment to the efficient performance of social roles, but it also requires interaction. Carrington's ideal model of society must seek to eradicate interaction in favour of a centrally-ordered system of control, and it is the struggle between interaction and domination which preoccupies this film.

Just as MacDonald and Mills argued that the new system of domination broke down interactive communities in order to bind individuals directly to the centres of power, so *The Thing from Another World* dramatises the conflict between these two modes of social organisation. It suggests that in the latter system, people are merely objects to be used, and this situation is dramatised through the film's presentation of the alien as a kind of modernist vampire. It feeds on human blood which it also needs to reproduce itself as a species. Marx had used the image of the vampire to describe the workings of capitalism, and argued that 'Capitalism is dead labour which, vampire-like, lives only by sucking living labour, and lives the more, the more it sucks.'[28] In a similar way, as Carlos Clarens puts it, *The Thing from Another World* suggests that 'superior science … will bleed us to death'.[29] Even Carrington is worried by this situation. If the alien only sees humans as a means of sustaining and reproducing itself, why should it want to communicate with them? As Carrington puts it: 'He regards us as important only for his nourishment. He has the same attitude towards us as we have towards a field of cabbages. That is our battle.' Unfortunately Carrington is as unable to influence the actions of the alien as ordinary people are able to influence the elites of mass society. He is as unsuccessful in persuading the alien to communicate with him as the soldiers are in trying to persuade him to interact with them.

The issue of communication is therefore central to the film, and it is partly dealt with through the different styles of speech which distinguish the film. While Carrington tends to give speeches or monologues, the soldiers tend to speak in overlapping dialogue, a feature common to those films associated with the director Howard Hawks who produced *The Thing from Another World*. The soldiers talk fast, bouncing ideas off one another, finishing each others' sentences as they add ideas and comments. In this kind of dialogue, meaning and ideas do not originate in the authority of any one individual, but develop out of communal interaction. Hendry may act as the leader, but instead of dictating to the group as Carrington does, he mainly acts to facilitate dialogue. Indeed, he is often given ideas and even orders by his subordinates, and in the final battle, he actually loses track of what is being planned. He becomes displaced from the centre of the group, which now no longer needs him to coordinate it, and moves to a place on the sidelines from which he keeps asking what is going on. However, this situation is not presented negatively, and Hendry does not resent it. In fact, the reverse is true: Hendry turns it into a joke because he is able to accept that his men know what they are doing, and may even be better equipped in certain areas than himself. Indeed, the group even involve themselves in his 'private life', and finally succeed in pushing Hendry and Nicky, his girlfriend, together. As she tells him, 'they know what's best for you'.

In contrast, Carrington gives monologues and speeches in which he sets himself up as an authority who hands down information and orders to others. Indeed, rather than interacting with others, he frequently withholds information in an attempt to control situations, and he shows little concern when this often endangers people. When he discovers that the alien is using the camp's greenhouse to reproduce itself, he refuses to tell Hendry and the others. Instead he leaves a couple of his fellow scientists to keep watch and so causes their deaths. He even begins secretly to breed the alien's seeds himself. Indeed, the more he tries to understand the alien and to communicate with it, the more he finds himself unable to communicate with other humans. His powers of speech start to deteriorate, and he frequently resorts to passing his notes over to Nicky, his secretary, who reads them for him. This technique is similar to the way in which experts often use press conferences to control and manage the flow of information to the rest of the population. He even finds it increasingly difficult to interpret the responses of others. When he explains to the other scientists that he has been breeding the alien seed pods, he mistakes their looks of horror and disapproval for disbelief. This situation is unsurprising given that their lives are unimportant to him, except as an aid to the further development of scientific knowledge. As Carrington puts it, 'knowledge is more important than life'.

The film's concerns with issues of interaction and communication are also dealt with through the figure of Scotty, the newspaper man who comes to the base with Hendry. In this film, the news media are not presented as a form of mass cultural manipulation, but as a democratic force. It is their role to disseminate information to the public. But when the soldiers find the alien spaceship, a conflict develops between Hendry and Scotty. Hendry will not let Scotty release the story of the discovery. He claims that the army radio cannot be used for 'private information', but when Scotty retorts that this information is not private, but belongs to the whole world, Hendry replies that he is not working for the whole world, but for the US army. This exchange is given a darker dimension later in the film when Scotty comments on the destruction of the spaceship and claims that the military will probably make Hendry a general for destroying embarrassing information. The implication of these comments should be clear. The film raises the issue of the military hierarchy's control and manipulation of information. If Scotty represents the democratic flow of information, the military, like Carrington, seek to dominate and control information for their own ends, rather than in the interests of the wider population.

However, Hendry is largely dissociated from this problem. He is clearly seen to be acting under orders, and he makes great efforts to get permission from his superiors for Scotty to release his story. Indeed, Hendry has been responsible for persuading his superior to allow Scotty to go to the North Pole in the first place. As the film progresses, Hendry also becomes distanced from the hierarchy and learns the importance of disobeying orders. Scotty seems to acknowledge this situation, and though he still complains, he is spontaneously included within the group. The group even makes him their spokesperson after the conflict. Scotty is given the radio and not only addresses the world, but also talks for the group. His speech even includes Carrington within the group under the assumption that he has probably learned his lesson and will now respect the interactive community.

If the film concerns a conflict between the interactive community and the authority of scientific-technical rationality which seeks to dominate and reconstruct this community, these issues are also dealt with in relation to sexuality and gender. Not only is the alien's mode of asexual reproduction that which is ultimately defined as monstrous, but in American culture, as linguistic theorists such as Deborah Tannen have claimed, overlapping dialogue and interaction are usually associated with the feminine, while monologue and rationality are usually associated with the masculine.[30] As a result, while it could be argued that the alien's association with reproduction defines it as feminine, its physical appearance and its association with rationality define it as male. Indeed, there is a long history of horror texts, dating back to the early Gothic novels, concerned with the patriarchal fantasy of producing life without interaction with women and define the attempt to realise this fantasy as that which is ultimately monstrous. Mary Shelley's *Frankenstein* is a particularly clear example, and like *The Thing from Another World*, this novel relates this fantasy to the logic of scientific rationality. Not only is it this asexual method of reproduction which

leads Carrington to associate the alien with technology and rationality, both of which are usually defined as masculine, but this method also leads him to distinguish it from those very qualities which are usually defined as feminine, qualities such as interaction and emotion.

Indeed, the film is highly critical not only of the distinction between rationality and irrationality, but also of the distinction between masculinity and femininity to which it is related. As a result, it not only contains a strong central female character, but also presents its male characters as emotionally weak. Not only does Nicky wear trousers throughout the film, she is often at least as capable as the men in traditionally masculine activities. She has been able to out-drink Hendry, and knows enough about science to understand Carrington's work and its implications. Indeed, the military team accept her as an equal within their group without question. At one point, she does turn up with coffee for the men, but this scene is particularly telling with regard to the film's self-conscious handling of gender roles. As the men are discussing how to combat the alien, Nicky arrives at the door with coffee and asks if anyone wants a cup. Recognising that this is an excuse, they say that they don't want any coffee, but that she can join them anyhow. Having already been accepted, she admits that she had only brought the coffee so that she could join them. Only at this point, once the men have made it clear that she has been welcomed into the group as an equal, and not in order to perform traditionally female roles, do they then agree to drink the coffee.

But if Nicky is skilled in traditionally masculine activities, she is not a surrogate male.[31] She does not distance herself from traditionally feminine qualities in order to achieve male approval. Indeed, her strength is that she embodies both masculine and feminine virtues, but is not confined to either one. If she does trouble and disturb the male characters, it is due to their own inadequacies. Hendry, for example, is quite capable in traditionally masculine activities, but he is unable to deal with his emotions and so finds it difficult to relate to women. In the film's terms, he is not only presented as immature, but this immaturity is also associated with the rationality of the scientists and the alien. These latter figures either lack or despise emotion, and the scientists are frequently claimed to be 'like kids with a new toy'. If, as Biskind argues, this situation implies that the alien is not just associated with rationality but also with Hendry's sexuality, it is not because it is associated with his id, or his sexual desire. After all, the alien has no sexual desire. Instead, the alien is associated with Hendry's masculinity, and his inability to deal with women as anything more than objects for sexual conquest. In the film's terms, he must grow up, but this does not mean that he must repress his sexuality. Quite the reverse, he must acknowledge his feelings, including his sexual feelings, and learn how to interact with women as equals. In short he must acquire traditionally feminine qualities.

Not only does Nicky call into question traditional gender roles, and gender distinctions, she is also for this very reason absolutely essential to the destruction of the alien. Indeed, she is the one who comes up with the comment from which the final plan is developed. As the group tries to work out how to kill a vegetable, she jokingly suggests cooking it. It is by combining her domestic knowledge with practical science that the group is finally able to destroy the alien by burning it to death with electricity. It is only when the distinctions between the masculine and the feminine, the rational and the irrational, the domestic and the scientific, are dispensed with that the threat represented by the alien can be finally eliminated.

The Day the Earth Stood Still

The Day the Earth Stood Still, on the other hand, is a far more authoritarian film. Its criticism of American society is simply that it is not rational enough, and it calls for the repression of individual feelings, interests and desires, all of which are simply defined as both irrational and destructive. This repression is necessary in order to ensure the efficient running of a state which is not merely national or even international, but a fully 'universal' order. Nor is this film any less violent in its values than The Thing from Another World. It is just more impersonal. Violence, or at least the threat of violence, is essential to the smooth running of the rational state. It has to be used to keep irrational elements repressed. Violence may be denied to individuals or nations, but only because it is given over to the rule of

technology and science embodied in the robot police force of which Gort is a member.

Klattu has been sent to Earth to inform us that the Earth's internal conflicts threaten the peace of the universe, but the language which he uses to describe humans and human society clearly defines these conflicts as simply the products of irrationality. He criticises humans for their 'unreasoning attitudes' and when he is asked by an interviewer (who does not know his identity) if he fears the alien's arrival, Klattu answers that he is only 'fearful when [he] sees people substituting fear for reason'. For Klattu, human emotions have no foundation or validity, and it is only rational thought which has any positive value. The problems of human societies and their conflicts are simply dismissed as the product of these irrational emotions. When the nations of the Earth refuse to meet one another in order to hear Klattu's message, he is angered by their 'childish jealousies and superstitions'. They are not based on a reasonable foundation and are merely described as 'petty squabbles'. For Klattu, and for the film, individual and national interests must be put aside in favour of the Universal, but the Universal is not an interactive community based on shared interests. It is an abstract, rational and totalising order to which individuals and nations must surrender themselves. It is vertical, rather than horizontal, in its organisation.

Indeed, rather than criticising the scientific-technical rationality of the American state, the film continually defends and even champions it. For example, the film is careful to emphasise that it is not the American state which is responsible for the conflicts between the nations of Earth. Henley, the diplomat who tries to organise the meeting of national representatives which Klattu demands, is presented as honest and sincere. He genuinely wants to help Klattu, but it is the other nations which cause problems. The American president has even tried to appease the Soviet Union by agreeing to their demand that the meeting should be held in Moscow, and it is the British government who complicates matters by refusing to attend the meeting if it is held there. If there are problems with American institutions, it is that they are not rational enough in their organisation.

Neither is the American military presented negatively as is often claimed. It is presented as a problem only in so far as it functions to defend the interests of an individual nation, rather than universal interests. Indeed, Klattu does not even disapprove of war itself, but only wars fought for supposedly 'petty interests'. Strangely, when Klattu is taken on a tour of Washington by the young Billy Benson, a young boy whom he befriends during the course of the film, he is awestruck by both the Lincoln Memorial and Arlington cemetery. Indeed Billy's father, who has given his life in World War Two, is not presented as a fool who died in a meaningless war. Instead, both the American Civil War and World War Two are implied to have been heroic struggles for grand universal values. Lincoln in particular is seen as a 'great man'. The Gettysburg address is not seen as a piece of propaganda designed to encourage men to fight in one of the bloodiest wars of American history, but rather as a heroic testament to the values of 'Union' over sectionalism, of universal over particularistic interests. Unfortunately for Biskind, and others who defend this film as a critic of Cold War ideology, it was this rhetoric of universalism over particularism which America used to justify its Cold War politics. America, it was claimed, was defending universal human values over the particularism of the Soviet Union. Indeed, at the beginning of the film, the military is not even presented as having been responsible for the shooting of Klattu. The shooting is the fault of an individual soldier who panics when his emotions get the better of him. It is a lack of military discipline which is the problem, not military discipline itself.

As a result, in *The Day the Earth Stood Still*, it is ordinary people who are the problem, and they are presented as needing the authority of experts in order to keep them in line. Throughout the film, people are presented as prone to irrational panic and in need of discipline. When the spaceship lands, they run in terror. Later they form crowds around the vessel and need to be controlled by the military and police. When Gort appears they react in horror, and flee once more. Indeed, while Klattu claims that his message is too important to be entrusted to any one individual or nation, he does not seek to address the ordinary people, but only their leaders. If he has the power to make the world stand still for half an hour, it is difficult to accept that the film cannot find a way for him to address all the peoples of the Earth (as the aliens do in *Earth Vs the Flying Saucers* [1956]). Indeed, while he does go amongst the

ordinary people, he explicitly states that he is doing so in order to discover the basis of the irrationalities which divide the world. It is the irrationality of ordinary people which causes problems at the higher levels of government, not vice versa. Furthermore, the film does not contradict Klattu's view of people. When he goes amongst the people, he takes a room in a boarding house in which everyone except a young woman, Helen Benson, and her son, Billy, display irrationality and panic. They either suspect the alien of being a Russian, or are just plain 'jittery'.

If Helen Benson and her son do not display these negative features, it is not because the film values the feminine qualities of interaction or emotion. Instead, Helen displays the traditionally maternal qualities of self-denial and self-sacrifice. She represses her own interests and defers to authority. This feature is particularly clear in her relationship with her boyfriend, David. When he finds out that Klattu is the alien, David decides to inform the Pentagon. However, Klattu has spoken to Helen and has persuaded her of the universal importance of his mission. She accepts his authority and tries to persuade David not to inform. Unfortunately, he is filled with dreams of individual power and heroism. He says that by informing he will become a 'big man' and that he will 'be able to write [his] own ticket'. In response, Helen asks him to consider the broader implications of his actions, but he only responds, 'I don't care about the rest of the world'. In this film, individualism is merely irrational selfishness, but all the film has to offer in its place is self-denial. It hardly offers the image of a society in which humans can live more fulfilling lives, and simply calls for the repression of individual desires before an authoritarian state.

Helen's son operates in much the same way as his mother. Children are seen as open to the wonders of the world, but in the film, the reason for their openness is that they look up to others. Indeed, their sense of wonder is almost entirely presented in relation to scientific achievements. While adults are terrified by the spaceship, the children are presented as being excited by, and in awe of, the vessel. Billy is also fascinated by Klattu's stories about the scientific wonders of his civilisation.

Indeed, science in general is presented as wondrous and benevolent. Not only does the film emphasise that the science of Klattu's society is more advanced than that of humans, it often associates it with medicine. It is claimed that due to their advanced medicine, the life expectancy on Klattu's planet is twice that on Earth. At another point, a doctor comments on the miraculous properties of an ointment which Klattu has brought with him, an ointment which has healed a bullet wound on Klattu's arm within one day. But the greatest display of the healing powers of science occurs at the end of the film when Gort uses technology to bring Klattu back from the dead after he has been shot by the army for the second time. Indeed, this sequence also gives science religious overtones. The film has a clear parallel with the New Testament, in which Klattu takes the role of Christ. He comes to Earth to save it from its follies; goes amongst the common people; is killed by human ignorance and intolerance; and eventually rises again before delivering a message to the world and ascending to the heavens. He even takes the name Carpenter while on Earth. Klattu does tell Helen that his resurrection is only temporary and that only God can give back life once it has been taken, but this only further associates technology and science with the powers of God. They become powers to be worshipped and adored.

The film also goes to great lengths to allay fears about science. For example, Klattu tells Billy that his spaceship is powered by atomic energy. Billy is surprised and claims that he thought atomic energy was only useful in the making of bombs. In response, Klattu explains that atomic energy is useful for a great many other things, too. The implication should be clear: science in general and atomic energy in particular are not bad in themselves, but only when used in an irrational and irresponsible manner.

Indeed, science is presented as the only potential saviour of humanity. When Klattu finds that the world's leaders will not meet with him, he tries to find an alternative way of delivering his message, and asks Billy who is the greatest person in America. Billy seems a bit confused, and well he might. Klattu really means: who is the most intellectually brilliant, or as Billy puts it, the 'smartest' person. There are many different ways of defining 'greatness', but for Klattu, as for the film, greatness means scientific genius. Billy decides that the answer is Professor Barnhardt, and Klattu decides that instead of addressing the world's political leaders, he

will address its scientists. His preference for science over politics is again related to issues of rationality. Politicians are associated with the defence of particular interests, while scientists are presented as objective and rational. They are supposedly above the 'petty squabbles' of politics and address universal truths in a logical and rational manner. For this reason, they can overcome the irrationality which divides the world and come together for the good of all.

Not only are scientists the best way of spreading the message, the message itself is that humanity must put aside its irrational behaviour and accept the rule of science in the form of a robot police force. These robots are the embodiment of super-rationality and Klattu informs the scientists that the peoples of the universe have given them 'absolute power over us'. They have incredible destructive powers and have been programmed to destroy any planet which behaves aggressively. Klattu claims that this solution to war does not involve any loss of freedom, except the freedom to behave 'irresponsibly'. But there is a problem with the word 'irresponsible': it is not as easy to define as Klattu implies. What may be irresponsible to one person may not be to another. It is also worth noting that instead of a solution to aggression, the justification for this scheme sounds very similar to the Mutually Assured Destruction (MAD) philosophy which was later used to justify the arms race. According to this philosophy, the stockpiling of nuclear weapons was an aid to world peace, not a threat. The combined destructive strength of these weapons, it was argued, would be so great that no nation would dare to act aggressively for fear of starting an atomic war which would destroy the planet. It would assure the mutual destruction of both sides. Klattu's proposal does not reject violence, but places it firmly within the hands of the state. Not is it presented as an option. He informs the scientists that there is no alternative. Earth must either accept the rule of robots such as Gort, or be destroyed. Instead of respecting difference, the film demands rigid conformity to the universal order, an order from which there can be no valid dissent.

Notes

1   Patrick Lucanio, *Them or Us: Archetypal Interpretations of Fifties Alien Invasion Films* (Bloomington: Indiana University

Press, 1987).

2 Peter Biskind, *Seeing is Believing: How Hollywood Taught Us to Stop Worrying and Love the Fifties* (London: Pluto, 1983), p. 134.

3 Carlos Clarens, *Horror Movies: An Illustrated Survey* (London: Secker and Warburg, 1967), p. 147.

4 Lucanio, *Them or Us.*

5 Even in texts such as *War of the Worlds* where the woman's role is far more peripheral to the action except as an object to be protected, the male scientist-hero eventually occupies the very same position which the woman has occupied throughout the film. He learns the futility of his science in the face of the alien invaders, and the world is only saved when he is finally stripped of his technology and dominance, and embraces the woman's Christian faith.

6 Biskind, *Seeing is Believing*, p. 133.

7 Betty Friedan, *The Feminine Mystique* (New York: Dell, 1963).

8 Mary Shelley, *Frankenstein: or the Modern Prometheus* (1818) (Oxford: Oxford University Press, 1969).

9 See my analysis of *Frankenstein* in Mark Jancovich, *Horror* (London: Batsford, 1992).

10 While there are considerable problems with the concept of 'interactive communities', what is important is that these films operated around very similar oppositions to those which can be found in the mass culture critics of their period, critics who were at best dismissive of these films. Indeed, even within contemporary criticism, the opposition between 'interaction' and 'domination' is often present, even if it assumes very different guises.

11 Friedan, *The Feminine Mystique.*

12 For a discussion of these issues, see Barbara Ehrenreich, *The Hearts of Men: American Dreams and the Flight from Commitment* (London: Pluto, 1983).

13 John Campbell, 'Who Goes There?' (1938), republished in *The Mammoth Book of Classic Science Fiction* (New York: Carroll and Graf, 1988).

14 Ray Bradbury, 'The Concrete Mixer' (1949), in *The Illustrated Man* (1951) (London: Corgi, 1955).

15 Bruce Kawin, 'The Mummy's Pool', in Barry K. Grant, ed., *Planks of Reason: Essays on the Horror Film* (Metuchan: Scarecrow, 1984), p. 5.

16 Ibid.

17 Ibid., p. 7.

18 Biskind, *Seeing is Believing*, p. 134.

19 Ibid., p. 132.

20 Ibid., p. 157.

21 Ibid., p. 153.

22 Ibid.

23 Ibid.

24 Ibid., p. 154.

25 Ibid., p. 158.

26 Ibid.

27 Georg Lukacs, 'Reification and the Consciousness of the Proletariat', in Lukacs, *History and Class Consciousness* (London: Merlin, 1971), p. 89.

28 Karl Marx, *Capital Vol. I* (Harmondsworth: Penguin, 1976), p. 342.

29 Clarens, *Horror Movies*, p. 182.

30 Deborah Tannen, 'Relative Focus on Involvement in Oral and Written Discourse', in David R. Olsen et al., eds, *Literacy, Language and Learning: The Nature and Consequences of Reading and Writing* (Cambridge: Cambridge University Press, 1985).

31 There is considerable debate over the representation of women within the films of Howard Hawks. For an alternative view to the one presented here, see Peter Wollen, *Signs and Meanings in the Cinema* (London: Secker and Warburg, 1972).

'We're the Martians Now': British SF Invasion Fantasies of the 1950s and 1960s

Peter Hutchings

An astronaut infected with an alien organism stumbles across London (*The Quatermass Experiment* [1955]); alien-controlled humans construct a sinister refinery in the English countryside (*Quatermass II* [1957]); a Martian space-craft is unearthed at a tube station (*Quatermass and the Pit* [1967]); an extraterrestrial masquerades as a housewife (*Unearthly Stranger* [1963]); aliens take over a country hospital (*Invasion* [1966]); a visitor from one of Jupiter's moons kidnaps young women and returns them to his planet for breeding purposes (*The Night Caller* [1965]).

In reality Britain has rarely been invaded. In its fantasies the opposite is true. It is perhaps fitting that a nation with such an expansive imperial past should have developed a rich tradition of narratives about itself being invaded, whether this be in the thriller, horror or science fiction genres. All the examples of invasion referred to above come from British science fiction movies of the 1950s and 1960s, an especially active time as far as imaginary invasions are concerned. Sometimes dismissed as lesser versions of or adjuncts to the better known US science fiction invasion films of the 1950s, these British films actually have a distinctive character of their own and this essay will seek to identify the nature of this distinctiveness. It will focus on the ways in which the films engage with issues to do with national identity that are quite different from those addressed by their American cousins. Also discussed will be the changes that occur in the British invasion fantasy as it moves from the 1950s to the 1960s.

Before embarking on this, however, it is worth considering some of the broader issues associated with the subject of imaginary invasion. A useful starting point is perhaps the most famous fantastic invasion of all.

Fears of invasion

No one would have believed, in the last years of the nineteenth century, that human affairs were being watched keenly and closely by intelligences greater than man's and yet as mortal as his own; that as men busied themselves about their affairs they were scrutinised and studied, perhaps almost as narrowly as a man with a microscope might scrutinise the transient creatures that swarm and multiply in a drop of water. With infinite complacency men went to and fro over this globe about their little affairs, serene in their assurance of their empire over matter. It is possible that the infusoria under the microscope do the same.

– H. G. Wells, *The War of the Worlds* (1898)

These resonant opening lines from *The War of the Worlds* – with the matter-of-fact sense they give of humanity being caught in the gaze of another race – constitute a founding moment in the history of the science fiction invasion fantasy, just as the novel in which they feature has proven to be something of a model for alien invasion narratives. It is also true to say that while Wells has secured a place for himself (albeit a marginal one) in the literary canon as the writer of 'popular classics', twentieth-century fantasies about alien invasion have generally received a bad critical press. It is as if the intelligence of Wells's anti-imperial work – with its full-scale assault on British complacency – has been betrayed by a pulp tradition which has assimilated only the sensational qualities of the story and discarded its more serious elements. Bug-eyed monsters wielding death-dealing ray guns and, more recently, the increasing public fascination with UFOs and alien abductions have all been insistently associated with a credulous, juvenile point of view. This has been so regardless of whether one is concerned with real life – and the alleged actual presence of extraterrestrials amongst us – or merely with fictions about alien assault and invasion. The audiences for the latter, it is assumed, are content, keen even, to see any culture that is different from their own presented as threatening simply because of that difference. Matters are made worse by the association of this us/them attitude with a politically reactionary point of view – whether this be the anti-communism of 1950s America or the gung ho nationalism of *Independence Day* (1996). The imperatives remain clear in all cases – we are good, they are bad, destroy them before they destroy us.

Film historians writing on 1950s American sf cinema – notably Peter Biskind (1983) and Mark Jancovich (1996) – have sought to dispel this prejudicial outlook through identifying a set of ambiguities and ambivalences apparent in a range of American invasion fantasies. In particular they have drawn our attention to the ways in which these films are as much about anxieties internal to America as they are about real or imagined fears of communist infiltration and invasion. As Jancovich notes, 'the concerns with the Soviet Union were often merely a displacement or a code which different sections of American society used in order to criticise those aspects of American life which they feared or opposed' (Jancovich 1996: 17).

While this is certainly true, the stress laid in many of these accounts on films which are especially distinguished and insightful in their exploration of the collective national psyche – *Invasion of the Body Snatchers* (1956) and the films of Jack Arnold – tends to cover over the fact that the alien invasion fantasy as a generic format is less straightforward than might be imagined. The transformation presented in *The War of the Worlds* of what were once transcendent and immutable values into a set of relative, contingent beliefs is actually a property of alien invasion fantasies in general, even (perhaps especially) those which seek most rigorously to deny it. This is because the mere imagining of an alien culture always involves an acknowledgement of Otherness and this in turn unsettles a certain complacency and racial self-centredness. Humanity's imaginary dominion, its sense of itself as being at the centre of things, is wounded – and the extraterrestrial origins of this means that the wounding is especially traumatic, inflicted as it is against humanity in general rather than any circumscribed section of it. Once it is realised that, to use a phrase firmly associated with the science fiction genre, 'we are not alone', and once humanity is forcibly made aware of the boundaries or frontiers between it and an Other, then humanity becomes limited and is rendered fragile and perpetually vulnerable.

Alien invasion fantasies rely on what might be termed a relativisation of culture and cultural values. The instabilities and anxieties inevitably involved in this are managed in a variety of ways. In Wells' case, for example, the day is saved via the intervention of germs, 'the humblest things that God, in His wisdom, has put upon this earth'. Thus God – God in man's image, so to speak – is restored to the centre, although this turns out only to be a provisional conclusion, for mankind is left in expectation of further possible attacks. Many readers might well be left suspicious that those helpful germs could in the end prove just as dangerous to humanity as they were to the Martians. One thing should be clear, however: there can be no going back to a life led in blissful – and, as far as Wells is concerned, complacent – ignorance of something which exists 'out there'. Bearing this in mind, it does seem that the Martians' lasting achievement is not their temporary occupation of Earth but rather their forcing humanity to acknowledge the existence of an alien culture and in effect to make mankind return the gaze directed against it at the novel's beginning. Inasmuch as they succeed in doing this, the Martians have won, for they have effectively destroyed once and for all a particular human-centred way of existing in and making sense of the universe. It does seem that this destructive mechanism, by which humanity is presented with an overwhelming sense of its own limitations, is constitutive of all invasion fantasies. Regardless of the narrative outcome, the war is always over before the invasion even begins simply because the mere existence of an alien culture is sufficient to do the damage. It could further be argued that the articulation of such fantasies is dependent on a social and cultural context which has become relativised and less sure of itself. Hence the 1950s was a prime decade for invasions, not only because of the tensions associated with the Cold War, but also because of a number of shifts and new trends in the West, most notably a growing affluence and materialism coupled with a widespread sense that traditional values were increasingly being brought into question. Importantly, these various changes did not manifest themselves uniformly across the Western world. Consumerism, for example, meant something different in America from alleged undue influence of American culture on the British way of life). It follows that any account of British sf, while needing to preserve a sense of the generic character of the alien invasion fantasy and how all such fantasies, regardless of their country of origin, share certain qualities, must at the same time take account of the socially and historically specific pressures exerted upon the fantasies by the context within which they were produced.

Quatermass and the aliens

Alongside the best-selling novels of John Wyndham (including *The Day of the Triffids* [1951], *The Kraken Wakes* [1953] and *The Midwich Cuckoos* [1957]), probably the best-known invasion stories to emerge from 1950s Britain featured the character Professor Bernard Quatermass. Making his first appearance (played by Reginald Tate) in *The Quatermass Experiment*, a highly successful BBC Television serial from 1953, he subsequently featured in two more serials, *Quatermass II* (1955, played by John Robinson) and *Quatermass and the Pit* (1958/1959, played by André Morell). All three were written by Manx writer Nigel Kneale (also responsible for the celebrated television adaptation of Orwell's *1984* (1954)). Each of them presents a narrative in which an alien threat to the Earth gradually escalates to a point of absolute crisis at which time the knowledgeable Quatermass acts decisively in order to save humanity. In 1955 Hammer released its film version of *The Quatermass Experiment*. Directed by Val Guest with the American actor Brian Donlevy in the title role, it proved to be the company's first major box-office hit and in many ways was a forerunner to the Gothic horror cycle that was shortly to follow. Film adaptations of *Quatermass II* (again directed by Guest with Donlevy as the scientist) and *Quatermass and the Pit* (directed by Roy Ward Baker with Andrew Keir as Quatermass) appeared in 1957 and 1967 respectively. (A fourth Quatermass television serial appeared in 1979. Known both as *Quatermass* and *The Quatermass Conclusion*, it featured John Mills as Quatermass. There was also a radio serial – *The Quatermass Memoirs* – in 1996.) Hammer's film versions are better known today than the original television serials, if only because the serials are much harder to see. In writing about Quatermass, however, it is necessary to consider both versions of each story. This is not only because the television versions often contain significant sequences omitted from the films, but also because film and television programme alike display a considerable media awareness. Each contains comments about the medium in which it appears as well as about other media, and this in turn has implications for the way in which the alien invasion itself is presented.

The film version of *The Quatermass Experiment* concludes with the monster being discovered in Westminster Abbey by a live television outside broadcast team who promptly cease transmission, thus cutting off the television audience – but not the cinema audience – from the sight of Quatermass dealing with the threat. Charles Barr has linked this break in transmission with other attempts by 1950s British cinema to distance itself from television, its main rival, by presenting itself as 'a more autonomous and full-blooded experience' (1986: 214). This insistence on the difference between the two media is also apparent in the film being sold on its initial release as *The Quatermass Xperiment*, a marketing device designed to draw a prospective audience's attention to its status as an 'X' certificate film. The 'X' certificate, denoting a film for adults only, had been introduced in 1951 and had rapidly become associated with a growing explicitness *vis-à-vis* the representation of sex and violence. As Barr notes, there is a certain irony attached to this given that the film had itself been adapted from a television serial. The irony is compounded when one realises that the 1953 television version of the story contains a sequence set in a cinema during a screening of an absurdly juvenile, pulp-like science fiction film. Here the television drama, with obvious aspirations to be a mature treatment of pre-existing generic themes, seeks to differentiate itself from what it perceives as the mindlessness of the mainstream, conventional science fiction product. One might add here that the television version of *Quatermass and the Pit* also contains a scene not unlike the film version of *The Quatermass Experiment* in which a television outside broadcast is interrupted. In the case of *Quatermass and the Pit*, this takes place at a press conference in front of the recently uncovered Martian spacecraft and is witnessed mainly from the viewpoint of some people watching television in a nearby pub. Yet again television is shown as inadequate as a means of representing some appalling alien threat, although it is noteworthy that this time it is the television version of the story itself which is announcing its own shortcomings.

In fact the more one looks at the Quatermass stories, the more one sees how both television and film versions exhibit a sense that the material with which they are dealing is not easily assimilated into traditional forms and mechanisms of representation. Hence all the distancing references in both television programmes and films as well as the fact that the camera on board the original Quatermass rocket in *The Quatermass Experiment* (a device meant to provide a reassuringly objective account of the space journey) is broken in the crash which initiates the story. Hence too the presence in both versions of *Quatermass and the Pit* of a new type of recording device which picks up brain waves and translates these into images which can then be projected and viewed by others. Such a device abolishes the distinction between the prosaic mundanity of the television broadcast and the vapid escapism of the space opera shown in the TV *Quatermass Experiment*, engaging instead with private mental processes. In *Quatermass and the Pit*, the knowledge this provides finally enables Quatermass to discover the truth about the Martian invasion of the Earth that took place five million years previously. What the use of this radically new device suggests is that a new way of seeing is required in order to counter the alien threat, one that goes beyond what is currently available in 1950s British society. More generally, such moments of modest self-reflexivity – where, if only for a few sequences, a particular technology of vision and/or representation is foregrounded in the narrative – point to a widespread sense in these stories of they themselves being something new and strange within British film and television culture, something which is in many respects quite alien to the pre-existing norms of representation and storytelling.

These narratives about alien invasion, and indeed the aliens themselves, are defined in their strangeness against what for 1950s Britain passes for reassuringly familiar contexts. This means that while many of the conventional trappings of the science fiction genre – rockets, extraterrestrials and the like – are present, they are invariably located in relation to a reasonably accurate approximation of the real, even humdrum, world. The opening of the film version of *The Quatermass Experiment*, in which a rocket crashes near a cottage in the country, neatly dramatises a much more widespread collision that takes place throughout this and the other Quatermass narratives between the fantastic regime of science fiction and the

'realism' of British everyday life. The climactic sequence in Westminster Abbey would have had a particular resonance in this respect, especially for the television audience who only a few months previously had witnessed the same location on their screens during the Coronation of Queen Elizabeth II. There is a kind of iconoclasm here, a furtive pleasure in seeing the Queen supplanted by a deadly alien monster about to reproduce, just as there is in *Quatermass II* (film), where the Shell Haven Refinery in Essex is transformed into an alien base, and in *Quatermass and the Pit* (TV), where the Martians and the surgically-altered apemen are discovered in, of all places, Knightsbridge. One consequence of this mixing of the familiar and the strange, with the strange often concealed within the familiar and close to home, is that audiences are invited to look at their own world in a different light, seeing it to a certain extent as itself an alien world.

A comment made by Kim Newman in a discussion of US anti-communist movies offers a useful way of thinking about the view of 1950s Britain found in the Quatermass stories. Newman states that unlike their American counter-parts, British sf invasion films of the 1950s seem to be 'still fighting World War Two' (1996: 79). It is certainly true that the Quatermass television programmes and films are replete with distancing references to a Cold War conflict. As the avuncular Inspector Lomax (played by Jack Warner) puts it in *The Quatermass Experiment* (film), 'No one wins a Cold War', an attitude fully endorsed by the discrediting of the views of the hawk-like militarist Colonel Breen and his cronies in *Quatermass and the Pit* (TV and film). It is also true that the Quatermass stories show Britain as a nation still bound to the experience of the Second World War. This manifests itself in a number of ways: examples include the workers at the alien factory in *Quatermass II* who seem to have been transplanted directly from a morale-boosting Second World War film and whose social club contains a poster boasting the war-like slogan 'Secrets Mean Sealed Lips'; the concern with wartime unexploded bombs in *Quatermass and the Pit* as well as the way in which the destruction visited upon London at the conclusion of that story very clearly re-enacts the Blitz. It does not follow from this, however, that these stories are simply nostalgic or backward-looking. Instead this attachment to a collective memory of the Second World War needs to be connected with another distinctive feature of the Quatermass stories – one which further separates them from the US invasion fantasy – and that is their marginalisation of romance and sexual desire and their general suppression of domestic matters.

In the 1950s Quatermass stories, Quatermass himself is someone who, while working to protect the nation, remains a curiously isolated figure, bereft of anything resembling a meaningful relationship. (In the 1979 Quatermass, he has acquired a granddaughter; possibly connected with this is the fact that here he seems a much weaker figure who can only defeat the aliens through the sacrifice of the lives of both himself and his granddaughter.) The standard, if not clichéd, figures of the clean-cut square-jawed hero and his girl, which are present in some form or other in most US sf films of this period and parodied in the film-within-a-TV-programme in *The Quatermass Experiment* (TV), are absent. The most likely candidates for such roles are Victor Caroon, the surviving astronaut in *The Quatermass Experiment*, and his wife, but in both film and television versions their relationship remains marginal to the main narrative and Caroon himself ends up converted into an alien monster. In addition to this, families – another notable signifier of normality in many US sf films – are few and far between in the 1950s Quatermass stories.

While US science fiction invasion fantasies generally proceed in the direction of a heterosexual and/or familial resolution, the Quatermass stories have a tendency to view individuals as existing primarily within and in relation to groups, institutions and collectives. In the world of Quatermass, there are scientists, soldiers, policemen, politicians, journalists, workers, but few lovers or families and, to a certain extent, no free-standing individuals either. What one finds instead is a mode of social existence that bears more than a passing resemblance to a notion of the people developed and circulated in Britain during the Second World War. This pervasive ideal of national identity was presented in a range of propagandistic material in which the people as a national collective absorbed and superseded the individual, where romance and desire were expendable, even frivolous, given Britain's troubled circumstances, and where

the nuclear family that had been disrupted by war was replaced by the group as the prime site of interaction and mutual support. The crucial difference between this wartime notion of the people and the Britain of Quatermass is the populist and hegemonic nature of the former. In the late 1930s the population, and especially a working class alienated from ideas of national unity after the experience of the Depression, had to be won over to the war and the accompanying need for sacrifice. This led to the propaganda for this position having a persuasive, concessionary quality to it, the constant message being that Britain would be a better, more just and integrated nation after the war than it was before (Hurd 1984).

The nation as it exists for Quatermass in the 1950s is certainly unified in that, initially at least, there seems to be no internal dissent or conflict (apart from that occasionally articulated by Quatermass himself). However, the nation in the films lacks any sense of a wartime urgency to bind it together; its unity – with everyone having a place in the collective – is superficial. On one level this registers in a mass complacency where the people seem unconcerned about the dire threat with which they are faced. So in *The Quatermass Experiment* (film), rubbernecking crowds stand idly by at both the beginning and the end while the police's only advice is for everyone to go home (where, presumably, they would all watch television until something disturbing appeared on screen, at which point transmission would be terminated) (Hutchings 1993: 41–50). Similarly in *Quatermass II* the community at Wynerton Flats seems extraordinarily blind to the weird events going on around them, while the nation in general is complacent to the point of culpability in not noticing that aliens have established a firm foothold in Britain. On another, more disturbing level, the superficiality of unity and consensus is apparent in the violence that suddenly – shockingly in the context of the 1950s – tears apart the social order. One thinks here of the worker uprising in *Quatermass II* where the managers and their agents are machine-gunned and the workers themselves fed into the factory machinery, and the riot that concludes *Quatermass and the Pit*, in which a kind of race war breaks out on the streets of London. In each case, the violence can be related to underlying social tensions to do with class and race conflict apparent in

Britain at this time; but because these tensions have only been faintly articulated within the respective dramas (for instance, there is a passing reference to a race riot in a radio news broadcast heard near the beginning of the TV version of *Quatermass and the Pit*) the violence has a frighteningly spontaneous, irrational quality to it.

Within such a context Quatermass himself tends to be viewed ambivalently. On the one hand, he is a boffin-like protector of a society which generally seems incapable of protecting itself. On the other, as a 1950s scientist he is also, more disturbingly, associated with advanced technologies that register as strange and alien in the 1950s world and which on occasion parallel the technologies used by the alien invaders. So in *The Quatermass Experiment* it is the scientist's own failed experiment, and the Frankenstein-like hubris embodied in it (emphasised, not surprisingly perhaps, in the Hammer version) which brings the alien infestation to Earth while in *Quatermass II* Quatermass's design for a moon colony is turned against the human race when it appears fully realised in the English countryside as the initial home for the invading aliens. In part this ambivalent treatment derives from a broader uncertainty at this time about the role of the scientist in the nuclear age, as someone who deals with a mysterious power that is both wonderful and immensely destructive. However, typical of the idiosyncratic slant taken on such matters by the Quatermass stories is the fact that the narrative most explicitly about the nuclear age – *Quatermass and the Pit* – is also the one where Professor Quatermass is at his most dove-like and socially responsible and where, for once, he is not made complicit with the alien invasion (this role is taken instead by Colonel Breen).

It should be clear by now that lurking beneath the appeal of the Quatermass stories to the virtues of the wartime collective is a sense that something is wrong with Britain and that this predates any alien invasion. To a certain extent the function of the aliens is to reveal and clarify something that is already there, with their subsequent destruction a means of dealing, if only temporarily, with internal social tensions. It is interesting in this respect that, on a superficial level, the Quatermass aliens tend to be associated with a particular sort of modernity – especially shiny, streamlined

artefacts such as the rocket in *The Quatermass Experiment*, the Wynerton Flats complex in *Quatermass II*, and the Martian spacecraft in *Quatermass and the Pit* (in which, ironically, the most modern-looking object turns out to be five million years old). However, once these smooth, futuristic surfaces are penetrated, the aliens themselves are revealed as ultra-natural, defiantly organic, even primordial. So in *The Quatermass Experiment* the alien infestation is a primitive biological organism that absorbs human bodies and eventually transforms Victor Caroon into a plant-like creature; in *Quatermass II* the aliens are yet again relatively primitive, jellyfish-like objects nourished by an ammoniacal substance; while in *Quatermass and the Pit* the spacecraft not only contains the insect Martians and the genetically altered apemen but itself seems to have organic qualities.

When seen in this way the aliens do not merely inaugurate a Darwinist struggle of the species but also raise the possibility of an evolutionary regression, whether this be characterised by the primordial creatures in the first and second Quatermass stories or the apemen in *Quatermass and the Pit*. (A more appropriate Wells reference than *The War of the Worlds* here might be *The Island of Dr Moreau* (1896). Significantly, these aliens are often also associated with a contaminating dirtiness – for example, the black slime in *Quatermass II* which nourishes the aliens but which besmirches everything else it touches, or the mud from which the spacecraft is dug in *Quatermass and the Pit*. This filth, and the disgust and revulsion that go with it, makes the invasion/possession of the body which precedes the attempted full-scale invasion in all three 1950s Quatermass stories especially traumatic. The polluting experience of bodily invasion is thereby equated with the messy eruption of biological processes, with this taking place in a society whose adherence to a collective unquestioning mode of existence and general censoriousness and conservatism render it singularly ill-equipped to deal with something quite so vulgar and shockingly physical.

Within this situation Professor Quatermass mounts a holding operation. Associated himself with an alienating modernity, he nevertheless works to protect the existing social order from both external and internal threats. Yet Quatermass's Britain is visibly weak and vulnerable, caught as it is in a kind of collective post-war doze. Clearly this state of affairs cannot continue indefinitely. Change must be recognised and assimilated while Quatermass, who in combining traditional and progressive qualities is very much a figure of transition, will have to step aside. Britain faces a different sort of invasion.

Closer to home

In a sequence near the beginning of John Krish's *Unearthly Stranger (1963)*, a scientist invites a male colleague home to meet his new wife. The scientist is concerned about his wife, because, as strange as it might seem, she never blinks. Everything seems normal, even clichéd, in this early 1960s household with the partially domesticated husband willing to do a share of menial chores while the sexy wife manages the major tasks in her smart kitchen. Then the husband's friend sees the wife remove a red hot casserole dish from the oven with her bare hands. Understandably shocked, he retreats without comment but during the meal he cannot help staring at her. She chides him gently for this. Then she blinks.

The housewife is an alien, of course, sent to interfere with the scientist's attempts to project humanity out into space. Unlike the earlier Quatermass invasions, however, the principal site for this alien invasion is the domestic household and the face the alien wears is that of the female. The refocusing apparent here on both domesticity and gender is a general characteristic of many of the post-Quatermass invasion fantasies. A consequence of this – in films such as *Unearthly Stranger*, *Invasion* (1966), *The Night Caller* (1965), *The Earth Dies Screaming* (1965) and *Night of the Big Heat* (1967) – is that invasions take on a smaller-scale, more intimate quality. The aliens are merely passing through (*Invasion*), have relatively limited strategic aims which do not include a full-scale invasion (*The Night Caller*, *Unearthly Stranger*) or are encountered in isolated settings that are never integrated into a national or international whole (*Invasion* again, *Night of the Big Heat*). To a certain extent the aliens' limited ambitions in these films might be assigned to low budgets and a consequent restriction to small casts and few sets, although the fact that the hardly high budget Quatermass television programmes and films still managed to convey a sense of the

whole nation being under threat, suggests that something other than financial constraints is at stake in these 1960s films. Arguably connected with this disappearance of an idea of the nation as an integrated whole is the foregrounding in these films of notions of sexual difference – whether this be female invaders (*Unearthly Stranger*, *Invasion*), male aliens seeking out human females (*The Night Caller*) or, more generally, the alien invasion highlighting gender divisions and tensions within a particular group of humans (most spectacularly, *Night of the Big Heat*).

Quatermass-like elements are still undoubtedly present, especially in the films' opening sequnces. *Invasion* begins with an ominous failure in a military radar system; *The Night Caller* with the descent of a mysterious extraterrestrial object to Earth and its subsequent investigation by a team of scientists (with both of these decidedly reminiscent of *Quatermass II*); and *Unearthly Stranger* with the unexplained death of a scientist working on a top secret government space project. Yet these various inaugural mysteries never really demonstrate the possibilities for escalation and proliferation found in all the Quatermass stories. Thus in *Invasion* the aliens are only interested in recapturing a fellow alien and once they have done this they leave; while in *The Night Caller* the alien escapes to Soho where instead of planning for an invasion he advertises for women in the improbably titled magazine *Bikini Girl*. More prosaically, *Unearthly Stranger* focuses its attention on an extremely bizarre marriage. Even those figures who appear most Quatermass-like – notably the scientist played by Maurice Denham in *The Night Caller* – turn out to be ineffective, compromised by their personal relationships or, in the case of Denham's scientist who is killed by the alien, just plain weak.

The view of the nation that emerges from this is also quite different from that offered by the Quatermass storis. Perhaps inevitably given the context within which they were produced, these invasion fantasies all register a general diminution in British national identity consequent upon the visible decline of Empire after the Suez affair in 1956. The idea that Britain had a world-wide sphere of influence – a precarious enough notion in the 1950s – was clearly no longer tenable in the 1960s and one gains the sense that underlying the

1960s invasion films is the strategic question of why anyone would bother to invade Britain at all. As far as internal matters are concerned, it seems from these films that Britain has lost its centre and become fragmented, its population scattered in isolated groups and its institutions and hierarchies no longer as efficacious as they once were. So, for example, the hospital in *Invasion* is a far cry from the hospitals that feature prominently in a whole range of 1950s films – including *White Corridors* (1957), *No Time for Tears* (1957), *Doctor in the House* (1954) and its sequels – and which there act as a kind of microcosm of the caring Welfare State. *Invasion*'s hospital, by contrast, is beset by internal squabbles and is eventually sealed off from the outside world by an alien force field. More comically, the unsuccessful attempts of the army officer in *The Night Caller* to explain over the phone the situation to his obviously less than intelligent superiors yet again points to the inadequacy of any higher authority.

Connected with this is the films' fascination with and anxiety about gender, and especially the changing role of the woman, something that hardly concerned Quatermass at all. In a sense, particular notions of femininity are central to the increasingly consumerist society that was Britain in the 1960s. On the one hand, the woman as embodied in the figure of the housewife is the prime organiser of domestic consumption; but on the other hand, she is also often presented as the sexualised object of male consumption (most notably in this period in the James Bond films). The kidnapped women in *The Night Caller*, which in many ways is the most reactionary of the films being discussed here, seem to fall into the latter category. Defined entirely by their physical appearance and their sexual attractiveness – their abductor presents all his victims with a photograph of them as if to underline their objectification – they are throughout the film completely under the control of the male alien. Surprisingly, they are not even rescued at the end. It is interesting in this respect, if also disturbing, that the most intelligent, self-assured and independent woman in the film, the scientist Ann Barlow, is identified by the alien as especially threatening and is brutally killed.

More complex in their treatment of women are *Invasion* and *Unearthly Stranger*. In the former, all three aliens – two women and one man – are played by oriental actors. At first glance

this might be seen as invoking fears of Chinese communist subversion, but *Invasion* also needs to be located in relation to a wider orientalist strain in British cinema in the 1960s – including the Fu Manchu movies starring Christopher Lee, *Battle Beneath the Earth* (1967) and even *Dr No* (1962) – which in their stress on warlord villains seemed to be more about nostalgia for a lost imperial age than more contemporary fears and anxieties. *Invasion* is certainly not nostalgic, but its treatment of race is far from straightforward. While it might use the race of its oriental actors in an arguably racist sense to accentuate the otherness of the aliens, it also features another oriental female as a nurse at the hospital. What this produces is a kind of racial ambiguity about the identity of the aliens so that they are not fully or easily distinguishable from the humans in the hospital, or, to be more precise, from the hospital's 'resident alien', i.e. non-white human. This ambiguity is carried over into the gender roles adopted by the aliens as well for while there is a good deal of evidence in the film to support the female aliens' account of themselves – namely that they are extraterrestrial police in search of an escaped male criminal – the male alien's claim that he is a dissident on the run from what presumably is a female-dominated society is never fully discounted. The authoritative identification and containment of the aliens that is enacted throughout the 1950s by Quatermass is clearly no longer achievable and what one is left with instead are some unanswered questions and a sense that the truly important drama is taking place elsewhere.

This failure to name and control the alien threat is developed further in *Unearthly Stranger* with particular reference to the figure of the housewife. The film works system-atically to make the image of the housewife appear strange, so that in effect it becomes a surface beyond which some otherness may be lurking. It does this through stressing the performativity of the role, the way in which housewifery seems to be defined via the carrying out of a series of actions – such as preparing the evening meal – under the benign gaze of the husband. Once this performance is recognised for what it actually is – as is the case in the kitchen scene – then immediately the woman becomes a threatening enigma for the male, who can no longer trust the evidence of his own eyes. Hence the film's stress on the transformation of the male gaze at the woman into something troubled and fearful; hence too the mounting male paranoia of its hero – such a traumatic revelation obviously puts male identity itself in a state of turmoil. *Unearthly Stranger* concludes in true paranoid style with the scientist discovering that not only his wife but the helpful secretary at his office are aliens. He is last seen surrounded by a group of women, any or all of whom might be aliens too. The cool gaze of the Martians at the beginning of *The War of the Worlds* has been transformed into the female gaze, a gaze that dispels male complacency. The scientist's self-confidence, which in the Quatermass stories saved the nation from disaster, has gone and all that is left is a state of perpetual uncertainty.

Quatermass revisited

Hammer's 1967 version of *Quatermass and the Pit* is something of an anachronism. Of all three film versions, it is the most faithful to the television original and yet the view of Britain it conjures up, with all its wartime resonances, surely belongs more to the 1950s than it does to the 1960s. Nevertheless there is something about the story it tells which has a significance that goes beyond the immediate circumstances of its original production and which clarifies some of the more general qualities of the British invasion fantasy. In the story it is discovered that five million years ago Martians mounted a successful invasion of Earth by proxy through altering selected humans to instil Martian-like behaviour in them. The consequences of this are startling for it means that, as one of Quatermass's associates remarks, 'We're the Martians now'. This statement of fact is also, of course, a statement of defeat, for how can one change the very essence of the human when it is revealed as being partly alien?

As was suggested at the beginning of this essay, the invasion fantasy generally can be seen as a narrative of defeat. In a sense, aliens always win. What is apparent in *Quatermass and the Pit*, however, and indeed in all the British sf invasion films discussed here, is how close to the surface this realisation actually is, certainly more so than in most of the contemporaneous American sf films. It is as if Britain, displaced from an imperial history and the glories of the Second World War and caught up in a series of bewildering social changes, is more open to self-doubts and an accompanying acknowledgement of its own limits. That such an acknowledgement is always fearful – and viewed in films such as *Unearthly Stranger* and *Invasion* as a kind of collapse – is hardly surprising given that the identities of both the nation and the individual are at stake. Yet the dispelling of a self-centred complacency can in itself be seen as a positive experience for, as Quatermass finally comes to realise in *Quatermass and the Pit* and as H. G. Wells understood all along, to know the alien more clearly is to know oneself as well.

Works Cited

Barr, Charles (1986) 'Broadcasting and cinema: 2: Screens within screens', in Barr (ed.) *All Our Yesterdays: 90 Years of British Cinema*. London: British Film Institute.

Biskind, Peter (1983) *Seeing is Believing: How Hollywood Taught Us to Stop Worrying and Love the Fifties*. London: Pluto Press.

Hurd, Geoff (ed.) (1984) *National Fictions*. London: British Film Institute.

Hutchings, Peter (1993) *Hammer and Beyond: The British Horror Film*. Manchester: Manchester University Press.

Jancovich, Mark (1996) *Rational Fears: American Horror in the 1950s*. Manchester: Manchester University Press.

Newman, Kim (1996) 'Are you now or have you ever been…?', in Stefan Jaworzyn (ed.) *Shock*. London: Titan.

Wells, H. G. (1993 [1898]) *The War of the Worlds*. London: Phoenix Mass Market Publications.

Index

the science fiction film reader

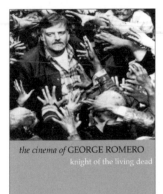

2003

£16.99 pbk   978-1-903364-73-4

£45.00 hbk   978-1-903364-62-8

208 pages

The Cinema of Gerorge A. Romero
Knight of the Living Dead

Tony Williams

The Cinema of George A. Romero: Knight of the Living Dead is the first in-depth study in English of the career of this foremost auteur working at the margins of the Hollywood mainstream. In placing Romero's oeuvre in the context of literary naturalism, the book explores the relevance of the director's films within American cultural traditions and thus explains the potency of such work beyond 'splatter movie' models. The author explores the roots of naturalism in the work of Emile Zola and traces this through to the EC Comics of the 1950s and on to the work of Stephen King.

"This thorough, searching and always intelligent overview does full justice to Romero's *Living Dead* trilogy and also at last rectifies the critical neglect of Romero's other work, fully establishing its complexity and cohesion."
> – Robin Wood, *CineAction!*

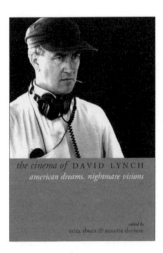

2004

£16.99 pbk   978-1-903364-85-7

£45.00 hbk   978-1-903364-86-4

208 pages

The Cinema of David Lynch
American Dreams, Nightmare Visions

Edited by Erica Sheen
and Annette Davison

David Lynch is an anomaly. A pioneer of the American 'indie' aesthetic, he also works in Hollywood and for network television. He has created some of the most disturbing images in contemporary cinema, and produced startlingly innovative work in sound. This collection offers a range of theoretically divergent readings that demonstrate not only the difficulty of locating interpretative positions for Lynch's work, but also the pleasure of finding new ways of thinking about it. Films discussed include *Blue Velvet*, *Wild at Heart*, *The Straight Story* and *Mulholland Drive*.

"A ground-breaking collection of new essays presenting a range of challenging theoretical perspectives on, and insightful readings of, Lynch's work."
> – Frank Krutnik, Sheffield Hallam University

Science Fiction Cinema
From Outerspace to Cyberspace

2000
£12.99 pbk
978-1-903364-03-1
144 pages

Geoff King and Tanya Krzywinska

From lurid comic-book blockbusters to dark dystopian visions, science fiction is seen as both a powerful cultural barometer of our times and the product of particular industrial and commercial frameworks. The authors outline the major themes of the genre, from representations of the mad scientist and computer hacker to the relationship between science fiction and postmodernism.

"The best overview of English-language science ficiton cinema published to date – thorough, clearly written and full of excellent examples. Highly recommended."
– Steve Neale, Sheffield Hallam University

The Horror Genre
From Beelzebub to Blair Witch

2000
£12.99 pbk
978-1-903364-00-0
144 pages

Paul Wells

The Horror Genre: From Beelzebub to Blair Witch provides a comprehensive introduction to the history and key themes of the horror film, the main issues and debates surrounding the genre, and the approaches and theories that have been applied to horror texts.

"A valuable contribution to the body of teaching texts available ... a book for all undergraduates starting on the subject."
– Linda Ruth Williams, University of
Southampton

Disaster Movies
The Cinema of Catastrophe (2nd edn)

2006
£12.99 pbk
978-1-905674-03-9
144 pages

Stephen Keane

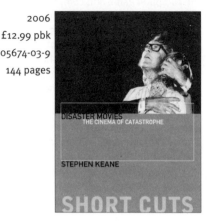

From 1950s sci-fi B-movies to high concept 1990s 'millenial movies', Stephen Keane looks at the ways in which the representation of disaster and its aftermath are borne out of both contextual considerations and the increasing commercial demands of Hollywood.

"Providing detailed consideration of key movies within their social and cultural context, this concise introduction serves its purpose well and should prove a useful teaching tool."
– Nick Roddick

Visions of the Apocalypse
Spectacles of Destruction in American Cinema
Wheeler Winston Dixon

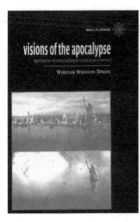

Visions of the Apocolypse examines the cinema's fascination with the prospect of nuclear and/or natural annihilation. The author discusses such topics as the political and social tensions that have made these visions of infinite destruction so appealing to the public.

'Dixon's knowledge of film is amazing ... This work relentlessly examines the monolithic and destructive character of media imperialism and documents the marginalisation of alternative modes of production and distribution.'
– Prof. Marcia Landy, University of Pittsburgh

'As money-fueled monsters from the military-industrial complex threaten cinema, civilisation and humanity itself, Dixon counter-attacks with a high-energy jolt of impeccably aimed scholarship. This is intellectual 'shock and awe' at their illuminating, life-affirming best.'
– Prof. David Sterritt, Long Island University

2003
£14.99 pbk   978-1-903364-74-1
£40.00 hbk   978-1-903364-38-3
192 pages

The Blade Runner Experience
The Legacy of a Science Fiction Classic
Edited by Will Brooker

Over twenty years after its original release, Ridley Scott's *Blade Runner* remains hugely popular and influential. This volume examines the film with original essays covering the depiction of the city, the nature of identity, fans, the computer game and comparisons with other films from Philip K. Dick's writings, including *Total Recall* and *Minority Report*. Placing the film in the contexts of cyberpunk, *film noir*, the detective genre and science fiction, the book explores these influences on the film as well as the influences it has had on other films.

Includes contributions by Dominic Alessio, Barry Atkins, Aaron Barlow, Peter Brooker, Christy Collins, Christine Cornea, John Cussans, Matthew Hills, Deborah Jermyn, Judith Kerman, Nick Lacey, Susana Pajares Tosca, Sean Redmond, Stephen Rowley.

2005
£16.99 pbk   978- 1-904764-30-4
£45.00 hbk   978-1-904764-31-1

The Matrix Trilogy
Cyberpunk Reloaded
Edited by Stacy Gillis

This book is a collection of new essays on the highly successful *Matrix* trilogy, as well as the computer game and the accompanying *Animatrix* series, and looks at the films in a way that no other book has done. Placing them in context within the cyberpunk genre, this timely volume looks at many of the theories and concepts used in the trilogy from Baudrillard to post-feminism, the use of special effects, and costume and design. A unique collection, *The Matrix Trilogy: Cyberpunk Reloaded* is set to be an unmissable authority on the *Matrix* phenomenon.

Includes contributions by Diane Carr, Pamela Church Gibson, Anne Cranny-Francis, Thomas Foster, Lisa Nakamura, Dan North, Kathleen O'Riordan, Andrew Shail, Paul Sheehan, Claudia Springer, Aylish Wood.

2005
£16.99 pbk   978-1-904764-32-8
£45.00 hbk   978-1-904764-33-5